WHERE SHOULD WE TAKE THE KIDS?

THE NORTHEAST
by Elin McCoy

Fodor's Travel Publications

New York • Toronto • London • Sydney • Auckland

First Edition

ISBN 0-679-02637-1

Fodor's Where Should We Take the Kids? The Northeast

Creative Director: Fabrizio La Rocca
Cover Photograph: Paul D'Innocenzo
Design: Guido Caroti

Special Sales

Fodor's Travel Publications are available at special discounts for bulk purchases for sales promotions or premiums. Special editions, including personalized covers, excerpts of existing guides, and corporate imprints, can be created in large quantities for special needs. For more information, contact your local bookseller or Special Markets, Fodor's Travel Publications, 201 East 50th Street, New York, NY 10022. Inquiries from Canada should be directed to your local Canadian bookseller or sent to Random House of Canada, Ltd., Marketing Department, 1265 Aerowood Drive, Mississauga, Ontario L4W 1B9. Inquiries from the United Kingdom should be sent to Fodor's Travel Publications, 20 Vauxhall Bridge Road, London SW1V 2SA, England.

MANUFACTURED IN THE UNITED STATES OF AMERICA

10 9 8 7 6 5 4 3 2 1

CONTENTS

Editors' Foreword

While every care has been taken to ensure the accuracy of the information in this guide, the passage of time will always bring change, and consequently the publisher cannot accept responsibility for errors that may occur.

All prices and opening times quoted here are based on information supplied to us at press time. Hours and admission fees may change, however, and the prudent traveler will avoid inconvenience by calling ahead.

Fodor's wants to hear about your travel experiences, both pleasant and unpleasant. When a hotel or restaurant fails to live up to its billing, let us know, and we will investigate the complaint and revise our entries where the facts warrant it.

Send your letters to the editors of Fodor's Travel Publications, 201 East 50th Street, New York, NY 10022.

Author's Acknowledgments

This book could not have been written without the cooperation of my family and the help of the many families—both friends and friends of friends—who shared their travel experiences in the Northeast with me. Very special thanks are due to Matthew Wool, whose research and help on Chapter 11 were essential.

I'd also like to single out Robbie Barnett; Rebecca Ballard; Sarah Jane and Krystyana Chelminski; Nancy Cherosnik; Mira Felner and Joshua Cutler; Abby and Eliza Fitzgerald; Mary Kay, Michael, and Matthew Flowers; Dan Ford; Sally, Stephen, Betsy, and Eric Fortlouis; Pam, John, Will, and Noah Gasner; Candace Gianetti; Betsy Goff; Bob and Carol Goldfeld; Betsy Hart and Marty O'Toole plus M.J., Teresa, and Emily; Susan Cohen and Peter, Jacob, and Kate Hellman; Jane and Andrew Holt; Sari Jubein; Nancy, Alison, Danny, Brendan, and John Kinchla; Susan, Eliza, and Caroline Kinsolving; Sue Kirber; Mark, Geri, Matt, and Dana Kupersmith; Larry Lindner; Justine McCabe and Jared Hudson; Carroll, Mike, Alexander, and Olivia Macdonald; Jim and Eileen McKay; Juliana May; Kristin Mellen-Smith; Wenda Harris Millard and her two kids; Vita, Arthur, and Owen Muir; Kathleen Heenan and Nicholas, Caitlin, and Jonathan Olmstead; Michelle Phelan and her two kids; Louise and Curtis Read; Connie, David, Andrea, and Sarah Rosengarten; Nancy and Malcolm Sandberg; Rosellen, Bob, Brian, and Michael Schnurr; Wendy and Brian Seeley; Frances and Peter Shocket; Judy and Jasper Speicher; Eddie Udel and his family; Tina Ujlaki and Nicholas and Chloe Marmet; the Van Hemerts; Sarah Van Fleet; Vanessa, Zoe, and Bridget Wool; Roberta, Jason, Matthew, and Richard Wool; Sally Zunino and her kids.

I'm also grateful to my editor at Fodor's, Nancy van Itallie, for her patience, and to all the staff at Fodor's for their efforts on this book. My agent, Joan Raines, deserves many thanks, too.

Last but not least, to John and Gavin, my heartfelt thanks for meals cooked, chapters read, trips taken, and much, much more.

Dedication

To the memory of my parents, Margaret and J.L. McCoy, who taught me the basics about family travel.

PART I

OPENERS

Information and Tips for Traveling with Children

ARE WE THERE YET?
GETTING STARTED IN THE NORTHEAST

My view of family travel is firmly rooted in my own childhood in western New York State and the Midwest. I am the child of parents who loved nothing better than climbing into the car on Friday night and heading off on a travel adventure for the weekend. For us a family vacation was a chance to step out of our normal daily routine (stay up late, eat ice cream every night) and have the exclusive attention of our parents, who, as we drove, listened to poems we wrote, shared tales of their own childhoods, and occasionally astonished us with their knowledge of some fascinating, obscure fact. Their main rules were simple: no fighting in the backseat and only one souvenir that cost over $1 on each trip.

Now there are three of us who travel together: my husband, John, a painter and writer, my 15-year-old son, Gavin, and me, though on many excursions our small band has also included cousins and friends, Cub Scouts and classmates. Our home base has been the Northeast—first in New York City, then in the small town in rural northwestern Connecticut where we now live—for more than 20 years. Over the past 15 years of short and long vacations with Gavin and some of his friends, John and I have most often discovered the pleasures *parents* glean from such travel scenarios when we could take the same relaxed attitude toward travel with kids as my parents did. This translated into being flexible, seeing the funny side of problems, and looking at things from a kid's perspective, whatever that was at different ages.

Then too, kids have the gift of instant friendships that make you part of a wider family community; Gavin's exuberance and questions have resulted more than once in an after-dinner invitation into the kitchen of a Chinese restaurant to meet the chef's family and try a few special treats. At playground and park stops we invariably met families who shared with us the name of the best local restaurant for kids, the most interesting biking spot, a tiny, just-opened bird sanctuary. Choosing activities that appeal to kids opens up new possibilities for you, too.

Traveling with a kid's perspective affects how you plan, where you go, where you stay, what you see and do when you get there, where and what you eat, and how you schedule a day's activities so that kids—and you—have fun. A morning in a museum can be boring, but not if you choose one that has displays of dinosaurs or real skeletons you can touch or an old boat where you can play lobsterman or dress up in a knight's armor and chain mail. Sightseeing as an end in itself is not a turn-on for any kids under 12 that I know. They want views of Quechee Gorge to culminate in action—like hiking down to the gorge itself on a narrow path for a swim or 15 minutes of tossing rocks into the stream.

Every family has its own set of likes and dislikes, and this book reflects ours and those of our friends, who were able to fill in our gaps. Lighthouses and forts have always appealed to us—and Gavin—more than historic houses; we're hikers and canoers more than bicyclists and horseback riders; as a family we prefer small hotels to big ones, and John and I have always heaved a sigh of relief that Gavin likes Chinese dim sum as much as fast food. We also have our individual passions. John is more a museum-goer than a sports-watcher (except for tennis). For me no trip is complete without a visit to a bookstore and a hike. Gavin's interests, like all kids', have changed and evolved from toddler to teenager: Skiing is a constant, but going to baseball games has not been; big machines and animals in zoos are no longer the delight they were when he was 6; a week in a city with a chance to skateboard and people-watch is more exciting to him now than a week camping and hiking in the mountains. Our vacations have had to evolve too. The 25 tips below are ones that have helped make our vacations and those of other traveling families we know work over a period of years.

One last thought: We've learned, not without effort, to give up the myth of the perfect vacation. Things will go wrong; kids will not coexist with you or each other in complete harmony; not all your planned activities will be as wonderful or exciting as you thought. But—hey—surprise! You can have fun anyway.

BEFORE YOU GO. Before you go, you can do a number of things to improve the chances of your trip's success.

• When choosing a destination, take into account the ages, likes, and dislikes of every member of the family, starting with the youngest—and including your own. If your 5-year-old gets bored with a constant round of museums or your teenager goes into a funk because he's cooped up with younger kids for days, no one will have a good time. Make sure the trip includes something special for everyone.

• Get your kids actively involved in planning your trip from the very beginning— that way older kids have a stake in making it work and you have a chance to allay younger kids' natural wariness of the unknown. Besides, it's fun. After poring over brochures and books (see suggestions, *below*), we each make a list of what we want to see and do. When Gavin was little, he used felt-tip markers to circle pictures of what appealed to him. From this we planned out what to do each day.

• Give kids information about where you are staying and distances in kid terms (i.e. it will take about as long as to drive to Grandma and Grandpa's), and don't take anything for granted with little kids. A family we know discussed their trip to a cottage in Cape Cod with their three kids for weeks, but as they climbed into the car, their 3-year-old wondered aloud nervously whether a cottage was "like cottage cheese."

• Start small. Try a one-night camp out in the backyard or a nearby state park before committing yourself to a weeklong trip, an afternoon hike as a trial run for a vacation in the mountains, a local museum visit before a weekend grand museum jaunt.

• Choose places to stay where families are welcome so you don't feel as though you have to apologize when your kids act like kids. We always pick somewhere with a pool if it's affordable.

• If your kids are under 8, pick one spot to stay and content yourself with occasional short day trips from there. It's hard for kids to adjust to new surroundings every night, and packing and repacking all their gear isn't much fun for parents either.

• Bring and plan small surprises you know your kids will like: new toys and books, an ice-cream picnic, an hour at a mall en route, fanny packs they've admired with $5 or $10 inside.

• Agree on a few basic behavior rules ahead of time and stick to them on your trip. This includes deciding what you plan to do to minimize sibling fights.

• With little kids, take pretend trips before you go. Gavin and his best friends loved packing a small suitcase, setting up rows of chairs as a plane, cutting up paper for play tickets, and taking turns being waiter and customer in a restaurant. Use this as an opportunity to warn kids about what to expect—that the plane may rock, for example.

EN ROUTE. En route, here are some strategies for smoother travel.

• Know what travel times work for your kids. Some families prefer traveling at night because their children will sleep.

• Though we've taken marathon car trips, we don't recommend them with kids, even older ones. Break the trip into smaller parts or better yet, fly as close to your destination as possible, then rent a car. When you do arrive, keep daily car travel to a minimum.

• Travel in comfortable clothes—sweat suits or T-shirts and shorts are best—and pack a small bag of backup duds that are easy to get to. On summer car trips keep a bag with bathing suits and towels handy for quick dips.

• Don't travel at peak hours on either airplanes or the road if any other option exists; otherwise tempers, including children's, can fray.

- On airplanes, get on last, rather than first (as most airlines suggest), so your kids can be active as long as possible and haven't tried all the activities they've brought before the plane even takes off.

- If you have kids over the age of 5, you can carry a cache of quarters for the video games and vending machines at highway plazas and gas stations.

- In the car, do not assume that kids over 9 want to sing "100 bottles of beer on the wall" or engage in any other (in Gavin's words) "dopey games" from your own childhood long, long ago. Do assume that whatever music you play will be torture to older kids' ears, especially if they are teenagers. Bring a headset and a small cassette player for each child.

- We stop frequently en route and include short adventures along the way by getting off the interstate to explore a town or arranging our route to pass state parks so we have more attractive spots for picnicking and even a swim. This takes longer but is much more fun and ensures that kids arrive at your ultimate destination still enthusiastic.

WHEN YOU ARRIVE. A couple of simple decisions can ease your first days at your destination.

- Arrive well before dark, preferably by 4 or 5 o'clock, so kids have time to explore and feel at home before they go to sleep. For us, jumping in a pool for a swim before dinner is the best start to a vacation.

- If you've traveled all day in a car or a plane, set aside most of the next day for action-oriented activities: swimming and digging at a beach, exploring a city park and playground, patting animals at a farm. Picnic instead of eating in restaurants, or splurge the first night by ordering from room service and watching a movie.

DAY BY DAY. Planning loosely and leaving room for spontaneity can improve your stay.

- Plan days to include a variety of activities: a morning at a terrific museum followed by a picnic in a park where kids can feed ducks and climb statues will work better than trying to pack all the museums into one day. Include time at playgrounds, parks, or other green spaces every day, and be back at your hotel or resort early enough for kids to chill out and relax, take a nap, or swim in the pool before dinner.

- Underplan. Schedules that are too tight don't leave time for those serendipities that are the delight of travel. Also, kids love to repeat what they've liked—go back to a great kids' museum, eat at the same restaurant two or three times, walk down a street or stop in a shop again.

- If your older kids are not that keen on historic sites—and there are many in the Northeast—focus on the gruesome ones where a massacre took place, six men were hanged, witches were stoned, skeletons were found. Many school-age kids respond to blood and gore.

● Build in time away from each other on longer vacations. Kids like to spend some time with others their own age instead of just siblings, and vacations should give parents a break too. Resorts and hotels that have children's programs offer the easiest solution.

SAVING MEMORIES. Think about ways to savor your trip after you get home.

● Part of the fun of a family trip is remembering later the wonderful, awful, and funny things that happened. Encourage kids to put together their own scrapbook and journal of the trip even if they can't write. We've always packed a spiral notebook or homemade notebook of stapled construction paper, a glue stick, tape, and locking plastic bags in which to collect souvenirs of the trip such as a subway token, a special leaf, menus, postcards, napkins, and so on. Each evening Gavin glued everything from that day into his book and dictated (later wrote) a sentence or two. Now it's fun to reread them and laugh.

● To most kids, part of the fun of travel is buying souvenirs. To keep this habit from becoming too expensive, a Boston family we know lets each child pick out a postcard at every stop. One year they wrote a few lines on each card, which they sent to themselves; when they returned home, they delighted in remembering the places they'd visited and what they most enjoyed at each. Other families encourage their kids to start collections: pencils, key chains, napkins, seashells, rocks, and leaves.

BONING UP: BOOKS AND VIDEOS BEFORE YOU GO. Two good books on general travel strategies with kids are: *Trouble-Free Travel with Children* by Vicki Lansky (1991, The Book Peddlers; available from Practical Parenting, Deephaven, MN 55391, tel. 800/255–3379, fax 612/475–1505); and *Traveling with Children and Enjoying It* by Arlene Kay Butler (Globe Pequot, 1991).

Getting kids interested in and knowledgeable about your travel destination in advance contributes to their enthusiasm for the trip and usually (we've found, anyway) makes it more successful because kids love seeing in person things they recognize from a book or movie. (I've also included specific book and video suggestions in individual chapters.) Available from *The Family Travel Guides Catalog* (see Gearing up to Go in Chapter 2) is a great resource: *Books on the Move: A Read-About-It-Go-There Guide to America's Best Family Destinations*, which lists dozens of children's titles (including fiction) related to many destinations in New England and topics such as animals, sports, nature, geography, and so on.

To help little kids grasp some basics: *Dinosaur's Travel: A Guide for Families on the Go* by Laurie Krasny Brown and Marc Brown (Little Brown; ages 3–8) covers aspects of vacationing such as getting ready for a trip, sleeping in an unfamiliar bed, and more, all from a kid's perspective; *Arthur's Family Vacation* by Marc Brown (Little, Brown; ages 3–8) is a humorous look at a vacation that includes six days of rain and how everyone had fun anyway. When Gavin was little, we also read books about whatever kind of transportation we would be using: *Your First Airplane Trip* by Pat and Joel Ross (libraries) and *The Car Trip* by Helen Oxenbury (Out & About Books, 1983) are two we particularly liked.

For older kids: *The Travel Bug: A Travel Journal for Kids 7 to 14, Creative Activities for Kids on the Go* by Linda Schwartz (Learning Works, tel. 800/235–5767) is full of games and projects to encourage kids to focus on their surroundings.

A trip to the library will turn up a surprising number of books for all ages related to some aspect of your trip. Some examples: If you're visiting Salem, Massachusetts, you might want to read books about witches and the history of the witch trials; if you're going to Maine, books about lobsters, lighthouses, and the classic *One Morning in Maine* (Robert McCloskey, Viking). Three books for kids in the 4 to 8 range that we've liked paint vivid pictures of outdoor action adventures: *Three Days on A River in a Red Canoe* by Vera Williams (Greenwillow), detailed enough to be a guide for planning a canoe trip; *Amelia Bedelia Goes Camping* by Peggy Parish (Avon), a humorous camping story for beginning readers; and *Tomorrow on Rocky Pond* by Lynn Reiser (Greenwillow), about an idyllic family fishing excursion.

Many resorts send short videos. Even if they sound like ads, they'll help kids picture where they're going. In our house, a screening of the hilarious National Lampoon's *Family Vacation* with Chevy Chase was a good starting point for discussion about how to ensure our trip didn't end up like that. Check individual chapters for videos that provide a preview of a specific location, such as New York City. Films based on events in American history or set in 18th- or 19th-century America (*The Last of the Mohicans*, for example) are good bets as they convey the flavor of the Northeast's past. Watching a movie such as *Free Willy* may interest your kids in whales in general, and by extension, a whale-watching trip.

PACKING THE ALL-IMPORTANT TOY-AND-BOOK BAG. Once kids turn 3 or so, they're ready to decide what toys and books *they* want to take—though I always reserved the right to make some suggestions and packed some additional toys in our regular luggage—and able to carry most of it themselves in a backpack or lightweight travel bag with lots of flaps, compartments, and zippered pockets. Some of our friends put a mesh bag behind each front seat so kids can see what toys and games they have. If we're going by car, we take a canvas bag of additional books and books on tape that we've borrowed from the library. (If you're traveling by plane, coloring books, playing cards, and kids' magazines are the most you can expect from the airline over and above the set of Junior Captain wings.) The following lists may serve as reminders of the objects children in your family consider essential.

These things can mean the difference between major crises and relatively peaceful traveling with infants and toddlers:

An essential stuffed toy and blanket; old baby rattles and teething toys (tie them with a string to the car seat so kids can drop them and pull them up); song tapes, including nursery rhymes, finger plays, lullabies; a toy telephone.

Preschoolers and up can create their own pastimes with washable felt-tip markers (crayons often melt if left in the sun); spiral notebooks or a clipboard and paper with a pencil on a string attached; a glue stick; a magic slate; playing cards and book of card games; books (preferably paperbacks), most brand-new but a few old favorites (keep a few of the new ones to dole out later in the trip); cassette tapes—of songs, novels, and children's books (let each kid—especially teens—bring his or her own tape player, tapes, and headset) and extra batteries; *Mad Libs* (pads of fill-in-the-blank stories that amuse kids from age 7) and fill-in activity books; sticker books, such as the *Where's Waldo Sticker Books* by Martin Handford (Candlewick Press); finger puppets, small toy people, or action figures of some kind; dolls; small cars and trucks; Legos in coffee cans or large zip-shut bags; hand-held video games; travel versions of popular games, such as Battleship, Yahtzee, and checkers; Klutz Press books, which come with jacks, juggling balls, and other toys; modeling compound; Brain Quest packages (each box contains 1,000 questions and answers designed for a specific age group, from preschoolers through grade 7); Etch-a-Sketch; disposable cameras; crocheting gear—or some other favorite craft; binoculars (for older kids); action toys for rest stops: bubble-liquid sets, Frisbee, inflatable beach ball, baseball bat, gloves, tennis ball, soccer ball, jump ropes.

Great Games for the Road

Most kids we know quickly get down to the basics: "I'm bo-o-o-red" and "How much longer before we get there?" One way to counteract that is with car games; the best ones don't require much in the way of equipment or props, relying instead on everyone's quick wits. Below are our favorites; some good books of others are: *Miles of Smiles: 101 Great Car Games and Activities* by Carole Terwilliger Meyers (Carousel Press); *The Usborne Book of Car Travel Games* by Tony Potter (Usborne, 1985) and *The Usborne Book of Air Travel Games* by Moira Butterfield (Usborne, 1986).

2–4 **WHAT'S IN THE CUP.** Take turns dropping a coin, key, crayon, grape, or other small object into a hard plastic cup. Shake it, then see if anyone can guess what's in it.

👪 4–8   **I SPY.** One child starts by "spying" something, such as a red barn, then announces, "I spy something red." Whoever guesses what it is becomes *It* next. Limit choices to inside or outside the car.

👪 4–12   **ANIMAL LOOKOUT.** Give points for animals spotted; the winner is the person with the highest total when you arrive at your destination. In our version dogs and cats were worth 1 point; chipmunks and squirrels, 2 points; farm animals (horses, cows, chickens, sheep), 3 points; deer, rabbits, and birds, 5 points; snakes, moose, and other unlikely specimens, 10 points.

👪 4–12   **COLLECT THE ALPHABET GAME.** We compete to see who can find all the letters of the alphabet, in sequence, first. We permit only one letter for each sign, billboard, license plate, and so on, per player. The letters q and z are the toughies.

👪 4–12   **PINK TOADS.** *It* must answer any question asked of her with the phrase "Pink Toads" without laughing. Other players try to provoke laughter by asking what her favorite breakfast is or what she always takes to bed with her or what she most hopes to get for her birthday. Whoever makes her laugh becomes *It* for the next round. Gavin and his friends found this a much more hilarious game than John and I did. For the most fun, use other silly phrases, changing frequently.

👪 4–12   **TIC-TAC-TOE.** This old favorite needs no description. We've always played it on a Magic Slate (you write on film, then lift it to erase), rather than relying on pencil and paper. As Gavin grew older, he preferred **Connections,** in which you make a square grid of dots in rows. Players take turns connecting two adjoining dots with a vertical or horizontal line, trying to be the one to complete a box. A player who does puts his initials inside it; the winner is the one who has the most initialed boxes at the end of the game.

👪 5+   **I'M TAKING A TRIP.** To us this is a classic. The first person says, "I'm taking a trip and packing an apron." The second person repeats the sentence and adds an item beginning with the letter b, and so on, until someone forgets one item.

👪 5+   **TREASURE HUNT.** With your kids, draw up a list of items to look for along the way. A few examples: a hay wagon, a cement mixer, a black dog, a bridge, and a waterfall. Twenty to 30 items are sufficient; if your kids are older, add in a few hard ones, such as a burned-down house or an auto graveyard. En route, check them off as they're spotted.

(👭 5–12) **COUNTING COWS.** One person counts the cows in fields on one side of the road; the other person counts those on the opposite side; when you pass a graveyard, the person whose side it is on must bury his or her cows and start again. To keep the game manageable, pick an end point—until you stop for lunch or reach a turnoff.

(👭 6–14) **ROUND-ROBIN STORY.** One person begins a tale, stopping after 10 sentences or an agreed-upon time limit (one or two minutes for little kids, longer for older ones). Then another storyteller adds to it, and so on until the last person has to wrap up a conclusion. We found it fun to tape these and play them later.

(👭 10+) **20 QUESTIONS.** You probably know how to play this game, but if not, read on. One player thinks of a person, place, or thing for others to guess. We sometimes mention one clue, as in "I'm thinking of something inside a house" or "I'm thinking of a place in New York City," to make it easy enough for younger kids. The other players can ask up to 20 questions (only those that can be answered with "yes" or "no") to help them guess.

(👭 10+) **GHOST.** Both John and I played this challenging game when we were kids, and Gavin likes it as much as we did then. The first player says the first letter of any word with more than four letters, but without saying the word. The next player adds a letter that would fit in a word he has in mind. Then the next player adds another letter, and so on. The point, however, is to add letters without completing any word. Whoever does (or can't think of a letter to add) is given the letter G. The next time it happens he or she gets an H, and so on until someone completes the word ghost and is out of the game. The last player in the game wins.

When Kids Have to Wait

Everyone in our family hates waiting in line or being stuck in traffic, and I don't know any kids who handle these situations with grace. The younger they are, the harder it is. Unfortunately, if you visit popular sights (the Statue of Liberty, for example) and resort areas in the Northeast on peak weekends and in summer, you'll have to face these problems sometimes, though lines and traffic will not compare to what our friends have encountered at Florida's Disney World. Our strategy is as follows. First, avoidance whenever possible. Throughout the book I've indicated the least crowded times for sights where you can expect a wait. As a general rule of thumb, arrive just before opening time on a weekday; for outdoor sights, aim for a cloudy but not actually rainy day. The hours between 11 and 3 on weekends are usually the most crowded no matter where you go, whether beaches or museums; at restaurants the least crowded times are early—11 for lunch; 5:30 to 6 for dinner, which is usually better for little kids anyway. Never visit any popular site on a free-admission day in summer. Traffic jams are most common on Friday and Sunday nights beginning with July 4th weekend. Our family decides together in advance how long we, including Gavin, are willing to wait to get into an attraction and we discuss how we can entertain ourselves. It's important to know your family's tolerance level, which will depend on both age and temperament. At most sites attendants can generally give you a fairly accurate estimate of waiting time; if it's too long, we leave. Another solution is for one parent to wait in line (this works best for paying entry fees) while the other whisks kids off for a nearby bench picnic or walk. Come prepared with books and game ideas, such as the car games above, and snacks.

Eating Out with Kids

THE PLEASURES OF PICNICS. One of the family trips I most enjoyed as a child was a car tour through New England because my sister and I had extracted a promise from my parents that we could picnic at every meal, including breakfast. They honored this promise even on a drizzly morning; as there was no park near our motel, we ate cereal and milk out of individual boxes while sitting on gravestones under a big overhanging tree. It was the highlight of our trip. When Gavin was little, he, too, considered picnicking the meal mode of choice because it is totally informal, you don't have to wait to be served, and you can jump around, make noise, and do all those things that are not considered "restaurant behavior" in our or any other family. And it's a way to save money.

On warm-weather trips, we usually scheduled a daily lunch picnic outside in a park (see Chapters 3, 4, 5, and 6 for suggestions) when Gavin was younger, but indoor picnics in a hotel room really made us feel as though we were on vacation, no matter what the season. A breakfast picnic of cereal and milk, fresh fruit, and boxed juices is easy to assemble (best if you have an in-room refrigerator) and ready more quickly than room service (older kids, however, love ordering by telephone even if they have to wait). The first night you arrive at a hotel or motel is a good time for a dinner picnic of sandwiches, chips, carrot and celery sticks, and cookies; most little kids don't perform well in any kind of restaurant when they're tired and cranky from being cooped up in a car or plane and welcome the chance to relax and explore the room, closets, and bathroom.

ON THE ROAD. Kids always seem to get hungry long before anything is served on a plane or in a restaurant, so I keep a bag of snacks in the car, in the backpack I carry while sightseeing, and let kids choose food to carry in theirs too. Our family is partial to bite-size crackers and cookies, trail mix, grapes (good when frozen), oranges, small boxes of raisins, granola bars, and pretzels. Bananas get too squishy and apples seem to develop bruises. When Gavin was a toddler, we tied a bagel on a string to his car seat so that he could pull it up and mouth it when he felt like chewing on something. For drinks we favor box juices, individual bottles of mineral water (these are expensive but can be refilled with tap water for hikes), and a few cans of soft drinks. If you freeze box juices the night before you leave, they'll stay cold for a long time. All these are easier to handle than pouring from a big jug or thermos while the car is moving (though not as ecologically desirable). For older kids, freeze a plastic squirt or sport bottle half full of water, then add cold water just before you leave.

IN RESTAURANTS. We extend our basic vacation travel principle—that everyone in the family should have fun—to restaurants. This means occasional, sometimes frequent, stops at fast-food restaurants, which have the added advantage of providing large, clean bathrooms that are usually more pleasant than those at service stations. All the restaurants listed in this book welcome children, but if yours are under 3, I advise frequenting those that offer booster seats or high chairs and whenever possible sitting in a booth or outdoor café section instead of in the middle of the restaurant's action. Though some do stock crayons for drawing on paper tablecloths, I always carried a restaurant survival kit of crackers and finger food to munch, washable markers and tablet, and sometimes finger puppets for the wait, as well as a damp washcloth in a ziplock bag. However, our best strategy was not sitting down until the food was on the table. This is easy if you eat in a restaurant in your hotel, as many will allow you to order from your room and tell you when your meal should be ready. Elsewhere, one parent can do the ordering while the other walks around with the kids outside.

Our solution when we want to eat something fancy but Gavin and his friend don't is staying at a hotel with an elegant restaurant; we eat there and order a pizza delivered to our hotel room for the kids. They love watching whatever they want on TV while eating with their fingers—and we are just downstairs in case they need us.

How to Use this Book

Part I, Openers, covers general strategies to make family travel fun, carefree, and rewarding for parents and kids alike and basic information on planning, packing, getting there, staying healthy, and what to expect in the way of weather and seasons in the Northeast.

Part II, Places, provides what you need to know for visiting the geographic areas in the Northeast most interesting for kids; each chapter includes the top kid-pleasing sights and stuff to do, the most family-friendly hotels, and restaurants that welcome kids. For Boston and New York I assembled panels of kids aged 2 to 15 and their parents who reside in or around the cities to assess sights, restaurants, and hotels. Chapters 3 and 4 explore the Northeast's two biggest cities, Boston and New York, both popular destinations, but for totally different reasons. Chapter 5, By the Sea, leads you to what our family considers the three best seaside resort areas: Block Island, Nantucket, and Cape Cod; In Chapter 6, we head inland to the mountains and hills of the Adirondacks in New York State, the Berkshires in Massachusetts, and the White Mountains of New Hampshire. Each of these areas offers a wide variety of things to do and see no matter what your kids' ages and interests—which is why they make such great family destinations.

The top sights listed in Part II are cross-referenced in Part III, Pleasures, which is organized by subjects. Chapters ranging from the most fascinating museums for kids (and why) to exciting opportunities for outdoor action adventures, all organized by state, go into more detail for each entry. If your kids are intrigued by science museums, for example, you can compare the Museum of Science in Boston with New York's Hall of Science and others included in Chapter 8 to see which they might like best.

As anyone who has traveled with kids knows, spots that appeal to 3-year-olds rarely interest teens and vice versa. On the basis of my experience with Gavin and friends' experiences with their kids, I've assessed sports, sights, hotels, restaurants, and more for their appeal to different age groups.

At the end of the book is a directory organized by location to make finding information on attractions as easy as possible, as well as an index.

Why the Northeast

Our home territory, the Northeast, includes all six states in New England—Connecticut, Maine, Massachusetts, New Hampshire, Rhode Island, and Vermont—and the eastern half of New York State—New York City, Long Island, and north, scooping in the Hudson Valley, the Catskills, and the Adirondacks. It's one of the best areas in the United States for family travel because such a wide variety of landscape, culture, history, and activity that's appropriate for families is packed into a small space just right for short trips or long. Here you and your kids can swim in warm ocean bays edged by perfect sand beaches, climb a mountain or ascend the world's most famous skyscraper, camp in the wilderness or visit unique historic sites of America's beginnings, like Paul Revere's House.

THE ESSENTIALS

2

Gearing up to Go

Visitor Services

Connecticut Department of Economic Development, 865 Brook St., Rocky Hill, CT 06067, tel. 203/258–4355 or 800/282–6863. **Maine Publicity Bureau,** Box 2300, Hallowell, ME 04347, tel. 207/623–0363 or 800/533–9595. **Maine Innkeepers Association,** 305 Commercial St., Portland, ME 04101, tel. 207/773–7670. **Massachusetts Office of Travel and Tourism,** 100 Cambridge St., Boston, MA 02202, tel. 617/727–3201 or 800/447–6277 (for Massachusetts Getaway Guide only). **New Hampshire Office of Travel and Tourism,** Box 856, Concord, NH 03302, tel. 603/271–2666 or 800/258–3608 (recorded message about seasonal events). **New York State Division of Tourism,** 1 Commerce Plaza, Albany, NY 12245, tel. 518/474–4116 or 800/225–5697. **Rhode Island Department of Economic Development, Tourism Division,** 7 Jackson Walkway, Providence, RI 02903, tel. 401/227–2601 or 800/556–2484. **Vermont Chamber of Commerce, Department of Travel and Tourism,** Box 37, Montpelier, VT 05601, tel. 802/223–3443. **Vermont Department of Travel and Tourism,** 134 State St., Montpelier, VT 05602, tel. 802/828–3236.

For cities' and local tourism offices, see Chapters 3, 4, 5, and 6.

The **Greater Boston Convention and Visitor's Bureau,** Box 490, Prudential Center, 800 Boylston St., Boston, MA 02199, tel. 617/536–4100, covers an area much wider than just Boston.

Family-Oriented Tour Agencies

Few general tour agencies organize regular tours in the Northeast for families; see Chapter 12 for specific nature, hiking, biking, and boating tours.

Adventure Guides, Inc. (7550 E. McDonald Dr., Scottsdale, AZ 85250, tel. 602/596–0226 or 800/252–7889) arranges adventure-type vacations all over the country, including the Northeast. Pat Dickerman, the owner, is known for her regularly published book, *Adventure Travel in North America.*

Traveling with Children (2313 Valley St., Berkeley, CA 94702, tel. 510/848–0929 or 800/499–0929), though located on the west coast, also offers consultation services to families planning trips to the Northeast and includes families in the Northeast among its clients.

Grandtravel (6900 Wisconsin Ave., Suite 706, Chevy Chase, MD 20815, tel. 301/986–0790 or 800/247–7651) offers tours for people traveling with their grandchildren, in a catalogue as charmingly written and illustrated as a children's book.

No travel agencies in the Northeast currently specialize in family travel or concentrate on planning itineraries in the Northeast. If you don't have an agency you use regularly, use one that belongs to ASTA (American Society of Travel Agents), as they have easy access to the entire network of agents in the organization, from whom they are able to obtain local information on an area to which you want to go.

Additional Resources

Family Travel Guides Catalogue (Carousel Press, Box 6061, Albany, CA 94706, tel. 510/527–5849; send $1 for postage and handling) publishes a catalogue of general and specialized travel guides that includes books of games and short "travel papers" on specific cities and areas, some in the Northeast.

Family Travel Times (45 W. 18th St., 7th Floor Tower, New York, NY 10011, tel. 212/206–0688; $55 per year) is a national newsletter that offers a wealth of helpful tips and up-to-date advice on traveling with children as well as periodic features on destinations in the Northeast.

Specialty Travel Index (305 San Anselmo Ave., San Anselmo, CA 94960, tel. 415/459–4900; $10 per year for 2 issues) lists a number of specialized family vacation offerings in the Northeast, including grandparent/grandchild tours, rafting trips, and more.

When to Go

New England and New York State are year-round destinations; the best seasons for visiting different areas depend on what you want to do. Summer, favored by most families with school-age kids, is pleasantly warm in mountain and coastal regions, but often muggy and very hot in cities. (Summer temperatures in northern coastal and mountain regions can vary as much as 40 degrees, however.) Even so, both New York and Boston attract families with a host of street fairs, festivals, and free outdoor entertainment. Memorial Day is the start of the summer season at mountain and beach resort areas, when festivals and outdoor concerts begin and seasonal museums open; serious summer tourist traffic usually commences only with July 4th weekend. Fall, when leaves begin to turn, is the most colorful season in the countryside. Be warned that many hotels and inns are booked far in advance for leaf peepers and that rates in places such as New Hampshire's White Mountains are

the very highest of the year. By the end of October, however, leaves are off the trees, hunting season begins, and the landscape is gray and bleak, so November is not a good month for family hiking. The early fall at beach resorts is lovely; if your kids are preschoolers this is an ideal vacation time as the water is still warm, but crowds disappear after Labor Day. In the Northeast's cities, fall is exciting: clear weather, pleasant temperatures, and new programs at museums and theaters. Winter is for downhill and cross-country skiing—and every state but Rhode Island is home to ski resorts that have snowmaking equipment. In December cities offer much entertainment specifically for kids and families, but they're usually not very pleasant from January through March—hotel rates reflect this. March is sugaring-off time in northern states. The spring is variable: You may see blizzards as late as April; otherwise it's mud season; avoid outdoor activities in the northern woods for the last two weeks in May and usually into early June because of black-fly season.

What to Pack

See Chapter 1 for information on packing toys, books, and games.

CLOTHING. The Northeast's changeable weather dictates bringing a wide variety of clothing. Even in warm weather be sure to pack sweatshirts, rain gear, long pants, and even a lightweight jacket, along with T-shirts, shorts, and bathing suits. In fall and spring, nights can be very cool; throw in hats, gloves, and jackets. Winters can be very, very cold. Plan on layers so you can add and subtract as needed and remember that all-cotton clothing takes a long time to dry. Let kids help select. Be sure everyone in the family takes comfortable walking shoes—nothing ruins the fun of sightseeing like blistered feet.

INFANTS. Make a list of what you think you'll need for your baby a few weeks, even a month ahead of time. That way you can add to your stacks of travel stuff gradually, during your baby's naps. Check off items as you go and leave basic necessities, like diapers and things you can't spare to pack away early (baby's favorite toy, for example) for the last minute.

OTHER ESSENTIALS. Some items we've found useful when traveling with Gavin are: flashlight (with extra batteries), can opener, Swiss army knife (any kind of folding knife will do), sewing kit, and almost the most important thing—all sizes of locking plastic bags, in which we've stashed everything from a wet bathing suit to soap to a snack to a precious collection of acorns. If your kids are little, bring safety plugs for electrical outlets and a small plug-in night-light.

Necessities like batteries, film, and sunscreen lotion are available almost anywhere, but if you end up buying them at shops on the tourist track, prices can be high. If your kids are still in diapers, buy them (along with wipes) at local supermarkets—hotel sundry shops usually don't sell them (and if they do they're too expensive). Bring an extra pair of your glasses, contact lenses, or prescription sunglasses, and pack any prescription medications you need regularly.

And we always pack a basic first-aid kit:

- bandages, gauze pads, and tape
- antiseptic cream
- thermometer and petroleum jelly
- needle and tweezers for splinters or removing ticks plus matches so we can sterilize
- children's acetaminophen
- small first-aid book

On airlines, the adult baggage allowance applies for children paying half or more of the adult fare. In general, you are entitled to check two bags—neither exceeding 62 inches, or 158 centimeters (length + width + height), or weighing more than 70

pounds (32 kilograms). A third piece may be brought aboard as a carryon; its total dimensions are generally limited to less than 45 inches (114 centimeters), so it will fit easily under the seat in front of you or in the overhead compartment. Diaper bags, like purses, are allowed in addition to carryons; strollers can be checked at the boarding gate and retrieved immediately upon arrival. The FAA details approved models in the free leaflet "**Child/Infant Safety Seats Recommended for Use in Aircraft**" (available from the Federal Aviation Administration, APA–200, 800 Independence Ave. SW, Washington, D.C. 20591, tel. 202/267–3479).

Money for the Road

Traveler's checks are preferable in metropolitan centers; the most widely recognized are **American Express, Citicorp, Diners Club, Thomas Cook,** and **Visa,** which are sold by major commercial banks. Both American Express and Thomas Cook issue checks that can be countersigned and used by you or your traveling companion. Typically the issuing company or the bank at which you make your purchase charges 1% to 3% of the checks' face value as a fee. Record the numbers of checks as you spend them, and keep this list separate from the checks.

Many **automated-teller machines (ATMs)** are tied to international networks such as **Cirrus** and **Plus.** You can use your bank card at ATMs away from home to withdraw money from your accounts or to get cash advances on a credit-card account (if your card has been programmed with a personal identification number, or PIN). There's usually a limit to how much you can get; check in advance. On cash advances you are charged interest from the day you receive the money. Transaction fees for ATM withdrawals outside your home turf may be higher than for withdrawals at home. For specific Cirrus locations in the United States and Canada, call 800/424–7787 (for U.S.

Plus locations, 800/843–7587) and press the area code and first three digits of the number you're calling from (or the calling area where you want an ATM).

Getting There

By Plane

Of all the airports in the Northeast, **Logan International Airport** in Boston (the biggest in New England) is the most kid-friendly. A special carpeted children's play area of climbing structures built to look like an airplane and a fuel truck, a view of the airfield, and kinetic sculptures is located in Terminal C. New York City is served by three major airports; **La Guardia** and **Newark** are cleaner and more pleasant and easier to get around with kids than **JFK. Bradley International Airport** in Windsor Locks, Connecticut, just north of Hartford, is in a central New England location, never crowded, and small. Other major airports are just outside Providence, Rhode Island and Portland, Maine. It's also possible to fly to many small airports in New Hampshire and Vermont and to Albany, New York.

The annual February/March issue of *Family Travel Times* details children's services on dozens of airlines ($10; see Gearing up to Go, *above*.). Many offer special meals for babies and older children if you request them when you reserve. On Delta flights, for example, kids may get a sugared cereal and bananas for breakfast, pizza, macaroni and cheese, chicken nuggets, or a turkey hot dog for lunch, and spaghetti and meatballs or cheeseburgers for dinner, all served with milk and cookies; jars of baby food are provided for the littlest ones. On United's flights into Boston and New York, McDonald's Happy Meals are the kids' choice; infants get baby food. If the airline has no children's meal, order a fruit plate. Playing cards, coloring books and crayons, games and puzzles are just some of the in-flight entertainment

provided. "Kids and Teens in Flight" (free from the U.S. Department of Transportation's Office of Consumer Affairs (R–25, Washington, D.C. 20590, tel. 202/366–2220) offers tips for children flying alone. For other useful tips on air travel with children from toddlers to teens, send for the free pamphlet, "When Kids Fly" put out by Boston's Logan Airport (Massport Public Information Program, Boutwell One, Logan International Airport, East Boston 02128, tel. 617/973–5500). Be sure to include a self-addressed stamped envelope.

KID DISCOUNTS. When you make plane reservations, be sure to state the ages of your children and ask about discounts and special packages available for families. Though it's no longer the norm, some airlines still offer children's discounts on certain flights, and infants under 2 generally fly free on domestic flights when they're held on a parent's lap. In recent years, the best family deals have been periodic "Kids Fly Free" promotions offered by several major airlines; these typically require an accompanying paying adult for each child. One of my friends purchased an American Express Platinum Card only because they so frequently offer free "Companion" tickets that can be used for kids.

BABY ON BOARD. If you'd like a bassinet—not available on all airlines—be sure to request one when you make a reservation. You'll need a bulkhead seat for a bassinet, but be warned—the seat trays in the bulkhead usually fold out of your chair arm and are impossible to use with a child on your lap. You can bring an FAA-approved car seat aboard, if you've bought a seat for your little one or if there's an unoccupied seat for it (your airline may charge for this—check). If you will want formula or baby food on the flight, be sure to request it when you reserve.

By Train

With room for fidgety kids to roam about, train travel can be a great alternative for vacationing families—so long as you have the time and the trains go where you need to go. Snack bars, rest rooms, and water fountains help kids fend off travel boredom; reclining seats, overhead luggage racks, and even sleeping compartments on long-distance routes make travel hours relatively comfortable. Call **Amtrak** (tel. 800/872–7245) for information and reservations.

Amtrak's Empire Corridor Service runs from New York City's Grand Central Terminal to upstate New York along the Hudson Valley; the *Adirondack* (Grand Central to Montreal) stops at points north such as Fort Ticonderoga. Frequent daily service traverses the Northeast Corridor Route from Washington and New York City to Boston, with stops in Connecticut and Rhode Island.

Children ages 2–15 ride for half-fare on Amtrak when accompanied by an adult paying full fare. Children under 2 ride free. For frequent train travelers, 15- and 30-day regional passes are a good value, allowing unlimited stopovers along the route. Peak season, when fares are highest, is from June through August. No reservations are required on Amtrak, but to avoid lines at departure time you can buy tickets in advance from a station agent or travel agent. For an Amtrak Travel Planner (*Amtrak's America*), which includes information on each train route as well as complete vacation packages, tips for traveling with children, and suggestions on what to do on board, call 800/321–8684.

By Car

The Northeast is a compact area with an excellent system of interstate highways, so traveling by car would be our choice throughout the region. However, be warned that in the summer, especially on Friday and Sunday nights, Route 1 up the coast of Maine, roads on Cape Cod, and highways on Long Island can be bumper to bumper. New York City and Boston are inhospitable to cars.

CAR SEATS. State laws require that children under age 4 or weighing less than 40 pounds (regardless of age) must be secured in a child safety seat, and everyone age 4 or older must wear seat belts. If you're renting a car, be sure to reserve a safety seat if needed when you make your reservation.

RENTAL CARS. All major car-rental agencies serve the Northeast. When you call, ask about seasonal promotions, discounts, and possible tie-ins with hotels, airlines, and family attractions. Here are toll-free numbers for some of the top agencies: **Alamo** (tel. 800/327–9633; but located at only the biggest airports); **Avis** (tel. 800/331–1212); **Budget** (tel. 800/527–0700); **Dollar** (tel. 800/800–4000); **Hertz** (tel. 800/654–3131); **National** (tel. 800/227–7368); and **Thrifty** (tel. 800/367–2277).

Be aware that picking up the car in one city and leaving it in another may entail substantial drop-off charges or one-way service fees. Some rental agencies will charge you extra if you return the car *before* the time specified on your contract, too—ask before making unscheduled drop-offs and get any changes in terms recorded in writing. Fill the tank when you turn in the vehicle to avoid being charged for refueling at what you'll swear is the most expensive pump in town.

In general, if you have an accident, you are responsible for the automobile. Car-rental companies may offer a collision damage waiver (CDW), which ranges in cost from $4 to $14 a day. You should decline the CDW only if you are certain you are covered through your personal insurer or credit card company. California, New York, and Illinois have outlawed the sale of CDW altogether.

ROAD CONDITIONS. When driving with kids we've always sought all the information we could get to avoid delays or dangerous road conditions (snow and ice, construction, and so on); in winter, sudden blizzards or freezing rain, and at other times, floods can create highly hazardous situations.

There is no one phone number in the Northeast to check on road conditions, and not all states' numbers include all roads. Connecticut (tel. 203/566–4880), Maine (tel. 800/675–7453, turnpike only, winter only), Massachusetts (tel. 617/374–1234, Smart Route Traveler line for Greater Boston area, Cape Cod, interstates to Rhode Island, New Hampshire and Maine coasts; tel. 800/828–9104, Massachusetts Turnpike), New Hampshire (tel. 603/485–9526), New York (tel. 518/456–2700 or 800/847–8929, Thruway only), Rhode Island (tel. 401/277–1362 or 800/354–9595), Vermont (tel. 802/828–2648, open 7–3:30, 24 hrs during blizzards, floods, other severe weather; in winter, also try 800/429–7623).

Once You're There

In Case of Illness

Before you leave home, ask your pediatrician for any prescriptions you think you may need for your children. Also check with your insurance company to see whether you are covered for hospital emergency room or doctors' visits while in the state you are visiting, and remember to bring insurance cards and forms for every member of the family.

If you're staying in a hotel, resort, or family camp, especially in a rural area, ask about the availability of health care there, including the location of the nearest hospital. Some resorts and camps have medical personnel on staff. Most hotels can furnish lists of local pediatricians and doctors or contact one for you.

To call for an **ambulance** or in the event of other medical emergencies, dial **911**. Some rural areas in the Northeast are not connected to the 911 system; check the front of the phone book for the local number. Regional **Poison Control Centers**: Con-

necticut (tel. 800/343–2722); Maine (tel. 207/871–2950; 800/442–6305 in Maine only); Massachusetts (tel. 617/232–2120 or 800/682–9211); New Hampshire (tel. 603/650–8000); New York, Hudson Valley (tel. 914/353–1000 or 800/336–6997), Long Island (tel. 516/542–2323, 542–2324, 542–2325), New York City (tel. 212/340–4494); Rhode Island (tel. 401/277–5727); Vermont (tel. 802/658–3456).

Staying Healthy

The two health risks common to many areas of the Northeast are poison ivy and Lyme disease. **Poison ivy,** a plant with three leaves on a stem ("leaflets three, let it be" is the rhyme we taught Gavin), flourishes in wooded areas, at the edge of rocks and dunes along the coast, and just about everywhere but city and town locations; it's also the name of the itchy rash caused by the plant's oil rubbing off on a child's (or grown-up's) skin. To prevent it, teach older kids to recognize the plant and avoid touching it, wear long-sleeved shirts and pants when hiking and walking, and wash exposed skin areas (not face!) with strong laundry soap such as Fels-Naphtha after the end of the hike. **Lyme disease,** communicated by deer ticks, is more serious and can lead to chronic arthritis and worse if left untreated. See Hiking *in* Chapter 12 for cautions and treatment.

Childproofing a Hotel Room

Rather than spend your time shrieking "no" every time your naturally curious toddler spies something unsafe to investigate, take a few moments to childproof a hotel room when you arrive (a few hotels now provide childproofed rooms). Bring electrical outlet covers and masking tape (to tape down lamp cords). Remove glasses, ashtrays, matches, and anything else on reachable surfaces. Move a bed against the wall and put pillows around your child so he or she won't fall out.

Places to Eat

In the Northeast, you certainly don't have to stick with fast-food spots to find meals appealing to kids. Many restaurants have special children's menus (usually limited to children age 12 and under), and some allow children to order from the adult menu for half price. Some hotels (*see below*) allow young guests to eat free from children's menus, though convincing a preteen to order from a "small fry" selection is usually tough; I could never get Gavin to do it after he turned 8. Anyway, children's menus are often limited to the burger/hot dog/chicken fingers/grilled cheese school of cuisine. Instead, ask if your kids can share an adult portion—most restaurants that welcome families will try to accommodate smaller appetites.

When you're on the road or in doubt, the reliable New England–based restaurant chain, **Friendly's,** is particularly welcoming to families, with regular special platters for kids that sometimes cost as little as $1.99 (and are superior to the usual kids' menu offerings or fast-food places), kid-size ice-cream desserts, and crayons for the games and pictures on the kids' place mat. You can count on booster seats and high chairs and pleasant, clean bathrooms.

Places to Stay

Among the kids I know, many prefer to stay in a chain hotel or motel rather than a very individual hotel. Part of that is knowing what to expect—one Howard Johnson's looks much like another, including the restaurants—and let's face it, kids are more comfortable with what's familiar. Many of these hotels and resorts now actively court family business, offering special deals such as allowing kids to stay free in a room with their parents. Others let families rent adjoining rooms at discounts, which is a great way for parents to have some privacy. You can get the same effect, often for less money, by staying at an all-suite hotel, an increasingly popular choice for families.

Here are some prominent chains with properties in the Northeast that have recently offered attractive children's programs and discounts. Some of these deals are strictly seasonal or aren't available at all sites, however, so be sure to call for current information:

Best Western (tel. 800/528–1234) allows kids to stay free in their parents' room in most locations, though the maximum age to qualify varies widely, from 2 to 17. Some locations let kids eat free from children's menus.

Choice Hotels (tel. 800/424–6423)—which includes Comfort, Clarion, Quality, Sleep, Rodeway, EconoLodge, and Friendship Inns—allows kids 18 and under to stay free with parents at most locations.

Days Inn (tel. 800/325–2525) allows all kids 12 and under to stay free in their parents' room; at some locations the maximum age extends to 16 or 18.

Four Seasons Hotels and Resorts (tel. 800/332–3442) features the V.I.K. (Very Important Kids) program, with amenity bags filled with goodies and other perks. Video games, toys, children's movies, baby supplies—even child-size furniture—are all available. Guest rooms can be childproofed upon request. Kids under 18 stay free with parents, and adjoining rooms are discounted for families.

Guest Quarters (tel. 800/424–2900) lets children 17 and under stay free with their parents. Some locations offer "Family-Friendly" suites—baby- and childproofed suites that come stocked with emergency baby supplies.

Holiday Inn (tel. 800/465–4329) allows kids 19 and under to stay free in their parents' room. In recent summers kids 12 and under have eaten free at most locations, a program expected to continue.

Howard Johnson Hotels (tel. 800/446–4656) lets kids under 18 stay free with their parents. The free summertime Kids Go HoJo Fun Pack contains crayons, puzzles, stickers, and games with a Sonic the Hedgehog theme.

Hyatt (tel. 800/233–1234) lets kids under 18 stay free in their parents' room and offers 50% discounts on second rooms year-round. At check-in kids are handed a welcoming pack, including a cap. "Frequent stay" kids can earn prizes.

Inter-Continental (tel. 800/327–0200) lets children under 14 stay free in their parents' room. In the northeast only New York City has a hotel in this chain.

Marriott (tel. 800/228–9290) lets kids 17 and under stay free at almost all locations. Recent seasonal promotions have included the "Family Room" program, offering discounts of up to 60% and free kids' meals for 21-day advance payment.

Radisson (tel. 800/333–3333) lets kids 17 and under stay free; a few locations let kids eat free; other packages depend on the individual hotel.

Ramada (tel. 800/272–6232) lets kids 18 and under stay free, and in some locations kids 12 and under eat free.

Ritz-Carlton Hotels (tel. 800/241–3333) allows kids up to age 12 or 18 (depending on location) to stay free; the Boston location has many unique kids' programs and events; see Chapter 3.

Sheraton (tel. 800/325–3535) lets kids 17 and under stay free in their parents' room. During occasional promotions and at some locations, kids 12 and under eat free or for 99¢.

Westin (tel. 800/228–3000) offers the year-round Westin Kids Club with planned activities for kids age 12 and under. Kids receive gifts at check-in; parents receive safety kits. Children under 18 stay free in their parents' room. The only Westin hotels in the Northeast are in New York City and Boston.

For ski resorts offering special kids' programs, see Chapter 13; for individual resorts,

lodges, and guest ranches with special kids' programs, see Chapter 14.

Finding bed-and-breakfasts that welcome young children can be difficult. Many are filled with fragile antiques, serve communal breakfasts of fruit, bran muffins, and yogurt (not exactly child-pleasers), and seldom have TV in the rooms. See Chapters 3, 4, 5, and 6 for B&Bs in specific areas. A few reservation services list B&Bs that welcome children and will match families with accommodations that fit their needs. Unfortunately no single service covers the entire Northeast. Here are two good ones: The American Country Collection–Bed & Breakfast Vermont (984 Gloucester Pl., Schenectady, NY 12309, tel. 518/439–7001) has visited all the more than 100 spots they list in Western Massachusetts, Vermont, and eastern New York State. Covered Bridge Bed & Breakfast Reservations (69 Maple Ave., Norfolk CT 06058, tel. 203/542–5944 or 800/488–3690) covers Connecticut and the Berkshires in Western Massachusetts; listings even include a working llama farm. Of special interest to families are cottages and apartments that come with fully equipped kitchens yet cost less than a downtown hotel room. For other possibilities, see Chapters 3, 4, 5, and 6.

Condo rentals are becoming increasingly popular for families because they usually offer more space for less money and the chance to save even more by cooking your own meals. Best bets for families are those at year-round ski resort areas, which usually offer children's and family programs, family discounts, and a wide variety of sports activities. For these see Chapters 6, 12, 13, and 14. For condos on Cape Cod, see Chapter 5.

Credit Cards

The following credit card abbreviations are used in this guide: AE, American Express; D, Discover; DC, Diners Club; MC, MasterCard; V, Visa.

PART II

PLACES

Major Cities and Family-Friendly Resort Areas

BOSTON

3

ON THE TRAIL OF PAUL REVERE, SWAN BOATS AND DUCKS, AND THE COUNTRY'S BEST ICE CREAM

To Gavin and my panel of kids who live in and around it, Boston is much more than a city where the country's history comes alive, even though its crooked streets are packed with sites they have learned about in school. To them, the home of the Boston Tea Party, Paul Revere's midnight ride, and the "shot heard round the world" is also a place of harbors and rivers and boats of all sizes tied up at wharves designed for walking and exploring. Kids like Boston's contrast of old and new, the many kid-oriented museums and theaters, and the fact that it's a small, clean, cheerful, cozy city.

Though our family loves New York City, we do find Boston more manageable and pleasant and welcoming to families. The one danger (for us, anyway) is concentrating too much on the educational possibilities of its historic sites and museums. You're missing much of Boston's pleasure if you don't picnic in one of the beautiful parks and stroll in one of its fascinating neighborhoods: the North End, the Waterfront, Beacon Hill, Downtown, Chinatown, Back Bay, Charlestown, and, across the Charles River, Cambridge. Each has a distinct flavor, and because Boston is so compact, you can visit more than one in a day if you wish. A weekend is barely enough time to get started; with a week you can begin to know the city.

Boston's suburbs, such as Brookline, have many attractions for kids and are easy to get to by public transportation. Several towns close to Boston are worth visiting for a day of your trip: Lexington and Concord for revolutionary sites; Salem for witch museums; Plymouth for Plimoth Plantation and, of course, the rock.

Boston feels safer than New York, but families should realize that they need to use the same kind of caution they would in any large city—stick to well-lighted streets at night, stay alert, and don't consider walking through Boston Common and the Boston Public Garden after dark. You will not see as many homeless people sleeping or begging for money as you do in New York City. I'm not sure that I would let young teenagers travel all around the city by themselves during the day, but I didn't feel worried when Gavin walked a few blocks back to the hotel himself or confined his explorations to busy Faneuil Hall Marketplace. With small children, your main concern is Boston's crazy drivers; when crossing streets, hang onto energetic little ones. Kids should know what to do and where to go in case they're separated from you.

The Basics

How to Find out What's Going On

The **Greater Boston Convention & Visitors Bureau** (800 Boylston St., Prudential Tower, Box 490, Dept. TPO, Boston 02199, tel. 617/536–4100 or 800/888–5515; open daily 8:30–6) is your best source of information on everything from events to maps to hotel packages; it's the most helpful and well-organized city visitor bureau I've ever dealt with. A free travel planner available by mail includes an events calendar and a folder on family hotel discount packages and restaurants that welcome children; for $4.95 they'll send you the more useful comprehensive travel kit; and for an additional $3.95, they'll put in *Kids Love Boston,* an entertaining large-type guidebook written for kids.

Boston by Phone (tel. 800/373–7400) is a telephone line sponsored by the Visitors Bureau that connects your call for free to restaurants, hotels, shops, attractions, theaters, and more.

VISITOR INFORMATION CENTERS. Boston Common Information Center (140 Tremont St., no phone; Park St. stop on Red Line T; open Mon.–Sat. 8:30–5; Sun. 9–5), on the Tremont Street side of Boston Common, has brochures, free maps, and information on sightseeing tours; here you can purchase subway and bus tourist passes (*see* subway and bus information, *below*). This also is where the Freedom Trail begins (*see* Historic Sites, *below*). **Prudential Center Visitor Kiosk** (800 Boylston St., tel. 617/ 536–4100; open weekdays 8:30–5), in the Center Court of the Prudential Center,

offers similar information. **Cambridge Discovery** (Box 1987, Harvard Sq., Cambridge 02238, tel. 617/497–1630; open Mon.–Sat. 9–6, Sun. 1–5) will help you plan your time in Cambridge with information on places of interest, food, hotels, shopping, and entertainment. At the **Boston National Historical Park Visitor Center** (15 State St., across from Old State House, tel. 617/242–5642, open daily 9–5) knowledgeable and patient park rangers can answer your questions about historic Boston; there are also very clean public bathrooms—highly important, as many of the old buildings on the Freedom Trail have no rest rooms.

NEWSPAPERS, MAGAZINES, AND BOOKS. The following publications are available on newsstands, in supermarkets, and in bookstores:

The Boston Globe (135 William T. Morrissey Blvd., tel. 617/929–2000), Boston's main newspaper, publishes a "Calendar" section every Thursday that highlights family-oriented activities.

The *Boston Parents' Paper* (Box 1777, Boston 02130, tel. 617/522–1515), published monthly, has a calendar of events and happenings for kids. It is available free at libraries, supermarkets, museums, and children's shops.

BOOKS FOR KIDS. *Kidding Around Boston* by Helen Byers (John Muir Publications, 1993), for kids about 8 to 12, contains simple maps and combines a history and sightseeing overview of the various neighborhoods, along with lots of interesting facts.

Kids Love Boston, published by the Greater Boston Convention and Visitors Bureau (*see above*) for the same age group, is shorter, organized by subject (museums, open space, cool for kids, and so on), and includes a short glossary of Boston lingo.

Boston's historic sites meant more to Gavin when he visited them because he'd read up on the Revolution. *Sam the Minuteman* by Nathaniel Benchley (HarperCollins) is an easy-to-read book for 4- to 8-year-olds. *And Then What Happened, Paul Revere?* by Jean Fritz (Scholastic), for kids 6 to 10, tells the story of Revere's life and famous ride in an amusing way. *Johnny Tremain* by Esther Forbes (Dell), for kids 8 to 13, is an exciting novel set in Boston at the time of the Revolution. Chances are your younger kids (3–7) have already read Robert McCloskey's beloved *Make Way for Ducklings* (Puffin Books), about a duck family's search for a home, which they find at the pond in Boston's Public Garden.

Getting into and out of Boston

BY PLANE. Some 50 major airlines fly to Boston's Logan International Airport, about 3 miles northeast of central Boston on the other side of Boston Harbor. If you can, choose a carrier that arrives at Terminal C (at press time, Delta, United, and TWA did) because of Kidport, a special kids' play space.

How to get into Boston: Because traffic through the two tunnels tends to jam up, the fastest and easiest (and most fun, according to Gavin) way to get into the city is the **Airport Water Shuttle** (tel. 617/330–8660 or 800/235–6426), comfortable commuter boats that take seven minutes to cross the harbor between the airport's Boat Dock and Rowes Wharf in downtown Boston. Buses from each terminal transport passengers to the water shuttle. The cost is $8 for adults; children under 12 travel free. A bargain choice is the **subway** (MBTA, the "T") from Airport Station to downtown, which costs only 85¢. Free shuttle buses (Nos. 22 and 33) connect terminals to the T station. Either of these is my choice over

taxis (available outside each terminal, tel. 617/561–1769), which cost about $15 if traffic is light. For general information on all ground transportation call Massachusetts Ground Transportation Information Line (tel. 800/235–6426).

BY TRAIN. On Amtrak (tel. 617/482–3660 or 800/872–7245), the northeast corridor route from Washington, D.C., New York, and Philadelphia ends at Boston's South Station (Atlantic Ave. and Summer St., tel. 617/345–7451), with its big, light-filled concourse busy with food vendors. The Lake Shore Limited, Amtrak's service to and from the Midwest and western New York state destinations, also terminates here. Some trains also stop at Back Bay Station. Commuter trains serving points north and west of the city come into North Station (Causeway and Friend Sts., tel. 617/722–3200).

BY BUS. Greyhound (2 South Station, tel. 800/231–2222) offers direct trips or connections to all major cities in North America. The **Peter Pan Trailways** terminal (555 Atlantic Ave., across from South Station, tel. 617/426–7838) connects Boston with cities in Massachusetts, Connecticut, New Hampshire, and New York.

BY CAR. Three major highways funnel into Boston. Interstate 95 links it with New York City, southern Connecticut, and Providence, and continues north through the city to New Hampshire and Maine. The Massachusetts Turnpike (a toll road known as the "Mass Pike"), I-90, runs east–west through the middle of the state, intersecting with I-91, which goes north to Vermont, and the New York Thruway. In Boston Mass Pike intersects with I-93, the main route from Boston to northwest New England.

Getting Around Boston

Forget driving a car in this city; the central downtown area consists of crooked, narrow streets, mostly one-way (many were originally cow paths leading to and from the

Boston Common). With the exception of several public garages, parking lots are expensive. (One central place to park is the underground garage at Boston Common, scheduled for completion in the fall of 1995.)

TAKE A WALK. Boston is relatively small and compact, with many parks, a long accessible harbor front, and several pedestrian-only marketplaces. Two walking routes are even marked on the sidewalk with a red stripe (the **Freedom Trail**) and a blue stripe (the **Harborwalk**). Sturdy shoes are a must, however, especially on the brick sidewalks of Beacon Hill and the cobblestones of open market spaces such as Faneuil Hall Marketplace. The other pedestrian problem here is the traffic. Beware of aggressive drivers when crossing streets, even if the light is with you.

The oldest part of Boston is a peninsula shaped like a fist, bounded by Boston Harbor to the north and east, the Fort Point Channel to the east, and the Charles River to the west, separating Boston from Cambridge. The focal point of the peninsula is Boston Common and the Public Garden, at the center. To the northeast lies the **North End,** the city's oldest section, whose hodge-podge of streets is the home of the Italian community, with colorful cafés, good-smelling bakeries, and frequent summer festivals. **Beacon Hill,** to the west, has cobblestone streets lined with trees and elegant brick town houses; it's largely a residential area. To the east, wedged between the Common and the waterfront, is **Downtown,** comprising several distinct areas—the department stores of Downtown Crossing, a pedestrian mall, historic sites on the Freedom Trail, Faneuil Hall Marketplace, and the financial district. Just south of it sits **Chinatown,** only a few blocks long, much smaller and less crowded than its New York City counterpart, yet still the third-largest in the United States. **The Waterfront,** with boats docked at every wharf, small parks, the aquarium, and several museums appealing

to kids, borders Boston Harbor. Trees, cafés, boutiques, elegant town houses, the library, Symphony Hall, and a couple of malls line the grid of fashionable **Back Bay,** which begins at the west end of the Public Garden and extends north to the Esplanade. To its west is the **Fenway,** a place of world-class museums, a sprawling park, and the Red Sox ballpark.

Charlestown, across the Charlestown Bridge from the North End, harbors one of the city's highlights for kids, the Charlestown Navy Yard, where the USS *Constitution* is permanently docked. Across the Charles River to the west is **Cambridge,** actually a separate city, home to Harvard University; it's good for people-watching and shopping, especially for teens.

RIDE THE T. Boston's subway is called the T (short for MBTA, Massachusetts Bay Transit Authority), and large signs with a black T in a circle mark the stations. The four lines—green, blue, orange, and red—radiate outward from central Boston, connecting at the hub of downtown stations. Tokens, available at booths or vending machines in each station, cost 85¢ for adults and 40¢ for children 5 to 11, but additional fares are charged for destinations outside a central zone. You may save money by buying 1-, 3-, or 7-day "Boston Passport" Tourist Passes ($5, $9, and $18 respectively, available at Visitor Information Centers, many downtown hotels, train stations, and the airport T station); they offer unlimited travel on the subway and local buses.

If you have a baby or toddler, be aware that on the Green Line trains you must climb several steps to board and must collapse strollers; on all other lines, you can wheel them right on. Note also that in some stations tracks are flush with the platform, so little kids don't realize when they are too close; hold their hands tightly and keep them well back.

Riding the T, except during rush hour, is our preferred way to get around Boston besides walking; kids find it nicer and more fun than the subway in New York. A large subway map is posted in each station, or pick up a pocket copy at the Park Street Station, visitor centers, and some hotels. Most stations seem safe, although, as in all cities, be alert, especially at night, and don't board deserted cars. In our experience the T's token clerks and other passengers are friendly and helpful. You can also call the Massachusetts Bay Transportation Authority's 24-hour travel information line (tel. 617/722–3200 or 800/392–6100) for trip planning directions.

TAKE THE BUS. Boston's bus system provides crosstown service and routes that extend farther into the suburbs than the T does; I find it relatively complicated, though efficient. Rather than poring over bus maps (available at Park Street T station information booth, Downtown Crossing and Government Center stations), call the MBTA's travel information line (see above) for bus numbers, schedules, and stop locations. Buses charge 60¢, 30¢ for kids 5 to 11; you must have exact change. The one-, three-, and seven-day tourist pass (see Ride the T, above) is also accepted on downtown buses.

HIRE A TAXI. Unlike New York, Boston is not a taxi town. You need to head for a hotel taxi stand or telephone for a cab. Two companies that offer 24-hour service are **Checker** (tel. 617/536–7000) and **ITOA** (Independent Taxi Operators Association; tel. 617/426–8700). Boston's one-way streets and tangled traffic make for convoluted routes that add up; the current rate is $1.50 when you get in the cab, $2.10 per mile thereafter.

Family-Friendly Tours

(**7–12**) **Boston by Little Feet.** Games, activities, and amazing facts (we learned that the City Hall Plaza contains 2½ million bricks) fill these one-hour downtown walking tours that introduce kids to history and architecture. Stops at both new and historic

buildings (some on the Freedom Trail) give kids a sense of more than just the "old stuff," as one 10-year-old puts it. Children must be accompanied by an adult.
Boston by Foot, 77 N. Washington St., tel. 617/367–2345. Meet on Congress St. at Statue of Samuel Adams in front of Faneuil Hall. Cost: $5. Reservations advised holidays and peak weekends. May–Oct., Sat. 10, Sun. 2.

(**7–15**) **Boston Harbor Tours.** Viewing Boston and all its piers and fishing boats from the water gave us a totally new sense of the city. For kids we favor one of the shortest tours: Bay State Cruise's 55-minute narrated trip around the inner harbor. You can get off at Charlestown Navy Yard to explore the USS *Constitution* (see below), then board another boat an hour or so later.
Bay State Cruise Company, 67 Long Wharf (red ticket booth near Marriott Hotel), Boston 02110, tel. 617/723–7800. Cost: $5 adults, $3 kids.

(**4–15**) **Charles River Boat Company Tours.** We boarded one of these single-deck boats for a 50-minute narrated ride up the Cambridge side of the Charles River and back down the Boston side. The views of the two skylines are truly special.
Pickup at Museum of Science or CambridgeSide Galleria Lagoon, tel. 617/621–3001. Cost: $6 adults, $4 kids 3–12. Open Apr.–Oct., daily noon–5.

(**7–15**) **Freedom Trail.** If your kids are history buffs, they may enjoy the free 90-minute guided tour of the most centrally located sites on the Freedom Trail (see Historic Sites, below) led by the National Park's rangers. How interesting it is to kids depends partly on the ranger leading the tour, but it *is* free.
National Historical Park Visitor Center, 15 State St. 02109, tel. 617/242–5642.

(**5–10**) **Historic Neighborhood Foundation.** Several 90-minute walking tours geared for kids focus on things like how cobblestone walks were built). The "Make Way for Ducklings" walk, our favorite (for kids between 5 and 8), follows the route taken by Mr. and Mrs. Mallard in Robert McCloskey's book from Boston Common through Beacon Hill and around to the Public Garden.

👪 2 Boylston St., tel. 617/426–1885. Cost: $5. Reservations advised. Mid-May–Aug., Sat.

(👫 7 – 15) Trolley Tours. Three different trolley companies offer 90-minute narrated city tours that are fun for kids. You can get on or off at any of the 14 to 17 stops, then board another trolley when you're ready to move on. A good starting point is Park Street, in front of the Boston Common.

👪 Boston Trolley Tours (blue trolleys), Box 267, Boston 02132, tel. 617/876–5539; Beantown Trolley (red trolleys), 435 High St., Randolph 02368, tel. 617/236–2148; Old Town Trolley (green and orange trolleys), 329 W. Second St., Boston 02127, tel. 617/269–7150. Cost: $14–$15 adults, $5 kids 6–12. 11 tours daily, 9–6.

Pit Stops

The best places to find clean, pleasant bathrooms: all museums, though only the Children's Museum and the Museum of Science have diaper-changing facilities; National Park Visitors' Centers at the Charlestown Navy Yard and along the Freedom Trail downtown (no bathrooms in most historic buildings along the trail); major department stores; shopping malls and markets such as the Prudential Center, Copley Place, City Place in the Transportation Building, CambridgeSide Galleria, and Faneuil Hall Marketplace; the Christian Science Center; the Boston Public Library on Boylston Street; and South Station. In Cambridge your best bet, outside of museums, are the second-floor rest rooms in the Coop in Harvard Square. If you're desperate, most shops will allow children to use their private facilities.

Emergency Treatment: Doctors, Dentists, and Hospitals

FOR MINOR PROBLEMS. Inn-House Doctor (tel. 617/859–1776) is a 24-hour, seven-day-a-week service that provides doctors (including pediatricians) who make house calls to hotels, apartments, and bed-and-breakfasts. A doctor returns your call in 15 minutes and arrives within an hour. Expect to pay between $150 and $250.

FOR SERIOUS EMERGENCIES. Children's Hospital (300 Longwood Ave., tel. 617/735–6000; emergency room tel. 617/735–6611) is the best place to call. Emergency dental services are available through Inn-House Doctor (see For Minor Problems, above) and through the Metropolitan District Dental Society (tel. 508/651–3521).

24-HOUR PHARMACY. Phillips Drug Store (155 Charles St., Boston, tel. 617/523–1028 or 617/523–4372).

Baby-Sitters

At many of Boston's hotels the concierge keeps a list of screened staff members willing to baby-sit when not on duty. Often this is the least expensive route to go. Two agencies are: Personal Touch (187 Summer St., tel. 617/451–2052), which uses screened college students and professional women and charges $12 per hour for one to three children, with a four-hour minimum, billed to your hotel room; and Parents in a Pinch (45 Bartlett Crescent, Brookline, tel. 617/739–5437), which has trained and screened sitters, many of them students, and charges about $60 (half-day or evening) to $100 (full-day) for two children.

When to Go

Boston has so many museums and indoor attractions for kids that there's plenty to do here even in the coldest winter months. In early April there's still a possibility of a blizzard. From mid-April, when the swan boats return to the Public Garden, through June, and in September and October, the temperature is generally delightful for walking around. For festivals, especially those in the North End, summer is the best time, though the city can be very hot and muggy, with occasional heat waves in the 90s. When that happens, there are many pleasant ways to get out on the water where it's cooler, or head for beaches.

Scoping out Boston

Serendipities

Of the sights my Boston kids' panel consider most "Boston," a surprising number turn out to be free or very inexpensive.

IN THE PUBLIC GARDEN AND ON THE COMMON

(0 – 8) **Ride on a Swan Boat.** The oldest and most famous children's attractions in the city are the pedal-powered Swan Boats (boatswains sit behind a swan shape) that circle the Public Garden's Lagoon, a hit ever since they debuted in 1877. Rides last 12 minutes, just long enough for little kids to want a second one. Other *Make Way for Ducklings* landmarks hereabouts: the shiny **bronze statues** of the Mallard brood just through the gates at the corner of Beacon and Charles streets; and the **banks of the Lagoon,** where well-behaved and well-fed ducks will soon gather if you arrive with a bag of bread crumbs (one prime spot is by the large weeping willow at the base of the bridge).
On the Lagoon, Boston Public Gardens, near Boylston and Charles Sts. Park St. stop on Red Line. Cost: $1.25 adults, 75¢ kids under 13. Open July–Aug., daily 10–5; mid-Apr.–June and late Aug.–mid-Sept., daily 10–4.

(1 – 10) **Wade in the Frog Pond.** On a hot summer day, it's a Boston tradition for kids to wade and splash in this large, shallow concrete depression in the Common below

the Soldiers and Sailors monument. Just about every little kid on my Boston panel listed this as one of the "most fun things to do" in the city.
North side of the Common, just in from Beacon St. and the State House.

BACK BAY

(6 – 13) **Stand inside a glass globe at the Mapparium.** We felt as though we were at the center of the world when we walked out on the glass catwalk across this unique 30-foot-diameter sphere that portrays the earth in stained glass. Constructed in the 1930s (the political boundaries are still those of the world in 1932), it has 608 panels of glass, each ¼ inch thick, illuminated from outside by 300 electric lights. Voices make intriguing echoes inside.
Christian Science Church Center, 1 Norway St. (Massachusetts and Huntington Aves.), tel. 617/450–3790 or 617/450–2000. Symphony or Prudential stops on Green Line. Free. Open Tues.–Fri. 9:30–4, Sat. 12–4.

(5 – 12) **Old John Hancock Building weather forecast.** A column of light panels on the Old John Hancock Building (not the new Hancock skyscraper) will give you the weather prediction if you can interpret the code. A simple rhyme helps kids remember it: "Steady blue, clear view/ Flashing blue, clouds due/Steady red, rain ahead/Flashing red, snow instead." In baseball season, flashing red means the Red Sox game is postponed.
Corner of Berkeley and Stuart Sts.

TRAINS AND SUBWAYS

(3 – 10) **Five-Minute Train Ride.** An incredibly cheap (85¢ adults, 45¢ kids 5–11, free under 5) and short real train excursion is the five-minute ride from refurbished South Station (near the Children's Museum) to Back Bay Station (not far from the Swan Boats at the Public Garden).

(2 – 13) **Ride in the First Subway Car.** Kids who've never traveled by subway usually find staring down the dark tunnel and glimpsing a lighted station ahead fun. Avoid rush hours if you can.

NEIGHBORHOODS

(**ii ALL**) **North End.** Boston's Italian-American district starts at Hanover Street or Salem Street and spreads north. Zigzag up the side streets until a good bakery smell draws you into a café. Food and festivals pull us to this neighborhood, along with a few Freedom Trail sites such as Paul Revere's House and Old North Church (see Historic sites, *below*). Hanover Street is lined with cafés, all with different atmospheres. Dairy Fresh Candies (57 Salem St.) displays all manner of sweets, and on Prince Street, one door in from Salem Street, Parizale's Bakery sells all shapes and sizes of bread. You can watch cheese being made at Purity Cheese (corner of Cross and Endicott Sts., Tues.–Fri. mornings). Don't come on a Sunday, when many shops are closed unless there's a festival on. Two of our favorites are the festivals of St. Joseph at the end of July and St. Anthony (the largest) at the end of August.

(**ii 11–15**) **Harvard Square, Cambridge.** The place where Gavin and his teenage friends hanker to hang out is around Harvard Square, which isn't a square at all but the chaotic intersection of Massachusetts Avenue, Brattle Street, and John F. Kennedy Street. It's right outside the gates of Harvard University, and the atmosphere is youthful and eccentric; teens may tell you, "Do you have to walk around with us? Couldn't we meet you someplace in an hour or two? ..." For funky used clothing and T-shirt shops, bookstores (we last counted 25), cafés, and street performers from bagpipers to magicians, it can't be beat. Don't miss the chess players at Au Bon Pain right on the Square; the zany Harvard Lampoon building on Mt. Auburn Street; or the Harvard Coop, across from the Red Line T station (see Shopping, *below*).

ALL AROUND THE TOWN

(**ii 3–12**) **"Sidewalk Sam's" artworks.** Every summer for more than 25 years Bob Guillemin has decorated Boston's sidewalks with pastel and paint reproductions of masterpieces. Look for them—and him—on Boston Common, City Hall Plaza, Copley Square, Downtown Crossing, Faneuil Hall Marketplace, or South Station.

(**ii 2–12**) **Animal statues.** Boston's public sculptures include many animals. In front of F.A.O. Schwarz (corner of Boylston and Berkeley Sts.; Arlington stop on Green Line T) you can't miss the 12-foot-tall **bronze bear,** which weighs 6,112 pounds. Atop Faneuil Hall (in Dock Square; State St. stop on Orange or Blue Line T) is a copper-gilded **grasshopper weathervane** that's been spinning since 1742, supposedly a symbol of good luck. The four huge **marble Foo dogs** (to us they look like lions) at the base of the 36-foot-high gate at the entrance to Chinatown (Beach and Edinboro Sts.) are said to guard Chinatown against evil spirits. And of course there are the **ducklings** in the Public Garden (see *above*).

Monuments, Markets, and Historic Sites

See the appropriate chapters in Part III, Pleasures, for sites whose costs and hours are not given below.

IN BOSTON

(**ii 10–15**) **African Meeting House and Black Heritage Trail.** The oldest African-American church in the United States helped escaped slaves find safe houses along the Underground Railroad. Boston has a surprising wealth of sites important in black history—in 1790, Massachusetts was the only state with free black citizens and no slaves—and the National Park Service offers a guided walking tour, called the Black Heritage Trail. 🏠 *8 Smith Court at Joy St., tel. 617/742–5415. Bowdoin stop on Blue Line T. Free.*

(**ii ALL**) **Boston Waterfront.** The renovated waterfront, where clipper ships once docked, is now a place for watching boats, sitting in cafés and parks, visiting the Aquarium (*see below*) and just strolling. The official HarborWalk route is marked with a blue line along the sidewalk (maps available at Boston Common Information Kiosk or National Park Service Visitor's Center at 15 State St.). See Chapter 7.

🏢 *Follow Atlantic Ave.*

(👫 ALL) Faneuil Hall Marketplace (also called **Quincy Market**). A shop-lined cobblestoned plaza in and around copperdomed Quincy Market, facing Faneuil Hall, is one of our favorite places for people-watching, free entertainment, and food stalls (*see* Eats and Shopping, *below*). See Chapter 7.

🏢 *State and Congress Sts., tel. 617/338–2323. State St. stop on Blue Line T.*

(👫 7 – 15) Freedom Trail. A prominent red line in the sidewalk marks a 3-mile walking route past 16 colonial or revolutionary landmarks. It's one of the city's chief attractions; we found the walk tiring, however. Focus on the sites that really interest kids (listed separately below). You can pick up brochures on the trail from the National Park Service Visitor Center (*see above*). See *also* Chapter 7.

(👫 5 – 15) John Hancock Tower Observatory. The observation deck on the 60th floor of the tallest skyscraper in New England is definitely the best place to get an overview of Boston. See Chapter 7. *200 Clarendon St, tel. 617/572–6429.*

(👫 8 – 15) Old Granary Burying Ground. Old shady graveyards appeal to my family; wedged between buildings on a busy modern street you'll find this historic one, where Paul Revere, Sam Adams, and John Hancock are buried. The tilting slate headstones, some from as early as 1660, are gruesomely decorated with old-fashioned skulls and crossbones (no rubbings permitted).

🏢 *at Tremont and Park Sts. Park St. stop on Red Line T.*

(👫 7 – 15) Old North Church. The code was "One if by land, two if by sea," and when two lanterns were hung in the steeple

of this church in April 1775, Paul Revere galloped off on his midnight ride, warning the militia that the British were arriving by sea. A brief stop to sit in the box pews here will interest even kids who aren't mad about history. Make sure you visit the small shop and museum next door, which displays an old musket actually fired in the battle at Lexington, and the little garden in back.

🏢 *193 Salem St., tel. 617/523–6676. Haymarket stop on Orange or Green Line T, then 10-min walk. Admission free. Open daily 9–5; Sun. services at 9, 11, and 4.*

(👫 10 – 15) Old South Meetinghouse. Built in 1729 as a Puritan Church, this meetinghouse was where issues of the day were argued in public; revolutionists gathered here to disguise themselves as "Indians" on the night of the Boston Tea Party. Older kids may like the dramatic recorded versions of the Tea Party debate, piped into the box pews via headphones; younger kids may only want to look at the model of Boston. The gift shop has many good kids' books about the Revolution. Prep your kids with some history before visiting here—and don't stay too long.

🏢 *310 Washington St., at Milk St., tel. 617/482–6439. State St. stop on Orange or Blue Line T. Cost: $2.50 adults; $1 kids 6–18. Open Apr.–Oct., daily 9:30–5; Nov.–Mar., daily 10–4.*

(👫 5 – 15) Paul Revere's House. The tiny house where Paul Revere lived when he made his famous ride—the oldest house in Boston—is worth a stop even for kids who aren't interested in famous houses. See Chapter 7.

🏢 *19 North Sq., tel. 617/523–1676.*

(👫 8 – 15) State House. Built in 1795 on land that was once John Hancock's pasture, this impressive gold-domed building with marble staircases is still Massachusetts' capitol building. Kids on my Boston panel, however, rated it "not very interesting" except when they could watch the legislature in session (for a schedule, call 617/727–2860). A huge wooden fish, called the Sacred Cod, hangs in the Senate Chamber. Self-guided tour brochures are available at the information desk; ask for the special children's guide. ᴁ *Beacon St. at Park St. (across from the Common), tel. 617/727–3676. Across from the Boston Common. Park St. stop on Red Line T. Admission free. Open weekdays 9–5.*

CHARLESTOWN

6+ **Bunker Hill Monument.** The site of the first major battle of the American Revolution, the Battle of Bunker Hill (a misnomer—the site is actually named Breed's Hill), offers a small museum and a panoramic view. If you can, visit during the annual live reenactment of the battle in mid-June (for information call 617/241–9511). See Chapter 7.
ᴁ *Breed's Hill, Monument Ave., Charlestown, tel. 617/242–5641.*

ALL **Charlestown Navy Yard.** At the Navy Yard, where warships were built for more than 170 years, you can spend a couple of hours savoring the waterfront sights and it won't be enough. The original Yard, now a National Park, is a virtual museum of American shipbuilding; the other 100 acres include gardens, old granite buildings converted to offices and condominiums, and a beautiful 1½–mile waterfront walk. Stop first at the National Park Service Visitor Center (good bathrooms) for a free map. Friendly park rangers will help you plan your time, or you can take their free 90-minute tour (it involves a lot of walking and seems geared to older kids.) You can go aboard two ships: the USS *Constitution,* Boston's number-one attraction (*see* Museums, *below*), and a World War II destroyer, the USS *Cassin Young,* which you can board. Also, don't miss the display of ship models at the **Boston Marine Society** in Building 32. The best place for lunch? The light-filled Atrium Cafe in Building 149 opposite the parking garage. In summer, "The Whites of Their Eyes," an exciting half-hour multimedia reenactment of the battle of Bunker Hill is presented in the **Bunker Hill Pavilion** not far from the USS *Constitution.* Between April and October

the easiest (and most enjoyable) way to get here is by water shuttles (run by Boston Harbor Cruises and Bay State Cruise Company) from Long Wharf, which cost just $1, or on Bus 93 from Haymarket. ᴁ *Constitution Rd., Charlestown, tel. 617/242–5601. Admission free, except for "The Whites of Their Eyes" ($3 adults, $1.50 under 16, $8 family) and U.S.S. Constitution Museum ($3 adults, $1.50 kids 6–16). Visitor Center and most attractions open daily 9–5. Parking.*

LEXINGTON AND CONCORD. The first battle of the American Revolution took place in these two towns, respectively 12 and 20 miles from Boston.

8–15 **Battle Green.** A number of sites are clustered in the center of Lexington, on Lexington Green: the **Minuteman Statue**; yellow wood-framed **Buckman Tavern** (tel. 617/862–5598), where the Minutemen met on April 19, 1775; and the small **Lexington Visitor Center** (1875 Massachusetts Ave., tel. 617/862–1450) with rest rooms and a diorama of the April 19th battle.

10–15 **Minuteman National Historical Park.** The first battles in the Revolution were fought along this 20-mile route. See Chapter 7.
ᴁ *Battle Road Visitors Center, 1 mi from Battle Green, off Rte. 2A, Concord, tel. 508/862–7753; North Bridge Visitor Center, 171 Liberty St., Concord, tel. 508/369–6993.*

8–14 **Orchard House.** Fans of Louisa May Alcott's books may want to make a pilgrimage to her home. Do take the informative tour. See Chapter 7.
ᴁ *399 Lexington Rd., Box 353, Concord, tel. 508/369–4118.*

10–15 **Walden Pond State Reservation.** Little of Thoreau's solitude is left: The nature trails are crowded, and in summer boaters, fishermen, and swimmers swarm over the pond. To our disappointment only a cairn of stones marks Thoreau's cabin site,

but we added to the pile, created by travelers from all corners of the globe.
🏠 *Rte. 126 off Rte. 2, Concord, tel. 508/369–3284. Cost: $5 per car. Mother's Day–Memorial Day and Labor Day–Columbus Day, weekends 8–7; Memorial Day–Labor Day, daily 8–7.*

SALEM. Twenty miles northeast of Boston (drive Rte. 1A north, or take Bus 450 or 455 from Haymarket, or Rockport train from North Station), Salem is a good place for a day trip. *See Museums, below,* for all the witch-related attractions, which are the real draw here for kids.

(👫 **12–15**) **House of the Seven Gables.** The inspiration for Nathaniel Hawthorne's famous novel of the same name, this dark, almost black house with imposing peaked gables is brooding and compelling from outside, cozy inside. The 10-minute audiovisual retelling of the novel that's presented is worthwhile even if you have read the book. Climbing up the twisting secret staircase is the main attraction for kids on my Boston panel.
🏠 *54 Turner St., tel. 508/744–0991. Cost: $6.50 adults, $4 kids 13–17, $3 kids 6–12. Combination ticket with Pioneer Village available. Open May–Dec., daily 10–4:30, July and Aug., daily 9:30–5:30; Jan.–Apr., Sun. 12:30–4:30.*

(👫 **5–13**) **Pioneer Village.** Some kids on my Boston panel prefer this smaller-scale living history village, with its intriguing dugout houses, to Plimoth Plantation (*see below*). *See Chapter 7.*
🏠 *Forest River Park, Salem, tel. 508/745–0525.*

PLYMOUTH. Expect to see many tour buses crammed into this small town 41 miles southeast of Boston. Cranberries, Pilgrim sites, unique living history museums, and tacky souvenir shops make up its wide appeal. The information booth on Water Street (tel. 508/746–4770) has walking tour maps. For information, write to **Destination**

Plymouth (Box 4001, Plymouth 02361, tel. 800/872–1620 or 508/747–4161).

(👫 **5–13**) **Cranberry World.** The Ocean Spray Visitor Center in the midst of the Massachusetts cranberry bogs turned out to be both fun and educational for us. The 45-minute tour ends with a juice-tasting. *See Chapter 7.*
🏠 *225 Water St., tel. 508/747–2350.*

(👫 **7–14**) **Plimoth Plantation, *Mayflower II*, and Hobbamock's Homesite.** More than any other living history museum in the Northeast, this village—thatched-roof dwellings, a replica of the *Mayflower,* and an Indian settlement—tries to be completely authentic. *See Chapter 7.*
🏠 *Warren Ave., Rte. 3A, tel. 508/746–1622. Take Rte. 3 south to exit 4, then follow signs.*

(👫 **5–15**) **Plymouth Rock.** The rock marking the spot where the Pilgrims landed is small and disappointing, but, says Gavin, "you have to see it." *See Chapter 7.*
🏠 *Water St., Plymouth, no phone.*

Museums

IN BOSTON

(👫 **4–10**) **Boston Tea Party Ship and Museum.** Anchored at the Congress Street bridge, the *Beaver II* is a fairly authentic replica of one of the British ships made famous by the Boston Tea Party in 1773. *See Chapter 8.*
🏠 *Congress St. Bridge, tel. 617/338–1773. South Station stop on Red Line T.*

(👫 **ALL**) **Children's Museum.** Plan on spending at least several hours in this, the very best children's museum in the Northeast, with four floors full of imaginative touch-look-discover-play exhibits (*see Chapter 8*). Most crowded on a rainy Sunday. The Computer Museum (*see below*) is next door.
🏠 *Museum Wharf, 300 Congress St., tel. 617/426–6500, 617/426–8855 for event info. South Station stop on Red Line T.*

👫 8+ Computer Museum. A converted wool warehouse next to the Children's Museum (*see above*) houses two floors of hands-on exhibits in the world's only museum devoted to the computer—a must for computer lovers, especially those over 10. See Chapter 8.

🏛 *Museum Wharf, 300 Congress St., tel. 617/426–2800. South Station stop on Red Line T.*

👫 7+ Isabella Stewart Gardner Museum. This museum, designed to look like a 15th-century Italian palace, has plenty of treasures that appeal to children, including a room with leather walls and paintings and ceramics of animals. See Chapter 8.

🏛 *280 The Fenway, tel. 617/566–1401. Ruggles/Museum stop on Green Line T.*

👫 13+ John F. Kennedy Library and Museum. Better than any other museum dedicated to a President, this one conveys the reality of an exciting election campaign and Kennedy's presidency—through televised commercials, speeches, and debates, displays of newspapers and magazines of the day, and re-created settings of campaign headquarters and offices. The building itself is spectacular, and beautiful willows shade the grounds on the University of Massachusetts campus.

🏛 *Columbia Point, tel. 617/929–4567. Cost: $5 adults, $1 kids 6–15. Open daily 9–5.*

👫 8+ Museum of Fine Arts. The MFA, Boston's counterpart to New York's Metropolitan Museum (though not quite as great), has almost 200 galleries of masterpieces and excellent art programs for kids and families. See Chapter 8.

🏛 *465 Huntington Ave., tel. 617/267–9300. Ruggles/Museum stop on Green Line T.*

👫 2+ Museum of Science. We spent about three hours at this huge museum of 400 interactive exhibits on the Charles River between Cambridge and Boston. We consider it the best science museum in the Northeast. See Chapter 8.

🏛 *Science Park, Boston, tel. 617/723–2500. Science Park stop on Green Line T.*

👫 6+ Sports Museum of New England, Cambridge. Located in the CambridgeSide Galleria (see Shopping, *below*), this new museum of interactive exhibits is well-placed for families with both sports aficionados and shoppers. See Chapter 8.

🏛 *100 CambridgeSide Pl., CambridgeSide Galleria, tel. 617/787–7678. Kendall Sq. stop on Red Line T (free shuttle to Galleria) or Lechmere stop on Green Line T.*

ACTON

👫 ALL Discovery Museums. Out front, Bessie, a green dinosaur sculpture, announces these two special museums 40 miles from Boston. The **Children's Museum** (ages 1–8), set in a converted Victorian house, is like a huge playhouse, with a whale video in a closet, a room full of Legos for building, and much more. The small, light-filled **Science Museum** (ages 6 and up) is modern, with an octagonal-windowed tower and a hands-on philosophy. Unfortunately the museums have different hours in winter, and at busy times there's a line to get in.

🏛 *177 Main St., Rte. 27, Acton, tel. 508/264–4200. Cost: $5 to visit one museum, $8 for both. Children's Museum open Tues.–Sun. 9–4:30; Science Museum open Tues.–Sun. 9–4:40.*

BROOKLINE

👫 5–12 Museum of Transportation. Inside a two-story carriage house with brick walls, wood beams, and archways, you'll find a museum of changing car exhibits that try to evoke the era in which the car was built. The vehicles include a police motorcycle, an old taxi, and a dune buggy that kids can actually climb into. Materials are provided for kids to design their own cars in the young inventors' workshops each weekend.

🏛 *15 Newton St., in Larz Anderson Park, Brookline, tel. 617/522–6547 or 617/522–6140. By car: Rte. 9 west to Lee St., then left. By T: Cleveland Circle stop on Green Line (then*

Bus 51 to museum. Cost: $4 adults, $2 kids under 12. Open Wed.–Sun. 10–5.

CHARLESTOWN

(👫 4+) USS *Constitution* and Museum, Charlestown. The USS *Constitution*, nick-named "Old Ironsides," is in dry dock for repairs until 1997, but a short tour is still given. The museum presents a video tour of the ship and hands-on exhibits. See Chapter 8; see *also* Charlestown Navy Yard under Historic Sites, *above*.
🏠 *Charlestown Navy Yard, Charlestown, tel. 617/426–1812.*

SALEM

(👫 8+) Salem Wax Museum of Witches and Seafarers. The most interest-ing wax museum in the Northeast offers activities for kids. See Chapter 8.
🏠 *Derby St., Salem, tel. 509/740–2929.*

(👫 7+) Salem Witch Museum. Figures in stage sets dramatize the history of the famous witch trials in this imposing museum. Not for little kids. The **Witch Dungeon Museum** nearby (16 Lynde St., tel. 508/744–9812) presents a live reenactment of a witch trial and tour of a dungeon. See Chapter 8.
🏠 *Washington Sq., off Washington St., Salem, tel. 508/744–1692.*

WENHAM

(👫 4–13) Wenham Museum. This collec-tion of dolls and dollhouses sponsors delightful special events for kids, such as a teddy bear parade. See Chapter 8.
🏠 *132 Main St. (Rte. 1A), Wenham, tel. 508/468–2377.*

Animals

IN BOSTON

(👫 ALL) Franklin Park Zoo. Covering 72 acres, this zoo has among its exhibits the world-class African Tropical Forest, with gorillas and hippos, baboons and crocodiles.

The Children's Zoo is best for kids 3–8. See Chapter 9.
🏠 *Circuit Dr., Franklin Park, Dorchester, tel. 617/442–2002.*

(👫 ALL) New England Aquarium. Located on the waterfront, the enormously popular aquarium is easy to get to, air-condi-tioned, and all indoors. Best features: the 4-story main tank, circled by spiraling ramps, and the touch tank. See Chapter 9.
🏠 *Central Wharf, Boston, tel. 607/973–5200.*

AROUND BOSTON

(👫 2–11) Drumlin Farm Education Cen-ter and Wildlife Sanctuary. This demonstra-tion farm and nature center 22 miles west of Boston, is a place to see farm animals as well as New England wildlife exhibits and has big grassy fields for running and kite-fly-ing. See Chapter 9.
🏠 *South Great Rd. (Rte. 117), South Lincoln, tel. 617/259–9807.*

(👫 1–12) New England Alive. Though treating injured and orphaned animals is the center's main purpose, kids can pat baby animals and view New England wildlife. See Chapter 9.
🏠 *185 High St. (Rtes. 1A and 133), Ipswich, tel. 508/356–7013.*

Green Space

A chain of parks stretching from Boston Common west, many of which were designed by Frederick Law Olmsted, are called the Emerald Necklace. For other parks outside but near the city, see Chapter 10.

IN BOSTON

(👫 ALL) Arnold Arboretum. More than 6,000 varieties of trees and shrubs (all labeled) adorn 265 beautiful acres of open spaces and ponds, hills, and ravines in this Harvard-run botanical garden designed by Frederick Law Olmsted. On a sunny day its roads (closed to cars) and paths are filled with families promenading and pushing strollers. Among the park's treasures is the huge 100-year old cork tree, whose massive low-slung branches sometimes hold as many as 10 climbers at once. (Sadly, the impact of kids jumping down and compacting the earth around its roots is killing the tree.) Best times to come are in May and June, especially on Lilac Sunday, when morris dancers perform.

🛍 *125 Arborway (Rtes. 1 and 203), Jamaica Plain 02310, tel. 617/524–1718 or 617/ 524–1717 (for recorded information). Forest Hills stop on Orange Line T, then walk 2 blocks northeast to main gate. Admission free. Open daily dawn–dusk.*

(**👫 ALL**) **Boston Common.** The 50-acre Common, the oldest public park in the United States (since 1634!), has big old trees and grass fields. It began as a cow pasture, and for nearly 200 years it was the site of public executions; today, the central downtown location makes it a traditional play spot for kids in all seasons. It felt small and cramped to our family, though, and it isn't as pretty as the Public Garden (see below) across Charles Street. A small fenced playground has picnic tables and a climber with a big blue tube to slide through; nearby, the Frog Pond lets kids splash and wade in summer, and there's a good sledding hill. This is not a place to walk after dark.

🛍 *Bounded by Beacon, Park, Tremont, Boylston, and Charles Sts. For information, call Boston Parks and Recreation Dept., tel. 617/ 635–4505. Park St. stop on Red Line T.*

(**👫 ALL**) **Boston Public Garden.** Across Charles Street from the Common lies the lovely 24-acre Public Garden. No child under 10 should miss riding in the Swan Boats (see Serendipities, above). Meandering short pathways under drooping willows, a miniature suspension bridge crossing over a 4-acre pond with ducks, and statues of ducks and George Washington make it ideal for small children.

🛍 *Bounded by Arlington, Boylston, Beacon, and Charles Sts. For information, call Boston*

Parks and Recreation Dept., tel. 617/635– 4505. Arlington stop on Green Line T.

(**👫 ALL**) **Boston Harbor Islands State Park.** Seventeen islands scattered across Boston Harbor constitute this park, where we love to picnic on a hot, muggy summer day. A pedestrian-only ferry from Long Wharf sails to the largest, Georges Island. See Chapter 10.

🛍 *Water taxis: Bay State Cruises, 67 Long Wharf, tel. 617/723–7800. The islands: Dept. of Environmental Management, 349 Lincoln St., Bldg. 45, Hingham 02043, tel. 617/740–1605.*

(**👫 ALL**) **Lower Basin and the Esplanade.** Along the Charles River from the Museum of Science to Harvard Bridge (Massachusetts Ave.) runs a stretch of grassy spaces, winding paths, duck-filled lagoons, and several playgrounds (see Action, below). In July the Boston Pops perform at Hatch Shell (see Entertainment and the Arts, below). From the open, grassy Cambridge side of the river you have a good view of Harvard's rowing crews skimming by; there's fine biking and in-line skating along the sidewalk. Take the Red Line T to either Charles Street on the Boston side or Harvard Square on the Cambridge side.

PLAYGROUNDS. Favorites of our family and my Boston panel: **Christopher Columbus/Waterfront Park** (Atlantic Ave. between Mercantile St. and Long Wharf), which has an excellent view of boats in the busy harbor, a long vine-covered colonnade that's fun to run through, wading in summer, and a clean, modern play area with a large boatlike wooden climbing structure; **Clarendon Street Playground** (corner of Commonwealth Ave. and Clarendon St., Back Bay), a small shady playground with a big wooden climbing structure and a grassy hill that's fun to roll down; **Charlestown Waterfront Playground** (facing Pier 4 across from USS *Constitution* Museum, Charlestown Navy Yard), a fabulous playground with an imaginatively designed wading pool and a ship-like wooden climbing structure that has decks, a steering wheel, and a slide; **Cambridge Common** (off Waterhouse St., between Massachusetts Ave. and Garden St., Cambridge), a delightful fenced playground that's accessible to people with disabilities.

AROUND BOSTON

(ȶȶ ALL) Blue Hills Reservation. Only about 10 miles south of the city in Milton, this 6,000-acre reservation is a haven for hikers, pond swimmers, berry pickers, cross-country skiers, and ice-skaters. The winding, steep, rocky trails are best for older kids with hiking experience. Don't miss the wigwam, or the Trailside Museum, where kids can see some animals.
🏠 Park headquarters: tel. 617/698–1802. Trailside Museum, 1904 Canton Ave., Milton, tel. 617/333–0690. By car: I–93 to Rte. 128, take exit 3 and follow signs for Houghton's Pond. Museum open Wed.–Sun., 10–5. Cost: $3 adults, $1.50 kids 3–12.

(ȶȶ ALL) Ipswich River Wildlife Sanctuary. This well-maintained Audubon Sanctuary just 24 miles from downtown Boston offers excellent kids' programs and guided hikes. See Chapter 10.
🏠 87 Perkins Row, Topsfield, tel. 508/887–9264.

(ȶȶ 2–15) Larz Anderson Park. The combination of hills and lawns, a pond with ducks to feed, picnic areas and playgrounds, and a museum filled with cars in an old carriage house (see Museum of Transportation under Museums, *above*) make this 63-acre park an excellent destination for an afternoon outing—and it's only 15 to 20 minutes from Boston. On a nice day the hill where the Anderson mansion once stood attracts kiteflyers; on a snowy one it's thick with sledders.
🏠 Entrances on Goddard Ave. and Newton St., Brookline, tel. 617/730–2083. By car: Rte. 9 west to Lee St., then turn left. By T: Cleveland Circle stop on Green Line T, then Bus 51 to museum.

Sports

Big Leagues

Spectator sports are a major obsession for many Bostonians, and they have unswerving loyalty to their home teams. Arrive early and don't cheer too loudly for the visitors, even if they're your own home team. (Definitely do *not* let your kids wear Yankees T-shirts at a Red Sox game.) When they're available, opt for seats in family sections where no alcohol is permitted. The *Boston Globe's* Friday edition lists college and professional sports schedules. *See also* Chapter 11.

BASEBALL. The baseball season runs from April to October.

Boston Red Sox. The Sox (American League) have played in charming, relatively small, old-fashioned Fenway Park since 1912. Tickets are usually easy to get, except when the Sox are playing the Yankees (their arch rival) or the Blue Jays.
🏠 4 Yawkey Way, tel. 617/267–8661 or 617/267–1700 for tickets. Fenway stop on Riverside/Green Line T.

BASKETBALL. Basketball season is late October through April.

Boston Celtics. Tickets to home games on the famous parquet floors of Boston Garden are very hard to get. Starting in 1996, the renowned Celtics will play in Shawmut Center, now under construction.
🏠 150 Causeway St., tel. 617/523–3030 or 617/720–3434 for tickets. North Station stop on Orange or Green Line T.

FOOTBALL. Football season is from early September through December. Pro games are usually on Sunday afternoons, college games on Saturday afternoons.

New England Patriots. Though the Patriots' home, Foxboro Stadium, is sometimes sold out, individual tickets do go on sale. Traffic is horrendous.

🏠 *Rte. 1 (25 mi south of Boston), Foxboro, tel. 508/543–1776 or 800/543–1776. Take Rte. 1 south off I–95 for 3 mi.*

Various college teams popular with Boston families include: the **Boston College Eagles** (Alumni Stadium, Chestnut Hill, Brookline, tel. 617/552–2000); the **Boston University Terriers** (Nickerson Field, off Commonwealth Ave., tel. 617/353–3838); **The Harvard University Crimson** (Harvard University Stadium, North Harvard St. and Soldiers Field Rd., Allston; tel. 617/495–2212).

HOCKEY. The season is from October through April, with games mostly on Thursday and Saturday evenings.

Boston Bruins. The Bruins share Boston Garden with the NBA's Celtics and will also move to Shawmut Center in 1996. Tickets are usually sold out by game time.
🏠 *150 Causeway St., tel. 617/227–3206 or 617/227–3223. North Station stop on Green and Orange Line T.*

RUNNING. The Boston Marathon. Held every year on Patriot's Day, the third Monday in April, this is one event that the families on my Boston panel love to watch. See Chapter 11.
🏠 *For information, contact Boston Athletic Association, 17 Main St., Hopkinton 01748, tel. 617/236–1652.*

Action

OUTDOORS

(👫 **8+**) **Bicycling.** The best place (with the nicest views) to ride bikes in the city is along both sides of the Charles River on the 18-mile-long **Dr. Paul Dudley White Bike Path,** which runs from the Museum of Science to Watertown Square and up to Cambridge. On Sundays in summer, when it's closed to traffic, we also like **Memorial Drive** on the Cambridge side of the river. For rentals, Community Bike Shop (490 Tremont St., tel. 617/542–8623) carries

bikes as small as 18 inches ($20 per day plus deposit) and helmets ($5 per day), and sells books detailing other city bike routes.

(👫 **6 – 15**) **Boating.** It's easy for a family to sail in Boston, on either the Charles River or Boston Harbor. On the **Charles River,** sailing dinghies can be rented at low rates through Community Boating (21 Embankment Rd. along the Esplanade just below Longfellow Bridge, tel. 617/523–1038, mid-June through Aug.). After passing a sailing test, experienced families can purchase two- or seven-day (or more) memberships allowing them to use boats; you can also hire an instructor. Summer group lessons for kids cost only $1. On **Boston Harbor,** the Courageous Sailing Center in Charlestown Navy Yard (1 First Ave., tel. 617/242–3821), with one of the best sailing schools in the northeast and dozens of boats of various sizes, offers classes, private lessons, and rentals in Boston Harbor. You can also row or sail on beautiful **Jamaica Pond** in Jamaica Plain, which is surrounded by shady trees and places to picnic. The Boathouse (tel. 617/522–6258) rents rowboats and sailboats by the hour.

(👫 **6 – 15**) **Ice-Skating.** On weekends in winter, skating on the **Lagoon** in the Public Garden (see Green Space, *above*) is a Boston family tradition. Though it can be crowded, we love skating under the bridge and around the island. Rental skates cost $3 for adults and $1 for kids under 16 (tel. 617/635–4505). See also Ice-Skating *under* Indoors, *below.*

(👫 **3+**) **Kite Flying.** Franklin Park's annual **kite festival** in mid-May (for information call Parks Dept., tel. 617/725–4006) draws thousands of kids and adults, as kites fill the sky in a mind-boggling array of shapes and sizes and colors. My Boston panelists also favor areas along the Cambridge side of the Charles River and the hill above the Museum of Transportation in Larz Anderson Park (see Green Space, *above*), both of which are open and usually breezy.

(👫 10+) Roller-Skating. In-line skating is a key spring, summer, and fall sport for kids in the city. One highly favored spot is the long paved paths through the **Esplanade** along the Charles River (wider than those across the river in Cambridge); around the **Christian Science Center** (intersection of Massachusetts Ave. and Huntington Ave.), the smooth brick pedestrian plaza by the reflecting pool is a good place for beginners to practice. For rentals, the Beacon Hill Skate Shop (135 Charles St., tel. 617/482–7400) near the Boston Common is the least expensive and has a limited selection of small sizes. Eric Flaim's Motion Sports (349B Newbury St., tel. 617/247–3284) rents only by the day, but also offers lessons.

(👫 12–15) Whale-Watching. Traveling out to the Stellwagen Bank in Massachusetts Bay to spot whales is a popular activity for families, particularly when the weather is hot and sticky, though it makes for a long trip, usually five to six hours. Of the regularly scheduled trips, we favor the New England Aquarium's trips aboard *The Voyager* (tel. 617/973–5277 or 617/973–5281). See Chapter 12.

INDOORS

(👫 3+) Bowling. Candlepin bowling, unique to New England and southern Canada, is much easier for little kids than regular bowling, because it uses a smaller and lighter ball. **Ryan's Fenway** (82 Lansdowne St., directly north of Fenway Park, tel. 617/267–8495), Boston's only bowling alley, has 20 lanes and makes playing even easier for kids by setting up bumpers so their balls don't end up in the gutter. There's no bar, but there are pool tables and a video game room, great for older kids.

(👫 13–15) Ice-Skating. The historic **Boston Skating Club** rink (1240 Soldiers Field Rd., Brighton, tel. 617/782–5900; skate rentals $3) has a big open dome, sunlight sifting through its many windows, a snack bar with homemade goodies, and plenty of heat; unfortunately, it's only open for public

skating on Saturday afternoon. Many fast-skating college kids come here then, so it may be best for older kids.

(👫 0–6) Indoor Playground. With two locations—one in Arlington and one in Salem—**Tot Stop** offers ride-on toys, special areas for toddlers and infants, and a snack bar. The Arlington site has a three-level play area, a large barn with nooks and crannies and slides, and an indoor "beach." The center of the smaller space in Salem is a large ship for climbing that leads to other play areas.
🏠 *41 Foster St., off Massachusetts Ave., E. Arlington, tel. 617/643–8687. Cost: $6. Open Mon.–Sat. 9:30–5:30 (Fri. until 8). Museum Plaza Mall, Salem, tel. 508/741–4913. Cost: $6. Open daily 9:30–5:30 (Thurs. until 8).*

(👫 9–15) Miniature Golf. Right by Fenway Park, the spectacular 18-hole course at **The Golf Club** (145 Ipswich St., corner of Lansdowne St., tel. 617/262–0300) even features waterfalls. I'd stick to afternoon times with kids.

(👫 12–15) Roller-Skating and Skate-Boarding. A huge old warehouse in Cambridge has been converted into **Maximus,** the indoor mecca for Boston area skateboarders and in-line skaters. No rentals, but helmets (required) can be borrowed for free. See Chapter 12.
🏠 *324 Rindge Ave. (off Massachusetts Ave.), Cambridge, tel. 617/576–4723.*

Shopping

Because of their significant population of college kids, Boston and Cambridge offer more than enough teen-appealing shops to occupy visitors for several weeks. It's also a book lover's heaven, with an amazing number of colorful, quirky, and often huge bookstores. Around **Harvard Square,** more than 100 shops are crammed into a several-block area, including lots of book and records stores, the best spots for antique clothing, and branches of chains such as the Body Shop and Urban Outfitters. The Back Bay's wide, elegant **Newbury Street** is another prime zone, starting from the stylish clothing boutiques at the Public Garden end and going on to the trendier, more youth-oriented clothing shops toward Massachusetts Avenue. Nearby, on Boylston Street, the **Prudential Center** also attracts clothes-browsing teenage girls.

Malls and Marketplaces

(**ALL**) **CambridgeSide Galleria.** This is a favored shopping and eating and just hanging-out spot. It's also the home of the Sports Museum of New England (see Museums, above). Among its 100 shops and restaurants, **Gap, J. Crew, Limited Express,** the **Original Levi's Store,** and **Banana Republic** are hot spots for clothes, **Pappa-Razzi** (see Eats, below) and the **Food Festival** on the Charles River for lunch or dinner. In summer, cruise boats dock here and paddleboats are for rent on the lagoon. The mall stays open until 9:30, and a free shuttle bus carries shoppers to and from the Kendall Square T station. The mall is also one block away from the Lechmere station on the Green Line T.
🏠 100 Cambridgeside Pl., tel. 617/621–8666.

(**ALL**) **Faneuil Hall Marketplace.** See Chapter 7. If you're going to shop in only one place in Boston, this is it. The 120 shops are joined by ranks of pushcarts under the canopies fanning out from the central building, Quincy Market. It's more a bustling open-air market than a mall. At **Purple Panache,** everything from stuffed animals to T-shirts is purple, **The Body Lab** has funky fun jewelry and wild hair accessories. Other favorite places are **Hog Wild,** which carries pig jewelry and wonderful pig mugs, sports shops such as **Hall of Fame Sports** and **Sports, etc.,** and for younger kids, **Tales with Tails** (books accompanied by wild stuffed animals), **Dinostaur** (dinosaur novelties), **The Nature Company** (books and

toys about wildlife and ecology), and **Kites of Boston** (you guessed it—kites). Peek in on the fantasy zoo of papier-mâché and metal animal sculptures at **Pavo Real Galeria.**
🏠 Between Commercial and Congress Sts., tel. 617/338–2323.

Books and Records

(**0–14**) **Children's Book Shop.** In contrast to those of most children's bookstores, this shop's large selection (some 20,000 books) includes plenty of young adult fiction and even a few racks of adult books where parents can browse.
🏠 238 Washington St., Brookline, tel. 617/734–7323.

(**11+**) **Harvard Coop.** This gigantic three-floor store of games, toys, and clothing also stocks an astonishing selection of books (100,000!), plus records, posters, and computer stuff in an annex just around the corner.
🏠 1400 Massachusetts Ave., Cambridge, tel. 617/499–2000.

(**12+**) **HMV.** The biggest record store in Cambridge, HMV attracts a diverse clientele with its huge stock (particularly of classical music), in-store DJ, and live performances.
🏠 1 Brattle St., Cambridge, tel. 617/868–9696.

(**13+**) **Newbury Comics.** Though the name makes it sound like a comic book shop (the store does have a few shelves of new comics, sold at a 20% discount), most of the business of this 12-store chain is rock CDs, especially those of alternative music groups. The Harvard Square store (36 JFK St., 2nd Floor of Garage Mall, Cambridge, tel. 617/491–0337), with its hip environment is a teen and student hangout, with occasional in-store concerts.

(**10+**) **Tower Records.** This chain's largest U.S. branch (three floors, 46,000 square feet) hums with electronic entertainment: TV monitors, listening posts, computer screens where you can punch up all sorts of music information. The music sections are on the second floor; the first floor sells books and videos.

🏠 *360 Newbury St. (corner of Massachusetts Ave.), tel. 617/247–5900.*

👫 ALL **Waterstone's Booksellers.** A charming castle playhouse and a huge selection of kids' books attract families to the store's second-floor children's section, a carpeted raised area marked off by gaily painted glass dividers and railings.

🏠 *26 Exeter St. (at Newbury St.), tel. 617/859–7300.*

Candy

👫 6–12 **Gourmet Chocolate by Design.** Here you'll find chocolates in whimsical shapes such as cars and swan boats, and jars of every color of jelly beans.

🏠 *134 Newbury St., tel. 617/424–1115.*

👫 3–15 **Sweet Stuff.** Artfully arranged in clear plastic bins are 150 varieties of sweets, from jelly beans to Hershey's kisses to hand-dipped chocolates in the form of seashells and sailboats.

🏠 *North Market Bldg., Faneuil Hall Marketplace, tel. 617/227–7560.*

Comics

👫 6–15 **Comicopia.** This clean, well-lighted store carries a comprehensive selection of new comics, plus comic book T-shirts and videos; there's even a special section at the front of the store with comics younger kids prefer.

🏠 *464 Commonwealth Ave., Kenmore Square, tel. 617/266–4266.*

👫 10+ **Million Year Picnic.** The collection—more than 25,000 comics, both new and vintage—is the biggest in New England, and the store also stocks comic-related T-shirts and posters.

🏠 *99 Mt. Auburn St., Harvard Sq., Cambridge, tel. 617/492–6763.*

Stuff to Wear

👫 12+ **Limited.** The trendsetter among the Limited's 958 U.S. stores is this branch, the favored clothes-grazing spot for several teenage girls on my Boston panel. A spiral staircase winds upward through nine floors that dazzle with weekly changing displays.

🏠 *1 Faneuil Hall Sq., Marketplace Center (across from Quincy Market), tel. 617/742–6837.*

👫 12+ **Mass Army Navy Store.** One room is devoted exclusively to worldwide military surplus goodies, but the rest of the two floors are stocked with a wide selection of teen staples: jeans, khakis, boots, and shirts.

🏠 *1436 Massachusetts Ave., Harvard Sq., Cambridge, tel. 617/497–1250.*

👫 12+ **Oona's Experienced Clothing.** Crammed onto racks in four tiny rooms is an excellent selection of the recycled clothes that are so appealing to many teens, all at relatively low prices.

🏠 *1210 Massachusetts Ave., Cambridge, tel. 617/491–2654.*

👫 8–15 **Reebok's.** Outside this hip shoe store, check out the footprints of various sports stars in the sidewalk (plaques identify them). Inside are high-tech graphics of players, a shoe-shaped ceiling, and TV monitors beaming ball games.

🏠 *344 Newbury St., tel. 617/266–2440.*

Toys and Games

👫 ALL **Children's Museum.** See Museums, *above*. The big first-floor museum shop sells new books, educational toys, and craft kits, but we gravitate instead to the Recycle shop on the second floor, where you can find wonderful cheap materials for craft projects. *300 Congress St., Museum Wharf, tel. 617/426–6500, ext. 203.*

👫 0–10 **Children's Workshop.** Puppet and magic shows, workshops, and holiday classes distinguish this friendly, air-conditioned toy shop run by a former teacher. Toys are set out on low shelves for touching and playing.

🏠 *1963 Massachusetts Ave., Cambridge, tel. 617/364-1633.*

👫 **10+** **Complete Strategist.** A mecca for kids who, like Gavin, are fascinated by role-playing games and miniatures, this small branch of the New York City store (see Chapter 4) is frequented by many college kids.

🏠 *201 Massachusetts Ave. (near the Christian Science Center), tel. 617/267-2451.*

👫 **6 – 12** **Enchanted Cottage.** Everything a dollhouse owner needs is on sale here. Thirty or more dollhouses decorated with miniature furnishings and light fixtures are usually set up for viewing.

🏠 *2512 Massachusetts Ave., Cambridge, tel. 617/491-8818.*

👫 **ALL** **F.A.O. Schwarz.** A huge bronze bear outside marks Boston's branch of the famous toy store, which is more cozy and fanciful in layout and design than the original in New York City. Its two floors brim with touch-and-play possibilities, wonderful animated displays, fabulous stuffed animals (some bigger than the little kids patting them!). The library section has an excellent selection of kids' books.

🏠 *440 Boylston St. (in Back Bay), tel. 617/266-5101.*

👫 **ALL** **Museum of Science.** See Museums, *above.* The gift shop stocks a wide selection of kids' science books and toys.

🏠 *Science Park, tel. 617/589-0320.*

Unusual Stores

👫 **8+** **Beadworks.** The Newbury Street store of this nationwide chain has one of the biggest (3,000 different beads) and most organized selections I've seen, enticingly sorted out in lovely oak boxes. There's a supervised worktable right in the store, and displays of sample projects hang

on the walls. The Cambridge branch is smaller and has no work area.

🏠 *349 Newbury St., tel. 617/247-7227; 23 Church St., Cambridge, tel. 868-9777.*

👫 **8 – 15** **Jack's Joke Shop.** This narrow shop across from Boston Common stocks all the appallingly corny stuff—hand buzzers, fake cockroaches and rats, crazy glasses, Halloween masks—that delights kids who are still in the practical joke stage.

🏠 *197 Tremont St., tel. 617/426-9640.*

👫 **8 – 15** **Nostalgia Factory.** Advertising collectibles, from Star Wars figures to old movie posters (at good prices), and other trendy trash are packed into this memorabilia shop.

🏠 *336 Newbury St., tel. 617/236-8754.*

👫 **ALL** **WGBH Learningsmith.** On the main floor, 12 different colorful "try it out" sections (crafts, games, astronomy, math, etc.) hold fascinating books, calendars, toys, and all manner of learning products to stimulate the mind. A carpeted area at the back of the store is just for the under-6 crowd. On the mezzanine eight computers let shoppers experiment with the latest in software.

🏠 *25 Brattle St., Harvard Sq., Cambridge, tel. 617/661-6008.*

Eats

Because about a third of the population of Boston and Cambridge are students, many of the city's restaurants are casual, inexpensive, and noisy—all of which make them appealing to families.

The biggest food specialty of Boston is fresh fish of all kinds: clams, fried and steamed and in chowder; baked scrod; codfish cakes; and lobsters every which way. Many of Boston's seafood restaurants offer kids' menus with appealing alternatives as well. Kids may be more interested in other quintessential Boston tastes: baked beans, Indian pudding, and apple pandowdy at Durgin-Park (see *below*), dim sum in Chinatown, Italian pastries and gelato in North End cafés, and marvelous ice cream, its quality kept high by fierce local competition.

Cambridge, with its diversity of students from every corner of the globe, is the place to try any ethnic cuisine that interests your kids, from Thai to Indian to Greek to Korean.

Boston's malls and indoor atriums contain food courts with many casual snacking spots: The concourse in light-filled **South Station,** where you can watch rushing people and see the train tracks; the Terrace Food Court in the **Prudential Center**; the brass-and-marble food court in upscale **Copley Place,** where kids can toss pennies into waterfalls; and the **CambridgeSide Galleria's** Food Festival court, overlooking the Charles River. You can eat alfresco at one of the city's two open-air markets. Colorful, untouristy **Haymarket Square** (bounded by Blackstone, Hanover, and North Sts.) teems with outdoor fruit and vegetable stalls and tiny shops behind opened shutters wafting the smell of fresh bread. It's open Friday and Saturday mornings. Haymarket Pizzeria (100 Blackstone St., tel. 617/723–8585) sells pizza slices that you can eat sitting at sawhorse tables under big skylights. At **Faneuil Hall Marketplace** (bounded by Commercial and Congress Sts.), head for the center building, Quincy Market, where more than three dozen food stalls compose an exotic buffet. A sampling: baked beans in a paper bowl at the Boston Beanery (tel. 617/227–2038); smoothies and nonalcohol coladas at the Monkey Bar (tel. 617/367–1333); mint brownies at Boston Brownie (tel. 617/227–8803); or New England chowder at the Bay State Chowda Co. (tel. 617/742–4441). Beware noontime, however, when the crowds fill the aisle between the stalls. Eat a picnic on a bench outside in the plaza, or head for one of the cafés under the canopies on either side.

Boston is a picnicker's paradise. In the **Public Garden,** we spread a blanket near the Lagoon and save our sandwich crusts for the ducks. Just below the **Science Museum** are lovely picnic tables overlooking the Charles River. In the plaza in front of the **Aquarium,** you can picnic by the wave pool near the cavorting harbor seals. From the grassy banks of the **Esplanade,** you can watch sailboats and Harvard's rowing shells. Along the harborfront are benches and views in **Christopher Columbus Park,** just beyond the **Charlestown Navy Yard,** and at the tip of **Long Wharf.** For a unique picnic spot try beautifully landscaped **Post Office Square Park** (bounded by Franklin, Pearl, Milk, and Congress Sts.), where atop a seven-story parking garage you'll find a wildflower garden, an expanse of grass, and chairs and tables by a café with take-out treats. Weekdays at lunchtime, it's crowded with office workers.

If your kids can't live without a Big Mac, try the McDonald's branch on the first floor of the Children's Museum (tel. 617/482–1746), which is usually crammed with families; if you get your burgers to go, you can picnic outside on benches by the water.

Category	Cost*
$$$	over $25
$$	$15–$25
$	under $15

per person for a three-course meal, excluding drinks, service, and sales tax

American Eclectic

(**ALL**) **Caffe Marino.** This cafeteria right off Harvard Square serves more interesting food than you'd expect—chicken grilled over a woodburning fire, an extensive salad bar and vegetable buffet, and a café section with one of Boston's best selections of all kinds of pastry.
 30 Dunster St., tel. 617/491–0222. Booster seats, high chairs. Dress: casual. Booster seats, high chairs. AE, DC, MC, V. $–$$

👪 12+ **Casablanca Restaurant.** This restaurant scores high for its inventive food and informal, with-it atmosphere. The booths in front are comfortable, but the back room, decorated with potted palms and a mural of Bogart and Bergman from *Casablanca,* is livelier. The food is an eclectic mix of juicy burgers, grilled pizza, and delicious Morroccan and Middle Eastern specialties.
🏠 *40 Brattle St., Harvard Sq., Cambridge, tel. 617/876–0999. Reservations advised. Dress: casual. MC, V. $$*

👪 ALL **Durgin-Park.** Climb a flight of wooden stairs to this Boston institution, here since 1827. The no-frills second-floor dining hall seats everybody at long communal tables. Waitresses treat you like family— which means they may exhort kids to finish their vegetables. Kids happily chow down on the good straightforward Yankee food: baked beans, prime rib, Indian pudding. Chicken fingers, franks and beans, and ice cream are on the menu also.
🏠 *340 Faneuil Hall Marketplace, North Market Bldg., tel. 617/227–2038. No reservations. Dress: casual. AE, MC, V. $$*

👪 9–15 **Hard Rock Cafe.** Outside, half a Cadillac thrusts out from the facade below the words Massachusetts Institute of Rock. Inside, rock-and-roll music plays loudly and rock memorabilia decorates the walls (look for Stevie Ray Vaughn's guitar). Besides the ubiquitous burgers and sandwiches, this member of the chain serves an okay New England Clam Chowder and Boston cream pie.
🏠 *131 Clarendon St. (between Columbus and Boylston Sts.), tel. 617/424–7625 or 617/353–1400. No reservations. Dress: casual. AE, DC, MC, V. $$*

👪 ALL **Marketplace Cafe.** An outdoor garden in front, a winter garden inside, and tables with paper tablecloths and crayons for the kids make this one of the most enjoyable lunch places in Faneuil Hall Marketplace. The chowder is spicy with cayenne

pepper; there's also a good selection of sandwiches and pastas.
🏠 *Faneuil Hall Marketplace, end of North Market Bldg., tel. 617/227–1272. Reservations advised. Dress: casual. AE, DC, MC, V. $–$$*

Chinese and Japanese

👪 ALL **Goemon's Japanese Noodle Restaurant.** The fun lies in choosing from a long list of meats and/or vegetables to top off your noodles (three kinds). Served in a big, deep bowl in steamy broth, it smells good, it's filling, and it's a bargain. At the counter, you can watch the chefs at work. The contemporary decor is sleek black lacquer, but relaxed and okay for kids.
🏠 *267 Huntington Ave., tel. 617/859–8669; 1 Kendall Sq., Cambridge, tel. 617/577–9595. Reservations for 6 or more. Dress: casual. AE, MC, V. $*

👪 ALL **Golden Palace.** This second-floor banquet hall in Chinatown has fancy pagoda-style overhangs, great golden dragons on the walls, an octagonal window into a fishtank with goldfish. Many families, mostly Chinese, come at lunchtime for *dim sum*: individual servings of tidbits or snacks (dumplings, spare ribs, spicy shrimp, and more) offered from wheeled carts. You pay for each serving you choose; most are around $1 to $2. Kids like the excitement of choosing and nibbling, though there can be a long wait on crowded Sundays.
🏠 *14 Tyler St. (between Beach and Kneeland Sts.), tel. 617/423–4565. Dim sum served 9–3. Reservations accepted. Dress: casual. AE, DC, MC, V. $–$$*

👪 ALL **Imperial Teahouse.** A rival to the Golden Palace (*see above*) for the best dim sum in Chinatown, this big, airy, noisy second-floor dining room has less in the way of decor, but its open fish tank is irresistible to kids. We give the dishes at the Golden Palace a slight edge, but the selection is larger here. Though the line moves fast, expect at least a 15-minute wait for dim sum on weekends.

🏠 *70–72 Beach St., tel. 617/426–8439. Reservations dinner only. Dress: casual. AE, CB, DC, MC, V. $–$$*

Fish

👫 3+ **Legal Sea Foods.** Fresh, fresh, fresh fish, as many as 30 varieties simply and deliciously prepared, keeps families coming back, despite the inevitable long waits. At the Arlington Street location, we skip the line for the dining room and sit in the bar, which is more informal—paper place mats on imitation-granite Formica; kids can color their place mats, hang out next to the saltwater aquarium, and watch sports on the TVs above the bar. There's even fish-shaped ravioli on the kids' menu.
🏠 *5 Cambridge Center, tel. 617/864–3400; 64 Arlington St. (in Boston Park Plaza Hotel), tel. 617/426–4444; a few other Boston locations. Children's menu. No reservations. Dress: casual. AE, DC, MC, V. $$*

👫 6–15 **Union Oyster House.** A friend tells me that Marshall House, a few doors down, is better for steamers and oysters, but the truth is I'm charmed by the history of this tourist-packed spot (a revolutionary newspaper was printed upstairs in the 1770s, and it claims to be the oldest restaurant in America, with the oldest wooden booths). Kids too young to appreciate history were nevertheless mesmerized by the big lobsters in the aquarium under the stairs.
🏠 *41 Union St., tel. 617/227–2750. Children's menu. Reservations accepted. Dress: casual. AE, DC, MC, V. $$*

Italian

👫 ALL **Cafe Paradiso.** Less colorful than the Vittoria (see below), this North End café has a downstairs espresso bar where you can get homemade spumoni, gelato, and Italian ices, and a sandwich if you're hungry. Tiny mirrored tables and hanging plants are the decor.
🏠 *255 Hanover St., tel. 617/742–1768. No reservations. Dress: casual. AE, MC, V. $$*

👫 ALL **Caffe Vittoria.** Despite the cramped seating, this North End café is worth a stop for great cappuccino, cannoli, and Italian ices that are tart but delicious. A massive polished espresso machine, marble floors, a mural of Italy, and lively music from the jukebox add up to what we think a café ought to be.
🏠 *296 Hanover St., tel. 617/227–7606. No reservations. Dress: casual. No credit cards. $*

👫 ALL **Florence's.** Every family we know in Boston seems to have a favorite "red-sauce" restaurant, serving the southern Italian specialties that usually please kids. This is one good choice, with moderate prices, a plain but homey atmosphere, large portions, and very, very good spaghetti.
🏠 *190 North St. (at Richmond St.), tel. 617/523–4480. Booster seats, high chairs. Reservations accepted. Dress: casual. AE, DC, MC, V. $$*

👫 ALL **La Piccola Venezia.** Reliable, filling, and authentic home-style pastas in large portions are served in this tiny, friendly, no-frills spot with a blackboard menu. Prices are exceptionally reasonable.
🏠 *63 Salem St., tel. 617/523–9802. No reservations. Dress: casual. No credit cards. $*

👫 ALL **Pappa-Razzi Trattoria/Bar.** These two branches of the chain are a step up from a pizza joint, with their wood-and-brass decor, low lighting, and casual, almost California-style atmosphere. There are pizzas, inventive pasta dishes (star and rocket pasta on the kids' menu), and Italian-style sandwiches.
🏠 *271 Dartmouth St., tel. 617/536–9200; CambridgeSide Galleria, Cambridge, tel. 617/577–0009. Booster seats, high chairs. Reservations accepted. Dress: casual. AE, DC, MC, V. $$*

Mexican

👫 9+ **Border Cafe.** Big portions of cheap but good burritos and other Tex-Mex specialties with Caribbean touches draw teens on my Boston panel. The chips and salsa are standard but good; bright advertis-

ing murals cover the walls. Expect hordes of students, noise, and slow service.
🏠 *32 Church St., Cambridge, tel. 617/864–6100. Booster seats, high chairs. No reservations. Dress: casual. AE, MC, V. $*

(👫 ALL) **Fajitas & 'Ritas.** It's easygoing, fun, and lively, and you can even write on the walls with crayons while sitting at your table. The menu offers assorted fajitas and a few other simple Mexican dishes. Service is fast. The Brookline branch has more kids.
🏠 *25 West St. (between Tremont and Washington Sts.), tel. 617/426–1222; 48 Boylston St., Brookline, tel. 617/566–1222. Booster seats, high chairs. No reservations. Dress: casual. AE, DC, MC, V. $–$$*

Mainly Hamburgers and Hot Dogs

(👫 4–15) **Fuddruckers.** Cheap burgers served with many toppings are just about all there is at this theater-district branch of a Texas-style chain.
🏠 *8 Park Pl. (at Stuart St.), tel. 617/723–3833. Booster seats, high chairs. No reservations. Dress: casual. AE, DC, MC, V. $*

(👫 ALL) **Hood Milk Bottle.** In front of the Children's Museum, this 40-foot-tall white wooden milk bottle is a Boston landmark. Salads, long hot dogs wrapped in a taco, and other to-go fare is dispensed from open windows hooded by red awnings.
🏠 *300 Congress St., Museum Wharf, no phone. Dress: casual. No credit cards. $*

Pizza Places

(👫 ALL) **Bertucci's Brick Oven Pizzeria.** At this friendly, informal chain, you can watch your pizza lifted out of the huge brick ovens with big wooden paddles. There's a floor-to-ceiling chalkboard to draw on, pizza playdough to mold, and at the Copley Square branch, a *bocce* court, where kids can try playing this old-fashioned Italian bowling game. The open kitchen produces

fair pastas, thin- and thick-crusted pizzas with a choice of 20-odd toppings; a kids' menu caters to finicky eaters with plain pasta with butter or a peanut-butter-and-jelly sandwich on an animal-shaped roll.
🏠 *Faneuil Hall Marketplace, 22 Merchant's Row, tel. 617/227–7889; 39–45 Stanhope St. (near Copley Sq.), tel. 617/247–6161; 21 Brattle St., Harvard Sq., Cambridge, tel. 617/864–4748. Booster seats, high chairs. No reservations. Dress: Casual. AE, DC, MC, V. $–$$*

(👫 5+) **Pizzeria Regina.** Gavin thought the pizza here was pretty good, and the pitchers of soft drinks are a plus. The original North End location is a Boston landmark, an authentic old-time pizza joint; neither the pizza nor the atmosphere at the Faneuil Hall branch are quite as good.
🏠 *11½ Thatcher St., tel. 617/227–0765; Faneuil Hall Marketplace, tel. 617/227–8180. Boosters, high chairs. No reservations. Dress: casual. No credit cards. $*

Sweet Stuff

(👫 6–12) **Emack & Bolio's.** Just a storefront in a Victorian town house, this place sells perhaps the best smoothies and ice-cream cake in town. We go for the hand-rolled cones filled with flavors like Chocolate Moose, dipped in chocolate sprinkles or coconut.
🏠 *290 Newbury St., tel. 617/247–8772. No credit cards. $*

(👫 ALL) **Herrell's Ice Cream.** A major player in Boston's competition for the best ice-cream shop, Herrell's is owned by Steve Herrell, founder and former owner of Steve's Ice Cream (*see below*). Come for the famed rich and creamy-smooth chocolate pudding ice cream. One room here used to be a bank vault—it still has a vault door with a dial that works.
🏠 *15 Dunster St., Harvard Sq., tel. 617/497–2179. High chairs. No credit cards. $*

(👫 3+) **Hing Shing Pastry.** On a visit to Chinatown, stop at this bakery store for a bag of freshly made fortune cookies for just $1, or some delicious almond cookies. 🏠 *67 Beach St., tel. 617/451–1162. No credit cards.* $

(🧑‍🧒 **ALL**) **Serendipity III.** This branch of the New York City spot carries the famous specialties: fabulous ice-cream treats and frozen hot chocolate so thick the straw stands up by itself. It doesn't have as much charm as the original, and it's ear-splittingly noisy. The long hot dogs make a good lunch. 🏠 *Faneuil Hall Marketplace, South Market Building, tel. 617/523–2339. Booster seats, high chairs. AE, D, MC, V.* $$

(🧑‍🧒 **ALL**) **Steve's Homemade Ice Cream.** This nationwide chain started locally in Somerville. It serves great ice cream with unusual mix-ins—M' & Ms, nuts, cookies, and more—but it's still not as great as the original one; we're partial to Herrell's (*see above*) ourselves. 🏠 *Faneuil Hall Marketplace, South Market Bldg., tel. 617/367–0569, and other Boston locations. No credit cards.* $

Outside the City

(🧑‍🧒 **3 – 12**) **Bonkers Fun House Pizza.** A good stop for energetic kids after visiting Salem's museums, this is a combination pizza-and-hot-dog place and noisy amusement park. 🏠 *Lowell St., Peabody, tel. 508/535–8355. Booster seats, high chairs. No reservations. Dress: casual. No credit cards.* $

(🧑‍🧒 **ALL**) **Clam Box of Ipswich.** With jaunty red-and-white striped awnings outside, this classic self-serve fish place has been selling fried clams and shrimp, lobsters, and more for 60 years. Portions are so large that two people can share one dinner. The outside deck, shaded by trees, draws families of noisy kids; the inside dining room has a wonderful mural of Wingersheek beach. 🏠 *245 High St., Rte. 1A, Ipswich, tel. 508/ 356–9707. Children's portions, booster seats, high chairs. No reservations. Dress: casual. No credit cards.* $

(🧑‍🧒 **ALL**) **Winter Island Grill.** Families we know come here for a view of the ocean from Salem Neck, a rocky beach and grassy slope for kids to frolic on, outdoor seating, and good grilled and battered fish as well as burgers. 🏠 *50 Winter Island Rd., tel. 508/744– 0203. No reservations. Dress: casual. No credit cards.* $

(🧑‍🧒 **ALL**) **Woodman's of Essex.** A road-side institution that opened in 1915, Wood-man's claims to have invented fried clams, for which it is now famous. Like the Clam Box (*see above*), it's a noisy, totally informal family place, with eat-in-the-rough seafood such as clam cakes and lobster; here you eat at picnic tables or in old scratched-up wooden booths. 🏠 *Main St. (Rte. 133), Essex, tel. 508/768– 6451. Booster seats, high chairs. No reservations. Dress: casual. No credit cards.* $

Where to Stay

As in New York, hotels here are expensive. The difference in Boston is that many more, including the luxurious ones, not only welcome families but cater to them with all manner of special treats: child-friendly rooms, story hours, game rooms with videos and Nintendo, and discount coupons to children's attractions. The Family Visitor Kit, available from the Greater Boston Convention and Visitors Bureau (see How to Find Out What's Going On, *above*), includes a "Kids Love Boston: Family-Friendly Hotel Packages" brochure that lists some 30 hotel family packages; be sure to ask specifically for the Kids Love Boston rate when you reserve.

There are practically no budget hotel alternatives in either Boston or Harvard Square. You can stay in an outlying area—convenient enough if you plan to spend time in Lexington and Concord, Salem, or the North Shore, but awkward if you plan to spend most of your time in the heart of the city. Boston can be hot in summer, so I've favored hotels with pools over those without. Because of the number of colleges and conventions in this city, hotels are often booked far in advance, including weekends, so prepare to be disappointed if you're calling at the last minute.

All of the hotels below offer some special family rate, which may cut as much as $100 off the posted rate. Expect all hotel rates to go up during the high season, May through October. Unless otherwise noted, parking will cost anywhere from $10 to $15 per night. The hotels listed below do not charge for cribs, but most charge $10 for a rollaway bed.

Category	Cost*
$$$$	over $250
$$$	$175–$250
$$	$100–$175
$	under $100

*All prices are for a standard double room, excluding 9.7% tax.

$$$$

Boston Harbor Hotel. Right on the water overlooking Boston Harbor, this striking hotel has the feel of a resort or a private club. It's convenient to many favorite family attractions (the Aquarium, Museum Wharf, Faneuil Hall Marketplace) and easy to reach from the airport on a fast water shuttle that docks in front. Exceptionally large rooms in chintz and Chippendale and flowers have great views of either the city skyline or the harbor. Kids also love the pool, but be warned: On weekdays, there are only certain hours they can use it. The family package includes a room with a foldout couch in the sitting area, discounts on area attractions, and free self-parking.
🏨 70 Rowes Wharf, Atlantic Ave., 02110, tel. 617/439–7000 or 800/752–7077, fax 617/330–9450. 204 rooms and 26 suites.

Kids under 19 free. Facilities: 1 restaurant, 1 café, 1 bar, 24-hr room service, pool, health club, concierge, water shuttle, marina, baby-sitting, parking. AE, DC, MC, V.

Four Seasons Hotel. A luxurious, 16-story brick hotel in a perfect location overlooking Boston Public Garden, this is one of the city's two best hotels for families (the other is the Ritz-Carlton, see below). The wonderful little luxuries for kids here include fluffy child-size bathrobes (a big hit with one well-traveled 6-year-old), bedtime milk, cookies, and balloons, kids' shampoo, complimentary VCR, and children's videos. It's less formal than the Ritz-Carlton, and the staff is friendly and considerate. The regular double rooms are large and elegant, but best bets for families are the corner rooms, which connect with a second room with twin beds (a special family rate is available), or the executive suites, consisting of a bedroom and a sitting area that can be closed off with French doors. The 51-foot-long pool on the eighth floor, which overlooks the garden, has a shallow end (2½ feet deep), unlike most hotel pools, and a full-time lifeguard; kids are welcome anytime it's open (6 AM to 10 PM).
🏨 200 Boylston St., 02116, tel. 617/338–4400 or 800/332–3442, fax 617/423–0154. 213 rooms, 75 suites. Children under 18 free. Facilities: 2 restaurants, pool, fitness center, concierge, no-smoking rooms, valet parking, complimentary limousine to waterfront. AE, DC, MC, V.

Ritz-Carlton. Rich with tradition and with impeccable service, this 16-story hotel facing the Public Garden exudes the air of an earlier era; I expect to see little girls in dresses with velvet collars and shiny Mary Jane shoes in the lobby. During the Christmas season, the lobby and restaurants are festively decorated; other kids' events year-round include lunches with kids' book authors, cooking classes, and a weekend of etiquette instruction. All rooms are grandly spacious and traditionally furnished, but the ultimate in family suites anywhere is the hotel's very expensive Junior Presidential

Suite, a colorful, child-proofed kids' bedroom/playroom filled with toys, books, stuffed animals, and a TV with video games, all connected to a room for parents. The Ritz, as befits a great hotel, provides everything families need, even lending ice skates to use on the pond in the Public Garden. The only big drawbacks are the lack of a swimming pool and the high price.
🏨 *15 Arlington St., 02117, tel. 617/536–5700 or 800/241–3333, fax 617/536–9340. 230 rooms, 48 suites, 8 non-smoking floors. Facilities: 4 restaurants, 24-hr room service, exercise room, no-smoking rooms, valet parking, concierge, baby-sitting. AE, DC, MC, V.*

$$$

Colonnade Hotel. To me, personal service and the large "baby-safe" rooms (rubber stops on table corners, covered electrical outlets, playpens) are the most appealing features of this small modern hotel across from the Prudential Center. The Cafe Promenade overlooking Prudential Plaza serves delicious food older kids like—a jumbo healthy hot dog on a soft roll with spicy fries, great chicken fingers, and gourmet pizza that's not too gourmet for kids. The family package, good any day of the week, brings it into this price range, and includes parking and Continental breakfast.
🏨 *120 Huntington Ave., 02116, tel. 617/242–4000 or 800/962–3030, fax 617/424–1717. 288 rooms, 15 suites. Facilities: 2 restaurants, room service, pool, fitness center, baby-sitting. AE, DC, MC, V.*

Guest Quarters Suite Hotels. This 16-story brick atrium hotel located along the Charles River offers all suites *and* an indoor swimming pool, something other suite hotels in town don't have. The one-bedroom suites, decorated in pale tan and salmon, have space for kids to cavort; the bathroom, with marble and mirrors and a telephone, is even luxurious. It's rather far off the downtown tourist path, but the amenities and family packages here make up for that.

🏨 *400 Soldiers Field Rd., 02134, tel. 617/783–0090 or 800/424–2900, fax 617/783–0897. 310 suites. Kids under 12 free. Facilities: restaurant, pool, baby-sitting, game room, courtesy van to downtown. AE, DC, MC, V.*

Marriott Long Wharf. For a summer weekend, this modern chain hotel on the waterfront would be our choice—first, because it's only a block from the shopping scene at Faneuil Hall Marketplace, and second, because it has a large shallow swimming pool, usually filled with kids of all ages, and a harborview sundeck where you can order poolside lunches. You have the Aquarium practically next door, Columbus/Waterfront Park just outside, and a T stop in front of the hotel. The Friday-night family rate and regular weekend special really bring down the price for a family of four. The mauve-and-green rooms are in traditional early American decor, with closets big enough to hide in.
🏨 *296 State St., Long Wharf, 02109, tel. 617/227–0800 or 800/228–9290, fax 617/227–2867. 400 rooms. Children under 18 free. Facilities: 2 restaurants, pool, health club, game room, in-room movies, refrigerators. AE, DC, MC, V.*

Royal Sonesta. This modern two-tower hotel is right on the Charles River in Cambridge. You can walk and bicycle along the riverside promenade right by the hotel, the Museum of Science (see Museums, *above*) is next door, and the CambridgeSide Galleria (see Shopping, *above*) is just across the street. It is far from other Boston attractions, though it does offer courtesy van service to and from many Boston and Cambridge points of interest. The summer family package gives you larger rooms but brings rates down into the next lower price range; extra amenities include use of bicycles, Polaroid cameras, boat rides on the Charles River, and all the ice cream you can eat from a cart in the lobby.
🏨 *5 Cambridge Pkwy., Cambridge 02142, tel. 617/491–3600 or 800/766–3782, fax 617/661–5956. 400 rooms. Children under*

12 free. Facilities: 2 restaurants, pool, health club, courtesy van, baby-sitting. AE, DC, MC, V.

$$

Boston Park Plaza Hotel & Towers. The location, just a block from the Public Garden, near the theater district and several kid-friendly restaurants, and close to one of the major T stations, is only one reason we liked staying here. It also has the hustle-and-bustle of a very big hotel, without the tour groups; instead, there's an old-fashioned high-ceilinged lobby with crystal chandeliers and comfy blue couches. The hotel welcomes families, offering a children's playroom, a 4 o'clock story hour in summer, a supervised pizza-and-movie party for kids on Saturday night, and cookies, milk, and a copy of *Make Way for Ducklings* at bedtime on the first night. Alas, there is no pool. The best rooms for families are those with two double beds offered with the family package (these have two bathrooms, though they are tiny); request an outside room, or else you may look out on a brick courtyard. ♨ *1 Park Plaza at Arlington St., 02117, tel. 617/426–2000 or 800/225–2008, fax 617/426–5545. 977 rooms, 21 suites. Children up to 17 stay free. Facilities: 3 restaurants, 24-hr room service, health club, in-room movies, free parking, airport shuttle, baby-sitting. AE, DC, MC, V.*

Eliot Suite Hotel. There's a warm, homey, European feeling to this small but elegant nine-floor suite hotel in the Back Bay, near Newbury Street shopping. The building is old, so the suites (one or two bedrooms) have slightly different layouts, but all are comfortable and spacious, with traditional decor and new marble baths. Corner suites have views of the Charles River. A typical family suite includes a bedroom, a large living room with a foldout queen-size sofa, a TV in both rooms, and a microwave, a small refrigerator, and a coffeemaker. The hotel serves breakfast in a lovely room off the lobby, and soup and sandwich fare is available through room service. The location on

Commonwealth Avenue makes it a good base for walking around town. ♨ *370 Commonwealth Ave., 02215, tel. 617/267–1607 or 800/443–5468, fax 617/536–9114. 93 suites. Children under 12 free (limit 2 to a family); over 12, $10. Facilities: baby-sitting, laundry room, no-smoking rooms. AE, DC, MC, V.*

Harvard Manor House. This modern five-story brick motel is right off Harvard Square—Gavin's idea of a perfect location—and the price goes below $100 a night in off-season. Rooms are smallish, decorated in standard contemporary motel style; if your family requires quiet, be sure to ask for a room that doesn't face the street. ♨ *110 Mt. Auburn St., tel. 617/864–5200 or 800/458–7777, fax 617/864–2409. 72 rooms. Children under 16 free. Facilities: coffee shop, parking. AE, DC, MC, V.*

$

Boston International AYH-Hostel. The five family rooms here are basic but clean—wood floors, a bunk bed (double below, single above) and an extra mattress, rental linens, and personal lockers—but that's a lot for the rock-bottom price of $40 (minus a discount if you're a member of American Youth Hostels). It's a lot of value, especially considering the central location, near Symphony Hall, the Museum of Fine Arts, and the Back Bay Fens park. Other accommodations are in dormitory-style rooms with three to six bunks. The staff is an exceptional resource for information on Boston and Cambridge. Reserve several weeks in advance if you can. ♨ *12 Hemenway St., 02115, tel. 617/536–9455. Accommodates 200; 5 family rooms. Facilities: shared kitchen and bath facilities. MC, V (for rooms reserved at least 48 hrs ahead).*

Susse Chalet Motor Lodge. There are two buildings here: a motor lodge fashioned after a ski lodge, where rooms have few frills, and a newer, more modern hotel-style inn next door. There's an outdoor pool, an indoor kids' center with video games and activities like the toddlers' ball crawl, and an adjacent bowling alley. Rooms are decent-sized, decorated in pleasant but bland motel style, and you can reserve a microwave and fridge. It's a 10-minute drive from the center of Boston, or you can get on the T (the Alewife stop on the Red Line is just under a mile away) to avoid taking your car into downtown. Ask for family package rates, offered year-round.

🏠 *800–900 Morrissey Blvd., Dorchester 02122, tel. 617/287–9200 or 800/524–2538, fax 617/265–9287. 306 rooms, 1 family suite. Children under 18 free. Facilities: restaurant, pool, free parking. AE, DC, MC, V.*

Terrace Motor Lodge Best Western. It looks like a highway motel plunked down on a city street, but the two-room family suites here, which include kitchenettes, are a big bargain. Close to Boston University and Boston College, it's only a few blocks from a public ice rink and a ball field, and within walking distance of the Green Line T.

🏠 *1650 Commonwealth Ave., 02135, tel. 617/566–6260 or 800/242–8377, fax 617/731–4543. 73 rooms. Children under 18 free. Facilities: free Continental breakfast, free parking. AE, CB, DC, MC, V.*

Bed-and-Breakfasts

Many B&Bs in Boston, unlike those in New York City, actually welcome children. **Bed and Breakfast Associates/Bay Colony Ltd** (Box 57–166, Babson Park Branch, Boston 02157–0166, tel. 617/449–5302, fax 617/449–5958) represents about 400 rooms throughout the city and surrounding area. If you stay in a house with two guest rooms sharing a bath, the second room is usually half-price for children. Expect to pay anywhere from $55 (if your kids are under 5 and stay in your room) to about $140 (for two rooms). When you reserve, ask detailed questions about locations, and check the deposit and refund policy.

Apartment Rentals

AAA Corporate Rentals. Totally furnished one- or two-bedroom condos with fully equipped kitchens and bathrooms—sometimes even fireplaces and cable TV—can be rented. For a weeklong stay, a family of four will spend about $130 per day.

🏠 *335 Beacon St., 02116, tel. 617/536–5020 or 800/487–5020, fax 617/536–2440.*

Entertainment and the Arts
Amusement Parks

(👫 2+) **Canobie Lake Park.** Only a 35-minute drive from Boston, this big shady park offers original turn-of-the-century buildings and 40 rides set against the backdrop of a lake. The exuberant spirit of the place hits you from the moment you park your car, and it has something for everyone, from the Yankee Cannonball, a classic old wooden roller coaster, to the Psycho-Drome, an indoor scrambler with light and sound effects (older kids only), a huge swimming pool, and 20-minute rides on a paddlewheeler. Throughout the summer puppet shows are presented daily; Saturday night means fireworks.

🏠 *North Policy St., Salem, NH, tel. 603/893–3506. Take exit 2 off Rte. 93, then left on Policy St. ½ mi. Cost: $14 adults, $8 kids under 48 inches. Open daily mid-April–Labor Day, noon–10.*

(👫 2+) **Salem Willows Park.** Beloved by several kids on my Boston panel, this oceanfront park is a nostalgic reminder of another era with a funky arcade, rides for little ones, best popcorn in the world, free concerts, and a pier for strolling and fishing.

🏠 *173 Fort Ave., Salem, tel. 508/745–0251.*

Film

(👫 3 – 6) **Boston Public Library.** A regular series of free films for younger kids is

held in this historic library filled with statues and paintings—don't miss the marble lions guarding the impressive main stairway.
🏠 *Copley Sq., tel. 617/536–5400. Sept.–June, 1st Fri. and Sat. of month, AM; July–Aug., Fri. AM.*

(👫 8+) **Hatch Shell on the Esplanade.** Bring a blanket and a picnic for the urban version of a drive-in: free Friday night flicks on a big screen (only in summer). Cross the Arthur Fiedler footbridge at Arlington and Beacon streets.
🏠 *Tel. 617/727–9547.*

(👫 6+) **Sony Theaters Copley Place.** Set in an upscale mall with expensive shops, this 11-screen theater always has at least a few films appropriate for younger kids.
🏠 *100 Huntington Ave., tel. 617/266–2533; ticket charge 617/333–5639 or 617/333–3456.*

Performing Spaces and Performers: Theater, Music, Dance

Considering its size, Boston and the surrounding towns have a significant number of performances for kids, many of them inexpensive events at college and university theaters. For folk music, Boston even beats out New York. The most complete listings appear in the Thursday edition of the *Boston Globe* and the monthly calendar in *Boston Parents' Paper* (see How to Find Out What's Going On, *above*).

DISCOUNT TICKETS

Bostix, Boston's best ticket source, sells half-price tickets for same-day performances at an octagonal booth by Faneuil Hall (tel. 617/723–5181; open Tues.–Sat. 11–6, Sun. 11–4; closed holidays). A "menu board" in front tells you which events are available. The line is always long on weekends, and you must pay cash. Advance half-price tickets are available by mail through **Arts/Boston** (100 Boylston St., tel. 617/423–0372).

THEATER AND PUPPET SHOWS

(👫 5–12) **Boston Children's Theatre.** Dramatizations of classic children's books are the specialty of this theater company of children and teenagers.
🏠 *93 Massachusetts Ave., Boston 02115, tel. 617/424–6634. Performances in The New England Hall, 225 Clarendon St.*

(👫 6+) **Children's Theatre in Residence at Maudslay State Park.** Innovative kids' theater is performed on weekends June through September in a gorgeous outdoor setting on an old estate.
🏠 *Curzon Mill Rd., Newburyport, tel. 508/465–2572. Take Exit 57 off Rte. 95, go right on Rte. 113, turn left at cemetery onto unmarked Noble St., then follow signs. Cost: $6 adults, $4 kids. First performance of each show free.*

(👫 6+) **Marco the Magi's "Le Grand David and his Own Spectacular Magic Company."** This lavish magic and vaudeville show takes place in suburban Beverly.
🏠 *Cabot Street Cinema Theatre, 286 Cabot St., Beverly, tel. 508/927–3677. Take Rte. 128, exit 22E to Rte. 62 and go 2½ mi to Cabot St.*

(👫 5+) **North Shore Music Theatre.** Celebrity concerts, Broadway musicals, and kids' plays and concerts are performed in the round, so you can see easily from any seat.
🏠 *62 Dunham Rd. (exit 19 off Rte. 128), Beverly, tel. 508/922–8500. Cost: $26 for regular shows, $6 kids' shows.*

(👫 5–12) **Puppet Showplace.** One of the best puppet theaters in the Northeast features two resident companies and visiting troupes.
🏠 *32 Station St., Brookline, tel. 617/731–6400. Brookline Village stop on Green Line T.*

(👫 9+) **Shear Madness.** A long-running humorous mystery play is performed cabaret-style.
🏠 *Charles Playhouse, 24 Warrentown St., tel. 617/426–5225.*

ALL **Wheelock Family Theatre.**
This college theater produces excellent
drama, musicals, and shows for both
younger and older children.
🏠 *Wheelock College, 200 The Riverway, tel.
617/734–5200.*

MUSIC

In summer, Boston rings with free outdoor
concerts in parks and plazas. To us the most
interesting concerts for kids are on Boston
Common, in City Hall Plaza (tel. 617/725–
4505) and on the Esplanade (*see below*). If
you have teenagers, check at Newbury
Comics (*see Shopping, above*) for information on store-sponsored rock music events.

8+ **Boston Pops.** The century-old
orchestra plays a crowd-pleasing mix of classical favorites and movie music in two locations—Symphony Hall in winter and the
Hatch Shell on the Esplanade in summer.
🏠 *301 Massachusetts Ave. tel. 617/266–
1492 or 617/266–2378.*

5 – 12 **Boston Symphony Orchestra.**
One of the country's great orchestras presents regular short youth concerts, with
activities before and after.
🏠 *301 Massachusetts Ave., tel. 617/638–
9375 (Youth Activities Office).*

8+ **Esplanade Concerts.** Picnicking
on the grass above the Charles River while
music wafts out from the Hatch Band Shell is
a summertime must for us. In addition to the
Boston Pops (*see above*), a range of internationally known dance, opera, and music
groups appears.
🏠 *Hatch Shell, tel. 617/727–0460.*

5+ **New England Conservatory.**
Boston's top-notch music college hosts per-
formances nearly every night.
🏠 *290 Huntington Ave., tel. 617/262–1120.
Concerts held in Jordan Hall, 30 Gainsborough
St.*

DANCE

5+ **Boston Ballet Company.** *The
Nutcracker, Cinderella,* and *Coppelia* are three

ballets performed by this generally excellent
company.
🏠 *19 Clarendon St., tel. 617/695–6950. Performances at the Wang Center for the Performing Arts, 270 Tremont St., tel. 617/482–9393.*

9+ **Dance Umbrella.** This organization, like Jacob's Pillow in the Berkshires,
presents the very best contemporary dance
troupes, such as the wild and acrobatic
Pilobolus.
🏠 *380 Green St., Cambridge, tel. 617/492–
7578. Many performances at the Emerson
Majestic Theatre, 219 Tremont St., tel. 617/
578–8727.*

CIRCUS

3 – 12 **Big Apple Circus.** In April and
May, this splendid one-ring show—possibly
the best circus in the world for younger
kids—performs in a heated tent near the
Children's Museum.
🏠 *Children's Museum, 300 Congress St.,
Museum Wharf, tel. 617/426–8855.*

6 – 15 **Ringling Bros. & Barnum and
Bailey Circus.** The three-ring big-top circus
plays at Boston Garden every October; on
arrival, a circus parade treks through the
North End.
🏠 *150 Causeway St., tel. 617/227–3200.*

MUSEUM PROGRAMS

2+ **Children's Museum.** Every
weekend there's something—a Japanese
mime, Puerto Rican dancers, a workshop to
learn hip-hop—and kids are invited to participate.
🏠 *300 Congress St., Museum Wharf, tel.
617/426–8855. Free with museum admission.*

4 – 12 **Museum of Fine Arts.** Two
regular year-round programs involve kids in
observing artworks and then creating something based on what they've seen. "The
Children's Room," for kids 6 to 12, is a free
drop-in workshop every weekday afternoon; "Family Place," held once a month on
a Sunday ($5 per family), is for kids 4 and
older with their parents.

🏛 *465 Huntington Ave., tel. 617/267–9300.
(See Museums, above, and Chapter 8).*

FESTIVALS AND STREET PERFORMERS

First Night (tel. 617/354–1340), a citywide,
no-alcohol New Year's Eve celebration of
250 performances, fireworks, and a special
kids' afternoon festival, is the oldest of these
events in the country. Every April, the **New
England Folk Festival** (tel. 617/354–1340)
attracts families for dance and music. On
weekends in late spring, summer, and early
fall **Faneuil Hall Marketplace** and **Harvard
Square** (particularly at Brattle Square,
where Mt. Auburn and Brattle Sts. join) are
thick with magicians, jugglers, musicians, and
acrobats. In late May, the **Street Performers
Festival** (tel. 617/523–1300) in Faneuil Hall
Marketplace is a time to stick bottle caps to
the bottom of your shoes and join the
marchers in the Kazoo Parade or simply
enjoy gazing at the continuous free entertainment. **The Revels** (Sanders Theater,
Cambridge, tel. 617/621–0505) is an annual
December pageant of folk traditions to cele-
brate the winter solstice, incorporating
music, dance, puppets, and exuberant audience participation.

NEW YORK CITY   ■ 4
SKYSCRAPERS, THE STATUE OF LIBERTY, AND THE BEST TOY STORE IN THE COUNTRY

My son Gavin, who grew up in New York and now visits regularly, has always thought of it as the most exciting city in the world—despite visits to Paris, Rome, Milan, Boston, and San Francisco. To him and my panel of 15 New York City kids it has the biggest and best of everything—skyscrapers and ferryboats, lights and crowds and energy, 7 million people that represent almost every nationality in the world, and tons of things to do that you can't do anywhere else. Here's what they love about New York: Chinese restaurants, climbing to the crown of the Statue of Liberty, the dinosaurs at the American Museum of Natural History, eating in tiny midtown parks with man-made waterfalls and at outdoor cafés, the Staten Island Ferry, the Paper Bag Players productions, flagging down taxis, the best bagels and the world's greatest pizza, the best toy store in the world, the daily rain-forest storm at the Bronx Zoo and the Knicks at Madison Square Garden, visiting a real aircraft carrier, making their own radio show at the Museum of Television and Radio . . . and on and on.

In fact, when we visit New York, choosing what to do is our family's biggest problem. I've learned that the most important thing you can do for your kids—and yourself— on a visit to this city is to resist the frenetic pace and slow down. Plan to see no more than two major attractions in one day and be flexible: To really enjoy this city with kids you have to build into your daily sightseeing plans a visit to a playground, a walk down just one street in a neighborhood, a stop for an ice cream at a café where you can watch people.

To most people, Manhattan is synonymous with New York City; that's where most of the city's attractions are. But the other four boroughs—Queens, Brooklyn, Staten Island, and the Bronx—are worth visiting too. Each offers something unique for families: the Bronx Zoo, the Brooklyn Botanical Garden, the New York Hall of Science in Queens, and Historic Richmond Town on Staten Island.

Manhattan is a collection of small neighborhoods: Greenwich Village, Chelsea, Murray Hill, the Upper East Side, the Upper West Side, Lincoln Center, Soho, Chinatown, Little Italy, the Lower East Side. Each has its own flavor, attractions, and restaurants. The best way to see and appreciate New York City with kids is to adopt a neighborhood for a day or a weekend and explore its sights, shops, restaurants, and parks.

The city also has its share of problems that families need to know about. The main question most families have is: Is it safe for children? My answer is: Most areas of Manhattan are as safe as—if not safer than—neighborhoods in any other major city. This means using the kind of caution required in any large city: sticking to well-lighted and well-traveled streets at night and being alert to what is going on wherever you are. I would not let young teenagers travel around the city by themselves even during the day, because they often don't have the street savvy to anticipate a problem. With small children, your main concern is street traffic and crowds. When crossing streets, watch out for bicyclists, who often ignore traffic lights, and hang onto rambunctious little kids in crowded stores, streets, and subways. Kids should know what to do and where to go in case they get separated from you.

Also anticipate the fact that you will see homeless people sleeping or begging for money on the street, in the subway, and in places like the Staten Island Ferry terminal. Some children are very upset by this and want to give money to them all. You may want to think about how to handle this situation with your own children.

The Basics

How to Find out What's Going On

Take a list of the attractions or events that most appeal to your kids, and make their first choice the highlight of your first day. **The New York Convention and Visitors Bureau** (2 Columbus Circle, New York, NY 10019, tel. 212/397–8222; open weekdays 10–6, weekends 10–6) has free information, bus and subway maps (be sure to get them here, as subway token booths often don't have them), a calendar of events, "The New York Hotel Guide," which lists 80 hotels that welcome children free or at a discount, "The New York Restaurant Guide," which lists restaurants with children's menus, a folder on seeing New York with children, and much more. Write for these before you come, or drop in here if you're in the neighborhood.

NEWSPAPERS, MAGAZINES, AND BOOKS. These publications are available on newsstands, in supermarkets, and in bookstores:

Big Apple Parents Paper (Family Communications, 36 E. 12th St., New York 10003; tel. 212/533–2277). This monthly newspaper includes a calendar of events as well as articles and reviews of restaurants.

Central Park Calendar of Events (Central Park Conservancy, 830 5th Ave. at 64th St., New York 10021, tel. 212/360–2766), published quarterly, lists walks, special activities, and performances for kids in Central Park.

New York City with Kids by Bubbles Fisher (Frommer, 1992) is the most complete guidebook to the city with kids; written from the point of view of a grandmother, it has a tone that's often hard to take, but it contains a lot of good information.

New York Family (Family Publishing Group, 141 Halstead Ave., Suite 3D, Mamaroneck 10543, tel. 914/381–7474) comes out monthly; it has the most detailed calendar of events and the most easy-to-use listings of current performances, museum exhibits, and the like.

New York Magazine (755 2nd Ave. at 40th St., New York 10016, tel. 212/880–0700) is published every week; check the sections "Other Events" and "Children."

New York Newsday (2 Park Ave., New York 10016, tel. 212/725–3600) has kids' features every day and events listings for kids on Friday.

The New York Times (229 W. 43rd St., New York 10036, tel. 212/556–1234) has a section on attractions for kids in the Friday Weekend Guide section.

ParentGuide (ParentGuide News, 475 Park Ave. S, New York 10016, tel. 212/213–8840) is also a monthly; their extensive listings cover all the boroughs.

BOOKS FOR KIDS. *Kidding Around New York City* by Sarah Lovett (John Muir Publications, 1993), for kids about 8 to 12, contains simple maps and provides a general overview of different areas and places that appeal to kids—like Chinatown.

A Kid's Guide to New York City (Gulliver's Travels series, Harcourt Brace, 1988), for ages 6 and up, includes much more historical information and the kind of amazing facts that usually appeal to kids.

If those don't get your children in the mood for New York, perhaps fiction will: *Eloise*, by Kay Thompson (ages 4–8), a classic humorous story of a little girl's life at the Plaza Hotel; *Harriet the Spy*, by Louise Fitzhugh (ages 8–12); *From the Mixed Up Files of Mrs. Basil E. Frankweiler*, by E. Konigsburg (ages 8–13), about children who hide out in the Metropolitan Museum of Art to solve an art mystery; and *Cricket in Times Square*, by George Selden (ages 8–12).

MOVIES. So many films have been set in New York that your child has probably seen one of them already, but if not, rent *Ghostbusters, Home Alone II, King Kong,* or *The Muppets Take Manhattan* to provide a preview of the city.

Getting into and out of New York

BY AIR. Try to land at LaGuardia Airport (in Queens) or Newark International Airport (in New Jersey) if you can; John F. Kennedy International Airport (in Queens) is a mess—many terminals are either in need of renovation or being renovated, the crowds are horrendous, and it's hard to get around. But all do have nurseries where you can easily change diapers, as well as a variety of restaurants, from Pizza Hut to cafeterias. If you're stuck at JFK, there's a great shop called Canyon Trading that features western headgear and jewelry.

How to get into Manhattan: Limousine services are the easiest way for your family to get to a hotel, as taxi lines are usually long. Limos can pick up riders only by prior arrangement; call at least 24 hours in advance. **Carmel Car and Limousine Service** (tel. 212/662–2222) and **Tel-Aviv Private Car & Limousine Service** (tel. 212/777–7777) often have station wagons that are larger but cost little or no more than taxis. If your children are over 12, an arranged limousine or taxi will actually cost your family less than an airport bus. Plan on $15–$23 plus tolls from LaGuardia; $24–$30 plus tolls from JFK; $25–$30 plus tolls from Newark. **Carey Airport Express buses** (tel. 718/632–0509 or 800/456–1012) go into Manhattan from JFK ($11) and LaGuardia ($8.50) frequently; as children under 12 ride free when accompanied by an adult, they're worth it for a single parent.

BY TRAIN. If you take **Amtrak** (tel. 800/872–7245), which offers frequent service between Washington, D.C., and New York, and Boston and New York, you will arrive at and depart from Pennsylvania Station (31st–33rd Sts. between 7th and 8th Aves.). Long Island Railroad trains (tel. 718/217–5477) and New Jersey Transit trains (tel. 201/762–5100) also come into this station. Metro-North Commuter Railroad (tel. 212/532–4900) serves the northern suburbs and Connecticut as far east as New Haven from Grand Central Terminal.

BY BUS. All lines arrive at and depart from Port Authority Bus Terminal. Prepare your kids to see a lot of vagrants and hustlers.

BY CAR. The major interstates that come into New York are I–495 from Long Island; I–95 from Connecticut and New England to the Bruckner Expressway (I–278) and across the Triborough Bridge; the Lincoln Tunnel (I–495), Holland Tunnel, and George Washington Bridge (I–95) connect New York City with New Jersey.

Getting Around New York

Take a cue from New Yorkers, who rarely use cars to get anywhere in the city. It's much easier (and more fun) to use public transportation or a taxi. While some hotels do offer parking, it is usually expensive (as much as $25 to $30 a day; see Lodging, *below,* for hotels that offer free parking), and many charge each time you take your car out. If you do drive to New York, plan to park your car for your entire stay.

TAKE A WALK. The easiest and most interesting way to see New York with children is on foot, provided that you have a stroller for children under 5. Do not try to go too far, and stop frequently. Sturdy shoes are important; pounding the pavement, stepping in potholes, and walking on cracked sidewalks is tiring. But walking offers kids a chance to notice typical New York sights: the man walking six huge dogs, bread shaped like a large turtle and an alligator in a bakery window, a juggler on a street corner. Our family likes to keep walking until we're all ready to go back to the hotel—then we take a taxi, subway, or bus and rest our feet.

The city streets above 14th Street are designed like a grid: Numbered streets run east and west, numbered and named avenues run north and south. Fifth Avenue divides the east side from the west side. The avenue west of Fifth is labeled Avenue of

the Americas, but no New Yorker calls it that. To us it's still Sixth Avenue. Below 14th Street the streets are a crooked hodgepodge, so you need a map. Manhattan is bounded on the west by the Hudson (or North) River and on the east by the East River.

Where to walk? Just explore a neighborhood. **Downtown** includes all the neighborhoods south of 14th Street. At the very tip of this island is **Lower Manhattan,** sometimes just called Wall Street or the Financial District. The oldest part of the city, it houses skyscrapers, the financial center, South Street Seaport, and parks right on the water. **Chinatown,** just north of it, has crowded streets filled with people speaking Chinese, fascinating shops, and dozens of Chinese restaurants. **Tribeca** and **Soho,** which border Chinatown on the west, are trendy and chic; you'll find the hippest art galleries, shops—especially clothing stores—and cafés here. Just north of Chinatown is **Little Italy,** a small neighborhood of Italian cafés, restaurants, and frequent festivals. Above these are **Greenwich Village** (called "the Village"), whose lovely tree-lined streets and brownstones, cafés, and shops reflect its history as home to writers and artists, and the **East Village,** whose funkier (and dirtier) streets spill over with a younger, more punk-looking crowd. **Chelsea** (on the west side) and **Gramercy Park** (on the east side) are largely residential. **Midtown,** bounded on the north by the bottom of Central Park, is like a big square in the center of the city that's primarily commercial—hotels, restaurants, department stores, and landmark office towers like the Empire State Building.

Everything above 59th Street is **Uptown.** On the west side of Central Park is the **Upper West Side,** a very family-oriented, primarily residential area with some important museums—the American Museum of Natural History, for example, as well as the Lincoln Center complex, and many family-welcoming restaurants. Just to the north of it is **Morningside Heights,** where Columbia

University is located, and above it is **Harlem**, a historic center for African-American culture, politics, and music for nearly a century, perhaps best explored on a tour (see Family-Friendly Tours, below). The **Upper East Side,** on the east side of Central Park, is dominated by expensive, elegant apartment buildings and shops and the greatest concentration of art museums in the city. Above it is **East Harlem** (or Spanish Harlem) where the population is almost entirely Latino.

RIDE THE SUBWAY. Subway tokens, available at booths or machines in each subway station, are $1.25; children under 6 ride free. Buy several at once. Put in a token to go through the turnstile; little kids under 6 just duck below it. The Metropolitan Transit Authority (MTA) is in the process of implementing an automated fare card system in which you slide a "MetroCard" through an electronic reader to pass through the turnstile; the reader deducts the fare from the card and displays how much remains. Many small stations still require tokens (and will until 1997). MetroCards are available at station token booths; they're good for a certain number of rides (from a $5 card for 4 rides up to an $80 card for 64 rides).

It's true that subways are noisy and often dirty, crowded, and—in some stations—filled with unsavory characters. It's also true that they are usually the quickest way to get somewhere and that many children—mine included—find them fun.

A few caveats. Avoid rush hours. Take a bus or taxi if you have a stroller and are alone; carrying a stroller up and down the flights of steps to the subway platforms is very tiring and dangerous—platforms slant toward the track and unattended strollers will roll. Hold tightly to your children's hands on the platform and stand well back from the edge. During off-peak hours wait in the designated safe area. Don't get into deserted cars.

Check the large subway maps by the token booth to figure out your route, ask the

token clerk or another passenger, or consult a folding map from the New York Convention and Visitor's Bureau. Most New Yorkers are friendly and are happy to help you. You can also call the Metropolitan Transit Authority's (MTA) information number, 718/330-1234, from 6 AM to 9 PM or its 24-hour number, 718/330-4847, for bus or subway directions in 140 languages and dialects.

TAKE THE BUS. Buses charge the same fare as the subway, $1.25; children under 6 ride free. You must have a subway token or exact change in coins; MetroCards are accepted on some buses beginning in spring 1995. Bus routes (the route number is displayed on the front of the bus) usually go north and south or east and west; if your route requires two buses, get a free transfer from the bus driver when you board. Before you wait at a bus stop, check to make sure the bus you want stops there, as not all buses stop at every stop along the route. It's important to have a bus map—get one at the New York Convention and Visitor's Bureau, Grand Central Station Information booth, or Penn Station Information booth, because buses never have them. You can call the MTA for route information (see Ride the Subway, above).

When traffic is heavy, buses are very slow, and during rush hours they're packed.

HAIL A TAXI. Because a family of four with two children over 6 will pay $5 for one ride on a subway or bus, if you're not going far, a taxi ride will actually cost less (they charge per ride, not per passenger—$1.50 for the first ⅕ mile, 25¢ for each additional ⅕ mile, and 25¢ for each 75 seconds you're not moving). Tip about 15%. It's usually pretty easy to find a taxi, but not when it's raining, at rush hour, or when theaters let out.

If your driver seems friendly, talk to him or her. Some were born in New York and know fascinating facts about the city. Most are new immigrants. One 11-year-old who delights in the power of flagging down a taxi finds out where the taxi driver is from; on one trip she learned how to say six words in Russian, on another she found out about life in New Delhi.

Family-Friendly Tours

Most kids I know do not like long tours on which adults drone on about events or buildings, so I've included only a few special tours.

👫 5+ **Circle Line Cruise.** New York is so packed with buildings that it's hard to get a picture of it as a whole, much less visualize it as an island. The best way is this classic 35-mile circumnavigation of Manhattan. The boats are big, so you don't feel cramped unless it's very crowded, as it is on holiday weekends when the weather is good. You can bring a lunch, but hot dogs and sodas are sold on board; there are bathrooms. Each guide has his own patter; some tell very funny jokes. Ours have always welcomed lots of questions from kids. Don't go unless it's a nice day, which means not too hot or too cold or too rainy, and don't go unless your child is up to a three-hour boat ride.
🏠 *Pier 83, 42nd St. at Hudson River, tel. 212/563–3200. Cost: $18 adults, $9 kids 2–12. Cruises Mar.–Dec. Tues.–Fri. 10, 1:30, weekends 10, 1:30, 5:30.*

👫 4+ **Express Navigation.** This hydroliner follows the same route as the Circle Line, but at a higher speed, taking only 1¼ hours.
🏠 *Pier 11, 2 blocks south of South Street Seaport, tel. 800/262–8743. Cost: $15 adults, $8 kids 5–11. Cruises Apr.–Sept., Mon.–Sat. at noon and 2.*

👫 4+ **Gray Line Trolley Tour.** This new tour in an old-fashioned trolley makes 16 stops around Manhattan, including the Intrepid Sea/Air/Space Museum and South Street Seaport, and takes about 2½ hours. What makes it great for families is that you can begin at any stop and get on or off the trolley as many times as you like; trolleys run

continuously every half hour, so you can walk around for an hour or two, then reboard a later one. The tour provides a guidebook with suggested walking tours and a good map for each stop, as well as commentary.
🏠 *1740 Broadway, tel. 212/397–2600. Cost: $16 adults, $8 kids 12 and under. Mar.–Oct. (Nov., if weather permits) daily 7:45 AM–6 PM.*

👫 9+ **Harlem Spirituals.** Of this friendly company's various bus tours in and around Harlem, those on Wednesday and Sunday, which include attending a vivid one-hour gospel service of music, singing, and clapping as well as stops at historic buildings such as the Apollo Theater, are best for kids. Soul-food lunches afterwards are optional and cost extra (but they're worth it). Tours begin at their midtown office.
🏠 *1697 Broadway, at 53rd St., tel. 212/757–0425. Cost: $30–$52 adults, $23–$45 kids 12 and under. Wed. and Sun. tours begin at 9 AM.*

👫 5+ **Island Helicopter.** The four helicopter tours are priced according to mileage; on the most expensive, you get to fly between the two towers of the World Trade Center, but all fly close to the Statue of Liberty and at least three skyscrapers. Not for kids who are scared of heights.
🏠 *E. 34th St. and East River, tel. 212/683–4575. Cost: $47–$119 per person. Apr.–Dec., daily 9–9, Jan.–Mar., daily 9–8.*

👫 5+ **Small Journeys, Inc.** If you are in New York with several other families, consider taking a custom tour with this group, which designs walking (and other) tours especially geared to children's interests. The guides are entertaining, flexible, and responsive to the group.
🏠 *114 W. 86th St., tel. 212/874–7300. Cost: $175 for 4 hrs., with a suggested maximum of 15 people.*

👫 5+ **Urban Park Rangers.** Rangers lead free walking tours every Saturday and Sunday at 11 or 2 (rain or shine) in Central Park. You need to reserve in advance. Be sure you ask what the suggested age range for the particular tour is. The tours last about 90 minutes and are full of action geared to kids—such as a Central Park "bug out" walk looking for insects beneath leaves and logs or an afternoon of Ranger nature games.

🏰 Belvedere Castle, Central Park, tel. 212/427–4040 or 212/772–0210. Admission free.

Pit Stops

The best places to find clean, pleasant bathrooms in New York City: all museums; major department stores, such as Saks Fifth Avenue, Bloomingdale's, Macy's, Lord & Taylor, Bergdorf Goodman, Tiffany's; lobbies of big hotels such as the Marriott Marquis in the theater district, which has rest rooms on each of its public levels; and public atriums, such as the Citicorp Center (53rd St. and Lexington Ave.), the Crystal Pavilion (805 3rd Ave. at 50th St.), Trump Tower (5th Ave. at 56th St.), or the World Trade Center or World Financial Center downtown. All of these rest rooms have enough space for you to change a diaper. If you're desperate, most shops will allow children to use their private facilities.

Now for a few don'ts: Don't plan on using the bathrooms prior to or during the intermission of any theater performance, no matter where it is. There are almost always long lines. The same is true of cinemas. Go before you leave for the theater. Don't use the bathrooms in railway terminals if you don't have to and don't use those in subway stations at all—they are usually filthy. Rest rooms in city parks can be iffy too; don't ever send a child in alone.

Emergencies

FOR MINOR PROBLEMS. Doctor's Walk-In (57 E. 34th St., tel. 212/683–1010); New York Hospital's Urgent Care Center (520 E. 70th St., tel. 212/746–0795) or Roosevelt Hospital's Urgent Care Center (58th St. at 9th Ave., tel. 212/523–6765).

FOR SERIOUS EMERGENCIES. Pediatricians are on duty in the emergency rooms at Bellevue Hospital Center (1st Ave. and 29th St., tel. 212/561–3025 or 212/561–4141) and at Columbia Presbyterian Medical Center (622 W. 168th St., tel. 212/305–6628 or 212/305–6000). In midtown there are 24-hour emergency rooms at St. Luke's–Roosevelt Hospital (58th St. at 9th Ave., tel. 212/523–6800) and St. Vincent's Hospital (7th Ave. and 11th St., tel. 212/790–7997).

Doctors on Call is a 24-hour house-call service (tel. 212/737–2333).

The Dental Emergency Service (tel. 212/679–3966; after 8 PM 212/679–4172) makes referrals.

24-hour Pharmacy: Duane Reade (485 Lexington Ave., tel. 212/682–5338).

Baby-Sitters

Most hotels have a list of baby-sitters or bonded baby-sitting agencies that they know and use regularly. The agency that many recommend is The Babysitter's Guild (60 E. 42nd St., Suite 912, tel. 212/682–0227), which has been in business for more than 50 years. Other baby-sitting agencies are listed in the Yellow Pages. Most charge $10 and up per hour, with a four-hour minimum.

When to Go

New York is a year-round destination, with special attractions indoors and outdoors during each season. In the coldest months, January and February (as well as any time the weather is miserable), New York's museums and indoor atriums provide plenty to occupy kids—and there's outdoor ice skating. December is exciting: The Christmas decorations are up, stores are crowded with shoppers, and there are free holiday concerts and performances all over the city that are geared toward children. But our favorite times are the early fall, late spring, and early summer, the most pleasant seasons for walking and outdoor sightseeing. These are also the seasons with the most parades and street fairs. Summer, especially July and August, can be brutally hot and humid; temperatures are often above 90°F, and though museums, buses, and shops are air-conditioned, just getting from place to place can be extremely unpleasant. On the plus side are the large number of free outdoor concerts, plays, and performances of all kinds.

Scoping out New York

Serendipities

Some of the sights our family views as "quintessentially New York" are free—or at least very inexpensive.

IN CENTRAL PARK

(👫 **2 – 6**) Climb on the Alice in Wonderland statue. You'll see little kids climbing all over this bronze statue of Alice sitting on a giant mushroom with a grinning Cheshire cat and flanked by the White Rabbit and the Mad Hatter.
🏛 *North side of Conservatory Water, near 5th Ave. and 76th St.*

(👫 **3 – 12**) Watch sailboats on the Conservatory Water. On Saturday at 10 you can watch people sailing very expensive and elaborate model boats on this small round pond many New Yorkers refer to as "the sailboat pond" (just in from 5th Ave. and 74th St.). You can bring your own toy sailboat to sail after the official races are over.

(👫 **2 – 10**) Listen to the Delacorte Music Clock. Near the Central Park Zoo is a whimsical clock (just in from 5th Ave. and E. 65th St.) set on top of a redbrick arch. Stand in front of it on the hour or half hour and you'll see and hear the six-animal band play a tune as they turn. The last time we were there the 4-year-old with us wanted to wait to see the hippo and hear the tune again and again and again.

(👫 **½ – 10**) Ride the carousel. This merry-go-round is a staple of childhood for many New York kids—an antique carousel with 58 painted, hand-carved horses and bouncy music. The carousel does go fast: Timid 2- and 3-year-olds may prefer to ride in one of the stationary sleighs.
🏛 *Midpark, off 65th St. transverse, tel. 212/879–0244. Cost: 90¢. Open May–Sept., weekdays 10:30–5:30, weekends and holidays 10:30–6:30; Oct.–Apr., daily 10:30–4:30, weather permitting.*

(👫 **ALL**) Feed the ducks on the pond. Bring a bag of bread crumbs to The Pond at the southeast corner of the park just off Grand Army Plaza (59th St. and 5th Ave.). Walk along the shore toward the bridge, and you'll see families of ducks eager to snap up your treats.

(👫 **ALL**) Horse-drawn carriages. Most kids are fascinated by the horse-drawn carriages at Grand Army Plaza at 59th Street (Central Park South) and 5th Avenue (you'll also find them along 59th St. and at 59th St. and Central Park West). All the carriages are different, some completely open, some covered; their drivers dress in top hats or other appropriate garb. You can hire a carriage for a ride through the park for $34 for 30 minutes; $10 for each additional 15 minutes (agree on a price in advance).

BOATS, TRAMS, AND SUBWAYS

(👫 **ALL**) Staten Island Ferry. One of New York City's major bargains is the 20- to-30-minute ferry ride from the tip of Manhattan across New York Harbor to Staten Island—it costs only 50¢. Make sure you wait for one of the high, old-fashioned ferries with outside deck space, so you can see the Statue of Liberty and the New York skyline. Our family likes to take the ferry on a warm summer night and see the city lit up; no matter how hot it is, there's usually a breeze on the water. Sometimes there are scheduled jazz concerts on board.

🏛 *Battery Park and Whitehall St. (Subway 1 or 9 to South Ferry), tel. 212/806–6940. Cost: 50¢. Open daily 24 hrs.*

👫 3+ **Roosevelt Island Tram.** Another way to get a splendid—and cheap—view of the Manhattan skyline is by riding the city's only aerial tram, from 59th Street to Roosevelt Island. It takes just a few minutes. Kids afraid of heights should avoid it, but those who like gondola rides or Ferris wheels think it's terrific.
🏛 *2nd Ave. between 59th and 60th Sts. (Subway 6, N, or R to 59th St.), tel. 212/832–4543. Cost: $1.40 each way. Open Mon.–Thurs. 6 AM–2 AM, Fri. and Sat. 6 AM–2:30 AM.*

👫 3–7 **Look down a subway grate.** There are 722 miles of tracks below the city, and you can see them when you look down an open subway grate. Hold your ears when a subway rushes through beneath you.

👫 2–13 Ride in the first subway car. Most kids love peering through the front window of the first subway car at the tracks and lighted tunnel, zooming through the darkness, and suddenly pulling into a lighted station.

NEIGHBORHOODS

👫 4–15 **Watch for murals on buildings.** New York is full of surprises. When you go to South Street Seaport or the Fulton Fish Market, walk north on Front Street to Peck's Slip, then face north and look at the trompe l'oeil mural of the Brooklyn Bridge by Richard Haas on the building opposite. When you're in Soho, find the "Knowledge is Power" graffiti mural (my son's favorite) at West Houston and Broadway and another Richard Haas mural of windows, one with a cat sitting on the windowsill, at the corner of Prince and Greene streets.

👫 ALL Neighborhoods. Our family is happy to spend an afternoon just wandering through one of New York's neighborhoods. Here are the two we like best:

In **Chinatown,** walk down Mott Street from Canal Street to Chatham Square. Gavin likes the pagoda-shape telephone kiosks and buildings, the twisty streets crammed with residents chattering Chinese with one another, and the restaurant windows where you can look in on chefs chopping and cooking. Kids can browse for Chinese toys and souvenirs displayed outside shops and markets. Chinatown Fair (8 Mott St.) is a video game arcade with more than 50 video and pinball games. It's a little dingy but filled with young kids having fun.

In **Soho,** walk down West Broadway, Wooster Street, and Prince Street. This 26-block gallery neighborhood of cast-iron buildings is especially entertaining on a crowded sunny Saturday. You'll see lots of New Yorkers with babies in strollers as well as teens and preteens.

Skyscrapers, Statues, and a Historic Seaport

👫 3–12 Castle Clinton National Monument. Built in the early 19th century to defend New York Harbor, this circular brick fortress is where you buy a ticket for the Statue of Liberty ferry. Surrounded by skyscrapers, it's a trip back in time.
🏛 *Battery Park. Admission free. Open daily 9–5.*

👫 5–15 Chrysler Building. Though not as tall as the Empire State Building, this shiny skyscraper, built as the home of the Chrysler Corporation, looks more like Flash Gordon's idea of a rocket. Look up at the car designs at each setback—the gargoyles at the fourth one are in the style of radiator caps—and the wheel designs carved right in the brick. If you go into the marble lobby, check out the ceiling mural.
🏛 *405 Lexington Ave., between 42nd and 43rd Sts. Open weekdays.*

👫 ALL Empire State Building. This 60-year-old landmark is probably the best known of the city's skyscrapers, even to kids. You can see 50-mile views and five states on a clear day from the 86th-floor outdoor promenade or the 102nd-floor observatory See also Chapter 7. In the lobby is the **Guinness World of Records Exhibit Hall** (see Museums, below).

🏛 34th St. and 5th Ave., tel. 212/736-3100.

(👫 8+) **Federal Hall National Memorial** and **Federal Hall Memorial Museum.** The big statue of George Washington on the steps of this building marks the spot where Washington took the oath of office as the first president. Gavin, like many kids, was surprised to hear that New York was once the country's capital and that Congress once met right here. If your kids are American history buffs, see the exhibits in the museum inside and buy a quill pen and paper.

🏛 26 Wall St., at Nassau St., tel. 212/264-8711. Admission free. Open weekdays 9-5.

(👫 5+) **Grand Central Terminal.** Of the two main train stations in Manhattan, this one's the more spectacular. In the main lobby, a map of the constellations covers the high ceiling, with stars marked in twinkling lights. Climb the wide marble stairs at rush hour and watch the commuters. Don't forget to try out the "whispering wall" near the Grand Central Oyster Bar on the lower level. Find the vaulted ceiling with four white tile square arches that come to the floor. Face the wall at the end of one arch; get another person to face the wall where the other end of that arch comes to the floor. When each of you whispers something into your respective corners, you'll hear what the other has said.

🏛 42nd St. and Lexington Ave., tel. 212/935-3960.

(👫 10+) **New York Stock Exchange.** The view from the visitor's gallery of brokers noisily trading shares on the 90-by-90-foot floor and the electronic screens on the walls were more interesting to kids we know than the exhibits and guided tours in the visitor's center. During school vacations, get in line early.

🏛 Visitor's Center, 20 Broad St. (Subway 2, 3, 4, or 5 to Wall St.; or J, M, or Z to Broad St.), 3rd Floor, tel. 212/656-5168. Free tickets distributed starting at 9; arrive before noon to be certain of getting in. Open weekdays 9:15-4.

(👫 8-15) **Old Merchant's House.** In this 19th-century residence you can see how a typical upper-middle-class merchant and his family in New York actually lived 125 years ago; my son loved imagining himself living there in 1880. This place is never crowded.

🏛 29 E. 4th St., tel. 212/777-1089. Cost: $3 adults, $1 kids 12 and under. Open Sun.-Thurs. 1-4.

(👫 ALL) **Rockefeller Center.** This complex of buildings, public plazas, and an ice rink on Fifth Avenue is a great place for walking around. (See also Chapter 7.) The Center also houses **Radio City Music Hall** (see Entertainment and the Arts, below) and the GE Building (on the west side of the Lower Plaza between 49th and 50th Sts.) where **NBC** is located. Tours of the NBC Studios ($7.75) leave from the GE Building's lobby (Mon.-Sat., plus Sun. in summer, every 15 minutes, 9:30-4:30). Kids especially like seeing the makeup rooms, special props, and the machinery in the studios.

🏛 47th-52nd Sts. between 5th and 6th Aves., tel. 212/632-4000.

(👫 ALL) **South Street Seaport.** Plan on spending a whole day in this 11-block district of restored seaport buildings, piers, and historic ships in lower Manhattan. They remind us of what New York was like in the 19th century when it was one of the great seaports of the world. It's also a center for boat rides, several dozen shops and eateries, and free entertainment and street performances every weekend. See also Chapter 7.

🏛 19 Fulton St., at East River, tel. 212/732-7678.

(👫 ALL) **Statue of Liberty.** This 151-foot-tall symbol of freedom, known to even very small children, is on all my New York kids' lists as one of the sights in the city they've liked best. It's a must-see, but wait for a nice day, go early to avoid crowds, and plan on at least four hours for your whole trip. *See also* Chapter 7.

🏛 *Liberty Island (ticket office at Castle Clinton for Statue of Liberty ferry), tel. 212/363–3200; ferry, 212/269–5755.*

(👫 9+) **Theodore Roosevelt Birthplace.** This small brownstone on a quiet street, now a national historic site run by the National Park Service, is a rebuilt version of President Theodore Roosevelt's childhood home. If your child is a Teddy Roosevelt fan, he or she may find all the memorabilia here, from bits of his baby clothing to tin campaign buttons, fascinating. Forget the teddy bear videos.

🏛 *28 E. 20th St., between Park Ave. and Broadway, tel. 212/260–1616. Open Wed.– Sun. 9–5. Cost: $1 adults, kids under 17 free.*

(👫 10+) **United Nations.** It's the flags of all the nations flying outside the Secretariat, one of the three main U.N. buildings, that appeal to kids under 10. Older kids like the meditation room in the main lobby; attending a meeting of the General Assembly, in session from September to Christmas (arrive early; only a limited number of seats are available each day); and the daily tours—in the Visitor's Gallery kids can listen on headphones and press a button to hear a translation into another language. The gift shops downstairs have international souvenirs, books of all countries, and U.N. stamp collections. The costumed, handmade dolls are especially colorful. Call before you go.

🏛 *East River between 45th and 46th Sts. (Subway 4, 5, 6, 7, or S to Grand Central Station, then walk east), tel. 212/963–7713; reservations, 212/963–4440. Cost: $6.50 adults, $4.50 students, $3.50 8th graders and under; no kids under 5. Tours daily 9:15–4:45.*

(👫 ALL) **World Financial Center.** The four buildings are joined by corridors lined with shops and restaurants; the Courtyard and Winter Garden Atrium overlooking the Hudson are places to run to in rainy weather or to buy take-out sandwiches or ice cream to eat while strolling on the

Esplanade (*see* Green Spaces, *below*). Weekends and holidays bring scheduled free entertainment, most of it for children.

🏛 *Battery Park City, on Hudson River at Liberty and Vesey Sts., tel. 212/945–0505.*

(👫 ALL) **World Trade Center** and **Observation Deck.** The view and the ride to the top of the city's two tallest skyscrapers still thrill us. *See also* Chapter 7.

🏛 *Church and Cortlandt Sts.; information and children's activities, tel. 212/435–4170; observation deck, tel. 212/435–7397.*

Museums

MANHATTAN

(👫 5+) **American Craft Museum.** Baskets, quilts, furniture, and objects made from fabric, clay, and glass are on display here. The exhibits are always imaginative. Check to see what's on.

🏛 *40 W. 53rd St., between 5th and 6th Aves., tel. 212/956–3535. Cost: $5 adults, $2.50 students over 12. Open Wed.–Sun. 10–5, Tues. 10–8.*

(👫 ALL) **American Museum of Natural History.** The best natural history museum in the country and the largest in the world, this is one of New York's must-see family sights. We don't know any kids, including toddlers, who don't love this huge place, filled with some 30 million specimens and artifacts. Dinosaur exhibits, lifelike animal dioramas, a hall of glittering minerals and gems—it would take a week to see everything that's here. The **Hayden Planetarium** has regular sky shows, including two specifically for children (reservations are needed). *See also* Chapter 8.

🏛 *Central Park West at 79th St., tel. 212/ 769–5100.*

(👫 1–10) **Children's Museum of Manhattan.** At this four-floor interactive museum of environments toddlers and preschoolers can explore colors, textures, nature, a sandy beach, and more in the Family Learning Center; older kids like the special exhibits, checking out recycling in the outdoor Sussman Environmental Center and Urban Tree House, and using a TV production studio where you can make your own video. *See also* Chapter 8.

🏠 *212 W. 83rd St. (Subway 1 or 9 to 79th St.), tel. 212/721–1223.*

👫 ALL **The Cloisters.** We've always loved walking around the medieval buildings, cloistered walkways, and gardens of this branch of the Metropolitan Museum of Art that looks like a medieval monastery. Toddlers gravitate to the flowers and statues in the small courtyards. Older kids enjoy the Unicorn tapestries and walking on the parapet. Quiet and peaceful, it has a wonderful view of the Hudson River.

🏠 *Fort Tryon Park (Bus M4 from midtown, or Subway A to 190th St.), tel. 212/923–3700. Suggested donation: $7 adults, $3.50 students, 12 and under free. Open Mar.–Oct., Tues.– Sun. 9:30–5:15; Nov.–Feb., Tues.–Sun. 9:30–4:45.*

👫 10+ **Ellis Island Immigration Museum.** An estimated 40% of all Americans today have at least one relative who was among the 12 million immigrants who came through Ellis Island between 1892 and 1954. The buildings here have been restored to what they looked like in 1918 and house exhibits of photographs and artifacts of that era. Go on a weekday if you can to avoid long lines. *See also* Chapter 8.

🏠 *Ellis Island (Statue of Liberty boat from Battery Park), tel. 212/363–3200.*

👫 4–12 **Forbes Magazine Galleries.** This museum in Greenwich Village is small and special, with a wonderful collection of 500 toy boats and 12,000 toy soldiers.

🏠 *62 5th Ave., at 12th St., tel. 212/206– 5548. Admission free. Open Tues., Wed., Fri., and Sat. 10–4.*

👫 4+ **Guggenheim Museum.** Though this Frank Lloyd Wright–designed museum has an extensive collection of European and American painting and sculpture, the real reason to see it with children is the build-

ing's spiral shape. Take the elevator to the top and follow the ¼-mile-long ramp past the paintings on the way down.

🏠 *1071 5th Ave., at 88th St. (Subway 4 or 6 to 86th St.), tel. 212/423–3500. Cost: $7 adults, $4 students, children 12 and under free. Open Sun.–Wed. 10–6, Fri. and Sat. 10–8.*

👫 8–15 **Guinness World Records Exhibit Hall.** Nearly 200 life-size displays, videos, and artifacts bring to life feats and facts from the *Guinness Book of World Records.* Two kids we know who are 13 and 15 thought this place was expensive, tacky, and a rip-off, but several others, who are fans of the book, thought it was great. The highlight for one was the World of Sports data bank, but his brother liked the videos best, especially the one of a man downing 32 eggs in 78 seconds.

🏠 *Empire State Building, 350 5th Ave., Concourse Level, tel. 212/947–2335. Cost: $6.95 adults, $3.50 kids under 12. Open daily 9 AM–8 PM.*

👫 4–15 **Intrepid Sea/Air/Space Museum.** When you board this World War II aircraft carrier, the USS *Intrepid,* you can see the fastest spy plane in the world and 40 other aircraft, space vehicles, and rockets. Across the pier are a guided missile submarine, a destroyer, and a 150-foot lightship that can be visited. A must-see on several boys' and girls' lists, this is the only museum in the world in an aircraft carrier. *See also* Chapter 8.

🏠 *Pier 86, W. 46th St. at 12th Ave. (Subway A, E, or C to 42nd St.; or Bus M42 to last stop), tel. 212/245–2533.*

👫 11–15 **Lower East Side Tenement Museum.** This urban living history museum on the Lower East Side portrays the lives of immigrants in New York City in the 19th and early 20th century. The gallery has several rooms of exhibits and displays of photographs of immigrants' living conditions. Taking a tour of the two restored apartments in the museum's actual tenement building at 97 Orchard Street is the most interesting part of a visit here. Guides acquaint you with the Italian and German families who really lived in these apartments and what their lives were like. They are full of facts about the hardships of immigrants' lives (so many people lived in an apartment that they had to sleep in shifts, for example). Sundays are crowded.

🏠 *90 Orchard St., between Broome and Delancey Sts. (Subway F to Delancey St.), tel. 212/431–0233 or 212/387–0341. Cost: $7 adults, $5 students, kids under 12 free. Open Tues.–Fri. 11–5, Sun. 11–6.*

(👫 4+) **Metropolitan Museum of Art.** Still the largest art museum in the Western Hemisphere and one of the greatest art museums in the world, the Met (as it's known to New Yorkers) is filled with gallery after gallery of masterpieces. Surprisingly many kids say they like this better than any other art museum in the city; don't miss the Temple of Dendur, the arms and armor collection, and one of the family programs. See *also* Chapter 8.

🏠 *1000 5th Ave., between 82nd and 84th Sts., tel. 212/535–7710.*

(👫 3+) **Museum of the City of New York.** A favorite destination of Gavin's, this family-friendly museum devoted to the history of New York City houses a permanent collection of fabulous dollhouses and antique toys on the third floor and models of ships and dioramas of life in early New York on the second floor. Their excellent once- or twice-a-month free family weekend workshops always include something hands-on related to an exhibit or collection—like learning to play old-fashioned stickball (during the Stickball Hall of Fame exhibit) or making dollhouse furniture from found objects.

🏠 *5th Ave. at 103rd St. (Subway 6 to 103rd St., or Bus M1, M3, or M4), tel. 212/534–1672. Suggested donation: $8 per family, $5 adults, $3 children. Open Wed.–Sat. 10–5, Sun. 1–5.*

(👫 7+) **Museum of Modern Art.** At this world-famous collection of modern paintings on Saturday mornings from 10 to 11 there's a special $5 per family (including a return pass) drop-in guided tour for kids 5 to 10 and their parents before the museum (known as MOMA to New Yorkers) opens; each week you explore a different aspect of the museum's collections (enter through the Edward John Noble Education Center at 18 W. 53rd; doors open at 9:30). Hour-long family movie programs are shown on Saturday at 12:30, and twice a year (spring and fall) the museum has a special family festival day that includes performances and art activities.

🏠 *11 W. 53rd St. (Subway E or F to 5th Ave.), tel. 212/708–9500. Cost: $8 adults, $5 students, kids under 16 free with adult; pay what you wish Thurs. and Fri. after 5:30. Open Sat.–Tues. 11–6, Thurs.–Fri. noon–8:30.*

(👫 5–15) **Museum of Television and Radio.** This library of television and radio has a collection of 25,000 TV programs and 15,000 radio programs for viewing and listening that spans broadcast history. The key attractions for children are exhibits like the one in 1993 on Star Trek, regular screenings, and the radio workshops. (See Chapter 8 and Entertainment and the Arts, *below*.)

🏠 *12 W. 52nd St., tel. 212/621–6600.*

(👫 ALL) **National Museum of the American Indian.** The largest collection of Native American artifacts in the world is now at the Heye Center on the lower floors of the ornate Alexander Hamilton Customs House in downtown Manhattan, which opened in fall 1994.

🏠 *1 Bowling Green, tel. 212/668–6624. Admission free. Open daily 10–5.*

(👫 3–10) **New York City Fire Museum.** The two floors of horse-drawn fire wagons, fire buckets, sliding poles, and fireproof uniforms in this turn-of-the-century firehouse fascinated Gavin and his friends when they were about 5. The collection here is the largest in the country. The only drawback is that you can't climb on any of the fire engines. Call to make sure a school tour isn't scheduled for the day of your visit or it's a madhouse.

🏠 *278 Spring St., between Hudson and Varick Sts., tel. 212/691–1303. Suggested donation: $3 adults, 50¢ children. Open Tues.–Sat. 10–4.*

👫 ALL **South Street Seaport Museum.** Only part of the whole seaport complex is an actual museum; it comprises the four historic ships, a gallery with changing exhibits, a working 19th-century print shop, and a children's center with hands-on workshops. Exploring aboard the sailing ships, especially the four-masted *Peking,* was a thrill for my son and his friends. *See also* Chapter 7.

🏠 *16 Fulton St., at East River, tel. 212/ 669–9400.*

👫 7+ **Studio Museum of Harlem.** The center of Harlem's art community, this small, but world-class 25-year-old museum features both paintings and sculpture of African-American, African, and Caribbean artists and exhibits of crafts that appeal to kids. Events like the December Kwaanza celebration attract many families. The gift shop has an excellent selection of books on African-Americans.

🏠 *144 W. 125th St., between Malcolm X and Adam Clayton Powell Blvds. (also called Lenox Ave. and 7th Ave.), tel. 212/864–4500. Cost: $5 adults, $3 students 12 and over, $1 children under 12. Open Wed.–Fri. 10–5, Sat.–Sun. 1–6.*

👫 3–10 **Ukrainian Museum.** We like to visit this small, unusual, out-of-the way museum during the two months before Easter to see their extensive collection of painted Easter eggs (called *pyansky*). There are workshops (for older kids) that will teach you how to copy the designs once used to ward off evil spirits.

🏠 *203 2nd Ave., between 12th and 13th Sts., tel. 212/228–0110. Cost: $1 adults, 50¢ students, children under 12 free. Open Wed.–Sun. 1–5.*

BROOKLYN

👫 2–12 **Brooklyn Children's Museum.** A multilevel hands-on play-and-learn museum with an imaginative tunnel entrance, this wildly exuberant place is hard to get to but worth it. Exhibits explore water (including a waterwheel kids can play with) and my son's favorite—the Walking Piano in the music studio. Other attractions include daylong group workshops on weekends and during holidays. *See also* Chapter 8.

🏠 *145 Brooklyn Ave., tel. 718/735–4400.*

👫 7+ **New York City Transit Museum.** Set in an actual 1930s subway station, the museum has 18 restored subway cars, some 90 years old. A group of Cub Scouts we know rated the scale model of the entire 460-station subway system the best sight.

🏠 *Beneath Boerum Pl. and Schermerhorn St., Brooklyn Heights (Subway G to Schermerhorn; A or F to Jay St./Borough Hall; M, N, or R to Court St.; or 2, 3, or 4 to Borough Hall), tel. 718/330–3060. Cost: $3 adults, $1.50 kids under 17. Open Tues.–Fri. 10–4, weekends noon–5.*

STATEN ISLAND

👫 ALL **Historic Richmondtown.** The 26 restored 17th- to 19th-century buildings in this 90-acre museum village include the oldest (300 years old) standing elementary school in the United States. From time to time craftsmen such as the harness-maker wearing period costumes give demonstrations and there are special seasonal events. A museum of childhood displays antique dolls and toys.

🏠 *441 Clarke Ave., Staten Island (Staten Island Ferry, then Bus S74), tel. 718/351– 1611.*

👫 1–10 **Staten Island Children's Museum.** Part of the Snug Harbor Cultural Center, a group of landmark buildings on 80 acres overlooking New York Harbor that offers concerts and art shows, this museum for children has several hands-on exhibits set up as environments to play in. In the "Building Buildings" environment they can build with blocks as well as examine exposed (not connected) wires and plumbing in a construction site; in another they can investigate the science behind magic tricks.

🏠 1000 Richmond Terr. (Staten Island Ferry, then Bus 40), tel. 718/273–2060. Cost: $3.25, kids under 2 free. Open Tues.–Sun., noon–5.

QUEENS

(👫 8+) **American Museum of the Moving Image.** For kids who are buffs, this is the only museum in the country devoted to film, television, and radio. In the permanent exhibit, Behind the Scenes, don't miss Tut's Fever Movie Palace, a spoof of 1920s movie palaces complete with life-size cutouts created by artist Red Grooms; the "Magic Mirror" that projects your image wearing famous stars' costumes; and one of the original Yoda puppets from *The Empire Strikes Back.* Among the great temporary exhibits we've seen here is the history of video games (you could play all of them). Check to see what's on.

🏠 35th Ave. and 36th St., Astoria, Queens (Subway N to Broadway, Queens), tel. 718/784–0077 or 718/784–4520. Cost: $5 adults, $2.50 children and students with ID, children under 4 free. Open Tues.–Fri. noon–4, weekends noon–6.

(👫 3 – 15) **New York Hall of Science.** New York City's only science museum, filled with two floors of hands-on exhibits, is worth the trek to Queens. Kids can learn about light, optical illusions, atoms, and, in an exhibit new in 1994, the science of sounds. Kids' favorites: blowing a bubble 2 feet across, watching a film of the dissection of a cow's eyeball, pedaling a bike to turn an airplane propeller, and looking at the video microscope. *See also* Chapter 8.

🏠 47-01 111th St., Flushing Meadows, Queens, tel. 718/699–0005.

Animals

New York is astonishing in having not just one, but four zoos and one aquarium, all managed by the New York Zoological Society's Wildlife Conservation Society. It's easy to think only of visiting the huge internationally famous Bronx Zoo, but for small children the others in Manhattan, Queens, and Brooklyn may be more appealing and manageable, especially if you don't want to spend an entire day looking at animals.

MANHATTAN

(👫 0 – 12) **Central Park Wildlife Conservation Center.** The 5½-acre Central Park zoo, small and encompassable, is a delight, especially for toddlers and preschoolers. The animals are arranged in areas representing three different climate zones—the Tropic Zone, the Temperate Territory, and the Polar Circle—interspersed with charming gardens. The gift shop, snack bar, and planned events are outstanding. *See also* Chapter 9.

🏠 64th St. and 5th Ave., tel. 212/861–6030.

THE BRONX

(👫 ALL) **Bronx Zoo/International Wildlife Park.** Plan to spend an entire day at the oldest and largest zoo in any United States city. Its naturalistic habitats, home to some 4,000 creatures, substitute moats for cages to separate people from the animals. Visit the indoor rain forest to watch the monkeys, journey to the Himalayas to see pandas and snow leopards, take a safari to Wild Asia by way of a monorail train and look down on Siberian tigers and elephants. In the Children's Zoo, kids can pet and feed domestic animals. *See also* Chapter 9.

🏠 Bronx Park, Bronx, tel. 718/367–1010.

BROOKLYN

(👫 ALL) **New York Aquarium for Wildlife Conservation.** After much renovation and new building in 1993 and 1994, this is one of the Northeast's top aquariums, with 300 species of fish and outdoor habi-

tats with penguins and seals. Make your visit part of a day-long excursion to Coney Island—walk along the beach and the 2½-mile boardwalk and stop at the Astroland Amusement Park. See also Chapter 9.
🏠 *Coney Island at W. 8th St., off Surf Ave., Brooklyn, tel. 718/265–3474.*

👫 **0–12** **Prospect Park Wildlife Conservation Center.** Opened in 1993, this zoo in Prospect Park is geared for children, with exhibits on animal lifestyles. Highlights are the baboon exhibit and the wallabies. It's best combined with a visit to lovely Prospect Park, the Brooklyn Botanic Garden (see Green Spaces, below), or a children's art program at the Brooklyn Museum (see Entertainment and the Arts, below).
🏠 *450 Flatbush Ave., Brooklyn, tel. 718/399–7339. Cost: $2.50 adults, 50¢ kids 3–12, free under 3. Open Apr.–Oct., weekdays 10–5, weekends 10–5:30; Nov.–Mar., daily 10–4:30.*

QUEENS

👫 **0–12** **Queens Wildlife Conservation Center.** This small, 11-acre zoo next to the Hall of Science specializes in North American animals, all cleverly arranged so you can see them close up, but in the surroundings they like best. The aviary is in Buckminster Fuller's geodesic dome, designed for the 1964 World's Fair. Most little kids like petting goats, rabbits, donkeys, and sheep.
🏠 *Flushing Meadows Park, 53-51 111th St., Queens, tel. 718/271–7761. Cost: $2.50 adults, 50¢ kids 3–12, free under 3. Open Apr.–Oct., weekdays 10–5, weekends 10–5:30; Nov.–Mar., daily 10–4:30.*

Green Spaces

👫 **ALL** **Battery Park Esplanade.** This 25-acre park along the Hudson River starts north of the World Financial Center (see Hudson River Park, below) and extends south of Battery Park City, a complex of apartments and shops. Strolling along on a nice day you'll see tugboats, ferries, and barges on the river, sailboats in the North

Cove harbor, and the Statue of Liberty from South Cove. The fences along the river are toddler-proof, and the small playground at the south side of North Cove is exceptionally clean. Skateboarding and rollerblading are permitted along one of the walkways.
🏠 *Battery Park City at World Financial Center, between West St. and Hudson River; enter through World Financial Center.*

👫 **ALL** **Central Park.** This 853-acre haven designed by Frederick Law Olmstead in the heart of Manhattan is one of the great city parks of the world. Home to a zoo, a model sailboat pond, a children's marionette theater, baseball fields, adventure playgrounds, a carousel, places to feed ducks, a rink for rollerblading and ice-skating, a lake for rowboating, statues to climb on, and bike and horseback riding, it provides so much for families that your visit to the city won't be complete without at least one stop. The playground at 67th Street and 5th Avenue has a tree house with a slide down into the huge sandbox area, a stone bridge, picnic tables, and a rock to climb. Others on the east side are at 71st, 77th, 85th, and 95th streets; on the west side you'll find good ones at 68th, 81st, 85th, and 93rd streets. The visitor center at the Dairy (64th St., midpark, tel. below) is the most convenient place to pick up a good map of the park, a calendar of events (there are many for kids), and try out some good hands-on exhibits. For the best people- (and skateboarder-) watching, head for Bethesda Terrace (72nd St., midpark).
🏠 *Bordered by 5th Ave., Central Park West, 59th St., and 110th St., tel. 212/794–6564.*

👫 **0–12** **Hudson River Park.** One of the nicest playgrounds in the city is along the Hudson River just north of the World Financial Center. Metal-chain climbing nets for the adventurous, miniature slides for toddlers, a pedal-driven carousel, even a raised sand-table for kids using wheelchairs, fill the enormous playground space.
🏠 *Between Chambers and Vesey Sts. at Hudson River. Special programs tel. 212/267–9700. Open daily dawn–dusk.*

Other Manhattan Parks and Playgrounds.
Among the small parks scattered all over
the borough, our favorites are: **Abingdon
Square Park** (in Greenwich Village at the
corner of Bleecker and Hudson Sts.), which
has a big sandbox and new climbing equipment; **Mercer St. Park** (also in the Village,
just north of Houston St.), which has a big
sand area, a climbing area with a bridge, and
a spray fountain when it's hot; the **P.S. 87
School Playground** (on the Upper West
Side at Amsterdam Ave. and 77th St.),
which has a fabulous, architect-designed,
parent-built climbing space. **Riverside Park**
(on the Upper West Side just west of Riverside Drive), a long narrow park along the
Hudson River, has a good playground at
91st Street. Some parts of this park are
cleaner and more pleasant than others.
Walk along the Promenade, a walkway that
goes north from 80th Street.

BROOKLYN

🏃🏃 ALL Brooklyn Botanic Garden.
When you need a break from the city environment, visit the garden's 52 acres with
more than 12,000 different kinds of plants.
For kids there's a Discovery Center and
Children's Garden, but most children also
like the ducks and bridges in the Japanese
Garden, where the pond (in the shape of
the Chinese character for "heart") has turtles and goldfish and a Japanese teahouse.
🏠 *1000 Washington Ave. (Subway 2 or 3 to
Eastern Pkwy., or D to Prospect Park), tel.
718/622–4433. Admission to garden free.
Cost for conservatory, $2 adults, $1 students
with ID and kids 3–11. Open Apr.–Sept.,
Tues.–Fri., 8–6, weekends and holidays, 10–6;
Oct.–Mar., Tues.–Fri., 8–4:30, weekends and
holidays, 10–4:30. Conservatory closes ½ hr.
earlier.*

🏃🏃 ALL Prospect Park. At 536 acres,
this stretch of green, also designed by Olmstead, is nearly two-thirds the size of Central
Park, on which it's modeled, though it has
no streets crossing it. The 90-acre Long
Meadow is great for picnics and kite-flying;

feed the ducks or paddle a boat on the 60-
acre lake; see puppet shows and more at
the Picnic House (tel. 718/788–0055) stage;
in winter, ice-skate on the rink; stop at the
zoo (see Animals, *above*). Right by the zoo
are a lovely old-fashioned carousel with
dragon chariots and giraffes; the Lefferts
Homestead, where kids can play with reproductions of 19th-century toys; and a playground with a tree house.
🏠 *Eastern Pkwy. and Grand Army Plaza
(Subway 2 or 3 to Grand Army Plaza, or D to
Prospect Park), tel. 718/965–8999. Open
daily dawn–midnight.*

THE BRONX

🏃🏃 ALL New York Botanical Garden.
One of the world's largest botanic gardens
(250 acres), with a huge, glass conservatory
filled with changing exhibits, this is reason to
make another trip to the Bronx.
🏠 *Bronx Park (Metro North train from Grand
Central Terminal to Botanical Garden station),
tel. 718/220–8700.*

ROOSEVELT ISLAND

🏃🏃 3 – 12 Lighthouse Park. Perched on
the northern tip of an island in the middle of
the East River, this lovely, clean small park
has picnic tables, lots of open space, a lighthouse, and a fine view of the Manhattan skyline, bridges, and tugboats. It's a good
excuse to take the tram, and it's fun for a
picnic on a warm day.
🏠 *Roosevelt Island tram from 2nd Ave.
between 59th and 60th Sts., then 10¢ bus trip
to park.*

Sports

Big Leagues

New York is home to six major-league
teams, but only two of them actually play in
Manhattan. When you buy tickets, check the
stadium diagrams near the front of the Man-

hattan Yellow Pages (see Chapter 11). Ticketmaster (tel. 212/307-7171) has tickets for all but football games.

BASEBALL. The baseball season runs from April to October.

New York Mets. The Mets (National League) play at Shea Stadium in Queens. Tickets are usually easy to get. *126th St. and Roosevelt Ave. (Subway 7 from 42nd St. to Willets Point/Shea Stadium stop), Flushing 11368, tel. 718/507-8499.*

New York Yankees. The home of the Yankees (American League) is Yankee Stadium in the Bronx, where they've played since 1923. Tickets are usually easy to get. *161st St. and River Ave. (Subway 4, C, or D to 161st St./Yankee Stadium), Bronx 10451, tel. 718/293-6000.*

BASKETBALL. Basketball season is late October to April.

New York Knickerbockers. The "Knicks," an NBA team, play at Madison Square Garden. Tickets are sometimes hard to get. *7th Ave. between 31st and 33rd Sts.; box office, tel. 212/465-6741; Knicks hot line, 212/465-5867; Ticketmaster, 212/307-7171.*

FOOTBALL. Football season is September to December.

The **New York Giants** (National Football Conference) and the **New York Jets,** (American Football Conference) both play at Meadowlands (East Rutherford, NJ 07073). It's nearly impossible to get tickets for either one, but a few individual Jets game tickets go on sale at the end of August. *Giants tel. 201/935-8111; Jets, 516/538-6600.*

HOCKEY. Hockey season is October to April.

New York Islanders. The Islanders (tel. 516/888-9000) play at Nassau Veterans Memorial Coliseum in Uniondale, Long Island.

New York Rangers. The Rangers (National Hockey League) play at Madison Square

Garden. *7th Ave. between 31st and 33rd Sts.; box office, tel. 212/465-6741; Rangers hot line, 212/308-6977.*

TENNIS. U. S. Open. One of United States tennis's four prime tournaments is held at the U.S.T.A. National Tennis Center in Flushing Meadows–Corona Park in Queens during the end of August and in early September. Tickets to early matches are sometimes easy to get; those for the semifinals and finals sell out as soon as they go on sale in May. *United States Tennis Association, Flushing Meadows–Corona Park, Flushing, Queens 11365, tel. 718/271-5100.*

Action

OUTDOORS

8+ **Bicycling.** The best place to ride bikes with kids is in **Central Park.** The long circular drive is closed to car traffic for several hours on weekdays and all weekends and on holidays. The most convenient place to rent bikes is AAA Bikes (Loeb Boathouse, mid-park near E. 74th St., tel. 212/861-4137). Expect to leave a credit card or a large deposit. If you have small children, consider renting a pedal carriage (they seat four) at the Tavern on the Green parking lot (Central Park West at 66th St., tel. 212/860-4619; $15 per hr). Brooklyn's **Prospect Park** is also a lovely place to bike; its winding roads are closed to cars.

3+ **Boating.** Rowing a boat on the 18-acre lake in the middle of Central Park is fun even when the lake is very crowded. My son still talks about seeing a fairly hefty man stand up, lose his balance, and go overboard, his arms waving while a dozen boatloads of people looked on. Let young teenagers have their own boat (if they can swim). Go early on a nice weekend morning or you'll wait and wait. *Loeb Boathouse*, mid-park near 74th St., tel. 212/517-4723.

4+ **Ice-Skating.** In winter, the two best places to skate outdoors are **Rockefeller Center** (50th St. at 5th Ave., lower plaza, tel. 212/757–5730) and the **Wollman Rink** (Central Park, midpark near 63rd St., tel. 212/517–4800). Both have lockers, skate rentals, music, and places to eat, and both are crowded on weekends. Wollman Rink is larger and has special teen rates. Don't go at night with little kids—the teens skate fast.

🚶 2+ Kite-Flying. The Sheep Meadow in **Central Park** near West 67th Street is a huge expanse of lawn. On a windy day, my son likes flying kites here along with bunches of other boys and girls.

🚶 5 – 13 Miniature Golf. New York is not really known for its mini golf courses, but at the nine-hole Gotham Miniature Golf (mid-park, near 64th St., tel. 212/517–4800) next to Wollman Rink in Central Park, open during warmer months, each hole is a scale model New York City landmark.

🚶 8+ Roller-Skating. The traditional spring, summer, and fall sport for kids 8 and up in New York City is rollerblading, and the best place to do it is in Central Park. Rent skates at **Peck & Goodies** (917 8th Ave. at 54th St., tel. 212/246–6123; 1414 2nd Ave. at 73rd St., tel. 212/249–3178; they also give lessons in Central Park); **Blades West** (120 W. 72nd St., tel. 212/787–3911); **Blades East** (160 E. 86th St., tel. 212/996–1644; they'll give you instructions and a carrying box); or at **Wollman Rink** (midpark at 63rd St., tel. 212/517–4800), where you can skate to music in the rink during the warm months—there are inexpensive special family nights here. You can also skate along the Riverside Park Esplanade and in Brooklyn's Prospect Park (see Green Spaces, *above*).

INDOORS

🚶 5+ Ice-Skating. The huge (200 foot by 85 foot) **Sky Rink** is a year-round ice surface on the 16th floor of a midtown building. Serious competitive skaters practice here, but it's fine for kids. You can rent skates.
🏠 *West St. at 23rd St., tel. 212/336–6100.*

🚶 ½ – 6 Indoor Playground. Mothers of very young children rave about **Playspace,** a new 4,000-square-foot indoor play area. It's clean, has safe climbing equipment, a huge sandbox, blocks and other toys, a snack bar, and is even air-conditioned. Parents must supervise their children.
🏠 *1504 3rd Ave., at 85th St., tel. 212/717–5200; 2473 Broadway, at 92nd St., tel. 212/769–2300. Cost: $8 for 3 hrs. Open Wed.–Mon. 10–6, Tues. 8–8.*

🚶 5+ Sports Center. At **Hackers, Hitters, and Hoops,** whether your kids want to play miniature golf, ping-pong, basketball, or bat a baseball in a batting cage, they can do it in this unique 23,000-square-foot sports center. It's expensive, but worth it if your kids are sports fanatics and you're here in winter.
🏠 *123 W. 18th St., tel. 212/929–7482.*

Shopping

New York is a shopper's paradise. This selection of stops represents a small fraction of places that appeal to kids. I've concentrated on the unique and unusual.

Flea Markets

A favorite activity of young New York teens is shopping for clothes and jewelry at some of the city's regular flea markets. Here are our family's picks:

The **Intermediate School 44 Flea Market** (Columbus Ave. between 76th and 77th Sts.) is held inside and outside this school building on Sundays from 10 to 5:30. There's a real teen scene here.

Tower Market (Broadway between W. 4th and Great Jones Sts.), on weekends from 10 to 7, is full of crafts and funky ethnic clothes.

Mall

👫 ALL South Street Seaport. The scores of shops in Pier 17, the Fulton Market Building, and the pedestrian extension of Fulton Street draw preteens and teens on weekends. Girls mention the clothing stores **Benetton, J. Crew, Gap,** and **Banana Republic.** My son always stops by the branch of **The Sharper Image,** filled with electronic gadgets. Other favorite places are **A to Z,** where you can custom-make a card, buy a lava lamp, or try on slippers that talk, and food shops like **Sweet Stuff/New York Egg Cream,** which has homemade candy and delicious egg creams. The highlight for several boys and girls we know is a stop at **Virtuality,** where you can put on head gear and try out virtual reality machines.

Comics and Baseball Cards

👫 6+ Forbidden Planet. When we lived in New York, no week was complete for my son without a trip to this store full of vintage and new comic books, a fabulous selection of science fiction and fantasy books and posters, and displays of games and collectible toy action figures, robots, and spaceships from the United States and Japan.
🏠 821 Broadway, at 12th St., tel. 212/ 473–1576.

👫 6+ New York Mets Clubhouse Shop (575 5th Ave., at 47th St., tel. 212/986–4887) and The **New York Yankees Clubhouse** (110 E. 59th St. between Park and Lexington Aves., tel. 212/758– 7844) both have baseball cards, memorabilia that belonged to former players, sweatshirts, hats, and so on. You can also purchase tickets for games in both shops.

👫 6+ Village Comics. Half of this second-floor comics store is full of new and collector comics, the other half has an outstanding selection of science fiction books and science fiction posters. Isaac Asimov's computer is on display—it was one of the first personal computers ever made.
🏠 163 Bleecker St., tel. 212/777–2770.

Books and Records

👫 2–10 Barnes & Noble Jr. A small, strictly children's branch of this citywide chain of huge bookstores, it has an excellent collection and offers regular story hours.
🏠 120 E. 86th St., between Lexington and Park Aves., tel. 212/427–0686.

👫 2+ Books of Wonder. Our favorite children's bookstore in New York is the largest, with 5,000 books including out-of-print bargains and any Oz book you want, but it doesn't feel like a warehouse. People who work here really like kids and know their books.
🏠 132 7th Ave., at 18th St., tel. 212/989– 3270.

👫 10+ HMV U.S.A. These huge CD, cassette, and record superstores with their high-tech decor are where my son and his friends like to buy—or to just sit in a booth and listen through headphones.
🏠 1280 Lexington Ave., at 86th St., tel. 212/ 348–0800; 201 Broadway, at 72nd St., tel. 212/721–5900.

👫 2–10 Storyland. In a well-stocked small bookstore you can enjoy children's story hours, usually with an author or illustrator.
🏠 1369 3rd Ave., at 78th St., tel. 212/517– 6951.

👫 10+ Tower Records. HMV's rival in terms of size, selection, and appeal to the preteen and teenage market, it's crowded, busy, noisy. The hip clientele of the Greenwich Village Tower Records makes for better people-watching than HMV. The selection of records for young children is better here, too.
🏠 692 Broadway, at 4th St., tel. 212/505– 1500; 1961 Broadway, at 66th St., tel. 212/ 799–2500.

Stuff to Wear

👫 12+ Antique Boutique. A number of 14-year-old girls we know recommend this place, with its racks and racks of recy-

cled clothing, including suede jackets, sweaters, prom dresses, Hawaiian shirts.
🏠 712–714 Broadway, at Washington Pl., tel. 212/460–8830.

(👫 12+) **Canal Jean.** Bins of inexpensive sweaters and jeans, motorcycle jackets, funky clothing from the '40s and '50s, plus a trendy Soho atmosphere attract lots of New York teenagers.
🏠 504 Broadway, near Spring St., tel. 212/226–3663.

(👫 5+) **Capezio Dance Theatre Shop.** Girls and boys taking dance lessons like to stop in this shop, which carries tights, leotards, and ballet shoes. You can dance on a tiny wooden dance floor overlooking Broadway.
🏠 1650 Broadway, at 51st St., tel. 212/245–2130.

(👫 8+) **Savage Unique Jewelry.** Their unusual and outrageous accessories and jewelry, like earrings shaped like candles, the sun, moon, and stars, are what draw girls we know back again and again.
🏠 267 Columbus Ave., at 72nd St., tel. 212/724–4662; 1007 Madison Ave., at 78th St., tel. 212/794–6463.

Toys and Games

(👫 4+) **Big City Kite Company.** This store for the enthusiast sponsors kite festivals and exhibitions and will help you choose something for a beginner. There are old-fashioned box kites, animal kites, and a kite that looks like a comet.
🏠 1201 Lexington Ave., at 82nd St., tel. 212/472–2623.

(👫 10+) **Compleat Strategist.** For role-playing games (Advanced Dungeons and Dragons, and such) and role-playing miniatures, this is a must-stop. The 33rd Street branch has the best collection of miniatures and paints; the 57th Street branch has the most extensive selection of role-playing kits.
🏠 11 E. 33rd St., at 5th Ave., tel. 212/685–3880; 320 W. 57th St., between 8th and 9th Aves., tel. 212/582–1272.

(👫 2+) **Dollhouse Antics.** Though serious dollhouse collectors shop here, the miniature furniture, rugs, lamps (complete with wiring), doll families, and dollhouses all on a 1-inch scale delighted some 8-year-old girls we know.
🏠 1343 Madison Ave., at 94th St., tel. 212/876–2288.

(👫 1+) **Enchanted Forest.** You have to push hard on the wooden door to enter this charming Soho store that looks like a whimsical theatrical stage set of a forest. Handmade stuffed animals in baskets stand on a treehouse-like platform. Even if you don't buy any of the handmade toys or books of fairy tales, this is an essential place to visit.
🏠 85 Mercer St, near Spring St., tel. 212/925–6677.

(👫 3 – 8) **R.H. Macy and Company.** The time to visit Macy's toy department is in December when Santaland on the 8th floor holds puppet shows and animated puppet displays, and Santa hears your Christmas wishes. Don't bother to come here during the rest of the year, as the toy selection is not terrific.
🏠 34th St. at Herald Sq., tel. 212/695–4400.

(👫 ALL) **F.A.O. Schwarz.** This is my son's—and most New York kids'—favorite toy store and a must-see place. Its two floors have everything from trains to dolls to baby toys arranged in small boutique shops. On the first floor, the collection of stuffed animals of all sizes, some twice as big as small children (or even grown-ups), is the best anywhere. When Gavin was 5 to 10 he loved the kid-size real car upstairs that you can climb in and the Lego section with a table of Legos to play with, but now he heads for the video game systems in the back of the first floor. The best part is that you can touch and try everything. Prices are very high, and weekends before Christmas it's jammed, with a line extending into the street by afternoon.

🏠 *767 5th Ave., at 58th St., tel. 212/644–9400.*

(👫 **4+**) **Tenzing & Pema Presents of Mind.** This has a fascinating selection of hundreds of unusual educational toys, including science kits and games.
🏠 *956 Madison Ave., at 75th St., tel. 212/288–8780.*

Unusual Stores

(👫 **7+**) **Bead Store.** Many kids. especially the preteen and teen girls that we know (and some boys too) love to make their own necklaces and earrings from beads. Here you'll find more than 1,500 different kinds, as well as leather and silk cording to string them on. They have special two-hour teen and children's classes, but someone will give you a design tray and help you put together a necklace at any time.
🏠 *1065 Lexington Ave., at 75th St., tel. 212/628–4383; 132 Spring St., tel. 212/941–6450.*

(👫 **5+**) **Louis Tannen's.** With more than 8,000 items, this is the world's largest magic store. Wands, crystal balls, top hats with rabbits—there are lots of things for kids. It publishes a catalog and sponsors a one-week summer magic camp.
🏠 *24 W. 25th St., 2nd Floor, tel. 212/929–4500.*

(👫 **6+**) **Maxilla & Mandible Ltd.** This is a strange store that intrigued my son when he was 9, 10, and 11 and collecting specimens. It's full of all kinds of animal skeletons, fossils, antlers, teeth, butterflies, and seashells. Most are too expensive for souvenirs, but the porcupine quills, fossil sand shark teeth, and fish vertebrae are less than $3.
🏠 *451–455 Columbus Ave., between 81st and 82nd Sts., tel. 212/724–6173.*

(👫 **5+**) **Star Magic.** The space-age environment—black ceiling, spacecraft-like walls, suspended spheres and spaceships—means just walking into these shops is fun. But there's plenty to buy: new-age futuristic

music tapes, high-tech toys, scientific items like minerals and prisms and star charts.
🏠 *745 Broadway, between 8th St. and Astor Pl., tel. 212/228–7770; 275 Amsterdam Ave., at 73rd St., tel. 212/769–2020; 1256 Lexington Ave., between 84th and 85th Sts., tel. 212/988–0300.*

(👫 **ALL**) **Think Big!** Most of the items in this amusing store are huge replicas of ordinary objects—a 7-foot-high pencil, a lightbulb the size of a chair. The little things—a tiny tennis ball, for example—are affordable.
🏠 *390 West Broadway, between Spring and Broome Sts., tel. 212/925–7300.*

(👫 **ALL**) **Warner Bros. Studio Store.** This is a cartoon lover's heaven—three floors of Bugs Bunny, Tweety Bird, Daffy Duck, and other Looney Tunes characters and DC comics heroes on clothes, in art work, on toys, posters, even golf balls.
🏠 *5th Ave. and 57th St., tel. 212/754–0300.*

Eats

Believe it or not, there are more than 17,000 restaurants in New York. I've chosen from among the many reasonably priced ones that welcome children. Though not all have high chairs, booster seats, or a children's menu, they do have food and atmosphere that my family and my New York City kids' panel (ages 2 to 15) and their parents like, and most represent something unique for kids in atmosphere, type of food, or history. (I'm not including regular McDonald's, Burger King, Pizza Hut; if your kids have to go there, check the Yellow Pages; however, if you're desperate, the McDonald's at 335 8th Ave., at 26th St., tel. 212/243–9594, has a large kiddie play area appropriate for toddlers and preschoolers. There is also a unique McDonald's in downtown Manhattan; see below.)

There are some New York food experiences that our family thinks no visitor should miss—eating bagels and drinking egg creams, going to a New York deli for a pastrami sandwich, buying a bag of hot roasted chestnuts or a big salty pretzel from a street vendor, eating an Italian ice, having dim sum in Chinatown and knishes at the Yonah Schimmel Knishery. In New York you can try food from almost any culture in the world—Italian, Jewish, Mexican, Ethiopian, Chinese, Korean, Thai, Indian—so if there is an ethnic cuisine your child has ever wanted to try, now is the time. The latest edition of Gerry Frank's *Where to Find It, Buy It, and Eat It in New York* (Gerry's Frankly Speaking, Box 2225, Salem, OR 97308; $12.95) is a good source.

But don't eat only at restaurants in New York. Among the eating places Gavin liked best when he was small, especially on a rainy day, were the city's indoor atriums. The **IBM Garden Plaza** (56th St. and Madison Ave.) has towering bamboo trees, tables, a snack bar that sells good sandwiches, and free concerts on Wednesdays at 12:30; the **Market at Citicorp** (Lexington Ave. and 53rd St., tel. 212/826–4088) has plenty of take-out food places in its three levels beneath a huge skylight, plus café chairs and tables where you can eat, and it often has musical entertainment for children at lunchtime on weekends. In the **World Financial Center** (across from the World Trade Center on the Hudson River between Liberty and Vesey Sts., tel. 212/945–0505) you can get take-out sandwiches or just ice cream to eat along the Esplanade or choose something simple at one of the Winter Garden's several cafés. At **Pier 17 in South Street Seaport** there is a "food fair" with dozens of selections similar to those in malls (see Shopping, *above*).

Despite the fact that New York is filled with skyscrapers, there are good places to picnic, even in midtown. In the city's outdoor "pocket parks," which are about the width of a small building, you'll see lots of parents and kids, especially on weekends. Our favorites are **Paley Park** (53rd St. between 5th and Madison Aves.), **Greenacre Park** (51st St. between 2nd and

3rd Aves.), and the **McGraw-Hill Park** (48th St. between 6th and 7th Aves.). All have waterfalls more than 20 feet high (you can walk under the one in the McGraw-Hill park), snack bars, and tables and chairs or benches.

Then there's **Central Park.** Our family loves to spread a picnic out by the baseball playing fields on the park's west side and eat while we watch one of the many weekend baseball games. We also like taking a picnic to the **Statue of Liberty** or to the **Lighthouse Park** on Roosevelt Island, which even has picnic tables.

A few restaurant hints: Remember that during the week midtown and Wall Street area restaurants will be jammed between noon and 2 PM; the same is true on weekends in more residential neighborhoods like the Upper West Side. If you have very small children, eat early.

Category	Cost*
$$$	over $25
$$	$12–$25
$	under $12

per person for a three-course meal, excluding drinks, service, and sales tax

American Eclectic

(**ALL**) **America.** Among our preteen friends, this noisy airplane hangar–size former carpet showroom is the favorite restaurant. Young, punk-looking waiters serve you from a menu of several hundred items—from pancakes to Buffalo chicken wings to New Mexican black bean cakes to New England roast turkey to hamburgers, pizza, and PB and J. On weekends they give kids coloring books and crayons, and sometimes a magician performs.
9 E. 18th St., between 5th Ave. and Broadway, tel. 212/505–2110. Reservations

advised. Dress: casual. Booster seats available. AE, MC, V. $

🧍🧍 4+ **American Festival Café.** Eat lunch or dinner here, right next to the Rockefeller Center skating rink, in winter; be sure to ask for a table by the window. Hamburgers and prime rib are your best bets, along with Sedutto's ice cream for dessert. Two bargains for families: the pre-theater dinner and our pick—the Skaters' Specials that include skate rentals and rink admission along with dinner and on weekends, with breakfast and lunch, too.
🏠 20 W. 50th St., between 5th and 6th Aves., tel. 212/246–6699. Reservations advised. Dress: casual. Booster seats available. AE, DC, MC, V. $$

🧍🧍 8+ **Mickey Mantle's.** No matter where you sit in this informal contemporary restaurant, you're surrounded by baseball. You can watch one of the eight oversized TV screens tuned to baseball games while you eat. The friendly, gregarious waiters wear baseball shirts. You can check out the hats and uniforms that belonged to baseball stars like Babe Ruth. Plus the food—burgers, Southern fried chicken fingers, chicken pot pie—is good and portions are large.
🏠 42 Central Park South, between 5th and 6th Aves., tel. 212/688–7777. Reservations required. Dress: casual. Children's menu and portions available. AE, DC, MC, V. $

🧍🧍 4+ **Museum Café.** This relaxed and casual place just behind the American Museum of Natural History is popular with both kids and adults. You can revel in the paper tablecloths and crayons, the Death by Chocolate dessert, the chicken wings, and the individual pizzas. Sit in the windowed area by the street so you can people-watch.
🏠 366 Columbus Ave., at 77th St., tel. 212/799–0150. Reservations advised. Dress: casual. Booster seats available. AE, V. $$

🧍🧍 6+ **Tavern on the Green.** If you want to take your children over 6 to one fancy restaurant in New York, this is the place. In Central Park, it's a magical extrava-

ganza of twinkling lights and glass that one 7-year-old we know dubs "the fairyland restaurant." My family prefers the glitzy Crystal Room with its glass walls and ceiling, but in warm weather some kids favor dining in the garden. The food is good, and there are hamburgers and delicious french fries for unadventurous kids. The pretheater and after-theater specials are the bargains.
🏠 Central Park West and 67th St., tel. 212/873–3200. Reservations required. Dress: casual but neat. AE, DC, MC, V. $$–$$$

🧍🧍 ALL **Two Boots.** They love kids here, and kids reciprocate the sentiment, but the crowd includes artists from this East Village neighborhood as well. The food is Cajun and Italian (the boot shapes of Louisiana and Italy are the inspiration for the name), and they are famous for their pizza and pasta jambalaya. Cups with animal handles, crayons, coloring books, paper tablecloths, and rides outside on stationary animals all have kid-appeal.
🏠 37 Ave. A, between 2nd and 3rd Sts., tel. 212/505–2276. Reservations advised. Dress: casual. Children's menu, high chairs, booster seats available. Diaper-changing table in rest room. AE. $–$$

🧍🧍 0–10 **West End Gate.** The reason to come here with kids, besides the kids' menu with grilled chicken, hamburgers, pizza, and ice cream, is the 1 PM Saturday kids' show featuring magicians, ventriloquists, and clowns. Eat lunch before or after the show.
🏠 2911 Broadway, at 114th St., tel. 212/662–8830. Reservations required for show. Dress: casual. High chairs, booster seats available. AE, MC, V. $

Bagels

🧍🧍 2+ **H & H Bagels.** Are these the best bagels in New York? Several kids we know think so. They recommend getting a hot one at these stores and munching on the street.
🏠 2239 Broadway, at 80th St., tel. 212/595–8000; 1551 2nd Ave., tel. 212/734–7441. $

Barbecue

(👫 **ALL**) **Brother Jimmy's BBQ.** At this authentic Southern barbecue place with great ribs kids 12 and under eat free on weekdays.
🏠 *1461 1st Ave., at 76th St., tel. 212/288–0999. No reservations. Dress: casual. AE. No lunch. $*

(👫 **ALL**) **Cowgirl Hall of Fame.** This place is a fantasy old-time Western saloon, with wooden booths and antler chandeliers with colored lights. The special here is Texas barbecue and a $9.95 all-you-can-eat catfish and chicken fry—kids eat for $4.95. There are crayons and paper to keep kids busy while you wait.
🏠 *519 Hudson St., at 10th St., tel. 212/633–1133. Reservations advised. Dress: casual. Children's menu, high chairs, booster seats available. AE. $*

(👫 **ALL**) **Dallas BBQ.** Big portions of good ribs, corn bread, and chili, and drinks in huge glasses keep several families we know coming back to this Texas-style barbecue chain. Food comes quickly, there's lots of noise, and specials (early-bird, two people eat for $7.95) make family eating cheap.
🏠 *1265 3rd Ave., at 73rd St., tel. 212/772–9393; 27 W. 72nd St., between Central Park West and Columbus Ave., tel. 212/873–2004; 21 University Pl. and 8th St., tel. 212/674–4450; 132 2nd Ave., at St. Mark's Pl., tel. 212/777–5574. No reservations. Dress: casual. AE, MC, DC, V. $*

Breakfast

(👫 **ALL**) **Royal Canadian Pancake House.** Big and friendly, these two locations are open for breakfast all day. Go for the 53 varieties of pancakes—flapjacks (three in a regular order!) are so big they drape over the huge plates. They also serve eggs, sausage, and omelets. There are crayons on the table. Expect a wait on weekends.
🏠 *1004 2nd Ave., at 53rd St., tel. 212/980–4131; 2286 Broadway, between 82nd and 83rd Sts., tel. 212/873–6052. Dress:*

casual. High chairs, booster seats available. No credit cards. $–$$

Chinese and Japanese

(👫 **5+**) **Benihana of Tokyo.** You sit around a big square table for nine with its own chef and center grill in this spacious, calm second-floor Japanese restaurant. Chefs dramatically chop and slice chicken and steak, twirling and tossing the knife in the air in between chops, and then cook the pieces on the grill. Everything is ready quickly, and you're entertained while you wait. The Japanese food isn't the best in the city, but it is good. If you tell them it's your child's birthday, they sing "Happy Birthday" in Japanese and bring ice cream with a candle in it—and take a Polaroid picture of the whole thing.
🏠 *47 W. 56th St., between 5th and 6th Aves., tel. 212/581–0930. Reservations advised. Dress: casual but neat. Boosters seats available. AE, DC, MC, V. $$*

(👫 **4+**) **Pig Heaven.** As well as being an excellent restaurant, this place appeals to small children because it has a giant pig holding the menus and pigs dancing around the walls and offers the chance to look through a glass window at the chefs preparing dishes in the kitchen. Some dishes are very spicy, so check before ordering. They have better desserts (like apple pie) than Chinese restaurants usually do.
🏠 *1540 2nd Ave., at 80th St., tel. 212/744–4333. Reservations advised. Dress: casual. AE, DC. $$*

(👫 **6+**) **Shun Lee West/Shun Lee Café.** These Lincoln Center area restaurants adjoining one another have superb Chinese food. Here a waiter actually describes the items on the rolling carts of dim sum; the finger food in the café also appeals to kids we know. The setting in the main restaurant is theatrically black, with golden Chinese dragons on the walls. In the café prices are lower and service is faster.
🏠 *43 W. 65th St., tel. 212/769–3888. Dress: casual but neat. AE, D, MC, V. $$*

ALL Golden Unicorn. You'll see lots of families, mostly Chinese, between 11 and 4 on weekends at this big, two-story restaurant that looks like a mess hall. The attraction is dim sum: individual servings of dumplings of all kinds, noodle and rice dishes, egg custards, and more. Chinese waiters wheel carts full of new things every 10 or 15 minutes, everyone points, choosing and trying different dishes, and you sit at a big round table with people you don't know. You pay according to the number of plates on your table at the end of the meal.
18 East Broadway, at Catherine St., tel. 212/941–0911. No reservations. Dress: casual. Booster seats available. AE, MC, V. $

3+ Ollie's Noodle Shop and Grille. Both branches look like busy luncheonettes; the one on Broadway and 84th Street, across the street from a good movie theater, attracts more families. The portions of mandarin noodle soup and other noodle dishes are large, and the good flavors even appeal to fussy eaters. Service is fast.
200 W. 44th St., between Broadway and 8th Ave., tel. 212/921–5988; 2315 Broadway, at 84th St., tel. 212/362–3111. Reservations advised. Dress: casual. AE, MC, V. $

3+ 20 Mott Street. For a quieter atmosphere we also like the Golden Unicorn's other restaurant, which has a fish tank to look at in the upstairs room, tables with tablecloths, and a wider variety of dim sum. Try the won ton soup, vegetable dumplings, and the sticky rice in a lotus leaf.
20 Mott St., tel. 212/964–0380. No reservations. Dress: casual. Booster seats available. AE, MC, V. $

Delicatessen/Jewish

ALL Carnegie Delicatessen and Restaurant. It's noisy and crowded and you have to wait in this quintessential New York deli with a take-out counter in front and small tables in the back. But we think it's a real slice of New York—and they like kids too. Try their egg creams. The best pastrami

sandwiches, chicken soup, and potato pancakes are what we go for, but they also have burgers and franks—and even Jell-O.
854 7th Ave., between 54th and 55th Sts., tel. 212/757–2245. Reservations not required. Dress: casual. Booster seats available. No credit cards. $

3+ Yonah Schimmel's Knishery. This lower East Side Jewish institution started out as a pushcart 100 years ago. Eating potato *latkes* (pancakes) here or any of their dozen delicious knishes (pastries stuffed with potatoes, cheese, fruit, or meat, then deep fried) is like entering the New York immigrant world of the early 20th century. If you go to the Lower East Side Tenement Museum, be sure to come here.
137 E. Houston St., near 2nd Ave., tel. 212/477–2858. Reservations not necessary. Dress: casual. No credit cards. $

Diners

ALL E J's Luncheonette. A '50s-style diner with funky plastic statues of Marilyn Monroe, mini jukeboxes that work at some tables, and old-fashioned chrome-rimmed counter stools, it's open for breakfast, lunch, and dinner every day. It's crowded for lunch on weekends.
447 Amsterdam Ave., near 81st St., tel. 212/873–3444. No reservations. Dress: casual. Booster seats available. No credit cards. $

5+ Ellen's Stardust Diner. This cramped '50s diner is loaded with memorabilia, but kids 6 to 11 groove on the loud doo-wop music, the black cow drink (a root beer float), the TV monitors with the black and white movies, and the waiters' cool nicknames—our last one was Boogaloo.
1377 6th Ave., at 56th St., tel. 212/307–7575. Reservations for 7 or more only. Dress: casual. AE, DC, MC, V. $

ALL Mayrose. This upscale corner diner with 25-foot windows has traditional black Formica tables rimmed in metal inside, as well as outdoor seating in warm weather. It's all food kids love and it's good: baked

macaroni and cheese, meatloaf, tuna casse-role, and grilled cheese.
🏠 *920 Broadway, at 22nd St., tel. 212/533–3663. Dress: casual. Booster and Sassy seats, children's portions available. AE, MC, V. $*

Italian

👫 **ALL** **Carmine's.** These big, informal, noisy Italian family restaurants are "like going to Grandma's" says one family that goes to one every Friday or Saturday night. Service is family style, with huge platters of old-fash-ioned Italian-American food like spaghetti and meatballs and chicken Parmesan. Six people, even hungry teenagers, can split three or four entrées and eat for about $80 to $90. You'll see more families at the upper West Side branch. So that you don't have to wait an hour or more at the smoky bar, put your name down, ask how long the wait will be, and then come back.
🏠 *2450 Broadway, between 90th and 91st Sts., tel. 212/362–2200 (reservations for 6 or more only); 200 W. 44th St., between 7th and 8th Aves., tel. 212/221–3800 (reservations required for lunch and pretheater before 6 PM). Dress: casual. Booster seats available. AE. $–$$*

Mainly Hamburgers and Hot Dogs and Sandwiches

👫 **6+** **Hard Rock Cafe.** This is a touristy place, but it is fun. The music is loud, the TV monitor is always tuned to MTV, and the walls of the multilevel dining area are full of signed guitars and other rock-and-roll memorabilia from stars such as Springsteen. The motorcycle from the Aerosmith video on the second floor that you can actually touch draws kid fans. Favorite items to eat: the BLT, hamburgers, cheeseburgers, Caesar salad, and the straw-berry virgin daiquiris. The desserts are yummy; hot fudge brownies and old-fash-ioned sodas and shakes please us. It's not for kids under 8 who aren't mad about rock and roll. During school breaks, there's always a long line to get in; the wait's shorter on Sunday than Saturday.

🏠 *221 W. 57th St., between Broadway and 7th Ave., tel. 212/489–6565. No reservations. Dress: casual. AE, DC, MC, V. $$*

👫 **5+** **Planet Hollywood.** The food is not the reason to come here—though they have better and cheaper food than does the Hard Rock Cafe. For kids the decorations—props from movies, like the saddle from *City Slickers* or the cryptkeeper from *Tales from the Crypt*, and the place mats with pictures of movie stars when they were teenagers, plus old movies being projected on the walls—are the real attraction. There are long lines on weekends. Your best bet is to line up at 11:30, so you can get in as soon as the restaurant opens at 12, or go about 5:30 for an early dinner. If you stay at the Parker Meridien hotel next door, you get a special pass. The menu is mainly pizzas, salads, pas-tas, fajitas, sandwiches. We thought the desserts were the best, especially the Snick-ers pie and the chocolate mousse in an Oreo crust.
🏠 *140 W. 57th St., between 6th and 7th Aves., tel. 212/333–7827. No reservations. Dress: casual. AE, MC, V. $–$$*

👫 **3+** **Hamburger Harry's.** It's busy, but the hamburgers are good, there are free french fries, and they do special things for children on weekends—like let them sit together at a "kids' table," pass out crayons and paper, balloons, and even give away Mets caps when kids order a sundae.
🏠 *157 Chambers St., between West Broad-way and Greenwich St., tel. 212/840–2756; 156 7th Ave., tel. 212/242–2612; 145 W. 45th St., between 6th and 7th Aves., tel. 212/840–0566. Dress: casual. Booster seats avail-able. $10 minimum. AE, MC, V. $*

👫 **ALL** **Jackson Hole Wyoming Burg-ers.** The five branches of this citywide chain not only have the very best—and maybe the broadest selection of—hamburgers in town, they're also hip, funky, and cheap, and have great fries, onion rings, salads, and real hot chocolate. Teenagers hang out at the Columbus Avenue branch (which looks like a café) and the 2nd Avenue and Madison

Avenue branches after school and on weekends.

🏠 232 E. 64th St., tel. 212/311–7187; 521 3rd Ave., at 35th St., tel. 212/679–3264; 1611 2nd Ave., at 84th St., tel. 212/737–8788; 517 Columbus Ave., at 85th St., tel. 212/362–5177; 1270 Madison Ave., at 91st St., tel. 212/427–2820. Reservations not required. Dress: casual. AE. $

(👫 3+)   McDonald's. This is the fanciest McDonald's in the world, a five-star example of the chain. Yes, you'll recognize a lot of the food, though they do have special soups and salads, as well as a more elaborate dessert menu (they use real whipped cream here) and even cappuccino. It's the setting and service that are special—a doorman, a pianist, marble tables, mirrors, real flowers, and table settings. (You still have to go to the counter to order your food.) The prices are no higher than at any other McDonald's, which makes this a bargain.

🏠 160 Broadway, between Maiden La. and Liberty St., tel. 212/385–2063. Reservations for 6 or more only. Dress: casual. AE, MC, V. $

(👫 ALL)   Hot dogs. You can get them from a street vendor and eat in a park, but we like **Gray's Papaya** (2090 Broadway) and the reliable **Papaya King** (179 E. 86th St. and 201 E. 59th St.). Both are just stand-up counters and very inexpensive.

Mexican

(👫 ALL)   Benny's Burritos. It's just a storefront with a few tables inside (and out, when the weather is nice), but as you walk by, the smell of Mexican beans and beef assaults you. Several families we know swear these are the best burritos in New York.

🏠 113 Greenwich St., near Jane St., tel. 212/727–0584; 93 Ave. A, at 6th St., tel. 212/254–3286. No reservations. Dress: casual. No credit cards. $

(👫 4+)   Manhattan Chili Company. My son likes to come here in summer when you can eat in the outdoor garden. The children's menu includes hot dogs, but our

whole family are chili aficionados, and this is our favorite place for it in the city. Be sure to inquire how spicy a particular dish is before you order.

🏠 1500 Broadway, at 43rd St., tel. 212/730–8666. Reservations advised. Dress: casual. MC, V. $

Pizza Places

In New York you can get several kinds of pizza—New York style with a puffy crust (also called Sicilian style), Roman style with a thin, crisp crust, and deep-dish Chicago style.

(👫 4+)   John's Pizzeria. The three branches make Roman style. The crust on John's pizza is crisp and slightly charred, there are 55 different topping choices, and the ingredients are truly fresh. Even the plain cheese with fresh tomatoes is a gourmet treat—and kids like it, too. You can't buy by the slice here and there are lines, but it's worth the wait. We prefer the downtown branch; the uptown ones are more like restaurants.

🏠 278 Bleecker St., between 6th and 7th Aves., tel. 212/243–1680; 408 E. 64th St., between 1st and York Aves., tel. 212/935–2895; 48–50 W. 65th St., between Broadway and Central Park West, tel. 212/721–7001. No reservations. Dress: casual. No credit cards. $–$$

(👫 2+)   PizzaPiazza. This is also worth a stop, particularly for its deep-dish pizza and its movie-plus-dinner bargains—$22.99 buys pasta or pizza, salad, and drinks for two, plus tickets that can be redeemed at any Sony theater for an entire year. It has high chairs and booster seats.

🏠 785 Broadway, at 10th St., tel. 212/505–0977. No reservations. Dress: casual. AE, MC, V. $–$$

(👫 ALL)   Ray's Pizza. For New York style this is our family's (especially Gavin's) favorite. Don't be fooled by all the other Ray's Pizzas you'll see around the city. This one is the real thing: your basic corner pizza joint with a few Formica tables in the back.

🏠 *465 6th Ave., at 11th St., tel. 212/243–2253. No reservations. Dress: casual. No credit cards. $*

Sweet Stuff

👫 ALL Ferrara's. My husband and I like the smaller, less touristy Caffé Roma down the block where many Italian families come after church on Sunday, but my son and his friends have always preferred this spacious, shiny, and expensive Italian café because of the long, fancy glass case where you can see the huge selection of cookies and pastries. Strollers are welcome; they do have booster seats. You can order plates of miniature versions of delicious pastries and gelato, Italian ice cream.
🏠 *195 Grand St., between Mulberry and Mott Sts., tel. 212/226–6150. No reservations. Dress: casual. AE, V, MC. $$*

👫 ALL Minter's in the Courtyard. A self-service waffle, sandwich, and ice-cream spot in one of the Financial Center's atriums, it has especially good ice cream.
🏠 *Courtyard, 4 World Financial Center, 250 Vesey St., tel. 212/945–4455. No credit cards. $$*

👫 3+ Original Chinatown Ice Cream Factory. This small store front is a must-stop place if you're touring Chinatown. There are 20 unusual ice-cream flavors, including lychee, taro, even red bean. The kids' favorite in our experience—green tea.
🏠 *65 Bayard St., near Elizabeth St., no phone. No credit cards. $*

👫 2+ Serendipity 3. This quaint, cozy, kid-size spot on the ground floor of a brownstone oozes charm. A variety of Tiffany lamps hangs from the ceiling; two boys we know about 4 and 6 opted to sit opposite the curved mirror on one white brick wall so they could watch their distorted reflection while they ate. Though it is noted for its fabulous desserts, foot-long hot dogs, and whimsical gifts and funky jewelry in the tiny shop in front, you can get a basic omelet, vegetable pizza, hamburgers,

crepes, and more. Try the huge old-fashioned drugstore sundaes and the frozen hot chocolate.
🏠 *225 E. 60th St., between 2nd and 3rd Aves., tel. 212/838–3531. Reservations advised. Dress: casual. Booster seats available. AE, DC, MC, V. $$*

Where to Stay

In New York City the ideal family hotel just doesn't exist; it's a matter of trade-offs. The biggest problem is price: Hotels here are very expensive. The best way to get a bargain is to take advantage of special weekend packages; many expensive ($$$) hotels listed below fall into the moderate ($$) category on weekends. Most hotels in New York charge $10 to $20 for cots, and few provide the family packages and amenities (story hour, kids' toiletries, and so on) that are a matter of course in Boston's hotels.

The following 10 hotels, however, offer families something special and actually want families to stay in them. For additional hotels, check the Sunday travel section of *The New York Times* for special family-rate packages tied to particular events.

Category	Cost*
$$$$	over $250
$$$	$185–$250
$$	$130–$185
$	under $130

All prices are for a standard double room, excluding $2 occupancy charge and 13¼% tax.

$$$$

U.N. Plaza–Park Hyatt. The kid-appeal at this modern, luxury hotel is the 22-by-44-foot glass-enclosed pool on the 27th floor (a lifeguard is on duty when it is open). What parents like is the exceptionally accommodating service, the children's menu of healthy items—whole wheat pizza, baked sole with cornflake topping—that their kids like, and the hotel's family plan, which allows them to rent a connecting room for the kids at 50% off, something I'd do as the rooms are not really big enough for two parents and two school-age children. The U.N. Plaza offers good weekend and holiday packages, but it will not recommend baby-sitters. Hotel rooms start on the 28th floor, so all have spectacular views; request one that has floor-to-ceiling windows. Our family calls the furnishings "plush contemporary."

🏨 *1 United Nations Plaza, 44th St. and 1st Ave., 10017, tel. 212/758–1234 or 800/ 228–9000, fax 212/702–5051. 428 rooms, 25 suites. Children under 16 free. Facilities: restaurant, 3 floors of no-smoking rooms, fitness center, pool, indoor tennis court, complimentary limousine to theater district, garage with unlimited access. AE, DC, MC, V.*

$$$

Guest Quarters Suites. Although this 43-story, all-suite hotel is in the slightly unsavory theater district (but right across from TKTS, the discount ticket office), it has so many features attractive to parents and children under 10 that staying here is worth it. The small street lobby has a staff member on duty at all times. The basic suite, with attractive modern, sturdy furnishings in blacks, grays, and blues, has a private bedroom, a living room with a queen-size sofa bed, a dining table and chairs, and a kitchenette with a sink, a microwave, and a small refrigerator. The bathrooms are basic and small, but new. Suites on the 8th floor (there are only 13 on each floor) are childproofed: electrical outlet covers, unbreakable dishes, furniture corner guards, and so on. The one drawback in all suites is the lack of closet space. It's the special services for families on request—stocking your refrigerator with milk or peanut butter and just putting it on your bill, providing a free stroller, a baby bathtub, and even diapers—and the Cool Kat Kids Club, a supervised kids' play center (open daily 9:30–5:30; Fri. and Sat. to 11),

that really set this hotel apart. Though the club is billed for 3- to 13-year-olds, older kids may find it tame.

🏨 *1568 Broadway, at 47th St., 10036, tel. 212/719–1600 or 800/424–2900, fax 212/921–5212. 460 suites. Children under 12 free; $20 older children. Facilities: restaurant, day care center; washer/dryer available. AE, DC, MC, V.*

Le Parker Meridien. This subdued but classic and elegant French hotel, with its soaring lobby linking 56th and 57th streets, has a 20-by-40-foot pool on the 42nd floor where you can order lunch or just ice cream; a sundeck with lounge chairs where you view the Hudson River; and a special pass that gets you into the restaurant Planet Hollywood (see Eats, above) next door without waiting in line. It's also centrally located—a short walk from Central Park, Rockefeller Center, and the F.A.O. Schwarz toy store. The regular double rooms are decorated in brown, black, and cream Biedermeyer with a touch of Art Deco; a family of four with two small children could fit, although it would be a little cramped. The best choice for families is an executive room, which contains a queen-size sofa and has lots of drawers and shelf space.

🏨 *118 W. 57th St., between 6th and 7th Aves., 10019, tel. 212/245–5000 or 800/ 543–4300, fax 212/708–7477. 700 rooms, 262 suites. Many no-smoking floors. Children under 12 free, $25 older children. Facilities: restaurant, lounge (with snacks), pool, swimming lessons, fitness center, VCR in suites, garage. AE, DC, MC, V.*

Manhattan East Suite Hotels. All the units in this group of small hotels (reviewed in the next three paragraphs) on Manhattan's east side are suites with real kitchens that contain a microwave, a four-burner stove, a full-size refrigerator, a toaster, a sink, a coffeemaker, a dishwasher, and all the dishes and cookware you need. Rooms are larger than usual hotel rooms, with plenty of space for kids to color, curl up and read, or have a snack. Staying in one is like having your own apartment in New York. Best of all, they offer families a wonderful weekend (Fri.–Sun.) package year-round that includes their own special guide to family restaurants, popcorn, discount admission to the Children's Museum of Manhattan, free parking, a babysitting referral service, a special rate on one- and two-bedroom suites, and much more. 🏨 *All hotels, tel. 800/637–8483. Facilities: concierge, coin-operated washers and dryers, fitness centers, fully equipped kitchens. AE, DC, MC, V.*

Dumont Plaza is the most modern, with a mirror-filled marble lobby, a green-and-burgundy color scheme with art deco–style lamps, and it has the largest rooms. Even the junior suite, with two club chairs and a pull-out sofa as well as a king-size bed, would easily be comfortable for a family of four. The one-bedrooms here and at the other hotels have a dining table and four chairs, as well as two TVs; some have bathrooms with a door into the living room as well as the bedroom. 🏨 *150 E. 34th St., at Lexington Ave., 10016, tel. 212/481–7600, fax 212/889–8856. 250 suites. Children under 12 free. Facilities: restaurant, outdoor café, room service, VCR on request (no charge).*

Plaza Fifty is sleek and shiny, with contemporary furnishings in blue and beige, as well as more modern bathrooms and kitchens than the other two Manhattan East Suite Hotels, large closets, and three nonsmoking floors. Though the hotel doesn't have a restaurant, two restaurants and a gourmet deli nearby deliver room service orders, and a supermarket will deliver until midnight. 🏨 *155 E. 50th St., 10022, tel. 212/751–5710, fax 212/753–1468. 206 rooms and suites.*

Shelburne Murray Hill is the most elegant, with Oriental rugs, chandeliers, reproduction Chippendale, and dark blue carpeting set off by pale yellow walls, yellow striped sofas, and flowered drapes and bedspreads in all the suites. The plus for kids here is the big roof garden.

🏨 *303 Lexington Ave., 10016, tel. 212/689–5200, fax 212/779–7068. 258 suites. Facilities: restaurant, bar, roof garden.*

$$

Mayflower on the Park. There's something stately and gracious yet warm and homey about this small (by New York standards), independently owned hotel just across the street from Central Park. The highlights of a Thanksgiving weekend here are a good view of the Thanksgiving Day parade (it goes right by the hotel) and a petting zoo and hot chocolate in the lobby. Most members of the staff have been here a long time and are very friendly to children. The concierge maintains a list of approved baby-sitters and restaurants in the area for kids. The rooms, even a basic double, are high ceilinged and exceptionally spacious, decorated with comfortable traditional American reproduction furniture upholstered in pinks and greens, with closets so big that one could—and did—double as a great hideout for kids with books and a pile of pillows. Most rooms have kitchenettes and you can get a hot plate on request. Some bathrooms are old fashioned; request a room with a renovated one. One-bedroom suites are enormous; ask for one with a large table and chairs. 🏨 *15 Central Park West, at 61st St., 10023, tel. 212/265–0060 or 800/223–4164, fax 212/265–5098. 577 rooms, 200 suites. Children under 15 free. Facilities: restaurant (high chairs available), fitness center with 45" TV, meeting rooms, no-smoking rooms. AE, DC, MC, V.*

Paramount. "A wild place" is a 13-year-old's description of this ultra-modern, sophisticated, and hip hotel just west of the theater district. Both the rooms and the public spaces are full of witty surprises: a strangely shaped stairway, curved and molded lounge chairs, cone-shaped stainless sinks. It's like staying in a theater set. While it appealed to young teens, it might disorient some small children. But it does have a whimsical children's playroom on the mezzanine that con-

tains a doghouse kids can crawl in and chairs made from stuffed animals, as well as lots of toys. The tape library has a good selection of kids' videos. The double room with two double beds is the best bet.
🏨 *235 W. 46th St., 10036, tel. 212/764–5500 or 800/225–7474, fax 212/354–5237. 610 rooms. Children under 14 free. Facilities: restaurant, café, gourmet take-out, fitness room, children's playroom, VCRs. AE, DC, MC, V.*

$

Excelsior. The key attractions to this hotel are its low price and excellent location for families in a neighborhood that my New York city kids' panel rates highly. This is also a street where they blow up the huge float balloons the night before the Macy's Thanksgiving Day parade. The one-bedroom suites (most appropriate for families; the double rooms are not really big enough for four people) have two good-size rooms (including two closets); the double bedroom and living room are filled with basic but pleasant Danish modern style furniture—a foldout couch and two chairs, a TV (no cable), a table and two chairs. The full kitchenette has a stove, a refrigerator, and a sink, and you can get pots, pans, and dishes from the housekeeper. Do make sure you reserve (three weeks to a month in advance) a park view—rooms that don't have one are dingy.
🏨 *45 W. 81st St., 10024, tel. 212/362–9200 or 800/368–4575, fax 212/721–2994. 160 rooms, 100 1-bedroom suites, 4 2-bedroom suites. Facilities: coffee shop. AE, DC, MC, V.*

Hotel Beacon. All the rooms in this small combined apartment house and hotel are large and pleasant, with warm pink-toned walls and attractive traditional style furnishings. Each has a kitchenette with a full-size refrigerator, a sink, and a four-burner stove, and individual air-conditioning. Suites are large enough to accommodate three or four children. The hotel is out of the bustle of midtown but convenient to many attrac-

tions for children. Although it's not as luxurious as the more expensive Manhattan East Suite hotels, its rooms and suites are an exceptional bargain, especially on weekends.
🏨 *2130 Broadway, at 75th St., 10023, tel. 212/787–1100 or 800/572–4969, fax 212/724–0839. 120 rooms, 45 suites. Children under 17 free. Facilities: coffee shop. AE, DC, MC, V.*

Skyline Manhattan. The best things about this hotel are the pool and the price. It looks and feels spacious but bland—just like lots of motels we've stayed at when driving on interstates; the rooms are good-sized and easily accommodate a four-person family. There are no special rates for the suites, so they're not worth it. The pool has a great view of Manhattan. Now for the bad news: location. This far-west area is not a neighborhood, and it is a long, not very pleasant walk to theaters. Buses one block away do go to Rockefeller Center, Lincoln Center, and the *Intrepid* Sea/Air/Space Museum; the nearest subway stop is farther. You may find yourself, as one family we know did, taking a lot of taxis back in the afternoon.
🏨 *725 10th Ave., between 49th and 50th Sts., 10019, tel. 212/586–3400 or 800/433–1982, fax 212/582–4604. 231 rooms, 11 suites. Children under 15 free. Facilities: restaurant, Olympic-size pool, coffee shop, fitness center, sauna, free on-site parking. AE, MC, V.*

Bed-and-Breakfasts

If your family wants to feel like natives and see what it's like to live in a Soho loft or a Village brownstone, or if you're planning a long stay in the city, you might want to try an "unhosted" apartment offered through a bed-and-breakfast referral service. (Unlike a regular B&B, the owner does not stay on the premises, and you are responsible for the housekeeping; few "hosted" apartments in New York City accept children.) Most apartments cost from $140 up for a family of four. Be as complete as possible in describing your family's requirements (if you have very small children, ask if the apartment has window guards, for example) when you reserve, and ask detailed questions about locations. Check the deposit and refund policy.

City Lights Bed & Breakfast Ltd. (Box 20355 Cherokee Station, 10028, tel. 212/ 737–7049, fax 212/535–2755; AE, DC, MC, V) is particularly accommodating to families and follows up with questionnaires.

Urban Ventures (306 W. 38th St., 10018, tel. 212/594–5650, fax 212/947–9320; AE, MC, DC, V), in business for 25 years, represents more than 300 unhosted apartments.

Home Exchanges

Several New York City families we know regularly exchange their apartment for one in another city or a house in the country. This is the cheapest solution to the hotel-cost problem.

Vacation Exchange Club (Box 650, Key West, FL 33041, tel. 800/638–3841) always lists some New York city apartments; a membership to receive directories and list your own home costs $50.

Entertainment and the Arts

Amusement Parks

(🕴🕴 3+) **Astroland Amusement Park.** Coney Island is where amusement parks started, and even though it's a bit shabby today, Astroland is worth a stop, particularly if you're visiting the New York Aquarium, which is just a short walk away. (Its parking lot is adjacent to Astroland.)
🏠 *1000 Surf Ave., Coney Island, Brooklyn, tel. 718/372–0275. By subway, F train to W. 8th St. and walk across overpass; by car, Exit 7, Ocean Pkwy., south from Belt Pkwy. onto Surf Ave.*

(🕴🕴 3+) **Deno's Wonder Wheel Park.** A short walk from Astroland is this smaller

park with 16 rides for kids. The beach is visible just across the boardwalk.
🏠 *1025 Boardwalk (adjacent to Astroland), Coney Island, Brooklyn, tel. 718/372–2592.*

Film

(🕴🕴 6+) **Bryant Park Summer Film Festival.** Every Monday evening in summer (from mid-June to Sept.) classic films, preceded by Looney Tunes cartoons, are projected onto a giant screen in this recently restored midtown park. In a city version of a drive-in, chairs are set up on the lawn. Seats are free; popcorn and hot dogs are available. Or you can bring a blanket and a picnic.
🏠 *42nd St. between 5th and 6th Aves., behind New York Public Library, tel. 212/ 512–5700.*

You don't have to wait in line to buy a ticket for any movie in New York. Just call **Movie-Fone** (tel. 212/777–3456) to charge a ticket to your credit card.

(🕴🕴 6+) **Sony 84th Street Theater.** Formerly a Loew's, this sixplex movie theater, one of the cleanest and friendliest in the city, according to several teenage patrons we know, is frequented by families, preteens, and teens. It has a good selection of video games.
🏠 *84th St. and Broadway, tel. 212/595–6397.*

(🕴🕴 6+) **Sony Theatres Lincoln Square.** So far this 12-screen theater complex, which opened in fall 1994, is the ultimate movie-viewing spot in New York City, a combination of modern comfort, new technology, and a dash of the ambience of old-style movie palaces. The top attraction for kids is the IMAX theater, with a screen eight stories high and super-advanced 3-D technology. Movie goers wear lightweight cordless headsets (sterilized after each use) whose liquid crystal lenses and special 3-D speakers seem to pull you right into the picture and make viewing a "virtual reality" experience that far surpasses those cardboard 3-D glasses I remember from my youth. The staff seem unduly concerned with crowd control.

🏛 *Broadway and 68th St., tel. 212/336–5000 or 212/595–6391.*

Performing Spaces and Performers

There are excellent performances just for children in New York City every weekend; be sure to check under "Activities for Children" in *New York Magazine* and in *New York Family* (see How to Find Out What's Going On, *above*).

DISCOUNT TICKETS. Bryant Park Ticket Booth. Half-price tickets for same-day music, dance, and sometimes opera performances are sold here Tuesday through Sunday, 12 to 2 and 3 to 7. *Off 42nd St., east of 6th Ave., tel. 212/382–2323.*

TKTS. This is the source for almost half-price tickets for same-day Broadway theater performances. Of the two locations, the Lower Manhattan booth is often better for families than the one centrally placed on Broadway. Downtown lines tend to be shorter, you can wait indoors, and tickets for Wednesday, Saturday, and Sunday matinees are sold a day in advance.

🏛 *Mezzanine level of 2 World Trade Center or Broadway at 47th St., tel. 212/768–1818.*

THEATER AND PUPPET SHOWS

👫 4+ Broadway and Off-Broadway. Kids often enjoy plays, performances, and especially musicals that are not intended for children. The big drawback for families is the cost; an orchestra ticket can be as much as $60 or more. Try to get half-price tickets the day of performance if you can (see *above*).

👫 5+ Brooklyn Academy of Music. BAM, as it's known to New Yorkers, sponsors wonderful performances for children in their Family Fun Series, which runs from March through June and includes puppet shows, productions with live actors, and the annual world music festival.

🏛 *30 Lafayette Ave., Brooklyn, tel. 718/636–4100.*

👫 3 – 8 Little People's Theater Company. Kids like these performances of classic fairy tales such as "Hansel and Gretel" and "Sleeping Beauty" because the 20-year-old company's versions of the stories contain lots of comic elements and give kids the opportunity to participate.

🏛 *Courtyard Playhouse, 39 Grove St., tel. 212/765–9540. Cost: $7. Performances weekends at 1:30 and 3.*

👫 4 – 9 Paper Bag Players. The original productions of this award-winning children's theater company are a must. The hour-long shows of skits, dances, mime, and music with the company's trademark—scenery and costumes ingeniously made from cardboard boxes and brown paper grocery bags—are innovative, hilarious, and fast-paced.

🏛 *50 Riverside Dr., tel. 212/362–0431; Sylvia and Danny Kaye Playhouse, 68th St. between Park and Lexington Aves., tel. 212/772–4448.*

👫 3 – 10 Puppet Playhouse. You'll see excellent puppet shows, magicians, dancers, and musicals by many different talented groups here at Friday, Saturday, and Sunday performances from October through May. The performances feature professional casts and directors.

🏛 *Mazur Theater at Asphalt Green, 555 E. 90th St., tel. 212/688–1740.*

👫 3 – 7 Puppetworks. This company, which puts on 45-minute shows of 19th-century fairy tales with classic, handmade marionettes on weekends year-round, has been performing since 1938. Just sitting in the theater is fascinating—on the walls hang hundreds of marionettes from earlier performances.

🏛 *338 6th Ave., Brooklyn, tel. 718/965–3391.*

👫 3+ Swedish Cottage Marionette Theater. This is a great place for an introduction to the theater. First of all, the small

(85 seats) theater is in a little cottage in the middle of Central Park behind the Delacorte Theater. The one-hour production (in 1994 it was *The True Story of Rumpelstiltskin*) uses large-size marionettes and has great costumes, fancy sets, and music. The weekend performances are very, very popular; reserve a week in advance if you can. Usually they take only school visits during the week, but sometimes there's an extra space or two.

🏠 *Near Central Park West and 79th St., tel. 212/988–9093.*

(👫 4+) **Tada! Youth Ensemble.** This unique musical theater group composed of New York City kids aged 6 to 17 puts on three to four lively original one-hour family productions during July and August and December and January. Some, like the hilarious one we saw about summer camp (its name, Camp Ichikawaooeemakohooyahoo, tells you something), are based on kids' experiences; others are adaptations of children's books—like one based on three books by Ezra Jack Keats. All have catchy songs and easily graspable plots.

🏠 *120 W. 28th St., tel. 212/627–1732. Cost: $9 adults, $5 kids. Performances July and Aug., Wed.–Fri. matinees (call for times); Dec. and Jan., Fri. 7:30, weekend matinees at 1 and 3. Reservations strongly advised.*

(👫 7+) **Taipei Theater.** In November and December, this theater sponsored by the Chinese Information and Culture Center presents performances by renowned Chinese puppet theaters at exceptionally reasonable prices ($7 for children, $10 for adults).

🏠 *1221 6th Ave., between 48th and 49th Sts., tel. 212/373–1800; box office, 212/373–1850.*

(👫 6–12) **Theatreworks USA.** Each year this award-winning producer puts on 13 different plays and musicals for children during its New York season—between October and March and during the month of July—in the small Promenade Theater (2162 Broadway at 76th St.).

🏠 *Office for information, 890 Broadway, 10003, tel. 212/677–5959.*

MUSIC. One of the great things about New York is the variety of free concerts, especially in summer, that are held in Central Park, at the World Financial Center, at South Street Seaport (*see below*), and at many other places around the city.

(👫 5+) **Arts Connection.** Just about every Saturday afternoon at 3 PM during the school year, this organization presents bargain ($5 per person) one-hour shows of famous dance, theater, or music groups or individual performers designed specifically for families. The New York City Opera's shortened version of *The Magic Flute* (complete with costumes and scenery but accompanied only by piano and sung in English) converted one 9-year-old we know to opera. The small 250-seat theater is just the right size for kids. Reserve at least a week or two in advance.

🏠 *120 W. 46th St., tel. 212/302–7433.*

(👫 8+) **Bryant Park Young Performers Series.** From May through September one-hour lunchtime concerts feature young, up-and-coming jazz and classical musicians playing with established artists.

🏠 *Bryant Park, W. 42nd St., east of 6th Ave., tel. 212/983–4142.*

(👫 8+) **Jazzmobile.** During July and August this group dedicated to introducing people to jazz performs about 40 concerts in the five boroughs.

🏠 *154 W. 127th St., tel. 212/866–4900.*

(👫 7+) **Juilliard School.** Great bargains for families are the free recitals and concerts given by pre-college students at this world-famous music school in Lincoln Center. On Saturdays from about 11 to 6, for example, you can hear one-hour recitals by students aged 7 to 17 in the main recital hall. There's a wide range of accomplishment; some of the older kids are already under management. The other advantage for families, besides the cost, is that attending is all very informal: You don't need tickets. Just walk in, listen as long as you like, then leave. The regular student orchestra concerts are also free, but you must pick up a ticket at the box office for some of them. Be prepared to see a few homeless people in the audience. The school will send you a schedule or tell you what is on over the phone, but you can also just check the bulletin board in the lobby.

fi *60 Lincoln Center Plaza, tel. 212/799–5000, ext. 241.*

(ǏǏ 3 – 12) **Little Orchestra Society.** Now in its 45th season, this organization presents especially wonderful concerts for children 3 to 5 and 6 to 12 at Avery Fisher Hall. There's lots of action along with the music, and the concerts are accessible without being condescending.

fi *220 W. 42nd St., tel. 212/704–2100.*

(ǏǏ 6 – 14) **Metropolitan Opera.** Most kids find opera hard to take, but the Growing Up with Opera special events and performances produced especially for families by the Metropolitan Opera Guild have enchanted our family and several kids we know. The operas are in English, shortened to 1½ hours including an intermission, use up-and-coming singers not always in period costumes, and take place in a smaller theater than the Met. After you reserve, the Guild sends your child an activity book that contains the story of the opera and drawings of all the characters so that he or she can follow the performance. Meeting the cast afterward and getting their photographs autographed can be a treat for kids. There's a 1½-hour backstage tour of the Met (daily except Sun., Sept.– June), in which kids over 9 will see the wig shop, the scenery shop, and the huge and fabulous sets for current productions; they may also get to hear a rehearsal.

fi *70 Lincoln Center Plaza; Growing up with Opera reservations, tel. 212/769–7022, $12–$25; backstage tour, tel. 212/769–7020. Cost: $8 adults, $4 students with valid ID.*

(ǏǏ 6+) **New York Philharmonic.** One of the great orchestras of the world, the Philharmonic, performs at Avery Fisher Hall in Lincoln Center and for free in various New York City parks in summer. The 4th of July concert in Central Park, accompanied by fireworks, is crowded but fun to attend if you have older children. The best bet for kids 7 to 14 are the Philharmonic's four annual Young People's Concerts and the children's Promenades that precede them. Or attend an inexpensive and informal rehearsal of a regular performance.

fi *10 Lincoln Center Plaza, tel. 212/875–5732.*

(ǏǏ 6+) **Radio City Music Hall.** I just can't leave out the Easter and Christmas shows at this huge 6,000-seat theater (the largest in the United States), despite the fact that our family isn't that crazy about them. But we do love the Art Deco interior of the theater, and if you like spectacles, you'll see one on the vast stage here. The costumes are lavish, there's lots of music and action, the new laser lighting effects are spectacular, and the Rockettes are as impressive as ever in their precision dancing.

fi *1260 6th Ave., tel. 212/247–4777.*

(ǏǏ 6+) **South Street Seaport.** Concerts of jazz, sea chanteys, folk music, and more are offered here for free (or sometimes at a nominal cost) in summer. They're usually pretty good. Check to see what's on and the suggested age range.

fi *Tel. 212/669–9400.*

(ǏǏ 10+) **SummerStage.** A wide variety of free concerts from rock to reggae to bagpipes and more appear here each summer. Have a picnic while you listen.

fi *Rumsey Playfield, Central Park, tel. 212/360–2777.*

DANCE. Besides performances in the museum programs, listed below, and at Arts Connection and the Taipei Theater, listed above, the following are good bets for kids.

(ǏǏ 6+) **American Ballet Theater.** The story ballets (*Swan Lake, Coppelia, Giselle,* and so on) for which this company's dancers are world-renowned tend to be more

accessible to kids. The costumes, dancing, and stage sets are uniformly superb. Unfortunately they perform in the huge Metropolitan Opera House; if you can't get seats in the front of the orchestra or in the grand tier, which are closer to the stage, don't bring younger kids. The company performs from April through June.
🏚 *70 Lincoln Center Plaza, tel. 212/362–6000.*

👫 8+ **Joyce Theater.** Many dance companies, some of them appealing to children, perform at this small theater each year, usually for one to three weeks each. The wild, acrobatic Pilobolus group and the American Indian Dance Theater troupe, whose traditional dances involve lots of colorful costumes and headdresses and sound, have runs at the theater. The tickets cost about half what you pay for good seats at the New York City Ballet.
🏚 *175 8th Ave., tel. 212/242–0800.*

👫 4+ **New York City Ballet.** The annual production of *The Nutcracker*—this company's is our favorite version of the ballet—is the reason to come here in December.
🏚 *New York State Theater at Lincoln Center, tel. 212/870–5570.*

👫 3 – 12 **New York Theater Ballet.** This small company's three annual one-hour productions, at Christmas, Easter, and the week of Mother's Day, are abridged versions of classic ballets geared just for families. The intimate theater where they perform has only 350 red velvet seats, so kids can really see no matter where you sit.
🏚 *Florence Gould Hall, 55 E. 59th St., tel. 212/679–0401.*

STORYTELLING. Barnes & Noble Jr., Books of Wonder, and Storyland bookstores (see Shopping, *above*) have regular story hours for kids.

👫 5 – 9 **Central Park's Hans Christian Andersen Statue.** During the late spring, summer, and early fall, storytellers entertain kids on Saturday from 11 to 12. If you can,

hear the beguiling Diane Wolkstein, author of several books of folktales. A storyteller will be there even if it's raining lightly.
🏚 *Near 72nd St. and 5th Ave. on west side of sailboat pond, tel. 212/794–6565.*

👫 3 – 12 **New York Public Library.** There's something for every kid at one of the world's largest branch library systems. The Central Children's Room at the Donnell Library Center (20 W. 53rd St. between 5th and 6th Aves., tel. 212/621–0636), the largest children's room in the system, always has a program.

CIRCUS

👫 1 – 12 **Big Apple Circus.** Attending this one-ring circus from October through January, when it's housed in a tent at Lincoln Center, is an annual event for many New York City families. We think this small circus, which has a long performing season in the city and then travels to New England, is the best one in the world for young kids.
🏚 *Administrative offices, 35 W. 35th St., tel. 212/268–0055.*

👫 6+ **Ringling Brothers and Barnum & Bailey Circus.** This huge three-ring circus arrives in New York in April for its annual visit to Madison Square Garden and usually stays until June. An extravaganza that has many more acts, animals, sequined costumes, and floats than the Big Apple Circus, it's not as much fun for little kids. The most unusual and exciting part of it is the Circus Walk of animals through the city the night before it opens.
🏚 *Madison Square Garden, 4 Penn Plaza, 7th Ave. between 31st and 33rd Sts., tel. 212/465–6741.*

MUSEUM PROGRAMS. Almost all museums in New York have regular events for children; some offer both performances and workshops that fall into more than one category. Those I've chosen are ones that we and my kids' panel have particularly enjoyed.

👫 6+ **American Museum of Natural History.** Check out what's on in the Leon-

hardt People Center on the 2nd floor. In this small theater space it's easy for kids to see and hear—and it's not hard to leave if you lose interest. Most of the performances involve dance or music from another culture. If you're in New York before Christmas, be sure to attend one of the museum's origami workshops. The 40-foot screen in the Naturmax Theater (cost: $5 adults, $2.50 kids) shows visually spectacular films such as one of the Grand Canyon in which you almost seem to be in a helicopter zooming down the canyon's sheer sides.
🏛 *Central Park West and 79th St., tel. 212/ 769–5315. (See Museums, above, and Chapter 8.)*

👫 **2 – 10** **Brooklyn Children's Museum.** In addition to all-day activities on weekends, there's usually a performance on Saturday or Sunday. We've seen the colorful Chinese Folk Dance company as well as a puppet show featuring African-American popular music. Workshops and performances here tend to be very multicultural.
🏛 *145 Brooklyn Ave., Brooklyn, tel. 718/ 735–4400. (See Museums, above, and Chapter 8.)*

👫 **2 – 10** **Children's Museum of Manhattan.** Weekends here are chock-a-block with activities for kids. Most performances are for ages 5 and up; the theater is small, participation is encouraged, and kids have a chance to talk with the performers. You'll see everything from an Irish music group playing bagpipes and harps to clog dancers. The Art Studio also has regular workshops.
🏛 *212 W. 83rd St., tel. 212/721–1234. (See Museums, above, and Chapter 8.)*

👫 **6+** **Metropolitan Museum of Art.** Every Friday and Saturday night the Met is open until 8:45. Between 4:30 and 5, the Great Hall Balcony Quintet begins playing on the 2nd floor balcony. While you can sit at small tables near the performers and order something to drink, children often just like to sit on benches across from the musicians, listen for a while, then explore the surrounding galleries. Stay to have dinner in

the museum cafeteria, then attend the excellent one-hour family lecture and sketching workshop for parents and kids 6 to 12 at 6 or at 7:30.
🏛 *1000 5th Ave., at 82nd St., tel. 212/ 535–7710. (See Museums, above, and Chapter 8.)*

👫 **6+** **Museum of the City of New York.** Nearly every Saturday there's a special family performance of dance, theater, or music or a workshop related to a special exhibit. We've found the puppet shows here among the very best in the city. There's a special family rate for performances.
🏛 *5th Ave. and 103rd St., tel. 212/534– 1672. (See Museums, above).*

CLASSES. There are an enormous number of classes in music, dance, and art for children in the city, but most of them require you to sign up for a certain number of sessions. Those below (and under Museum Programs, above) do not; though some of them don't require reservations, it's best to call before going.

👫 **5+** **Arts Connection.** From 12:30 to 2:30 on Saturday afternoon, prior to the regular 3 PM performance (see Music, above), there's always a fascinating, activity-packed family workshop—you might make Mexican masks for the Day of the Dead, learn to hula, or build instruments from paper tubes and bottles. The artists, architects, musicians, and dancers who lead them are adept at finding ways to involve kids of all ages and parents. Cost is $2 per person, but make sure to reserve.
🏛 *120 W. 46th St., tel. 212/302–7433.*

👫 **7+** **Bead Store.** At tables in this shop there are regular classes for kids and adults in jewelry-making.
🏛 *1065 Lexington Ave. at 75th St., tel. 212/ 628–4383; 132 Spring St., tel. 212/941– 6450. (See Shopping, above.)*

👫 **4 – 12** **Brooklyn Museum.** This huge museum offers free weekend art classes. "Arty Facts" is a 1½-hour family workshop

(kids 4–7) in which you view some aspect of an exhibition, then create related artworks. "What's Up?" is a drop-in program for kids 6 to 12 with the same focus. The instructors here are especially tuned in to kids.
🏛 *Eastern Pkwy., Brooklyn, tel. 718/638–5000.*

⚲ 2 – 10 **Children's Museum of the Arts.** The space in this ground-floor Soho loft is an environment for making art rather than a traditional museum. When there's a special "exhibit" kids make art related to it. The atmosphere is informal and fun; the highlight for a 6-year-old we know was decorating a vest with buttons and beads in a costume collage workshop.
🏛 *72 Spring St., tel. 212/941–9198. Cost: $4. Open Tues.–Sun. 11–5, Thurs. 11–7.*

⚲ 7 – 17 **City Lights Youth Theater.** One of the few places that has single workshops in different aspects of acting, this theater has four Saturday workshops a term, each for a different age group. Stage Combat, for kids 13 and up, offered in 1994, taught kids how to fake a realistic fight on stage.
🏛 *130 W. 56th St., tel. 212/262–0200.*

⚲ 3 – 12 **Staten Island Children's Museum.** The regular art workshops here, usually on Saturdays and holidays, are highly imaginative. Many involve creating things and learning unusual techniques such as making marbleized designs with acrylic paint. Listings usually say all ages, but ask when you reserve.
🏛 *1000 Richmond Terr., tel. 718/273–2060.*

Like most American families, we love visiting beaches every summer. We do have strong prejudices and preferences, though. First of all, we like beach resort areas that seem cut off from the world, that offer a real sense of retreat. Then there's the matter of water temperature: We've been to grand Maine beaches where we couldn't step in the water past our knees—and that's not for us.

Using those criteria, I've picked three areas that our family feels passionately about, each for different reasons: the beach-ringed peninsula of Cape Cod, Massachusetts, and two offshore islands, upscale Nantucket and more relaxed Block Island.

Cape Cod

Cape Cod is an especially great place for kids of all ages, from babies to teens. This 70-mile-long arm of land has an amazingly diverse assortment of beautiful white-sand beaches and dunes, and its several towns each have their own personality. You'll find wonderful playgrounds, shops, miniature golf, day camps, and nature programs for kids all over the place. Concerts and movies prevent the boring-evening syndrome that dooms many beach areas.

The Cape's summer traffic jams are legendary. It can sometimes take two hours just to cross the bridge over the canal that separates the Cape from mainland Massachusetts. To us, braving the traffic is definitely worth it.

Though there is undeniably a commercial, shopping-mall side to the Cape, at least in its bustling larger towns, the creation of the Cape Cod National Seashore preserved most of the land in what's known as the Lower Cape—from the "elbow" of the arm, around Chatham, up to the "fist" at Provincetown. Families we know with young kids may prefer the south shore beaches,

where the water is warmest. No matter where we're based, we always end up driving around to attractions elsewhere on the Cape. Distances are not great, but there can be traffic tie-ups in summer.

The Basics

HOW TO FIND OUT WHAT'S GOING ON. The **Cape Cod Chamber of Commerce** (Rtes. 6 and 132, Box 16, Hyannis 02601, tel. 508/362–3225) is open year-round. Besides the main location, look for information booths at the Sagamore Bridge rotary (tel. 508/888–2438), just over the Bourne Bridge on Route 28 (tel. 508/759–3814) heading toward Falmouth, and a large center on Route 3, exit 5. Local chambers of commerce include: **Brewster** (Old Town Hall, Box 1241, 02631, tel. 508/896–8088); **Chatham** (533 Main St., Box 793, 02633-0793, tel. 508/945–0342); **Dennis** (Jct. Rtes. 28 and 134, West Dennis; Box 275, South Dennis 02660; tel. 508/398–3568 or 800/243–9920); **Eastham** (Rte. 6 at Fort Hill Rd., Box 1329, 02642, tel. 508/255–3444); **Orleans** (Rte. 6A and Eldredge Pkwy., Box 153, 02653, tel. 508/255–1386 or 508/240–2474); **Truro** (Rte. 6 at Head of the Meadow Rd., Box 26, North Truro 02652, tel. 508/487–1288); and **Wellfleet** (Rte. 6, Box 571, 02667, tel. 508/349–2510).

Kids on the Cape (Sandcastle Publishing Co., Box 183, Chatham, MA 02633, tel. 508/945–0436), a free booklet published four times during the summer season, is the best resource for families on current activities, events, and sights on the Cape.

GETTING IN AND OUT OF CAPE COD.

By air: Barnstable Municipal Airport (Rte. 28 rotary, Hyannis, tel. 508/775–2020) offers service from Boston year-round via Delta Connection; in summer there's also service from New York City area airports.

By train: Amtrak (tel. 800/872–7245) has limited weekend service to the Cape in summer. The *Cape Codder* travels from Washington, D.C., through Philadelphia and New York City to Hyannis; some routes stop at several towns on the Cape, but these may change from year to year. Trains to Boston's South Station connect with a Bonanza bus (*see* By Bus, *below*) to the Cape, a long and tiring haul for kids.

By bus: Bonanza Bus Lines (tel. 508/548–7588 or 800/556–3815) offers direct and frequent service to Falmouth, Bourne, Woods Hole, and Hyannis from Boston and Logan Airport, as well as daily service from New York, Connecticut, and Providence. **Plymouth & Brockton Company** (tel. 508/775–5524 or 508/746–0378) runs buses from Boston to a number of Cape communities, including Provincetown. The **Cape Cod Regional Transit Authority** (tel. 800/352–7155) provides local service, including a route between Hyannis and Woods Hole that stops, conveniently for those with teens, at the Cape Cod Mall.

By boat: Bay State Cruise Company (tel. 617/723–7800) runs a three-hour trip by ferry from Boston to Provincetown (summer only). This is too long for all but older kids.

By car: Route 6 (the Mid-Cape Highway), which connects to Route 3 from Boston, runs the length of the Cape to Province-

town, but it has no view of the water. Route 28, which connects to Route 195 and then to I–95, goes along the south shore and is usually full of traffic. Route 6A along the north shore is the scenic route. On all roads in summer, eastbound lanes are jammed afternoons and evening on Friday, and westbound traffic is jammed from noon to 9 on Sunday. The big tie-up is at the bridges across the Cape Cod Canal.

FAMILY-FRIENDLY TOURS

(4+) **Cape Cod Scenic Railroad.** This can be a treat: a 1¾-hour, 42-mile round-trip excursion between Hyannis and Sagamore, stopping at Sandwich depot and the Cape Cod Canal, offering views of cranberry bogs, marshes, sand dunes, villages, Cape Cod Bay, and more.
Main and Center Sts., Hyannis, tel. 508/771–3788. Cost: $10.50 adults, $6.50 kids 3–12. June–Oct., Tues.–Sun. at 10, 12:30, and 3; also weekends in May.

(4 – 13) **P-Town Trolley Tour.** If your kids have never traveled on an old-fashioned trolley, they might enjoy this 45-minute narrated tour of Provincetown. You can get on and off at four locations (including the national seashore's visitor center), wander around, then board another trolley a half-hour later.
In front of Town Hall, Provincetown, tel. 508/487–9483. Cost: $6 adults, $4 kids under 13. May–Oct., daily 10:30–5:30.

(2 – 12) **Rambling Rose Carriage Rides.** These 10- to 20-minute rides in a fancy horse-drawn carriage through Provincetown in summer are just the right length for little kids.
Commercial St. in front of Town Hall, Provincetown, tel. 508/487–4246. Rates vary; short ride for a family of 4 costs $17.

EMERGENCIES.
Cape Cod Hospital (27 Park St., Hyannis 02601, tel. 508/771–1800) and **Falmouth Hospital** (100 Ter Heun Dr., Falmouth 02540, tel. 508/457–3524) both have 24-hour emergency rooms, though these are jammed in summer. For **fire** or

ambulance anywhere on the Cape, call 800/352–7141 or check the front page of the telephone book for a local number. **Omni Dentix** (Cape Cod Mall, Hyannis 02601, tel. 508/778–1200) is a dental clinic that accepts emergency walk-ins. Most of the Cape's 20 **CVS** drugstores (there's one in the Cape Cod Mall, Hyannis, tel. 508/771–1774) are open until 9 PM Monday through Saturday, Sunday until 6; the **Stop 'n Shop Pharmacy** (65 Independence Dr., Hyannis, tel. 508/790–2149) is open until 9 PM on Sunday.

BABY-SITTERS. Most resorts keep a list of baby-sitters they have used previously. If you are staying somewhere on the outer Cape, Provincetown's **Council on Aging** (tel. 508/487–9906) offers baby-sitting services; **Tot Drop** (64 Enterprise Rd., Hyannis, tel. 508/778-6777), a baby-sitting service by the Cape Cod Mall, offers drop-off service.

WHEN TO GO. As the main reason to go to the Cape with kids is for the beach, the water, and outdoor action, summer is the time to be here. Tourists swarm in July and August, however; the last half of June and early September would be a better choice if it doesn't conflict with your kids' school calendar. Early fall is still balmy, the water is warmer than it is in June, and prices drop dramatically. Most attractions on the Cape are open from Memorial Day through September, sometimes to the end of October.

Scoping out Cape Cod

Cape Cod is commonly divided into three sections: the Upper Cape (the first section you drive through as you come from the mainland), Mid-Cape, and the Lower Cape. The Upper Cape includes such towns as quaint **Sandwich** on the north shore or, on the south shore, New England-y **Falmouth** and **Woods Hole** (home of the famous oceanographic institute and docking point for ferries to the island of Martha's Vineyard). In the Mid-Cape, **Hyannis,** a village

made famous by the Kennedys, is the business hub of the Cape. Though it's crowded and noisy, families usually end up here at some point or other, either to visit attractions, go shopping, or catch a ferry to Martha's Vineyard or Nantucket. **Dennis,** with its charming colonial center, encompasses four towns and some 15 beaches on both Cape Cod Bay and the south shore.

The Lower Cape begins where the peninsula abruptly hooks northward. On the bay, **Brewster,** an old New England town of shade trees, captain's houses, and country roads, is a good place for outdoor action, including freshwater swimming, camping, and miles of tidal flats. We love **Chatham,** situated on the elbow of the Cape and surrounded by water on three sides; it has gray-shingled cottages and the smell of honeysuckle and the sea. Pleasant, unassuming **Orleans** has activities such as roller-skating, sailing, kayaking, and swimming at beaches on both the bay and ocean. At **Eastham** the Cape becomes wilder and less populated, a place of high dunes and windswept ocean beaches. Uncrowded **Wellfleet,** tucked into a sheltered spot on Cape Cod Bay, has a meandering coastline of watery green salt marshes, hidden freshwater ponds, a wildlife sanctuary, and the national seashore. **Truro** is also untouristy, surrounded by high dunes, rolling moors, and houses in tiny valleys. **Provincetown,** nestled on a hill above the bay at the Cape's tip, has a diverse mix of people—families, fishermen, flamboyant gays, assorted sightseers. We come to shop, to climb the Pilgrim monument, go on a whale watch, people-watch on the wharf, and marvel at the 60-foot-high dunes.

Attractions below have been grouped by town, beginning at the Cape Cod Canal and proceeding out along the Cape to its tip.

6 – 13 Pairpoint Crystal Glass Works. Cups, plates, and much else in beautiful colors are created in the oldest glass factory in America. From a gallery, kids can watch as a craftsman heats glass to the melting point, then blows it into shapes.

🏠 *851 Sandwich Rd., Rte. 6A, Sagamore, tel. 508/888–2344 or 800/899–0953. Admission free. Open daily 9–6; demonstrations weekdays 8:30–4:30.*

(👫 **3–13**) **Heritage Plantation.** The Shaker round barn is full of classic and historic cars, including a 1931 yellow and green Duesenberg built for Gary Cooper. There's also a collection of 2,000 hand-painted miniature soldiers and an old-fashioned carousel with hand-carved horses. The museum complex is set on 76 acres of gardens and wooded groves along Shawme Pond.
🏠 *Grove and Pine Sts., Sandwich, tel. 508/888–3300. Cost: $7 adults, $3.50 kids 6–18. Open mid-May–Oct., daily 10–5.*

(👫 **3–10**) **Thornton W. Burgess Museum.** This homey little cottage by a willow-edged duck pond houses books and memorabilia of children's book author Thornton Burgess. See Chapter 8.
🏠 *4 Water St., edge of Shawme Pond, Sandwich, tel. 508/888–6870.*

(👫 **4–10**) **Green Briar Nature Center and Jam Kitchen.** In the Center, you'll find live frogs, turtles, a rabbit in a hutch, shells, and aquariums; the gardens and an adjoining 57 acres dubbed the Old Briar Patch are laced with the finest nature paths in this part of the Cape. You can also visit the old-fashioned kitchen nestled in the woods next to a pond, where you can buy some beach-plum jelly.
🏠 *6 Discovery Hill Rd., off Rte. 6A, East Sandwich, tel. 508/888–6870. Donation requested. Open Apr.–Dec., Mon.–Sat. 10–4, Sun. 1–4.*

(👫 **3–12**) **Fisheries Aquarium.** Kids can touch and see lobsters, starfish, and other species native to Cape Cod's waters here at the public aquarium of the Northeast Fisheries Science Center. The highlights in summer are the two harbor seals. See Chapter 9.
🏠 *Albatross and Water Sts., Woods Hole, tel. 508/548–7684.*

(👫 **2–12**) **ZooQuarium.** This combination petting zoo, discovery center, aquarium, and sea lion show also offers regular education programs. See Chapter 9.
🏠 *Rte. 28, West Yarmouth, tel. 508/775–8883.*

(👫 **0–9**) **Discovery Days Children's Museum.** There are 4,000 square feet of interactive exhibits here, including Jakes International Diner, where kids can pretend to be waiters, waitresses, and chefs.
🏠 *444 Main St. (Rte. 28), Dennisport, tel. 508/398–1600. Cost: $4.50 adults, $4 kids under 17. Open mid-June–Labor Day, daily 9:30–7:30; Labor Day–early June, Wed.–Mon. 10–5.*

(👫 **3–12**) **Cape Cod Museum of Natural History.** This museum set on 82 acres taught us much about how the Cape's native creatures survive, with exhibits, programs, and short nature trails through marshes. The museum also organizes family excursions to Momomoy wildlife refuge (see below).
🏠 *896 Main St., Brewster, tel. 508/896–3867. Cost: $3.50 adults, $1.50 kids 6–14. Open May–mid-Oct., Mon.–Sat. 9:30–4:30, Sun. 12:30–4:30; mid-Oct.–May, Tues.–Sat. 9:30–4:30, Sun. 12:30–4:30.*

(👫 **3–12**) **New England Fire and History Museum.** Kids can climb on engines and a fireboat here, at one of the world's biggest collections of fire engines and memorabilia. The museum's six buildings on Brewster's common also house a historic blacksmith shop and an animated diorama of the Great Chicago Fire.
🏠 *Rte. 6A, Brewster, tel. 508/896–5711. Cost: $4.50 adults, $2.50 kids 5–12. Open Memorial Day–Labor Day, weekdays 10–4, weekends noon–4.*

(👫 **3–8**) **Brewster Mill.** At this weathered-shingle mill with turning waterwheel, little kids like to clatter across the small wooden bridges out back. Inside you can watch cornmeal being ground and a weaver working at a loom.

🏛 *Stoney Brook Rd., Brewster, tel. 508/896–6745. Donations accepted. Open July and Aug., Thurs.–Sat. 2–5.*

👫 2 – 10 Bassett Wild Animal Farm. When Gavin was little, no trip was complete without a stop to see exotic wild critters and pet domestic animals. Here you can do both, but don't expect anything like a major zoo. See Chapter 9.

🏛 *620 Tubman Rd. between Rtes. 124 and 137, Brewster, tel. 508/896–3224.*

👫 ALL Chatham Fish Pier. After 2 in the afternoon, wiggly little kids and grown-ups crowd the pier's observation deck to watch the returning fishing boats unload their catch; the action reaches its peak between 4 and 5.

🏛 *Shore Rd. and Barcliff Ave., Chatham.*

👫 6 – 14 Monomoy National Wildlife Refuge. This 2,750-acre preserve on Monomoy Island, a barrier beach of tidal flats, dunes, marshes, and ponds, provides a resting and nesting place for migrating birds. On the mainland, a ¾-mile interpretive trail around Morris Island by the visitor center is fun for kids: You have a good view of the refuge and its birds.

🏛 *Morris Island, Chatham, tel. 508/945–0594.*

👫 5 – 12 Railroad Museum. In a restored depot, an old caboose and thousands of train models are on display.

🏛 *Depot Rd., Chatham, no phone. Donations accepted. Open mid-June–mid-Sept., Tues.–Sat. 10–4.*

👫 ALL Wellfleet Bay Wildlife Sanctuary. The appeal of this 750-acre haven of salt marshes, moors, ponds, and woods are the animals (muskrats, turtles) and 250 species of birds, which appear even when kids are making lots of noise. We like the mile-long Goose Pond Trail; an inexpensive guide shows the birds and plants you will see on it. A new nature center has hands-on exhibits; regularly scheduled activities for kids include walks, workshops, evening slide shows, and a day camp. It's run by the Mas-

sachusetts Audubon Society; if you've been an Audubon member for at least a year, you can camp here.

🏛 *West side of Rte. 6, off West Rd., Box 236, South Wellfleet, tel. 508/349–2615. Cost: $3 adults, $2 kids under 16. Open daily dawn–dusk.*

👫 6 – 15 Highland Light. The Cape's oldest lighthouse, Highland Light is still active, and you can even drive right up to it. The treacherous sandbars to its north have caused hundreds of shipwrecks.

🏛 *Off Lighthouse Rd., off Rte. 6, North Truro.*

👫 6 – 15 Pilgrim Monument and Museum. A granite tower honors the Pilgrims, who landed here in 1620 before pushing on to Plymouth. See Chapter 7.

🏛 *High-pole Hill on Winslow St., off Bradford St., Provincetown, tel. 508/487–1310.*

BEACHES. The Cape's 150 salt- and fresh-water beaches provide an amazing variety of sand, water, and amenities. The Cape Cod Visitor's Guide details costs; hefty parking fees ranging from $5 to $10 per day are charged at town beaches unless you purchase a weekly or season-long sticker, which is even more expensive (check at individual town halls). Parking lots at the most popular beaches fill up quickly.

The **Cape Cod National Seashore** (headquarters in South Wellfleet, MA 02663, tel. 508/349–3785) stretches 40 miles from Chatham to Provincetown, offering beaches, dunes, hiking paths, bike trails, and beachcombing. Two visitor centers—the Salt Pond Visitor's Center (tel. 508/255–3421), off Route 6 just outside Eastham, and the Province Lands Area Visitor's Center (tel. 508/487–1256), on Race Point Road, off Route 6 in Provincetown—provide information and some of the best guided walks and family nature programs on the Cape. A National Seashore season pass is $15.

The beaches facing the Atlantic Ocean along the national seashore are beautiful and less crowded, but they're not for young kids; serious, rough surf rolls in, sometimes with a strong undertow, and the water temperature is cold. Instead, head for the gentle swells and dune landscape of beaches along Cape Cod Bay, or the big, wide south Cape beaches facing Nantucket Sound, where the water is warmed by the gulf stream. A caveat: It's easy for kids to sunburn here, as the light reflects off the water and few beaches have shade. Bring an umbrella and slather skin with sunblock. See Swimming in Chapter 12 for the Cape's best beaches; here is a town-by-town rundown of kid-friendly spots.

North Falmouth. See Chapter 12.

West Barnstable. See Chapter 12.

Hyannis. Wide **Kalmus Beach** (Ocean Street), nearly a mile long, has fine sand, warm water, no undertow, a very gradual drop-off, and a sheltered area good for little kids; you'll find a snack bar, showers, lifeguards, and rest rooms. Along Lewis Bay, smaller **Veteran's Park Beach** (Ocean Street) is also good for little kids, with similar water and wave conditions and a tree-shaded picnic table. It has rest rooms, lifeguards, and a snack bar. Active young teens may prefer **Craigville Beach** (see Chapter 12).

West Dennis. See Chapter 12.

Harwich. On the Sound, **Red River Beach** has amenities, a pleasant expanse of sand, and stone jetties, or fishing.

Brewster. Eight miles of bay beach here are washed with calm, warm water, and tidal flats stretch as far as a mile into the bay. At **Paine's Creek Beach** a gentle stream winds through a salt marsh meadow to a small beach surrounded by coves and inlets (no rest rooms), but keep an eye out for the incoming tide. **Breakwater Beach** has the largest parking area, better swimming, and rest rooms. For freshwater swimming, as well as boating and windsurfing, try **Flax Pond** in Nickerson State Park (see Chapter 12).

Chatham. A curving strip of barrier beach that protects Chatham's harbor, **South**

Beach can be reached only by a five-minute water taxi shuttle (Outermost Harbor Marine, Morris Island Rd., tel. 508/945–3030). On the ocean side of the sandbar, surf crashes in; currents on the bay side create shallow pools for wading. There are no rest rooms. Straight, long **Hardings Beach** attracts lots of kids; it has small dunes crisscrossed by paths winding down to the beach. Water is in the 70° range, with no undertow and gentle surf; there are rest rooms, lifeguards, and a snack bar.

Orleans. With its large tidal flats and warm water, **Skaket Beach** is one of best beaches for kids on the Lower Cape. The snack bar sells butterfly and minnow catching nets.

Eastham. On the spot where the Mayflower Pilgrims first met the local Indians, **First Encounter Beach** is a lovely quiet beach on the bay, bordered by a vast marsh meadow. There are rest rooms. The national seashore's beaches begin in Eastham, with **Coast Guard Beach** and **Nauset Light Beach.** Their imposing cliffs, long rolling waves, and roaring surf draw avid body-surfers and board surfers; though riptides and cold waters make them unsuitable for smaller kids to swim, the beach is wide and the sand inviting, and they're conveniently close to the Salt Pond Visitor Center. There are lifeguards, showers, and a food concession.

Wellfleet. A small sand beach on freshwater **Long Pond** (take Long Pond Road off East Main Street) is a lovely place for younger kids to swim; it has a shaded grassy area with picnic tables, a float to swim to, and good fishing. You need a town sticker to park at any of Wellfleet's beaches, and to get one you have to prove you are staying in Wellfleet.

Truro. On the bay, **Corn Hill Beach** is where the Pilgrims first found corn. It's a good place for shelling. Off-road vehicles take over after 5 PM.

Provincetown. Two national seashore beaches here are great for families: **Herring**

Cove and **Race Point Beach,** both near easy hiking trails and equipped with showers, lifeguards, and rest rooms. Parking lots fill early. Herring Cove has slightly warmer bayside water, gentler waves, a snack bar, and a parking lot closer to the beach; It draws both a gay crowd and families. We prefer Race Point Beach because it's near massive sand dunes and feels more remote.

Action

Recreation departments and public libraries in towns all over the Cape offer a profusion of day camps and town activity programs for kids, including tennis, swimming, and sailing lessons; if you're going to be here at least a week, they're well worth checking out, especially if your kids want to get together with other kids. Also try the nature programs offered by the Cape Cod National Seashore and Wellfleet Bay Wildlife Sanctuary (see Scoping out Cape Cod, *above*).

AMUSEMENTS. Much of the arcade and minigolf action is clustered along Route 28 between Yarmouth and Harwich Port.

Cape Cod Storyland Golf. This 2-acre 18-hole miniature-golf course is set up as a mini–Cape Cod; each hole is a town on the Cape, with reproductions of historic buildings, ponds, waterfalls, and a mill.
🏠 *70 Center St., by railroad depot, Hyannis, tel. 508/778–4339. Cost: $5 adults, $4 kids under 12. Open mid-Apr.–Oct., daily 8 AM–midnight.*

Pirate's Cove. The most elaborate of the Cape's dozen minigolf emporiums, this place has a great pirate ship in a fake pond surrounded by cliffs and waterfalls.
🏠 *723 Main St. (Rte. 28), South Yarmouth, tel. 508/394–6200. Cost: $5 adults, $4 kids under 13. Open Apr.–June, Sept., and Oct., daily 10–7; July and Aug., daily 9 AM–11 PM.*

Charles Moore Arena. Roller skating goes on here Tuesday and Wednesday nights in the summer. Friday night is Rock Night, just for kids 9–14 (no parents) from 8 to 10.

🏠 *O'Connor Way, Orleans, tel. 508/255–2971. Cost: $4, $3 kids under 13, $2 skate rentals. Open June–Aug.*

Ryan Family Amusement Centers. Everything from candlepin bowling (using a lighter ball) to pinball to video games is offered at five locations on the Cape.
🏠 *Capetown Mall, Rte. 132, Hyannis, tel. 508/775–5566; 441 Main St., Hyannis, tel. 508/775–3411; Cape Bowl, Rte. 28, South Yarmouth, tel. 508/394–5644. $2 per game. Open daily 9:30 AM–10 PM, bowling, weekdays 4–6, all day weekends.*

Trampoline Center. At this outdoor fenced-in area the 12 6-by-12-foot trampolines are set at ground level over pits, so little kids don't have far to fall. Parents can jump with kids under 7.
🏠 *Rte. 28, across from A&W restaurant, Harwich, tel. 508/432–8717. Cost: $3 for 10 min. Open mid-June–Labor Day, daily 9 AM–11 PM.*

BASEBALL. Cape Cod Baseball League. Teams play regularly in 10 towns, including Hyannis, Chatham, Brewster, Harwich, and Orleans, at hours early enough for even little kids to enjoy the games. *See* Chapter 11.
🏠 *Box 164, South Harwich 02661, tel. 508/362–3036.*

BIKING. What a great place Cape Cod is for family biking! The paths on the Lower Cape are mostly flat, some ideal even for kids with training wheels, and lead to beaches, picnic spots, and wonderful views. The 20-mile Cape Cod Rail Trail, the longest, runs from South Dennis to Eastham. For the best trails, books of paths, and rentals, see Bike Paths *in* Chapter 12.

BIRD-WATCHING. The **Wellfleet Bay Wildlife Sanctuary** (*see* Scoping out Cape Cod, *above*) has extensive kids' birding activities. For books and bird paraphernalia, check out the **Bird Watcher's General Store** (*see* Shopping, *below*).

BOATING. The Cape's calm ocean bays and kettle ponds are prime locations for all types of boating, and instruction for kids is readily available, both on a one-time lesson basis and as part of a series. **Nickerson State Park** off Route 6A in Brewster (tel. 508/896–3491; see Chapter 10), a large, forested park that almost seems more like the Berkshires than Cape Cod, is dotted with kettle ponds for swimming, fishing, and boating, including windsurfing. Chatham, Wellfleet, and Eastham also offer good windsurfing; sailing is best in South Orleans (see Sailing and Windsurfing in Chapter 12). **Canoe Eco-Tours,** offered through Jack's Boat Rentals in Wellfleet (tel. 508/349–9808), tour connecting kettle ponds in search of wildlife.

FISHING. The Friday *Cape Cod Times* Fishing Around column tells the latest on what's being caught and where. Gavin found clam digging and catching blue crabs most absorbing, but he enjoyed casting his line off busy MacMillan Wharf in Provincetown, too. The bridge on Mill Pond in Chatham is another spot for kids to drop in a line. For clam digging, we head for Wellfleet. See *also* Chapter 12.

A treat even for very small kids is hermit crabbing. Just put some small empty shells in a bucket of sand and water, then add shells with hermit crabs inside. If you touch the back of the hermit crab's shell, it will crawl out and investigate one of the empty shells.

HIKES AND WALKS. We think the best hikes in the Lower Cape are in the **Cape Cod National Seashore, Wellfleet Bay Wildlife Sanctuary,** and at the **Cape Cod Museum of Natural History** (see Scoping out Cape Cod, *above*). Another of our favorites is the half-mile **Parmet Cranberry Bog Trail** off North Parmet Road in Truro, where a wooden boardwalk and trail lead past a pond, the cranberry vines grow down to the sea, and bird song fills the air. **Nickerson State Park** in Brewster (Rte. 6A, tel. 508/896–3491; see Chapter 10) has regular nature walks geared for kids.

PLAYGROUNDS. The Lower Cape has three splendid playgrounds—in Harwich, Chatham, and Orleans, each adjacent to the local elementary school.

WHALE-WATCHING. Taking kids on a whale watch is easier on Cape Cod than anywhere else in the Northeast because you don't have to go far to get to prime whale-watching waters. See Watching for Whales *in* Chapter 12.

Shopping

In Hyannis, **Main Street** is lined with touristy T-shirt shops, ice-cream and candy stores, cheerful eating places, souvenir shops, and minigolf, the kind of atmosphere favored by teens. In a brick courtyard off Main Street, look for **Lions & Tigers & Bears** (599 Main St., tel. 508/790–4146), a charming toy store with a good selection of stuffed animals, games, and a great selection of stickers. The air-conditioned **Cape Cod Mall** (between Rtes. 132 and 28, Hyannis, tel. 508/771–0200) is the Cape's largest, with 90 shops, a food court, and stroller rentals.

Orleans has several good stores for young shoppers. The **Baseball Shop** (26 Main St., tel. 508/240–1063) sells everything related to baseball (and other sports) including baseball cards, hats, and clothing. **Compass Rose Book Shop** (45 Main St., tel. 508/255–1545), owned by a mother of young children, has an excellent selection of kids' titles plus toys and games, and in summer it offers children's programs. The **Bird Watcher's General Store** (36 Rte. 6A. tel. 508/255–6974 or 800/562–1512) is full of neat bird-related stuff.

Throughout July and August, the **Wellfleet Drive-In Theater** (Rte. 6, Eastham–Wellfleet line, tel. 508/349–2520) becomes a giant flea market on Mondays, Wednesdays, Thursdays, weekends, and holidays (hours 8–4). A snack bar and playground and a carnival atmosphere make it a worthy destination for a family with kids of widely varying ages.

In Provincetown, **Commercial Street,** the main drag, has shops of nostalgic memorabilia and oddball items jammed alongside restaurants and cafés; it's great for people-watching. Stop by the **Provincetown Fudge Factory** (210 Commercial St., tel. 508/487–2850), which sells what we believe are the best peanut-butter cups in the world, among other sweet treats. The barn-like **Marine Specialties** (235 Commercial St., tel. 508/487–1730) is loaded with odd inexpensive items kids like to collect. Head down to the honky-tonk wharf, off Commercial Street for T-shirt and souvenir outlets.

Eats

Chowder, clams, lobster (try lobster rolls), scallops, and fish of all kinds are the Cape's specialties, though most seafood restaurants offer alternatives; ideal for families with young kids are the many informal clam shacks where you can sit outside at picnic tables. Several restaurants have early-bird specials—low-priced dinners in early evening, usually before 6. A local chain that can be counted on for good home cooking, friendly service, and informality is **Hearth & Kettle,** which serves breakfast, lunch, and dinner.

(ALL) Barbyann's. Tasty Mexican dishes, pizza, burgers, and homemade chili at low prices can be a nice change of pace from seafood. Decor is comfortable—exposed beams and a green-pink-and-red color scheme—but not special. *120 Airport Rd., Hyannis, tel. 508/775–9795. Children's menu, booster seats, high chairs. No reservations. Dress: casual. AE, D, DC, MC, V. $*

(ALL) Baxter's Fish N' Chips. Sitting at picnic tables on an outdoor deck, you can watch the boats on busy Lewis Bay as you eat delicious fresh fish and maybe the best fried clams on the Cape. Occasionally a seaplane lands nearby, to the delight of kids. The menu includes burgers as well. *117 Pleasant St. Wharf, Hyannis, tel. 508/775–4490. Booster seats and high chairs. No*

reservations. *Dress: casual. MC, V. Closed Oct.–Apr. $–$$*

(ALL) Bayside Lobster Hutt. At this noisy, friendly place on a country road leading to the harbor, everyone sits at long picnic tables. The fish is fresh and good; cheeseburgers and hot dogs are also available. *Commercial St., Wellfleet, tel. 508/349–6333. Dress: casual. $*

(ALL) Box Lunch of Cape Cod. We rate this small chain of conveniently located take-out spots the best choice for instant picnic fare on the Cape. Its main claim to fame is the "rollwich," pita bread covered with various ingredients of your choice, then rolled up and heated in a microwave. The kids' menu includes a mini-ham-and-cheese "piglet" sandwich. *353 Commercial St., Provincetown, tel. 508/487–6026; Briar La., Wellfleet, tel. 508/349–2178; Seatoiler Shops, North Eastham, tel. 508/255–0799; Patriot Square Mall, South Dennis, tel. 508/394–2202; 217 Main St., East Orleans, tel. 508/240–3278; Underpass Rd., Brewster, tel. 508/896–6682; 357 Main St., Hyannis Center, tel. 508/790–5855. Children's menu. Dress: casual. $*

(ALL) Lobster Claw. A step up from lobster-in-the-rough places, this popular rustic spot with a menu shaped like a lobster claw is generally considered the best family restaurant on Cape Cod. Fish dinners, lobster, mussels, steamers, and superior fried clams are the best bets. Come early (before 5:30) to beat the crowds—and save money with the early-bird menu. *Rte. 6A, Orleans, tel. 508/255–1800. Children's menu; booster seats, high chairs. Dress: casual. AE, D, MC, V. $*

SWEET STUFF

(ALL) Four Seas. Eating homemade ice cream (35 flavors) in this old-fashioned parlor has been a Cape tradition since 1934. *360 S. Main St., Centerville, tel. 508/775–1394. Booster seats, high chairs. Dress: casual. No credit cards. $*

⚭ ALL Sundae School Ice Cream Parlor. The working nickelodeon and other memorabilia in this 19th-century barn capture kids' interest while they wait for their cones. Dollops of real whipped cream and homemade ice cream plus toppings are served from an antique marble soda fountain. ⚭ 210 E. Main St., Dennisport, tel. 508/394–9122. Dress: casual. $

FOR PICNICS. The Lower Cape has literally hundreds of picnicking places with views, tables, beaches, and rest rooms, easily accessible to car or bike; there's a good list in every issue of *Kids on the Cape* (see How to Find out What's Going On, *above*). **Pilgrim Lake,** off Monument Road in Orleans, has plenty of parking, warm swimming waters, and picnic tables. **Doane Rock Picnic Area** in Eastham, off the Cape Cod Rail Trail bike path, is marked by a huge glacial boulder. Gavin loved the view of both bay and ocean from the **Pilgrim Heights** picnic area off Route 6 in North Truro. The **Castle in the Clouds playground** at Harwich Elementary School (corner of Parallel and South Sts., Harwich) has a picnic area next to it. Off the beaten path, crowd-free **North Beach,** a barrier beach off Chatham reached by water taxi from Chatham Harbor (tel. 508/945–9378), is one of our favorites. For dinner picnics we head to one of the Cape Cod Baseball League's games (see Sports, *above*).

Where to Stay

The Cape Cod Chamber of Commerce's *Resort Directory* lists hundreds of accommodations, plus real-estate agencies. For summer stays the most popular cottages must be booked far, far in advance; most accommodations insist on weeklong minimums. The Chamber's information booths (see How to Find out What's Going On, *above*) can help with last-minute accommodations. After Labor Day, rates drop markedly.

The price categories that follow are based on summer-season rates and reflect what a family of four would spend for one night in a double room or the smallest appropriate accommodation available (sometimes a cottage): $$$$, over $160; $$$, $110–$160; $$, $70–$110; $, under $70. When resorts are MAP or AP, categories are $$$$, over $450; $$$, $350–$450; $$, $200–$350; $, under $200. Prices do not include 9.7% tax.

Capt. Gosnold Village. The gray-shingle one- to three-bedroom cottages and motel buildings stand in a shady complex. The colonial-country and knotty-pine cottages are simple and pleasant and have private porches or picnic tables; the three-bedroom cottages have three TVs and three baths. It's on a quiet street, safe for biking, and only a short walk from two beaches. The fenced-in pool has a lifeguard. ⚭ 230 Gosnold St., Hyannis 02601, tel. 508/775–9111, fax 508/775–8221 (call first). 18 cottages. Facilities: pool, basketball court, game nets, picnic areas, gas grills, daily maid service, baby-sitting. MC, V. Closed Nov.–Apr. $$–$$$

Chatham Bars Inn. The luxurious gray-shingled inn and cottages facing Pleasant Bay make up a total resort on the ocean, with kids' programs, tennis, golf, a pool, a private beach, and a soothing atmosphere. See Chapter 14. ⚭ Chatham 02633, tel. 508/945–0096 or 800/527–4884, fax 508/945–5491. 152 rooms. Facilities: pool, golf course, 4 tennis courts, 3 restaurants. AE, MC, V. $$$–$$$$

Kalmar Village. Set on a quiet strip of bayfront south of Provincetown, close to dunes and grassy hills and wide open spaces, this family-owned cottage resort is a great place for swimming in the bay and communing with nature. The housekeeping cottages, grouped around green lawns with picnic tables and a large pool, are authentically Cape Cod—cheerful, white-and-bright, with lots of windows and blond wood. The newer two-bedroom cottages, closest to the water, are the nicest.

🏠 *Shore Rd., Rte. 6A, Box 745, North Truro 02652, tel. 508/487–0585, fax 617/247–0211. Winter mailing address: 246 Newbury St., Boston 02116, tel. 617/247–0211. 50 cottages, 6 efficiencies, 4 motel rooms. Facilities: pool, private beach, laundry, daily maid service, picnic tables, hibachis, baby-sitting. D, MC, V. Closed Columbus Day–Memorial Day. $$*

Lighthouse Inn. This sprawling, friendly, unpretentious resort on the ocean offers many family sports options. Though it has its own beach, West Dennis Beach (see Swimming *in* Chapter 12) is close, as is the Bass River for canoeing. See Chapter 14.
🏠 *Box 128, West Dennis 02690, tel. 508/398-2244, fax 508/398–5658. 61 units. Facilities: pool, miniature golf course, 2 tennis courts, game room. MC, V. $$–$$$*

Mid-Cape Hostel. Two cozy family cabins are part of this 60-bed hostel surrounded by woods. It's just a step up from camping, at a rock-bottom price. The location is a plus: close to the Salt Pond Visitors' Center and only 4 miles from the national seashore's ocean beaches.
🏠 *75 Goody Hallet Rd., Eastham 02642, tel. 508/255–2785, fax 508/255–9752. Facilities: bike rentals, ping-pong, volleyball, sailing instruction and rentals, kitchen privileges. Reservations essential July and Aug. Kids 5–10 half-price. MC, V. $*

New Seabury Resort. A 2,000-acre complex of tasteful small villas and private homes by Nantucket Sound offers beaches, a day camp, golf, tennis, pools, and its own little shopping area. See Chapter 14.
🏠 *Box 550, Rock Landing Rd., New Seabury 02649, tel. 508/477–9111 or 800/999–9033; in MA, 800/752–9700; fax 508/477–9790. $$*

CAMPING. There are nine private family campgrounds on the Lower Cape; the Chamber of Commerce has a brochure listing them.

Nickerson State Park Campground. Just outside your tent flap (or RV door) are all the recreational opportunities of this beauti-

ful 2,000-acre park (see Chapter 10). Breakwater Beach in Brewster and Skaket Beach in Orleans (see Beaches, *above*) are not far.
🏠 *Rte. 6A, Brewster 02631, tel. 508/896–3491. 420 sites; no hookups. Facilities: showers, water, flush toilets, dumping station. No reservations. Closed late Oct.–early Apr. Cost: $12 per night.*

Entertainment and the Arts

For nighttime activities, don't ignore the many outdoor options—beach walks, bat walks, campfires with sing-alongs, and concerts under velvety black skies. Check out the programs offered by **The Wellfleet Bay Wildlife Sanctuary** and the **Cape Cod National Seashore** (see Scoping out Cape Cod, *above*).

👫 **4 – 10** Cape Playhouse. This renowned and historic theater presents children's concerts, plays, and puppet shows by the best touring performers on Friday mornings in July and August.
🏠 *Rte. 6A, East Dennis 02641, tel. 508/385–3838.*

👫 **ALL** Chatham Band Concerts. These traditional free Friday evening band concerts feel like a lively town party. Families carrying sweatshirts (it gets cold), blankets, folding chairs, and picnic baskets spread out their dinner beforehand. Then the 40-piece band, resplendent in blue and red uniforms, plays while folks keep time on the roped-off dance floor. Younger kids energetically join the sing-alongs and special children's dances; when they get too sleepy, their parents carry them off to the car. Come early to get a parking space.
🏠 *Kate Gould Park, Main St., tel. 508/945–0342.*

👫 **4+** Harwich Junior Theatre. Founded in 1952 by the then drama director of the Wheelock Family Theatre in Boston (see Entertainment and the Arts *in* Chapter 3), this theater offers kids a chance to participate in productions through acting, dancing,

and set construction classes with professionals—or you can just watch the plays.
🏠 Division St., Harwich Box 168, West Harwich 02671, tel. 508/432-2002.

👫 3 – 10 Village Green Movies. Ben & Jerry's Ice Cream Shop sponsors big-screen family movies such as *Aladdin* on the town green Thursday nights.
🏠 Main St., Hyannis. Admission free.

👫 ALL Wellfleet Drive-In Theater. This is the last drive-in left on the Cape. There's also a minigolf course (which appealed to Gavin), a playground, and a snack bar.
🏠 Rte. 6, tel. 508/349-7176 or 508/255-9619. Cost: $6 adults, $3.50 kids over 5 and senior citizens, kids under 5 free. Open June–Sept.

Nantucket

It's the postcard-perfect summer vacation spot: an island removed from time, guarding its historic cobblestone streets, quaint gray-shingle cottages, proud whaling captain's houses, and miles of clean white-sand beaches, to serve them up annually to visiting summer families. This 12-by-3-mile island 30 miles from Cape Cod is self-contained and cozy—big enough to offer activities for every age group, but small enough that everything is easy to get to. Older kids can be independent, biking off in the morning to the beach, going to the movies by themselves, learning to sail and windsurf—and you don't have to drive them. The water is warm, the broad flat beaches invite sand castles and bare feet, and the land is delightfully breezy and wide open.

There's also lots of history here. This little island was the foremost whaling port in the world in the mid-19th century; the town of Nantucket preserves the atmosphere of that past almost too faithfully. Little kids may enjoy reading the Obediah books by Brinton Turkle (published by Puffin/Penguin), about a boy who lived on Nantucket at that time;

older kids may have read or seen the movie *Moby Dick*, the story of a whaling captain who lived on Nantucket.

Summer crowds can be a problem, as honking traffic clogs the town's streets and people flood the beaches. Everything is expensive, in keeping with the upscale group who summer here regularly and the fact that all must be ferried from the mainland. Still, it's a marvelous island.

The Basics

HOW TO FIND OUT WHAT'S GOING ON. The **Chamber of Commerce** (Pacific Club Bldg., 48 Main St., tel. 508/228-1700; open Memorial Day–Labor Day, weekdays 9–5, Sat. 11–5; weekdays only rest of year) publishes *The Official Guide to Nantucket* and pamphlets on seasonal events. **The Nantucket Information Bureau** (25 Federal St., tel. 508/228-0925, open daily 9–5 July–Labor Day, Mon.–Sat. 9–4 rest of year) will provide a free *Nantucket Vacation Guide* and help you find a room for the night if you have not reserved, but will not make advance reservations for you. Call **The Helpline,** tel. 508/228-7227, for information on health services, activities, and transportation.

Guide to Nantucket by Polly Burroughs (Globe Pequot) has good historic information on the island and the island's buildings. *What's So Special About Nantucket* by Mary Miles (available from Mitchells Book Corner, see Shopping, *below*) introduces kids 4–8 to all Nantucket's sights through a story about a little boy who visits.

GETTING IN AND OUT OF NANTUCKET. **By air:** A number of airlines fly year-round into **Nantucket Memorial Airport** (tel. 508/325-5300) from Boston, Hyannis, Martha's Vineyard, and New Bedford; in summer there is direct service from New York (LaGuardia and Newark), Philadelphia, and Baltimore. Business Express/Delta Connection (tel. 800/345-3400) and Northwest Airlink (tel. 800/225-2525) fly from Boston and New York; Continental (tel. 800/525-

0280) flies from Newark. The airport is about 3½ miles from town; your kids may know the place from the TV series *Wings,* which is set here.

By ferry: You MUST have reservations far, far in advance if you want to bring your car over in summer; we know people who have shaped their entire vacation around the dates of their ferry reservations. The highway distance to Hyannis from New York City is 271 miles (6 hours or more), from Boston, 80 miles (2 hours or more); be sure to account for summer traffic jams on the Cape (we know people who have missed their precious car reservation because of them). It's much easier if you only bring people and bicycles on the boat.

The **Steamship Authority**'s car-and-passenger ferries leave South Street dock in Hyannis year-round. The trip takes 2¼ hours. *For reservations, call 508/477–8600 (Hyannis) or 508/228–0262 (Nantucket). One-way fare: $10 adults, $5 kids 5–12, cars $180 (May–mid-Oct.), $100 (mid-Oct.–May).*

Hy-Line ferries carry only passengers (and bikes) and operate from May through October, leaving from Ocean Street dock in Hyannis; their trip is shorter, 1¾ or 2 hours. *For information and reservations, call 508/775–7185 (Hyannis) or 508/228–3949 (Nantucket). One-way fare: $11 adults, $5.50 kids 3–12; $20 for first-class ticket.*

By car: Not only are ferry reservations hard to get for a car, Nantucket's main streets are clogged with traffic in summer. For short visits of a weekend or several days, it's best not to bring a car; for longer vacations when you're staying farther out, you may want one, but it's easier to rent a car on the island than bring your own (just make sure you reserve a car in advance). Besides, there are some neat beaches you can get to only in a four-wheel-drive vehicle (you must have a permit to drive off-road; check with the Chamber of Commerce for current regulations). Both cars and Jeeps can be rented at the airport from **Budget** (tel. 508/228–5656 or 800/486–5666), **Hertz** (tel. 508/228–9421 or 800/654–3131), **Thrifty** (tel. 508/325–4616 or 800/367–2277), and **Nantucket Windmill** (tel. 508/228–1227). **Nantucket Jeep Rental** (tel. 508/228–1618) and **Preston's Rent a Car** (tel. 508/228–0047) deliver cars to wherever you're staying. **Young's Bicycle Shop** (Steamship Wharf, tel. 508/228–1151), which also rents cars and Jeeps, is right in town.

By bike: Everyone on the island seems to bike—we've seen whole families strung out along paths, their descending bike sizes making them resemble a family of ducks. Good paved paths lead to most beaches, and rentals are readily available. An energetic family could bike around the entire island in one day. *See* Biking, *below,* for bike paths. Helmets must be worn by kids under 12.

By bus: See Cape Cod, *above,* for bus services that connect with the ferries at Hyannis. On Nantucket, regular shuttle buses run from town to Jetties, Surfside, and Madaket Beaches, and 'Sconset village, mid-June through Labor Day; **Barrett's Tours** (20 Federal St., tel. 508/228–0174) charges $1–$4 one-way, depending on destination; kids pay half fare to Surfside and 'Sconset.

By taxi: You can usually find a taxi waiting at the airport or at the foot of Main Street by the ferry, or call one of the many taxi companies, such as **Atlantic Cab** (tel. 508/228–1112), **All Points Taxi** (tel. 508/228–5779), and **B.G.'s Taxi & Tours** (tel. 508/228–4146). Fares are flat fee, based on one person, and are not cheap: $3–$15, plus $1 for each additional passenger.

FAMILY-FRIENDLY TOURS. Most taxi companies also provide private guided tours.

8+ **Gail's Tours.** Gail Johnson, a seventh-generation native, is knowledgeable, lively and enthusiastic, flexible enough to stop for photos and a picnic, and likes kids. Regular 1½-hour van tours are scheduled. This is a great way for kids to get a sense of the whole island.

🏨 *Tel. 508/257–6557. Cost: $10 per person. Departures in season, daily 10, 1, and 3. Open year-round.*

For whale-watching tours, see Sports, *below.*

PIT STOPS. You'll find public bathrooms at the end of Main Street on Straight Wharf, on the waterfront at Children's Beach, and at the Nantucket Information Bureau (see How to Find out What's Going On, *above*). Almost all beaches have rest rooms.

EMERGENCIES. The **Nantucket Cottage Hospital** (S. Prospect St., tel. 508/228–1200) has a 24-hour emergency room. **Congdon's** pharmacy (47 Main St., tel. 508/228–0020) is open until 10 PM mid-June–September; **Nantucket Pharmacy** (45 Main St., tel. 508/228–0180) stays open until 10 PM Memorial Day–Labor Day; and **Island Pharmacy** (Finast Plaza, Sparks Ave., tel. 508/228–6400) is open until 8 or 9 PM year-round.

BABY-SITTERS. Most resorts and hotels maintain lists of baby-sitters. **Nantucket Babysitters' Service** (tel. 508/228–4970) provides well-screened student baby-sitters for either summer-long jobs or evenings.

WHEN TO GO. Summer is the prime season here, with July and August the most crowded; more kids seem to be here in July than in August. The sun's heat is tempered by ocean breezes, making the island more pleasant than mainland beaches in summer. Nantucket's waters are warm enough for swimming as early as mid-June and sometimes as late as October, though the waves get rough after Labor Day. Biking, hiking, hanging out in town are all pleasant long after the tourist crush has left after Labor Day; museums and restaurants usually stay open until Columbus Day. The spring is iffy, often wet and dreary. The Chamber of Commerce (tel. 508/228–1700) is your best source of information for the following events.

(🧒 **4+**) **Harborfest.** Three days of performances, parades, a chowder-eating con-

test, and family games take place at Children's Beach over Father's Day weekend in June.

(🧒 **ALL**) **Fourth of July.** It's fun to join the crowds at Jetties Beach for games, then a band concert, then fireworks at dusk.

(🧒 **3+**) **Sandcastle Sculpture Day.** In August, the most unusual and fun-filled family event on the island includes competitions for kids and adults.

(🧒 **ALL**) **Christmas Stroll.** This old-fashioned town-wide celebration on the first weekend of December includes Santa arriving by boat; reserve well in advance for accommodations.

Scoping out Nantucket

Nantucket is basically a one-town island, with all the shops and most restaurants clustered in a few blocks by the waterfront at the entrance to Nantucket harbor. The twisting lanes and brick alleyways of Nantucket town are best explored on foot; sneakers are best for little kids to wear because of the bumpy cobblestones and high curbs. Fourteen historic buildings are open to the public; you can buy a visitor pass that admits you to all, at a cost much lower than paying separate admissions. A guide is available from the Nantucket Historical Association (tel. 508/228–1894). Most kids pick up plenty of history just from strolling around and absorbing the 17th- and 18th-century atmosphere.

Roads and bike paths lead from this hub off across the island's moors to small villages near beaches to the west, east, and south. The biggest of these is Siasconset, called 'Sconset, 7 miles from town—mostly a summer community with a post office, a few stores, restaurants, and cottages. The village of Madaket has not much more than a restaurant and good sunsets.

(🧒 **8 – 12**) **First Congregational Church,** or **Old North Church.** When you climb the 92 steps to the tower of Nantucket's largest church, you have the best view of the island—ponds, beaches, winding streets, and rooftops.

🏠 *62 Centre St., tel. 508/228–0950. Cost: $1.50 adults, 50¢ kids under 15. Open Mon.– Sat. 10–4.*

👫 **3 – 14** **Maria Mitchell Science Center.** Nantucket-born Maria Mitchell in 1847 was the first person to discover a comet with a telescope. She went on to become the first woman astronomy professor in the United States at Vassar College. The center named for her includes an observatory (open Wednesday night in summer), a library, the house in which she lived, an **aquarium** on the wharf (28 Washington St., tel. 508/228–5387 or 508/228–0898; cost $1), and a natural history museum, **Hinchman House** (7 Milk St., tel. 508/228–0898; $3 adults, $1 kids under 13), with a collection of live reptiles and a huge insect display.

🏠 *1 Vestal St., tel. 508/228–2896; Mitchell Association, tel. 508/228–9198. Combined admission ticket $5 adults, $2 children. Open mid-June–Aug., Tues.–Sat. 10–4.*

👫 **5 – 12** **Old Mill.** This red-and-gray shingled mill is one of the last working wind-powered mills in the country, still grinding corn to cornmeal when the wind is blowing. Once a month in summer kids can help grind the cornmeal, then take it to the oldest house on the island to bake it into cornbread.

🏠 *Prospect, W. York, and S. Mill Sts., tel. 508/228–1894. Cost: $2 adults, $1 kids under 15. Open May–mid-June, Sept., and Oct., daily 11–3; mid-June–Sept., daily 10–5.*

👫 **5+** **Sanford Farm/Ram Pasture and the Woods.** Much of Nantucket is flat heath that blooms with wildflowers in summer; on these 900 acres at the island's west end a meandering trail passes Hummock Pond, a long silvery finger of water where you can spot turtles and, at dusk, deer.

🏠 *Off Madaket Rd. near intersection of Cliff Rd.*

👫 **ALL** **Straight Wharf.** At the foot of Main Street, along a wharf where some fer-

ries from Hyannis and Martha's Vineyard pull in, gift shops and restaurants are crammed side by side and teens hang out—shopping, eating ice cream, sitting on the benches, talking, and performing for each other.

👫 **6 – 15** **Whaling Museum.** It's set in a historic factory built for refining spermaceti (a wax made from whale oil) and making candles; the enthusiastic guides (call for tour times) give vivid descriptions of whaling days. The rustic old building holds a whale skeleton, harpoons, a rigged whaleboat, and a replica of a full-scale tryworks (where they processed whale oil on the ship), giving kids a real feel for Nantucket's whaling past.

🏠 *Broad St., head of Steamboat Wharf, tel. 508/228–1736. Cost: $4 adults, $3 kids 5–14. Visitor passes to 14 historic buildings permit 1 visit to each: $8 adults, $5 kids 5–14. Open summer, daily 10–5; spring and fall, daily 11–3.*

BEACHES. Nantucket's long wide beaches circle the island like a big golden wreath, one overlapping the other; kids can bike or take a shuttle bus to almost all of them, and all are open to any visitor—no parking permits are required. Beaches on the north shore facing Nantucket Sound have the calmest and warmest water; the best waves for surfing roll into the popular south shore beaches and those to the east, where the undertow is stronger.

North Shore Beaches: Great for the littlest kids, **Children's Beach** has lovely sand for sand castles and calm, warm water. Close to town—just a short walk down South Beach Street from Steamboat Wharf—it's next to a grassy park with benches and picnic tables, a playground, rest rooms, a bandstand, take-out food, lifeguards, and showers. Dune-sheltered **Dionis Beach** (3 miles west of town via the Madaket bike path and Eel Point Road; look for a white rock pointing to the entrance) has calm water and a long sandbar stretching out during low tide, which make it good for swimming, picnicking, and shell collecting; it does, however, have pebbly areas and occasional seaweed. There are life-guards and rest rooms. **Jetties Beach,** just a mile north of town, is the all-around family beach, with the most activities for all ages: windsurfing, sailing, tennis, volleyball, swim lessons for little kids, and a playground. There are lifeguards, changing rooms, rest rooms, showers, phones, restaurant and take-out food, a boardwalk to the beach, and water-sports rentals—but on a sunny day it is busy, busy, busy. Scenic **Brant Point** (take Hulbert Ave. from Jetties Beach), by a lighthouse where you can watch boats, is best for picnicking and shell collecting; the current is strong, the drop-off sudden, and there are no lifeguards.

South Shore Beaches: One of the most popular beaches with teens is **Surfside Beach,** which has the best surf on the island; little kids like exploring the small rolling dunes and playing on the long, wide beach. A 3-mile bike or bus ride south from town, it gets crowded in summer (to escape, walk east toward 'Sconset). There are lifeguards, rest rooms, showers, phones, swings, and a snack bar. Just west of Surfside is **Miacomet Pond,** a small, warm freshwater pond separated from the ocean by a strip of sand where little kids can wade. At out-of-the-way **Cisco Beach** (4 miles from town via Hummock Pond Rd.) you can walk for miles, surf in the big waves, fish, and feel the wind. About the only facilities here are lifeguards. **Madaket Beach** is my idea of a perfect beach—clean white sand, humongous waves, and the best sunsets on the island, all reached by a scenic 6-mile bike path over gentle hills. It has lifeguards, rest rooms, and a gourmet take-out shop on the bike path.

Other Beaches: Seven miles east of town, **'Sconset Beach** makes for a full day's outing, with its grassy dunes and cliffs, the picturesque nearby village, and the Sankaty Lighthouse. It's not always good for swimming—the surf can be heavy and the wind blows in seaweed—but it has lifeguards and a playground.

Coatue-Coskata–Great Point is an empty spit of dune and beach separating Nantucket Harbor from Nantucket Sound; you have to take a boat or four-wheel-drive car (permits at Wauwinet Gate House, tel. 508/228–0006).

Action

AMUSEMENTS. J. J. Clammps. In such a carefully preserved, picturesque environment you eventually end up saying "Thank God for Clammps"—an 18-hole minigolf course set in a garden and other fun and games such as remote-control boats on ponds and splash-gun target-shooting. There's a free shuttle from downtown and a casual restaurant on site.
🏠 *Nobadeer Farm and Sun Island Rds., off Milestone Rd., tel. 508/228–8977. Open July and Aug., daily 10 AM–midnight; June–Sept., hrs vary.*

BIKING. For kids, Nantucket is nicer than the Cape for biking, because they can safely bike to all the best beaches themselves. In the busy summer months they should stick to the four paved official bike paths, described below, which are only open to foot and bicycle traffic. It's possible to ride on the island's many dirt roads if you rent a mountain bike, but these are also open to speedy mopeds. A rudimentary bike trail map is in the *Official Guide to Nantucket,* but it's better to get the detailed maps available from rental places.

The 6-mile-long **Milestone Bike Path** parallels Milestone Road across the center of the island to the village of 'Sconset and 'Sconset Beach. **Surfside Bike Path,** 3 miles of flat terrain ending at Surfside Beach, is the easiest for young kids; along the way, stop at The Shack, a snack bar with hot dogs and picnic baskets. **Cliff Road Bike Path,** 2½ miles of rolling terrain, takes you alongside Cliff Road, past a small pond. The 5-mile-long **Madaket Bike Path** is the most beautiful—a winding path traversing gentle hills, skirting Long Pond (picnic tables), and ending at spectacular Madaket Beach. You can rent bikes at **Nantucket Bike Shops** (Steamboat Wharf and on Straight Wharf, Nantucket 02554, tel. 508/228–1999; daily bike price, $16–$20 adults, $12–$16 kids).

BIRD-WATCHING. The Natural History Museum at **Hinchman House** (see Scoping out Nantucket, *above*) sponsors bird walks for kids and adults in summer. The best place to see many different kinds easily is at **Eel Point,** on the northern side of Madaket Harbor, where the humps of a long sandbar create little islands on which gulls rest and scores of other birds perch, fly up, chatter and sing to one another.

🚶 *Follow trail from Eel Point Rd. Cars must be left about ½ mi from beach on dirt road. Map available from Maria Mitchell Association (see Scoping out Nantucket, above).*

BOATING. The best destination for kayaking and sailing is deserted **Coatue Beach** (see Beaches, *above*). Kids can windsurf, sail sunfish, or kayak at **Jetties Beach** (see Sailing and Windsurfing *in* Chapter 12), where you can get both rentals and lessons.

Sea Nantucket (Washington St. Extension, tel. 508/228–7499) rents kayaks and sailboats and **Indian Summer Sports** (Steamboat Wharf, tel. 508/228–3632) rents kayaks; both also provide lessons. **Skip Willauer** (tel. 508/228–7669) gives private sailing lessons and cruises for all ages. On Straight and Steamboat wharves you'll find many charter sailboats to take you out for a few hours or the whole day. Our pick is the Friendship sloop *The Endeavor* (Straight Wharf, tel. 508/228–7448), which also offers Pirate Adventures (see Entertainment and the Arts, *below*).

FISHING. The main island catch in summer is bluefish—if you go out on a small fishing boat, you can look down and see the fish just lying in the waves. Charter boats dock at Straight Wharf; Ray DeCosta, owner of the *Albacore* (Straight Wharf, tel. 508/228–1439) schedules trips so you start fishing just 10 to 20 minutes from the dock.

Younger kids we know enjoy catching flounder from the dock; just drop in a line, using a quahog for bait. What you catch, you can eat. **Bill Fisher Tackle** (14 New La., tel. 508/228–2261) and **Barry Thurston Fishing Tackle** (at the Marina, tel. 508/228–9595) rent equipment and welcome kids.

HIKES AND WALKS. The most magical places for quiet walks are the beaches, especially just before dusk, and the long trail in the **Sanford Farm/Ram Pasture** conservation area (see Scoping out Nantucket, *above*). The **Nantucket Conservation Foundation** (Larsen-Sanford Center, 118 Cliff Rd., tel. 508/228–2884) owns thousands of acres of open land, marked by maroon signs with a wave-and-seagull logo.

INDOOR SWIMMING. The Nantucket Community School has a big pool with a lifeguard where kids congregate on rainy days. Much is going on, from water aerobics to kids' swim lessons, so check the schedule. 🚶 *10 Surfside Rd., tel. 508/228–7257. Basic rate is $3–$4 per session.*

TENNIS. At Jetties Beach (see Beaches, *above*), the local parks and recreation department sponsors regular tennis clinics at their six courts (for adults too).

Shopping

In downtown Nantucket, **Mitchell's Book Corner** (54 Main St., tel. 508/228–1080) is a cozy, very personal bookstore noted for its huge collection of books on Nantucket and big children's corner. If you write before you come, they'll send you a brochure listing kid and adult books related to the island. **Seven Seas Gifts** (46 Centre St., tel. 508/228–0958) is filled with inexpensive gift and souvenir items such as shells, Nantucket jigsaw puzzles, and jewelry. Some older teens may be fascinated by **The Fragrance Bar (a.k.a. Essence Natural)** (5 Centre St., tel. 508/325–4740), an all-natural perfume oils store carrying 420 different essences, which you can test on yourself to find your own special scent. For clothing, **Vis a Vis, Ltd.** (34 Main

St., tel. 508/228–5527) has dresses and
shoes that teens approve of.

Along touristy Straight Wharf, check out
Four Winds Gifts (tel. 508/288–1597), a
shop in a two-story barn that provides good
browsing for everyone in the family: toys,
reproduction lightship baskets and fine pottery, inexpensive jewelry, and a slew of high-
end sports stuff. **The Toy Boat** (tel. 508/
228–4552) has lots of handmade toy boats.
Aunt Leah's (Straight Wharf Courtyard, tel.
508/228–1017) sells over 20 varieties of
fudge and imaginatively packed goodies.

Eats

As at any beach resort in the northeast,
seafood is the specialty—chowder, bluefish,
and, starting in the late fall, scallops.
Gourmet take-out shops and deceptively
simple white-walled restaurants serve
sophisticated things like ravioli with chutney.
Those below are tried and true.

(ALL) **Atlantic Cafe.** Of the various
burger spots, we'd pick this casual, sometimes noisy place with nautical art, wood
beams, and a good menu—finger food, salads, sandwiches, simple chicken and fish
dishes, and of course burgers. Most families
head for the hand-carved wooden booths
in the quieter back room rather than the
tables around the bar in front.
*15 S. Water St., tel. 508/228–0570. Chil-
dren's menu, booster seats, high chairs. No
reservations. Dress: casual. AE, D, DC, MC, V. $*

(ALL) **Downey Flake.** A large
doughnut-shape sign leads you to the best
breakfast in town. Famous for homemade
doughnuts, pancakes with blueberry or
cranberry syrup, and pastries, the Downey
Flake is also a good source of take-out sandwiches for a picnic lunch at the beach.
*Children's Beach, tel. 508/228–4533. No
reservations. Dress: casual. No credit cards. No
dinner. Closed Nov.–Mar. $*

(ALL) **Espresso Cafe.** A popular
hangout for teens and college kids, this old-

fashioned ice-cream soda fountain serves
the best cappuccino, chewy brownies, and
ice cream, along with soup, pasta, sandwiches, and thick gourmet pizza. Inside, you
sit under paddle fans at round tables; you
can also take a number, order, then eat
under sea-green umbrellas on the tree-
shaded brick patio.
*40 Main St., tel. 508/228–6930. Booster
seats. No reservations. Dress: casual. No credit
cards. $–$$*

(ALL) **Hearth at the Harbor House.**
Special early-evening dinner bargains draw
families to this pretty, high-ceilinged restaurant with exposed wood beams and upholstered chairs in the 1860s Harbor House Inn.
Expect simply prepared New England fare—
lamb chops, flounder stuffed with crab, and
surf-and-turf combinations. With kids we'd
eat on the outdoor patio. The four-course
Sunset Special, served 5–7 PM, lets kids under
13 dine free with their parents.
*S. Beach St., tel. 508/228–1500. Chil-
dren's menu, booster seats, high chairs. Reservations required for Sun. brunch; advised for
other meals. Dress: casual. AE, DC, MC, V. No
lunch. $$*

(ALL) **Juice Bar.** Right on the wharf,
it's a runner-up to the Espresso Cafe *(see
above)* for the best ice cream on Nan-
tucket, as the long lines will testify. Home-
made flavors are served in waffle cones
with lots of toppings. There are also
yummy fresh-squeezed juices (try the
guava) or coffee or muffins.
*12 Broad St., tel. 508/228–5799. Dress:
casual. No credit cards. Closed mid-Dec.–Mar. $*

(ALL) **Nantucket Lobster Trap.** Very
casual and down home, this place has walls
draped with fish nets and a big patio with a
canopy. The lobster dinners are among the
best on the island.
*23 Washington St., tel. 508/228–4200.
Booster seats. Reservations advised. Dress:
casual. AE, MC, V. Closed Nov.–Apr. $$*

(ALL) **Something Natural.** For a
lunch stop en route to Madaket Beach, try

this store's thick, delicious sandwiches (go for the turkey) on a variety of homemade breads, along with chocolate-chip muffins and regular or organic sodas. You can eat at the picnic tables here or have your food packed to take to the beach.

🏠 *50 Cliff Rd., next to bike path to Madaket Beach, tel. 508/228–0504. No credit cards. No dinner. Closed Tues. and late Oct.–early May. $*

FOR PICNICS. North shore beaches (*see Beaches, above*) are better for picnics, as they have less wind to blow sand on your food. For little kids, try the picnic tables at **Children's Beach**; at uncrowded **Brant Point** you can watch boats while you eat; and on **Long Pond,** which is right off the Madaket Bike Path, there are picnic tables by the water. For a major picnic expedition rent a boat to cart family, food, and Frisbees over to **Coatue Beach.**

Where to Stay

The majority of accommodations on Nantucket are small inns and bed-and-breakfasts, better suited for romantic honeymooners or older couples than they are for families. (The *Official Guide to Nantucket* highlights with a baby-shaped symbol the places that do welcome kids.) The B&Bs that welcome children usually have at least one separate apartment or ground-floor suite that separates you from the guests looking for romance.

If you'd prefer to stay in a cottage, remember that on Nantucket in summer, weeklong stays are the minimum. **House Guests Cape Cod and the Islands** (Box 1881, Orleans 02653, tel. 508/896–7053 or 800/666–4678) books B&Bs, cottages, and efficiencies for families (among others). Realtors who handle rental houses and apartments are listed in the *Official Guide to Nantucket;* the **Maury People** (35 Main St., 02554, tel. 508/228–1881) is one company that's happy to work with families. For prime dates, reserve well in advance. In season, The Nantucket Information Bureau (see How to

Find out What's Going On, *above*), keeps a current list of rooms available for last-minute bookings.

Most lodgings, except for some of the cottages, are in or close to town (handy to Children's and Jetties beaches). Kids are likely to prefer staying in town, or out toward Surfside and Madaket beaches, to 'Sconset, where the great attractions are peace, solitude, and the company of gulls.

The price categories that follow are based on summer-season rates and reflect what a family of four would spend for one night in a double room or the smallest appropriate accommodation available (sometimes a cottage): $$$$, over $225; $$$, $175–$225; $$, $120–$175; $, under $120. Prices do not include 9.7% tax.

Few places comfortable for families are available for much under $100 a night—which makes a $1,000-a-week cottage, where you can spread out and do your own cooking, look pretty good. There are no campgrounds on the island. If you're looking for rock-bottom budget accommodations, wait until 1996, when the **Nantucket Youth Hostel** (31 Western Ave. at Surfside, 02554, tel. 508/228–0433) will open several new family rooms costing under $50 per night for a family of four.

Harbor House. A warm, friendly atmosphere, good service, and large rooms are the draw here. The complex includes a main 1886 inn and several town houses around a flower-filled quadrangle in the town's historic district. Go for the larger town house rooms that look out on the pool; decks, sofa beds, and cathedral ceilings make them more like a condo than a hotel. 🏠 *S. Beach St., Box 1048, 02554-1048, tel. 508/228–1500; reservations, 800/485–2638; fax 508/228–3639. 111 rooms. Facilities: restaurant, pool, room service, concierge, putting green. AE, D, DC, MC, V. $$$*

Eighteen Gardner Street. Though it's a little away from the downtown action, this traditional Nantucket house built by a whaling captain (his portrait is over the fireplace) is nice for families who want to try a B&B—a family with two kids lives here, and it has three spacious yet cozy suites, two of which have TVs. One thoughtful touch that kids like is the fresh-baked cookies always on hand. Breakfast is to youngsters' taste and bigger than the usual sparse Continental fare: fresh fruit, muffins, juice, cereal. 🏠 *18 Gardner St., 02554, tel. 508/228–1155. 14 rooms, 3 suites, some with fireplaces. Facilities: breakfast included in rate, in-room refrigerators, bikes, beach towels, parking, picnic baskets available, honor bar for sodas and snacks. Kids under 12 free; no charge for older kids in suites. No smoking. MC, V. $$*

Periwinkle Guest House and Cottage. On North Water Street, not far from the Whaling Museum and Children's Beach, stands this big old Nantucket house and a small cottage. The family who owns them rents rooms in six buildings in town; they've set these particular properties aside for families, along with another cottage a little farther away. There's a backyard and a homey shared kitchen where you can warm a bottle or make a late-night snack. 🏠 *Accommodations Et Al, 11 India St., Box 1436, 02554-1436, tel. 508/228–9009 or 800/992–2899. 18 rooms (some share baths), 1 cottage. Facilities: picnic tables, kitchen, complimentary Continental breakfast. MC, V. $–$$*

White Elephant. This grand old-style resort away from the noisy wharf is separated from Nantucket harbor only by a wide grassy lawn. Decks with bright white tables, chairs, and umbrellas wrap around the main hotel and look out on a swimming pool and boats bobbing in the bay. Gray-shingled cottages, done up in English country style—some with a small kitchen—are good for families. Here you can have privacy, super resort amenities, and top-notch service. 🏠 *Easton St., Box 359, 02554-0359, tel. 508/228–2500; reservations, 800/485–2638; fax 508/228–3639. 48 rooms, 32*

1- to 3-bedroom cottages. Facilities: restaurant, complimentary Continental breakfast, room service, pool, croquet, putting green, minirefrigerators, kitchens in some cottages, concierge. AE, D, DC, MC, V. Closed mid-Sept.–Memorial Day. $$$$

Entertainment and the Arts

👫 4+ Actor's Theater of Nantucket. The early afternoon kids' shows here are mostly short musicals, magic, and plays. 🏠 *2 Centre St., tel. 508/228–6325 or 508/228–5387. Cost: $10. Open July–Aug.*

👫 4 – 15 Nantucket Island School of Design and the Arts. In a funky old converted cow barn, this school holds kid-friendly classes in painting, collage, and more. 🏠 *23 Wauwinet Rd., tel. 508/228–9248.*

👫 4 – 8 Pirate Adventures. This pretend pirate adventure takes place on *The Endeavor*, a Friendship sloop docked at Straight Wharf that also schedules harbor sails (see Boating, above). Before boarding, little kids have their faces painted and eye patches, hooks, and hats are handed out; then they climb on for the 45-minute participatory play—firing fake cannons that boom, and so on. Adults must accompany kids. 🏠 *Straight Wharf, tel. 508/228-5585. Reservations required. Daily 11:30 and 12:45. Open July–Labor Day.*

👫 10 – 15 White Dog Cafe & the Gaslight Theater. A tiny, intimate movie theater with old-time atmosphere is something few kids see anymore, and they usually like this one. Upstairs is a pretty café serving hamburgers and pasta; Gaslight theater, showing recent films, is downstairs. 🏠 *N. Union St., tel. 508/228–4435.*

Block Island

Nature-loving families looking for an old-fashioned, unsophisticated beach vacation gravitate to this small island 13 miles off the

Rhode Island coast. All you really need are bikes, bathing suits, and a fishing rod, plus maybe a sweatshirt for a cold night. The Nature Conservancy calls it "one of the 12 last great places in the western hemisphere," and you can see why: though the island's only 7 miles long by 3 miles wide, its landscape is varied and dramatic—200-foot-high bluffs and cliffs, golden sand beaches, 365 freshwater ponds, high moors, rolling dunes, and gentle surf as well as ferocious waves.

The options at Block Island are limited— which is why it's not great for teens—but happily, everything is kid-sized. The hikes are truly special but short; the bike rides are easy; the cliffs are an adventure to climb, but hardly El Capitan. Its two towns, Old Harbor and New Harbor, are tiny, low-key, and relaxed. Kids can walk down the street with a bucket of bait and go barefoot just about everywhere. Restaurants have big decks where kids can watch boats and make noise without bothering other customers. You don't need a car to get around unless you are staying far from the towns; distances are so small that even kids get used to walking or biking everywhere. And despite the summer crowds who flow off the ferry each day, Block Island is still less crowded—and less expensive—than practically any other beach area in the Northeast.

The Basics

HOW TO FIND OUT WHAT'S GOING ON. The **Block Island Chamber of Commerce** (23 Water St., Old Harbor, Block Island 02807, tel. 401/466–2982 or 800/383–2474) has an information booth right at the ferry landing and a larger office just up the hill. Their Official Visitor's Map is essential.

The *Block Island Times* (Box 278, Block Island 02807, tel. 401/466–5533), published biweekly in summer, lists community activities and special events and carries ads that alert you to dinner bargains. The map on the inside of the back page is highly detailed and useful. Pick up a free copy in town or

send $1 plus your address to receive a copy before you arrive.

GETTING IN AND OUT OF BLOCK ISLAND. By air: Block Island State Airport (tel. 401/466–5511) is a short distance from both Old and New Harbor, off Center Road. Two airlines serve the island: New England Airlines (tel. 401/596–2460 or 800/243–2460) leaves hourly in summer from Westerly, Rhode Island, arriving in a mere 12 minutes; Action Airlines (tel. 203/448–1646 or 800/243–8623) flies a summer schedule from Easthampton on Long Island, LaGuardia Airport in New York City, and the airport in Groton, Connecticut. In foggy or stormy weather, flights will probably be canceled; schedule your flight so that you can catch a ferry if that happens. Some hotels offer van pickup at the airport; taxis are available there, too.

By ferry: This is the easiest—and most enjoyable—way to get here, though if you want to bring your car in the summer, make reservations very, very far in advance. Block Island is 9 miles from Rhode Island's coast and 13 miles from the tip of Long Island. The shortest trip is from Point Judith, Rhode Island (1 hour and 10 minutes), operated year-round by **Interstate Navigation Co.** (Galilee State Pier, Point Judith, tel. 401/783–4613; one-way fare $6.60 adults, $3.15 kids under 12, $20.25 per car). In summer, Interstate also runs passenger-only ferry boats from Newport and Providence, Rhode Island, and passenger-and-car service on the two-hour trip from New London, Connecticut (tel. 203/442–7891). **Viking Ferry Lines** (tel. 516/668–5709) takes passengers and bicycles (no cars) in summer from Montauk, Long Island (1 hour and 45 minutes). There are always lots of taxis waiting at the ferry landing; it's worth it to take one to your hotel if you have lots of gear and kids. Two to call are: **O. J.'s Taxi** (see *Family-Friendly Tours, below*) and **Wolfie's Taxi Service** (tel. 401/466–5550).

By train: To take **Amtrak** (tel. 800/872–7245) to the ferry, the easiest connection is at New London; it's also possible to take the train to Kingston, Rhode Island, and then get a cab to the Point Judith ferry pier.

By car: A car is not essential unless you're staying in a house far from town. If you don't bring your own car over on the ferry, you can rent one from **Old Harbor Bike Shop** (tel. 401/466–2029), **Block Island Car Rental** (tel. 401/466–2297), or **Boat Basin Rentals** in New Harbor (tel. 401/466–2631).

FAMILY-FRIENDLY TOURS. O. J.'s Taxi (tel. 401/782–5826) gives a lively tour around the island filled with anecdotes about the island's history. It's a good way to get an overview, especially with tots.

PIT STOPS. You'll find public rest rooms on the Old Harbor ferry dock, at the town dock, at Town Hall on Old Town Road, at the public library, at North Light, and at Benson Beach Pavilion at State Beach.

EMERGENCIES. There is no hospital on Block Island; serious medical emergencies require a flight to Westerly, Rhode Island, arranged through the Block Island Medical Center (Box 919, Payne Rd., tel. 401/466–2974), which has a resident physician. **Block Island Pharmacy** (High St., tel. 401/466–5825), the island's only drugstore, is open daily, 8 AM–10 PM.

BABY-SITTERS. Most resorts keep lists of individuals they've used before. The Chamber of Commerce also has a list of potential baby-sitters, but no one on it has been screened.

WHEN TO GO. The prime summer season here is from the end of June through Labor Day, and most hotels, many restaurants, and other businesses close for the winter after Labor Day or by the end of October. In autumn, the island is a famous stopover for many different migrating small birds. Check with the Block Island Chamber of Commerce (tel. 401/466–2982) for information on the following events.

(**ALL**) Taste of Block Island Seafood Festival and Chowder Cookoff. Lots of food to taste and vote on and a small circus are the highlights of this June event, along with arts and crafts and kids' face painting.

(**ALL**) Fourth of July. A real small-town celebration in a spectacular and unique setting, it's the island's biggest event, with the usual concerts, picnics, parades, and fireworks.

Scoping out Block Island

The two towns are in the center of the island, barely a mile apart. Old Harbor, the larger, is a cluster of streets around the water; New Harbor, facing onto Great Salt Pond, is just a grouping of restaurants, hotels, boat docks, and marinas. There is one lighthouse at each end of the island.

Outside the two towns, most of the island is open space: dunes and hummocks of grass, beach and high bluffs, salt ponds and sparkling kettle holes scraped out by glaciers 10,000 years ago. About one-third of it is preserved in several conservation areas; there are five wildlife refuges, some mainly dunes and grass and beach, some high bluffs and meadows. The three most interesting ones to us are **Clay Head,** along the north shore, **Rodman's Hollow,** a wildlife refuge in the center of the southern part of the island, and the **Greenway,** a network of trails in the island's center, west of Old Harbor. **Andy's Way,** a shallow tidal area and small beach on Great Salt Pond, is a favored place for younger kids to squish their feet in tidal flats. The Nature Conservancy (Ocean Rd., New Harbor, tel. 401/466–2129) can tell you everything you want to know, provides a map, and takes kids 5 to 10 on hands-on exploring walks.

(**5+**) Block Island Historical Society. Once a hotel, this rambling structure is filled with permanent and special exhibits, some of which appeal to kids—such as Manissean Indian arrowheads.

🏛 *Old Town Rd., tel. 401/466–2481. Cost: $2 adults, $1 kids. Open late June–Sept., daily 10–4; spring and fall, weekends 10–4.*

👫 **4 – 12** **Block Island National Wildlife Refuge.** This stretch of dunes and grass at the northern tip of the island next to North Lighthouse is a primary summer nesting area for gulls. See Chapter 10.

🏛 *Corn Neck Rd., Block Island 02807. Call the Nature Conservancy (tel. 410/466–2129) for information. Admission free. Open daily dawn–dusk.*

👫 **4 – 14** **Great Salt Pond Channel.** As boats pass through this narrow channel by the Coast Guard Station to enter Great Salt Pond, it's fun to wave at the passengers and fish in the churned-up water.

🏛 *Follow Coast Guard Rd. past Charleston Beach.*

👫 **ALL** **North Light** and **North Light Interpretive Center.** Sturdy granite-block North Light looks more like a stone church; it stands lonely and deserted amid dune grass at the northernmost tip of Block Island. Inside is the island's most fascinating museum for kids. The first floor is an interpretive center of old lifesaving equipment—boats, ropes and pulleys—and huge photos of past storms, wrecks, and lifesaving expeditions. The original Fresnel lens used in the tower is displayed on a pedestal at kid height.

🏛 *Corn Neck Rd., tel. 401/466–3200. Cost: $1. Open daily June–Sept.; check interpretive center hrs.*

👫 **4 – 15** **Southeast Light and Mohegan Bluffs.** Mohegan Bluffs is the most spectacular natural site on the island, with views of Montauk and big waves crashing impressively on the rocky shore far below. A sandy path through roses and daisies ends at the bluffs. Agile older kids can take the narrow stairway 200 feet down the cliff face (easier than the slog back up; expect groans) to the rock-strewn beach—standing there by the surging surf is awe-inspiring. From the bluffs you can walk to the working lighthouse, a picturesque brick house, though you can't go inside.

🏛 *Southeast Light Rd., tel. 401/466–5009.*

BEACHES. You could practically walk all the way around the island on beach, but most areas are not for swimming or sand-castle building. Jellyfish, debris, and seaweed are swept onto the west coast by prevailing winds; the pebbly beaches below the Mohegan bluffs and the Spring House Hotel are better for collecting rocks and beachcombing; and off the stretches of sand at the northernmost point of the island are dangerous currents that have swept people away.

Nestled into the curve of the island's eastern shore, however, from Old Harbor to Jerry's Point, is a 2-mile-long string of perfect sand beaches collectively called **Crescent Beach,** the best on the island for swimming. Corn Neck Road roughly parallels them. **State Beach**, also called Fred Benson Town Beach (tel. 401/466–2611), just north of the harbor, is often crowded with day-trippers straight off the ferry, but it has good amenities—a snack bar, picnic tables, rest rooms, and lifeguards. Above State Beach, **Scotch Beach** draws many young teens because a volleyball net is set up here and the waves are bigger. Farther north lies **Mansion Beach,** the island's prettiest beach, where the tang of the sea mingles with the scent of beach roses and bayberry bushes. It's good for little kids because the sandy bottom stays shallow a long way out; for older kids, the waves are big enough for good body-surfing and boogieboarding. Tidal pools here are fun to explore; just north of the beach, rocky areas called Pots and Kettles attract many different kinds of fish, making it the top local spot for snorkeling. (Rent or buy snorkeling equipment from Island Dive Shop on Ocean Avenue, tel. 401/466–5502.) Parking is limited.

Ballard's Beach, a ½-mile stretch just below Ballard's Inn in Old Harbor (see Eats, *below*), teems with action—lifeguards, volleyball, a self-service food court—but the crowd tends to be older. It's a fine place for kids to play while you are eating dinner.

Action

BASEBALL. Visiting kids ages 6 to 12 are welcome to play at the regular summer baseball games two nights a week. Check game schedules in the *Block Island Times*.

BEACH CLUB. Block Island Club. To plug into a local community of families, get a short-term membership to this low-key club, which offers a lifeguarded beach on calm Great Salt Pond, sailing, boating, swimming, tennis lessons, and barbecues and picnics for kids and grown-ups. You can join for a week, fortnight, month, or summer.
🏠 *Corn Neck Rd., tel. 401/466–5939.*

BICYCLING. A bicycle ride on a black-berry-bordered lane past a tiny sparkling pond is a typical Block Island outing. All kinds of roads and paths suitable for bikes, from paved to dirt, traverse the fairly hilly terrain, though there are no paved paths set aside just for bikes. Watch out for traffic between about 11 and 3 on the roads around town; on the island's west side, hills are steeper but car traffic is lighter. If you want to explore dirt roads, you should rent a mountain bike. You can get maps at the Chamber of Commerce or from your bike rental stores.
Moped Man (245 Main St., Box 125, Old Harbor 02807, tel. 401/466–5011), right across from the Point Judith ferry, has a wide variety of types; helmets are included in the price. **Old Harbor Bike Shop** (Box 338, Old Harbor 02807, tel. 401/466–2029) has adults' and children's bikes and baby seats; helmets are included in the price.

BIRD-WATCHING. The Atlantic Flyway, the path thousands of birds—more than 200 species—take in their migration along the Atlantic coast, passes right over Block Island. For perching birds, look near the ponds on the trails at **Clay Head** (see Hikes and Walks, *below*).

BOATING. The calm Great Salt Pond has good conditions for kids to learn any kind of boating. Kayaks are stable enough to be used at the beach. The **Block Island Club** (see Beach Club, *above*) teaches sailing and windsurfing and sponsors races for kids and adults. **The Boatworks** (Corn Neck Rd., tel. 401/466–2033; see Shopping, *below*) rents canoes and kayaks at $15 per hour and offers some lessons. **Oceans and Ponds** (Ocean Ave., Old Harbor, tel. 401/466–5131) has a larger selection of canoes and kayaks and will pick up and deliver. Surf-boards, boogie boards, and sailboards can be rented from **Island Sports Shop** (995 Weldon's Way, tel. 401/466–5001) and the Boatworks.

FISHING. Fishing is big here, and much of it is the kind of fishing kids like—where they can catch a fish right away. **Payne's Dock,** which juts out into the Great Salt Pond in New Harbor, is a good spot to drop a line (nearby Payne's Dock Take Out has picnic tables where you can eat lunch). Some kids may prefer to go out on the water to fish from a rowboat; **Twin Maples** (Beach Ave. by New Harbor, tel. 401/466–5547) rents rowboats ($15 per hour), fishing equipment, and tackle, and sells bait.

Thick populations of striped bass, bluefish, cod, and flounder hide in the ledges just off shore in Block Island Sound, and many families come to this island to catch them. Among charter boat operators, **Captain Bill Gould** and his crew provide equipment and instruction for hour-long, half-day, and full-day trips, April to October, on the *G. Willie Makit* (Old Harbor, Box 1010, tel. 401/466–5151).

HIKES AND WALKS. See also Hikes, Walks, and Climbs *in* Chapter 12. Hiking on Block Island is tailor-made for kids—trails in nature areas are short but eventful, winding by ponds, opening up to sudden ocean views, skirting thickets where you can glimpse deer, passing an old stone wall strung with juicy blackberries. At **Clay Head,** one of the best places in North America to observe songbirds in the fall, we wandered a series of densely wooded paths called The Maze, and then emerged at the top of a dramatic bluff above the beach. The Chamber of Commerce (see How to Find out What's Going On, *above*) has several maps of hiking trails; from the Nature Conservancy (see Scoping out Block Island, *above*), get a copy of "Block Island Walking Trails." Wherever you hike, be aware that Lyme disease (see Hikes, Walks, and Climbs *in* Chapter 12) is endemic to Block Island.

HORSEBACK RIDING

👫 6 – 15 **Rustic Rides Farm.** This stable offers an appealing guided trail ride of the rocky west coast, as well as pony rides for little kids.
🏠 *West Side Rd., tel. 617/466–5060.*

KITE-FLYING. At the end of the day, when swimmers leave the beach, kids of all ages fly kites above the silvery water. Other breezy locations are the grassy field by Southeast Lighthouse above the Mohegan Bluffs (see Scoping out Block Island, *above*) or on the Spring House Hotel's property (see Where to Stay, *below*), if you're staying there. To buy kites, head for **Block Island Kite Company** (Corn Neck Rd., tel. 401/466–2033).

PARASAILING. Cheaper than hot-air ballooning, parasailing looks like an even more exciting way to go aloft. You launch and land on a boat deck, spending about 12 to 20 minutes in the air at 400 to 600 feet above the water. **Block Island Parasail** (Box 727, tel. 401/466–2474) offers daily trips from Old Harbor Dock. Cost: $35–$45.

Shopping

Water Street in Old Harbor is the main shopping drag. **Esta's at Old Harbor** (tel. 401/466–2651) is filled with junky souvenirs and a slew of beach toys and supplies; teen girls should check out the jewelry. **Star Department Store** (tel. 401/466–2651), an old and wonderful "everything" store, keeps many kids, including mine, happy on a rainy

day. **The Book Nook** (tel. 401/466–2993), the only bookstore on the island, has a small selection of kids' books plus comic books, along with magazines, posters, and so on. **Strings 'n Things** (Water St. at Fountain Sq., tel. 401/466–5666) has a craft room where older kids can put together necklaces and earrings from the large assortment of beads.

Block Island Kite Company and **Boatworks** (tel. 401/466–2033), two stores in adjacent buildings on Corn Neck Road across from Crescent Beach, are a must-stop for families. The kite store is the third oldest in New England and has one of the best selections, plus all kinds of essential air and sand toys for the beach. The Boatworks has everything you need to buy or rent for sand and water, including sandals and swim suits.

Eats

Specialties on the island are Block Island Chowder and fresh fish. Some of the restaurants in the grand old wooden hotels perched above the harbor serve elegant—and expensive—gourmet fare, but we also found many inexpensive, down-home establishments with booster seats.

👫 ALL **Aldo's Italian Seafood Restaurant.** This family-style refuge behind Esta's (see Shopping, *above*) serves good pasta and gourmet pizza and has a video arcade. You can eat outside.
🏠 *Weldon's Way, tel. 401/466–5871. Booster seats, high chairs. No reservations. Dress: casual. MC, V. $–$$.*

👫 ALL **Ballard's Inn.** It's an island landmark, a place where the motto truly is "Bring the kids and come as you are." Huge family lobster dinners (there's also Italian food) are served up in stainless-steel bowls on oilcloth-covered tables in a noisy, lively dining room or out on a deck overlooking the beach where kids run when they finish eating, returning just in time for the family-style entertainment that includes silly songs. This is not for sophisticates, but it's great fun.

42 Water St., Old Harbor, tel. 401/466–2231. Children's menu, booster seats, high chairs. No reservations. Dress: casual. MC, V. $$

(ALL) **Bethany's Airport Diner.** Right next to the runway of the Block Island Airport, this diner is decorated with model airplanes, propellers, and other flying gear, and kids can watch planes take off while they eat. *State Airport, tel. 401/466–3100. Booster seats, high chairs. No reservations. Dress: casual. No credit cards. $*

(ALL) **Ernie's Old Harbor Restaurant.** Breakfast at this local hangout is a tradition among kids who summer here. Sitting on the broad deck, you can watch the ferries arrive. *Water St., Old Harbor, tel. 401/466–2473. No reservations. Dress: casual. No credit cards. No dinner. $–$$.*

(ALL) **Finn's Seafood Restaurant.** Eat outside on the deck, where the panorama of the harbor keeps kids constantly entertained. The menu includes fish dinners, lobster rolls, smoked bluefish pâté, and fish-and-chips fresh from Finn's fish market next door, as well as burgers. There's also a take-out window. *Ferry Landing, Water St., Old Harbor, tel. 401/466–2473. No reservations. Dress: casual. AE, MC, V. $$*

(ALL) **Ice Cream Place.** We think the best stuff in town is this shop's French Silk flavor, which tastes like frozen chocolate mousse. *Weldon's Way, tel. 401/466–2145. No reservations. Dress: casual. No credit cards. $–$$.*

FOR PICNICS. We usually choose to picnic at the beach. **State Beach** has picnic tables crowded with day-trippers. Head for scenic **Mansion Beach** farther north. **Negus Park,** a 2-acre square of green downtown behind the Fire Barn, is one of the few places on the island for a picnic under shade trees. At **Settler's Rock,** on the road to the North Light (see Scoping out Block Island, *above*),

there are some picnic tables with great views and bird-watching. A big grassy field by the **Southeast Light** (see Scoping out Block Island, *above*) is a good spot for picnicking and flying kites. For take-out delis, try **Payne's Dock Take Out** (tel. 401/466–5572) on Great Salt Pond in New Harbor or **Old Harbor Take Out** (tel. 401/466–2933) at the Ferry Landing in Old Harbor, which also has blue picnic tables with a prime view of the ferry dock.

Where to Stay

Block Island's lodging choices include sprawling wooden Victorian hotels (some refurbished and some not), smaller inns and B&Bs (sometimes with very thin walls), and clusters of small cottages, most close to the towns of New or Old Harbor. Many do not take children; each of the three listed below has something special for families. For stays of a week or more, consider renting a house (several months in advance). **Phelan Real Estate** (Payne Rd./Water St., 02807, tel. 401/466–2816) has many rentals; the Phelans have two school-age children themselves and know about lots of activities. **Sullivan Real Estate** (Water St., 02807, tel. 401/466–5521) also has extensive listings. There is no camping on the island.

The price categories that follow are based on summer-season rates and reflect what a family of four would spend for one night in a double room or the smallest appropriate accommodation available (sometimes a cottage): $$$, over $150; $$, $100–$150; $, under $100. Prices do not include 12% hotel-and-sales tax.

Bellevue House. This property offers two-bedroom apartments and a cottage, a location about five minutes above the town and harbor, and grassy spaces for kids to run around. The rooms have a beachy look, airy and pleasant, but they aren't big; the cottage is unheated. I lean toward the third-floor two-bedroom apartment, which has light coming in on all four sides. Small stoves and big refrigerators allow families to save some money on restaurant meals.

🏨 *Box 1198, 356 High St., 02807, tel. 401/466–2912. 19 rooms (B&B rooms, 5 apartments, 3-bed cottage, house). Facilities: croquet, picnic table, grills, MC, V. $$*

Spring House Hotel. High on a hill above the ocean, but only a five-minute walk from town, the Spring House is a grand white Victorian hotel that's both warm and elegant. Staying here, you feel like part of the island's past. Big two-room suites are furnished with solid Victorian replicas; the wide green lawns are great for kite-flying or sprawling in Adirondack chairs. A regular all-you-can-eat family barbecue is laid out on the veranda in summer; in the dining room, parents can enjoy a truly gourmet meal while kids play flashlight tag outside. One drawback: Instead of the deep Victorian bathtubs you'd expect, the bathrooms here have stingy shower stalls.

🏨 *Spring St., 02807, tel. 401/466–5844 or 800/234–9263, fax 401/231–2266. 39 rooms, 10 suites. Facilities: restaurant, complimentary Continental breakfast, private beach, volleyball, croquet. Kids under 12 free; over 12, $20. AE, MC, V. $$$*

Surf Hotel. Casual and funky, the Surf is a rambling old Victorian inn with white verandas and cupolas; painted rockers on the front porch look out on Old Harbor. It's filled with kid-friendly touches—a playground with a basketball hoop, a parakeet and dogs in the lobby, grills for barbecuing on the porch. Run out the back door and down a few steps and you're at the beach. The clean, colorful rooms line long corridors; most share baths. There is a six-night minimum in July and August.

🏨 *Dodge St., 02807, tel. 401/466–2241 or 401/466–2240. 47 rooms, all with sink; 3 rooms with private bath. Facilities: complimentary Continental breakfast, barbecue grills, playground, bicycle rentals, communal refrigerator. Kids in parents' room, $!5. MC, V. Closed Nov.–Apr. $–$$*

Entertainment and the Arts

👫 3 – 15 **Empire Theater.** Exposed beams and rafters make this former roller-skating rink, built in 1882, look like a big barn dressed up as a theater. Families come here for more than just rainy day matinees and evening screenings of first-run features. In summer there are weeklong kids' theater workshops and productions that are easy to sign up for. Also on site, the **Empire Cafe** makes a good stop for breakfast or lunch.

🏨 *Water St., tel. 401/466–2555. Closed Oct.–Apr.*

HIGH IN THE HILLS AND MOUNTAINS

6

The Northeast's mountains and hills offer families action, a chance to get back into the natural world, and something that's increasingly hard to find on a family vacation: ways to get far from crowds.

Ideal mountain destinations for families in the Northeast are those that offer a variety of things to do, not only for the inevitable rainy day, but to accommodate the varying interests of parents and children. Among the mountainous areas of the East, I'd have to single out the Berkshires of Massachusetts, the Adirondacks of New York, and the White Mountains of New Hampshire as tops. Each has its own flavor—the Berkshires are loaded with art and culture, the Adirondacks offer everything from wilderness canoeing to time-warp 1950s amusement parks, and the White Mountains harbor spectacular but accessible hiking in classic New England surroundings.

The Berkshires, Massachusetts

The Berkshires' green hills, spread over western Massachusetts, beckon families with an unsurpassed variety of cultural events, a landscape of kid-size New England towns, and ample recreational opportunities, from spying a beaver to dipping a candle to exploring a round stone barn. Moreover, all these attractions are within an hour's drive of one another. Each of the area's attractive towns has one or two—sometimes several—attractions for kids, but again, some towns have more to offer than others. My pick? Great Barrington, Lenox, and Williamstown.

The Basics

HOW TO FIND OUT WHAT'S GOING ON. Berkshire Visitor's Bureau (Berkshire Common, Pittsfield 01201, tel. 413/443–9186 or 800/237–5747) provides an essential and excellent map, a free official guide to the region that includes restaurants and lodging options, locations of information booths, and various touring guides and brochures. The lodging list in the official guide indicates whether or not children are welcome at each spot. **Lenox Chamber of Commerce** (Lenox Academy Bldg., 75 Main St., 01240, tel. 413/637–3646) has guides to local restaurants, shops, lodging, and cultural events as well as information on area attractions. **Mohawk Trail Association** (Box 722, Charlemont 01339, tel. 413/664–6256) publishes a Visitor's Guide to the region.

The *Berkshire Eagle* (75 S. Church St., Pittsfield 01201, tel. 800/245–0254) is the area's main newspaper with ads for house rentals. It publishes a regular supplement in summer, *Berkshires Week*, that contains a calendar of events. *The Berkshire Book: A Complete Guide* by Jonathan Sternfield (Berkshire

House) is the most detailed guide to the region. *Adventures in the Berkshires: Places to Go with Children* by Patti Silver and Vivienne Jaffe (The Berkshire Country Day School, Box 867, Lenox, MA 01240; 1991) is a terrific resource for visiting families, including everything from museums to berry farms to libraries. *A Guide to Natural Places in the Berkshire Hills* by Rene Laubach, *Hikes & Walks in the Berkshire Hills* by Lauren Stevens, and *Bike Rides in the Berkshire Hills* by Lewis C. Cuyler, all published by Berkshire House, are very detailed guides.

GETTING TO AND FROM THE BERK-SHIRES. **By air:** Bradley International Airport (Windsor Locks, CT, tel. 203/627–3000), between Hartford, Connecticut, and Springfield, Massachusetts, is the closest major airport to the Berkshires, about an hour by car. All major car-rental firms have desks at the airport. **Albany Airport** (*see* Adirondacks, *below*), just west of the Berkshires, is also an access point.

By train: It's possible to reach Pittsfield on **Amtrak's** (tel. 800/872–7245) once-a-day Lake Shore Limited from Boston to Chicago, or to reach Hudson, New York, on the north–south line.

By bus: **Peter Pan Bus Lines** (tel. 413/442–4451) links Boston and Albany with Pittsfield and Lee; **Bonanza Bus Lines** (tel. 800/556–3815) connects New York City, Vermont, and Providence, Rhode Island, with the Berkshires and stops at several towns in the region.

By car: The Massachusetts Turnpike (I–90) connects Boston with the central Berkshires area of Stockbridge and Lenox, continuing on to link with the New York State Thruway. From Boston the trip takes about 2½ hours. The fastest route from New York City is on the Taconic State Parkway, which joins the Berkshire section of the Thruway at Chatham; to the central area around Lenox, it's about three hours. The main north–south highway through the Berkshires is Route 7, which runs south into

Connecticut and north into Vermont. Route 23 cuts across the region in the south; Route 2 (the Mohawk Trail) is the main east–west route in the north.

GETTING AROUND THE BERKSHIRES. **By car:** Having a car is essential for visiting the area's back roads and attractions with kids. Towns are best explored on foot, especially during the trafficky summer months. Route 7 links all the major towns, from Great Barrington in the south to Williamstown in the north.

FAMILY-FRIENDLY TOURS. You can get an overview of the region or a special insight into a particular aspect of it.

(ẅ ALL) Berkshire Tour Company. Nancy Henriques designs individual tours for families or just kids to fit kids' ages and interests.
🏠 *Box 383, Pittsfield 01202, tel. 413/443–5017.*

(ẅ 8+) Berkshire Hiking Holidays. Tours by these experienced guides vary widely, both in hike length and difficulty (some include canoeing and biking) and in types of overnight accommodations, so be sure to let them know how old your kids are and how much hiking experience they've had.
🏠 *Box 2231, Lenox 01240, tel. 413/637–4442.*

PIT STOPS. Besides local gas stations, which can always be counted on, the town hall in each community has bathrooms open to the public. Another good bet is the Chamber of Commerce in Lenox (*see above*). Shops are generally understanding.

EMERGENCIES. The basic emergency number for police, fire, and ambulance is 911. **Berkshire Medical Center** (725 North St., Pittsfield, tel. 413/499–4161) is the largest and best-equipped hospital in the Berkshires. **Patrick's Pharmacy** (200 West St., Pittsfield, tel. 413/499–4063) maintains a 24-hour emergency service. The **CVS** in the Lenox Mall (Rtes. 7 and 20, tel. 413/499–

3430) stays open Monday to Saturday until 9, Sunday until 6.

BABY-SITTERS. Most resorts and inns maintain a list of baby-sitters they've used before.

WHEN TO GO. The Berkshires have something for families during every season. In winter, when it's cold and snowy, but not as icy as farther north in New England, downhill and cross-country skiing at one of the several ski areas and excellent outdoor ice-skating on small lakes are favored activities. March is maple sugaring time at several farms and at Hancock Shaker Village. Skip a visit in April, when wet weather and mud are the norm and ski areas are slush. The beginning of May can be iffy outdoors, but is the month for kids' fishing derbies. During June, especially the last half, you can enjoy all outdoor activities, including baseball, but without the crowds. July and August, the best time for all music, dance, and theater events and country fairs, but also traffic, crowds, and very high prices, are hot and muggy during the day. From September through October, when the leaves are a riot of color, is ideal for hiking and hayrides.

The following events are worth planning for:

(👫 5–15) Indian powwows of dancing and native food are held May–August regularly at Indian Plaza in Charlemont (tel. 413/339–4096).

(👫 3–15) Pittsfield Mets baseball season starts in June (tel. 413/499–6387).

(👫 5–15) The **Fourth of July** musical extravaganza at Tanglewood ends with fireworks over the waters of Stockbridge Bowl (tel. 413/637–1940).

(👫 8–15) Josh Billings RunAground in September is the Berkshires' greatest one-day party. Hundreds of teams compete in the oldest triathlon (bicycle, canoe, and running race) in New England (tel. 413/443–5674).

Scoping out the Berkshires

Great Barrington is the southern Berkshires' big town, the place where families go to walk down a wide main street, see a matinee at an antique movie theater with painted loges and boxes, play indoor miniature golf on a rainy day, and eat at one of its many, many family-friendly restaurants. Lodgings here are less expensive and more available in the prime summer months.

What always strikes me about **Lenox** and **Stockbridge** is the contrast between the number of things for families to do and the number of antiques-filled bed-and-breakfasts and restaurants that really don't want their business. Still, within a 15-mile radius is the greatest concentration of attractions for families in the Berkshires, from museums to parks and sanctuaries with short walks and much wildlife to the most scenic stretch of river canoeing to our favorite place to watch baseball, to, above all, the many, many performing spaces where kids can attend music, dance, and theater events free. Lenox has more historic mansions as well as more kids' activities; Stockbridge is glossy, a Norman Rockwell New England–postcard place jammed with summer tourists.

Colonial **Williamstown,** dominated by Williams College, doesn't exude the touristy coziness of Stockbridge or the hum of culture of Lenox. This is a center for some of the most challenging hiking and canoeing, and the only white-water rafting, in the region. Spectacular views, a natural stone bridge to cross, Indian powwows, uncrowded swimming, the best state forest camping, a theater with great kids' programs, and a couple of first-rate museums are all good reasons to come here.

Attractions below have been grouped by town, beginning in the south around Great Barrington and proceeding north to the Williamstown area.

(👫 3–10) Tyringham Gingerbread House and Gallery. When Gavin was little,

we used to stop just to look at this thatched-roof cottage that reminded us of something from Hansel and Gretel and walk on the paths through the surrounding woods and gardens.
🏠 *Tyringham Rd., Tyringham 01264, tel. 413/243–3260.*

👫 3 – 15 **Norman Rockwell Museum.** Norman Rockwell's lively paintings of an earlier small-town New England peopled with freckle-faced kids skating, batting a ball, ordering dinner on a train, tell humorous stories that kids I know respond to readily. This large building set on 36 acres above the Housatonic River holds the largest collection of his work in the world. It also houses his studio—he lived the last 25 years of his life in Stockbridge and plumbed its people and streets for subject matter. The beautiful grounds are dotted with sculptures designed for kids to climb on; we like the monster surrounded by monster benches.
🏠 *Rte. 183, Stockbridge 01262, tel. 413/298–4100. Cost: $8 adults, $2 kids. Open May–Oct., daily 10–5; Nov.–Apr., daily 11–4.*

👫 0 – 8 **Berkshire Botanical Garden.** The 15 acres of the Berkshires' only botanical garden are a series of kid-size landscapes where little ones can let go of your hand and run freely and you can wander paths and trails with a stroller. The growing vegetables, small ponds holding water lilies and frogs, fragrances of blooming flowers, and the enclosed herb garden all leave lasting impressions. Among the best events for kids of all ages are the scarecrow-making workshop and the wonderful fall Harvest Festival.
🏠 *Rtes. 102 and 183, Stockbridge 01262, tel. 413/298–3926. Cost: $5 adults, kids under 12 free. Open May–Oct., daily.*

👫 5 – 10 **Berkshire Scenic Railway and Museum.** Two operating model railroads are the centerpiece of a museum in the old Lenox Station. You can take a short trip in a shiny 1920s Erie Lackawanna coach on the museum grounds.
🏠 *Willow Creek Rd., Lenox 01240, tel. 413/637–2210. Museum free; train ride,*

$1.50 adults, $1 kids. Open weekends and holidays Memorial Day–Oct. and several weekends in Dec.

👫 ALL **Pleasant Valley Wildlife Sanctuary.** Here along Yokun Brook kids can see animals in natural settings, hike short trails to meadows and ponds, and participate in outdoor nature activities. There's a garden planted with red flowers that attracts hummingbirds from May to October. A small trailside museum houses displays and live exhibits. The regular family canoe trips are a bargain.
🏠 *472 W. Mountain Rd., Lenox 01240, tel. 413/637–0320. Cost: $3 adults, $2 kids. Open Tues.–Sun. dawn–dusk.*

👫 5 – 12 **Yankee Candle Company.** On the second floor is a fascinating **candle-making** exhibit showing how candles are dipped from start to finish. At the end kids can color their own (for $1) by dipping already-formed white paraffin candles into tanks of melted colored beeswax. It's quick, but very satisfying to younger kids.
🏠 *639 Pittsfield–Lenox Rd., Lenox 01237, tel. 413/499–3626.*

👫 4 – 12 **Berkshire Museum.** Everything from glass made in the town of Berkshire to American Indian artifacts to abstract and Chinese paintings to aquariums and live animals is on display here. This one is better and more family-focused than most regional museums. There are behind-the-scenes tours, camping in an Indian tepee in summer, and daily activities. Don't miss the room filled with miniature dioramas of animals of the world.
🏠 *Rte. 7, Pittsfield 01201, tel. 413/443–7171. Cost: $3 adults, $1 kids 12–18, under 12 free; free Wed. and Sat. 10–noon. Open Sept.–June, Tues.–Sat. 10–5, Sun. 1–5; July and Aug., Mon.–Sat. 10–5, Sun. 1–5.*

👫 8 – 13 **Hancock Shaker Village.** This restored village, one of 18 farming communities the Shakers founded in America in the 18th century, conveys the simple and peaceful Shaker way of life through cooking and

blacksmith demonstrations and visits to cows and sheep in the barn. *See Chapter 7.*
🏠 *Rte. 20, 5 mi west of Pittsfield, at junction of Rtes. 41 and 20, Box 898, Pittsfield 01202, tel. 413/443–0188.*

👫 2 – 10 **Fairfields Dairy Farm and Bed & Breakfast.** Many kids look forward to visiting a farm. For insurance reasons, fewer and fewer allow it. You can see cows being milked here and take a half-hour picnic trek with a llama if you call in advance.
🏠 *954 Greenriver Rd., Williamstown 01267, tel. 413/458–3321. Cost for trek: $10 adults, kids free. Open Apr.–Oct., weather permitting.*

👫 7 – 14 **Williams College Museum of Art.** Curved cut-out doorways, angled walls with interior windows, and the catwalk to a stairway in the three-story atrium make it seem like a stage set of surprises. The temporary exhibits can be highly unusual and colorful. On special family days you can do gallery sketching and other activities.
🏠 *Main St., Williamstown 01267, tel. 413/596–2429. Admission free. Open Tues.–Sat. 10–5, Sun. 1–5.*

👫 3 – 13 **Western Gateway Heritage State Park.** The big attraction for kids we know is "The Tunnel Experience," a sight-and-sound-effects display about how the 4½-mile-long Hoosac Tunnel was built more than a century ago. Inside several railroad boxcars the sound of pickaxes striking stone, the feel of dripping water, and simulated explosions convey the drama. This is one of eight Heritage Parks in Massachusetts designed to preserve urban areas.
🏠 *B & M Freightyard, Rte. 8, North Adams 01247, tel. 413/663–8059. Donation requested. Open daily 10–5.*

👫 ALL **Mohawk Trail (Route 2).** A portion of the highway that follows the historic footpath known to the Indians in early American times passes through the northern Berkshires. Indian powwows of traditional dances, costumes, and food held periodically throughout the summer in Charlemont and

the "trading post" stores of kitschy Indian souvenirs may interest your kids more than the marked historic spots where Indian treaties were signed. If you go, stop at the Hail to the Sunrise monument to the Five Indian Nations of the Mohawk Trail.

Action

AMUSEMENTS. Route 7 has a wide variety of good places for fun on rainy days.

👫 4 – 15 **Cove Lanes.** This recreation center offers all sorts of great indoor entertainment for families, including Rainbow's End, an indoor miniature golf course (*see* Indoor Action High Spots *in* Chapter 12).
🏠 *Rte. 7, north of Great Barrington 01230, tel. 413/528–1220. Open daily 9 AM–midnight.*

👫 4 – 15 **Par-4 Mini-Golf.** This is a large and elaborate outdoor miniature golf course.
🏠 *Rte. 7, Lanesborough 01237, tel. 413/499–0051. Open mid-May–mid-Oct.*

👫 8 – 15 **Roller Magic Roller Skating Rink.** A DJ and a light show are added attractions at the 9,000-square-foot skate rink. Skates can be rented.
🏠 *Colonial Shopping Center, Rte. 2, Williamstown 01267, tel. 413/458–3659. Cost: $3 ($5 Fri. and Sat. nights), $1 skate rentals. Open Fri. 7:30–11 PM; Sat. 10:30–1, 2–4:30, and 7:30–11 PM; Sun. (Sept.–Apr. only) 2–4:30, 7–9 PM.*

👫 2 – 11 **Kids' World Playground.** The large, multilevel wooden structure with a tower and a bridge is the most imaginative outdoor playspace in the Berkshires. Check on hours when school is in session.
🏠 *96 School St., Williamstown 01267, tel. 413/499–5707.*

BASEBALL. The Berkshires are home to the ideal baseball experience for young fans.

👫 3+ **Pittsfield Mets.** The cozy, old-fashioned field in Wahconah Park where this minor league team plays charms us all with its family atmosphere and kids' contests between innings. Attend a game on a warm summer night even if you think your kids are too little. See Chapter 11.

🏠 *Box 328 (North St. ½ mi to Wahconah St. and turn left), Pittsfield 01202, tel. 413/499–6387. Open mid-June–Sept.*

BIKING. Though the Berkshires have no paved bike paths like Cape Cod's, the back-country roads through rolling farmland just outside Lenox—and elsewhere in the Berkshires—offer good family biking. In Lee, for example, most children ride their bikes downtown. **Main Street Sports & Leisure** (48 Main St., Lenox, tel. 413/637–4407; $20 per day) rents mountain and hybrid bikes in all sizes and includes helmets, bike locks, and a detailed map of routes they have checked out themselves. Reserve in advance for busy weekends. **In-line skates** (they have kids' sizes) are $10 per day; the staff know all the parking lots that are empty on weekends.

BOATING. For the best powerboating and sailing in the Berkshires, head for the huge **Otis Reservoir** (Rte. 8, Otis). **Miller Marine** (Reservoir Rd., Otis, tel. 413/269–6358) rents both sailboats and speedboats. Pretty little **Lake Garfield** in South County is a good size for short boat ventures with kids—there are swimming ducks to feed as you go. **Kinne's Grove** (Rte. 23, Monterey, tel. 413/528–5417), right on the lake, rents rowboats and a canoe as well as motors and kid-size life jackets. Though you can canoe south on the Housatonic River from Great Barrington, I still prefer the stretch above Lenox.

The 7-mile-long flat-water stretch of the meandering **Housatonic River** north of Lenox passes farms and wetlands. Unfortunately, you can't swim, as there are PCBs in the water. At picturesque **Stockbridge Bowl**, ringed with summer houses and shady willows and birches, a small island makes a good lunch destination. **Main Street Sports & Leisure** (48 Main St., Lenox 01240, tel. 413/637–4407), which rents

canoes, provides shuttle service to launching sites for both the Housatonic and Stockbridge Bowl. **Onota Lake Boat Livery** (455 Pecks Rd., Pittsfield 01201, tel. 413/442–1724) is the main place to rent motorboats or canoes by the hour for use on Onota Lake.

FISHING. Kids under 15 don't need fishing licenses in Massachusetts; older kids and adults can obtain them from town clerks and most outdoor sports stores. Bass, pickerel, several kinds of trout, and perch are some of the fish hiding in lakes, ponds, and streams. The **Green River** (stocked with trout) off Rte. 23 west of Great Barrington is easy to get to. **Benedict Pond** in Beartown State Forest (*see* Green Spaces, *below*) has an open, grassy bank. For easy pier fishing, try Burbank Park on **Onota Lake** west of Pittsfield. Shops do not rent equipment, but in summer **Onota Boat Livery** (*see* Boating, *above*) sells a $10 rod, reel, and tackle package that's perfect for kids, as well as bait. At **Berry Pond** in Pittsfield State Forest (Cascade St., Pittsfield, tel. 413/442–8992) kids can throw in a line. Only kids aged 6 to 14 are permitted to fish **Wild Acres** (South Mountain Rd., Pittsfield, tel. 413/499–9344), a well-stocked trout pond in a pristine location near the Pittsfield Airport.

👫 **4 – 14** Jiminy Peak. The easiest place for kids to fish in the entire Berkshire area is in this resort's stocked trout pond because rental poles, buckets, and bait are right here. 🏠 *Corey Rd. off Rte. 7, Hancock 01237, tel. 413/738–5500.*

GREEN SPACES. The Berkshires are rich with parks and forests for exploring and enjoying nature.

👫 **ALL** Beartown State Forest. Outdoor family activities, from swimming and canoeing, to camping, to fishing in flowing brooks to hiking woodsy trails, are more easily accessible—even to families with little kids—in this state forest's thousands of acres than in others nearby.

🏕 *Blue Hill Rd. off Rte. 17 (access also from Beartown Mountain Rd. off Rte. 102 and Meadow Rd.), Monterey 01245, tel. 413/ 528–0904. Cost: $2 parking. Activities: boating, camping, fishing, hiking, picnicking, cross-country skiing in winter.*

(6+) Mt. Greylock State Reservation. From Massachusetts' highest peak you have a more spectacular view than from any other mountaintop in the Berkshires—and you can drive to it. Hiking trails wind through evergreen forests; a lodge at the top offers guided hikes, breakfast, and lodging. The hikes and walks guided by the Appalachian Mountain Club here are challenging, best for older kids with experience and good hiking shoes. A map of trails is available at the Visitor Center. (See Chapter 10.)

🏕 *Rockwell Rd. (Mass. Pike to exit 2, Rte. 20 west, Rte. 7 north to Lanesboro, follow signs to visitor center), Lanesboro 01237, tel. 413/ 499–4262 (visitor center).*

(7+) Natural Bridge State Park. A geologic wonder, the 30-foot marble bridge stretches across a narrow gorge through which the water of Hudson Brook rushes. A series of fenced walkways leads right down into the chasm. (See Chapter 10.)

🏕 *Rte. 8 (Rte. 2 to Rte. 8 north, follow signs), North Adams 01247, tel. 413/663–6392.*

(ALL) Savoy Mountain State Forest. The wild and beautiful forested landscape of this 11,000 acres is similar to Mt. Greylock's, but families with younger kids prefer it because of the uncrowded beaches on North and South Pond. Of the many hiking trails, the short route through a cool, dark forest ends at Tannery Falls, one of the prettiest in the Berkshires.

🏕 *Rte. 116, Savoy 01247, tel. 413/663– 8469. Cost: $2 parking, $12 camping. Activities: boating, fishing, camping, hiking, nature center, picnicking, swimming, snowmobiling, cross-country skiing.*

HIKING AND WALKING. One of the pleasures of this area with younger kids and babies in strollers is walking the rolling lawns

and gardens of historic houses such as **Arrowhead** (780 Holmes Rd., Pittsfield 01201, tel. 413/442–1793) and **Chesterwood** (off Rte. 183 between Glendale and Stockbridge 01262, tel. 413/298–3579), which has a short nature trail and large sculptures kids climb on.

(3 – 12) Bartholomew's Cobble. Short, easy trails with rounded rocks to climb, wildflowers and ferns, and well-organized family hikes make this National Natural Landmark a delight for families with young kids to explore. It's almost at the Connecticut border. See Chapter 12.

🏕 *Weatogue Rd. (from Rte. 7A, turn right on Rannapo Rd. 1½ mi to Weatogue Rd.; turn right; entrance on left), Ashley Falls 01222, tel. 413/229–8600.*

(4+) Bash Bish Falls. This cascade plunges 60 feet into a deep pool surrounded by flat rocks. The hike from the lower parking lot (actually in New York state) follows a gravel road to the falls (less than 1 mile) where you must climb down some stone steps to the view, which always seems a surprise. Guard rails keep you on the trails; swimming is not allowed, nor is picnicking.

🏕 *Mt. Washington State Forest (Rte. 41 to Bash Bish Rd., which becomes Rte. 344), Mt. Washington 01223, tel. 413/528–0330. Admission free. Open daily.*

(5 – 15) Benedict Pond Trail. Following the perimeter of the quiet small pond, the trail skirts a mix of boulders and hemlocks and blueberry bushes. The Pond Loop Trail, just 1½ miles, lies right next to the shore, but is rough in spots; a longer route follows an old road. End at the beach with a swim.

🏕 *Beartown State Forest (see Green Spaces, above).*

(8 – 15) Ice Glen Trail. A clattery wooden suspension footbridge across the Housatonic River takes you to a shadowy trail through a mysterious boulder-strewn ravine edged with droopy hemlocks. The maze of rocks creates caves and crevices that retain ice long into spring and impart cool air even on a hot summer day. Climbing over these is difficult; make sure your kids are up to it and are wearing proper footwear.

🏔 *End of Park St., off Rte. 7, 2 mi south of Stockbridge.*

👬 **7 – 15** Monument Mountain Reservation. This is a real mountain with a short (2.7-mile), circular trail to the Squaw Peak summit that's easy enough for young children to climb yet has everything a hike should have: spectacular views, a waterfall and a stream, open rocky ledges to scramble on, and rock towers, cliffs, and huge, jumbled white quartzite boulders at the top that glisten in the sun. It's one of the most memorable short hikes in the Berkshires, but unfortunately, on summer weekends, it feels like everyone else is appreciating it, too. Beat the crowds by going early or on a weekday. Be sure to wear hiking shoes, not sneakers. Check the trail map displayed in the parking lot.

🏔 *Parking area off Rte. 7, about 3 mi south of Stockbridge.*

👬 **5 – 15** Tyringham Cobble. A rewarding 2-mile loop leads up to rocky outcrops (a perfect picnic site) where you have views of the white church, the town, and Goose Pond. Follow white, then blue blazes through a hillside meadow of blackberries (bring a plastic bucket in summer) and woods to the top.

🏔 *Jerusalem Rd. (watch for* TRUSTEES OF RESERVATIONS *sign), Tyringham 01262, tel. 413/298–3239. Open daily sunrise–sunset.*

HORSEBACK RIDING. There are more horseback riding stables in Lenox than in any other Berkshire town; the one at **Undermountain Farm** (Undermountain Rd., Lenox, tel. 413/637–3365) holds kid-oriented horse shows and gives lessons and trail rides.

ICE SKATING. When the weather turns icy, the town floods the field behind the **Lenox Community Center** for ice-skating;

Main Street Sports & Leisure (see Biking, *above*) rents skates.

SKIING. Butternut Basin (see Chapter 13), a friendly but crowded mountain, is a 10-minute drive from Great Barrington. For a day's outing with young kids who aren't hotshots, we prefer the tiny **Otis Ridge Ski Area** (tel. 413/269–4444), whose 10 trails lie a bit farther east along Route 23. It has the intimate family atmosphere of a club and is much less expensive. We'd rather ski at **Jiminy Peak Ski Area** (see Chapter 13) than elsewhere in the Berkshires because of the more challenging trails and clean, spacious, uncrowded atmosphere.

SWIMMING. Despite the number of lakes in the Berkshires, it's surprisingly hard to find a public lake beach with really good swimming. **Onota Lake,** west of Pittsfield (tel. 413/499–9344), has a variety of beaches, some very shallow, and lifeguards, bathhouses, picnic tables and grills; for mountain ponds untouched by noisy power boats, we prefer **Benedict Pond** (in Beartown State Forest), which we consider mountain pond swimming at its best—a small sandy beach, a sprinkling of picnic tables, no houses, and big pines, boulders, and mountain views.

👬 **4 – 15** Green River Swimming Hole. Here you can enjoy river swimming, with clear, albeit quite, quite chilly water and a spot for sunbathing, but no lifeguards.

🏔 *Off Rte. 23 (1 mi west of town; watch for other cars parked on road), Great Barrington 01230.*

👬 **ALL** Lake Mansfield. Tucked into the northwest edge of Great Barrington, this lake has a pretty charm, plus warm water, a playground, and lifeguards.

🏔 *Off Christian Hill Rd., Great Barrington 01230, tel. 413/528–3140.*

👬 **3 – 15** North Pond. Uncrowded pond swimming in a beautiful forest environment draws families to this intimate, unspoiled pond in Savoy State Forest (see Green Spaces, *above*). The water lapping onto the sandy beach is chilly and clear. Picnic tables and barbecue grills make this a good daylong destination.

ⁱⁱ ALL Otis Reservoir. Sailboats and motorboats and very clean, clear water are the attractions here. The beach in Tolland State Forest is sandy.

🏠 *Rte. 8, Otis 01253, tel. 413/269–7268.*

ⁱⁱ ALL Sand Springs Pool and Spa. The friendly atmosphere at these thermal mineral springs is more laid-back family club than resort attraction. The naturally warm springs, a steady 74° year-round, have been known since the mid-18th century when Indian tribes gathered here. Now they're channeled into a huge 50-by-75-foot swimming pool, an outdoor family-size hot tub with a shallow end for little ones, and a toddlers' pool with a cute, splashy fountain. Big old trees and umbrellas shade the pool edge and picnic area.

🏠 *Sand Springs Rd., Williamstown 01267, tel. 413/458–8281. Cost: $7.50 adults, $6.50 kids under 14, $3.50 kids 4–6, free under 4. Open Memorial Day–mid-Sept., weekdays 11–8, weekends 10–8.*

WHITE-WATER RAFTING. It's rare in the region, but you can do it.

ⁱⁱ 8 – 15 Deerfield River. The only place for white-water rafting in Massachusetts, about 25 miles west of Williamstown, is also one of the best spots in the Northeast for families to try it. See White Water Rafting in Chapter 12.

🏠 *Charlemont 01339.*

Shopping

Much of the Berkshires' shopping is antiques. Of the rest, most is not for kids.

MALLS AND MAIN STREETS. Berkshire Mall (Rte. 7 and Berkshire Mall Dr., Lanesboro 01237, tel. 413/445–4400) is the only enclosed shopping center in the Berkshires; favored stores are The Gap, KayBee Toys, Record Town, A & W Hot Dogs in the food court, a cineplex with 11 movie choices, and more. Great Barrington's **Railroad Street**,

almost a pedestrian street in summer, has many shops worth kids' browsing.

STORES. Among the many stores in the Berkshires, these are especially interesting for children:

ⁱⁱ 4+ The Bookstore. Little kids like to read in the tiny cave-like play area in the midst of a wide selection of great kids' books.

🏠 *9 Housatonic St., Lenox 01240, tel. 413/637–3390.*

ⁱⁱ 0 – 8 Gifted Child. A selection of educational toys, craft kits, dolls, clothes, and accessories for infants fills the shelves.

🏠 *72 Church St., Lenox 01240, tel. 413/ 637–1191.*

ⁱⁱ 13+ Glad Rags. It's the neat accessories in the Berkshires' hippest clothing emporium that attract teens.

🏠 *76 Church St., Lenox 01240, tel. 413/ 637–0088.*

ⁱⁱ 3+ Nature of Things. When kids walk into this fabulous, two-story hands-on nature and science store, they have a hard time deciding what to do first: climb into a kaleidoscope? crawl in the red and blue rocket? or try out the tornado tube?

🏠 *36 Pittsfield Rd. (on Rte. 7), Lenox 01240, tel. 413/637–4373.*

ⁱⁱ 13 – 15 Purple Plume. Gifty stuff, like inexpensive antique-y looking earrings, incense, candles in the shape of unicorns, and good-smelling soap, are irresistible to young teenage girls I know.

🏠 *35 Church St., Lenox 01240, tel. 413/ 637–3442.*

ⁱⁱ ALL Where Did You Get That? A sense of humor and fun permeates this store carrying both hands-on educational toys and a big corner of wonderful junky novelty items—like the talking "portable Mom and Dad."

🏠 *Colonial Shopping Center, Rte. 2 (1 mi east of town), Williamstown 01267, tel. 413/ 458–2206.*

Eats

Our family has eaten more dinner picnics in the Berkshires, I think, than just about anywhere else. With kids along, the best seats for a concert at Tanglewood or a Shakespeare play at The Mount are on a blanket spread on the grass with a picnic on top. From the picnic tables by the Inside/Out stage at Jacob's Pillow you have a good view of dance works-in-progress performed before the main evening event. Picnic caterers (some too elegant for kids) will pack one for you: The **Store at Five Corners** (Rtes. 7 and 43, Williamstown, tel. 413/458–3176) is a gourmet shop whose sandwiches and salads satisfy adults and kids—and don't forget the creamy homemade fudge. In Lenox, head for **Crosby's** (62 Church St., tel. 413/637–3396), but put together your own choices. For a hefty price they'll pack plates and utensils too. **The Deli** in Great Barrington (343 Main St., tel. 413/528–1482) is more our picnic style—sandwiches, each named for a famous person, as in a Jacques Cousteau shrimp sandwich that's our favorite.

Throughout the region we've found picnic tables attractively placed for family meals— in the Berkshire Botanical Garden, in state parks by ponds, and on the rolling grassy lawns and gardens of the Clark Art Institute (225 South St., tel. 413/458–9545) in Williamstown, from which you can hike a pretty footpath up Stone Hill for a vista of the town.

Dress is casual in all the restaurants below. See introduction to Eats in Chapter 3, Boston, for price categories.

(ALL) Bogie's at the Barn Club. Inside the big wood barn you get the food: sandwiches, unusual gourmet (and plain) pizza, and even prime ribs. Outside is the action—a swimming pool, a kiddie pool, a playground, and a golf driving range in summer, an ice-skating rink in winter. *935 S. Main St., Great Barrington, tel. 413/528–5959. Kids' menu, high chairs. AE, MC, V. $$*

(4–15) Cheesecake Charlie's. The 50 flavors of light but creamy cheesecake—the best our family has ever eaten—are the reason to come here. You can also have a sandwich at one of the tables clustered in the shop's center. *72 Main St., Village Shopping Center, Lenox, tel. 413/637–3411. MC, V. $–$$.*

(5+) Dakota. You feel here as though you are in a grand but rustic hunting lodge. Moose and elk heads gaze down from the pine walls and a birch-bark canoe hangs from the ceiling. The fare is steaks and chicken and mesquite-grilled fish. *Rtes. 7 and 20, Pittsfield, tel. 413/499–7900. Kids' menu, booster seats, high chairs. Reservations advised. AE, DC, MC, V. No lunch. $–$$.*

(ALL) Dos Amigos. Mexican fare at this relaxed restaurant in a yellow cottagey building you can't miss ranges from simple tacos to a sophisticated seafood quesadilla. Inside it's open beams, dark wood, low lighting, and lively music. For little kids, the best time to go is every other Wednesday, when a singer entertains them with songs from 5:30 to 6:30. The kids' menu items are less spicy, smaller portions of just what's on the menu. *250 Stockbridge Rd. (Rte. 7), Great Barrington, tel. 413/528–0084. Kids' menu, booster seats, high chairs. Reservations advised. AE, MC. $–$$*

(ALL) Hobson's Choice. Good grilled steaks, seafood, chicken, and Cajun specialties for the adventurous, a homey, rustic atmosphere (barn-board walls and beams), and a salad bar where you can look into the kitchen to see the food being cooked and talk to the chef about your own order appeal to us. You can get half orders for kids. *15 Water St., Williamstown, tel. 413/458–9101. Booster seats, high chairs. Reservations advised. AE, MC, V. Closed Mon. $$*

(ALL) Miss Adams Diner. This shiny 1949 Worcester Lunch Car in downtown

North Adams serves breakfast and lunch. The menu is classic (meat loaf) with modern touches (granola). Our pick is the homemade chili or crisp fish and homemade chips with cole slaw for lunch; malted waffles with thick, glossy syrup for breakfast.
🏨 *53 Park St., North Adams, tel. 413/743–5300. Booster seats. No reservations. No credit cards. No dinner.* $

(👫 9–15) Red Lion Inn. Even if you don't stay at the most famous inn in the Berkshires, one dinner in its shady Courtyard of white tables under green-and-white umbrellas (casual dress okay here) or a cold drink with scones and biscuits on its wide, rocker-filled veranda is a must in summer. The regular weekly Courtyard barbecues are a treat; otherwise the food is solid, traditional New England.
🏨 *Main St., Stockbridge, tel. 413/298–5545. Kids' menu, booster seats, high chairs. Reservations advised. AE, DC, MC, V.* $$$

(👫 5+) Shaker Mill Tavern. Along with the Red Lion Inn, this is one of the few restaurants in the Lenox/Stockbridge area where a casual atmosphere, good food beyond the burger category, and kid- and adult-pleasing surroundings come together. The restaurant, once an old stagecoach inn and still full of that wood-and-antique ambience, is just across the Williams River from the little town of West Stockbridge.
🏨 *Rte. 102, West Stockbridge, tel. 413/232–8565. Kids' menu, booster seats, high chairs. Reservations accepted for 6 or more. AE, MC, V.* $$

Where to Stay

The full range of condo resorts, inns, motels, individual homes and cottages, and above all bed-and-breakfasts can be found throughout the region. Route 7 is lined with motels, especially between Great Barrington and Stockbridge, north of Lenox, and just south of Williamstown. Most seem very ordinary and just too close to the road and the noise of trucks. Three inexpensive ones that offer something special: in Great Bar-

rington, **Monument Mountain Motel** (tel. 413/528–3272) has a pool, woods, and family rooms; outside Lenox, **Susse Chalet** (tel. 413/637–3560) has a pool; in Williamstown, the **Maple Terrace Motel** (tel. 413/458–9677) is right on Main Street but has a secluded pool.

Renting a house for a week or two can be difficult if you go through realtors. You may have better luck checking the ads in the *Berkshire Eagle* (see The Basics, *above*).

Bed-and-breakfast reservation services listed in Chapter 2 are your best bet for finding a B&B that welcomes families because they know these places intimately.

In July and August, the prices for rooms in Lenox and Stockbridge soar, and many inns and B&Bs insist on a several-night minimum stay at weekends, causing families to look south to Great Barrington and north toward Williamstown for cheaper accommodations. Do not come without reservations in summer. The price categories that follow are based on summer-season rates and reflect what a family of four would spend for one night in a double room or the smallest appropriate accommodation available (sometimes a cottage): $$$$, over $160; $$$, $110–$160; $$, $70–$110; $, under $70. For Eastover, where prices are MAP, the price category $$ is equivalent to $200–$350. Prices do not include 9.7% sales tax.

(👫 6–15) AMC Bascom Lodge. When you stay at this rustic Appalachian Mountain Club lodge atop Mt. Greylock with its hand-hewn beams and stone fireplace, you feel cut off from everything but views and woods when night falls. It's best for a hiking and sports-minded family who want to make only a few treks to local cultural activities, preferably in nearby Williamstown.
🏨 *Box 1602, Lanesboro 01237, tel. 413/743–1591 or 413/443–0011; Oct.–May, 413/684–3900. 4 private double rooms, 4 bunk rooms for 6 or 8, all with shared bath. Facilities: 3 meals daily, guided hikes, hiking*

trails, nature workshops. MC, V. Closed Oct.–mid-May. $

★★ ALL Eastover Resort. Staying at this informal resort is like being on a cruise ship on land. It offers just about every activity a family might want from horseback riding to nightly dances at which kids join in; the atmosphere can get a bit noisy and corny, like glorified summer camp. It's a place you either love or hate. Totally kid-friendly, it has a thousand acres to roam, built-in playmates, all-you-can-eat buffets, and buffalo to feed. Despite the exterior grand-estate appearance, accommodations are very basic motel, with no phone, TV, or air-conditioning.

East St., off Rte. 7, Box 2160, Lenox 01240, tel. 413/637–0625, fax 413/637–4939. 165 rooms, 120 with bath. Family weeks. Facilities: dining room, kids' programs and activities, tennis, indoor and outdoor pools, driving range, softball, volleyball, archery, skeet shooting, cross-country and downhill skiing, tobogganing, exercise room, shuffleboard, badminton, live music, dancing, free local transport, horseback riding, baby-sitting. AE, D, DC, MC, V. Rates include 3 meals daily and all activities but horseback riding. Family weeks offered. Closed Apr. $$

★★ ALL Jiminy Peak. The tasteful gray clapboard country inn and condos nestled attractively at the base of the mountain have a ski resort flavor even in summer—massive stone fireplaces, bright wood, views of hills, angled roofs, and a clock tower. There is a certain blandness to the decor, but rooms are light-filled, and in winter the restaurants and public lounges always seem cleaner and brighter than other Berkshires ski areas.

Corey Rd. off Rte. 7, Hancock 01237, tel. 413/738–5500 or 800/882–8859. 212 rooms. Facilities: restaurant, pool, miniature golf, trout pond, tennis, Alpine slide, mountain biking (no rentals), baby-sitting. AE, D, DC, MC, V. $$–$$$$

★★ ALL Oak 'n Spruce Resort. This former farm still feels like it's out in the country, but the rooms and condos are

more high-quality motel-modern than quaint farmhouse: good sturdy blond wood furniture and large rooms with TV and an anonymous flavor. This is a good spot for families with active kids who want to be fairly close to theater, music, and museums but have lots of outdoor action possibilities right out their door.

Meadow St., Box 237, South Lee 01260, tel. 413/243–3500 or 800/424–3003, fax 413/243–3500. 175 units (rooms, suites, 1- and 2-bedroom condos with kitchens). Facilities: restaurant; indoor and outdoor pools; health club; basketball; tennis; volleyball; hiking; badminton; shuffleboard; supervised kids' games, movies, and planned activities; kids' recreation building; 9-hole golf course; sledding; cross-country skiing. Kids under 12 free in parents' room. Family packages. AE, MC, V. $$–$$$

★★ 6 – 15 Red Lion Inn. It's the classic rambling New England inn, immortalized by Norman Rockwell, with a genteel small-town, Main Street flavor and rooms with antiques and colonial charm. In August it's expensive and hectic in town. Rooms in the main inn vary in size and decor; for families our pick are the sets of two rooms connected through a bath or the larger suites in the annexes, some of which even have kitchens. They do welcome families. Come in the spring or early summer.

Main St., Stockbridge 01262, tel. 413/298–5545, fax 413/298–5130. 108 rooms (78 with bath), 17 suites, 8 connecting rooms. Facilities: dining rooms, lounge, outdoor pool, baby-sitting. AE, D, DC, MC, V. $$$–$$$$

★★ 0 – 11 Rookwood Inn. This striking Victorian inn a half block from the center of Lenox has turret rooms and gables and heavy carved couches, striped wallpaper, bedrooms with fireplaces, and love seats tucked in an alcove under windows. Many of the larger rooms have small sitting areas with daybeds for kids; the ultimate for those with a dream of sleeping in a tower is the two-level turret room on the top floor. The big screened porch does perfectly for card games on a still night.

🏠 *Old Stockbridge Rd., Box 1717, Lenox 01240, tel. 413/637–9750. 19 rooms, 2 suites. Facilities: breakfast room, lounge. No smoking. AE. Rates include breakfast and afternoon tea. $$$–$$$$*

👪 ALL **Sunset Farm Inn.** This friendly place, which produces maple syrup and sugar in its own sugarhouse, has a real farm feel even though the only animals left are 15 chickens and a mean-tempered rooster. Trails and a brook where kids can fish are out back. The farmhouse, filled with antiques that don't look worrisome for kids, also has a 10-table restaurant where lunch and dinner are served. The best unit for families is the apartment attached to the main house with an upstairs bedroom, a huge downstairs living room, and a full-size kitchen.

🏠 *Tyringham Rd. (HC63, Tyringham Rd., Lee 01238), Tyringham, tel. 413/243–3329, fax 413/243–3229. 4 rooms with shared baths, 1 apartment. Facilities: restaurant, trails, fishing, sugarhouse, chickens. AE, D, MC, V. $$*

Entertainment and the Arts

Among the paramount attractions of the Berkshires are the performing arts—no other summer resort area in the Northeast can rival the excellence of music, theater, and dance performances here, for both adults and kids, some of which are free for kids under 12 when you sit outside.

👪 12 – 15 **Berkshire Opera Company** productions highlight the funny and exciting elements of the scores and librettos.

🏠 *Cranwell Opera House, Rte. 20, Lenox 01238, tel. 413/243–1343.*

👪 8 – 14 The **Berkshire Theatre Festival** puts on hilarious plays written by kids who are middle-school age acted by professionals under a tent, as well as off-Broadway fare that older kids sometimes like.

🏠 *Main St., Stockbridge, tel. 413/298–5536; in summer, 413/298–5576.*

👪 6 – 15 **Jacob's Pillow** dance events include free works-in-progress and wandering through the studios to watch dancers at work through one-way mirrors.

🏠 *Rte. 20, Becket, tel. 413/243–0745.*

👪 5 – 9 **Mac-Haydn Theatre**, just over the New York state line, presents musicals for kids and adults.

🏠 *Rte. 203, Chatham, NY, tel. 518/392–9292.*

👪 3 – 8 **Robbins-Zust Marionettes** present familiar fairy tales and allow kids to touch the puppets and see how they work firsthand.

🏠 *Berkshire Public Theatre, 30 Union St., Pittsfield 01202, tel. 413/445–4634.*

👪 13+ **Shakespeare & Co.** performs the bard's works with zany humor outdoors.

🏠 *The Mount, Plunkett St., Lenox 01240, tel. 413/637–3353.*

👪 3 – 15 **Tanglewood** concerts draw kids of all ages, especially when the Boston Pops play or fireworks cap the music.

🏠 *West St., Lenox 01240, tel. in summer, 413/637–1600; in winter, 617/266–1492.*

👪 ALL **Williamstown Theater Festival** is for adults, but the actors put on regular kids' programs (ages 5–10) outside under a tent.

🏠 *Adams Memorial Theatre, Main St., Williamstown 01267, tel. 413/597–3399; in summer, 413/597–3400.*

The Adirondacks, New York

Entering the Adirondacks can be a bit like revisiting the 1950s. An inexpensive, uncrowded outdoorsy vacation is still here. In many ways, the region is refreshingly unsophisticated, even in the most touristy areas, and has little of the restored-village/trendy-franchise syndrome that infects many parts of New England.

Much of the Adirondacks' landscape is rugged, dramatic, and wild (yes, there are bears) forests and mountains, but it also has nearly 3,000 lakes that range from 32-mile-long Lake George to small pristine wilderness ponds. That makes it not only great hiking territory, but also the place we've come for some of the best canoeing, fishing, and lake swimming in the East. Civilization, including its tackier aspects, is never far away. Even families with toddlers can find the ideal mix of activities. (See also Adirondack Park in Chapter 10.)

The Basics

HOW TO FIND OUT WHAT'S GOING ON. For the entire Adirondack region, the **I Love NY Tourism Office** (1 Commerce Plaza, Albany, NY 12245, tel. 518/225–5698) and the **Adirondack Regional Tourism Council** (Box 51, West Chazy, NY 12992, tel. 518/846–8016) provide general information and travel guides. We've always found the **Department of Conservation** (50 Wolf Rd., Albany, NY 12233, tel. 518/457–3521 or 800/487–6867), which is in charge of the Adirondack Park, to be the most helpful. From the **Warren County Tourism Department** (2750 Municipal Center, Lake George, NY 12845, tel. 518/761–6366 or 800/365–1050) and the **Lake George Chamber of Commerce** (Box 272, Lake George, NY 12845, tel. 518/668–5755) you can get a four-season travel guide that includes hotels and special events. **Hamilton County Tourism** (County Office Bldg., White Birch La., Box 771, Indian Lake, NY 12842, tel. 518/648–5239) can provide information on lodging, canoeing, fishing, and more. Be sure to ask for the "Blue Mountain Lake Information" and lodging, food, services brochures. Also a source of useful information is the **Indian Lake Chamber of Commerce** (Box 18, Indian Lake, NY 12842, tel. 518/648–5112). A guide we found useful for local hiking, fishing, and canoeing spots is the "Woods and Waters" booklet published by the **Town of Long Lake Department of Parks, Recreation, and Tourism** (Long Lake,

NY 12847, tel. 518/624–3077). **Lake Placid-Essex County Visitors Bureau** (Olympic Center, Lake Placid, NY 12946, tel. 518/523–2445 or 800/447–5224) has travel planner booklets, regional guides, and information on the latest family packages.

The Adirondack Book by Elizabeth Folwell (Berkshire House) is the most complete guide to the entire region, and a good resource when traveling with children.

The New York State Atlas & Gazetteer (DeLorme Mapping, Freeport, ME) is essential if you want to get off the beaten path. The best single road-map I've found to the whole park is published by The Adirondack North Country Association (ANCA) (183 Broadway, Saranac Lake, NY 12983, tel. 518/891–6200).

GETTING IN AND OUT OF THE ADIRONDACKS. **By air:** The major airport closest to the entire region is Albany International Airport (tel. 518/869–9611), 50 miles south of Lake George, which is served by most airlines. The only commercial airport in the area is the Adirondack Airport (tel. 518/891–4600) at Lake Clear, about 30 minutes from Lake Placid. Car rentals are available at both airports.

By train: Amtrak (tel. 800/872–7245) runs trains between New York City and Montreal with a stop in Westport, about 40 miles from Lake Placid. You have to arrange shuttle service (tel. 518/523–4431) in advance, and you'll have to rent a car when you get there.

By bus: Though you can get to Lake Placid on Adirondack Trailways buses from Albany that connect to service from New York City, it's a hassle with kids.

By car: The Adirondack Northway (I–87), which runs north and south on the eastern edge of the region, is the continuation of the New York State Thruway from New York City and is toll-free beyond Albany. It travels north just west of Lake George; for Lake Placid, take the exit for 9N and 73. Lake George is roughly four hours from New

York City; Lake Placid, 5½. Route 30 is the north–south road through the center of the region. The two primary east–west roads are Route 28 in the south (from Lake George to Blue Mountain Lake) and Routes 3 and 73 in the north. If you're coming from Vermont, ferries cross Lake Champlain at Ft. Ticonderoga and Burlington, and a bridge at Crown Point.

GETTING AROUND. No matter where you base your family in the Adirondacks, a car is a must. Blue Mountain Lake is roughly in the center of the Adirondack Park, a little more than 50 miles northwest of Lake George and about 50 miles southwest of Lake Placid.

FAMILY-FRIENDLY TOURS. Overlook Tours (tel. 518/793–7914) puts together theme tours in the Lake George region. Lake Placid Carriage Rides (1 Main St., Lake Placid, tel. 518/523–2483) offers a ride around Mirror Lake that's especially fun right before it turns dark when the lights of the hotels are reflected on the water.

PIT STOPS. At the corner of Canada Street (the main drag) and Beach Road in Lake George village are public bathrooms, and most public beaches also have them. Otherwise, head for a gas station. The municipal parking lot off Main Street in Lake Placid has public bathrooms.

EMERGENCIES. Glens Falls Hospital (100 Park St., Glens Falls, tel. 518/792–3151; 518/761–5261 emergency room) has a 24-hour emergency room. Hudson Headwaters Health Network (Indian Lake, Rte. 28, tel. 518/648–5707) has a physician or physician's assistant on duty. Adirondack Medical Center (Church St., Lake Placid, tel. 518/523–3311) maintains a 24-hour emergency service with physicians on call. For ambulance and fire: call 911 in Lake George, 518/352–7711 in Blue Mountain Lake, and 911 in Lake Placid. For police call 911 in Lake George, 518/585–6200 in Blue Mountain Lake, and 911 in Lake Placid. For poison control: tel. 518/761–5261 in Lake George.

Pharmacy Associates (tel. 518/792–1195) in Glens Falls responds to emergency calls from doctors after hours.

BABY-SITTERS. Most resorts—or any kind of accommodation—have a list of baby-sitters they've used before.

WHEN TO GO. Beginning at the end of June, the summer is prime boating, swimming, and hiking time in and around the region's lakes, but you're likely to find even the touristy places less crowded than the coast. Temperatures can be pleasantly warm, rarely too warm during the day, but they cool off considerably at night. The early fall is even better for hiking than the summer, with fewer mosquitos and less humidity. In winter, the region comes alive with carnivals, snowmobiling, skiing, and ice-skating, but be prepared for very, very cold temperatures and a ton of snow. The spring is the one season not to come: It's basically mud and then black flies, which last into mid-June.

The following holiday events are worth planning for:

3+ Winter Carnival, Saranac Lake. The highlight of the February nine-day winter festival is the ice palace. Tel. 518/891–1990 or 800/347–1992.

ALL The July 4th Fireworks over Mirror Lake in Lake Placid are the highlight after an afternoon and evening of music at the band shell and a parade.

ALL Ice Shows and Figure Skating Competitions take place at the Olympic Arena and Ski Jumping Competitions and demonstrations at the Ski Jumping Complex in July and August. Tel. 518/523–1655.

ALL Lake George Family Festival Week in August at Lake George's Shepard Park includes concerts, puppet shows, and general festivities just for families. Tel. 518/668–5755.

Scoping out the Adirondacks

The Adirondack Park has several distinct regions, but among those, three in particular stand out: busy, yet beautiful Lake George, with its mixture of amusement park attractions and superlative boating; Blue Mountain Lake, ideal for canoeing, a quiet lake vacation, and centrally located for exploration of the park; and Lake Placid, with its spectacular Olympic complex and proximity to high peak hiking.

The lower end of **Lake George** is like an 8-year-old boy's idea of heaven: eight minigolf courses, boat rides, a boardwalk with every conceivable kind of confection and junk food, games and corny gewgaws. This is the most developed part of the Adirondacks, but the rest of the huge lake is still wonderful to explore by motorboat or sail.

For a lake vacation, **Blue Mountain Lake** is the opposite of Lake George, with just enough outdoor activity—short hikes, easy but diverse canoeing, a sprinkle of islands on a small lake, clear, clean but chilly swimming—to occupy families for at least a week. With its many connected lakes and ponds not too far from civilization, it is one of the best areas in the Adirondacks for family canoeing.

Lake Placid has hosted the Winter Olympics twice, in 1932 and in 1980, and the complex, extensively used for training, is open to visitors. It's also on the edge of the High Peak country, the center for not only some of the most difficult and challenging climbing in the East, but also easygoing, simple climbs to great views that families with young kids can enjoy. Unlike Blue Mountain Lake and Lake George, it doesn't shut down on Columbus Day.

Attractions below have been grouped by region, starting with Lake George and ending with Lake Placid.

(ŤŤ 2–15) Fort Ticonderoga. At the other end of Lake George from the village (about 30 miles), this huge stone fort has booming cannon demonstrations and colorful marching music as well as a gift shop with bins of souvenir peace pipes and headdresses. (See Chapter 7.)
Rte. 74 (18 mi east of exit 28 off I-87), Box 390B, Ticonderoga 12883, tel. 518/585-2821.

(ŤŤ 5–15) Fort William Henry. At this re-created log fort, site of the French and Indian War massacre portrayed in *The Last of the Mohicans*, the tour guides give detailed accounts of the gruesome hardships and slaughter of the inhabitants. (See Chapter 7.)
Canada St., Beach Rd. and Rte. 9 entrances, Lake George, tel. 518/668-5471.

(ŤŤ 6+) Saratoga Racetrack. Just 30 miles south of Lake George is the oldest and most famous thoroughbred racetrack in the United States, open only in August.
Rte. 9P, Saratoga Springs, tel. in Aug., 518/584-6200.

(ŤŤ 6+) National Museum of Racing. The short film re-creates the excitement of a day at the races with lots of noise and color but not too much information for young kids to absorb. The gallery exhibits are arranged in an oval to resemble a racecourse; at the entrance you walk through a starting gate. At the Oklahoma Track next door, there's a demonstration of how to brush and curry a racehorse, as well as a screening of the classic film, *National Velvet*.
191 Union Ave., Saratoga Springs, tel. 518/584-0400. Cost: $3 adults, $3 students, under 5 free. Open Mon.–Sat. 10–4:30, Sun. noon–4:30.

(ŤŤ 5–15) Painted Pony Rodeo. The Friday night atmosphere at the country's oldest weekly rodeo seems pretty authentic—steer roping, fantastic trick riding, a few clowns, and a chance to get close to the horses.
Route 9N, Lake Luzerne 02846, tel. 518/696-2421.

(ŤŤ 3–12) Lake George Steamboat Cruises. A cruise on the lake is a must. The

one-hour trip around the Lake George village end of the lake aboard the classic and colorful paddle wheeler, the *Minne-Ha-Ha*, is about the right length for young kids.
🏠 *Beach Rd., tel. 518/668–5777 or 800/553–2628. May–Oct., 6 1-hr trips daily.*

(👫 3+) **Adirondack Museum.** The magic for Gavin at this great regional museum of Adirondack life is its layout: To get to the 22 exhibit areas that overlook the lake you walk down dirt paths to buildings that don't look alike—one is an old Adirondack log cottage filled with twig furniture, and there's an old locomotive you can climb on. (*See* Chapter 8.)
🏠 *Rtes. 28N and 30 (past town), Blue Mountain Lake, tel. 518/352–7311.*

(👫 4–15) **Newcomb Adirondack Visitor Interpretive Center.** Much more than a source of travel information, it is worth visiting for an introduction to the nature and history of the region through guided walks (some for kids) and exhibits. Some of the lovely nature trails have paved surfaces convenient if you have a baby in a stroller.
🏠 *Rte. 28N (exit 29 off I–87), Box 101, Newcomb 12852, tel. 518/582–2000. Open Oct.–Apr., daily 9–5; May–Sept., daily 9–7.*

(👫 4–12) **Bird's Boat Livery Mail Boat.** Tagging along on the pontoon boat that delivers mail to various cottages around Racquette Lake is the best way to get to know it. All you have to do is show up before it leaves—usually about 10 AM, but double check.
🏠 *Bird's Marina, Rte. 28, Raquette Lake, tel. 315/354–4441.*

(👫 4–15) **Paul Smiths Adirondack Interpretive Center.** This is a good stop to get an overview of the Lake Placid region's plants and animals that's really geared to kids. (*See also* Chapter 10.)
🏠 *Adirondack Park Visitor Center, Rte. 30, 12 mi north of Saranac Lake, Box 3000, Paul Smiths 12970, tel. 518/327–3000.*

(👫 6–15) **Olympic Site Tour and Events.** For kids to whom skiing and all winter

sports are more important than the World Series, a visit to the sites of the Olympic facilities in Lake Placid is vital.

The **Olympic Jumping Complex and Kodak Sports Park** (Rte. 73, tel. 518/523–2202) wowed Gavin more than anything else. A glass elevator takes you up 26 stories to an enclosed observation deck at the top of the jump tower. From there the jump looks like a giant's roller coaster that only goes down. Definitely visit it before you watch skiers training and competing; the freestyle aerialists zoom down jumps with special plastic matting and land skis first in a huge pool of water. It's much better than watching the Olympics on TV. The self-guided auto tour package is the best bet: We saved money and were able to spread our visits over two days. Expect lines and start early. The **Olympic Center and Museum** (Main St., tel. 518/523–1655; $3 adults, $2 kids 5–12) is not included in the tour price. *See also* Chapter 11.
🏠 *Olympic Regional Development Authority, Olympic Center, Lake Placid 12946, tel. 518/523–1655 or 800/462–6236; in eastern Canada, 800/858–7782. Tour package (excluding admission on competition days): $15 adults, $12 kids 5–12. Open daily 9–4.*

(👫 5–15) **International Winter Sports Museum.** Typical of the new interactive sports museums where you can use simulators to see how skating or ski jumping would feel, this shiny, technology-packed space absorbs visitors.
🏠 *130 Main St., Lake Placid 12946, tel. 518/523–4100. Cost: $5 adults, $3.50 kids 7–12. Open Oct.–Apr., daily 10–6; May–Sept., daily 10–9.*

(👫 ALL) **Whiteface Mountain.** This is to the Adirondacks what Mt. Washington is to New Hampshire's White Mountains—a must, even though it's not the highest peak here. You can drive the 8-mile highway and climb the steep stone stairs to the summit, or you can take an elevator inside the mountain (better for little kids), reached by a long tunnel. The open summit seemed covered with tourists when we were there, but the view of so many lakes is impressive. The cost, $10 + $3 for each additional person in the car, is included in the Olympic site tour package (see above), as is a ride on the chair lifts over the Olympic Racing Trails.

Action

AMUSEMENTS. Cheerful honky-tonk sums up Lake George village. Its huge variety of fun parks, arcades, and wax museums have the advantage of small crowds and little expense. With 162 holes of miniature golf, Lake George has to be the capital of the sport in the Northeast; even the oldest miniature golf course in the world is right here.

(ALL) Great Escape Fun Park. One hundred rides, shows, and attractions and six themed areas on 140 acres: It's the biggest amusement park in New York state and one of the oldest. Story Town and Jungle Land provide plenty of tame rides far from the screams of those strapped into the incredible Comet roller coaster. The only long lines were for the wet-and-wild attractions.
Rte. 9, between exits 19 and 20 off I-87, Lake George 12845, tel. 518/792-6568.

(6+) Leonelli's Playland Arcade North. We liked this one the best of the crop on Canada Street. It's not the biggest (that's Fun World, at 127), but it had more kids Gavin's age.
227 Canada St., tel. 518/668-5255. Cost: 50¢-$1 for most games. Open daily 9 AM-1 AM.

(2-9) Magic Forest Family Fun Park. A 40-foot statue of Uncle Sam benignly oversees this smaller, calmer park, where kids stick their heads into the mouth of a huge lion's head sculpture for a drink of water and clap their hands on the train ride through a jungle of ferocious animal sculptures to keep the "beasts" from attacking.
Rte. 9, Lake George, tel. 518/668-2448.

(2-10) Santa's Workshop. This Santa's village of buildings and rides has been here since 1949 and has the flavor of the 1950s.
North Pole (near Lake Placid), tel. 518/946-2211.

(ALL) Water Slide World. It's a mix of terrifyingly high looping water-slick slides, a sweet toddler lagoon, a giant wave pool, and the Lazy Adventure River, down which you float on huge tire tubes until the waterfall dunks you. Compared with some other water parks we've been to, this one was clean and the staff friendly. Expect long lines for the slides.
Rtes. 9 and 9L, Lake George, tel. 518/668-4407.

BEACHES. There's a wide selection of beaches in the Adirondacks, from sandy lakesides to secluded islands.

(5-15) Lake George Islands. Forty-eight islands in the lake are open to the public for swimming, picnicking, and (on a few) camping, but you must have a boat to get there and obtain a permit. The Department of Environmental Conservation (Hudson Ave., Warrensburg, NY 12884, tel. 518/668-5441) has season permits ($4.50-$7.50) and information; stop at island headquarters, Glen Island, Narrow Island, or Long Island the day you plan to picnic.

(8-15) Million Dollar Beach. The largest and most famous beach, so-called because of the cost of construction back in the early days of the resort, has more action (volleyball) for older kids, as well as lifeguards, picnic tables, and so on. In back of it is a park with the remains of an old fort.
Beach Rd., east of U.S. 9, tel. 518/668-3352. Cost: $1 adults, 75¢ kids.

(ALL) Shepard Park. This is the family beach: a dock and a diving board, an enclosed swimming area, and so much free family entertainment in summer—regular movies on Thursday night, puppet shows, and the special Family Fun Week concerts in August—that you end up coming here even if you're staying somewhere with a private beach.

🏛 *Canada St., Lake George, tel. 518/668–2864. Admission free.*

BOATING. The boats on Lake George are primarily powerboats and sailboats. The waves on the lake when a wind comes up and the big wakes of the large and numerous speedboats make canoeing with kids a scary enterprise. You can explore some of the lake's many islands (see Lake George Islands, *above,* for information on obtaining permits to land on the islands). Rent a boat from a marina farther up the lake so you don't start out in a traffic jam. **Yankee Yacht Sales** (Rte. 9N, Diamond Point, tel. 518/668–2862) rents both motorboats and sailboats and even offers weekend sailing courses in June and July and private sailing lessons throughout the summer. Even farther north, **Water's Edge Marina** (Sagamore Rd., Bolton Landing, tel. 518/644–2511) rents ski boats.

CAMPING. The campsites nearest to Blue Mountain Lake are on **Lake Durant** (Rte. 28 about 3 mi east of Blue Mountain Lake, tel. 518/352–7797). These have a swimming beach, canoe rentals, and showers. But the most beautiful primitive campsites (best with older kids) are the island sites on **Indian Lake** (off Rte. 30, 11 mi south of Indian Lake hamlet, tel. 518/648–5300). **Fish Creek Pond Campground** (Rte. 30, west of Saranac Lake, tel. 518/891–4560) feels like a wilderness but has all the amenities of showers and canoe rentals at the center of a short, easy canoe route (see *below*), and it is one of the New York state campgrounds that offers camping gear to borrow free through the Camper Assistance Program (see Chapter 12). **Saranac Lake Islands Campsites** are beautiful and primitive, but not far from shore. (See Chapter 12.) The Department of Environmental Conservation (tel. 518/457–2500) will provide site maps and brochures. To reserve campsites, call 800/456–2267.

CANOEING. I can't imagine staying at Blue Mountain Lake and not spending some time in a canoe exploring the lake and its small, uninhabited islands of rock and pine. Most of the resorts provide canoes, but you can rent them from **Blue Mountain Outfitters** (see Canoeing in Chapter 12). With little kids just paddling to an island is a big deal; older kids with some canoeing experience might like to try the route through the connected lakes and camp out one night. Lake Durant (2 miles east on Route 28) is good for younger kids and beginning canoers because no motorboats are permitted on it. Around Blue Mountain Lake are a host of other lakes and chains of lakes to explore in a canoe; it's possible to travel all the way to Old Forge or to the St. Regis canoe area north of here.

👫 **6 – 15**) **Fish Creek Ponds Loop.** Seven different ponds and a creek make up this 12-mile canoe loop west of Saranac Lake, where you'll see lots of wildlife. Any part of this is good with younger kids. You can even spend a day with a guide here. **St. Regis Canoe Outfitters** (Box 318, Lake Clear 12945, tel. 518/891–1838) has experience with families; they run a regular introduction to canoeing for kids.

FISHING. The **Steel Pier in Lake George,** where all the cruise boats dock, is a neat place for kids to throw in a line, something they can also do along the boardwalk. **Beach Road Outdoor Supply** (Beach Rd., Lake George, tel. 518/668–4040) sells bait.

Check with the **Pumpkin Mountain Gun Shop** (Rtes. 28 and 30, Blue Mountain Lake, tel. 518/352–7772) or **Blue Mountain Lake Boat Livery** (tel. 518/352–7351), which sell bait and fishing tackle, for the best fishing spots. At Long Lake, we pulled in some sunfish and perch fairly quickly at the Town Dock behind the Post Office.

There are so many ponds and lakes and rivers around Lake Placid that the most-up-to-date tips on what is biting where are important. **All Seasons Outfitters** (168

Lake Flower Ave., Saranac Lake 12983, tel. 518/891–6159) guides stream and pond float fishing trips for families and has gear.

👫 5 – 15 **High Peaks Base Camp, Fish Farm, and the Wood Parlor Restaurant.** For non-fishing families in the Lake Placid region, a stop here is an easy way for kids to fish and then eat their catch without your having to clean it. The spring-fed pond is stocked; equipment is available. Be warned that service from the kitchen is sometimes slow.
🏠 *Springfield Rd., Wilmington, tel. 518/946–2133. Reservations advised. AE, MC, V. $–$$*

HIKES AND WALKS. Lake George. With little kids, strolling Lake George's boardwalk from the docks holds the delights of ducks to feed and benches to rest on and boats to watch. The Adirondack Mountain Club (Luzerne Rd., Lake George, tel. 518/668–4447) has an office that schedules guided hiking trips, The Adirondack Mountain Club guidebook, *An Adirondack Sampler,* lists easy to moderately difficult hikes in the whole region. The Department of Environmental Conservation (Hudson Ave., Warrensburg, tel. 518/623–3671) has free individual trail brochures.

👫 8+ **Prospect Mountain.** The view from the 2,100-foot summit is spectacular, but it tends to get crowded. If you have little kids and don't want to climb, free trams run regularly to the top, where you can see 100 miles into Vermont and New Hampshire.
🏠 *Prospect Mountain Memorial Hwy., off Rte. 9 (5½-mi drive from parking area to summit; trailhead begins on Montcalm St.), Lake George, tel. 518/668–5198. Cost: $5. Open daily 9–6.*

👫 4+ **Pack Forest.** For little kids the diverse nature trails to ponds and by a river in this experimental forest may be much more interesting than the Prospect Mountain climb and vista.
🏠 *Rte. 9, past Rte. 28 junction, Warrensburg. Admission free.*

Blue Mountain Lake. Of the eight trails near Blue Mountain Lake, four are 1 mile or less. Forget the trail to Blue Mountain's summit (2½ miles each way) with little ones; it is very steep, with rocky patches tough to navigate on the way down. The two easiest and most level are the trails off Route 28 to Rock Lake. The free "Woodland Trails of Blue Mountain Lake" map is available from shops in the town.

Lake Placid. One of the easiest walks in the Lake Placid region, ideal if you're pushing a stroller or eating ice-cream cones, is the 2½-mile sidewalk around Mirror Lake. Early in the morning you may glimpse U.S. Olympic rowing and kayaking teams working out.

The High Peaks district directly south of Lake Placid has some rugged trails, but we've tried several short ones even younger kids can manage. **Owls Head** (off Rte. 73 between Lake Placid and Keene; watch for sign about 3 mi past Cascade Lake) is a rocky peak with views and blueberries to pick along the ½-mile trail to the summit. It takes about 40 minutes to an hour to climb to **Balanced Boulder** (off Rte. 73, 8 mi south of Lake Placid by Cascade Lake), a spectacular rock formation that looks just the way it sounds. We finished off with a dip in Cascades Lake.

The **Adirondack Mountain Club** (off Rte. 73, Box 867, Lake Placid 12946, tel. 518/523–3441) has trail maps, good suggestions, and great guided hikes and programs for families (see Chapter 12); from the Chamber of Commerce you can get a free list of good hikes put out by the ADK.

HORSEBACK RIDING. Warren County, right around Lake George, is noted for dude ranches and trail rides. The best bet for families who want to ride frequently is staying at a ranch resort (see Where to Stay, below).

MINIATURE GOLF. Our family usually can't bear to pass up a miniature golf course, no matter how uninteresting-looking. In Lake George you can quickly become a connoisseur: Out of the six right in town, two appealed to us especially. Costs for one round of golf range from $3.50 to $5.

👥 5 – 15 Around the World in 18 Holes Mini-Golf. A huge statue of Paul Bunyan towers over a course where each hole is one of the world's landmark buildings. It's old and a classic.
🏠 *Beach Rd., Lake George 12845, tel. 518/ 668–2531. Open mid-Apr.–Sept., daily.*

👥 5+ Magic Castle Indoor Golf. Our mainstay when it rained was this unique course inside a building shaped like a castle.
🏠 *275 Canada St., Lake George, tel. 518/ 668–3777. Open daily.*

MOUNTAIN BIKING. A new Mountain Bike Center at the Mt. Van Hoevenberg Olympic Cross-Country Area uses the network of ski trails through forest and by streams for mountain biking; many are easy family fun. **High Peaks Cyclery** (331 Main St., Lake Placid 12946, tel. 518/523–3764), which runs the Mountain Bike Center, rents bikes and helmets, including youth sizes, and has pamphlets of good road and off-road trails in the area.

ROCK HOUNDING. Rock lovers can find good pickings halfway between Blue Mountain Lake and Lake George.

👥 6 – 13 Barton Garnet Mines. A 45-minute drive brings you to an open-pit mine where kids can pick up garnets and visit a great mineral shop. (See Chapter 12.)
🏠 *Rte. 28, North Creek 12853, tel. 518/ 251–2706.*

SWIMMING. The Adirondacks' lakes, whether surrounded by cottages or wilderness, provide refreshing, sometimes chilly, swimming. All the recommended lodging spots are next to water. For the **Lake George area,** see Beaches, *above,* and Where to Stay, *below.* For **Blue Mountain Lake,** see Where to Stay, *below.* In the **Lake Placid** region, calm **Mirror Lake** is fine for little kids, especially as it does not permit

motorboats. For more remote swimming, **Heart Lake,** next to the Adirondack Mountain Club's lodge (see Where to Stay, *below*) is just at the edge of wilderness. The deep, chilly **Cascade Lakes** off Route 73, nestled into the chasm between Cascade and Pitchoff Mountain, are so narrow you can almost throw a stone across. It's a bit of a drive from Lake Placid to **Chapel Pond,** south of Keene Valley on Route 73, but above this glacial pond with good rocks to climb and sit on are crags favored by rock climbers.

WHITE-WATER RAFTING. In this region most of the rafting trips, on the Upper Hudson River, are too dangerous for kids.

👥 8 – 15 Sacandaga River. This short, safe trip on an easy river is the only one in the region I can recommend for families. (*See Chapter 12.*) **W.I.L.D. W.A.T.E.R.S.** (Rte. 28, Box 197A, HCR01, Warrensburg, 12885, tel. 518/494–7478) runs regular trips daily and offers instruction in canoeing and kayaking.

WINTER SPORTS. For skiing at Whiteface Mountain, cross-country skiing, and ice-skating, see Chapter 13.

Shopping

MALLS AND MAIN STREETS. The Adirondacks are not primarily shopping destinations, but you can find some interesting stores here.

👥 ALL Canada Street is souvenir street: T-shirt shops galore, Indian headdress schlock, kitschy postcards.
🏠 *Lake George.*

👥 13 – 15 Million Dollar Half-Mile Factory Outlets. More than 70 outlet stores are arranged in four separate plazas next to and across the road from one another.
🏠 *Rte. 9, north of exit 20 off I–87, Lake George.*

You might as well comb all the shops in **Blue Mountain Lake:** There are only three. We bought a birch-bark origami bird at the tiny **Adirondack Lakes Center for the Arts shop** (tel. 518/352–7715; see Entertainment and the Arts, *below*). The biggest shop is at the **Adirondack Museum** (see Scoping out the Adirondacks, *above*), which carries tapes of famous Adirondack storytellers who we heard at the Adirondack Lakes Center for the Arts.

In nearby **Long Lake, Hoss's Country Corner** (Rtes. 28N and 30, tel. 518/624–2481) has ice cream, worms, and a game room, not to mention a few magazines, books, and general picnic supplies.

Lake Placid's Main Street has some kitsch, and kids we know happily spend evenings walking it while their parents finish dinner. **Parajax** (tel. 518/523–9399) has the best selection of T-shirts, odd games, and stuffed animals. At **Adirondack Trading Company** (tel. 518/523–3651), full of doodads like cedar sachets, you can find bear-foot slippers. **Where'd You Get That Hat?** (tel. 518/523–3101) has wacky new and used hats. At the **U.S. Olympic Committee Gift Shop** (U.S. Olympic Training Center, 421 Old Military Rd., Lake Placid, tel. 518/523–4856) you can use the discount coupon in the brochure from the Visitors Bureau.

Eats

Adirondacks restaurants range from old-timey roadside diners to gourmet establishments with ironed white tablecloths, including lots of fairly good family restaurants. Local food specialties are trout and game (along with Adirondack Bear Claw candy, see *below*); atmosphere is what makes most of the restaurants listed below special. Dress is casual unless otherwise indicated.

Picnicking on a Lake George island can mean a picnic on a slab of rock, your boat rocking gently at anchor, and swimming afterward. To us Blue Mountain Lake's many tiny islands, where you can beach a canoe on flat rocks and spread a blanket under pine trees, hold the best picnic places. At Buttermilk Falls, several miles north of town on North Point Road (left off Rte. 28N), you'll find picnic tables and fireplaces within a short walk of the falls.

4 – 15 **Boathouse.** The wraparound deck above Mirror Lake and a sandy beach below plus food that pleases both kids and grown-ups (even a wine list) are reasons to come here. Pasta servings can be ordered in three sizes. The building actually used to be a boathouse.
Lake Placid Club Dr., Lake Placid, tel. 518/523–4822. Reservations advised. MC, V. $–$$

ALL **Log Jam Restaurant.** It looks like a log cabin inside and out, and the atmosphere is just as casual. It serves solid American fare with a few fish choices.
Rtes. 9 and 149, Lake George, tel. 518/798–1155. Kids' menu, booster seats, high chairs. Reservations advised. AE, DC, MC, V. $$–$$$

ALL **Mary T's.** The quintessential deli, with fresh-baked bread and the best sandwiches to go, this Lake Placid institution is a base for picnickers.
89 Saranac Lake Ave., Lake Placid, tel. 518/523–9750. No reservations. $

ALL **Noon Mark Diner.** The dining room of this friendly two-room diner has big windows that let in the sun. It's usually filled with hikers with backpacks, tourists, families with wiggly kids, and a couple of business folk in suits. Breakfast is served all day, along with hamburgers, chili, small steaks, and great ice-cream sundaes.
Main St., Rte. 73, Keene Valley, tel. 518/576–4499. No reservations. No credit cards. $

ALL **Potter's Restaurant.** The food is not fabulous, but the atmosphere is pure Adirondack—a birch-bark canoe under the rafters, a collection of stuffed animals on the walls, a view of the lake, where you can watch families arrive by boat. Lunch—burgers and French dip sandwiches—is the better bet.

🏠 *Rtes. 28 and 30, Blue Mountain Lake, tel. 518/352–7664. Reservations advised for dinner. AE, D, MC, V. $$*

(👫 ALL) **Shoreline Restaurant and Marina.** From the wraparound deck (a blue canopy screens the sun) you see busy boats and the public docks and water. Food is okay steaks and ribs and pasta, with chicken wings and other dishes with kid appeal. This is one of many similar lakefront restaurants.
🏠 *4 Kurosaka La., behind post office, Lake George, tel. 518/668–2875. Kids' menu. Reservations advised. AE, MC, V. $$*

(👫 ALL) **Tail o' the Pup.** When we spied the chrome-based stools at outside counters hanging off a squat little building flying the stars and stripes, we knew we'd found a classic roadside restaurant. For 50 years it's been serving great American road food, chicken and ribs in tangy barbecue sauce with waffle fries and cole slaw.
🏠 *Rte. 86, halfway between Lake Placid and Saranac Lake, Ray Brook, tel. 518/891–5092. Kids' menu, booster seats, high chairs. No reservations. No credit cards. $*

(👫 ALL) **Wagar's Soda Fountain & Candy Factory.** They do have inexpensive sandwiches and burgers, but we come for the ice-cream concoctions (thick hot fudge on sundaes) and the chocolate cigarettes with great labels like "Old Toad—Smoke Till You Croak" that reminded John and me of our own childhoods. Don't leave without trying their specialty: Adirondack bear claws—caramel covered with dark chocolate and spiked with nuts.
🏠 *327 Canada St., Lake George, tel. 518/ 668–2693. No reservations. $*

Where to Stay

The motels cramming the main road through Lake George village are a bit depressing. Try staying outside the town where you can really experience the lake—either farther up the lake in Diamond Point or Bolton Landing, or at an inexpensive lake-side cottage in nearby Lake Luzerne. See also Chapter 14 for resorts.

The tiny hamlet of Blue Mountain Lake has a handful of accommodations, most clustered around the eastern end of the lake alongside a few churches, a post office, a store, a boat livery, and a public beach. There is no campground. See also Chapter 14.

A wide variety of inexpensive-to-expensive lodging in individual houses, condos, lodges, hotels, cabins, motels, and bed-and-breakfasts is available in Lake Placid; lists are available from The Lake Placid Visitors Bureau (see The Basics, above).

The price categories that follow are based on summer-season rates and reflect what a family of four would spend for one night in a double room or the smallest appropriate accommodation available (sometimes a cottage): $$$, over $125; $$, $60–$125; $, under $60. When resorts are MAP or AP, categories are: $$$$, over $450; $$$, $350–$450; $$, $200–$350; $, under $200. Prices do not include 7% sales tax.

(👫 ALL) **Adirondack Loj.** The bed-and-breakfast lodge run by the Adirondack Mountain Club is a rustic, comfortable place perched at the edge of the wilderness with hiking trails up the high peaks and lake swimming right outside the door. We like the cozy bunk rooms with four built-in log beds that make you feel you're on board a ship. Meals are family style in a pine dining room at picnic tables.
🏠 *Adirondack Loj Rd., Lake Placid 12946, tel. 518/523–3441. 14 family, double, and bunk rooms with shared bath; campground. Kids under 2 free. Facilities: dining room, beach, swimming, fishing, hiking trails, High Peaks information center, nature museum and program, guided walks and talks, kids' nature programs. Rates include breakfast. MC, V. $*

(👫 0 – 13) **Best Western Golden Arrow Hotel.** European modern right on the lake, it's casual and comfortable, with more atmosphere than most motels in the chain, within walking distance of everything in town (across from the Olympic Center), yet still with great views.

🏠 *150 Main St., Lake Placid 12946, tel. 518/523–3353 or 800/582–5540. 125 rooms, 4 with kitchen, 7 with fireplace. Facilities: cable, indoor heated pool, kiddie pool, private beach, boats and dock, baby-sitting. Kids under 13 stay free. AE, D, DC, MC, V. $$*

👫 5–15 Canoe Island Lodge. What attracts us most about this lodge and assorted cottages on a Lake George hillside are the boating and the 4-mile-long private island for swimming and water sports. Flotillas of launches manned by college kids ferry families back and forth, a treat in itself. An air of casual elegance coexists with kids scrambling about the complex network of stone stairways and bridges and paths.

🏠 *Lake Shore Dr., Diamond Point, 12824, tel. 518/668–5592. 65 rooms. Facilities: island, sandy beach, sailboats, rowboats, Windsurfers, tennis courts, small playground, game room with ping-pong and TV. Rates include breakfast and dinner. Reduced rates for kids. No credit cards. $$$–$$$$*

👫 0–12 Curry's Cottages. We were charmed 20 years ago by these cute but simple barn-red cottages (some with fireplaces) with a straight line of white Adirondack chairs by their sandy beach; toddlers splashed in the shallow water then just as they do now. The cottages on the water are better for families than those across the road at the edge of the woods.

🏠 *Rte. 28, Blue Mountain Lake 12812, tel. 518/352–7354; in winter, 518/352–7355. 10 1- to 3-bedroom cottages. Facilities: sand beach. No credit cards. $–$$*

👫 ALL Lakeview Fireplace Cottages. The log-sided cabins with their big screened-in porches sit comfortably under pines by the shore of tiny Lake Vanare. The beach is a sunny peninsula with shallow water and canoes; a roped-in swimming area keeps kids safe. Furnishings are sturdy. Unlike many cottages in the Lake George vicinity, all have big fireplaces and stacks of logs.

🏠 *3199 Lake Ave., Box 174, Lake Luzerne 12846, tel. 518/696–3197. 6 1-, 2-, and 3-bedroom cottages. Facilities: boats, beach. Rates include linens and firewood. Rentals by week only. AE, D, MC, V. $–$$*

👫 0–12 Prospect Point Cottages. Away from the road on a private point with a big sandy beach, these cottages have fantastic views of the lake and a wide green lawn yet are within walking distance of town.

🏠 *Rte. 28, Blue Mountain Lake 12812, tel. 518/352–7378. 10 2- and 3-bedroom cottages. Facilities: private beach, boats, dock, playground. No credit cards. $$*

👫 ALL Rydin' Hy Ranch Resort. One of the several dude ranches in Warren County, it's the least refined, the most kid-friendly, and the only one with its own shallow, sand-bottom lake and activities to match. A couple of ponies are tied to a tree outside the main lodge so little kids can climb on and be led around any time. Kids whoop and holler in the lobby. If you want to ride morning and afternoon, you can. Beware Boy Scout troops.

🏠 *Sherman Lake, Warrensburg 12885, tel. 518/494–2742. 12 cabins, 24 rooms in motel units, 4 2-room suites, 8 rooms in main lodge. Rooms are child-proofed. Facilities: 800 acres with trails, trail and horseback riding, pony rides, indoor pool, lake beach, waterskiing, boating, fishing, tennis, volleyball, shuffleboard, game room, horseshoes, rodeos, supervised kids' program, baby-sitting. Rooms are child-proof. Many family packages. Rates include 3 meals daily. AE, D, MC, V. $$–$$$*

👫 6+ Timberlock. This is a place for sophisticated families who want the authentic, unpretentious flavor of a small rustic Adirondack lake camp (unheated cabins have only propane lanterns and wood stoves; the oilcloth-topped dining table is on an open porch with plastic shades for bad weather) in a beautiful setting, but also the myriad water sports for kids, including teens, that you usually find only at a bigger resort. It's 10 miles from Blue Mountain Lake but worth the trek. Here you'll find good hearty food, nightly campfires, boats, horses for trail rides, and other kid stuff that's great, like the rope swing that drops kids into the water.

🏠 *Indian Lake, Sabael 12864, tel. 518/648–5494; in winter, 802/457–1621. 10 2- and 3-bedroom cottages, 4 1-room cabins with bath, 7 1-room cabins with shared bath; no electricity. Facilities: sand beach (with swings), canoes, kayaks, rowboats, Windsurfers, horseback riding, tennis, children's lodge with toys and ping-pong, nature programs, adventure camp for teens, waterskiing, baby-sitting. Rate includes 3 meals daily. No credit cards. $$–$$$*

Entertainment and the Arts

(👫 4 – 15) **Adirondack Lakes Center for the Arts.** It's the coziest-looking art center you can imagine—a former garage painted blue with a long box of pink and white flowers edging the porch. Few other vacation communities the size of Blue Mountain Lake can offer regular performances of everything from movies to zydeco music to fiddle jamborees along with family arts and crafts workshops and storytelling.

🏠 *Rte. 28, Box 101, Blue Mountain Lake 12812, tel. 518/352–7715.*

(👫 ALL) **Lake Placid Center for the Arts.** A regular Family Fun series features the classic staples of good summer kids' theater programs (like the Mettawee Theater Company's larger-than-life puppet shows of myths) and a few comedy surprises.

🏠 *Saranac Ave., Lake Placid, tel. 518/523–2512.*

(👫 0 – 12) **Lake Placid Sinfonietta.** The free Wednesday night orchestra concerts at the village park band shell on the shore of Mirror Lake are a family affair. Adults sit on folding chairs, kids on the grass, and teens glide by in paddleboats with their dates. Bring insect repellent.

🏠 *Box 1303, Lake Placid, tel. 518/523–2051.*

(👫 8+) **Saratoga Performing Arts Center.** The summer home of the New York City Ballet, it's one of the best places to see first-class dance and music performances in July and August, and it's only a 30-minute drive from Lake George. If you plan to attend a dance matinee (best for younger kids), call the National Museum of the Dance (South Broadway, Saratoga Springs, tel. 518/584–2225) to reserve a spot on the special behind-the-scenes tour offered to kids.

🏠 *Saratoga Springs 12866, tel. 518/587–3330.*

The White Mountains, New Hampshire

Vistas of bare peaks roll on for miles, as though you're on a vast bumpy sea. Among the region's many other pleasures are pulling in a fish from an icy pool, riding the world's oldest mountain railway, canoeing a slow river, sleeping in a tent serenaded by owls, picnicking on a rock ledge, spotting a moose by a boggy pond. Less spread out than the Adirondack region, it offers the same wild, mountainous terrain, but with a New England flavor.

The western White Mountains (see Chapter 10 for outdoor highlights around the towns of Lincoln, North Woodstock, and Franconia Notch) is linked to the less crowded, more diverse Mt. Washington Valley area to the east by the scenic Kancamagus Highway. My pick as the ideal base for a family stay in the White Mountains is the Mt. Washington Valley, especially the unspoiled village of **Jackson** and dramatic **Pinkham Notch**, near Mt. Washington itself.

The Basics

HOW TO FIND OUT WHAT'S GOING ON.
Mt. Washington Valley Visitors Bureau (Box 2300, North Conway 03860, tel. 603/356–3171) puts out the *Official Guide to Mt. Washington Valley* and a "Tips and

Tours" planning guide that lists everything from accommodations to where to find covered bridges. **Jackson Resort Association** (Box 304, Jackson 03846, tel. 603/383–9356 or 800/866–3334 except New Hampshire and Canada) publishes a free travel guide and will book accommodations. For camping, biking and hiking trails, and canoeing, check with the **White Mountain National Forest** (Box 638, Laconia 03246, tel. 603/528–8721), which also publishes a regular newsletter, and when you arrive, the **Saco Ranger Station** (on the Kancamagus Hwy. just off Rte. 16, Conway, tel. 603/447–5448), which not only has comprehensive information, but much experience in assessing White Mountains hikes and activities in terms of children. The **New Hampshire Division of Parks and Recreation** (Box 856, Concord 03301, tel. 603/271–3556, parks, or 603/271–3627, recreation office) has information on state parks. For other trail maps and hiking information see Hikes, Walks, and Climbs in Sports and Activities, below.

The *Mountain Ear* (Conway, tel. 603/447–6336) is the local weekly newspaper; it lists happenings and events of interest to families and carries restaurant ads.

The *New Hampshire Atlas and Gazetteer* (DeLorme Publishing, Freeport, ME 04032) has detailed maps of the region, a good fishing guide, plus listings of campgrounds, covered bridges, nature areas, and much more.

GETTING TO AND FROM THE WHITE MOUNTAINS. By air: The major airport closest to Jackson is **Portland Jetport** in Portland, Maine (tel. 207/774–3941), about a 90-minute drive to the southwest. Major airlines flying to the **Manchester, New Hampshire, Municipal Airport** (tel. 603/624–6556) include United, USAir, Delta Connection, Northwest, and several commuter links. It is about 100 miles south of Jackson. Both airports have major car-rental agencies.

By car: The interstate nearest the Mt. Washington area, I–93, runs north and

south through the western White Mountains; Route 112, the scenic Kancamagus Highway, links it with Route 16, the primary north–south highway through the Mt. Washington Valley; Route 302, which joins it for a short distance, branches off to the west and is always less crowded.

By bus: Concord Trailways (tel. 800/639–3317) runs from Boston to various points in the valley.

GETTING AROUND THE WHITE MOUNTAINS. By car: To travel around the Mt. Washington and Jackson areas comfortably with a family, you must have a car. All airports have most major car-rental agencies, including the small regional airport at Conway. Be warned that Route 16 between Conway and North Conway is often a matter of stopping and starting in traffic on weekends. You can try to bypass it by using the West Side Road in Conway to River Road, then Route 16 or Route 32.

EMERGENCIES. Memorial Hospital (Rte. 16, North Conway; emergency room tel. 603/356–5461). For **ambulance, fire,** and **police** in North Conway and Conway: call 911. For **ambulance** in other towns, tel. 603/539–6119. For **poison control** tel. 800/562–8236. **CVS Pharmacy** (Shaw's North Way Plaza, Rte. 16, North Conway, tel. 603/356–6916) is centrally located and open until 8 PM in summer.

WHEN TO GO. The White Mountains have family appeal in winter for skiing and in summer and early fall for hiking, canoeing, and everything else. Avoid arriving before mid-June because of the black fly season.

The following celebrations are worth planning for:

Winter carnivals and family ski weeks fill February in most of Mt. Washington Valley's five ski resorts.

Blueberry Festival (Attitash, tel. 603/374–2368), in August, features a blueberry olympics, picking blueberries, and trying everything from blueberry syrup to muffins and pie.

Scoping out the White Mountains

The Mt. Washington Valley has attractions, action, and lodging to entertain families four seasons of the year. **Conway** and **North Conway** at its southern end are the commercial hub, with factory outlets, outdoor-equipment shops, minigolf, and movie theaters—plus access to fine canoeing and a lake with a sandy beach. Farther north are **Glen**, which has several commercial attractions that appeal to kids, and **Jackson** (see Chapter 13), where we most like to stay. Still farther north is dramatic, less developed **Pinkham Notch**, home of the Appalachian Mountain Club, wonderful hiking, and the road up Mt. Washington. To the northwest of Jackson is **Crawford Notch**, the least developed and most magnificent of the White Mountains' narrow high passes, with the area's most scenic waterfalls, views, and more hikes; **Bretton Woods** to the north, a center for skiing, has the region's grandest hotel, and one of the world's oldest railways.

(6 – 15) **Mt. Washington.** At 6,288 feet, New Hampshire's highest peak is a real mountain even in Western terms. From the distance it looks impressive, the summit often in clouds. Even if you don't get to the top—you should—it's omnipresent as you drive and hike in the valley. It has incredible views (as far as the Atlantic Ocean) from the summit—if you're not fogged in, as happens 300 days of the year.

About 100 people have died on Mt. Washington, mostly because of extreme changes in weather conditions in summer for which they were unprepared. Temperatures can drop drastically within hours and the wind has been clocked at 231 miles per hour, the world record. In fact, even though Mt. Washington is not nearly as high as many peaks out West, it's considered to have the

worst combination of wind, cold, and ice of any regularly inhabited place on earth— worse than anywhere outside of the regions at the North and South Pole.

There are three ways to get to the top: hike, which is not recommended for families—it's a tough slog and the weather is too unpredictable and dangerous; take the 19th-century cog railway, the second steepest railway in the world (see below); or drive the steep 8-mile-long Auto Road (Rte. 16, Pinkham Notch, Gorham, tel. 603/466–3988; see Chapter 10) that climbs all the way up.

(7+) **Mt. Washington Cog Railway.** The train trestles and tracks snaking up to the top of Mt. Washington were the world's first mountain-climbing cog railway, built in 1869. The one-car train is pulled by a cute green and red coal-burning engine. On the way back, the engine backs down the steep 37% grade in front of the car to act as a brake. The cog wheels fit into slots between the rails. The round trip takes three hours, with a break at the top to visit the observation center. *Rte. 302, Bretton Woods 03575, tel. 603/846–5404 or 800/922–8825, Ext. 7. Reservations advised. Cost (round-trip): $32 adults, $22 kids, under 6 free; 8 AM fares discounted. Open May–Oct.*

(3 – 12) **Conway Scenic Railroad.** In contrast to the cog railway, this is a soothing rather than exciting ride, best for younger kids. You can eat a meal in the dining car. The hour-long trip includes a short layover in Conway. In 1995, another similar old-fashioned train starts runs up to Crawford Notch. *Main St., North Conway 03860, tel. 603/356–5251 or 800/232–5251. Cost: $7.50–$9.50 adults, $5–$7 kids 4–12. Open May–Oct.*

(4 – 15) **Wildcat Mountain Gondola.** To us the ride was worth it even though we'd already been to the top of Mt. Washington because the view of the peaks of the Presidential Range. Little kids who can't climb a mountain this high (and older kids who don't want to) may enjoy the ride and the nature trails the most.

🏔 *Rte. 16, Jackson, tel. 603/466–3326. Cost: $8 adults, $4 kids 6–12. Open mid-May–July 4, weekends 10–4; July 4–Columbus Day, daily 10–4.*

Action

AMUSEMENTS. Places to go on rainy days or just for fun are sprinkled throughout the region.

👫 **6+** **Attitash Alpine Slide and Outdoor Amusements.** This is one-stop amusement shopping with an all-you-can-eat price. An all-day ticket allows kids to ride the water slides, the ¾-mile alpine slide, and the chair lift up and down until they really are tired of it. The ticket doesn't include the pony rides or the golf driving range.

🏔 *Rte. 302, Bartlett 03812, tel. 603/374–2368. Cost: $16, single rides $6.50. Open mid-June–Labor Day, daily 10–6; Memorial Day–mid-June and Labor Day–Columbus Day, weekends 10–5.*

👫 **5 – 15** **Fun Factory Amusement Park.** Go for the video arcade if you feel deprived, not the miniature golf, is Gavin's advice. The giant double water slide is not much compared with the Water World park in Lake George, but it is something.

🏔 *Rte. 16, south of North Conway center, tel. 603/356–6541. Fees for individual activities. Minigolf open May–Oct.; water slide open Memorial Day–Labor Day; arcade open weekdays 5–10, weekends 10 AM–11 PM.*

👫 **4 – 13** **Heritage New Hampshire.** A portrayal of New Hampshire's history through scenes and special effects is touristy but fun for an hour and a half on a rainy day.

🏔 *Rte. 16 (6 mi north of North Conway), Glen, tel. 603/383–9776.*

👫 **4+** **Pirate's Cove Adventure Golf.** Definitely the best minigolf in the area, say Gavin and his friend, who could have done it over and over.

🏔 *Rte. 16, North Conway 03860, tel. 603/356–8807. Cost: $5.50 adults, $5 kids under 13. Open mid-May–Oct., daily.*

👫 **2 – 11** **Story Land.** This nursery rhyme and fairy-tale theme park in the woods has much more charm than most such places. The price includes all rides, shows, parking, strollers, even a kennel service and loaner camera.

🏔 *Rte. 16 (6 mi north of Conway), Glen, tel. 603/383–4293.*

CAMPING. The White Mountains' wealth of camping opportunities includes a site especially suited to families:

👫 **6 – 13** **Crawford Notch General Store and Campground.** This is secluded wilderness camping in the most beautiful section of the Mt. Washington valley. Unlike the primitive tent sites in Crawford Notch State Park, these have a store and showers. Sites are along the Saco River.

🏔 *Rte. 302, Hart's Location 03812, tel. 603/374–2779. 70 sites. Kids under 16 free with parents. Facilities: camp store, hot showers, swimming, fishing, mountain biking, hiking trails, shuttle service. Reservations advised. MC, V.*

CANOEING AND KAYAKING. Of the White Mountains' many waterways, one in particular offers good conditions.

👫 **3+** **Saco River.** This shallow, sandy-bottomed river is one of the most perfect in the Northeast for both short and long family canoe or kayak trips no matter how old your kids. Take a short route from River Road in North Conway to a long sandy beach just after the covered bridge. Reserve rentals far in advance. (See Canoeing in Chapter 12.) **Saco Bound** (Center Conway, tel. 603/447–2177) has rentals.

CLIMBING. North Conway is one of the two major centers for learning to rock climb in the Northeast. **Mt. Cranmore Recreation Center** (North Conway, tel. 603/356–6301) offers two-hour instruction sessions to a family of four for $100 using a large indoor climbing wall.

FISHING. The cold, deep ponds, wide rivers, and winding streams in the White Mountains hold brown and brook trout, lake trout, bass and salmon. You are more likely to actually catch fish on the Swift River along the Kancamagus Highway just west of North Conway, the Saco River, especially off West Side Road past Humphrey's Ledge and route 302 in Harts Location and Crawford Notch, and the Wildcat River just past the iron bridge in Jackson. Tiny Saco Lake in Crawford Notch, where we've been lucky, is very easy to get to and usually not crowded. For fly-fishing information and gear, **North Country Angler** (North Main St., Conway, tel. 603/356–6000) rents rods ($25 a day) and teaches fly fishing to kids (10 and up) as well as adults. For other types of bait and equipment, try **Patch's Gun Shop** (Glen, tel. 603/383–6545).

Kids 12 to 15 need a junior fishing license, which costs $5, available at the North Country Angler. The New Hampshire Fish and Game Department (tel. 603/271–3421) can give you additional information. If your kids (and you) are really serious about fishing, *New Hampshire Fishing Maps*, published by DeLorme Publishing (Freeport, ME 04032) give detailed information on 100 prime spots.

(**†† 3+**) Hill's Nursery Pond. Down a private road behind this florist and nursery is a field with a few big trees and a pond stocked with rainbow trout for fishing that looks like it belongs on a farm; families bring picnics and blankets and make an afternoon of it.
🏠 *Rtes. 16 and 302, Intervale 03845, tel. 800/640–5750. Cost: $2 kids over 10, $1 kids 4–10; pole rental, $1; worms, $1.75; fish, 30¢ per inch. Open daily 10–4.*

HIKES, WALKS, AND CLIMBS. Mt. Washington Valley's trails range from easygoing to highly challenging, up many peaks over 4,000 feet, as well as to waterfalls, along streams and rivers, to high mountain lakes. The mountains here have more of an alpine feel than the dense woods of the

Adirondacks. For families, the Appalachian Mountain Club's system of huts, guided hikes, lodges, and family programs helps even those with small children feel comfortable hiking farther afield. The AMC has the best information on trails and trail conditions; we always stop at the **Pinkham Notch Visitor Center** (Rte. 16, Pinkham Notch Visitor Center, Box 29, Gorham 03581, tel. 603/466–2727; see *also* Chapters 13 and 15) for advice, encouragement, and maps, and sometimes come back to have dinner. (See *also* Hiking *in* Chapter 12.) A few more:

When Gavin was small, he was captivated by the **sidewalk loop in Jackson** frequented by joggers that goes through town and the covered bridge. The **Rob Brook Road Trail** (on left off Bear Notch Rd., 12 mi west of Conway off Kancamagus Highway) is great for viewing wildlife. **Crystal Cascade/Tuckerman Ravine Trail** (under 1 mile round-trip) begins from the AMC Pinkham Notch Camp; in less than half a mile you see the spectacular falls.

Arethusa Falls and Frankenstein Cliff trails (off Rte. 302; look for signs about 15 mi from Rte. 16 and 302 junction), a 4½-hour loop, take you to Arethusa Falls, the state's highest waterfall, 200-foot ribbons of water that plunge to a pool. You can lunch on Frankenstein Cliffs.

(**†† ALL**) White Mountain National Forest. Covering most of the upper half of New Hampshire and reaching in to Maine, the forest contains 750 miles of streams, 22 campgrounds, 50 lakes and ponds, and 1,200 miles of hiking trails. The Mt. Washington Valley section is in its eastern half. (See Chapters 10 and 12.)
🏠 *Forest Supervisor, Box 638, White Mountain National Forest, Laconia 03247, tel. 603/ 528–8721.*

(**†† 1+**) Echo Lake State Park. There's good swimming at the base of a dramatic rock cliff and hiking or biking on a scenic trail. (See Chapter 10.)

🏠 *Rte. 302 off Rte. 16, North Conway 03860, tel. 603/356–2672.*

🏕 6 – 15 **Crawford Notch State Park.** This pass harbors the highest waterfalls in the state and some of the most untamed forests and mountains in New Hampshire. (See Chapter 10.)
🏠 *Rte. 302, Bartlett 03812, tel. 603/ 374–2272.*

MOUNTAIN BIKING. There's a surprising amount of fairly easy biking in this area of 82 peaks. In **Conway** a single sandy track parallels the Saco River. Start at the footbridge at the right end of the picnic area. In **Jackson,** the **Carter Notch Trail,** which crosses several brooks, begins at the end of Carter Notch Road off Route 16A. Cycle shops have a pamphlet listing easy rides.

The **national forest** is crisscrossed with **logging roads** mountain bikers can use. For bike rentals, **Joe Jones Shop** (Main St., North Conway, tel. 603/356–9411; $25 per day; $4 for helmets) has sizes as small as 14 inches plus helmets and a pamphlet of routes. **North Conway Athletic Club** (tel. 603/356–5774) is a source of information on good routes and has some organized outings fine for families with teens.

PLAYGROUND. On Main Street in North Conway, next to the Conway Railroad Station, are monkey bars, slides, climbers, swings.

SWIMMING. You don't come to the White Mountains for great swimming of the serene, blue mountain lake kind. Here it's mostly cold, rocky pools under waterfalls. The ones we go back to are at **Jackson Falls** just above Jackson Village, where the Wildcat River, has scoured out a series of fair-sized pools and slides in a sunny spot.

Other favorites are the pools and slabs of rock for jumping above **Rocky Gorge** about 9 miles west of Conway on the Kancamagus Highway. Watch for the Rocky Gorge Picnic Area. The beach at **Echo Lake State Park** (see *above* and Chapter 10) can get very crowded at noon, but even tots can enjoy it.

WINTER SPORTS. For downhill and cross-country skiing in Jackson and at Black Mountain, Bretton Woods, and Waterville Valley, and sleigh rides and skating in the region, see Chapter 13.

Shopping

From Conway to North Conway 200-odd factory outlets are divided up among a series of centers like boxed chocolates, attracting tourists and teens with shopping addictions by the prospect of low prices and no sales tax on clothing. You can even outfit everyone for school in a day. **OVP** (Settler's Green Outlet Village Plus, Rte. 16, North Conway, tel. 603/356–7031) is nice for kids because it's set around a large courtyard with grassy lawns, benches, and a gazebo. The highlight among the stores here is **L.L. Bean** (tel. 603/356–2100), the only store besides the big one in Maine, but it's not as neat as the original.

🏕 7 – 12 **North Conway Baseball Card Shop** also carries every kind of assorted baseball memorabilia—jackets, caps, sweatshirts, and more.
🏠 *Rte. 16, North Conway, tel. 603/356– 3349.*

🏕 6+ **White Mountain Puzzles** designs and manufactures souvenir jigsaw puzzles with maps and scenic views of not just the White Mountains but also Stowe, New York City, and other famous places.
🏠 *5 Mile Circuit Rd., Jackson, tel. 603/383– 4346.*

Eats

Our picnics are mostly on hikes—we try for a peak with a view or a waterfall, and the promise of food keeps us going. Down in the valley we found picnicking in the rain an unusual treat at the picnic tables inside the restored Swift River Covered Bridge (off West Side Road in Conway Village), now only used as a footbridge. Among the coziest eateries are those in the family farms and inns in the area (see Where to Stay, *below,* and Chapter 14). North Conway has a number of kid-friendly cafés, pizzerias, and burger spots. See introduction to Eats in Chapter 4, New York City, for price categories.

(ᵗᵗ ALL) Elvio's Pizzeria. Three types of pizza—thin crust baked in a stone deck oven, thick crust Sicilian, and white pizza with cheese but no tomato sauce—are the fare. Our vote goes to the thin crust. 🏠 *Main St., North Conway Village, tel. 603/ 356–3307. MC, V. $*

(ᵗᵗ 4+) Fabyans Station. Here you can feast on burgers and sandwiches in an old railroad depot next to the Cog Railway. 🏠 *Rte. 302, Bretton Woods, tel. 603/846– 2222. MC, V. $*

(ᵗᵗ ALL) Grammy MacIntosh Village Cafe. We always know we'll like the food if the air is full of good smells the way it is in this second-floor restaurant. Home-baked treats like potato pancakes and crisp waffles with ice cream do for either an indulgent breakfast (us) or dessert. Lunch and dinner are burgers, sandwiches, salads. 🏠 *151 Main St., Conway Village, tel. 603/ 447–5050. AE, D, MC, V. $*

(ᵗᵗ ALL) Red Parka Pub. The bar scene here is lively, but there's also a terrific and huge salad bar where kids can fill up plates and start eating immediately. A corny sense of humor that kids understand pervades—a menu in the form of a newspaper, chicken dishes listed as "Top Hen Hits," and appetizers like spudskins. 🏠 *Rte. 302, Glen, tel. 603/383–4344. Kids' menu. AE, MC, V. $–$$*

Where to Stay

This region has a wider range of places to stay than most resort areas, from hostel hiking lodges to grand hotel complexes. We'd rather be out of the busyness of North Conway in summer, so all my choices, except the least expensive, are in the smaller, more New England-y towns farther north in the valley. See also Chapter 14.

The price categories that follow are based on summer-season rates and reflect what a family of four would spend for one night in a double room or the smallest appropriate accommodation available (sometimes a cottage): For the hostel, $ is under $70. When resorts are MAP or AP, categories are: $$$$, over $450; $$$, $350–$450; $$, $200–$350; $, under $200.

(ᵗᵗ ALL) Christmas Farm Inn. The suites in the barn and the cottages are the best accommodations for families at this cheery country inn that has the facilities of a resort but the atmosphere of an intimate, friendly farm. Kids are welcome. In winter cross-country ski trails are just outside the door. 🏠 *Rte. 16B, Jackson 03846, tel. 603/ 383–4313 or 800/443–5837, fax 603/ 383–6495. 37 rooms, 4 suites, 6 cottages with fireplaces. Facilities: restaurant, heated outdoor pool, game room, tennis, golf, kids' play area, putting green, volleyball, cross-country ski trails, baby-sitting. Rates include breakfast and dinner. AE, MC, V. $$–$$$*

(ᵗᵗ ALL) Hostelling International. The Albert B. Lester Memorial Hostel. More like a jolly do-it-yourself bed-and-breakfast in a country Victorian inn than the sometimes drear and rustic dormitory atmosphere of many hostels, this is a renovated 100-year-old house with both family rooms and small bunk rooms where families can save additional money by cooking their own dinners in the communal kitchen. 🏠 *36 Washington St., Conway 03813, tel. 603/447–1001, fax 617/734–7614. 10 rooms with shared bath. Kids under 12 ½-price. Facilities: kitchen, common room, covered area for bikes. Rate includes breakfast. MC, V. $$–$$$*

(ᵗᵗ ALL) Mount Washington Hotel. From a distance—and you can see it from miles away—the mammoth white building with its red roof framed by the highest peaks of the Presidential Range looks like a remote summer palace, every inch the grand resort it was at the turn of the century. Lawns are smoothly manicured, horse-drawn carriages roll past; everything, including all the activities and facilities, is on such a grand scale that it's hard to picture yourself going off to hike a mountain. Kids love exploring all this and don't find the formality oppressive. The rooms range from simple to extravagant.

🏨 *Rte. 302, Bretton Woods 03575, tel. 603/278–1000 or 800/258–0330. 200 rooms and suites in hotel (closed fall–spring), plus 34 in Bretton Arms Country Inn, 50 in Bretton Woods Motor Inn; all use resort facilities. Facilities: restaurant, golf, indoor and outdoor pools, bicycles, game room, fly-fishing, playground, tennis, horseback riding, kids' program and dinner, baby-sitting. Family packages. Kids under 4 stay free in hotel; kids under 18 stay free in Bretton Arms. Rates at hotel include breakfast and dinner. AE, D, DC, MC, V. $$$*

Entertainment and the Arts

Compared to the Berkshires or the Adirondacks, the arts are a minor attraction here. For families, the best is the **Arts Jubilee's** (Box 647, North Conway 03860, tel. 603/356–9393; check location of performances) once-a-week summer family entertainment programs, which always feature something fairly active—magicians or acrobats or rollicking country music. It's laid-back, so kids can join in and ask questions afterward. Their regular outdoor concerts for adults are fine for kids too—picnic dinner on the grass is the way to go.

The fine children's theater troupe at the **Paper Mill Playhouse** (tel. 603/745–2141) at Loon Mountain performs short fairy-tale musicals; some years they travel to North Conway for a performance. For movies, there are seven theaters among Conway Village, North Conway, and the Mountain Valley Mall.

PART III

PLEASURES

Top Family Activities and Destinations by Category

FORTS, LIGHTHOUSES, SKYSCRAPERS, HISTORIC VILLAGES, AND OTHER FAMOUS SITES

7

The Northeast's landscape is saturated with famous and historic sites, not surprising when you consider that this is where the Pilgrims landed, the American Revolution unfolded, and the Industrial Revolution came to the states. Take advantage of this cornucopia of exploration possibilities by seeking out places that interest everyone in the family. It's not just the biggest and most famous places that are worth seeing. Smaller houses, forts, and villages are more fun for young children—they don't seem so overwhelming.

The Northeast's historic sites certainly offer an education, but kids absorb more just from taking in the atmosphere of a place; in the Northeast many are staffed by costumed interpreters who invite kids to join in. Reading *Johnny Tremain, The Courage of Sarah Noble, The Witch of Blackbird Pond,* and Jean Fritz's books for young readers about Sam Adams and Paul Revere may spark even more interest. I've mentioned other pre-trip movie and book possibilities under individual sites.

Connecticut

Gillette Castle State Park

 ALL

This 24-room, oak-and-fieldstone medieval-looking structure, perched high on a cliff overlooking the Connecticut River, combines the odd, the outrageous, and the tacky—all the more fun for kids to explore. A 15-minute history of the castle, given hourly by a guide on the main floor, includes amusing stories about eccentric cat- and frog-loving William Gillette, the actor (noted for his portrayal of Sherlock Holmes) who built it in 1919. Kids can search for Gillette's cat memorabilia (including cat-shape salt and pepper shakers, black cat bookends, and 100 scrapbooks with pictures of cats) in the castle's rooms. You get the best view of the castle coming over the river on the Chester-Hadlyme Ferry. It runs every day but Sunday (follow Rte. 148 to the river, where the ferry leaves every hour; $2.25 for car and driver, 75¢ each additional person), and the trip takes a mere five minutes.
🏠 *67 River Rd. (off Rte. 82), East Haddam 06423, tel. 203/526–2336. Cost: $4 adults, $2 kids 6–11. Open Memorial Day–Columbus Day, daily 10–5; Columbus Day–weekend before Christmas, weekends 10–4.*

Mystic Seaport

(👫 ALL)

Mystic Seaport, a re-creation of a 19th-century coastal village, is one of three living history museums in the Northeast that our family considers a must-see (see Plimoth Plantation and Old Sturbridge Village, in Massachusetts, below). Its 17 riverfront acres contain some 60 shops, homes, and workplaces, including a shipyard and docks filled with historic tall ships and fishing craft. Of the three tall ships you can board, Gavin's favorite is the Charles W. Morgan, the last of America's wooden whalers. In some historic houses and shops of the maritime village craftspeople give demonstrations. At the Children's Museum, kids under 8 can dress in sailor's garb, climb into a bunk, peek out a porthole, swab a deck, and climb on rigging.

You can spend an entire day here, no matter what your kids' ages. Mystic's one drawback is the lack of protective railings along wharves and waterfront streets. Bringing an energetic and unpredictable 2-year-old may doom you to a day of nervous vigilance and constantly grabbing hands. If you hate crowds, avoid big weekends such as 4th of July and consider visiting off-season. The Taste of History Festival, at which we savored 19th-century delicacies, and the Lantern Light Tours during December (for kids 10 and up), in which you are part of a Victorian Christmas drama, are the two Mystic events we've liked best.
🏠 Mystic Seaport (1 mi south of I–95 on Rte. 27, exit 90), Box 6000, Mystic 06355, tel. 203/572–0711 or 203/572–5315. Cost: $15 adults, $7.50 kids 6–15. Open Nov.–Mar., daily 9–4; Apr.–June and Sept.–Oct., daily 9–5; July–Aug., daily 9–8.

Old Newgate Prison and Copper Mine

(👫 7 – 15)

You descend the tunnel stairway into the dark, dank underground chambers and passageways of the colonial mine that later served as a prison for burglars, horse thieves, and British sympathizers. The guides posted along the way tell stories of prisoners' ingenious escapes. The journey takes about 20 minutes if you don't linger. The atmosphere is cold (bring a sweater) and creepy. The aboveground guardhouse can also be explored, and there are places to picnic and a nature trail around a pond nearby. All explorations are self-guided.
🏠 Newgate Rd., East Granby 06026, tel. 203/653–3563. Take exit 40 off I–91 to Rte. 20, then west to East Granby. Cost: $3 adults, $1.50 kids 6–17. Open mid-May–Oct., Wed.–Sun. 9:30–4:30.

Sheffield Island Lighthouse

(👫 6 – 13)

My husband is fascinated by island lighthouses, but few are open to the public. A regularly scheduled half-hour ferry ride takes you to this one—a two-story cut-stone keeper's house with a two-story lighthouse on top—on a 50-acre island in Long Island Sound. You can walk up to the light room and observation platform, from which you can see the tops of buildings in New York City (only on a clear day). Most of the island is a National Wildlife Refuge filled with birds; you can picnic and walk.
🏠 Sheffield Island ferry service (Norwalk Seaport Association, 132 Water St., South Norwalk 06854, tel. 203/838–9444; cost $9 adults, $7 kids under 12) from Hope Dock, corner of Washington and North Water Sts. Open weekends and holidays Memorial Day–June; ferries leave at 10, noon, 2; daily July–Labor Day, ferries 9:30 and 1:30 on

weekdays, 9:30, 1:30, 3:30 on weekends and holidays.

Maine

Ft. Knox State Park

(👫 3 – 15)

Bring flashlights on your visit to this impressive, enormous granite fort perched on a bluff above the Penobscot River; the dark underground tunnel (Long Alley) and massive, now-empty, gunpowder storage rooms stemming off it are the most exciting parts to explore. Start with the 45-minute guided tour (best for kids 6 and up), on which you learn the story of the building of the fort, Maine's largest, in the 1830s to keep the British from sailing up the river during the Aroostook War. In either of the two granite spiral staircases that wind up to the roof you can test out the fort's echo potential. At Civil War encampments held the last weekend of July and August, tents, colorful flags, and soldiers fill the parade ground. Picnic tables, fireplaces, a snack bar, and nature trails are outside the fort.

🏠 *Rte. 174 (just off Rte. 1), Prospect Harbor 04669, tel. 207/469–7719. Cost: $2 adults, 50¢ kids 5–11. Open May–Nov., daily 9–5; Memorial Day–Labor Day, daily 9–sunset.*

Ft. Popham

(👫 4 – 13)

For pretending a flotilla of ships is about to attack and you're defending the coast, unfinished Ft. Popham can't be beat. The 500-foot-long, 30-foot-high granite crescent of archways and spiral staircases was erected during the Civil War to guard the mouth of the Kennebec River and the shipyards upriver at Bath. It's right on the water at the tip of a flat peninsula, with clear views of

boats on both sides and an old cannon pointing out to sea.

🏠 *Ft. Popham State Park, Rte. 209, Phippsburg 04562, tel. 207/389–1335. Admission free. Open Memorial Day–Labor Day, daily 9–sunset.*

Ft. William Henry and Colonial Pemaquid Restoration

(👫 5 – 12)

A round brick-and-stone tower fort is great for climbing (as are the stone walls outside it for jumping off). You can fish from the dock by the small riverside restaurant. In addition, there's an ongoing archaeological excavation of a 1625 fishing village, with a small museum displaying some of the finds. A miniature model of the village in the museum, plus some 75,000 artifacts (ask for the kids' guidebook), helped us picture the original buildings; and the resident archaeologist told us some of the history of the village and the three forts built to protect it.

🏠 *Entrance on Rte. 130, about 13 mi south of Rte. 1 (no street address), New Harbor 04554, tel. 207/677–2423. Cost: $2 adults, 50¢ kids 5–12. Open Memorial Day–Labor Day, daily 9:30–5:30.*

Pemaquid Point Lighthouse and Fisherman's Museum

(👫 5 – 15)

At the tip of the Pemaquid peninsula stand the charming little lighthouse keeper's house that's now a museum, a grove of tall pointed firs, and the picturesque lighthouse built in 1827. What makes this site so special is the long, ½-mile-wide finger of spectacular exposed rock ledges that leads, almost like a stairway, down to the crashing surf. The rocks form smooth, polished tables, tempting spots for spreading a picnic lunch, and they have just the right number of notches and crevices to make them perfect for climbing. Wear sneakers, avoid wet rocks (they're slippery), and don't go too close to the surf, where a wave can catch kids off balance and pull them into the water.

The lighthouse tower can't be visited, but stop in the adjoining museum for a look at one of the largest lobsters caught in Maine and some old-time photographs.

 End of Rte. 130, Pemaquid 04554, tel. 207/677-2494 or 203/677-2726. Cost: park, $1 adults, free kids 12 and under; museum, donation. Open Memorial Day– Columbus Day, Mon.–Sat. 10–5, Sun. 11–5.

Massachusetts

Boston Waterfront

To get the full flavor of Boston, you have to walk along the wharves and piers that jut into its busy harbor. On the historic waterfront, renovated and rehabilitated, you can gaze at ferries and cruise boats, sit in cafés and parks, visit the world-class aquarium, and just stroll.

The official HarborWalk route, the blue line prominently marked on the pavement from Christopher Columbus Park to the Children's Museum and across the Congress Street Bridge, takes you past four wharves. If you have young children, start by spending some time at the Christopher Columbus Park playground and fountain. Long Wharf, Boston's oldest, has a breezy small park (perfect for a picnic), where kids can take a look at boats in the harbor through free telescopes. Families munching lunch cluster around the wave fountain and harbor seals in front of the Aquarium (see Chapter 10) on Central Wharf. India and Rowes wharves have brick apartment towers and a hotel with cupolas, colonnades, and oddly shaped steps, as well as a ferry

terminal and an outdoor café. At the James Hook Lobster Company next to Northern Bridge, you can ogle huge lobsters in a salt-water tank.

 Waterfront between Christopher Columbus Park and Northern Ave. Bridge. Maps at Boston Common Information Kiosk, tel. 617/426-3115. Open Mon.–Sat. 8:30–5, Sun. 9–5, or National Park Service Visitor's Center, 15 State St., tel. 617/223-5200. Open daily 9–5.

Bunker Hill Monument

A towering obelisk marks the site of the first major battle of the American Revolution. The battle, a defeat for the colonists, is most remembered for Colonel William Prescott's command to the citizen's militia, "Don't fire till you see the whites of their eyes." You can climb 294 steps to the top for a good view of the city. A reenactment of the battle takes place each year on June 15. In the museum, 15-minute talks and dioramas relate the history of the battle.

 Breed's Hill, Monument Ave. (Bus 93 from Haymarket), Charlestown 02129, tel. 617/ 242-5641. Admission free. Open daily 9–5; last climb, 4:30.

Cranberry World

At the Ocean Spray Visitor Center, in the midst of the Massachusetts cranberry bogs, the 45-minute run-through of everything you ever wanted to know about cranberries ends in tastes of cranberry juice. It's not for everyone, particularly not teens. Little kids, however, seemed entranced with the buttons to push on the interactive displays and with the little machine that demonstrates how cranberries are bounced to determine their quality.

 225 Water St. (overlooking Plymouth Harbor), Plymouth 02360, tel. 508/747-2350.

*Admission free. Open May–Nov., daily
9:30–5:30.*

Faneuil Hall Marketplace

(👫 **ALL**)

This is what malls try to be but aren't. Boutiques, restaurants, food stalls, and flower
stands spill out of three refurbished buildings
onto cobblestone, traffic-free plazas. The
place is filled with color, exotic food aromas,
and swarms of adults and kids watching jugglers balance spinning plates, listening to gui-
tarists play the blues, and just chowing
down. If you have teens, this is the one place
in Boston where I can confidently predict
they will be happy.

The copper-domed center building has
been known as Quincy Market since the
1830s. Restored in 1976, the inner hall is a
prime food stall-browsing territory, where
we tried everything from baked beans to
gourmet fudge. It's flanked by canopies and
pushcarts selling jewelry and all kinds of
stuffed toys. Facing it is colonial Fanueil Hall,
where the virtues and drawbacks of the
Revolution were argued in town meetings
more than 200 years ago. Check out the
grasshopper weathervane on top. Threaded
throughout the two other buildings are 75
shops and 22 restaurants. Walking on cobblestones is tiring. Wear sturdy shoes and
think twice about bringing a stroller.
🏠 *Between Congress and Commercial Sts.
(Information booth tel. 617/338–2323: Summer, South Market St., Entrance 3; winter, South
Canopy, Quincy Market). Limited parking. Free
entertainment Apr.–Oct., daily 11–11, more on
weekends (schedule at Information Booth);
shops open Mon.–Sat. 10–9, Sun. noon–6;
restaurants open later.*

Freedom Trail

(👫 **7 – 15**)

Unless your kids are avid American history
buffs, visit only the highlights of the 3-mile

Freedom Trail, a self-guided walk that winds
its way past 16 of Boston's most important
historic sites: The Paul Revere House (*see
below*), the Old Granary Burial Ground
(Tremont St., next to Park Street Church,
tel. 617/542–3071), the Old North Church
(193 Salem St., tel. 617/523–6676; the
enthusiastic guide here makes the stories
come alive, and you can sit in the box
pews), Old South Meetinghouse (*see Monuments in Chapter 3*), and the USS *Constitution* in Charlestown (*see Chapter 8*).
🏠 *Freedom Trail Information Center, Tremont
St. side of Boston Common. (Brochures also at
National Park Service Visitor Center, 15 State
St., Boston 02109, tel. 617/242–5642.) Open
daily 9–5.*

Hammond Castle Museum

(👫 **6 – 15**)

Inventor John Hayes Hammond, Jr., who
made a fortune from his more than 400
patents (only Thomas Edison held more),
built this version of a medieval castle in
1926. It sits on a steep rock ledge above
Gloucester Harbor and has a moat, a draw-
bridge, parapets, and turrets. Like Gillette
Castle in Connecticut (*see above*), it's a mix
of the awe-inspiring and the wacky, and it
seems to be just what kids have in mind
when they imagine living in a castle. Partway up the winding stairway to one 85-foot
tower, you can peer into a small but not
too creepy dungeon. In the interior courtyard, a deep, curved stone swimming pool
was designed so that Dr. Hammond could
dive into it from his bedroom window, and
pipes in the skylight enabled him to create a
mild drizzle or a teeming downpour. During
October, the castle's rooms are decorated
as stage sets from spooky movies such as
Little Shop of Horrors.
🏠 *80 Hesperus Ave. (off Rte. 123), Gloucester 01930, tel. 508/283–2080 or 508/283–
7673. Cost: $5.50 adults, $3.50 kids 4–12.
Open Memorial Day–Oct. 1, daily 10–5, Oct.
(many special events) and Nov.–Memorial
Day, weekends 10–5.*

Hancock Shaker Village

(👫 8 – 13)

Hancock, the largest restored Shaker farming community in the Northeast, is one of the few historic sites in the Berkshires that appeals to kids. The round stone barn and 20 other buildings here have none of the hustle-bustle, almost hectic quality of such restorations as Sturbridge. Guides explain, and often demonstrate, the traditions of Shaker life, and kids love visiting the laundry and the machine shop to hear about Shaker inventions such as the clothespin. In the Family Discovery Room, kids can dress up in Shaker clothes and experiment with a quill pen. Throughout the year the special events are superb—especially the maple sugaring, when kids can help collect the buckets of syrup and, in the summer, the special tours for 5- to 12-year-olds. **🏠** *Rte. 20 (at Rte. 41, 5 mi west of Pittsfield), Box 898, Pittsfield 01202, tel. 413/443–0188. Admission: $10 adults, $5 kids 6–17, $25 family rate. Open May–Oct., daily 9:30–5.*

HMS *Bounty*

(👫 8 – 15)

We're familiar with the story of the 1787 mutiny on the English ship, HMS *Bounty*, because my father collected books on the subject and shared his knowledge over many dinners. When this replica of the ship, which starred in the 1962 movie along with Marlon Brando and Trevor Howard, moved to Massachusetts in 1993, our visit became almost a pilgrimage. On the 40-minute tour, the actor who greets you plays Captain Bligh, then mutiny leader Fletcher Christian takes you below. Each confides his side of the story, which kids may follow better if they've screened the movie first. **🏠** *State Pier, Battleship Cove, Fall River 02722, tel. 508/673–3886 (information also*

from Chamber of Commerce Bounty Foundation, 200 Pocasset St., Fall River 02722, tel. 508/676–8226). Cost: $4 adults, $2 kids 4–11. Open Memorial Day–Labor Day, Sun.–Tues. and Thurs. 10–6, Fri. and Sat. 10–8; closed Wed.

John Hancock Tower Observatory

(👫 5 – 15)

On a clear day you can see to New Hampshire, Vermont, and the Berkshires, as well as a spectacular bird's-eye view of the city's buildings, parks, and bridges, and waters. Boston 1775, a dramatic presentation on the revolution, played out on a circular, waist-high map model in an adjoining room, is worth seeing (if your kids are over 8). The 60-story tower is the tallest in New England. **🏠** *John Hancock Tower, 200 Clarendon St. (observatory ticket office, corner Trinity Pl. and St. James Ave.), Boston 02116, tel. 617/572–6429. Cost: $3.50 adults, $2.75 students and kids 5–15. Open Mon.–Sat. 9 AM–11 PM; May–Oct., Sun. 10 AM–11 PM; Nov.–Apr., Sun. noon–11 PM.*

Lowell National Historical Park

(👫 8 – 15)

It's fitting that the nation's first urban national park is in the nation's first industrial city. The squared-off redbrick mill buildings and peaceful canals of Lowell National Historical Park offer families an unusual perspective on America's industrial revolution through hands-on exhibits, complete with churning noisy machinery and action-oriented tours. The 10-block area in downtown Lowell is a mix of old restored buildings housing exhibits and contemporary restaurants and shops. You can explore the park yourself by foot on brick promenades or by turn-of-the-century trolley (year-round and free), or on one of the many guided tours, some by boat through the 5½ miles of canals, others by a combination of boat, trolley, and walking. The park isn't a well-defined geographic area, so stop at the Visitor Center for the film, a good map, and a list of good lunch spots.

The essential stops: the Boott Cotton Mills Museum, where 88 power looms clatter and vibrate, and the Tsongas Industrial History Center in the same building, where kids can try out looms and play with a model of the canal system.

🏛 *Visitor Center, Market Mills, 246 Market St. (Lowell Connector of I–495 to exit 5N for Thorndike St., then follow national park signs), Lowell 01852, tel. 508/970–5000. Cost: boat-and-trolley tour $3 adults, $1 kids 6–16; Boott Museum $3 adults, $1 kids 6–16. Open daily 8:30–5.*

Minuteman National Historical Park

👨‍👧 10 – 15

The heart of this park is the 20-mile winding, hilly road along which the first battles in the Revolution took place. You can drive the route, hopping in and out of the car to visit historic houses and sites, but it's hard to picture the bloody battles at these now peaceful spots. For us the most interesting part was following the wide path to the Old North Bridge, where the "shot heard round the world" was fired. Several visitor centers have maps and staff to answer questions. The Battle Road Center also has a film, exhibits, and a large diorama of the battle on April 19, 1975. On your way there you can stop at the Battle Green in Lexington, where the revolution began. Each year the anniversary is marked with a colorful reenactment.

🏛 *Battle Road Visitors Center, 1 mi from Battle Green, off Rte. 2A, Concord 01742, tel. 617/862–7753. Admission free. Open Apr.–Dec., daily 8:30–5.*

Old Sturbridge Village

👨‍👧 4 – 13

One of the country's largest living history museums sprawls over a rolling 200-acre country landscape just like a real rural agricultural community of the 1830s. Shops and houses are clustered around a village green, while farther out are a working farm, several mills, a pottery, and a blacksmith shop. Costumed interpreters busily engage in 19th-century chores; talking to the printer and cooper we felt we had been transported back in time.

There's too much here to see and do in just one day, and on the map everything looks closer together than it really is. Fortunately a horse-drawn wagon rolls back and forth between the village and the outlying area. Don't miss a session at the district school, even if you have to wait in line. A costumed teacher treats visitors as pupils, giving you a vivid picture of what a day at school was like in the 1800s. Among the special events here, sheepshearing and the Harvest Weekends are great fun for kids. Reading The *Witch of Blackbird Pond* or *Halfway down Paddy's Lane* (both for ages 8–12) will give your kids some sense of the period.

🏛 *1 Old Sturbridge Village Rd., Sturbridge 01566, tel. 508/347–3362. Take Mass. Tpke. (I–90) to exit 9, then Rte. 20 west. Cost: $14 adults, $7 kids 6–15. Open Tues.–Sun. 10–4.*

Orchard House

👨‍👧 8 – 14

Two girls we know who are fans of Louisa May Alcott's *Little Women* delighted in the 40-minute tour of the house the author shared with her father, Bronson. None of the rooms is roped off, so kids can pretend they've come for an afternoon visit. If they've read *Little Women* or seen the 1995 movie, they will undoubtedly spot items that

are mentioned. The tour reveals little-known aspects of Alcott's life, such as her involvement in the women's rights movement. Extensive programs for young kids include games and hoop rolling.
🏠 *399 Lexington Rd., Box 353, Concord 01742, tel. 508/369–4118. Cost: $4 adults, $3.50 kids 13–18, $2.50 ages 6–12. Family rates available. Open Apr.–Oct., Mon.–Sat. 10–4:30 and Sun. 1–4:30; Nov. and Mar., weekends only 10–4:30 and 1–4:30.*

Paper House

👫 5 – 12

All the furniture in the house—lamps, chairs, grandfather clock—is made from paper. The walls are 215 sheets thick, the writing desk is made only from newspaper reports of Charles Lindbergh's 1927 flight, and the bookcase consists of only foreign papers. The project started as a lark back in 1924 and finally drew so many tourists that the owners, a Boston couple, moved into another house next door.
🏠 *50 Pigeon Hill St. (across from Pigeon Cove Post Office), Rockport 01966, tel. 508/546–2629. Cost: $1 adults, 50¢ kids 6–14. Open July and Aug., daily 10–5.*

Paul Revere's House

👫 5 – 15

This small, gray-green, lopsided frame structure with tiny diamond-paned windows, in the midst of the larger buildings in Boston's North End, is the house from which the Boston silversmith made his famous ride to warn patriots in Middlesex County that the British were coming. It's the oldest building in Boston. Its cozy size (just four rooms) and crooked walls, and the brick courtyard and tiny garden outside have a special charm. Though you can't touch anything, the museum guides are quick to show you rope supports on the beds, point out Paul Revere's

rocker, and tell you about bedbugs in the straw mattresses. It helps to read the information on the kiosk outside or the "Kid's Guide to the Paul Revere House," available from the ticket office, before you go in.
🏠 *19 North Sq., Boston 02113, tel. 617/523–1676. Cost: $2 adults, 75¢ kids 5–17. Open mid-Apr.–Oct., daily 9:30–5:15; Nov.–mid-Apr., Tues–Sun. 9:30–4:15.*

Pilgrim Monument and Museum

👫 6 – 15

The Pilgrims landed first in what's now Provincetown and even stayed here a month and signed the Mayflower Compact before sailing on to Plymouth. With its arches and turrets, the 252-foot-high granite tower built to commemorate the first landing is certainly more impressive than the official rock in Plymouth. The 116 steps (60 ramps) to the very top bring you to a view of dunes, harbor and boats, and, if you squint, Boston's skyscrapers. Be sure to see the exhibit in the museum of the pirate ship, *Whydah*, wrecked in the 18th century and recovered in the 1980s, and the coins, jewelry, and weapons from it.
🏠 *High-pole Hill on Winslow St., off Bradford St., Provincetown 02657–1125, tel. 508/487–1310. Cost: $5 adults, $3 kids 4–12 (includes monument, museum, and special exhibit). Open Sept.–June, daily 9–5, July and Aug., daily 9–7.*

Pioneer Village

👫 5 – 13

The year in the country's oldest living history village is 1630, when Salem was a Puritan fishing settlement. Small in scale, less well known and less crowded, it also has some unusual features, such as replicas of dugout houses—the kind the settlers lived in the first winter—and a few cottages with real thatch. The daily activities kids can join in are simple but fun, like helping to wash clothes in a stream. You can swim and picnic in the park.

🏛 *Forest River Park, Salem 01970, tel 508/ 745–0525 (mailing address c/o House of Seven Gables Historic Site, 54 Turner St., Salem 01970). Take Rte. 114 to West St., 2 mi from Salem State College. Cost: $4.50 adults, $3.50 kids 13–17, $2.50 kids 6–12, $12 family rate. Open Mon.–Sat. 10–5, Sun. 12–5.*

Plimoth Plantation, *Mayflower II*, and Hobbamock's Homesite

(👫 7 – 14)

More than at any other such museum in the Northeast, it's as though you've actually been transported back in time to the year 1627. The essential 12-minute presentation at the Visitor Center tells you what to expect. Compared to Old Sturbridge and Mystic, the village of 20 humble, thatched-roof dwellings, barns, and storehouses, on a gentle slope above Cape Cod Bay, is simple and untouristy (though sometimes crowded). Paths are rough and dusty, and the smells of hay and farm animals fill the air as you walk around. Each actor (including children) in the village takes on the name, dress, and role of a specific Pilgrim who came from England on the Mayflower. They play their parts so completely that if you ask about anything that happened after 1627, they stay in character, look puzzled, and reply in a variety of dialects. Initially the kids with us felt shy, but they soon discovered that to have the most fun they had to wander into homes and barnyards and chat with the Pilgrims as they baked bread, thatched a roof, repaired a fence, and fed the chickens running around. Soon they were offering to help the Pilgrims, just as though they lived there too.

Be sure to visit Hobbamock's Homesite, a small Indian community of bark houses a short walk away, to see the contrast between the two cultures, especially in how they treat children. Two and a half miles away, moored at State Pier in Plymouth Harbor, is the *Mayflower II*, a too-brightly painted replica of the famous ship, with actors playing passengers and crew.

🏛 *Warren Ave., Rte. 3A, Plymouth, 02362, tel. 508/746–1622 (mailing address: Box 1620, Plymouth 02362). Take Rte. 3 south to exit 4, then follow signs. Cost: $18.50 adults, $11 kids 5–12; Mayflower II only: June–Nov., $5.75 adults, $3.75 kids 5–12. Open Apr.–late June and Sept.–Nov., daily 9–5; July–Aug., daily 9–7.*

Plymouth Rock, Plymouth

(👫 5 – 15)

Though we'd warned Gavin that the rock the Pilgrims supposedly stepped on as they disembarked from the *Mayflower* in 1620 looks quite small (most of it is actually underground, and over 3,000 pounds was chipped away by tourists in the past), at 9 he was still expecting something akin to the Rock of Gibraltar. Instead the rock has a crack running through it and the date 1620 carved in its side; the white-columned portico and iron bars around it look grander. But if you've come to visit Plimoth Plantation and *Mayflower II*, nearby, it might be worth five minutes so you can say you've seen it—along with the other 1.5 million yearly visitors.

🏛 *Water St. (overlooking harbor, near Mayflower II), Plymouth 02362, no phone. Admisison free. Open daily.*

New Hampshire

Fort No. 4

(👫 4 – 12)

Fort No. 4 gives you a taste of life on the frontier during the French and Indian Wars.

The reproduction of the first tiny settlement at Charlestown, with a 10-foot-high wooden stockade, a lookout tower you can climb into, and simple cabins and lean-tos like the ones in which the original settlers lived, sits on a meadow on the Connecticut River. Costumed guides give cooking, candle-dipping, woodworking, and musketball-molding demonstrations, and barns and a blacksmith shop stand outside the fence. None of this is as impressive as Mystic or Sturbridge or Ft. Ticonderoga, even during one of the frequent militia musters, but its simplicity may be more appealing to young kids.

🏠 Rte. 11, Springfield Rd., Charlestown 03603, tel. 603/826–5700. Cost: $6 adults, $4 kids 6–11. Open late May.–Oct., Wed.–Mon. 10–4.

Strawbery Banke

(👫 7 – 14)

At the 42 historic buildings in this 10-acre area of downtown Portsmouth restoration is an on-going process. You can watch archaeologists, carpenters, gardeners, and others actively at work on projects in different stages of completion. The nine furnished houses you can visit are not all from the same period; each one illustrates a different time period, from the 1600s to the 1950s, so it's fun to compare them and talk with the appropriately costumed role players. The Visitor Center has walking guides and posts times of demonstrations.

🏠 Marcy and Hancock Sts. (opposite Prescott Park and Portsmouth waterfront), Portsmouth 03802, tel. 603/433–1100 or 603/433–1106 (mailing address: Box 300, Portsmouth 03802). Cost: $10 adults, $7 kids 7–17, $25 family; tickets good for 2 days. Open May–Oct., daily 10–5.

New York

Empire State Building

(👫 ALL)

This 60-year-old skyscraper, a New York City landmark, probably needs no introduction, even to kids. Those who've never been to New York still know it from King Kong, Sleepless in Seattle, and countless other movies. Built in 1931, it's no longer the world's tallest building, but to us its shape has more character than the ubiquitous glass-walled towers. More than 2½ million people visit each year, and you can see 50-mile views and five states on a clear day from the 86th floor outdoor promenade or the 102nd-floor observatory. We like to come at sunset to watch the city light up.

🏠 350 5th Ave. at 34th St., New York 10001, tel. 212/736–3100. Cost: $3.75 adults, $1.75 kids under 12. Open daily 9:30 AM–11:30 PM.

Farmer's Museum and Village Crossroads

(👫 5 – 13)

Compared with such museum villages as Sturbridge and Mystic, the Village Crossroads at the Farmer's Museum, representing a typical upstate New York farming village in the late 19th century, is small, eclectic, and laid-back, and it may be more fun for little kids. Sheep, chickens, and geese run around freely. The printer's shop, doctor's office, and so on are staffed by guides giving demonstrations. The museum itself, through which you enter the village, is a huge stone barn, where you can see spinning, weaving, and other demonstrations, with a wonderful re-creation of an old-fashioned curiosity museum downstairs. Don't miss the stone carving that was passed off by a farmer/con artist as a petrified giant in one of the most famous hoaxes of the 19th century. This is a place to come while you're here to visit the nearby Baseball Hall of Fame (combined tickets are available), not a destination in its own right.

 Lake Rd. (off Rte. 80, 1 mi north of Cooperstown), Cooperstown 13326, tel. 607/547–2593. Cost: $8 adults, $3 kids 7–12; combined tickets (include Fenimore House Museum and Baseball Hall of Fame); $17.50 adults, $7 kids 7–12. Open June–Sept., daily 10–4; Oct.–Nov. and Jan.–May, Tues.–Sun. 10–4; closed Dec.

Ft. Ticonderoga

👫 2 – 15

Everything about this restored 18th-century stone fort that figured so prominently in both the French and Indian Wars and the American Revolution struck us as impressive and imposing: the way it sits high, high above the southern end of Lake Champlain, the varied flags flying from the ramparts, its star shape of stone bastions, the dozens of bronze cannon poking out. Kids can watch booming cannon demonstrations and join in the fife and drum corps parades. We got a stronger sense of life at a fort here than at any other fort in the Northeast. The 20- to 40-minute tours are a good introduction to the fort's basic structure and history; experienced guides tailor each one to the ages of those in the group. There's much to explore and do—a dungeon, exhibits of muskets, swords, and pistols, an underground bakery, and running on the parade ground.

 Rte. 74, Box 390B, Ticonderoga 12883, tel. 518/585–2821. Take I–87 to exit 28, continue east 18 mi. Cost: $7 adults, $5 kids 10–13. Open early May–June and Sept.–mid.-Oct., daily 9–5, July and Aug. 9–6.

Ft. William Henry

👫 5 – 15

In the mid-18th century, this now-restored log fortress high above Lake George was an important wilderness outpost in the French and Indian Wars. The massacres that occurred when French troops seized it were the basis for James Fenimore Cooper's *Last of the Mohicans*. The fort, now owned by a corporation, makes an interesting contrast to the grander stone Ticonderoga farther north, but be warned that it has a hokier, somewhat commercial flavor. The short tour includes musket and cannon firings, a grenadier bomb toss, a musketball molding demonstration, and exploring the underground powder magazine and dungeon. You can also watch the 1930s movie version of *Last of the Mohicans* or screen the 1992 version before you come.

Canada St., Beach Rd., and Rte. 9 entrances, Lake George 12845, tel. 518/668–5471. Cost: $8 adults, $6 kids 4–11. Open May–mid-June and Labor Day–mid-Oct., daily 10–5; mid-June–Labor Day, daily 9 AM–10 PM.

Philipsburg Manor

👫 ALL

A working water-powered gristmill that grinds corn and wheat every day, a farmyard of animals, and an old restored barn are the prime attractions for us at this 17th-century historic manor, on the Potanico River near the Hudson River. Once the commercial center of a 52,000-acre estate owned by Frederick Philipse, it shipped flour down the Hudson to New York City. The costumed miller lets in the water and recruits kids to help pour the corn; the cornmeal can be purchased in the gift shop. Costumed interpreters are stationed throughout to answer questions and perform demonstrations. You may want to combine your visit to Philipsburg with trips to nearby Sunnyside and Van Cortlandt Manor (combined tickets are available). If you have time for only one, Philipsburg appeals to the widest age group. This is also the place to come on Halloween for spooky stories and a visit to the Old Dutch Church graveyard nearby.

🏛 *Rte. 9 (2 mi north of Tappan Zee Bridge), North Tarrytown 10591, tel. 914/631–8200 (mailing address: Historic Hudson Valley, 150 White Plains Rd., Tarrytown 10591). Cost: $6 adults, $3 kids 6–17; combined admission (includes Sunnyside and Van Cortlandt Manor), $17 adults, $9 kids 6–17. Open Wed.–Mon. 10–5.*

Rockefeller Center

 ALL

This complex of buildings and public plazas on Fifth Avenue is a great place for strolling around, window-shopping, and people-watching. On the upper level, the Channel Gardens have flowers and pools; water jets spray a gold-leaf statue of Prometheus, and flags of the states and the United Nations members wave. In winter skaters twirl on the lower level's ice rink. Don't miss the huge Christmas tree during the holidays. The Center also houses Radio City Music Hall and the GE Building (on the west side of the Lower Plaza between 49th and 50th Sts.), where NBC is located. (*See also* Chapter 4.)

🏛 *47th–52nd Sts. between 5th and 6th Aves. (Subway B, D, F, or Q to Rockefeller Center), New York, tel. 212/698–8901.*

South Street Seaport

 ALL

Unlike Mystic Seaport (see Connecticut, *above*), the 11-block South Street Seaport district of historic ships and restored buildings in lower Manhattan is as much commercial as it is educational. Parts of the Seaport remind us of what New York must have looked like in the 19th century, when it was one of the great ports of the world. It also has a bustling atmosphere, much like the port must have had back then, but the action now comes from a shopping mall, with trendy boutiques, restaurants, pubs and a food court, and a constant stream of street

performers and free entertainment. The effect is somewhat like Faneuil Hall Marketplace in Boston, which was designed by the same team. Plan to stay for most of a day.

To get a map and find out what's going on, stop at the Museum Visitor Center on Fulton Street. Be sure to explore the sailing ships moored at Pier 16, especially the four-masted 347-foot *Peking*. Stop by the Maritime Crafts Center to watch craftspeople work on models, and the boat building shop, where small wooden boats are being restored. The Children's Center offers excellent hands-on workshops with a maritime focus.

The fast-food stalls in the Fulton Market Building across from the Visitor's Center and the Promenade Food Court on the third floor of Pier 17 have places to get burgers and hot dogs as well as more unusual fare. See Chapter 4.

Steamers and a paddleboat make scheduled sails on the harbor in summer (check at the Visitor's Center), and tours of the historic Fulton Fish Market, the oldest fish market in the United States, take place year-round. If you can rally the troops by 6 AM for the market tour, you'll see 600 varieties of fish while you soak in the frenetic atmosphere of people, pushcarts, and forklifts.

🏛 *19 Fulton St. (at East River; Subway 2, 3, 4, 5, J, M, or Z to Fulton St. or A or C to Broadway–Nassau), New York 10002, tel. 212/669–9400 (museum) or 212/732–7078 (marketplace). Cost: (museum) $5 adults, $2 kids 5–12, $4 students; open Memorial Day–Labor Day, daily 10–6; all other times daily 10–5. South Street Seaport open year-round.*

Statue of Liberty

 4 – 15

This symbol of freedom on an island in New York Harbor is probably the best-recognized statue in the world. It was rated among New York's top 10 sights by every kid over 5 on my New York panel, and among the top 10 in the world (!) by several. All insist that for the full effect it's necessary to climb the 365 steps (the equivalent of 22 stories) from the statue's pedestal to the crown. You go in a spiral, so it's easy to get dizzy (if you can move fast enough), especially on the last six or seven flights. Because of crowds, the pace can be agonizingly slow, and the climb may take as much as two hours. You can ride an elevator to the top of the pedestal (10 stories), where, from the balcony, I think you get the best view of Manhattan. If you start climbing at this point, it's only 168 steps to the top. At the base of the statue is the American Museum of Immigration, whose exhibits about what people have gone through to reach America are best for kids over 8.

The ticket office for the ferry is in the center of Castle Clinton, a restored brick fortress in Manhattan's Battery Park. It takes the ferry only a few minutes to get to Liberty Island, where you can debark and visit the statue, then reboard any ferry to go on to Ellis Island (see Chapter 8), boarding another boat to return. Sounds simple. The problem is the crowds. Ask how long the wait is to get to the crown before you buy your ferry ticket. Forget a sunny summer weekend, unless you arrive before the ticket office opens at 8:30 and get on the very first boat. In any case, plan on about four hours for your trip.

🏠 *Liberty Island, tel. 212/363–3200; ferry tel. 212/269–5755. Take Subway 1 or 9 to South Ferry or 4 or 5 to Bowling Green and Battery Park, then cross Battery Park to Circle Line office at Castle Clinton. Cost (ferry): $6 adults, $3 kids 3–17. Departures daily every 45 min, 9:15–3:30.*

Sunnyside

(👫 6 – 14)

Author Washington Irving, best known for "The Legend of Sleepy Hollow" and "Rip Van Winkle," lived and worked in this romantic 17-room house he described as "full of angles and corners as an old cocked hat." You can enjoy its cozy-cottage, slightly mysterious, fairy-tale quality, a picnic by the swan pond, and the walking path with views of the Hudson River designed by Irving himself. For younger kids, a previsit screening of the Disney version of *The Legend of Sleepy Hollow* can be useful.

Combine a visit here with trips to Philipsburg Manor (3 miles north, *see above*) and Van Cortlandt Manor (9 miles north of Philipsburg Manor, *see below*), for which an all-in-one ticket is available. In summer, you can take a special boat tour from New York City and New Jersey to Tarrytown, where a waiting bus transports you first to Philipsburg Manor, then to Sunnyside (NY Waterway, tel. 800/533–3779).

🏠 *Rte. 9 (1 mi south of Tappan Zee Bridge), Tarrytown 10591, tel. 914/631–8200 (mailing address: Historic Hudson Valley, 150 White Plains Rd., Tarrytown 10591). Cost: $6 adults, $3 kids 6–17; combined cost (includes Philipsburg Manor and Van Cortlandt Manor), $17 adults, $9 kids 6–17. Open Mar.–Dec. Wed.–Mon., 10–5.*

Van Cortlandt Manor

(👫 3 – 14)

This estate was occupied by the wealthy Dutch-American Van Cortlandt family for 300 years, and touring the grounds and several buildings gives kids a picture of family life around the time of the American Revolution. During that war, soldiers bivouacked here and left behind graffiti you can still see. At the Ferry House, a tavern on the estate, we learned that the price of accommodations in the 1700s was based on sharing a bed with as many as five strangers. A blacksmith gives demonstrations, the kitchen in the tenant house is always good for a few cookies made from old Dutch recipes, and kids can help mix clay with their bare feet in the brickmaking pit—if you let them. Lovely gardens and brick paths provide exploring space.

🏠 *Croton Point exit from Rte. 9 (9 mi north of Tappan Zee bridge, accessible by Metro North trains), Croton-on-Hudson 10520, tel. 914/631–8200 (mailing address, Historic Hudson Valley, 150 White Plains Rd., Tarrytown 10591). Cost: $6 adults, $3 kids 6–17; combined cost (includes Philipsburg Manor and Sunnyside), $17 adults, $9 kids 6–17. Open Apr.–Dec., Wed.–Mon. 10–5.*

West Point (United States Military Academy)

👬 7 – 15

America's oldest and most distinguished military academy, perched on bluffs above the Hudson River, is also a historic military site with statues, monuments, cannons, a museum, and restored forts that appeal to many kids. If you can, time a visit to coincide with a football game (see Chapter 11) preceded by dress parades of cadets in colorful uniforms and brass bands.

🏠 *U.S. Military Academy, Visitors Center, West Point 10996, tel. 914/938–2638; West Point Tours, tel. 914/446–4724. Take Rte. 9W to Highland Falls, then follow signs. Admission free; tours, $3.50 adults, $2 kids under 12. Visitor Center open Mar–Dec., daily 9–4:45, Jan.–Feb., Wed.–Sun. 9–4:45.*

World Trade Center and Observation Deck

👬 ALL

At 110 floors, these two skyscrapers are New York City's tallest towers. On a clear day the view from the open-air Rooftop Promenade at the top of Two World Trade Center (still the world's highest outdoor observation platform), or the indoor observation deck on the 107th floor, is fantastic. Check the visibility before you buy your tickets, but even if it's a little cloudy it's still fun; kids can look down on clouds clustered around the towers. The ear-popping elevator ride to the top, with the wind howling down the elevator shaft, is also a thrill.

The plaza between the two towers has shops and restaurants, and there's often free entertainment, much specifically for children, on weekends and during the winter holidays.

🏠 *Church St. and Cortlandt St. (Subway 1, N, or 9 to Cortlandt St. or A, C, or E to Chambers St.), New York 10047, tel. 212/435–4170, 212/435–7000 for information on children's activities and observation center. Cost: $6 adults, $3 kids 6–12. Open daily 9:30 AM–9:30 PM.*

Rhode Island

Astors' Beechwood

👬 8+

While seeing The Breakers is a matter of oohing and aahing on a formal tour, visiting The Astors' Beechwood, the summer cottage of "The Mrs. Astor" (as she wished to be called) is like entering a Newport version of the TV series "Upstairs Downstairs," and much more fun for younger kids. The Beechwood Theatre Company assume the roles of the Astors' gossipy servants and eccentric guests getting ready for an anniversary ball; they welcome you as a guest, gossiping to you about their mistress as they show you through the mansion. The tour lasts about an hour and ends with Mrs. Astor's strawberry tea.

🏠 *580 Bellevue Ave., Newport 02840, tel. 401/846–3772. Cost: $8 adults, $6 kids 6–12. Open late May–Oct., daily 10–5.*

The Breakers

👬 8+

Cornelius Vanderbilt II built his 70-room, four-story summer "cottage," the Breakers, on the Atlantic Ocean in 1895. No other mansion we've seen in the Northeast is so magnificent. In this American version of a Northern Italian palace, gilt and painted ceilings, grand staircases, massive carved archways, ornate paneling, and bathrooms with both salt- and freshwater taps evoke the era appropriately called The Gilded Age. You can buy a combination ticket that admits you to additional mansions, but a little of this goes a long way with kids.

🏠 *Ochre Point Ave., Newport 02840, tel. 401/847-1000 or 401/847-6543. Cost: $8 adults, $3.50 kids 6–11. Open late Mar.–Oct., daily 10–5; extended Sat. to 6 June–Aug.*

Flying Horse Carousel, Watch Hill Lighthouse, and Napatree Point

(👫 3 – 10)

In a town full of Victorian houses is the oldest and prettiest merry-go-round in America. It's now a National Historic Landmark and may be the lone site in the Northeast that's just for kids. The horses of the ride have real tails and manes, leather saddles, agate eyes, and swing out on chains when they're in motion, rather than just going up and down on a pole. A short walk away on Lighthouse Road is a charming lighthouse, which has nice views from its tower but is hot on a sunny day (tel. 401/596-1182; open daily 8–dusk). Still farther is Napatree Point, a long sandy spit of land that's one of the nicest beach walks around.

🏠 *Bay St., Watch Hill, no phone. Cost: 25¢. Open June 15–Labor Day, weekdays 1–9; weekends and holidays 11–9.*

Vermont

Ben & Jerry's Ice Cream Factory

(👫 3 – 15)

This factory is where 9 million gallons of this ice cream are made each year. If your kids have never seen an ice-cream or candy factory and you're nearby, the short tour and the gift shop—black-and-white cow hats, socks, mugs, sweatshirts, glasses, T-shirts, and so on—are worth a visit. Be prepared for unbelievably corny jokes during the slide show. Don't miss the miniature model of the factory.

🏠 *Rte. 100 (exit 10 off I–89), Waterbury 05676, tel. 802/244-5641. Cost: $1 adults and kids over 12. Open daily 9–5.*

Billings Farm and Museum

(👫 ALL)

This 350-acre historic working dairy farm illustrates to kids what living on a farm was like in the 19th century, in a more personal and intimate way than most living history villages. You can walk anywhere you like in the rambling 1890s farmhouse, for example, just as though you were a friend of the family, and join any of the staff in their 19th-century tasks. In the kitchen, where workers (who are not in costume, as at Plimoth Plantation) are always cooking something, kids can peel apples with an old mechanical peeler. In the basement creamery, even toddlers can help make the butter in old-fashioned churns—and taste it spread on crackers. If you come during cider-making season, you can help press and drink. The farm life museum in four connected barns houses both exhibits and demonstrations.

🏠 *Rte. 12, Woodstock 05091, tel. 802/457-2355. Cost: $6 adults, $3 kids 6–17, $17 families (2 adults and all accompanying children). Open May–Oct., daily 10–5; Nov.–Dec., weekends 10–4.*

Rock of Ages Granite Quarry

(👫 6 – 13)

One of the most unusual and imposing sights in the Northeast is the view of the world's largest granite quarry from an observation platform. Huge 40-ton blocks of stone are being carved out by machines, then hauled up from a pit the size of a football field by derricks so big they reminded us of dinosaurs. On the guided walking tour the noise assaults you. At the Visitor Center, besides checking out the exhibits, you can purchase tickets for a 25-minute bus ride right into the work areas farther uphill. Perhaps most interesting of all is watching men and machines polish, shape, and carve the blocks into finished products, from the observation deck above the Craftsman Center.

🏠 *Exit 6 off I–89, Box 482, Barre 05641, tel. 802/476–3119. Admission free, bus tour: $3.50 adults, $1 kids 6–12, kids under 6 free. Open May–Oct., daily 8:30–5; bus tour June–mid-Oct., weekdays 9–3.*

DINOSAURS, MUMMIES, ROBOTS, AND HALLS OF FAME

8

ART, HISTORY, SCIENCE, SPORTS, AND CHILDREN'S MUSEUMS

An Italian palazzo filled with paintings, the country's finest dinosaur display, a theater where you can watch a machine create lightning, the world's first nuclear-powered submarine, the history of baseball on three floors: The Northeast's numerous museums cover subjects appealing to both children and adults. The trouble is that if you're not careful about how you see them, kids come to regard museums as those places parents think kids should go to get the required dose of culture and to be "exposed" to the finer things of life.

In our experience, hands-on museums, natural history museums with stuffed animals, and history museums on board ships are those that most appeal to kids until they're nearly teens. Almost all the museums I've included below have at least some participatory exhibits. A good book that lists many children's museums is *Doing Children's Museums* by Joanne Cleaver (Williamson). For additional museums, see Chapters 3 to 6 in Part II, Places.

No matter what their age, pick a museum with at least some objects your kids are already interested in—whether dinosaurs or dolls or robots, or paintings of some of these subjects. Do talk with kids in advance about what you're going to see. If you're visiting an art museum, it's worth reading a book on a particular artist, or *The Usborne History of Painting* (for kids 8–12) or *Visiting the Art Museum* by Laurie Krasny Brown and Marc Brown. We go early, when museums are usually least crowded. When our son was under 6, we used to let him run around outside and blow off steam before going in. Plan on spending no more than two hours before you head for something to eat (less if your kids are under 6). If the museum has no cafeteria, bring snacks or determine the location of the nearest restaurant or coffee shop. Make sure what you want to view will be on display the day you plan to be there.

We stop first at the Information Desk for the following:

● A floor plan and directions to exhibits, bathrooms, and the cafeteria (plus the hours it is least crowded). Nothing so ruins a museum visit for our family as wandering about aimlessly.

● Museum pamphlets or guides for kids or families (ask, as they're not always displayed).

● Tickets for scheduled events—puppet show, discovery room, planetarium, music show—or family tours or workshops. Often these fill up and sell out early in the day. (Generally take only tours designed for kids unless yours are over 10; older kids we know often enjoy self-guided audio tours.)

Games can keep interest from flagging, especially in art and history museums. We have two favorites. In "picture hunt," kids pick out several postcards of related paintings or sculptures in the museum's gift shop when you first come in, then hunt for them in the galleries. Hint: Ask the staff person in the gift shop if these items are on display now. In "animal hunt," kids look for paintings or objects that have some particular item in them—animals or dragons or angels or babies or, hey, even body parts—whatever works.

Connecticut

Barnum Museum

(👫 3 – 13)

This museum about the life of showman P. T. Barnum, who is best known for founding the Barnum and Bailey Circus, "The Greatest Show on Earth" is a must for circus-lovers. We immediately head for the third-floor gallery to see the hand-carved moving miniature three-ring circus that covers 1,000 square feet and to marvel at its 3,000 tiny figures and models of animals and performers, boxcars and wagons, big tents, even carpenters building platforms and cooks stirring up dinner. In the Clown Corner, you'll find baggy pants, crazy hats, and makeup mirrors; if you put your face up to them, you can check out how you'd look as a clown. Did I forget to mention the circus music and sounds that greet your ears as soon as you enter? Combine a visit here with a stop at the Beardsley Zoo (see Chapter 10) or the Discovery Museum (see below).
🏠 820 Main St. (exit 27 off I–91), Bridgeport 06604, tel. 203/331–1104. Cost: $5 adults, $3 kids 4–18. Open Tues.–Sat. 10–4:30, Sun. 12–4:30.

Children's Museum of Southeastern Connecticut

(👫 2 – 7)

Though tiny in comparison with places like the Children's Museum in Boston—the single-story white building covers only 5,000 square feet—this museum has a couple of intriguing and unusual exhibits. One is the small-size working pipe organ in the Discovery Room, complete with stainless steel pipes. A panel of Plexiglas covers the inner pump and valves so kids can view the way air moves the parts to create sounds when they play. In addition, temporary exhibits convey the excitement of historical events to small kids and spark conversations between them and their parents. In 1995, the topic is the Underground Railroad.
🏠 409 Main St. (exit 74 off I–95), Niantic 06357, tel. 203/691–1255. Cost: $3; kids under 1 free. Open Mon.–Sat., 9–4, Sun. noon–4; Sept.–May, closed Mon.

Discovery Museum

(👫 3+)

At the largest and best hands-on museum in Connecticut's Challenger Learning Center, you can spend a Saturday being part of a once-a-month simulated space mission. The computer-filled mission control room looks just like a simplified version of the real ones we've seen on TV, as does the space module joined to it by a long, dark hallway. The morning training session teaches you to work the computer programs, monitors, and video cameras you'll need to use in the afternoon as you work together with other participants, each taking a different role, to perform the mission. Regardless of the emergencies you have to deal with, all missions end successfully. If you don't want to spend a whole day, you can go on a half-hour minimission tour. The artist's studio here has interactive exhibits about how artists view art.

🏛 *4450 Park Ave. (exit 27 off I–95), Bridgeport 06604, tel. 203/372–3521. Cost: $6 adults, $4 kids 4–18; $3 for minimission; $25 for all-day Challenger program. Open Sept.–June, Tues.–Sat. 10–5, Sun. noon–5; July–Aug., Mon.–Sat. 10–5, Sun. noon–5.*

Peabody Museum of Natural History

🏃🏃 6 – 15

We've always thought of this museum on the Yale University campus as a miniversion of the American Museum of Natural History in New York City, but more staid and static. Go for the dinosaurs, as we used to: It has the best display in southern New England, including an impressive 65-foot-tall brontosaurus, as well as a huge dinosaur mural in the Hall of Dinosaurs.

🏛 *Yale University (exit 3 off I–91), 170 Whitney Ave., New Haven 06519, tel. 203/432–5050. Cost: $4 adults, $2.50 kids 3–15; free weekdays 3–5. Open Tues.–Sat. 10–5, Sun. and holidays noon–5.*

U.S.S. *Nautilus* Memorial Museum

🏃🏃 6 – 15

The first nuclear-powered U.S. submarine floats just outside the entrance to the U.S. Submarine base in Groton. Only 60 people at a time are allowed aboard, so you'll probably have to wait at least a short time for the self-guided tour unless you get here first thing in the morning or on a weekday. It's hard to believe that 116 men could live in a space just 319 feet long and 28 feet wide, once cruising over 3,000 miles without surfacing. You carry electronic wands to activate narration at each point. The bunk room is stacked with rows of cots; each enlisted man had only a small white bag to hold his personal possessions. In the museum, connected to the submarine by a walkway, the three working periscopes fascinate kids. You can focus them on the Nautilus or just catch glimpses of people who don't know they're being watched. You can see the sub and nearby U.S. submarine base by boat. The *River Queen II* (tel. 203/445–9516), which departs from the Thames River Inn, conducts sightseeing cruises.

🏛 *U.S. Naval Submarine Base (exit 86 off I–95 to Rte. 12, then left at Crystal Lake Rd.), Groton 06349, tel. 800/343–0079 or 203/449–3174. Admission free. Open mid-Apr.–mid-Oct., Wed.–Mon. 9–5; mid-Oct.–mid-Apr., Wed.–Mon. 9–4. Closed 1st full week in May and Dec.*

Maine

Lumberman's Museum

🏃🏃 6 – 15

This unusual nine-building museum up by huge, rugged Baxter State Park traces the history of the logging industry. It captures a feeling of a wild and almost frontier past and a present far removed from urban life. You can picture the lumbermen of the 1800s when you view the diorama of a miniature logging camp and full-size exhibits of bunkhouses and cookhouses here.

🏛 *Rte. 159 (at the northern entrance to Baxter State Park), Patten 04765, tel. 207/ 528–2650. Cost: $2.50 adults, $1.50 kids under 12. Open Memorial Day–Labor Day, Tues.–Sat. 9–4, Sun. 11–4; Labor Day– Columbus Day, weekends 11–4.*

Maine Maritime Museum

👫 4 – 15

Once there were nearly 100 shipyards on the banks of the Kennebec River. Now these old, white clapboard buildings and the new Maritime History Building are a museum filled with exhibits illustrating Maine's nearly 400-year-old shipbuilding, fishing, and lobstering past. In the main building you'll find some hands-on exhibits (you can try tapping out Morse code, for example). At the lobstering exhibit, you can learn exactly how lobster traps work and why lobstermen never paint their boats blue or utter the word "pig" aboard. The best time to come is in summer when there are demonstrations of seafaring techniques and weekly lobster bakes, and you can go aboard the vessels outdoors.

🏛 *243 Washington St. (Washington St. exit off Rte. 1), Bath 04530, tel. 207/443–1316. Cost: $6 adults, $2.50 kids 6–19. Open daily 9:30–5.*

Railway Village

👫 3 – 9

At this re-created turn-of-the-century museum village you can ride the Boothbay Central, pulled by a real steam-engine loco-motive over a narrow-gauge railroad just like the one that used to go through nearby Wis-casset. Stop in the old-fashioned ticket office and take the 1½-mile ride by a little red

schoolhouse, a doll museum, a bank, a barber shop, and 25 other buildings. On the village green, you can pet sheep and feed ducks.

🏛 *Rte. 27, Boothbay 04537, tel 207/633– 4727. Cost: $6 adults, $3 kids 12 and under. Open mid-June–mid-Sept., daily 9:30–5; mid-Sept.–Columbus Day weekends 9:30–5.*

Massachusetts

Basketball Hall of Fame

👫 5 – 15

Basketball was invented in Springfield in 1891 by Dr. James Naismith for his students at the School for Christian Workers, so it's entirely fitting that this 56,000-square-foot shrine documenting and celebrating all lev-els of the game, from high-school amateur to international professional, is located here. To us its atmosphere is more intense and action-oriented than that of any other sports museum, and like most families we left tired and perspiring. Again and again we took the moving sidewalk through the Shoot Out Hall and tried to beat our records for sinking baskets in 15 hoops set at different heights and distances. You can see a floor-to-ceiling arch of basketball shoes at the entrance to the professional section and a huge blowup of Hall of Famer Oscar Robertson dribbling a ball. Don't miss Bob Lanier's bronzed size-22 basket-ball shoes.

🏛 *1150 W. Columbus Ave. (exit 4 on I–91 N or exit 7 on I–91 S), Springfield 01101, tel. 413/781–6500. Cost: $7 adults, $4 kids 7–14. Open Sept.–June, daily 9–5; July and Aug., daily 9–6.*

Battleship *Massachusetts*

👫 7 – 15

This complex of six big and small U.S. Navy warships from World War II is special. If you've ever visited a submarine, skip the tour of the USS *Lionfish*'s bleak, confined quarters. Concentrate instead on the huge USS *Massachusetts*, a World War II battleship nicknamed "Big Mamie," whose main deck is twice the length of a football field. We saw more of what life was like on a ship for the 2,000 men aboard than we could on the *Intrepid* (see New York, below), because you can explore nine decks on your own (better than taking the tour); buttons at different stations activate information tapes. You can aim the battleship guns, climb the turrets, try out one of the 500 Navy bunks hung on chains, and eat in the air-conditioned snack bar aboard ship (it used to be the wardroom). Make sure you take a brochure with the plan and keep your kids close. Kids under 6 have legs that are too short for some of the climbing. You can combine a visit here with one to the New Bedford Whaling Museum (see below).

🏠 *Battleship Cove (exit 7 off Rte. 24), Fall River 02721, tel. 508/678–1100 or 800/ 533–3194. Cost: $8 adults, $4 kids 6–14. Open daily 9–5.*

Boston Tea Party Ship and Museum

👫 4 – 10

Most school-age kids know the story of how, in 1773, American revolutionists disguised as Indians crept aboard several ships in Boston Harbor loaded with tea from Britain, smashed the 340 tea chests, and threw them overboard to protest the newly imposed British taxes on tea. The small museum and fairly authentic replica of one of the ships, the *Beaver*, moored beside it, with crew members dressed in typical Colonial attire seemed an expensive, hokey, and commercial attraction to us. The best part was just looking at the *Beaver II* from the Congress Street bridge.

🏠 *Congress St. Bridge (South Station stop on Red Line T), Boston 02210, tel. 617/338–*

1773. Cost: $6 adults, $3 kids 5–15. Open Mar.–Memorial Day and Labor Day–Nov., daily 9–5; Memorial Day–Labor Day, daily 9–6; closed Dec.–Feb.

Children's Museum

👫 ALL

You can't miss it: a take-out snack bar in the shape of a giant white milk bottle with red trim and awnings stands on the wharf in front of a converted warehouse that houses the very best children's museum in the Northeast, the one that pioneered hands-on exhibits back in 1962 and became the model all the others copied. If you have preschoolers, ask at the Information desk for the booklet on exploring the museum with under-5s; there is even a section for kids under 2.

The multilevel spaces fill with kids under 12 and their parents making noise and playing—dancing with a skeleton, dressing up as a clown, wiggling in front of a giant color screen, climbing up the popular two-story open cagelike sculpture. Teen Tokyo on the top floor is designed to introduce American kids to what it would be like to be a teenager in Japan through contemporary music, biographies and photos of Japanese teenagers, comic books, Japanese animated films, and more. Standing in footprints on a real Japanese subway car and looking in on a teenager's room gave all of us a sense of how crowded everything there is. Also be sure to take your kids into the two-story Japanese silk merchant's house on the floor below.

🏠 *Museum Wharf, 300 Congress St. (South Station stop on Red Line T), Boston 02210, tel. 617/426–6500; What's Up line, 617/426–8855. Cost: $7 adults, $6 kids 2–15, $2 1-year-olds, $1 for all Fri. 5–9 PM. Open Tues.–Thurs. and weekends 10–5, Fri. 10–9.*

Computer Museum

 8+

For many kids, these two floors of hands-on, easy-to-use exhibits in the world's only Computer Museum (next to the Children's Museum) are like a technological playground. The giant working walk-through computer with a mouse and keyboard 50 times larger than life is overrated as a family attraction. The best part for families is Tools & Toys, seven jazzily designed environments with several dozen computer stations in which you can do everything from make your own cartoon to use a joystick to compose new songs from digitized sound samples to pretend to be an ant in a simulated ant colony, fending off invaders. We had a hard time pulling ourselves away from The Talking Computer, which explains how voice synthesis works and reads out sentences you type in, and the virtual reality chair.

Younger kids need parents to work with them. I'd think twice about bringing kids under 7 here (most of the kids we saw having fun here were over 10), but if you do, be sure to get the flyer, "Making the Most of Your Visit with Children," which is available at the Admission Desk.

🏛 *Museum Wharf, 300 Congress St. (South Station stop on Red Line T), Boston 02210, tel. 617/426–2800. Cost: $7 adults, $5 kids 5–17. Open Sept.–June, Tues.–Sun. 10–5; July–Aug., daily 10–6.*

Essex Shipbuilding Museum

 6 – 13

From 1650 to 1950 Essex was the Detroit of the shipbuilding industry. More wooden ships were built here than in any other place in the entire world—more than 4,000, mostly two-masted schooners—and this small museum tracks both how the work affected the people in the village and exactly how the ships were built, from the keel up.

Kids can try aspects of the building process themselves with real (not replica) shipbuilding tools at workstations in front of exhibits.
🏛 *Rte. 133W, Essex, tel. 508/786–7541. Cost: $3. Open May–Oct., Thurs.–Sun. 12–5.*

Higgins Armory Museum

6 – 15

The Higgins collection of medieval and Renaissance armor, originally put together in the 1920s and 1930s by steel magnate John Higgins, is even more exciting for kids than the arms and armor collection at New York City's Metropolitan Museum of Art. When we stood in the Great Hall during one of the regular sound-and-light shows, for example, we heard the clatter of dueling swords. During the engaging weekend presentations (daily in summer) kid volunteers are asked up on stage to try on chain mail (over a padded doublet, which answered many kids' questions about what knights wore underneath their armor) and helmets. Don't miss the armor for dogs.
🏛 *100 Barber Ave. (exit 1 from I–90 to Rte. 12N), Worcester 01616, tel. 508/853–6015. Cost: $4.75 adults, $3.75 kids 6–16. Open Sept.–June, Tues.–Sat. 10–4, Sun. 12–4; July–Aug., Mon.–Sat. 11–4, Sun. noon–4.*

Isabella Stewart Gardner Museum

7+

Just two blocks from Boston's Museum of Fine Arts is a mansion in the style of a Venetian palazzo built in 1903 by the eccentric socialite Isabella Stewart Gardner after her husband's death. Now it houses only her collection of artworks, but for a time the top two floors were also her home. Our favorite place in the museum is the Great Court, a reconstruction of a 15th-century Venetian Gothic palace court with hanging balconies, a mosaic floor, and a glass skylight

that feels like an indoor garden and looks like a set for *Romeo and Juliet*. (Stop at The Gardner Café, which overlooks the court, for an elegant dessert.) If your kids are curious about Mrs. Gardner, who once walked her pet ocelot down Tremont Street, there's a fine portrait of her, painted by John Singer Sargent, in the third-floor Gothic Room. In 1990 13 priceless art works were stolen from the museum in the largest art theft ever; they have yet to be recovered.
280 The Fenway, Boston 02199, tel. 617/566-1401. Cost: $6 adults, $3 students, kids under 12 free. Open year-round, Tues.–Sun. 11–5.

Museum of Fine Arts

8+

MFA (as it's called by Bostonians) contains gallery after gallery of masterpieces. It has a formal, gray-stone, Greek-columned look, plus a dramatic wing for contemporary art that also holds the cafeteria, which is full of light and open space. Kids like this museum for the silver pieces actually made by Paul Revere and the portraits of Revolutionary War heroes they've read about: George Washington (the famous painting by Gilbert Stuart), Paul Revere, John Hancock, Sam Adams, and John Quincy Adams. The collections of Egyptian art (the key attraction for kids are the mummies, which are more interesting than those in New York) and Asian art (visit the Japanese Garden) are among the most extensive in the world. The best bets for families are the self-guided tours using one of the Family Activity Booklets (they include sketch pads) available at the Information Center, and two drop-in programs. In the once-a-month Family Place (for kids 4 and up) families explore the museum's collections together through scavenger hunts, sketching, and games. In the Children's Room, weekly dramatics and art workshops for ages 6 to 12 (no parents) highlight the museum's collections.

465 Huntington Ave. (Ruggles/Museum stop on the E Green Line T), Boston 02115, tel. 617/267-9300. Cost: $8 adults, $3.50 kids 6–17, free Wed. 4–9:45. Open Tues. 10–4:45, Wed. 10–9:45, Thurs.–Sun. 10–4:45.

Museum of Science

2+

Almost as soon as we entered the largest science museum in the Northeast we got lost in its complicated layout of east and west wings on three floors, which are not all accessible to one another without backtracking. Carrying a floor plan with you is essential. On a plot of land that straddles the Charles River between Boston and Cambridge, this museum of interactive exhibits is a favorite place of all the kids on my Boston panel, including preschoolers, who head for the two-level Discovery Center to touch and hold bones, huge shells, and rocks and to watch mice in glass tanks. But the other 400-plus exhibits are a mixed bag. Concentrate on the Human Body Discovery Space, where kids take turns riding on a bike and see the skeleton opposite mimic them; the holograms; the Rube Goldberg–like autokinetic sculpture in which bells ring, balls go around, and buzzers go off; the sound stairs, which play a different note on each step as you walk up; the electron microscope and observatory; and most spectacular, the two-story Theater of Electricity. An Omni Theater and Planetarium have regular shows.
Science Park (Science Park stop on Green Line T), Boston 02114, tel. 617/723-2500. Cost: $7 adults, $5 kids 3–14; free Wed. PM. Open Mon.–Thurs. and weekends 9–5, Fri. 9–9.

New England Science Center

3 – 15

This large, catch-all center on 60 acres has everything from a wildlife center (see Chapter 10) to old-fashioned, fairly ordinary natural history dioramas to more modern, interactive question-oriented exhibits to a narrow-gauge railroad and nature trails. Some of what's here is fascinating, some not, but the regular Sky Watch programs at the Norton Observatory, during which you first get acquainted with stars, planets, or the moon through a planetarium show, then view the same thing from several sizes of telescopes are something most museums don't offer; these are best for 12 and up. 🏛 *222 Harrington Way (off Rte. 9), Worcester 01604, tel. 508/791–9211. Cost: $6 adults, $4 kids 3–16 and college students with ID. $12 Sky Watch evening program. Open Mon.–Sat. 10–5, Sun. 12–5.*

Salem Wax Museum of Witches and Seafarers

👫 8+

It's not one of the official museum stops in Salem, even though its 13 stage sets with 50 figures (not all gruesome) convey different aspects of Salem's colorful past. Among the things that make it more interesting than other such museums is that it has a section where kids can learn how wax figures are produced and make a gravestone rubbing. 🏛 *Derby St., Salem 01970, tel. 508/740–2929. Cost: $4 adults, $2.50 kids under 14. Open Nov.–June, daily 10–4:30; July–Aug., 10–6; Oct.–Nov. weekends, late hrs.*

Salem Witch Museum

👫 7+

Salem was a major seaport from which ships sailed to China and the East Indies in the 17th and 18th centuries, but everyone remembers it for the "witch trials" that took place here in 1692. The museum, an imposing, heavy stone structure that resembles a church, across from the town Common, seems a fittingly solemn setting for the subject from the outside, but it may disappoint

you. The exhibits consist of just 13 stage sets with life-size figures built into the walls of the auditorium. The room is dark when you enter for the half-hour presentation that uses the stage sets, sound effects, and narration of accusations, court proceedings, and hangings to dramatize what happened and why. I found all the eerie music and facts gruesome, but tourists off the bus and older kids in the audience seemed to revel in it all; some little kids were scared and had to leave. 🏛 *Washington Sq. (off Washington St.), Salem 01970, tel. 508/744–1692. Cost: $4 adults, $2.50 kids 6–14. Open Sept.–June, daily 10–5; July–Aug., daily 10–7.*

Sports Museum of New England

👫 6+

This museum in Cambridge celebrates all sports from baseball and candlepin bowling to marathon running and sailing. Besides displaying sports memorabilia, though, many exhibits here attempt to tell a story, which makes the information easier for kids to grasp, while others imaginatively let you take part in the actual experience of playing or watching. At "Catching Clemens" you put your face into a catcher's mask, your hand into a glove, call Roger Clemens's pitch, and feel the sting of the ball in your mitt. When you relive the greatest moments of a particular sport on video, you'll sit on real stadium seats in a small room painted to look like a local football or baseball stadium. But what makes it a great family stop is its location in one of Boston's most family-oriented shopping malls. Family members less interested in sports can shop while the fanatics immerse themselves in sports history. 🏛 *100 CambridgeSide Pl., CambridgeSide Galleria (Red Line T to Kendall Square stop, then pick up the free CambridgeSide Galleria shuttle), Cambridge 02141, tel. 617/787–7678. Cost: $6 adults, $4.50 kids 4–7. Open Mon.–Sat. 10–9:30, Sun. 12–6.*

Thornton Burgess Museum

👫 3 – 10

If your kids have read the Mother West Wind stories by Thornton Burgess about Reddy Fox, Paddy the Beaver, and other animals, as my son—and my husband before him—did, they may be as taken with this picture-book perfect museum memorial as we were. Burgess visited his aunt Arabella Eldred Burgess in this typical 19th-century house, where you can look at original illustrations for Burgess's books (most interesting to adults) and try on animal costumes (most interesting to kids). But what felt most special was sitting under a shady tree for the Story Hour featuring live animals corresponding to those in the stories and feeding swans and ducks on the pond afterwards.
🏠 4 Water St. (edge of Shawme Pond), Sandwich 02537, tel. 508/888–6870. Cost: donation. Open Apr.–Dec., daily 10–4, Sun. 1–4; story hr daily July and Aug. and most holidays.

U.S.S. *Constitution* and Museum

👫 4+

At the Charlestown Navy Yard, Boston's number-one historical attraction, across the Charles River from Boston proper, we got a real sense of early United States maritime history from just walking around. It's big: The grounds include a National Historical Park Visitor's center, two ships you can board, a couple of museums, a grand waterfront walk, and more. Much is free. But what we most wanted to see was the USS *Constitution*, nicknamed "Old Ironsides," a wooden 44-gun three-masted ship built in 1797. It got its nickname because during the War of 1812 even British cannon balls bounced off its 2-foot-thick oak hull. (A good book: *The Story of Old Ironsides* by Norman Richards, Children's Press.) Unfortunately, the ship is in dry dock for repairs until 1997 (a video tour of the ship is in the museum). The sailor guides tell entertaining stories about hardships aboard—such as the fact that men aboard only bathed every five or six months. Until the ship is refloated, kids may have more fun in the *Constitution* Museum's exhibits about the ship's history, especially in "Life at Sea," where they can swing in a sailor's hammock, hoist sails, and take a crew member's role in a computerized video of the War of 1812.
🏠 Charlestown Navy Yard (Bus 93 from Haymarket; tel. 617/722–3200 for schedule), Charlestown 02129, tel. 617/426–1812. Cost: museum only, $4 adults, $2 kids 6–16. Admission to Navy Yard free. Open: ship daily 9:30–sunset, tours to 3:30; museum, Dec.–Feb. 10–3, Mar.–May 10–5, June–Aug. 10–5:30, Sept.–Nov. 10–5.

Wenham Museum

👫 4 – 13

Seeing the world-class collection of 1,000 dolls made from wood, china, cloth, rubber, leather, even metal, in this 17th-century house 25 miles north of Boston is a must for doll lovers. It's the most appealing doll museum I've seen (though it's not all dolls). The intricate dollhouses are fascinating: A Victorian mansion even has parquet floors and stained-glass windows. Also in the museum are tools once used to cut ice in Wenham lake for shipment to India and Australia.
🏠 132 Main St. (Rte. 1A), Wenham 01984, tel. 508/468–2377. Cost: $3 adults, $1 kids 6–14. Open weekdays 11–4, Sat. 1–4, Sun. 2–5.

Whaling Museum

👫 6 – 15

You might want to screen the movie version of the book, *Moby Dick*, before you come to this museum in the world's most famous whaling port. Historic New Bedford is the city from which Captain Ahab set off in his quest for the great white whale. Of all the whaling museums in the Northeast, this one best re-creates that world for kids. It's not just the collection, which includes an 89-foot-long model of a full-rigged whaling bark kids can climb aboard, and real harpoons and blubber hooks to touch. It's also that the museum is in what was once the world's whaling capital. Just looking at the buildings and wharves nearby recalls that past. The museum's 25-minute silent film of an actual whale voyage is action-packed, but when they captured the whale in the end, it upset some 5-year-olds in the audience. The kids with us were fascinated by the story of scrimshaw and bought souvenir examples in the shop.

🏛 *18 Johnny Cake Hill (exit 15 off I–95 to "Downtown" exit, then right on Elm St., left on Bethel), New Bedford 02740, tel. 508/997–0046. Cost: $4.50 adults, $3 kids 6–14. Open Mon.–Sat. 9–5, Sun. 1–5 (July and Aug., Sun. hrs. 11–5).*

New Hampshire

Children's Metamorphosis Museum

👫 1 – 7

What sets this small children's museum apart from others its size is how light and bright and clean it is and the fact that kids can play with everything they see. From the outside the museum looks like a ranch house, and inside it's a series of small rooms, each with one exhibit, such as the "Sticky Room" of Velcro boards and magnets.

🏛 *217 Rockingham Rd., Londonderry 03053, tel. 603/425–2560. Cost: $3.50, kids under 1 free. Open Tues.–Thurs. and Sat. 9:30–5, Fri. 9:30–8, Sun. 1–5.*

Christa McAuliffe Planetarium

👫 3+

Named for the Concord, New Hampshire, teacher who perished on the *Challenger* space mission, this small planetarium is one of the most appealing in the Northeast for kids because of its intimate size (just 92 seats), the way shows make you feel as though you are traveling through space (an effect of the Digistar projector), and the box of interactive buttons on each seat that allow kids to participate in choosing what you'll see in the show. A small exhibit area houses hands-on activities, but don't come here unless you plan to see the show. There are special shows for preschoolers.

🏛 *3 Institute Dr. (Exit 15E off I–93), Concord 03301, tel. 603/271–2842. Cost: $5 adults, $3 kids 3–17. Open Sept.–mid-June, Thurs.–Sun.; mid-June–Labor Day and during school vacations, Tues.–Sun. Hrs and show times vary; call first. Reservations advised.*

Heritage New Hampshire

👫 4 – 13

Strictly speaking, this crash course in 300 years of New Hampshire's history is a commercial attraction, not a museum; the 25 scenes showing different periods and events in the state's history are full of the kinds of special effects kids (mine included) love. Despite a touristy flavor, it's fairly authentic. When we boarded the ship *Reliance* for our 60-day "voyage" from England to Mason's Grant in the New World, we smelled codfish (it's in a barrel), heard seagulls squawk, saw lightning flash and sails billow, and felt the ship roll while the captain gave us some sobering facts. Not all scenes were quite so involving, and some of the speeches given by mechanized mannequins may impress little kids more than cynical teenagers, but real trout swim in the Amoskeag Falls, and the woodsman carves spoons and gives them to kids as souvenirs.

🏠 *Rte. 16 (6 mi north of North Conway), Glen 03838, tel. 603/383–9776. Cost: $7.50 adults, $4.50 kids 6–12. Open mid-May–mid-Oct., daily 9–5; mid-June–Labor Day, daily 9–6.*

New York

Adirondack Museum

👫 **3+**

This outstanding outdoor museum devoted to the social history of the region perches on the side of Blue Mountain. Just dipping in and out of the 22 buildings on this "campus" with spectacular views of lakes and mountains gave our family a picture of and feeling for what the Adirondacks were like in the past—from the days of mining and logging camps, fishing, trapping, and boatbuilding, to the Gilded Age in the 19th and early 20th century, when robber barons arrived on private railway cars at their huge log "Great Camps," and upper-class city dwellers took launches to fancy "rustic" hotels on remote islands.

In a massive, wood-columned pavilion in the center of the campus you'll find an old steamboat and the short Marion River Carry locomotive, which took travelers on the shortest stretch of railroad track in the country—from one side of an island in Racquette Lake to the other. Kids can climb aboard. Other exhibits include the luxurious private railroad car that once belonged to financier Austin Corbin, with its mahogany-paneled, red-plush sitting area and casual club car.

🏠 *On Rtes. 28 N and 30, Blue Mountain Lake 12812, tel. 518/352–7311. Cost: $10 adults, $6 kids 7–16. Open late May–Oct., daily 9:30–5:30.*

American Museum of Natural History

👫 **ALL**

This is the best natural history museum in the Northeast—in fact, in the entire country—with 30 million artifacts and specimens displayed on four floors. One of the country's "must-see" museums for families, it's on the top-10 list of every kid on my New York City panel, regardless of age.

The building, set in its own four-block park, has several entrances, but we still like to go in the main one, across from Central Park, because as soon as you walk in, you see the tallest freestanding dinosaur exhibit in the world—a five-story tall Barosaurus rearing up to defend its baby from an Allosaurus—right there in the rotunda. For some of the kids we consulted, especially those 5 and up, the museum's world-renowned collection of dinosaurs are *the* highlight.

Other kids, including mine, prefer the meticulously crafted lifelike dioramas with stuffed animal specimens. Those in the two-story Hall of African Mammals with the realistic elephant herd displayed in its center and the Hall of North American Mammals are his favorites. Because the glass goes almost to the floor, even tikes in strollers can see. If you have a toddler or preschooler, spend some time in the dimly lighted Hall of Ocean Life (the blue whale model is suspended from the ceiling), a large self-contained space down a flight of stairs, with dioramas of walruses, seals, and sharks.

The museum has excellent family workshops (once we helped carve a Tibetan butter sculpture) and dance, music, and storytelling programs for children. The attached **Hayden Planetarium** (for kids 3 and up) has two sky shows specifically for children: Wonderful Sky with the Sesame Street Muppets, intended for 3- to 6-year-olds, and Robots in Space, a "tour of the universe" for 7- to 12-year-olds. (Reservations are needed for these.)

🏛 *Central Park West between 77th and 81st Sts. (Subway C or B to 81st St.), tel. 212/ 769–5100. Cost: $6 adults, $3 kids. Open Sun.–Thurs. 10–5:45, Fri.–Sat. 10–8:45; Hayden Planetarium, $5 adults, $2.50 kids. Open Oct.–June, weekdays 12:30–4:45, Sat. 10– 5:45, Sun. noon–5:45; July–Sept., weekdays 12:30–4:45, weekends noon–4:45.*

Brooklyn Children's Museum

(👫 0 – 12)

A corrugated metal tunnel entrance leads into this multilevel hands-on play-and-learn museum, which tells you that this will be an unusual and exuberant place. Though it is small compared with the huge Boston Children's Museum and difficult to get to, it's worth it. Not only is it the oldest children's museum in the country (nearly 100 years old), but it's also unique among those we've been to in terms of imaginative graphics and museum design. The tunnel, lighted by bands of neon, is the museum's central core. Kids run up and down the ramp inside it to get to all the exhibits, stopping to put their hands in the raised water trough, complete with waterwheel, that flows down its center. The graphics of the exhibits are particularly wild, like brightly painted stage sets inside an old factory.

All the exhibits try to link the business of a museum—displaying artifacts and collections to inform people—with kids' lives and concerns. In the Night Journeys exhibit about sleep, beds, and dreams, kids can try out a life-size re-creation of an Egyptian leather-strap bed and the hard headrests or write down bad dreams and push them into the mouth of a wooden monster, Baku, the Dream Eater. In the Music Room, you can make music by dancing on huge piano keys on the floor (even parents can't resist this).

Be sure to check the day's big information board: There's an excellent short workshop or program for some age group going on just about every half hour.

🏛 *145 Brooklyn Ave. (take Subway 3 to Kingston Ave.; walk 6 blocks on Kingston to St. Mark's Ave., then left 1 block to the museum), Brooklyn 11213, tel. 718/735–4400. Cost: $3 suggested contribution. Open Wed.–Fri. 2–5; weekends and holiday weeks 12–5.*

Ellis Island and Immigration Museum

(👫 10+)

Touring this national museum on a historic island in New York Harbor can be a moving experience for families, but I'm convinced it's primarily for kids over 12 who are beginning to be interested in their own identities and where they come from. Between 1892 and 1954 about 12 million immigrants from all over the world, many fleeing poverty or political or religious persecution, came through the immigration-processing center on Ellis Island, which reopened as a museum in 1990. An estimated 40% of all Americans have at least one relative or ancestor who was among these immigrants. The restored buildings include the great hall where newcomers were questioned as well as exhibit galleries with photographs, maps, posters, and objects telling the story of what happened to them. Taped personal stories of real people bombard you as you walk through. To us the most moving exhibit was the display of precious items people brought with them, entitled "Treasures from Home," which prompted a discussion of what we would take with us if we had to leave our home behind.

Coming here with a grandparent or a relative who actually immigrated and can explain why he or she came to America would make the experience even more meaningful for kids. Bring a picnic. This is among the most heavily visited national monuments, so go on a weekday if you can or on the earliest morning boat on a weekend to avoid long lines.

🏛 *Ellis Island, New York 10004, tel. 212/ 363–8340. Take Statue of Liberty boat that* stops at both Liberty and Ellis Islands from Battery Park; tickets at Castle Clinton in park, tel. 212/269–5755; cost: $7 adults, $3 kids 3–17; boats depart every 45 min 9:30–3:30, every ½-hr May–Labor Day. Museum free. Open Sept.–June, daily 9:30–5; July–Aug., daily 9:30–5:30.

Intrepid Sea/Air/Space Museum

👫 4 – 15

When you board the USS *Intrepid,* an aircraft carrier used in World War II that is permanently moored at a pier in the Hudson River, you can see the fastest spy plane in the world and 40 other aircraft, space vehicles, and rockets. This is the only museum in the world in an aircraft carrier and the world's largest naval museum (owned and maintained by the U.S. Navy). It includes the USS *Growler,* a guided missile submarine, and the USS *Edson,* a destroyer, moored on the other side of the pier.

See the short film in the main exhibit hall, which shows how planes take off and land on a carrier's deck, before you walk around. Inside the carrier several huge halls have displays of photographs, videos, and battleship and airplane models, each focusing on a different war period. Most kids want to head for things you can climb on or peer into, like the cockpit of a fighter plane, or just explore the ship's passageways and walk around the deck looking at the planes. The naval personnel on the navigation bridge answer questions and explain how officers guided the carrier and why it is painted "battleship gray."

As you can't explore cabins and the engine room on the *Intrepid,* be sure to take the 25-minute tour of the USS *Edson.* Everything is impressively compact, especially the stacked, curtained bunks for enlisted men with not even enough space to sit up.

The lines for the 20-minute tour of the USS *Growler* submarine have always been long

when we've been here. Only 13 people at a time can board, so you'll almost always have to wait at least half an hour.
🏫 *Pier 86, W. 46th St. at 12th Ave. (Subway A, E, or C to 42nd St.; Bus M42 to last stop), New York 10036, tel. 212/245–0072. Cost: $7 adults, $4 kids 6–11. Open early Sept.– May, Wed.–Sun. 10–5; Memorial Day–Labor Day, daily 10–5.*

Metropolitan Museum of Art

👫 4+

The Met (as it's known to New Yorkers) is the largest art museum in the Western Hemisphere and feels like it. With kids, this is one museum where it's essential to get a map, pick only a few exhibits or rooms to see, and not stay too long before you head for lunch in the cafeteria or a walk in Central Park behind the museum.

Kids like the full suits of armor for people and horses and the swords in the hall of arms and armor. The collection of mummies in the Egyptian galleries is also a hit, but seeing the Temple of Dendur, a real Egyptian temple moved here because it would have been submerged after the Aswan Dam was built, eclipses them for us. It's set on a platform and illuminated by a full wall of glass. Another exhibit we always have to visit is the Ming Dynasty Chinese Garden Court on the second floor. Walking through the circular entrance is like entering an area outside an old Chinese home to discover a tiny goldfish pool, plants, rocks and seats. At Christmas, don't miss the decorated tree and crèche display in the medieval hall.

Check at the information desk for the "Museum Hunt" and family gallery guides. Among the best times to go on weekends are Friday and Saturday evenings, when there are also concerts (see Entertainment and the Arts in Chapter 4), and the first thing Sunday morning.
🏫 *1000 5th Ave., between 82nd and 84th Sts. (Subway 4, 5, or 6 to 86th St.), New York*

10028, tel. 212/879–5500. Cost: suggested donation $6 adults, $3 students, kids under 12 free. Open Tues.–Sun. 9:30–5:15, Fri.–Sat. 9:30–8:45.

Museum of Television and Radio

5 – 15

Unlike the subjects of most museums, TV is something kids consider important in their own lives. What they don't know is its history. The museum's collection of 25,000 TV programs and 15,000 radio programs that span broadcast history is bound to contain some of your favorites. The museum has temporary exhibits that appeal very much to kids. One was a new technology exhibit in which kids could try out real-time animation to control a cartoon character; another displayed masks and costumes from Star Trek and provided a behind-the-scenes look at characters' makeup. The Saturday morning screenings, annual Children's Television Festival (more for kids 4–10), and radio workshops for kids 8 to 13 in which they learn how to re-create the sound effects and performances from radio shows of the 30s and 40s are terrific.

12 W. 52nd St. (Subway B, D, F, or Q to Rockefeller Center), New York 10019, tel. 212/621–6600. Cost: $5 adults, $4 kids. Open Tues.–Sun. 12–6, Thurs. 12–8, Fri. 12–9.

National Baseball Hall of Fame

6+

If your kids are baseball fans, this is mecca—*the* place they simply have to visit once in a lifetime. Everything you ever wanted to see and know about baseball except a live game is on these three floors of memorabilia, equipment, clothing, cards, photos, videos, and books, with life-size carved wooden statues of great stars greeting you as you enter. Don't skip the short introductory film

of baseball-movie and great-player clips. Half the fun is sitting in ballpark seats in a movie theater painted to look like a stadium while sound effects re-create hawkers' offers of hot dogs and peanuts.

In the records room you can check out how today's players compare with those in the past or call up information about Hall of Famers on video machines. You can see how a baseball is manufactured, and displays on early Negro baseball leagues and old equipment (baseball gloves used in the mid-1800s looked just like ordinary winter gloves). Trailers of baseball movies like *A League of Their Own, Field of Dreams,* and *The Natural* run continuously on a screen near the library alongside an exhibit of baseball-movie props. Don't even consider joining the hordes on July 4th or when the Hall of Fame inductions are held in early spring.

Main St., Cooperstown 13326, tel. 607/547–7200. Cost: $8 adults, $3 kids 7–12. Open May–Oct., daily 9–9; Nov.–Apr., daily 9–5.

New York Hall of Science

3 – 15

Although it can't compete with Boston's Museum of Science in terms of sheer size, the Hall of Science is one of the 10 best science museums in the United States in terms of the quality of its exhibits. It has the added virtue of feeling encompassable, intimate, and unusually friendly, something due partly to the museum's circular interior and partly to the group of young college student "explainers," who can answer kids' questions. The newest permanent exhibit, SoundSensations, in a musical chamber, took the mystery out of CDs and tapes for Gavin and gave him the chance to mix tracks, arrange synthesized music sources with just his hands, and even become the electrical link between one of the several music sources and a speaker. Other major exhibits explore color, optical illusions, light, microorganisms, and the atom. The only drawbacks are weekend crowds; the best time we had here was when Gavin's Cub Scout den and 200 other Scouts camped overnight on the mezzanine, because no one had to wait to try anything, even the popular bubble table on the main floor where you can blow bubbles 2 feet across or the video microscope center where you view tiny insects on a TV screen.

🏛 *47–01 111th St. (Subway 7 to 111th St.), Flushing Meadows, Queens 11368, tel. 718/ 699–0005. Cost: $3.50 adults, $2.50 kids (free parking). Open Wed.–Sun. 10–5.*

Old Rhinebeck Aerodrome

👫 6+

Of the several airplane museums in the Northeast, this one is a favorite because of its colorful but corny weekend airshows. Battles of World War I are reenacted in costume as crowds cheer for the good guys and announcers explain just what is going on. Other demonstrations range from thrilling aerobatics to funny comedy routines, but all of it takes you back to the exciting Red Baron era of flying. Though the walking tour of restored airplanes in several hangars is led by enthusiastic guides who can—and will—tell mechanically inclined kids as much as they want to know, the air shows here are the real treat. You view the shows from outdoor bleachers; take hats in summer and jackets in the fall.

🏛 *U.S. 9 (U.S. 9 north from Rhinebeck to Stone Church Rd., then watch for signs), Rhinebeck 12572, tel. 914/758–8610. Cost: $10 adults, $5 kids 6–10. Open mid-May–Oct., daily 10–5; air shows weekends only mid-June–mid-Oct.*

Rhode Island

Of this state's few museums, only two appeal to kids. If you're visiting: The lively Children's Museum of Rhode Island in a Vic-

torian mansion in Pawtucket (tel. 401/726–2590) and the small Museum of Natural History (for 9 and up) in Roger Williams Park in Providence (tel. 401/985–9450). Check Chapter 7 for listings of the many famous houses and sites to view.

Vermont

Fairbanks Museum and Planetarium

👫 5 – 13

Remember when natural history museums were vast collections of curious treasures in big old buildings where you felt as though you should whisper? That's just how we felt in the 130-foot long great hall of this ornate, red sandstone Victorian structure right on Main Street that manages to be wonderfully old-fashioned, cozy, and grandly impressive all at the same time. Four large stuffed bears, one an immense standing Kodiak bear, greet you by the entrance. The exhibits have character: stuffed specimens and strange artifacts neatly displayed behind oak-trimmed glass cases, everything from a giant clam to paper made from the bark of a mulberry tree.

The shows in the small 50-seat planetarium have the same personal, eclectic flavor—each of the six staff interpreters stresses what she or he is interested in. Ours told Indian stories about the constellations. The weather center in the basement lets you watch weather forecasters prepare maps, consult computer data, and make their broadcast. In summer a children's nature room is staffed by kids 10 to 15.

🏛 *Main St., St. Johnsbury 05819, tel. 802/ 748–2372. Cost: $4 adults, $2.50 kids under 12, $10 families. Open Sept.–June, Mon.–Sat. 10–4, Sun. 1–5; July and Aug., Mon.–Sat. 10–6, Sun. 1–5.*

Montshire Museum of Science

 2+

This is the complete opposite of the Fairbanks Museum (see above). A cathedral-ceilinged, open, modern space on 100 peaceful acres above the Connecticut River, it hums with the noise and activity of kids launching pennies to spiral down into the dark hole of the "gravity well" or watching 250,000 leaf-cutter ants or playing around with the other natural and physical science exhibits or taking a nature trail. It's a miniversion of Boston's Museum of Science transplanted to the country, but it has one thing that huge museum doesn't: a physics playground. The equipment is typical playground stuff, but set up so you can experiment; the seesaw has adjustable weights underneath so two kids of widely differing weights can balance out. Of all their special weekend events, the most unusual is the annual igloo-building workshop in February.

🏠 *Rte. 10A, Norwich 05055, tel. 802/649–2200. Cost: $5 adults, $3 kids 3–17. Open daily 10–5.*

Shelburne Museum

 5+

Imagine a great collection of all the very best American folk art, artifacts, and architecture gathered up on 45 acres to make one perfect small Vermont village of 37 19th-century houses and shops, a round barn, and a covered bridge, where the smell of one of the finest lilac gardens in New England greets visitors in May. That's the Shelburne Museum. It's slightly stiff and proper, with quilts and weathervanes, dolls and toys, furniture and pewter pitchers, sleighs and carriages, less a living history center than Sturbridge Village, where kids can be more involved. A jitney service helps those whose legs get tired. "Owl Cottage," the family activity center, offers tours, workshops (register in advance; tel. 802/985–3346, ext. 395), and games to involve kids more directly in the historical era. Time a visit for one of the special events weekends, such as July 4th or Lilac Sunday or the December Christmas celebration.

🏠 *Rte. 7, Shelburne 05482, tel. 802/985–3344. Cost: $17.50 adults, $7 kids 6–14. Open May–Oct., daily 10–5; Nov.–Apr., daily at 1: 2-hr guided tour ($6 adults, $2 kids 6–14) only.*

ANIMALS, ANIMALS
ZOOS, AQUARIUMS, GAME FARMS, AND WILDLIFE SANCTUARIES

9

Are there any kids who don't like to pet or just watch animals? Not among the ones I know, even 1-year-olds and those in their teens, who all put visiting zoos and aquariums high on their lists of favorite things to do. As Gavin is no exception, we've always tried to work in an animal visit on any trip. In the Northeast you can see all kinds, from baby animals to pet at a charming farm in New Hampshire to the exotic species at one of the world's greatest zoos—the Bronx Zoo in New York City—and the sea life at several terrific aquariums—in Boston, New York City, and Mystic, Connecticut. But don't neglect smaller places: As befits a region with a long coastline on the Atlantic Ocean, the Northeast has some small aquariums right next to the water that provide opportunities for kids to handle crabs and jellyfish (see also Chapter 5). Inland you'll find everything from a game farm that raises exotic animals and sells them to the country's zoos to science centers that introduce kids to species native to the Northeast such as beavers and deer (see also Chapter 6). Many children's museums (see Chapter 8) have petting areas and small aquariums. In our experience most of the region's wildlife sanctuaries and Audubon centers are more appealing as places to hike than to see animals (see Chapters 10 and 12); I've included here only a couple that have special live-animal exhibits or injured animal programs that appeal to kids.

Uncomfortable with the image of just being menageries for viewing animals in cages, people who run zoos and aquariums in the Northeast have taken a strong conservation tack in the past few years, actively working to preserve and breed endangered species. They're spreading word with interactive exhibits and educational programs for kids.

We've found that age often makes a big difference in the kinds of animals kids are interested in. When Gavin was a toddler, he was just as excited about feeding chickens in a barnyard as he was about looking at sea lions and giraffes. At age 7 it was monkeys of all kinds that appealed, and the idea of petting farm animals was pronounced babyish. Now, at 15, he's more taken with the whole idea of complete environments—like a tropical rain forest—and more concerned about whether or not a friend is along. For him, as with most kids, having a chance to interact with animals—feed, hold, pet, or at least get as close as possible—has always been the real highlight, so my choices for this chapter are heavily weighted toward places where kids can do all those things.

Connecticut

Beardsley Park and Zoological Gardens

👫 ALL

Connecticut's only zoo, 36 acres in a 180-acre park, has the only South American rain forest in New England in the zoo's New World Tropics building, which opened in 1992. Its four main viewing areas, separated by bamboo and glass walls and lighted by skylights, are home to four different kinds of monkey, small crocodilelike creatures called caimans, ocelots, toucans, macaws, and other exotic animals. If you stop for a break next to a glass barrier, a curious woolly monkey may even peer through it at you and tap on the glass.

The zoo has been gradually moving its animals from old-style cages to natural habitats and plans a number of buildings for indoor exhibits. Most of the hoofed animals graze in a field set off by a moat. Little kids we know gravitate toward the children's zoo—a New England farm setting where you can feed unusual species of farm animals and walk through a covered bridge.

🏠 Noble Ave., Bridgeport 06608, tel. 203/576–8082. Cost: $4 adults, $2 kids 3–15; parking $3. Open daily 9–4.

Hungerford Outdoor Education Center

👫 3 – 12

Housed in a restored horse stable set on 27 acres, Hungerford has a range of animals that kids can get close to, from a capuchin monkey to rabbits and tarantulas inside, and geese, turkeys, goats, sheep, ducks, chickens, and even a bull outside. Exhibits focus on teaching respect for animals and on wildlife rehabilitation. Regular animal talks are particularly good, with lots of questions from kids and a chance to touch animals.

🏠 191 Farmington Ave., Rte. 372, Kensington 06037, tel. 203/827–9064. Cost: $2 adults, $1 kids 2–18. Open Labor Day–mid-June, Tues.–Fri. 1–5, Sat. 10–5; July and Aug., Tues.–Fri. 11–5, Sat. 10–5.

Maritime Center at Norwalk

👫 ALL

This complex, opened in 1988 in a restored 19th-century foundry, includes a maritime museum, the only IMAX theater in Connecticut, two seagoing boats for cruises, and a working boat shop in addition to a wonderful aquarium devoted to the marine life of Long Island Sound and the Atlantic Ocean. Because it's less well known and smaller than Mystic's aquarium (it has a mere 1,100 specimens), the Center is also less crowded, even on weekends. What's special in this aquarium is the ingenious way the 20 marine environments are arranged: You progress from a shallow salt marsh with sand shrimp and mussels through each successive level of habitat to the depths of the ocean. A 110,000-gallon tank houses the Center's sand tiger sharks and sandbar sharks, some of which are 9 feet long. The viewing windows (they are 4 inches thick, so you're safe) go almost to the floor; even little kids can easily watch the sharks swimming by. A tank in the "Communities beneath the Sound" section shows which kinds of fish live around a shipwreck.

If your kids are between 4 and 11, be sure to try out the "Waterworks" display in which they can build toy dams and maneuver lighthouses, boats, and bridges to understand about water and waves. If you plan to see an IMAX show (for kids over 5), buy your tickets as soon as you arrive or reserve in advance; we've sometimes missed out because they are usually sold out by showtime. The two research cruises in the Sound are appropriate for interested older (8 and up) kids; participants get to help collect animals and record data. Regular (weekends in May and June, daily in summer) 45-minute walk-in kids' programs are great.

🏠 *10 N. Water St., Norwalk 06854, tel. 203/852–0700. Exit 14 northbound or 15 southbound off I–95. Cost: $7.50 adults, $6.50 kids 2–12; IMAX theater, $6 adults, $4.50 kids 2–12. Open daily 10–5.*

Mystic Marinelife Aquarium

(👫 ALL)

Along with the Mystic Seaport Museum (see Chapter 7) nearby, this great aquarium is one of our favorite places in the Northeast, a must-see for traveling families. It's also Connecticut's number-one tourist attraction, drawing hordes of people in summer (though not as many as the New England Aquarium in Boston); if you can, come in spring or fall.

Mystic Marinelife has the largest collection of marine mammals in the Northeast, including three beluga whales, dolphins, and more than 50 seals and sea lions. You can see (and hear) four kinds of seals as you walk around the huge 2½-acre outdoor Seal Island complex, which re-creates New England, California, and Pacific Northwest rocky coastal habitats. The penguins in the outdoor Penguin Pavilion nearby don't look like the ones from the Antarctic; these are African blackfooted penguins. Don't miss watching them swim underwater from inside one of the glass bubbles that jut into the tank.

Inside are nearly 50 more exhibits, including a shark tank with 16 viewing windows where you can see the sand and nurse sharks swim around an Atlantic coral reef with lots of colorful fish; it's nowhere near as impressive as the saltwater tank at the Aquarium in Boston. Among the interactive exhibits you can look through a series of lenses to see what a fish sees and learn how to estimate a fish's age.

At the daily 30-minute shows in the Marine Theater you'll see dolphins leap 20 feet into the air, vocalize, swim in formation, and walk on the water on their tails. The large-screen film, *The Deep Frontier*, is for kids 8 and up.

🏠 *55 Coogan Blvd., Mystic 06355, tel. 203/572–5955 or 203/536–9631. Exit 90 off I–95. Cost: $9.50 adults, $6 kids 5–12. Open Labor Day–July 1, daily 9–4:30 (grounds close at 6); July 1–Labor Day, daily 9–7 (grounds close at 8).*

Science Center of Connecticut

(👫 3 – 12)

The only zoo in Hartford is part of this center filled with many other kinds of science exhibits. The indoor/outdoor Live Animal Center, though very small, includes 30 different species (including cougars, reptiles, birds, and small mammals) and a touch tank. The talking macaws, who can imitate the way different members of the staff say hello and even the way they sneeze, are hilarious. Each day there's a short talk about one kind of animal, which includes the story of how it came to the museum. Kids get to touch the animals at the end of the talk.

🏠 *950 Trout Brook Dr., West Hartford 06119, tel. 203/231–2824. Cost: $5 adults, $4 kids 3–15. Open Sept.–June, Tues.–Fri. 10–4, Sat. 10–5, Sun. noon–5; July and Aug., weekdays 10–4, Sat. 10–5, Sun. noon–5.*

Maine

Acadia Zoological Park

(👫 1 – 12)

The most interesting exhibit at this small collection of 40 species just 16 miles north of Bar Harbor is the large barn full of rainforest creatures. Black and white colobus monkeys, rare golden lion tamarins (the zoo is part of a worldwide effort to save and reintroduce to the wild this endangered species), lemurs, poison-arrow frogs, 2-inch-long hissing cockroaches, and more inhabit this space. Outside are moose and reindeer and some farm animals to pet. In July and August, an elephant comes to visit.

🏠 RFD 1, Box 113 (on Rte. 3), Trenton 04605, tel. 207/667–3244. Cost: $5 adults, $4 kids 3–12. Open May–Columbus Day, daily 9:30–5.

Baxter State Park

(👫 3+)

This huge wilderness park is a fine place for animal watching. Moose, deer, nearly 200 species of birds, and the usual small forest mammals live here in abundance. The best places to see moose are at Elbow and Daicey ponds at twilight or in the early morning; crouch somewhere off the easy trail around the latter and wait very quietly. Wear insect repellent. Ask at the park office for the guide to where to see the park's wildlife. (See also Chapter 10.)

🏠 664 Balsam Rd. (18 mi north of Millinocket), Millinocket 04462, tel. 207/723–5140. Parking free for Maine residents, $8 for out-of-state vehicles. Open daily 6–10.

Maine Aquarium

(👫 2 – 14)

This small building with just 26 tanks is the way aquariums used to be, without the sophistication of more modern institutions. We still enjoyed seeing the sharks and the two harbor seals who put on demonstrations three times a day—they open and close their door, dive for objects, and balance balls. Little kids go to the duck pond where they can feed the ducks. As the building is crammed with beachgoers on rainy days (Old Orchard Beach is only a few miles away), try to stop by on a sunny one.

🏠 Rte. 1 (exit 5 from I–95), Box 859, Saco 04072, tel. 207/284–4511. Cost: $6.50 adults, $4.50 kids 5–12, $2.50 kids 2–4. Open Oct.–May, daily 9–4; June–Sept., daily 9–9.

Maine Department of Marine Resources Public Aquarium

(👫 2 – 12)

If you're in the area, take the time to visit this small (1,800 square feet) but interesting aquarium tacked onto a fisheries research lab and perched on a lovely point overlooking the ocean. Totally rebuilt in 1994, it introduces people to the marine life of this part of Maine. The touch pool, designed by the same people who designed the one at the New England Aquarium, is a three-sided, 16-foot-long naturalistic rocky habitat filled with sea urchins, starfish, periwinkles, and other creatures clinging to rocks that kids can reach in and touch. What one adventurous 6-year-old we know always wants to do here, though, is pat the huge dogfish and the skate in the open 1,000-gallon tank in the middle of the room. A standing platform around it enables even 3-year-olds to reach easily into the tank. All the fish are indoors, but the large wraparound deck outside with views of boats and the harbor has displays of maps, shells, models of fish, and more.

🏠 McKown Pt., West Boothbay Harbor 04575, tel. 207/633–9500. Admission free. Open Memorial Day–Columbus Day, daily 9–5; mid-Oct.–May by appointment.

Mt. Desert Oceanarium

(👫 ALL)

One of the nicest things about this small, cozy, low-key 25-tank aquarium (called "The Living Room") and museum of local marine life is the staff of college students, who wander around the exhibits answering questions and just pointing out something special about whatever you happen to be looking at. Hits here are the touch tank with 12 animals kids can hold and the scallop demonstration. The museum's interactive exhibits about sea life and the fishing industry include games to play to answer questions such as How does the tide happen? Why is the ocean salty? This place is jammed on a rainy day; come before 10:30 or after 3.

The same family also runs an oceanarium and a lobster hatchery in Bar Harbor; a combined ticket to all three can be used over a several-day period. At **The Oceanarium,** a combination indoor lobster museum, outdoor salt marsh, and harbor seal pool, you can find out in an interactive exhibit that you can't squeeze as hard as a lobster can. On the guided walk through the 13-acre salt marsh, you see ponds, lots of birds, and maybe even a great blue heron. Displays in the tiny **Lobster Hatchery** on the waterfront will tell you everything you ever wanted to know about how Maine lobsters grow. You'll see mothers with eggs on their tails, babies at different stages, and about 5,000 tiny lobsters.
🐾 *Mt. Desert Oceanarium: Clark Point Rd. (off Rte. 102), Southwest Harbor 04679, tel. 207/244–7330. Oceanarium in Bar Harbor: Rte. 3, Bar Harbor 04609, tel. 207/288–5005. Lobster Hatchery: 1 West St., Bar Harbor 04609, tel. 207/288–2334. Cost: $4.95 adults, $3.95 kids 4–12; Lobster Hatchery, $3 adults, $2 kids; three-location ticket, $9.60 adults, $7.40 kids. Open mid-May–mid-Oct., Mon.–Sat. 9–5.*

Scarborough Marsh Nature Center

(👫 7+)

In this 3,000-acre marsh, the largest in Maine, we saw snowy egrets, osprey, herons, ducks, gulls, cormorants, river otters, and seals. It's hard to spot some of these creatures; your kids are more likely to see something if you take a naturalist-

guided tour. The most enjoyable way to see animals here is to get out on the marsh in one of the center's rental canoes. Paddles, life jackets, and maps are provided.
🐾 *Rte. 9 (south of Portland), Scarborough 04074, tel. 207/883–5100. Donation requested; naturalist-led tours $4. Open mid-June–Labor Day, daily 9:30–5:30.*

Massachusetts

Bassett Wild Animal Farm

(👫 2 – 10)

Stop only if you really want to see some exotic animals instead of hanging out on a Cape Cod beach. Tigers, lions, monkeys, lemurs, and more are displayed in a cluster of old-fashioned chain-link cages. You can pet goats (40 altogether) and lambs and walk among chickens, ducks, and peacocks on the farm's 20 acres. Go on a hayride, ride a pony, or have a picnic.
🐾 *620 Tubman Rd. (between Rtes. 124 and 137), Brewster 02631, tel. 508/896–3224. Cost: $5.75 adults, $3.75 kids 2–11. Open mid-May–mid-Sept., daily 10–5.*

Butterfly Place at Papillon Park

(👫 4 – 12)

About 500 butterflies (24 different species) flutter freely in this 3,000-square-foot plant-filled atrium of wood and glass, one of the only butterfly farms in the Northeast. Walking around it, we felt transported to some exotic jungle. A 15-minute video introduces the life cycle of the butterfly, and display cases explain more, but we just enjoyed walking on the brick pathway and asking the staff person on duty for specific information. Don't come on a morning during the school year, when school groups are scheduled.

⛺ *120 Tyngsboro Rd. (40 mi north of Boston), Westford 01886, tel. 508/392–0955. Cost: $6 adults, $5 kids 3–12. Open mid-Apr.–Columbus Day, daily 10–5.*

Drumlin Farm Education Center and Wildlife Sanctuary

(**👫 2 – 11**)

The horses, pigs, cows, owls, chickens, and special demonstrations are the main attractions at this large working farm and nature center run by the Massachusetts Audubon Society just outside Boston. Sunday afternoons, when cow milking or sheep shearing takes place and kids can actually pat the animals, are the best times. Check out the outdoor New England wildlife exhibits too, especially the one on hibernation where during the winter we peered into fox, skunk, groundhog, and rabbit dens and caught a glimpse of sleeping animals—something we'd never seen anywhere else. There are fields to run in, short, easy trails to hike, and ponds for exploring. Alas, no picnicking is allowed.
⛺ *208 S. Great Rd. (Rte. 117), South Lincoln 01773, tel. 617/259–9807. Cost: $6 adults, $4 kids 3–15. Open Tues.–Sun. 9–5.*

Fisheries Aquarium

(**👫 3 – 12**)

The 16 display tanks with marine specimens in the public aquarium at Woods Hole's Northeast Fisheries Science Center include a large tank with eels, but our favorite part is the laboratory room behind the scenes where you can reach into three large child-height touch-tanks and pick up lobsters, starfish, and other creatures, look at tiny specimens under a microscope, and peer down into the display tanks. Student volunteers answer questions. The purpose of this center is to help the commercial fish industry, so they provide all sorts of information on local fish, including recipes.

⛺ *Albatross and Water Sts., Woods Hole 02543, tel. 508/548–7684. Admission free. Open mid-Sept.–mid-June, weekdays 10–4; mid-June–mid-Sept., daily 10–4.*

Franklin Park Zoo

(**👫 ALL**)

This 72-acre enclosed zoo in a huge Boston park is in the process of being revitalized (as is Franklin Park itself), and each year is likely to see more improvements. Currently, the world-class African Tropical Forest, North America's largest freestanding enclosed tropical forest, is the main reason to make the trek—we found its warmth and light especially welcome on a cold, rainy day. As you walk through the gorilla area, put your face against the glass at overlook no. 2, as Gavin did. Chances are a gorilla will amble over, sit on the other side, stare at you, and put his face up to yours. Walking along the meandering path, we saw pygmy hippos underwater, listened to the sound of waterfalls, observed birds building nests, and stopped to watch baboons, crocodiles, and leopards. On the other side of the zoo, at the Children's Zoo, the best time to come is in spring, when area farms bring in baby goats, lambs, chicks, and calves for kids to pet. Parking lots at each end of the zoo are monitored. Pierpont Road parking is closest to the Tropical Forest, Blue Hill to the Children's Zoo.
⛺ *Circuit Dr., Franklin Park, Boston 02543, tel. 617/442–2002. Rte. 203 east from Rte. 1 to Circuit Dr. Cost: $5 adults, $2.50 kids 4–11. Open weekdays 9–5:30, weekends and holidays 9:30–6.*

New England Alive

(**👫 1 – 12**)

Kids can hold newly hatched chicks and newborn bunnies and feed goats, lambs, and calves at this barnyard and nature center on 6 wooded acres that feature 250 specimens of New England wildlife. It's special because it's also a licensed rehabilitation center that treats as many as 700 injured and orphaned animals every year. Coyotes, turtles, frogs, black bears, snakes, a bobcat, hawks and owls, and more are in natural enclosures, and there's a brook with a waterfall, a pond, flower gardens, a snack bar, and tables with white-and-red-checked tablecloths at which to picnic (you can bring your own). Paved paths are ideal for strollers.

 189 High St. (Rtes. 1A and 133), Ipswich 01938, tel. 508/356–7013. Cost: $5 adults, $3 kids 2–12. Open Apr.–Nov., weekdays 9–5, weekends 9:30–6.

New England Aquarium

🚹🚺 ALL

One great thing about this world-class aquarium is its easy-to-reach location right on Boston's historic waterfront overlooking the harbor; it's much more accessible to the city than New York's aquarium is to New York. Virtually all the exhibits are inside, including ground-level pools with jackass penguins that bray like donkeys and rock-hopper penguins with head feathers that resemble punk hairdos. The most spectacular exhibit is the glass-enclosed, four-story saltwater Giant Ocean Tank (one of the largest in the world) at the center of the building, which brings several species of sharks, huge sea turtles, and hundreds of fish just inches from your face. When the diver descends five times a day to feed them, the fish get excited, gobbling up drifting bits of food, darting here and there, and they even eat from his hand. Kids seem to find just running up and down the ramp that spirals around the tank irresistible. When the aquarium is crowded, the line of visitors winding up the ramp seems almost claustrophobic—kids press their noses to the windows and don't move on. (Kids as young as 4 or 5 can use the step-ups at the windows along the ramp to see into and across the tank, but the best place for tod-

dlers is at the open top, which has to-the-floor windows.) Crowds are worst between 11 and 3 on weekends and during school vacations.

Another highlight is the "Edge of the Sea" hands-on tidal pool, a re-creation of a rocky shore in Maine, where you can learn from encouraging Aquarium employees how to turn over a horseshoe crab, even lift up a sea urchin.

At the sea lion shows aboard the floating pavilion next to the aquarium (admission is included in your aquarium ticket) you'll get wet if you sit in the front rows. From April to October the aquarium also sponsors its own excellent whale-watching expeditions (see Chapter 12) and 45-minute tours of Boston Harbor (best for little kids) on which kids can help pull up lobster traps and look at plankton under microscopes. *Central Wharf (Aquarium T stop on the Blue Line), Boston 02110, tel. 617/973–5200. Cost: $8.50 adults, $4.50 kids 3–11. Open Mon., Tues., and Fri. 9–6; Wed. and Thurs. 9–8; weekends and holidays 9–6.*

New England Science Center

🚹🚺 2+

What's unique in this large, three-story building in Worcester packed with science exhibits is the way live animals are interspersed among natural history, energy, and microbe exhibits (see Chapter 8). The small indoor zoo in one section of the first floor includes three 440-gallon aquariums. On the second floor are lizards and macaws. Outside, polar bears, bobcats, river otters, and snowy owls live in mostly chain-link fence enclosures on the Center's 60 acres. One of the nicest ways to see them is on the leisurely 20-minute train ride ($1) past all the animals. *222 Harrington Way (off Rte. 9), Worcester 02110, tel. 508/791–9211. Cost: $6 adults, $4 kids 3–college students with I.D. Open Mon.–Sat. 10–5, Sun. noon–5.*

Southwick's Wild Animal Farm

👫 ALL

One of several family-owned game farms in the Northeast, Southwick's has more than 100 different species, including giraffes, rhinos, lions, and tigers, making it the largest zoo in New England. Like New York's Catskill Game Farm (see below), Southwick's doesn't have the atmosphere or conservation-oriented philosophy of the Bronx Zoo and other members of the American Zoological Society. Though it has a countryish feeling and wide, winding paths good for strollers, some of the animals here are still in old-fashioned small cages with chain-link fencing. There are daily animal shows and elephant rides. Though this bothered me, it didn't trouble my son or his two friends, who were happy to be able to feed and stroke the llamas and walk among a herd of deer.
🏠 2 Southwick St. (off Rte. 16), Mendon 01756, tel. 508/883–9182 or 800/258–9182. Cost: $7.50 adults, $5.50 kids 3–12. Open Apr.–May and Sept.–Oct., daily 10–5; Memorial Day–Labor Day, daily 10–5.

ZooQuarium

👫 2 – 12

The small group of buildings and outdoor environments used to have a circus-y atmosphere, but the owners now stress conservation in their exhibits, which focus on aquatic creatures native to the waters of Cape Cod (inside in tanks) and species that flourish in Massachusetts like bobcats, fox, raccoons, and so on (outdoors in small but naturalistic environments). There are still llamas, pigs, sheep, and other domestic animals that you can pet. The Children's Discovery Center has displays teaching about different aspects of animal life. Daily seal and sea lion shows and short live animal presentations take place all summer.

🏠 674 Rte. 28, West Yarmouth 02673, tel. 508/775–8883. Cost: $7.50 adults, $4.50 kids 2–10. Open mid-Feb.–Nov., daily 9:30–5; Memorial Day–Labor Day, daily 9:30–6:30.

New Hampshire

Friendly Farm

👫 1 – 7

We spent hours at this charming New England farm with more than 100 baby animals in a barn, henhouse, and fenced pens outdoors during Gavin's first three summers. In the henhouse you'll usually see chicks hatching and you can cuddle a baby chick. Other highlights are the fat sow reclining in dirt as she feeds her tiny pink piglets, a pen of baby bunnies, and the honking geese, who draw a crowd when they hiss and attack each other.

If you can, visit at the beginning of the season and then again later so you can see how much the animals have grown.
🏠 Rte. 101 (½ mi west of Dublin Lake), Dublin 03444, tel. 603/563–8444. Cost: $4.75 adults, $3.75 kids 1–12. Open late Apr.–Labor Day, daily (weather permitting) 10–5, Labor Day–Columbus Day, weekends 10–5.

Science Center of New Hampshire

👫 3 – 14

All the animals in this 200-acre complex of indoor and outdoor exhibits devoted to native New Hampshire wildlife have been either orphaned or injured and can no longer survive in the wild. The black bears, bobcats, deer, red fox, otters, turtles, birds, and more live in spacious natural woodland and marsh habitat enclosures along an easy-to-walk, ¾-mile exhibit trail. The otter exhibit has an underwater viewing window where we watched these playful creatures swimming; and we hung over the stone wall that surrounds Turtle Island with lots of other families to spot the snapping turtles sunning themselves. There's a real effort here to introduce kids to the science behind these animal and plant environments through interactive exhibits, puzzles, and games. In summer staff members amble along the trail stopping to answer questions and give regular 15-minute minitalks about animal and plant life. At the Children's Activity Center in a two-story barn kids three to eight find out what it feels like to be an animal by going down a groundhog hole, climbing a giant spiderweb, and walking through a two-story hollow tree. Don't miss one of the 45-minute "Up Close to Animals" live-animal programs given twice a day in summer. The Center also offers nature cruises on Squam Lake for older kids.

🏠 *Rte. 113, Box 173, Holderness 03245, tel. 603/968–7194. Cost: $6 adults ($7 July and Aug.), $3 kids 5–15 ($3.50 July and Aug.). Open May–Oct., daily 9:30–4:30 (live animal programs July and Aug. only).*

New York

Bronx Zoo/International Wildlife Park

(👫 ALL)

Everyone in our family has always loved this internationally famous 265-acre zoo, the oldest and largest in any North American city. You simply won't be able to see all the 4,000 creatures here in a single day. The Zoo has self-guided tour maps that show the quickest routes to specific animals. (Your best bet is to call or write for a map before you come.) If your children are toddlers or preschoolers, it's essential to bring a stroller or rent one at a park entrance (to reserve in advance, call 718/220–5188; $5 plus $20 deposit; you can't take the strollers

into buildings). Even older kids may need to rest their feet on the Zoo Shuttle, which follows the perimeter path.

Paved paths from the several parking lots pass large and small outdoor naturalistic habitats that are interspersed with buildings. Birds, sea lions, monkeys, the Children's Zoo, and the Zoo Center (buildings around this are being renovated) cluster in the northeastern part of the zoo; African, Asian, and a few South American animals spread over the western half. We head first to the monorail around Wild Asia because lines waiting to board it grow very long in the afternoon; riding it is as much fun as looking down on the elephants, rhinoceros, and other Asian creatures you pass. The daily rainstorm in the indoor rain forest in World of Birds is another of our favorite things, as is The World of Darkness, which seems quite dark even after your eyes adjust. It's best for kids over 8. Be sure to see the bats and the amazing Naked Mole-Rats exhibit (new in 1994), which features cross-section views of mole-rat tunnel systems; miniature TV cameras provide close-ups. If your family are snake aficionados, the reptile house has the longest snake in the United States (a python). Kids can pet and feed domestic animals in the Children's Zoo and climb the rope spiderweb, try on the turtle shell, sit in the kid-size bird nest, and go down the slide in a hollow tree—all designed to illustrate what it might feel like to be an animal. This area is often very crowded on sunny weekends; skip it if your kids are over 9.

We favor eating in the African Market, a cluster of mud buildings designed to look like a village in West Africa, where you can munch pizza while overlooking the baboon reserve. The more centrally located Lakeside Café, next to a pond with ducks, has more extensive food choices, including hot dogs and hamburgers.

🏠 *Fordham Rd. (Subway 2 to Pelham Pkwy. or Express Bus BxM11), Bronx 10460, tel. 718/367–1010 or 718/220–5100. Cost: $5.75 adults, $2 kids 2–12; free Wed.; park-*

ing $5. Open Mar.–Oct., weekdays 10–5, weekends and holidays 10–5:30; Nov.–Feb., daily 10–4:30.

Catskill Game Farm

 ALL

Seeing, patting, and bottle-feeding rare and exotic baby animals (like baby camels and Vietnamese potbellied pigs) in the animal nursery are among the highlights of a visit to this 240-acre game farm, the first privately owned zoo in the United States. Kids can walk among, pat, and feed the friendly deer and llamas. Animal food is expensive—$2.75 for 40 crackers. Among the more than 2,000 animals to see are zebras, African antelopes, crocodiles, rhinos, lions, and bears, and you can get fairly close to all of them, especially those still in old-fashioned cages. Paved pathways ideal for strollers connect all the areas; from the petting zoo you can take a train through the bird section—the best bet with little kids. Exciting and excellent animal shows featuring dancing elephants and bicycle-riding bears, and elephant and amusement park rides reflect a more entertainment-oriented philosophy than the one prevalent at zoos today.

 400 Game Farm Rd. (off Rte. 32), Catskill 12414, tel. 518/678–9595 or 518/678–9030. Cost: $11.75 adults, $7.50 kids 4–12. Open early May–Oct., daily 9–6.

Central Park Wildlife Conservation Center

 0 – 12

Central Park's 5½-acre zoo is one of the most charming small city zoos I've ever seen, the perfect size for toddlers and preschoolers or just for a one-hour stroll to see animals. The sea lion pool (feeding times are 11:30, 2, and 4) lies at the center (you can glimpse these popular animals without actually going into the zoo). There are Victorian-style green metal fences and

gates, walkways, benches, four large, fierce-looking stone eagles, and gardens around it, and buildings and areas representing three different climate zones beyond. A surprising number of animals, from red pandas to penguins, are housed in these miniature environments. The indoor Tropic Zone has a small rain forest; the outdoor Temperate Territory has snow monkeys scampering on an island; the Polar Circle has polar bears in a big pool. Toddlers can see into the pool from a stroller. It's easy for preschoolers to walk around the whole zoo. Occasional events, like the Go Batty Halloween celebration, are always well planned.

 64th St. and 5th Ave., New York 10021, tel. 212/861–6030. Cost: $2.50 adults, 50¢ kids 3–12. Open Apr.–Oct., weekdays 10–5, weekends and holidays 10:30–5:30; Nov.–Mar., daily 10–4:30.

Jamaica Bay Wildlife Refuge

 10+

For kids who are interested in birds, this nearly 10,000-acre tidal wetlands and uplands nature preserve on Long Island Sound is a treat to visit. Late summer is an especially good time to glimpse migrating birds—the refuge's two ponds are at the crossroads of two migratory routes, and one of them is in the area open to the public. On Sundays National Park Service rangers offer slide and film shows about birds and a tour of the refuge.

 Visitor's Center, Crossbay Blvd., Broad Channel, Queens, tel. 718/318–4340. For information, write to Gateway National Recreation Area, Floyd Bennett Field, Brooklyn 11234, tel. 718/338–3338. Admission free. Open daily 8:30–5.

Long Island Game Farm

 2 – 12

There are not many places to see animals on Long Island; at this combined petting zoo and 45-acre family park that's been around since 1970 kids can cuddle and bottle-feed baby animals at the Nursery and hand-feed deer in Bambiland as well as see llamas, zebras, camels, monkeys, bears, peacocks, and more. Paved pathways suitable for strollers link the themed sections. Kids we know also head for Old MacDonald's Farm, where farm animals live in a cluster of big red barns, and for the swing rides in the Play Park. Get an overview of all the animals aboard the 1860s train around the park. At the "Animal Wonderland" shows kids can touch pythons, lizards, and an iguana.

🏠 *Chapman Blvd., Manorville 11949, tel. 516/878-6644. Exit 70 off Long Island Expwy. (LIE). Cost: $11.95 plus tax for adults, $8.95 plus tax for kids 2–11. Open mid-Apr.–mid-Oct., weekdays 10–5, weekends 10–6.*

New York Aquarium

The best time to visit this aquarium is on a nice day in spring, summer, or fall. That's because it's adjacent to the Coney Island boardwalk and beach, and because unlike the New England Aquarium, the most exciting part of it is outside—the 300-foot-long Pacific rocky coast habitat, "Sea Cliffs," a series of five environments where penguins, seals, walruses, and otters live. Even toddlers in strollers can easily see the animals because the all-glass barriers go all the way down to the walkway, and the animals swim right up to them. From inside an adjoining building you have an underwater view of each animal (we saw the fur seals playing and kissing), as well as many other exhibits, including the "Living in Water" room, where we compared our weight with those of different animals. The shark exhibit is the best we've seen; we dug up shark fossils and touched a cow-nose ray, a cousin of the shark, as it swam by. Do visit the Discovery Cove building filled with interactive exhibits.

🏠 *W. 8th St. off Surf Ave., Coney Island, Brooklyn 11224, tel. 718/265-3400. Subway F or D to W. 8th st. stop in Brooklyn, then pedestrian overpass. Cost: $6.75 adults, $2 kids 2–12. Open Labor Day–Memorial Day, daily 10–5; Memorial Day–Labor Day, weekdays 10–5, weekends and holidays 10–7.*

Rhode Island

Roger Williams Park and Zoo

It's easy to see why the *Boston Globe* rated this 40-acre haven for 600 domestic and exotic animals the best zoo in New England. Set in the middle of a beautiful large Providence park with ponds, lakes, expanses of lawn, and walkways designed in the 19th century, the inexpensive-to-visit zoo still has some charming historic Victorian buildings as well as many exhibits revamped in 1993 and 1994. Most of the large animals are now in outdoor naturalistic settings. As you can easily walk the whole zoo in a couple of hours, you can combine a visit here with time in the adjacent park (see the Greenhouse, rent a boat, or ride the carousel) or before a trip to see the Pawtucket Red Sox (see Chapter 11).

The Plains of Africa habitats have giraffes, zebras, bongos, elephants, and cheetahs; the underwater viewing window lets you see the Polar Bear pool; and the International Farmyard has storybook-style signs telling about donkeys, goats, pigs, sheep, a pair of adorable miniature horses, and the famous state chicken, the Rhode Island Red. Look in on the new-in-1994 two-level Tropical America building with very active monkeys.

🏠 *1000 Elmwood Ave. (off I-95), Providence 02907, tel. 401/785-9450. Cost: $3.50 adults, $1.50 kids 3–12; parking free. Open Nov.–Apr., daily 9–5; May–Oct., weekdays 9–5, weekends and holidays 9–6.*

Vermont

Billings Farm and Museum

(👪 1 – 13)

This large, historic working dairy farm illustrates what farm life was like in the 19th century. You can even help hand-milk the cows. Besides the L-shape dairy and livestock barns and pens that house prize Jersey cows, chickens, oxen, super woolly Southdown sheep, and a newborn calf nursery, you can also wander through a farm-life museum and a rambling 1890s farmhouse, which has a dairy bar with farm-made ice cream attached. The kinds of demonstrations and special events you see depend on the weather and the time of year and day you visit—you might see teams of oxen pulling plows just the way they did in the past and learn how farmers trained these huge animals. The best time to come is in the afternoon. There's lots to do to fill a morning or afternoon here, plus places to picnic.

🏠 Rte. 12, Woodstock 05091, tel. 802/457-2355. Cost: $6 adults, $3 kids 6–17, $17 families (2 adults and accompanying kids). Open May–Oct., daily 10–5; Nov.–Dec., weekends 10–4.

Shelburne Farms

(👪 2 – 10)

We came here on a warm, sunny summer afternoon to see goats, cows, sheep, chickens, and all the usual farm animals at this former estate high above Lake Champlain. It's about a 10-minute walk on a mowed-grass path from the Visitor Center at the entrance to the Children's Farmyard, an open area bounded by traditional New England red barns and outbuildings that's designed so kids can run around among the animals, but we rode on a hay wagon along with several families with small children.

Before long all the kids, including ours, were learning how to milk a cow, collect eggs, and make butter. The Farmyard is more appealing to toddlers and preschoolers than is the Billings Farm. At the main barn the farm's prizewinning (and delicious) cheddar cheese is made; you can visit and taste. Skip the slide show and the historic gardens (boring, Mom). A 3½-mile walking trail around the property has wonderful views of Lake Champlain from Lone Tree Hill.

🏠 Bay and Harbor Rds. (off Rte. 7), Shelburne 05482, tel. 802/985-8686. Cost: $6.50 adults, $3.50 kids 2–15. Open late May–mid-Oct., daily 10–5.

UVM Morgan Horse Farm

(👪 4+)

This working farm, one of the centers where purebred Morgan horses were developed in the 19th century and now operated by the University of Vermont, is worth a stop for kids who are keen horse lovers (especially if they've read Justin Morgan Had a Horse by Marguerite Henry). Stroll around the spacious grounds, hang over a fence to see horses being trained for riding, and poke your head into the Victorian barn to see the horses in their stalls. The 20-minute guided tours of the stables and the 15-minute audiovisual presentation will educate you about this breed. You can't pat or feed the horses, but they will come up to the fence to check you out.

🏠 Morgan Horse Farm Rd., Middlebury 05753, tel. 802/388-2011. Cost: $3.50 adults, $2 kids 13–19. Open May–Oct., daily 9–4.

Vermont Institute of Natural Science

(👪 3 – 15)

The Raptor Center at this research institute has 26 species of owls, falcons, hawks, bald eagles, and more who have been injured and rehabilitated. The most intriguing part to us was the way the large naturalistic flight cages have been customized to suit each bird's injury; one for a bird with injured feet had branches wrapped with carpeting. In summer stay for a live-animal presentation or miniprogram, like the one on what to do if you find a baby bird. The Institute also has two short, self-guided nature trails on its 77 acres.

🏠 *Church Hill Rd., Woodstock 05482, tel. 802/457–2779. Cost: $5 adults, $1 kids 5–15. Open May–Oct., daily 10–4; Nov.–Apr., Mon.–Sat. 10–4.*

GREEN SPACES FROM HARRIMAN TO ACADIA
STATE AND NATIONAL PARKS, NATURAL WONDERS, AND A SPECIAL GARDEN

10

The Northeast has national parks, forests, seashores, and wildlife refuges, and state parks, forests, and recreation areas, as well as lands that are preserved by national organizations such as the Audubon Society and the Nature Conservancy, all with different purposes. **National and state parks** almost always have the most facilities. The largest, like Acadia National Park in Maine, have visitor centers that offer nature programs and guided hikes for families and kids; campgrounds and picnic areas are well equipped. Even the smaller parks on lakes usually provide a lifeguard, bathhouses, and a snack bar. **National and state forests** extend over much larger areas and tend to have fewer amenities. I have to admit that these are what my husband and I prefer, and sometimes my son has agreed. Swimming in rock pools or rivers or ponds without lifeguards and floats can be exciting. **Wilderness areas** in the Northeast are as wild as any in the West; they're for families with older kids who like to backpack, hike, and canoe. **National seashores,** like the one on Cape Cod, are similar to national forests in terms of facilities, but offer beaches and swimming and have more educational programs.

Wildlife refuges and sanctuaries have attracted us because we've found our enthusiasm for birds and animals and nature activities rarely wanes, as long as the programs don't get too didactic. For information on National Wildlife Refuges in the Northeast contact the United States Fish and Wildlife Service (Northeast Regional Office, 300 Westgate Center Dr., Hadley, MA 01035, tel. 413/253–8322). Audubon Centers in particular are a wonderful combination of short, well-laid-out hikes, wildlife viewing, and very strong but interesting-to-kids educational programs—we learned how bees swarm at one—that are particularly appealing for a one-day visit. For our family a park has to offer more than woods and a view, and the parks and places listed below reflect that preference.

July and August are the most crowded months in all parks; that's also when most planned activities occur. The early fall is our favorite time to explore woods. (Be aware that Lyme disease, caused by the tiny deer tick, is a problem in the Northeast. When exploring parks during the summer, check yourself and your children daily for ticks.) For information on camping, hiking, and canoeing, see Chapter 12. More parks are listed in Chapters 3, 4, 5, and 6; city parks are listed only in Chapters 3 and 4.

Connecticut

Connecticut has more than 100 state parks and forests, many quite similar to one another, with the woodland, stream, and pond landscape that characterizes much of Connecticut; you'll find others along the state's two most scenic rivers, the Housatonic and the Connecticut, along the shores of lakes, and at a few saltwater beaches on Long Island Sound. For more information, contact the Bureau of Outdoor Recreation (State Parks Division, Connecticut Dept. of Environmental Protection, 79 Elm St., Hartford 06106, tel. 203/566–2304).

Lake Waramaug State Park

👫 0 – 12

Lake Waramaug, surrounded by nicely forested hills and lake inns, has a meandering, winding coastline and a road that follows it. The park lies along a sheltered finger of water; shady trees, picnic tables, and grass edge a wide sand beach; across the road and down a bit among the trees are campsites that all have a view of the water. For little kids the swimming area is just the right size; the grassy spots are good places to stand and throw in a fishing line; and the lake is calm enough for easy canoeing and paddle-boating even with young kids. Rarely crowded except on holiday weekends, the park attracts families and kids. The only drawbacks: Kids have to cross the road to get to the snack bar, and in the early fall the beach attracts lots of messy geese.

🏠 30 Lake Waramaug Rd., New Preston 06777, tel. 203/868–2592. Free weekdays; $8 nonresident parking fee weekends. Open daily 8–sunset. Facilities: camping, canoe and paddleboat rentals, fishing, hiking, picnicking, snack bar, swimming.

Rocky Neck State Park

👫 2+

Though we prefer the coastal beaches of Rhode Island, Cape Cod, and Long Island, this mile-long crescent beach is our preferred public saltwater bathing site in Connecticut.

🏠 Rte. 156 (exit 72 off I-95), Niantic 06357, tel. 203/739–5471. Cost: $5 weekdays, $8 weekends for CT vehicles; $8 weekdays, $12 weekends for out-of-state vehicles. Open daily 8–sunset. Facilities: bathhouses, family campground, fishing, picnicking, snack bar.

Sharon Audubon Center

👫 4 – 12

This center's 684 acres are essentially rural Connecticut countryside, but the woodlands, ponds, stream, marsh, meadow, and swamp crisscrossed by trails and wildlife seem to have been perfectly arranged by nature for young kids and families who want to spend an afternoon or the whole day outdoors. Trails go along the edge of ponds with ducks, out on a boardwalk above a bog, by big rocks to climb on. Kids' nature programs are offered on many weekends (call to check).

🏠 Rte. 4, 93 West Cornwall Rd., Sharon 06069, tel. 203/364–0520. Cost: $3 adults, $1.50 kids. Trails open daily dawn–dusk; museum open Mon.–Sat. 9–5, Sun. 1–5.

White Memorial Foundation

👫 3 – 12

The 4,000 acres of Connecticut's largest nature center and wildlife sanctuary used to be a private estate. What drew our family back weekend after weekend were the easy walks, ponds where you can catch tadpoles and spot sunning turtles, wide meadows and grassy areas for running and spreading a blanket for a picnic, and a terrific selection of kids'

books in the nature library on the second floor of the Conservation Center Building.
🏠 *Rte. 202, Litchfield 06759, tel. 203/567–0857. Grounds admission free; nature center, $2 adults, $1 kids 6–12. Grounds open daily 24 hrs; nature center, Apr.–Nov., Mon.–Sat. 9–5, Sun. noon–4; Nov.–Apr., Mon.–Sat. 8:30–4:30, Sun. noon–4. Facilities: bird-watching, cross-country skiing, camping, fishing, gift shop, hiking, horseback riding, nature center, library.*

Maine

Maine's parks are the most diverse in the Northeast, from sandy beaches and rocky promontories along the Atlantic to freshwater lakes inland to a wilderness of mountains and gorges in the vast, forested, remote northern region. I haven't included any of the state's southern beach state parks; Maine's northern rocky coast, unique in the Northeast, is what we prefer. One warning: No matter where you go, bring insect repellent especially in June, which is black-fly season. For general information contact the Maine Bureau of Parks and Recreation (State House Station 22, Augusta 04333, tel. 207/287–3821). The state Department of Conservation publishes "Outdoors in Maine," a map and guide to 30 state parks. Family season passes allowing unlimited daytime use of Maine's state parks are available for $30 by mail from the Bureau. *The Maine Atlas and Gazetteer* (DeLorme Mapping Company, Box 298, Freeport, ME 04032, tel. 207/865–4171) has a complete listing of Maine's city, state, and national parks and recreation areas, plus nature preserves, natural areas, waterfalls, and beaches.

Acadia National Park

(👫 2+)

Acadia is one of the country's most popular national parks, and no wonder: Its 22 square miles, which include most of Mount Desert Island (and the Schoodic Peninsula,

Isle au Haut, and some small islands), capture in one spot all that our family loves about Maine's coast—a ragged shoreline of fingers of rock; craggy, towering cliffs with pounding surf at the bottom; fragrant pines; perfect blue lakes; pink granite mountains and shallow mountain streams; and over all of it misty fog streaming in. Mount Desert Island's first settlers were the Abnaki Indians. The explorer Samuel de Champlain named it, and Woodrow Wilson set aside much of it as a park in 1919. What makes Mount Desert Island so attractive to us as a place for a family vacation is the unique combination of beautiful scenery, a wide range of activities—you can bike, hike, swim, canoe, ride horseback, camp, and participate in some of the best kids' nature programs around—and proximity to several towns, especially the lively village of Bar Harbor, which is full of shops, museums, and restaurants. Plus, it's an island, and that makes it seem cut off from ordinary life.

Stop first at the Visitor's Center at Hulls Cove. The free 15-minute film gives kids a quick introduction to the park's history, geology, flora, and fauna. Pick up information on hiking trails, campgrounds, and especially the "Acadia Beaver Log," which lists free daily naturalist programs for kids (and adults).

Next, for an overview, drive the 20-mile loop road around one small portion of the park, finishing off with the Cadillac Mountain Summit Road (come back at sunrise to be the first people in the United States to see the sun that day). The views of the whole island and the bay from the top are simply stunning, though on most days this has to be the most densely populated spot on the island.

If your kids are old enough, rent bikes and explore the 57 miles of car-free carriage paths; this is a way to get to more remote spots without hiking (see *also* Chapter 12). Even younger kids can handle the paved paths around Eagle Lake and Witch Hole Pond. Do take one of the park naturalist cruises; you won't always see a seal (we didn't), but you'll probably see porpoises. The best place to swim is in freshwater Echo Lake, near Southwest Harbor, which has a sandy beach and lifeguards. The water at Sand Beach is so frigid our legs went numb.

Head for the famous sights—Thunder Hole (a chasm that gets its name from the boom of waves rushing in and compressing pockets of trapped air), Sand Beach—before 10 or after 4:30 and concentrate on hiking (see Chapter 12) on the western side of the island during the middle of the day. (For camping information, see Chapter 12; the Sierra Club offers a yearly "Toddler Tromp" camping and hiking experience for families with small children.) Warm clothes and rain gear are essential.

The best guide to the park is The AMC Guide to Mount Desert Island and Acadia National Park (Appalachian Mountain Club, 1993). The best descriptions of appropriate hikes for kids in the park is in Best Hikes With Children in Vermont, New Hampshire & Maine (Lewis and Lewis).

Δ Superintendent, Box 177, Bar Harbor 04609, tel. 207/288-3338. Park Headquarters, Rte. 233, Eagle Lake; open year-round, daily 8–4:30. Visitor's Center, Rte. 3, Hulls Cove, tel. 207/288-4932. Cost: $5 per car for 1 week. Park open daily 24 hrs. (Cadillac Mt. closed midnight–dawn). Facilities: biking, boat cruises, camping, canoeing, hiking trails, horseback riding, carriage roads, nature programs, rock climbing, swimming.

Baxter State Park

ΔΔ 8+

This is a place for families who want a great wilderness experience where they can stay in a primitive cabin instead of pitching a tent. It's best for kids who have already done some primitive camping and really love hiking and fishing. Why? Baxter's unspoiled 201,018 acres in Maine's remote northwest region, dominated by mile-high Mt. Katahdin, is as

close to wilderness as you'll get in the Northeast. That means no running water, electricity, food, or supplies in the park. On the other hand, it offers some of the best canoeing and fishing in the country on truly pristine ponds and lakes, as well as the chance to see bear, moose, deer, and other wildlife; and you will not find crowds on the easy trails.

The park has only nine campgrounds, and people start reserving space in January. The best site for families is Daicey Pond, which has primitive cabins with bunks and mattresses, a stove, a table, and chairs. It is near many easy trails and has views of Katahdin. The essential complete guidebook to the park (and other camping possibilities nearby) is Katahdin: A Guide to Baxter State Park & Katahdin by Stephen Clark (North Country Press).

Δ Baxter Park Headquarters, 64 Balsam Dr., Millinocket 04462, tel. 207/723-5140. Open mid-May–mid-Oct., daily 6 AM–10 PM; mid-Oct.–mid-May, daily dawn–dusk. Facilities: backpacking, camping, fishing, hiking, moose-watching.

Desert of Maine

ΔΔ 5 – 14

This unique, 50-acre sandy desert environment surrounded by lush trees and wildflowers has an intriguing story: During the last ice age, glaciers left behind sand and mineral deposits that were eventually covered over with soil, then trees; finally it became farmland. After years of tree-cutting and overgrazing, the topsoil eroded, exposing the sand underneath. Now it's both a privately owned tourist attraction and a natural wonder: a small desert with dunes higher than trees and buildings and occasional sandstorms. On the sand, it's sometimes more than 100°F; when you step into the pine woods at the desert's edge it's like walking into air-conditioning.

Δ Desert Rd. (exit 19 off I-95), Freeport 04032, tel. 207/865-6962. Cost: $4.95 adults, $2.75 kids 6–12. Open May 15–Oct. 15, daily 9–sunset.

Grafton Notch State Park

(🏃🏃 7+)

Waterfalls and gorges are the attractions of this end of the Mahoosuc range not far from the Sunday River ski resort. Several of these impressive sights are almost roadside stops along Route 26, so they're easy to explore with kids. Both 900-foot-long Mother Walker Falls Gorge and Screw Auger Falls Gorge have natural bridges at their upper end; each has rocks to climb on and pools to wade in. Moose Cave Gorge has large mossy boulders. If you want to hike, head for Table Rock; underneath its ledges are a labyrinth of slab caves and tunnels to explore, but with caution. Don't miss Step Falls, just outside the south end of the park on Nature Conservancy land; a trail along the brook leads to icy pools for a dip and rocks to slide down; the sound of the rushing water drowns out even the ordinary chirps of birds and rustling of trees. (See Chapter 12.)
🏞 *Rte. 26 (14 mi north of Bethel), between Upton and Newry, Newry 04261, tel. 207/ 824–2912. Cost: $1 adults, 50¢ kids 5–11. Open mid-May–mid-Oct., daily 9–sunset. Facilities: fishing, hiking, picnicking.*

Lily Bay State Park

(🏃🏃 5+)

This park's 924 acres on the shores of Moosehead Lake, Maine's largest lake, are almost but not quite in the wilderness. The spacious, well-laid-out campsites among pine trees make you feel you're in back country, but amenities like a playground, a nice small beach with good but cold swimming, and a place to rent canoes make it a bit more comfortable. It's best as a center from which to explore the bays and inlets and islands of undeveloped Moosehead Lake. Forty miles long and 10 wide, the lake is surrounded by rugged mountains and dense forest, where some 10,000

moose live. The best time to see them is at dawn or dusk in some of the secluded bogs not too far from the park. From Greenville, you can board the S.S. *Katahdin* for a boat trip to spectacular Mt. Kineo. (See *also* Chapter 12.)
🏞 *Beaver Cove, Moosehead Lake (about 8 mi north of Greenville), Greenville 14441, tel. 207/695–2700. Cost: $1.50 adults; 50¢ kids 5–11. Open early May–mid-Oct., daily 8 AM–10 PM. Facilities: boat launch, camping, fishing, freshwater swimming, hiking, moose-watching, picnicking.*

Mt. Blue State Park

(🏃🏃 6+)

Mt. Blue is one of those large (more than 4,000 acres) parks that has everything: good campsites, a lake for swimming, a recreation hall, scenic hiking with relatively easy climbs to views of Mt. Washington in New Hampshire, and deep gorges with rocky walls. But it's the unusual ranger-naturalist program here that makes the park so special for kids, especially the trips to pan for gold and pick blueberries growing on the ledges of Bald Mountain. (See Chapter 12.)
🏞 *15 mi off Rte. 2 from Wilton or Dixfield, Weld 04285, tel. 207/585–2347. Cost: $1.50 adults, 50¢ kids 5–11. Open mid-May–Sept., daily 24 hrs. Facilities: boat launch, camping, canoe and boat rentals, freshwater swimming, hiking, nature trails, picnicking.*

Reid State Park

(🏃🏃 ALL)

This park's two long stretches of sand beach and dunes lie at the tip of the Georgetown peninsula, but it's the other natural features that appealed to Gavin. The saltwater lagoon is safe for swimming and deliciously warm compared to the icy Atlantic, so our warm-water-loving family could actually swim. At low tide, we walked on a sandbar to an island in the Sheepscot River and watched shore birds who come in to feed at the far end of the beach by Little River.

 Rte. 127 (14 mi south of Rte. 1 in Woolwich), Georgetown 05448, tel. 207/371–2303. Cost: $2 adults, 50¢ kids 5–11. Open daily 9–sunset. Facilities: bathhouses, freshwater showers, sand beach, fireplaces, fishing, picnicking, snack bar, swimming.

Scarborough Marsh Nature Center

👫 5+

Scarborough, the largest salt marsh in Maine, is 3,000 acres of tidal marshes, salt creeks, cattails, and marsh grasses that teem with animal and bird life (see *also* Chapter 10). From a distance, a salt marsh doesn't have the immediate spectacular appeal to kids (at least not to mine) of a waterfall pool or a stretch of sand beach; you need to get close. In most sanctuaries you can't do that. Here you can: through nature center activities (on one program you can sample cattail pancakes) and by renting a canoe. As you glide, using a paddle to test the water depth, along the edges of the Dunstan River as it winds through the marsh, you notice all sorts of creatures. Be sure to head for the sea on an outgoing tide and return on an incoming tide unless you want to work hard. Bring lots of bug repellent and sunblock, and wear old canvas shoes that you won't mind getting wet and mucky. The 90-minute guided canoe tours are best for older kids.

 Pine Point Rd., Scarborough 04074, tel. 207/781–2330. Nature center, mid-June– Labor Day, daily 9–5. Facilities: canoeing and rentals, children's nature programs, hiking, guided tours, nature center, nature tours.

Sebago Lake State Park

👫 ALL

Sebago Lake, the state's second-largest lake and only 32 miles from Portland, hums with

boating and swimming activity. At its north end this 1,300-acre wooded park has one of the only public beaches on the lake and the nicest; it's long, sandy, well supervised, and backed by a shady picnic grove; one camping area is on the waterfront near it. Boat-launching sites and nearby places to rent boats and sailboards mean it is easy for families to sail, canoe, windsurf, waterski or fish. The working lock on the Songo River raises the water so boats from Long Lake can pass into Sebago. Besides watching the action, kids can help close and open it time after time for the lines of small pleasure boats waiting to go through. As the park is not too far from civilization it sometimes closes to day users by mid-morning on a hot weekend. (See Chapter 12.)

 RFD 1, Box 101 (off U.S. Rte. 302 between Naples and South Casco), Naples 04055, tel. 207/693–6615. Cost: $2.50 adults, 50¢ kids 5–11. Open early May–mid-Oct., daily 8–sunset. Facilities: bathhouses, boating, camping, fishing, hiking, nature programs, sand beach, swimming, hot showers, snack bar.

White Mountain National Forest

👫 7+

More than 49,000 acres of this forest are in Maine along the New Hampshire border. For a description, see New Hampshire, *below.*

 Evans Notch Ranger District, RFD 2, Box 2270, Bethel 04217, tel. 207/824–2134.

Massachusetts

Massachusetts has the ninth-largest forest and park system in the country, with more than 100 state parks and forests. My family gravitates toward parks in the east along the coast, which are mostly beaches, and those in the west in the rounded, forested Berkshire hills. The few I've listed here are only some of our favorites; others are mentioned in Chapters 3, 5, and 6. For further information, contact the Massachusetts Department of Environmental Management (Division of Forests and Parks, 100 Cambridge St., 19th Floor, Boston, MA 02202, tel. 617/727–3180) or the Massachusetts Audubon Society (South Great Road, Lincoln, MA 01773, tel. 617/259–9500).

Boston Harbor Islands State Park

 ALL

It may be apparent by now that our family likes islands. Well, 17 islands in Boston Harbor constitute this park. Part of the fun is going to the largest and most developed, Georges Island, in a water taxi (*see below*) that holds 49 people, then island-hopping on the free daily water taxi to others. On Georges you'll find an old fort, Fort Warren, with tunnels and parapets (bring a flashlight!) to explore on your own (kids must be accompanied by an adult) or on a guided tour. Lovells has good beaches (though no lifeguards), walking trails through dunes, and a salt marsh. Both have picnic tables and shade. If you have kids in strollers, you might want to stop on Thompson Island (open to visitors only on weekends), because many of the paths are roadways. Bring a picnic, as there is only a refreshment stand on Georges Island, and no water on any of the others.

 Water taxis: Bay State Cruises, 67 Long Wharf, Boston 02210 (red ticket booth on wharf beyond Marriott Hotel), tel. 617/723–7800. Cost: $6 adults, $4 kids under 12. The islands: Dept. of Environmental Management, 349 Lincoln St., Bldg. 45, Hingham 02043, tel. 617/740–1605. Facilities: camping, fishing, hiking, guided walks, snack bar.

Cape Cod National Seashore

ALL

To our family this 40-mile-long national seashore that extends from Chatham to

Provincetown on Cape Cod (the elbow-to-fist portion of the peninsula shaped like a flexed arm) is the ultimate stretch of beach and dunes, at least on the East Coast. Established in 1961 to preserve the Outer Cape's natural resources from commercial development, it encompasses sandy white beaches, nature trails, bicycle paths, rolling dunes as high as 100 feet, salt marshes, and kettle ponds, those deep round dips of freshwater tucked behind ocean beaches. The government owns more than half the land in the seashore; the rest is private or commercial land in the six towns that have boundaries in it. Though the setting is beach and dunes, the National Seashore reminds me of Acadia National Park (*see above*) in what it offers families: a combination of swimming (much better here), biking, hiking, and extensive naturalist programs for kids and families along with proximity to charming towns with shopping, baseball, and concerts that I'm discovering is essential if you have teenagers. It's more diverse both as an environment and in terms of activities than the Fire Island National Seashore (*see New York, below*).

You can stop first at the Salt Pond Visitor's Center just beyond the village of Eastham or the Province Lands Visitor's Center in Provincetown, where you can pick up information and trail maps, see short audiovisual programs about the area, and look at some exhibits. Be sure to get a list of the regular guided walks, demonstrations, children's and evening nature films and programs held at both centers' amphitheaters during the summer; the walks designated for children 5 to 10 are shorter and more hands-on, with scavenger hunts and games. On the Fort Hill Trail you get to walk under a whalebone archway in front of the historic home of a whaleship captain, and on the Sunset Beach Walk guides tell stories around a campfire and help the young ones to see the shapes in the stars.

For beachcombing, the ocean beaches are best: sea urchins, sand dollars, starfish are what you'll find. For swimming, the ocean beaches have the highest, roughest surf (with a strong undertow) good for boogie-boarding and strong swimmers; the best ones for younger families are Race Point and protected and warm Herring Cove on Cape Cod Bay (both in Provincetown). See Chapter 12.

🏠 *National Seashore Headquarters, South Wellfleet, MA 02663, tel. 508/349–3785. Salt Pond Visitor's Center, off Rte. 6, Eastham, MA 02663, tel. 508/255–3421. Province Lands Area Visitor's Center, Race Point Rd., off Rte. 6, Provincetown, tel. 508/487–1256. Beach-area parking $5 in summer. Open mid-June–Labor Day, daily 9–4:30; July and Aug., daily 9–6.*

Halibut Point Reservation and State Park

👫 5+

Basically this small park at the very top of Cape Ann is a place to picnic and explore, though there is a good 90-minute guided tour most Saturdays at 9:30. Do pick up a self-guided tour brochure. Some of the magnificent tide pools are surrounded by big rocks good for climbing. There's an old granite quarry filled with greenish water to walk around (hang on to little kids' hands), blueberries to pick in late July, views of lobstermen hauling up their traps, and huge open sheets of granite to sit on while you admire the view. Make sure the kids wear sneakers, bring jackets because it gets windy, and watch out for poison ivy.

🏠 *Gott Ave. (via Rte. 127), Rockport 01966, tel. 508/546–2297. Cost: $5 per car. Open daily 8–sunset. Facilities: bird-watching, hiking, picnicking.*

Ipswich River Wildlife Sanctuary

👫 4+

The rockery at the largest Audubon sanctuary in the state is what draws several Boston families on my panel back to these 2,800 acres again and again. The series of stone stairways, tunnels, and bridges built nearly a century ago is an intricate maze of boulders to explore. It took nine years to construct it all; the rocks were hauled here by horse and cart. Set on a section of the Ipswich River, the sanctuary has many other enticing sites—rustic bridges, boardwalks, abundant wildlife, the remains of early colonial settlements, an observation tower, an island, and a very special Japanese garden.

🏠 *87 Perkins Row, Topsfield 01983, tel. 508/887–9264. Rte. 1 north to Rte. 97 south at lights; 2nd left onto Perkins Row. Cost: $3 adults, $2 kids. Open Tues.–Sun. dawn–dusk. Facilities: bird-watching, camping (for members), canoeing, hiking, library, nature programs.*

Mt. Greylock State Reservation

👫 6+

At 3,491 feet, Mt. Greylock is the highest peak in Massachusetts, a monadnock (single peak) surrounded by 10,000 acres of red spruce and balsam forests, streams, and waterfalls. The Appalachian Trail crosses the park. The woods have a near-wilderness look and feel, but we go for the view, especially during fall foliage time. This isn't just any old view: An 8-mile winding road leads to the summit, then there are the 89 steps to the top of the war memorial tower for a view of five states on a clear day—you can even see Mt. Monadnock in New Hampshire (*see below*). A 360° map identifies the peaks. The views may not be as spectacular or the summit as high as those of New Hampshire's Mt. Washington (*see below*), but Greylock is less crowded. At the top, the Appalachian Mountain Club offers guided hikes, slide shows, and exhibits at Bascom Lodge (tel. 413/743–1591; see Chapter 6), a rustic stone house where you can stay overnight or just eat lunch, as we did, on the big porch that overlooks the mountains to the west.

鼎 Rockwell Rd., Lanesborough 01237, tel. 413/499–4262. MA Turnpike to exit 2, Rte. 20 west, then Rte. 7 north to Lanesborough; follow signs to Visitor's Center on Rockwell Rd. Cost: $2 per car. Open mid-May–mid-Oct., daily 9–sunset. Facilities: camping, canoeing, cross-country skiing, hiking, naturalist programs, picnicking.

Natural Bridge State Park

 7+

The natural light-gray marble bridge that extends 30 feet across a gorge 45 feet deep in this tiny state park is a one-of-a-kind site. What was most exciting to Gavin was actually walking across the bridge (an easy trek to get to it) and looking down at the rushing water and the length of the gorge. The bridge is 15 feet thick and is made of marble 500 million years old. It was formed about 10,000 years ago during the last ice age; Hudson Brook flowed both down and across and gradually eroded the layers of rock covering the marble.

鼎 Rte. 8, North Adams 01247, tel. 413/663–6392. Rte. 2 to Rte. 8 north, then follow signs. Cost: $2 per car. Open May–Oct., weekdays 10–8, weekends 10–6. Facilities: picnicking.

Nickerson State Park

 ALL

This 1,955-acre forested state park near the Cape Cod National Seashore is dotted with eight freshwater kettle ponds but has no ocean or bay frontage. It both complements activities on the Seashore and provides a good camping center for exploring the best

part of the Cape. Toddlers can splash happily in the warm, calm waters of the kettle ponds (some have lifeguards). Flax Pond is the ideal place for slightly older kids to experiment with boating; you can rent kid-size sailboards (and pedal boats, kayaks, and sailboats). Several ponds are stocked with trout. (See Chapters 5 and 12.)

鼎 Rte. 6A, Brewster 02631, tel. 508/896–3491. Rte. 6 east to exit 12, Rte. 6A west, then follow signs. Admission free. Open daily 8–8. Facilities: biking, bird-watching, camping, canoeing, fishing, sailing, swimming.

New Hampshire

What most draws us to this state's green spaces are the White Mountains, higher than any others in the northeast, including New York's Adirondacks. They offer better views and easier climbs—but they're also more crowded. Many state parks are fairly large, but the White Mountain National Forest (see below) dwarfs them all. Avoid May through mid-June, which is black-fly season. For information on state parks contact New Hampshire Division of Parks (Box 1856, Concord, NH 03302, tel. 603/271–3254). The New Hampshire Atlas and Gazetteer (DeLorme Mapping, Box 298, Freeport, ME 04032, tel. 207/865–4171) has the most complete listing of parks and national areas.

Bear Brook State Park

 ALL

A large (9,300-acre), heavily forested park with ponds and streams for fishing and swimming, Bear Brook offers some highly unusual features: a family camping and snowmobile museum, with tents, RVs and snowmobiles kids can climb into. The nature center sponsors family field trips and evening movies. Teens bike, families with little kids laugh as they learn how to canoe on a calm pond, and parents bait kids' fishhooks alongside a stream. Hikes range from short to serious. The one drawback: The only swimming is in a small pond.

🏠 *Off Rte. 28, Allenstown 03275, tel. 603/ 485–9874. Cost: $2.50 over 12. Open daily sunset–sunrise. Facilities: biking, boat rentals, camping, canoeing, cross-country skiing, fishing, hiking, museums, nature center and trails, park store, picnicking, showers, snowmobiling, swimming.*

Crawford Notch State Park

(👫 5+)

This rugged mountain-pass park near Mt. Washington resembles Franconia Notch State Park (see *below*) in size but is much less crowded, with none of Franconia's commercialism. It too has splendid waterfalls visible from the road, but there aren't as many buses and cars parked at the turnoffs, and my husband and I didn't feel as though we were standing in line to look at a tree. To my mind it has the edge in scenery and laid-back, peaceful mountain atmosphere, but my son prefers Franconia's action and people-watching. The campground has only a few sites spread out in the woods, and the hiking trails are just as superb, especially the one to Arethusa Falls, New Hampshire's highest. The one thing it doesn't have is a lake for swimming.

🏠 *Rte. 302 (12 mi north of Bartlett), Harts Location 03596, tel. 603/374–2272. Admission free; fee for camping. Open mid-May– Columbus Day, daily 24 hrs.*

Echo Lake State Park

(👫 1 – 15)

Set below White Horse Ledge, a dramatic sheer rock face in the White Mountains, small Echo Lake has a beach and a shallow swimming area good for toddlers as well as a raft for older kids. A 1-mile trail leads around the lake, if you want to walk, but don't miss the road that leads to 700-foot-high Cathedral Ledge, from which we could watch rock

climbers inching their way up and sky divers coming down. Picnic tables and fireplaces are set attractively among pine trees. It's least crowded before noon and after 4.

🏠 *Rte. 302 off Rte. 16, North Conway 03860, tel. 603/356–2672. Cost: $2.50 per person over 12. Open Memorial Day–Labor Day. Facilities: camping, hiking, picnicking, swimming.*

Franconia Notch State Park

(👫 ALL)

This may be the state park with the most easy-to-get-to famous natural sights in New England; but it has, on weekends, too many people. Along Route 3, which parallels the Pemigewasset River through the center of the park's 6,440 acres, you can find **The Basin,** a 20-foot-wide glacial pothole at the bottom of a waterfall; **The Flume** (tel. 603/ 745–8391; open mid-May–mid-Oct., daily 9–4:30; $6 adults, $3 kids 6–12), an 800-foot-long gorge 70 feet deep and only 12 to 20 feet wide that you can explore on boardwalks and trails; **The Old Man of the Mountains,** a granite outcropping formed 200 million years ago that resembles a man's face, above Profile Lake (overrated; it's worth two minutes, tops); and the **Cannon Aerial Tramway** (tel. 603/823–5563; open Memorial Day–end June and Sept.–mid-Oct., daily 9–4:30, July and Aug., daily 9–7; $8 adults, $4 kids 6–12), a huge gondola that whisks you to the top of Cannon Mountain in five minutes—it's definitely worth it.

Franconia's other attractions are incredible natural beauty, wonderful family hikes (our favorite is Lonesome Lake), the comfortable, developed Lafayette Campground, a 9-mile biking path, excellent nature programs for kids, swimming in another Echo Lake, and fishing in Profile Lake. (See Chapter 12.)

🏠 *Rte. 3, Franconia Notch 03580, tel. 603/ 745–8391. Cost: $2.50 over 12. Open daily. Facilities: biking, camping, fishing, hiking, nature center and programs, swimming.*

Lost River Reservation

♟♟ 7+

Our family was damp and dirty after we followed the riverbed of the Lost River for ¾ mile through a narrow, steep-walled gorge, caverns, and crevasses formed in the Ice Age. But this one-hour self-guided tour is definitely fun. You can stick to the boardwalks and bridges by the tumbling falls and skip the caves, but 10-year-olds are likely to slither through the "Dungeon," a cave where you have to pull yourself through on your stomach. Climbing up and down ladders and stairs and navigating the caves is more involving here than it is at Ausable Chasm or Howe Caverns (see New York, below). It's important to wear sneakers and it would help to have a flashlight. Forget bringing preschoolers because you'll have to hang on to them every minute. There is a snack bar and picnic area and a lovely nature garden. Friday is the least crowded.
🏠 *Rte. 112, Kinsman Notch, North Woodstock 03262, tel. 603/745–8031. Cost: $6.50 adults, $3.50 kids 6–12. Open mid-May–mid-Oct., daily 9–5.*

Mt. Monadnock State Park

♟♟ 8+

We first spied Mt. Monadnock from far away across a pond while on Route 101 between Keene and Dublin. In eastern terms, it's impressive; a solitary mountain whose upper slopes, unlike most mountains this size (just 3,165 feet) in the Northeast, are bare, craggy rock, burned off by massive fires in the last century. The reason to come to the park is to climb this famous mountain, a national landmark and the second most climbed mountain in the world after Japan's Mt. Fuji. It has been scaled by Thoreau, Emerson, and many other writers and artists. (See also Chapter 12.) When the air is crisp and clear and blue you can see Boston's skyscrapers from the summit (so

they say; we never have). The least crowded times are weekdays and the first two weeks of September.
🏠 *Off Rte. 124 (4 mi north of Jaffrey), Jaffrey Center 03452, tel. 603/532–8862. Cost: $2.50 over 12. Open daily 24 hrs. Facilities: camping, hiking, picnicking, ski touring.*

Mt. Washington State Park

♟♟ 4+

At the summit of the highest peak in the Northeast (6,288 feet) the record was set for the highest wind speed in the world—231 miles per hour. You can see the Atlantic Ocean from here. (We were lucky; 60% of the time it's fogged in.) The guided tour of Tip Top House, the huge stone hotel built in the 1800s and now restored, includes many fascinating historical facts about the mountain, but it's for older kids. If you drive up the 8-mile, 12%-grade winding road, you can stop periodically above the treeline to snap photos or explore. For the most excitement, take the three-hour Cog Railway trip from Mt. Washington Hotel (see Chapter 6). Expect it to be 20 to 30 degrees colder at the summit and very windy.
🏠 *Visitor Center at summit: Sargents Purchase 03581, tel. 603/466–3347. Facilities: museum, cafeteria, gift shop. Auto road: Glenn House 03581 (off Rte. 16, 8 mi south of Gorham), tel. 603/466–3988. Cost: $14 driver and car, $5 additional adults, $3 kids 5–12. Open mid-May–late Oct., weather permitting. Facilities: gift shop, cafeteria, guided van tours.*

White Mountain National Forest

♟♟ ALL

The 773,000 acres of national forest here cover about 80% of the White Mountains, sprawling through the middle of the state from west to east and into a chunk of Maine. If we want mountain hiking in the Northeast, we'd rather do it on the

National Forest's 1,200 miles of trails than anywhere else (see Chapter 12 for some good family hikes). The peaks are sharper, higher, rockier, and more vivid, with more open vistas than Vermont's Green Mountains or even the Adirondacks.

For families, the Appalachian Mountain Club's camping programs and comfortable huts (see Chapters 12 and 14) in prime scenic locations are especially attractive. The AMC is the source of the best guidebooks and maps for the White Mountains (available at Pinkham Notch Visitor Center, tel. 603/466–2727; or from AMC, Box 298, Gorham NH 03581, tel. 800/262–4455). The National Forest also maintains a system of campgrounds and primitive huts.

We're hikers, but energetic, athletic teens we know say the National Forest's old roads are great for mountain biking. Swimming here is in icy cold ponds and rivers (no lifeguards); fishing is good, but can't compare with the Adirondacks for the sheer number and variety of lakes, ponds, streams, and rivers. The most scenic route through the forest is the east–west Kancamagus Highway, Route 112, from Conway to Lincoln, which is lined with campgrounds. (See Chapter 6.)

🏚 *Forest Supervisor, Box 638, White Mountain National Forest, Laconia 03247, tel. 603/ 528–8721. Office open weekdays, 8–4. Facilities: camping, hiking, picnicking, swimming.*

New York

There is an amazing amount of green parkland in the eastern part of this state, much of it concentrated in the north in huge tracts of forests, high mountains, and lakes that provide some of the best family hiking, canoeing, and fishing in the Northeast—and some of the most remote wilderness outside of Maine. This is the state with the most caves to explore. Its coastline on Long Island is where you'll find parks with perfect sand beaches. For further information con-

tact New York State Parks, Recreation and Historic Preservation Office (Empire State Plaza, Agency Building 1, Albany 12238, tel. 518/474–0456) or the Department of Conservation (50 Wolf Rd., Albany 12233, tel. 518/457–3521 or 800/487–6867). The most complete listing of parks and natural wonders is in *The New York State Atlas and Gazetteer* (DeLorme Mapping, Box 298, Freeport, ME 04032, tel. 207/865–4171).

Adirondack Park and Forest Preserve

 4+

This vast 6-million-acre park, ⅔ of upper New York State, is the Northeast's Yellowstone or Yosemite, though it's much bigger than any national park in the lower 48 states. Unlike other state parks, it is a patchwork of public and private land, a combination of the most remote wilderness east of the Mississippi (except for Maine), the noisy amusement parks and pop-culture activities of Lake George, and developed ski areas like Whiteface Mountain. Motels and restaurants on private land coexist with statemaintained campgrounds and hiking trails, which means families have many more options than they do in the remote reaches of northern Maine. No matter what outdoor activity you are interested in, you can probably do it somewhere in this park, though I wouldn't take a bike trip here because it's so mountainous.

To me, much of the park's landscape and its 42 mountains over 4,000 feet seem rugged, dramatic, and wild, a place of mysterious dark forests and the calls of loons, with challenging hiking, climbing, and cross-country skiing best suited to families with kids over 10. What makes this pine-forested range so different from Vermont's Green Mountains and New Hampshire's Whites, however, is the number of lakes and ponds—nearly 3,000—and the hundreds of miles of streams, ideal for family swimming, camping, canoeing, and fishing even with very young kids.

The park has several distinct regions (*see* Chapter 6). Nearly everywhere live significant populations of bear, moose, deer, beavers, and many other animals. If you climb Mt. Marcy, the highest peak, don't expect your family to be alone, communing with nature; on the trail and summit it seems as though just about everyone wants to bag the biggest peak.

Our advice: don't try to see the whole park; pick one area. Distances are greater than you think, and the best way to get to know this park with kids is on foot or in a canoe rather than by car.

The two visitor centers, Paul Smiths (just north of Saranac Lake) and Newcomb (about ½ hour from Blue Mountain Lake), have exhibits on the park's colorful history, flora and fauna, and special programs and walks for kids.

The Northway (I–87) runs north and south on the eastern edge of the park; Route 30 is the central north–south road. Route 28 in the south and routes 3 and 73 in the north are the primary east–west roads. (*See* Chapters 6 and 12.) Because of the size and nature of the park, there is, unfortunately, no single place to obtain information. For general information, contact the I Love NY Tourism Office (1 Commerce Plaza, Albany 12245, tel. 518/225–5698). For the best information on camping, hiking, and canoeing, including trail maps, write the Department of Conservation (50 Wolf Rd., Albany 12233, tel. 518/457–3521 or 800/487–6867) and the Adirondack Mountain Club (RR 3, Box 3055, Lake George 12845, tel. 518/668–4447). For an excellent free map of the whole park, contact ANCA (183 Broadway, Saranac Lake 12983, tel. 518/891–6200).

🏠 *Adirondack Park Visitor Centers: Box 3000, Paul Smiths 12970, tel. 518/327–3000 (Rte. 30, 12 mi north of Saranac Lake); Box 101, Newcomb 12852, tel. 518/582–2000 (Rte. 28N, exit 29 off I–87). Open Oct.–Apr., daily 9–5; May–Sept., daily 9–7. Activities: backpacking, biking, boating, camping, canoeing, fishing, hiking, rafting, swimming, sailing.*

Ausable Chasm

Don't be put off too much by the tour buses and touristy surroundings; this gorge has drama, especially if you've never been to one before. The layered sandstone cliffs, several hundred feet high and at some points a mere 20 feet apart, were carved out by the swiftly flowing Ausable River 500 million years ago. In the first half of the 1½-mile gorge tour you walk down into and along the gorge itself on natural stone walkways and steps and across the river on steel walkways where you can look down at the falls and rapids below. The 20-minute boat ride through the second half glides in the cool dim section of the Grand Flume, where towering cliffs are only 20 feet apart. A bus takes you back to the parking lot, where there are picnic tables, a playground, and food.

🏠 *Box 390, Rte. 9, Ausable Chasm 12911, tel. 518/834–7454. Exit 34 or 35 off I–87 or I–89 and ferry from Burlington, VT. Boat and walk, $12.95 adults, $7.95 kids 6–11; walk only, $9.07 adults, $5.57 kids. Open mid-May–early Oct., daily 9–4.*

Bear Mountain/Harriman State Park

We've always preferred the less-crowded, western section of the park (Harriman) along and off Seven Lakes Parkway, where you'll find more than seven lakes and the most interesting trails. Of the three sand beaches, we head for Lake Tiorati's small one, the least crowded because no buses can park here. Of the 200-odd trails, our favorites are those leading to higher hidden and deserted lakes like Pine Meadow, where we skip stones from long flat ledges that hang over the water, or to one of the abandoned 18th-century iron mines that dot the hillsides. Bear Mountain Park, to the east bordering the Hudson River, is the more civilized area and very crowded on weekends; a distinctly urban crowd hangs around the jammed swimming pool, lunches on the inn's deck, and strolls the walkways by the slightly shabby zoo, and along dramatically rocky Hessian Lake, filled with paddleboats. The walkways are good if you're pushing a stroller. Be sure to get a map ($2) from the Administration Building right across the parking lot from the inn.

ft *Palisades Interstate Park Commission, Bear Mountain 10911, tel. 914/786–2701. Palisades Pkwy. to Rte. 9W or Rte. 6, or bus from New York City's Port Authority Bus Terminal. Parking at Bear Mountain Inn $3, at beaches $4. Open daily dawn–dusk; swimming weekdays 10–6, weekends 9–7. Facilities: boating (and rentals), camping, fishing, hiking, ice-skating, cross-country skiing, nature museum, nature programs, swimming (lifeguards), zoo.*

Catskill Park and State Forest Preserve

(**ЖЖ ALL**)

It took our family years to discover the Catskills as a green space because our image of it was huge resort hotels with aging crooners singing every night. In truth, it does have many hokey attractions on the kitschy side, which appeal more to a lot of kids than do the magnificent landscapes. The Catskills are both a region just west of the central Hudson Valley and a mountain range. The Catskill Park (705,000 acres of public and fairly developed private land) and the Catskill State Forest Preserve (386,000 unspoiled state-owned acres), like a smaller version of the Adirondacks (lower peaks and fewer lakes), are spread over several counties—Ulster, Sullivan, Delaware, and Greene. All have good hiking, and fishing and tubing on rivers; there are a number of downhill ski areas. We favor the Greene County part of the park, which has 100 waterfalls with pools for swimming, the best

family campground and day-use area—North–South Lakes (Rte. 18, Haines Falls, tel. 518/382–0680), within easy hiking distance of the state's highest waterfall, Kaaterskill Falls. Ulster's mountains are still said to be haunted by ghosts and goblins of centuries past; in that county we prefer other parks in the Shawangunk Mountains (*see* Minnewaska, *below*). Sullivan is best for fishing and canoeing. As with the Adirondack Park, there's no convenient central Catskill Park and Forest Preserve office for information. Check with the I Love NY Tourism Office (I Commerce Plaza, Albany 12245, tel. 518/474–4116); for camping and hiking, the Department of Environmental Conservation (50 Wolf Rd., Albany 12233, tel. 518/457–3521 or 800/487–6867), and The Adirondack Mountain Club (RR 3, Box 3055, Lake George 12845, tel. 518/668–4447). *Other useful sources of information are Catskill Association for Tourism Services (Box 449TG, Catskill, NY 12414, tel. 800/882–2287; Greene County, tel. 518/943–3223 or 800/542–2414; Ulster County, tel. 800/342–5826; Delaware County, tel. 607/746–2281 or 800/642–4443; and Sullivan County, tel. 914/794–3000, ext. 5010 or 800/882–2287). See also Chapter 12.*

Fire Island National Seashore

(**ЖЖ 4 – 12**)

One of the East Coast's great barrier beaches, Fire Island is simply a 32-mile-long strip of sand, dune, and beach grass no more than a ½-mile wide off Long Island's south shore, between the Great South Bay and the Atlantic. It has good swimming, sand, beach-walking and not much else, which is why it appeals to us. You can go for the day. All the visitor center areas have splendid beaches; the best swimming for little kids is at high tide when shallow water extends far, far out into the Atlantic. We give a slight edge to the Watch Hill Visitor Center, especially for older kids: It's got camping, an 8-mile wilderness area for hiking, and (on the bay side) the most active marina, where kids can watch boats or fish at one end of the cove.

You can get to know the seashore by staying in one of the small resort communities (of the 17, several are very family-oriented, with planned kids' activities) interspersed amid protected land, as we did. Part of the fun was hauling our groceries home in a red wagon because there are no cars or roads, only boardwalks and sandy paths. Don't miss exploring the Sunken Forest (a self-guided trail map is available at Sailors Haven Visitor Center) hidden behind the dunes, where you can walk on boardwalks through a primeval forest that includes 200-year-old holly trees. *See also* Chapter 12.

🏠 *National Park Service, U.S. Dept of the Interior, Park Headquarters, 120 Laurel St., Patchogue 11772, tel. 516/289–4810. Sailors Haven Visitor Center, tel. 516/597–6183 (ferry from Sayville, tel. 516/589–8980; round-trip tickets, $8 adults, $4.50 kids under 11). Watch Hill Visitor Center, tel. 516/597–6455 (ferry from Patchogue, tel. 516/475–1665; round-trip, $10 adults, $6 kids). Smith Point West Visitor Center, tel. 516/281–3010 (William Floyd Pkwy. to Smith Point Bridge). Admission free. Visitor centers open late June–Labor Day; ferries May–Oct. Facilities: kids' activities and programs, bathhouses, camping, fishing, groceries, picnic tables, snack bars, swimming (lifeguards).*

Howe Caverns/Secret Caverns

(👫 5 – 15)

The elevator in the visitor center at Howe Caverns descends 156 feet into the earth to this series of cool limestone caverns, the biggest in the Northeast, carved out by streams millions of years ago. The tour lasts 1½ hours, so if you or your kids are claustrophobic, think twice before you climb in. The paved walkways are lighted; the colored lights playing across the strange, contorted rock formations make them seem like stage sets for an Indiana Jones movie. It's all very developed and organized. Be sure to listen to the

"Stone Organ," from which weird sounds emanate. Bring sweaters even in hot weather; the caves are always 52°F and damp. If you want a cave experience that has a more adventurous flavor, head for smaller Secret Caverns nearby (Cavern Rd., between Rtes. 7 and 20, tel. 518/296–8558). Here you walk down 130 steps to the underground river and see a 100-foot-high waterfall.

🏠 *Rte. 7 (between Central Bridge and Cobleskill), Howes Cave 12092, tel. 518/296–8900. Cost: $10.50 adults, $6 kids 7–12. Open daily 9–6.*

Ice Caves Mountain

 (👫 3+)

The self-guided drive-and-walk tour of hidden caves, secret grottoes, ice that never melts, and weird rock formations like Balanced Rock takes about 90 minutes, and we were intrigued throughout. This is a good place to take little kids: Nature trail walkways slope gently and on even a short walk you see many sights.

🏠 *Rte. 52, Ellenville 12464, tel. 914/647–7989. Cost: $6 adults, $4 kids 6–12. Open mid-May–early Nov., daily 9–dusk.*

Minnewaska State Park

(👫 6+)

Two glacial lakes, one remote and one not, a misty waterfall where you can see rainbows, easy biking on old carriage roads that pass ruins of old hotels, and good picnic spots are just some of the reasons we'll go back to this relatively undeveloped 11,600-acre park in the Shawangunk Mountains in southern Ulster County.

🏠 *U.S. 44, New Paltz 12561, tel. 914/255–0752. Cost: $4 per car. Park open mid-May–Labor Day, daily 9–9; swimming area daily 10–5:30; Labor Day–mid-May, weekends and holidays 9–5. Facilities: cross-country skiing, hiking, horseback riding, picnicking (tables and grills), swimming.*

Rhode Island

Although there are green spaces in many parts of this tiny state, the ones that most appeal to us are on or near the ocean along the stretch of coast from Westerly to Narragansett called South County, on the islands of Jamestown and Block Island, and on little headlands and points that reach out from the Newport peninsula. This is the land of white sand beaches, pine barrens, salt ponds, the sound of birds, and mists coming in from the sea. State park beaches tend to be interspersed among town beaches (see Chapter 12). For general information, check with the Rhode Island Tourism Division Department of Economic Development (7 Jackson Walkway, Providence 02903, tel. 401/277–2601 or 800/556–2484). The Rhode Island Visitor's Map lists all state parks, sanctuaries, and preserves; for a copy, contact the Rhode Island Tourism Division Department of Environmental Management (Information Office, 9 Hayes St., Providence 02908, tel. 401/277–2632).

Block Island National Wildlife Refuge

(👫 4 – 12)

Of Block Island's five wildlife refuges—some mainly dunes and grass and beach, some high bluffs and meadows—we especially like this stretch of dunes and grass at the northern tip of the island because it's next to North Lighthouse, which now houses a museum you can visit (ghostly when it's misty out). We also like the fact that it borders another preserve on calm Sachem Pond where you can find crabs, and that it's a primary summer nesting area for gulls by the thousands. Don't go too close, because protective parent gulls may dive at you. The refuge is administered by the U.S. Fish and Wildlife Service (Box 307, Charlestown 02813, tel. 401/364–9124). The Nature Conservancy (Ocean Rd., New Harbor, tel. 401/466–2129), however, can tell you all you want to know and has trail maps and special kids' walks in this and other areas. 🏠 *Corn Neck Rd., Block Island 02807. Admission free. Open daily dawn–dusk.*

Burlingame State Park

(👫 3 – 14)

This 2,100-acre, pinewooded park is just across Route 1 from beaches and the Ninigret Wildlife Refuge. The park is a big circle of land covered with reddish-trunked skinny pines around pretty, freshwater Watchaug Pond, which has a couple of pleasant small, sandy beaches with nice shade and lifeguards. The woods feel light and open and smell good, and a circular 8-mile trail rings the park. But the camping (755 sites) is the primary reason to come here. Everything is particularly clean and well-cared for (see Chapter 12). The best bet for an inexpensive vacation: camp here; swim and hike here; and make visits to Ninigret Wildlife Refuge and East Beach–Ninigret Conservation Area (see below). Day-users are relegated to a tiny beach and picnic area. 🏠 *Burlingame Park Rd., Charlestown 02813, tel. 401/322–7337; picnic area, 401/364–8910. For more information, write to Division of Parks and Recreation, 2321 Hartford Ave., Johnston 02919, tel. 401/277–2632. Day-use parking $4; camping $12. Open mid-Apr.–Oct., daily 24 hrs. Facilities: boating, camping, fishing, picnicking, freshwater swimming, playground, store.*

Ft. Adams State Park

(👫 3+)

Finding a park for watching boats is not as easy as you might think, but sailboats of all sizes and fishing boats regularly pass the narrow neck between this point overlooking Narragansett Bay and Jamestown Island. The beach on the south side of Brenton Cove has a roped-off area for young swimmers, a lifeguard, and lots of green space for running around.

🏛 *Ocean Dr., Newport 02480, tel. 401/ 847–2400. Admission free. Open daily dawn–dusk.*

Green Animals

👫 2 – 12

What makes this garden different is that it is a garden of topiary—trees and shrubs pruned to create living sculptures. Twenty-one of the 80 shapes are animal figures to hunt for on the mazelike winding paths. It's a humorous search. If you visit on a day when there are several families, you suddenly hear shouts naming an animal, and kids scurry to see a giraffe standing on top of a trimmed round platform looming over them or seat themselves between the happily out-stretched legs of a clipped teddy bear; don't miss the camel.

🏛 *Cory's Lane (off Rte. 114), Portsmouth 02871, tel. 401/847–1000. Cost: $6.50 adults, $3 kids 5–11. Open May–Oct., daily 10–5.*

Misquamicut State Beach and Atlantic Beach

👫 5+

Boom boxes, wall-to-wall people, the smell of suntan lotion—this 7-mile-long beach park has everything East Beach (*see below*) doesn't, including an amusement park next to it. The surf at Atlantic Beach is good for body surfing. For teens who want action and people-watching, these two beaches are fine places. The water is very clean, surf is moderate, and there's little undertow.

🏛 *Atlantic Ave. (off Rte. 1; follow signs), Westerly 02891, tel. 401/596–9097. Facilities: bathhouses, lifeguard, snack bar, nearby amusement park.*

Ninigret Conservation Area (East Beach)

👫 6+

This long barrier of low dunes and a 3½-mile swath of perfect, flat, windswept sand beach lies between Ninigret Pond, Rhode Island's largest salt pond, and Block Island Sound, and borders the Ninigret National Wildlife Refuge. Here you can walk and walk along the water's edge without seeing hundreds of people and play frisbee or fly a kite without hitting anyone. Though there are no high dunes to climb, small paths lead to the Salt Pond. It's not a place for kids who crave the excitement of lots of action or for families with little kids who must have bathhouses, showers, a snack bar, and lots of other kids. On the other hand, it's never very crowded because there are only 100 parking spaces in the lot. (On weekends, the lot is filled by 8:30 in the morning.) Bring a beach umbrella and plenty of sunblock, as there is no shade, and a cooler with snacks and drinks. If you crave more amenities and more kids, go to 4-mile-long Blue Shutters Town Beach, which you pass on East Road, and which has a snack bar and showers; its parking lot fills about an hour later (also $10).

🏛 *Conservation Area, end of East Beach Rd. (off Rte. 1), Charlestown 12813, tel. 401/ 277–2632). For more information, write to Division of Parks and Recreation, 2321 Hartford Ave., Johnston 02919. Parking $10, camping $12. Open daily dawn–dusk. Facilities: lifeguard, portable toilets, windsurfing.*

Norman Bird Sanctuary

👫 7 – 12

This 450-acre bird sanctuary has more diverse terrain than other refuges along the coast, and one of its key attractions is Hanging Rock, a rock formation with views of marsh, pond, and ocean that will appeal to parents. Kids have a chance to scramble up bumpy cliff walls like rock climbers. Legend has it that criminals were once hanged on top. Bring binoculars and a bird book, as birds are easy to spot here, even for noisy kids; there's a constant sound of birdsong and chatter. A museum on the second floor of the large barn has specimens of local birds, and cages near the main building house a few injured ones. Trail maps are available at the headquarters.

 583 Third Beach Rd., Middletown 02842, tel. 401/846–2577. Cost: $2 over 12. Open Memorial Day–Labor Day, daily 9–5; Labor Day–Memorial Day, Tues.–Sun. 9–5. Facilities: bird-watching, hiking, natural history museum.

Vermont

Vermont's landscape is tamer than New Hampshire's or New York's; the mountains are (mostly) rounder and forested. We usually head for the two large tracts of the Green Mountain National Forest; state parks tend to be small and neat, huddled by a tiny lake or one mountain or along Lake Champlain's shore; many offer on-site naturalists, annual arts and entertainment programs for kids, even cabins and cottages (see Chapter 12). All state parks charge $1.50 for adults and $1 for kids 4 to 13 for day use. Vermont Department of Forests, Parks, and Recreation (103 S. Main St., Waterbury 05676, tel. 802/244–8711) publishes "Vermont State Parks & Forest Recreation Areas." The Vermont Atlas and Gazetteer (DeLorme Mapping, Box 298, Freeport, ME 04032, tel. 207/865–4171) has descriptive listings of natural phenomena and a brief listing of all the parks.

Burton Island State Park

Near Canada, in the northernmost part of Lake Champlain, the largest lake in the Northeast (112 miles long), lies 253-acre Burton Island. You can get here only by ferry—something that always appeals to our

family. The park is an unusual combination of isolation (no cars or houses on the island), comfortable camping (hot showers), and wonderful boating and fishing, especially if you bring your own boat to keep at the large marina. It's a big enough island not to be boring after one day. The nearby chain of unspoiled Lake Champlain Islands, ideal for exploring by bike, is easy to get to for a day or overnight trip; a ferry from the state park goes to Knight Point on North Hero. The island's woods-and-fields terrain is fairly flat, good for short, easy hikes and bike rides with kids. Kids can roam and explore by themselves, fish in the marina and watch boats, swim at the shale beach with its nice gradual drop, make an Indian dreamcatcher at the nature center. The only drawback is no sand beach; but there is one at Knight's Point.

 Box 123 (Rte. 36 and Point Rd. to Kamp Kill Kare State Park, then passenger ferry), St. Alban's Bay 05481, tel. 802/524–6353. Cost: $1.50 adults, $1 kids 4–13. Open mid-May–Labor Day, daily 8–4:30. Facilities: beach, biking, boating (canoe and rowboat rentals), camping, fishing, marina, nature program and trails, picnic tables, playground, swimming.

Emerald Lake State Park

🧍🧍 0 – 13

Emerald Lake is a busy, family-filled park at the foot of Dorset Mountain, hidden from Route 7. The small, round, placid lake has charm, warm water, a short sand beach with grass and trees near it, and an island of rocks and a couple of trees to swim to. You can stop for the day or camp up on the mountain for several days, especially if you have little kids who want short, easy trails (try the one to the natural bridge) and swimming.

 RD Box 485 (off Rte. 7 in North Dorset), East Dorset 05253, tel. 802/362–1655. Cost: $1.50 adults, $1 kids 4–13. Open mid-May–mid-Oct. Facilities: boating (and rentals), camping, canoeing, fishing, hiking, picnic tables, playground, snack bar, swimming.

Green Mountain National Forest

 ALL

Vermont's mountains, green in summer, white in winter, cluster in the center of the state to form a wide, forested ridge with tidy farms on either side. On much of the ridge lies the 300,000 acres of the National Forest, which is broken into north and south sections that stretch over two-thirds the length of Vermont and include six wilderness areas. Route 100, the ski road our family knows well, is its boundary to the east, but five ski areas are actually in the forest. In winter the forest is a fine place for cross-country skiing and snowmobiling.

In summer, we find the Green Mountains friendlier and less rugged than New Hampshire's Whites, a place for hiking through trees and picking berries instead of climbing up rock faces (though there's some of that). Hiking, fishing, biking, and camping (and swimming in a few ponds) draw families here. But what we come to explore—and what's most unique—are the forest's special recreation areas, which make back-country experiences more accessible to families whether for a day or overnight. Picnic areas at the ends of roads serve as base points, and easy-to-read map brochures highlight features appealing to kids. The White Rocks are a slope of huge shattered quartzite boulders that harbor ice and snow in their crevasses all summer long. Our other favorite areas are Hapgood Pond, Texas Falls, and Grout Pond. There are also developed campgrounds; some have nature programs for kids. Information is available from the Forest Supervisor (Green Mountain National Forest, 231 N. Main St., Rutland 05702, tel. 802/773–0300 or 802/773–0324). The Green Mountain Club (RR1, Box 650, Waterbury Center 05677, tel. 802/244–7037) publishes helpful guides and maps and offers advice on where to go.

🏠 *For information, contact district office in Manchester (RR1, Box 1940, Manchester Cen-*

ter 05255, tel. 802/362–2307), Middlebury (Rte. 7, RR4, Box 1260, Middlebury 05753, tel. 802/388–4362), or Rochester (Rte. 100, RD1, Box 108, Rochester 05767, tel. 802/767–4261). Facilities: backpacking, camping, canoeing, cross-country skiing, fishing, hiking, picnicking, scenic drives, snowmobiling, swimming.

Merck Forest and Farmland Center

 3 – 12

A unique combination of old hilltop farm, wildlife sanctuary, environmental education center, and just plain beautiful near-wilderness hilly land with meadows and spectacular views, this 2,800-acre nonprofit foundation is open year-round for day-use or camping. Beyond the demonstration farm of animals and barns and visitor's center near the entrance, there are no cars, just 28 trails through woods and meadows that pass scattered primitive camping cabins (including one in a field by a clump of birch trees) and shelters, views of the Adirondacks, and a spring-fed swimming and fishing pond. Bears have been sighted. Coyotes too. The family nature programs include getting to know llamas or helping to make maple sugar.

🏠 *Rte. 315, Rupert 05768, tel. 802/394–7836. Admission free; fee for camping. Open mid-May–mid-Oct., daily. Facilities: camping, farm, fishing, hiking, nature programs, swimming.*

Quechee Gorge and Quechee State Park

6+

There are two ways to see Vermont's prime natural wonder, a mile-long, 200-foot-wide gorge that's 165 feet deep: Just park and stare down at it and the falls from either side of the bridge or take one of the trails to viewing spots by the Ottauquechee River. My family's vote; the falls from the bridge; the sheer, straight rock walls and rushing water of the gorge from the trails.

Quechee's gorge and falls are five to 10 times wider than New Hampshire's Flume (which is almost like a deep brook by comparison) or New York's Ausable Chasm, and the site is less touristy (no charge!). But it doesn't have an extensive network of walkways and bridges in the gorge itself.

🏛 *Gorge: Box Q, Rte. 4, Quechee 05059, tel. 802/295–7600. Exit 1 off I–89, then west on Rte. 4. Admission free. Open daily. Facilities: gift shop, snack bar. State park: 190 Dewey Mills Rd. off Rte. 4, White River Junction 05001, tel. 802/295–2990, mid-May–early Oct.; 802/886–2434, early Oct.–mid-May. Exit 1 off I–89, then 3 mi west on Rte. 4. Cost: $1.50 adults, $1 kids 4–13. Open mid-May–early Oct., 802/886–2434.*

HOOPS, HITS, HAT TRICKS, AND TOUCHDOWNS
BIG-LEAGUE SPORTS

The Northeast has some of the best teams and players in the country, some of the most historic stadiums and arenas, such as Yankee Stadium and the Boston Garden, and a wide variety of sports to view, from baseball to horse racing. For a fanatic fan's take on these subjects, I've asked some of Gavin's sports-loving teenage friends, notably a New York City high school journalist, Matt Wool, to add their expertise to this chapter.

We've always had the most successful sports outings when we take Gavin's age and current sports passions into account, not just our own. Though I've seen 2-year-olds at major-league baseball games and have some football-fanatic friends who always take their twin 5-year-olds along, I found that before Gavin and his friends turned 7 and 8 they weren't all that interested in watching sports at stadiums and arenas with enormous crowds and they rarely understood the intricacies of game rules. (Hockey and baseball seem easiest for kids to understand.) The four years from 10 through 13 were when he most wanted to attend just about any sports event; now he and his friends prefer seeing a sport they like to play themselves.

Minor-league baseball games and Ivy League college football are usually more fun than major-league events for little kids—the seats are much cheaper, the smaller stadiums have better viewing and more places to run around when kids have what my son calls "seatitis," the players are friendlier and more approachable, and the crowd is rarely combative or rowdy. Also check out the demonstration game schedules at such sports museums as the Baseball Hall of Fame (see Chapter 8); many of these games draw lots of families and can be combined with a museum visit.

When Gavin was little, we sat as close as possible to the action in the bigger stadiums to keep his interest, we made sure he knew what he was going to see before we went, and we aimed for events that had something special—such as baseball games on promotional days so he would leave with a special souvenir like a helmet, a poster, or his favorite, a bat.

Expect what happens on the rink or field in the Northeast to trigger strong passions among adult fans and players. We've seen plenty of drinking and obnoxious behavior at both baseball and hockey games—in Madison Square Garden players and spectators sometimes draw applause for starting fights. Many stadiums have family-oriented, alcohol-free sections.

Connecticut

Auto Racing

 5+

LIME ROCK PARK. We live only about 20 minutes from this racetrack, considered the best road racing in the Northeast, and our family has spent many sunny weekend afternoons watching races here. Perhaps the two most exciting race weekends for families are Memorial Day and the BMW Vintage Festival with historic sports car races and a swap meet on Labor Day. What's unique here is the parklike atmosphere. Along with many other families, we bring picnics and view the events from the natural amphitheater seating of the grassy spectator hillsides while the little kids roll down the gentle incline. Kids under 12 are admitted free, and families are welcome to camp for free (inside the track) and explore the park's 300 acres in the rolling Litchfield Hills.
🏠 *Rte. 112, Lakeville 06039, tel. 203/435–2571, 203/435–0896, or 800/722–3577. Cost: $5–$40, parking free. Season: mid-Apr.–mid-Oct. (not all weekends).*

Hockey

 8+

HARTFORD WHALERS. For hockey fans, the problem with the Hartford Whalers is that they have been one of the most consistently bad teams in the National Hockey League, losing twice as often as they've won. For younger kids we know, who frequently don't care whether the home team wins or not, the action keeps their interest, and some Whalers do sign autographs. Tickets are easy to get.
🏠 *Hartford Civic Center, Hartford 06103, tel. 203/728–6637. Cost: $20–$35. Season: Oct.–Apr.*

Massachusetts

Baseball

 7+

BOSTON RED SOX. I think seeing a game at Fenway Park, where the Boston Red Sox (American League) have played since 1912, is more fun for kids than at any other major sports stadium in the Northeast because it's small and idiosyncratic. Afternoon games here capture the spirit of baseball as it should be. No matter where you sit, whether box seats or bleachers, you have a good view of the action—though we favor the left side, where much of the action takes place. Fenway also has a quirky, personal, offbeat charm that even young kids seem to pick up on; its unique many-sided shape, the 37-foot-high green cement wall nicknamed "The Green Monster" in left field, the old-fashioned scoreboard, the Citgo sign all make it special to us. Along with the Yankees, the Boston Red Sox have had some of the most famous players in baseball, such as Ted Williams, Mo Vaughn, and Roger Clemens. Fenway welcomes families, offering regular family discount days (listed on ticket brochure), "Youth" days on which kids 15 and under get free promotion items, no-alcohol seating areas, and in 1994, even a special kid's opening day with kids' music. For autographs, arrive about an hour before the game and hang out by the dugout. Tickets are usually easy to get, even just before game time, except when the Red Sox are playing the Yankees (their arch rival) or the Blue Jays.
🏠 *Fenway Park, 4 Yawkey Way (Fenway stop on Green Line T), Boston 02215, tel. 617/267–8661 or 617/267–1700. Cost: $8–$20. Tickets also at BOSTIX and Ticketron. Season: 1st week of Apr.–early Oct.; day games 2 PM, night games 7:35 PM.*

👫 3 – 14

CAPE COD BASEBALL LEAGUE. The nation's most talented college baseball players are recruited to make up the 10 town teams of the oldest summer league in the country. Major-league scouts are at all the games; 80% of the Cape League players go on to play ball professionally—the way Carlton Fisk, Ron Darling, and Will Clark did. There are games most days of the week at 4, 5, 6, or 7 o'clock, usually at high school ball fields in the various towns, which conveniently solves the problem of what to do in the evening on a beach vacation. Wherever you happen to be staying, you'll find a game near you. Admission is pass-the-hat. Players also hold baseball clinics for kids on a weekly basis.

🏠 *Box 164, S. Harwich 02661, tel. 508/362–3036. Season: mid-June–Sept.*

👫 3+

PITTSFIELD METS. To us a baseball game at Wahconah Park on a warm summer night is the perfect place to introduce young kids to the sport. Cozy, charming, and intimate, with a backdrop of mountains, this old-fashioned ball field where minor leagues have played since 1919 has no AstroTurf, electronic scoreboard, or grandstand seating 50,000 people. Instead, plastic owls swing from the rafters to scare away pigeons, and the wooden seats are so close to the field you feel as if you could touch the players. You can even get (and afford) front-row seats. Though the Mets are a short season Class A New York–Penn League team, the first rung for rookies on their route to the major leagues, you'll see lots of talent at these games: Curtis Pride, Jeromy Burnitz, David Telcheder, Tito Navarro, are just some of the Pittsfield Mets who have made it to the majors.

Kids rush down for the on-field contests between innings, have time to shake hands with and get autographs from the ballplayers,

and meet Mr. Met, the mascot costumed as a huge baseball. Home games are held three or four times a week, mostly at 7 PM.

🏠 *Wahconah St., Box 328, Pittsfield 01202, tel. 413/499–6387. North St. ½ mi then left to Wahconah St. Cost: $3–$6. Season: mid-June–Sept.*

Basketball

👫 8+

BOSTON CELTICS. Going to a Celtics game in Boston Garden is one of the more exciting experiences in sports viewing. The famous parquet wood floor has irregularities only the home team knows. Colorful championship banners and numbers of all the retired stars hang from the rafters in this historic arena. Starting in 1996, however, the Celtics will be playing at the larger Shawmut Center, now under construction. The Celtics have been the National Basketball Association's top team 15 times, world champions 16 times. The electricity in the atmosphere is partly because of the enthusiasm of Boston's basketball fans, who are among the most knowledgeable and pleasant around. If you ask them about any player, you're likely to hear a complete biography. Tickets are very difficult to get, especially to games with the most popular teams. Your best bet is to call as soon as they go on sale in October.

🏠 *Boston Garden, 150 Causeway St. (North Station stop on Green Line T), Boston 02114, tel. 617/523–3030; tickets, 617/720–3434. Cost: $12–$45. Season: Nov.–Apr., sometimes as late as June.*

Football

👫 7+

COLLEGE TEAMS. Though the **Boston College Eagles** (Alumni Stadium, Chestnut Hill, Brookline, tel. 617/552–2000) have a long tradition of playing great football, our favorite place to see football in Boston is at

Harvard University's Soldier's Field on a Saturday afternoon. We like to come here for the atmosphere; though the stands are rarely full we find the energy and enthusiasm of the almost totally youthful crowd more appealing than the audience at a professional Patriots' game. The stadium is smaller, easier to get to, and the tickets are less expensive. The Yale–Harvard game is still the most exciting.

🏛 *North Harvard St. and Soldier's Field Rd., Allston, tel. 617/495–2212. Cost: $5–$10; Harvard-Yale game, $25. Season: Sept.–Nov.*

 9+

NEW ENGLAND PATRIOTS. Boston's professional football team plays at the Foxboro Stadium 25 miles from Boston. There are no tiers, poles or pillars, so you can see well from everywhere, and there is a special no-alcohol, patrolled family section. The giant scoreboard shows replays and more. On the other hand, bathrooms and water fountains are few. Traffic on Route 1 for the two hours before and after the game is horrendous (there are buses during the season, but no subway line). That may be the reason for the tradition of tailgate picnics before and after the game in the huge parking lot. Though the stadium is sometimes sold out, individual tickets do go on sale.

🏛 *Foxboro Stadium, Rte. 1, Foxboro 02035, tel. 508/543–1776 or 800/543–1776. Cost: $32–$35. Season: Sun.-afternoon games Sept.–Dec.*

Hockey

 9+

BOSTON BRUINS. One of the National Hockey League's most consistently good teams, the Bruins share the Boston Garden with the NBA's Celtics and will move to Shawmut Center in 1996. Two Hall of Famers, Phil Esposito and Bobby Orr, were once on the team, and two excellent current players are Adam Oakes and Ray

Borque. There's an undeniable excitement to a Bruins game, partly because most of the audience are total hockey buffs and devout fans who are ready to share their knowledge with kids, and partly because of the banners and atmosphere of the Garden itself. As at most hockey games, there's sometimes as much action in the stands as on the ice, which usually means fights. Games are usually sold out by game time, but you can get tickets if you call far enough in advance.

🏛 *Boston Garden, 150 Causeway St. (North Station stop on Green Line T), Boston 02114, tel. 617/227–3206 or 617/227–3223. Cost: $16–$40. Season: Oct.–Mar.*

Polo

 5+

MYOPIA HUNT CLUB. A polo match has many things kids find exciting—there's lots of speed and action as the horses thunder up and down the field and bump one another, and kids can jump up and down as they watch from a grassy sideline. For two horse-loving kids on my Boston panel, the big treat at half-time is stamping down the divots of turf kicked up by the horses on the field. Bring an elegant picnic, not fast food. The grounds open at 1 PM if you want to picnic first.

🏛 *Polo Productions, Rte. 1A (exit 20N off Rte. 128), Box 2103, South Hamilton 01928, tel. 203/468–4433. Cost: $5 adults; free under 13. Season: late May–Oct.*

Running

 6+

BOSTON MARATHON. Since 1897, the country's oldest marathon has been run annually on the third Monday in April—Patriot's Day—drawing both world-class runners and amateurs. To our way of thinking this marathon is the one in the Northeast that's most fun for families to watch.

That's because of the celebratory atmosphere generated by the spectators, including lots of kids, who regard this day as the
beginning of spring. Boston families we
know traditionally gather early at the starting point on the Common in Hopkinton, the
finish in Copley Square (our favorite), or
other good viewing points—along Commonwealth Avenue, Boylston Street, or Beacon Street, or at Wellesley College or on
Heartbreak Hill in Newton, 6 miles from
the finish. Many kids enjoy handing out cups
of water, which most runners accept grate-
fully. Front runners reach the finish at about
2 PM; an awards ceremony and live entertainment start at 6 PM. The route of the
marathon is printed in the *Boston Globe*.
🏠 *Boston Athletic Association, 17 Main St.,
Hopkinton 01748, tel. 617/236–1652.*

New Hampshire

Auto Racing

👫 8+

**NEW HAMPSHIRE INTERNATIONAL
SPEEDWAY.** One of New England's two
auto racetracks, the Speedway is not as picturesque or countryish a setting for families
as is Lime Rock (*see above*). But the track
does try to encourage family attendance at
their events—there's a smaller family grandstand, children 11 and under are usually
free, RV camping is allowed on the Speedway's 250 acres, and there are a great number of spacious and very clean rest rooms,
numerous concession stands, and even go-
kart racing weekends in which children as
young as 10 can compete.
🏠 *Rte. 106, Box 788, Loudon 03301, tel.
603/783–4744. Cost: $10–$60. Season:
Apr.–Oct.*

New York

Baseball

👫 7+

NEW YORK METS. If you live in New York
City, you're a Mets or a Yankees fan, not
both. In contrast to the Yankees, the Mets
are a relatively new team who started out in
1962 with a collection of losers—players
tossed out by other teams. In fact they were
perennial losers for seven years until they
finally won the World Series in 1969 (they
were nicknamed the Miracle Mets for that
year). Since then they've only won again in
1986—though the sixth game in that series
(versus the Boston Red Sox) has become
one of the most famous games in history
because of an error by a Red Sox player
that allowed the Mets to win that game, the
next game, and the Series. One problem
with Shea Stadium, however, is the noise
from low-flying planes bound to or from
nearby LaGuardia Airport. The horseshoe-
shaped stadium with no centerfield seats
seems more family-oriented than Yankee
Stadium, with no-alcohol and picnic sections
scattered around the stands. My son didn't
have much trouble getting a baseball card
autographed before the game. Tickets are
usually available right up until game time for
virtually all games.
🏠 *Shea Stadium, 126th St. and Roosevelt
Ave. (Willets Point/Shea Stadium stop on Subway Line 7), Flushing 11368, tel. 718/507–
8499. Cost: $6.50–$15. Season: Apr.–Oct.*

👫 7+

NEW YORK YANKEES. The history of
great baseball in America is filled with the
Yankees, as many of the sport's most
famous names—Babe Ruth, Lou Gehrig, Joe
DiMaggio, Mickey Mantle, Yogi Berra—have
played for the team. Watching a game at
Yankee Stadium, where the team has played

since 1923, is exciting partly because of its past. Just for your information, the Yankees have won more World Series—22—than any other team. The stadium is huge and impressive; we find night games more exciting because of the lights. If your kids are autograph seekers, get here an hour or two before the gates open because the only time the players will sign baseballs or cards (if they do at all) is as they're coming off the field during batting practice. Consumption of alcohol is prohibited in several sections of the stands; these are best for families. Though Yankee Stadium is not in a great neighborhood, riding the subway to this location is okay even for night games if you go home with the crowd.

🏠 *Yankee Stadium, 161st St. and River Ave. (Subway 4, D, or C to 161st St./Yankee Stadium), Bronx 10451, tel. 718/293–6000. Cost: $6.50–$17. Season: Apr.–Oct.*

Basketball

 9+

NEW YORK KNICKERBOCKERS. Going to a New York Knicks game in Madison Square Garden is exciting. The team is one of the leaders in the NBA, with a long list of previous players now in the Hall of Fame—Walt "Clyde" Frazier, Earl "the Pearl" Monroe, Bill Bradley, Harry Gallatin, Willis Reed—and current stars like Patrick Ewing. The fast-paced games are full of action but last just over two hours (less than football, baseball, or hockey). During time-outs and half-time the Knicks City Dancers perform short routines to music. Knicks games rarely become rowdy, and the fans, though wild about the team, are more sedate. The only problems are the high price of tickets and how to get seats close to the action. Center court is where we like to sit, but we've rarely been able to. Your best bet is to order tickets as far in advance as possible. Tickets for the play-offs are almost impossible to get, even if you're willing to pay scalpers' prices of as much as $125 a ticket.

🏠 *Madison Square Garden, 7th Ave. (between 31st and 33rd Sts.), New York 10001; box office, tel. 212/465–6741; Knicks' hot line, 212/465–5867; Ticketmaster, 212/307–7171. Cost: $13–$35.50. Season: late Oct.–Apr.*

Football

 9+

NEW YORK GIANTS. Ranked among the major NFL teams ever since their start in 1925, the Giants have won two Super Bowls. **The New York Jets** (American Football League) had their heyday in the '60s and early '70s when Joe Namath was their big star. Neither of these teams is easy to see. The trouble is that all seats for Giants games and most of the Jets games at this huge 77,000 seat stadium are sold on a season-ticket basis, and there's a waiting list for those. Every family we know who has attended a game has a friend or an employer with a season pass; individual Jets tickets are snapped up as soon as they go on sale in August. Giants tickets are sometimes available on the day of the game. If you go at the beginning of the season, get there early to see the team warm up. At half-time, high school bands play and dogs chase Frisbees. The Giants and the Jets play at Giants Stadium alternate weeks depending on the leagues' schedules.

🏠 *Giants Stadium (off Rte. 3), East Rutherford, NJ 07073; Giants, tel. 201/935–8111; Jets, 516/538–7200. Cost: $35–$40. Season: Sept.–Dec.*

 8+

WEST POINT. Michie Stadium at the United States Military Academy is among the most beautiful stadiums in the country. It's also a great place for families to see a football game. There's a pre-game parade of bands and hundreds of cadets in full dress uniforms, complete with tall hats and feathers, and four army mules run up and down the end zone each time the Black Knights make a touchdown. Before or after the game, there's plenty to see at this historic military site (see Chapter 7).

 U.S. Military Academy, Information Center, West Point 10999, tel. 914/938–2638; tickets, 914/446–4996. Cost: $18–$22. Season: Sept.–Nov.

Hockey

 9+

NEW YORK ISLANDERS. The Islanders games simply do not have the same excitement as the Rangers games in Madison Square Garden, unless the team is playing exceptionally well (as it did in the 1992–1993 season, when they went to the play-offs), nor is Nassau Coliseum, on Long Island, easy to get to except by car. But because tickets are sold out only when the Islanders are playing one of the league's star teams, you're more likely to be able to get tickets. It's also easier for kid fans to get autographs here before the game. The Islanders haven't yet equaled their incredible team of the early 1980s when they won four Stanley Cup trophies, but they do have one of the league's most exciting players, high-scoring forward Pierre Turgeon.

 Nassau Veterans Memorial Coliseum, Uniondale, Long Island 11553, tel. 516/888–9000. Cost: $16–$40. Season: Oct.–Apr.

 9+

NEW YORK RANGERS. The Rangers, who share Madison Square Garden with the NBA's Knicks, are exciting to watch. The crowd at Ranger games is sometimes rowdy, shouting and chanting obscenities at opposing teams or specific players—this upsets some kids and delights others. If you see a fan wearing a Ranger jersey, ask any hockey questions you have; in our experience the more obscure the better. Tickets are usually available up to two days before

game time, but may not be now that the Rangers have won the Stanley Cup.

 Madison Square Garden, 7th Ave. (between 31st and 33rd Sts.), New York 10001; box office, tel. 212/465–6741; Rangers' hot line, 212/308–6977. Cost: $13–$35.50. Season: Oct.–Apr.

Horse Racing

 6+

SARATOGA RACETRACK. Saratoga's 24-day thoroughbred racing season each August has the best atmosphere for families of any racetrack in the Northeast; it's the cleanest and most pleasant, and children are welcome despite the fact that the season is a major social as well as sporting event. Kids who already love horses have the most fun, but you may be able to inspire enthusiasm in any who don't by reading one of Marguerite Henry's stories about horses, especially *King of the Wind.* Post time for the first race is 1 PM, but a horse-loving family we know likes eating breakfast here (it's offered daily from 7 to 9:30) so they can watch horses work out. Soak up the atmosphere on a free tour of the barn and paddock areas on a "people train" (no strollers), where grooms, trainers, jockeys, and owners care for the horses. Whatever races you attend will be fast, exciting, and colorful. The best place for families to sit, especially those with little ones in strollers and small kids who need to run around, is the big open picnic area near the grandstand where you can see the race on the closed-circuit TVs on every tree. On big festival days the atmosphere is like a fair, with clog dancers and other entertainment.

 Rte. 9P, Saratoga Springs 12866; Aug., tel. 518/584–6200; Sept.–July, 718/641–4700. Cost: $2 grandstand; $5 clubhouse (dress code). Season: last week in July and Aug.

Tennis

 10+

U.S. OPEN. Everyone in our family is a passionate tennis player, so we grab any chance to see incredible playing up close. It's very difficult to get tickets to the U.S. Open, one of U. S. tennis's four prime tournaments, unless you're a season subscriber (members of the U.S.T.A. have priority for remaining tickets), but we think attending the qualifying matches the week before it starts (the third week in August) is even more fun for families, anyway—and they're free. Besides the matches between the hottest players in the two stadiums, there are matches on all the side courts; you can wander from one to another, stopping to watch whoever catches your fancy. The Sunday before the Open, now called Arthur Ashe Day, features matches with celebrities like Bill Cosby. The setting is pretty, near the New York Hall of Science (see Chapter 8). All kinds of food are available; we like the outdoor café. Tickets to early matches are easier to get; those for the semifinals and finals sell out as soon as they go on sale in May.

🏛 *United States Tennis Association, Flushing Meadows–Corona Park, Flushing 11365, tel. 718/271–5100. Cost: $25 day, $18 evenings. Season: late Aug.–early Sept.*

Winter Sports

 7+

OLYMPIC REGIONAL DEVELOPMENT AUTHORITY. Watching Olympic-caliber athletes in figure skating, ski jumping, and freestyle skiing competitions is more thrilling to our family than seeing most other sports—but maybe that's because we're mad about skiing. If your kids are, the Lake Placid area, the only official U.S. Olympic training site in the Northeast, is the place to see both national and international winter sports competitions at almost

any time of year. One major freestyle skiing event is even held at the end of August—the twisting and somersaulting jumps from the 70-meter jump south of town. Figure skaters and hockey teams compete in the Olympic ice arena in Lake Placid; bobsledders and lugers (for older kids who are really interested) race at Mt. Van Hoevenberg.

🏛 *Olympic Regional Development Authority, Lake Placid 12946, tel. 518/5230–1655 or 800/462–6236.*

Rhode Island

Baseball

 4+

PAWTUCKET RED SOX. The playing is pretty close to what you'd see at any major-league ballpark (this Class AAA affiliate of the Boston Red Sox is the last step on the minor-league ladder before the major leagues and it sends about 60% of its players to the majors; Ellis Burks and Mike Greenwell are alumni). The communal atmosphere at small, cozy 6,000-seat McCoy stadium draws everyone in. Regular promotional nights, with such giveaways for kids as posters, baseball cards, caps, and coloring books, are scheduled throughout the summer, as are free baseball clinics for kids on the baseball field with hands-on instruction from PawSox players. If you attend a summer evening game, sit on the first-base side so you don't face the sometimes blinding setting sun.

🏛 *McCoy Stadium, Pawtucket 02861, tel. 401/724–7300; Ticketmaster, 401/331–2211. I–95 south to exit 2A; Newport Ave. 2 mi, then right on Columbus Ave. at light. Cost: general admission $4 adults, $3 kids 12 and under; box seats $5.50 adults, $4.50 kids 12 and under. Season: Apr.–Sept.*

Football

BROWN UNIVERSITY. If you want to sit in the cold, scream till you're hoarse, and watch mediocre but enthusiastic play, there's always the autumn joy of Ivy League football at this university. The half-time show may appeal more to your kids than the game.

Brown University Stadium, Elmgrove and Sessions Sts., Providence 02906, tel. 401/863–2236.

TREKS, TRAIL RIDES, CANOE TRIPS, AND OTHER ACTION OUTDOORS

12

Our best vacations and outings, like those of other families we know, nearly always involve outdoor sports and activities. The Northeast's diverse terrain and coastline have allowed us to try just about any outdoor activity that interests us. We've canoed on lakes and rivers, swum in Atlantic surf and freshwater ponds, played tennis in the shade of mountains, climbed several peaks, hiked short paths and long trails, bicycled on backcountry roads, camped on islands, sailed into harbors, picked fruit on farms and mountaintops, and more, and we certainly haven't exhausted all the possibilities.

On guided hikes where we've joined other families, the kids enjoyed each other's company, our guide knew the precise places to spot moose and stop to fish, educated us about the natural sights of the area in an entertaining way, and spared us the drudgery of making lunch. If you're neophyte canoers or kayakers, a guided trip can be much safer and more enjoyable than going on your own because you won't have so much to plan and do. Learning to sail or canoe or windsurf as a family draws everyone together in a special way and ensures kids (not to mention the adults) will know how to do it safely. One organization that leads exceptional trips in several different categories is the Chewonki Foundation (RR 2, Box 1200, Wiscasset, ME 04578, tel. 207/882–7323; see Chapter 14), whose weeklong programs vary from year to year but usually include canoe, kayak, sailing, and hiking trips for families with kids 8 and up. *Wilderness with Children* by Michael Hodgson (Stackpole Books, 1992) is a useful book with extensive advice on family camping, canoeing, biking, and skiing.

Apples and Berries: Fruit-Picking

Filling up bushels of apples or baskets of berries can be a satisfying and inexpensive outdoor excursion, one that is available at many farms and orchards in every state in the Northeast. Besides a few unusual places listed below that we've particularly enjoyed, you can pick at farms throughout the Northeast. All states (see Chapter 2) publish lists of "pick your own" producers. One warning: bees, while not usually aggressive, also like berries. If one of your children is allergic, opt for apple-picking.

Connecticut

Buell's Orchards

(👫 4 – 13)

Buell's has an attraction highly appealing to kids, but not quite as healthy as the apples you can pick. It's a candy apple factory in which a Rube Goldbergesque contraption manages to produce 20,000 cases of these sticky treats a year. Yes, you can watch and buy samples. Besides blueberry-picking in summer, the old cider mill, the Saturday hayrides in fall out to the apple orchard, and pumpkin-picking, there's a Columbus Day weekend open house with free doughnuts and cider.

🏠 *108 Crystal Pond Rd., Eastford 06242, tel. 203/974–1150. Open for picking and special events July–Oct.; call for schedule.*

Massachusetts

Goodale Orchards

(👫 2 – 12)

Goodale's is a family-friendly New England farm where you feel like spending a whole day. There's an antique barn with a kids' swing, hayrides, the small pond where you can picnic, a barnyard with animals to pet, a kids' book corner by a big stone fireplace. You can pick strawberries and blueberries in summer, apples and pumpkins in the fall. The prime draw at Goodale's are the homemade cider doughnuts.

🏠 *Argilla Rd. off Rte. 1A, Ipswich, tel. 508/356–5366. Open Apr., weekends 9–6, mid-May–Dec., daily 9–6.*

New Hampshire

Pitcher Mountain

(👫 4 – 12)

Just off Route 123, between Marlow and Stoddard, is a turnoff and parking area for the ¼-mile trail to the top of Pitcher Mountain (*see also* Hikes, Walks, and Climbs, *below*), where you'll find some of the best, most concentrated mountain blueberries in the Northeast. Bring a few plastic containers. Pitcher Mountain is actually private land, so during blueberry season, you'll usually find someone in the parking area who'll weigh what you haven't eaten at the summit and charge you an outrageously small sum.

🏠 *Rte. 123, between Marlow and Stoddard. No phone. Blueberry season, late July–Aug.*

New York

Montgomery Place

(👫 5 – 12)

Five thousand trees fill the orchard on this grand estate above the Hudson River that once belonged to Revolutionary War hero General Richard Montgomery. After you pick apples, take some time to check out the views and roam around the trails through gardens, in woodlands, and by waterfalls.

🏠 *River Rd. (corner of Rtes. 9G and 199, just outside Rhinebeck), Annandale-on-Hudson 12504, tel. 914/758–5461. Open mid-June–Oct., daily 10–6.*

Bike Paths by Dunes and Forests

There are three essentials for a pleasant biking excursion in our family. Relatively flat terrain is important. Interesting places to stop and swim, picnic, or climb on rocks, or a goal such as strawberry- or apple-picking keep us going. Minimum car traffic has always been essential to my enjoyment, for reasons obvious to any parent who has watched speeding cars come dangerously close to defenseless bikers at the side of a road. I'm happiest on recreational paths designated just for bicycles or on backcountry dirt roads. It's hard to separate road and mountain biking because while some biking routes are paved, others, such as dirt roads, are best explored on mountain bikes, and many bike-rental shops rent hybrid bikes designed for both. For mountain biking strictly off-road in the mountains, see below. Besides state parks (see Chapter 10), a few locations stand out for the sheer number of biking possibilities within a small area as well as the easy availability of rental bikes in all sizes. Some shops do not have a large selection of bikes or helmets in small sizes or passenger seats for toddlers, so you might want to reserve one well in advance for major holiday weekends. Some include helmets in the rental price; others charge extra. Most states require children 12 and under to wear a helmet when biking, but even if they don't, I advise it, as helmets reduce the risk of serious injury from accidents by as much as 85%.

It's not too difficult to take a child under 3 or over 9 along on an extended bike trip, but few tour companies that plan and guide several-day bicycling tours cater to families. **Vermont Bicycle Touring** (Box 711, Bristol, VT 05443, tel. 802/453–4811; $350 per person, discounts for kids), one of the oldest and best-organized touring companies in the Northeast, offers special three-day family-only bicycle tours that include activities for several age ranges of kids, even very young ones. **Brooks Country Cycling Tours** (140 W. 83rd St., New York 10024, tel. 212/874–5151; day trips $25–$48 per person, weekend trips $209–$450 per person, plus rental bikes) offers guided day trips and several-day easy-to-moderate bicycle tours in Nantucket, Martha's Vineyard, the tip of Long Island, along the Delaware River, and

elsewhere in the Northeast on which they welcome families; when children are along, they add activities such as swimming or fruit-picking. Be sure to inquire about the trip guide, as I have had reports that not all tours are organized equally well.

Maine

Many of Maine's islands, such as the Casco Bay Islands, Vinalhaven, and Isleboro, are ideal for bike exploring, especially for kids over 10, but the one with the most car-free biking is Mount Desert Island (see below). For information on biking in Maine, especially with older kids, see *Bicycling* (Delorme Publishing; part of its "Maine Geographic" series) or *25 Bicycle Tours in Maine* by Howard Stone (Backcountry Publications).

Acadia National Park

👫 5 – 15

The park's 57 miles of car-free carriage paths, laid out by landscape architect Frederick Law Olmstead and built in the early 1920s and '30s, pass lakes, rocky coastline, beaches, woods, and the park's prime sights, and cross over 16 stone bridges. The easiest and most level, around Eagle Lake and near Witch Hole Pond (both okay for little kids), have a fine-grained gravel surface suitable for even small road bikes; most of the others have softer surfaces. Roads on the less-trafficked western side of the island and the 7 miles of paved roads on Swan's Island, accessible by ferry (40-minute ride) from Bass Harbor, are even more fun. **Acadia Bike & Canoe/Coastal Kayaking Company** (48 Cottage St., Box 405, Bar Harbor 04609, tel. 207/288–5483; full day, $16 adults, $10 kids) has a good selection of all types of bikes for children and adults and includes trail maps, advice on the best trails considering your kids' ages, instructions, and helmets in the price. For young kids, they also rent trailer bikes that can be attached to an adult bike.

Massachusetts

Besides bike paths on Cape Cod and Nantucket (*see below*) and Martha's Vineyard, families on my Boston panel like the 18 miles of looped and interlocking paved trails in **Myles Standish State Forest** (tel. 508/866–2526) in South Carver. Be aware that there is a law requiring helmets on children 12 and under. The Massachusetts Office of Tourism (*see* Chapter 2) maintains lists of bicycle-rental shops, organizations, and state parks with bike trails.

Cape Cod

 6 – 15

To us, the Cape, especially the Lower and Outer Cape from Dennis to Provincetown, is one of the best places for family biking in the Northeast because of the variety of long, relatively easy, and mostly flat bike paths that are never very far from a beach in case we want to stop for a swim or a picnic overlooking the ocean. (Even kids with training wheels maneuver them.) Considering the traffic on the Cape during the summer, biking is by far the most pleasant way to get around, though bike paths too can suffer from crowding. Besides maps and pamphlets available from the Chambers of Commerce in Dennis and Wellfleet (*see* Chapter 5), two books detail the best routes: *Short Bike Rides on Cape Cod, Martha's Vineyard, and Nantucket* (Globe Pequot Press) describes 19 rides on the Cape; *The Cape Cod Bike Book*, available in Cape bookstores and some bike shops or by mail (Box 627, South Dennis 02660; $3.25), is a booklet of both marked and unmarked bike trails. The **Cape Cod Rail Trail**, once a railroad track bed, is now a 20-mile-long paved path that winds through scrub pine forests, cranberry marshes, and fields from South Dennis (beginning at the parking lot off Rte. 134 near Theophilus Smith Rd.) to Eastham, where it ends at the entrance to the Salt Pond Visitor's Center. In Brewster it hooks up with bike paths in Nickerson State Park (trail maps are available at the park office; *see* Chapter 10). Though it's wide and safe, warn your kids not to weave suddenly from side to side and to watch out for hikers.

Of the three bike paths in the Cape Cod National Seashore, **Nauset Trail,** which ends at Coast Guard Beach, is shortest, a little more than 1½ miles. **Province Lands Trail,** a 5½-mile loop that starts in Provincetown, passes dunes and marshes and offers spectacular views. For trail maps, check at Salt Pond Visitor's Center (off Rte. 6, Eastham 02663, tel. 508/255–3421) or Province Lands Area Visitor's Center (Race Point Rd, off Rte. 6, Provincetown, tel. 508/487–1256).

On either side of the **Cape Cod Canal,** a waterway that separates the Cape from mainland Massachusetts, is an easy, straight, wide trail from which you have great views of freighters and tugboats. A fish pier along the way and Scusset Beach at the north end provide goals. You might want to stick to the path on just one side, as we found trying to cross the bridges (both busy highways with practically no space for bicyclists) was extremely dangerous. The **Shining Sea Bikeway,** an easy 3½-mile route, follows the coast along the ocean from Falmouth to the Woods Hole ferry parking lot.

Bike-rental shops in every community on the Cape offer bikes on an hourly, half-day, full-day, or weekly basis. Those that follow are conveniently located near a major bike path and have kids' bikes as small as 16 inches as well as a good supply of small-sized helmets, though these cost extra. **Idle Times** (Rte. 6A, Brewster 02631, tel. 508/896–9242; full-day price, $15 adults, $8 kids; helmets $3), is ideally situated at Nickerson State Park just off the Rail Trail; you must rent for at least four hours. **Arnold's** (329 Commercial St., Provincetown 02657, tel. 508/487–0844; full-day price, $10–$15 adults, $10 kids; helmets $2), also rents bikes with training wheels, baby carriers, and trailers that hold two small kids (up to 100 pounds, total) and fasten to the back of an adult bike; the staff is especially friendly. **The Little Capistrano** (Rte. 6, Eastham 02642, tel. 508/255–6515; 2-hr price, $8 adults, $5 kids), right across from the Salt Pond Visitor Center and by the Rail Trail, offers training wheels and baby carriers. **P & M Cycles** (29 Main St., Buzzard's Bay 02532, tel. 508/759–2830; 2-hr price, $8 adults and kids, including helmet), on the bike path along the Cape Cod Canal, has a wide range of bikes and training wheels, baby carriers, and attachable carts for two kids.

Nantucket

 5 – 15

Four bike paths, ranging in length from 2½ to 6 miles, lead to beaches and picnic areas and by dunes and ponds. The longer ones have drinking fountains en route (see Chapter 5). **Nantucket Bike Shops** (Steamboat Wharf and on Straight Wharf across from Hy-Line ferry, Nantucket 02554, tel. 508/228–1999; daily bike price, $16–$20 adults, $12–$16 kids) is Nantucket's largest bike-rental shop, with baby seats, kiddie carts, and kids' bikes.

Rhode Island

Besides the island biking (see below) that always appeals to our family, Rhode Island families we know recommend the peaceful, low-traffic village of Little Compton and one of the most interesting-to-kids bike paths in the northeast: The **East Bay Bike Path**; it's a 14½-mile scenic paved bikeway from Bristol to Providence that passes through two state parks, by a pond and a carousel, and even close to restaurants. In the Rhode Island Visitor's Guide published by the Rhode Island Tourism Division (see Chapter 2) is a map of the trail.

Block Island

 9 – 15

All kinds of roads and paths suitable for biking, from paved to dirt, traverse the hilly terrain on this island of moors, beaches, and bluffs; we've found traveling by bike is the easiest and most fun-filled way to explore. In summer the roads are crowded with cars and that bane of family bicyclists, noisy mopeds. Dirt roads from which mopeds are banned are frequently dead ends, so you have to spend some time on paved roads. Maps available at bike-rental shops tend to be sketchy. Biking is best here for kids 9 and up who have some experience. **Moped Man** (245 Main St., Box 125, Old Harbor 02807, tel. 401/466–5011; helmets included), right across from the Point Judith ferry, has a wide variety of bikes, starting with 20-inch BMXs for kids. **Old Harbor Bike Shop** (Box 338, Old Harbor O2807, tel. 401/466–2029; price per day, $15, per hr, $3; helmets included) has both children's bikes (as small as 16 inches) and baby seats.

Vermont

Many Vermont communities have paved and gravel recreational bike paths that are safe even for younger kids, but so far none of these link together to create loops. For information, contact the Vermont State Department of Forest, Parks and Recreation (Montpelier 05602, tel. 802/244–8713).

Stowe Recreation Path

5 – 15

This 5.3-mile-long scenic path along the West Branch of the Little River seems perfectly designed for kids: It starts in town, isn't too long, crosses 10 bridges, has views of Mt. Mansfield, and passes close enough to McDonald's that we could stop for lunch. It is frequented by hikers, rollerbladers, and people with strollers in addition to bicyclists. **Mountain Bike** (Mountain Rd., Stowe

05662, tel. 802/253–7919; price $6 first hr; $4 each additional hr adults, $4 first hr; $2 each additional hr kids; helmets included), rents bikes as small as 16 inches; they will suggest and arrange bike tours and routes for families with older kids.

Camping: From Cozy to Wild

We've tried just about every type of camping experience in the Northeast, from a cozy family campground with planned activities and oodles of kids running around to a wilderness site on a remote island with only the sound of a loon for company. A campground equipped with hot showers, a store to bike to, a swimming beach, boats to rent, and some organized nature activities for kids is easier when you have young kids along. We've generally opted for those in state parks and national forests that have some of what he wants, but where we can still feel as though we are out in the wild. One of the big advantages of the Northeast is how close so many scenic campgrounds in state parks and forests are to civilization; if it rains continuously and hiking begins to pall, a movie and shops are not that far away. Changeable weather is the worst aspect of family camping in this region; we've experienced sudden and severe thunderstorms, temperature drops of as much as 40 degrees in the mountains, and, on the Maine coast, awakening to a thick blanket of fog that lasted most of the day. A highly waterproof tent is essential, as is planning for indoor entertainment. Private campgrounds and those in some state parks have the most creature comforts; camping in state forests is usually more primitive, but most have a picnic table and fireplace at each site, plus flush toilets.

We have a couple of prejudices that may be apparent. We're tent, rather than RV, people, and private campgrounds that practically resemble a resort do not interest us.

Listed below are sites we've liked that have something unusual or are particularly scenic; see Chapter 10 for additional parks with good campgrounds. For families just starting out, the Appalachian Mountain Club's (AMC's) family camping programs in huts (see Hiking in New Hampshire, below) and New York State's Camper Assistance and Novice Camper programs are ideal. One friend of ours also raves about the AMC's weekend introduction to family backpacking and camping at the Valley View Lodge (Oliverea, NY, tel. 607/746–2737; mailing address. 3 Woolerton St., Delhi, NY 13753, June–Sept.; Box 366, Long Lake, NY 12847, Sept–June) in the Catskills, for which all you have to bring are sleeping bags; tents and backpacks are for rent (kids are welcome). Throughout the Northeast, campgrounds in national and state parks and forests cost between $9 and $20 per night, depending on location and facilities.

Connecticut

Most state campgrounds are open from mid-April to September 30, with reservations, by mail only, accepted from mid-January. Obtain a "Camping in Connecticut" brochure from the Bureau of Parks and Forests (CT Dept. of Environmental Protection, 165 Capitol Ave., Hartford 06106, tel. 203/566–2305), then write to the campground of your choice for a camping permit and site map.

Housatonic Meadows State Park

(7 – 15)

Sheltered among pine trees above the rushing and beautiful Housatonic River, the campsites at this park in the state's sparsely populated northwest corner make a fine base for family canoeing, rafting, and hiking. The park is the take-out point for shops in the area that rent water craft. The Appalachian Trail as well as several short hiking trails pass near the campground, which is also within a few miles' drive of several interesting towns. Only fly-fishing is permitted from the banks of the river in the park. Try to reserve one of the scenic 22 sites right on the water.

🏕 *Off Rte. 7 just north of town, Cornwall Bridge 06754, tel. 203/672–6772 or 203/ 927–3238. Facilities: 97 sites, flush toilets, showers, kayaking, canoeing, hiking, fishing.*

Rocky Neck State Park

(👫 4 – 15)

For beach camping that offers a pleasant retreat from the generally touristy and trafficky coast of Long Island Sound, yet still has many comfortable amenities, we'd pick one of Rocky Neck's open or wooded sites. Besides swimming, you can climb on the rocky peninsula that juts into the Sound, fish from a jetty, explore the wooded trails, and join a sing-along at one of the campground's communal bonfire rings.

🏕 *Box 676 (exit 18 from I–95), Niantic 06357, tel. 203/739–5471. Facilities: 169 sites, beach, bike paths, concessions, hiking trails, nature programs and guided walks, showers, toilets.*

Maine

Acadia Toddler Tromp

(👫 1 – 5)

Demanding and noisy, but also curious and social, toddlers are not easy to travel with, let alone take on a camping trip. I wish we'd known about the Sierra Club's annual week-long base camp on Echo Lake at Acadia National Park (see Chapter 10) designed for the interests and capabilities of families with kids this age when Gavin was little. The leader plans the meals and many activities for the six or seven families, so you don't feel exhausted.

🏕 *Sierra Club Outing Dept., 730 Polk St., San Francisco, CA 94109, tel. 415/923–5630. Cost: $470 adults, $315 kids under 14. Aug.*

Lily Bay State Park

(👫 5+)

The campground on the shores of Moosehead Lake is a combination of backcountry wilderness and family amenities (see Chapter 10).

🏕 *Beaver Cove, Moosehead Lake, Greenville 04441, tel. 207/695–2700.*

Mt. Blue State Park

(👫 6+)

To take full advantage of Mt. Blue's excellent mountain hiking (many short hikes to summits), swimming, and naturalist programs (they even include gold panning), you have to camp here. Tent sites are beachside and views of towering Mt. Blue resemble the Paramount Pictures opening peak. Yet because the park is not well known, it is one of the few state camping facilities that usually has openings (see Chapter 10).

🏕 *15 mi from Dixfield off Rte. 142, Weld 02485, tel. 207/585–2347.*

Sebago Lake State Park

(👫 2 – 15)

The park's campsites spread out through the woods and along the shore of this gigantic lake with beautiful sand beaches and clear water. There's easy access to windsurfing and boating. The Songo Locks, where boats pass into Sebago Lake, fascinate many kids; they're right next to one sector of the campground. (See Chapter 10.)

🏕 *Off U.S. Rte. 302 (between Naples and South Casco), Naples 04055, tel. 207/693– 6615. Facilities: bathhouses, hot showers, snack bar. Open early May–mid-Oct.*

New Hampshire

Appalachian Mountain Club

(👫 5 – 15)

We love the Appalachian Mountain Club's high mountain huts strung along and near 56 miles of the Appalachian Trail for "camping" because they feel adventurous yet safe and comfortable. Part of the fun of staying in these large bunkhouses that provide dinner, breakfast, wool blankets, pillows, and hot and cold running water is all the other people staying here. You need to bring only a sleeping bag. The Lonesome Lake and Zealand Falls Huts are the easiest to hike to and attract the most families. The AMC also offers family camping programs and maintains shelters, primitive tent campgrounds (meaning no showers or nature programs, but also no crowds), and lodges and hostels in the White Mountains. On the Saco River, we like Moose Campground, a combination of riverbank, woods, and open fields, with good swimming; it's a welcome respite from the North Conway crowds only a few miles away.
🏠 *Pinkham Notch Visitor Center, Pinkham's Grant (Box 298, Gorham 03581), tel. 603/466–2727.*

Lafayette Campground

(👫 ALL)

Though the campsites are tucked back into the woods and some have a feeling of privacy, the location in the heart of the White Mountains near superlative hiking and the profusion of amenities are what attract families—and Gavin. A paved, 9-mile bike path runs through it. New Hampshire's state parks do not take campground reservations, so you must arrive first thing in the morning in summer.
🏠 *Franconia Notch State Park, Rte. 3, Franconia Notch 03580, tel. 603/823–9513.*

Facilities: biking, camping, fishing, hiking, nature center and programs, swimming.

New York

A microcosm of the entire region, with campsites by perfect ocean beaches as well as in remote wilderness, New York turns out to be a particularly good place for families who are new to camping.

The Camper Assistance Program in some state parks and the Novice Camper Program in the Adirondacks and the Catskills (*see below*) were created for them. In the Adirondacks you're liable to hear the snuffle of a scavenging bear if you don't suspend your food from a tree limb at least 12 feet above the ground or in your closed and locked car—even if you camp in a developed campground. A number of state parks also have cabins and primitive lean-tos. For a booklet on camping in New York's state parks, write: Guide, State Parks (Empire State Plaza, Albany, NY 12238). Call 518/474–0456 or individual state parks for information about the Camper Assistance Program. For camping in the Catskills or the Adirondacks, write or call: Camping, New York State Department of Environmental Conservation (50 Wolf Rd., Room 623, Albany, NY 12233, tel. 518/457–2500). D.E.C. campsites are open from Memorial Day to Labor Day and range in price from $10 to $15, depending on the camp's facilities and the season. The most complete listing of parks is in *The New York State Atlas and Gazetteer* (DeLorme Mapping, Box 298, Freeport, ME 04032, tel. 207/865–4171). To make a reservation in any New York state campground, call 800/456–2267.

Hither Hills State Park

(👫 5 – 15)

This is the only oceanfront campground located in a beach resort area in the entire Northeast. It's also a bargain place to stay at this expensive tip of Long Island. Camping is right in the dunes near a beach with a remote and wild feeling. The only way to get a space is to call the state reservation number (see above) at 8 in the morning exactly 90 days before the date you want to arrive. Spots are filled in a mere 20 to 25 minutes. There are amenities and views, but the sites are open, interspersed with low, scrub vegetation. Rough surf and a strong undertow mean swimming here is best for older kids, but nearby, in Montauk Downs State Park, an Olympic-size pool and a little kids' pool are open to campers, as are the tennis courts and golf course. Volunteer expert campers help put up tents, answer questions and give advice, and teach an especially good nature program.

🏠 *Rte. 217, Montauk 11954, tel. 516/668–2461 or 516/668–3781. Facilities: beach, biking, bathhouse, camping, fishing, hiking, playground, restaurant, showers, store.*

Mongaup Pond Campground

(🧍🧒 **3 – 13**)

In the Novice Camper Program at this campground on a large pond edged with sandy beaches, all you have to bring are clothes and food; a tent, sleeping bags, air mattresses, a camping stove, a cooler, a lantern, day packs, even flashlights and batteries, will be waiting for you, and a friendly ranger will help you set up your tent. The rangers act as a support group for beginning campers, stopping by periodically to offer advice and encouragement. Everything in this park is on a small-kids' scale: the hiking trails are short and well marked, the pond is calm, the other campers are friendly families with young kids.

🏠 *Off Fish Hatchery Rd., Livingston Manor 12758, tel. 914/439–4233. Take Rte. 17 to exit 96, then 6½ mi northeast to DeBruce Rd., left onto Mongaup Rd. for 3 mi north to sign. Facilities: boating, fireplaces, fishing, hiking, picnic areas, showers, swimming. Open mid-May–mid-Dec.*

Saranac Lake and Indian Lake Islands

(🧍🧒 **5 – 15**)

The Adirondacks, with myriad lakes, have more developed island campsites that fit my fantasies than anywhere else in the Northeast; 500 spread over 48 islands on three lakes. Lake George is huge, with powerboating and wave action that are dangerous for family canoers with young kids or those less experienced. Less-trafficked Lower Saranac Lake, our preference, with a host of bays and points that are easy to explore in a canoe, boasts lovely island campsites, a particularly good outfitter (see Canoeing, below), and excellent fishing. Indian Lake, farther south, also has a few island campsites.

🏠 *Department of Environmental Conservation (see above for address), tel. 518/457–2500 for detailed site maps and brochures; 800/456–2267 for reservations.*

Rhode Island

Burlingame State Park

(🧍🧒 **ALL**)

Other than Nickerson State Park on Cape Cod (see Chapters 5 and 11), I don't know of any large campground (it has 755 sites) that is as well kept and well run as this one. It also has easy access to both fresh and salt water warm enough for swimming. Winding roads loop through open stands of tall pines to level campsites that are spacious, private, and woodsy with cushions of pine needles. Only the campsites by the small campers-only beach on Wachaug Pond feel crowded. Kids of all ages swim, fish from boats on the pond, and ride their bikes on the paved loop roads. Yet the camping area is also an easy 10-minute drive from the long coastline of sandy beaches on the other side of Route 1.

🏠 *Kings Factory Rd., Charlestown, tel. 401/322–7337 or 401/322–7337 (mailing address: Div. Parks & Recreation, 2321 Hart-*

ford Ave., Johnston, RI 02919). Facilities: biking, boating, fishing, picnicking, freshwater swimming; playground; store.

Vermont

A significant number of Vermont's state parks with campgrounds have summer naturalist programs, resident naturalists, and summer entertainment series of puppet shows, concerts, and storytellers geared to children. You can reserve sites with the Department of Forests, Parks and Recreation (103 S. Main St., Bldg. 10 South, Waterbury 05671, tel. 802/241–3655).

Burton Island State Park

(👫 ALL)

On Lake Champlain, Burton Island is one of the few state campgrounds with a marina where you can keep any kind—or size—of powerboat and even camp aboard. (See Chapter 10.)
🏠 *Box 123, St. Alban's Bay 05481, tel. 802/ 524–6353. Take Rte. 36 and Point Rd. to Kamp Kill Kare State Park, then passenger ferry. Facilities: beach, biking, boating (canoe and rowboat rentals), fishing, marina, nature program and trails, picnic tables, playground, showers, swimming.*

Canoeing, Kayaking, and Paddle Rafting

We're boosters of family canoeing because a canoe is light enough for two people to heft but big enough to hold several people and gear, close to the water, easy to nose into shallow places you want to explore, and able to be pulled up just about anywhere when everyone needs a break. The problem when you take small kids is the lack of stability. We favor smaller lakes that don't attract large motorboats whose wake can swamp us and where strong winds don't whip up waves. Our choices below have

canoe-rental shops nearby. Our rule: Everyone (including grown-ups) must wear a life jacket.

If you've never canoed, it's worth reading *Canoe Tripping with Children,* by David and Judy Harrison (ICS Books, 1990). The best guidebooks to canoeing in the Northeast are those published by the Appalachian Mountain Club; the two *Quiet Water Canoe Guides* by Alex Wilson contain detailed observations about each pond and lake with much helpful information for families, though not, unfortunately, places near each to rent canoes. The best seasons to canoe are summer and early fall. Carry warmer clothes in a waterproof bag, and don't forget sunscreen, hats, and something to drink.

Kayaks come in several different designs, including craft that seat two. Lake touring kayaks can travel on flat water anywhere canoes can (almost all outfitters below also rent them); sea kayaking (using heavier, more stable boats designed to plow into waves and carry more gear) is a safer way of edging around a rocky coastline, though it's best to go with a guide. In addition to the coast of Mount Desert Island (*see below*), Maine's Penobscot Bay and the coast of Connecticut near the Thimble Islands are fun to explore. Paddling a kayak is tricky, so I advise taking a course or going on a guided trip. Kids need to be about 10 or 12 and weigh about 100 pounds to be able to maneuver a kayak properly alone. W.I.L.D. W.A.T.E.R.S. (Rte. 28, Box 197AHCR01, Warrensburg, NY 12885, tel. 518/494–7478) offers regular family canoeing and kayaking clinics and workshops and guided tours.

Connecticut

Farmington River

(👫 4 – 15)

This 9-mile section of the Farmington between Avon and Simsbury, all peaceful flat water with vistas of lovely old trees, is only waist-deep, with sandy banks and a bottom that reminds me of the Saco River's (see below). The first 3 miles make an ideal beginning canoe trip for small children. The Pinchot Sycamore, the tree with the largest circumference in Connecticut (23½ feet around), stands near the picnic area at the 3-mile take-out spot. **Huck Finn Adventures** (9 Gemstone Dr., Collinsville 06022, tel. 203/693–0385; $40 per canoe per day), specializes in renting canoes (large ones will hold as many as three kids) and necessary equipment—even sling seats for kids—to families and conveniently picks up at 3-mile, 6-mile, and 9-mile intervals. With small kids and stops for swimming, 3 miles will take a couple of hours.

Housatonic River

🏃 8 – 15

A forested, well-traveled 12-mile section of this noted trout river from Falls Village to Cornwall Bridge is one of our favorite day-long canoe and raft runs; the trip takes about four hours if you stop to swim at one of the several good spots. Outfitters insist kids must be at least 7 for either canoes or rafts. **Riverrunning Expeditions** (Main St., Falls Village 06031, tel. 203/824–5579 or 203/824–5286), rents canoes ($45), rafts ($20–$25 per person), kayaks, and tubes ($10, no pickup) by the day, provides life vests and paddles and some brief instruction, transport to the river, and pickup service at Housatonic Meadows State Park.

Maine

Saco River flows from New Hampshire into Maine, so I've listed it under New Hampshire, below.

Mount Desert Island

🏃 9 – 15

Sea kayaking is the best way to explore the coastline's rocky ledges, much more fascinat-

ing to us than canoeing on Acadia National Park's freshwater lakes. I recommend guided tours, as guides know the safest and most interesting spots to take kids and provide a running commentary on bird and sea life. **Acadia Bike & Canoe/Coastal Kayaking** (43 Cottage St., Bar Harbor 04609, tel. 207/288–5483; $43 per person for 4-hr guided tour) offers tours geared to families that go at a slower pace and stress discoveries.

New Hampshire

Saco River

🏃 3 – 15

The Saco between North Conway, New Hampshire, and Hiram Falls, Maine, is the most perfect river I know in the Northeast for a family canoe trip, whether for one day or for several, with small kids or older ones. Because the Saco is one of the two most popular family canoeing rivers east of the Mississippi, on July and August weekends it can almost seem crowded. Inviting sand beaches and rocky ledges on the shore lure swimmers and picnickers. Because of the current, paddling is easy. Unlike on most rivers, camping is permitted anywhere along the Saco's banks for a stretch of 45 miles from just below Center Conway to the falls at Hiram, Maine. A fire permit, available at outfitters who rent canoes, is required if you wish to cook at your campsite. The best months are July and August, when mosquitoes are less pesty and the water is warm, but you must reserve weekend rentals several weeks in advance. Two good places to enter the river are just below Center Conway or across the border in Fryeburg, Maine. If you have a young teenager in your family, let him or her rent a kayak to paddle alongside you.

Saco Bound (Box 119, Rte. 302, Center Conway 03813, tel. 603/447–2177, and Main St., North Conway 03860, tel. 603/447–3801), has equipment, life jackets, maps, instructions, and shuttle service. On

Tuesday and Thursday in July and August, they guide day-long trips ($35.50 including shuttle service), which are excellent for families just starting out in canoeing. **Saco River Canoe & Kayak** (188 Main St., Rte. 5, Box 111, Fryeburg, ME 04037, tel. 207/935–2369; $35.50 per day, including shuttle service) rents sturdy, heavy Old Town Canoes, which have stability and plenty of space for a family and gear.

White Lake

When kids want to attempt canoeing on their own, you need a small, round lake with a completely visible shoreline, just like this one, which permits motorboats with only 6-horsepower motors. White Lake State Park, with a campground, a clean white-sand beach with shallow water, and canoe rentals, makes a good base.

🏠 *White Lake State Park, Box 273, Tamworth; office, West Ossipee 03890, tel. 603/323–7350. Canoe rentals.*

New York

The Adirondacks

This region draws us with its many blue, blue, island-dotted lakes that connect in long chains. Pulling up on a slab of rock on an uninhabited island sparks kids' sense of adventure; they quickly become explorers or pirates. Paddling from island to island also breaks up a trip, whether it's several hours or a day or longer. At many lakeside resorts (see Chapters 6 and 14), use of canoes is free.

👫 4 – 15

Blue Mountain Lake. Small and smooth, yet dotted with islands, this lake surrounded by shoulders of mountains that appear faintly blue from the water seems tame and wild at the same time. Just noodling around the lake is fun, but the 15-mile route through Eagle

and Utowana Lakes to the west, which ends up, after a short portage, in Racquette Lake, is easy enough for beginning canoers. **Blue Mountain Outfitters** (Box 144, Blue Mountain Lake 12812, tel. 518/352–7306 or 518/352–7675), rents sturdy Old Town canoes by the day ($20) or week ($115) and provides life jackets for adults and kids and shuttle service; they also have canoe carts ($5 per day), which are essential for families who want to portage a canoe across short stretches of land from one lake to another.

👫 9 – 15

Delaware River. Besides the Saco, this wide National Scenic and Recreational River protected by the National Park Service is the most popular waterway in the Northeast for canoeing, kayaking, tubing, and rafting (*see below*). It has much more drama than the Saco—easy rapids, steep shale cliffs, lush forested mountains, and abundant wildlife—but not such nice sandy beaches, and you have to camp at designated campgrounds. The 79-mile section that borders Pennsylvania has many access points. Kittatinny Canoes (Dingmans Ferry, PA 18328, tel. 800/356–2852) has several bases in New York state where you can pick up canoes ($45 per day) and kayaks ($29 per day) and offers special learn-to-canoe days for families.

🏠 *Sullivan County, the Catskills.*

👫 6 – 15

Saranac Lake. This is really three lakes: upper, middle, and lower. Larger and in parts wilder than Blue Mountain Lake and with more islands (including some where you can camp; see Camping, *above*) it has a more meandering shoreline to explore. **All Seasons Outfitters** (168 Flower Ave., Saranac Lake 12983, tel. 518/891–6159) rents canoes ($20–$33 per day), gives flatwater canoe lessons and transport to launch sites, and offers guided day and overnight trips.

Vermont

Battenkill River

(🚹🚺 5 – 15)

Known for trout fishing, the Battenkill seems more civilized than the Saco (see above), with gentle stretches and riffly patches flowing by white steepled churches, under covered bridges painted red, alongside quiet, open meadows of grass and flowers and deep woods with sunlight filtering through the trees. It's a good river for canoeing inn-to-inn. A prime reason to canoe on this river, however, is for the outfitter's special trips for families. **Battenkill Canoe** (Box 65, Historic Rte. 7A, Arlington, 05250, tel. 802/362–2800 or 800/421–5268) provides maps and information on all the best spots to picnic, swim, and explore, along with rental canoes ($45 per day) for day trips on the river, and offers three guided canoe trips ($200–$600)—overnighting at inns or camping—specially designed for families with kids under 13.

Fishing

There are three basic kinds of fishing in the Northeast—fly-fishing, ocean fishing from the shore or a boat, and bait fishing in lakes and streams, all of which abound in every state except Vermont. The attraction for most young kids and plenty of older ones, is baiting the hook, throwing in the line, and pulling out a fish, no matter what its size, as soon as possible. Our most satisfactory hauls have been from small, stocked ponds and trout hatcheries or preserves where you are almost guaranteed a bite. On the coast, fish usually cluster at the bottom of rock jetties, another place to be sure of catching something fairly quickly. Fly-fishing, best for kids 11 to 12 and up, requires patience, technique, and muscle control. Instruction for kids is available in both of the

Northeast's most famous trout river areas—the Battenkill in Vermont and New York's Catskills (see below). For a good book on the subject, see Fly-Fishing with Children by Philip Brunquelle (Countryman Press). Usually trout hatcheries and preserves rent simple poles, but shops only rent more expensive fly-fishing or surf-casting rods. The most inexpensive introductions to fishing for families are the free fishing days in each state, usually on a weekend in the beginning of June during or just before National Fishing Week, when state fish and wildlife divisions offer family instructional clinics and free use of equipment at several sites, and waive the license requirement for adults. In the Northeast, kids under 15 need a fishing license only in New Hampshire, where the license for kids 12 to 15 is $5.

Connecticut

The 500 lakes and ponds, 300 miles of streams, and 250 miles of coastline in the state ensure ample nooks and crannies for all kinds of fishing. For ocean fishing, we recommend the stone jetty in Rocky Neck State Park (see Camping, above, and Chapter 10). For easy and accessible pond fishing, Maltby Lakes (Rte. 34, West Haven, tel. 203/562–4020), three ponds filled with native sunfish and stocked trout and surrounded by hiking trails, are in the southwestern part of the state.

Massachusetts

Cape Cod

(🚹🚺 4 – 15)

Just about everyone we know on the Cape has a favorite fishing hole among the hundreds of freshwater ponds ideal for family fishing. The ponds are easy to get to and are stocked with fish; kids can fish from the shore, which my son likes best, as well as from a boat. Wellfleet's Gull Pond, loaded with trout, native perch, pickerel, and sunfish, and Cliff Pond in Nickerson State Park in Brewster (see Chapter 10), which also boasts "land-locked" salmon, are currently considered the best spots on the Outer and Lower Cape. **Goose Hummock Shop** (Rte. 6A, Orleans 02653, tel. 508/255–0455), has licenses, gear, tackle, and maps of the best fishing holes in the area and sells bait. Licenses for older kids are also available at the town halls in Wellfleet and Brewster. Ocean fishing is good from the jetties at Red River Beach in Harwich, but for safety, parents should accompany kids.

At low tide, feet squishing in the shellfish beds along the shoreline in Wellfleet, you can dig up steamers and mussels, oysters and scallops. Bring a bucket and invest in an inexpensive clam rake. You need a license from the town shellfish offices near Mayo Beach or from the town hall, where they'll give you advice on where to dig. To catch blue crabs, head for the public dock on North Dennis Road in Yarmouth. Tie a length of string around a chicken bone with some meat on it, lower it into the water, and wait for a bite.

Red-Wind Meadow Farm Trout Hatchery

👫 3 – 14

This private fish hatchery with four calm ponds in a big grassy meadow offers just about the simplest way possible for families (especially with little kids) to start fishing because you don't have to bring anything except a picnic. You can rent fishing rods (75¢), purchase nightcrawlers ($2 per dozen), and obtain fishing pointers from a staff member if you or your kids need it. Well-kept picnic tables are placed to catch sun and shade. You must purchase all trout you catch at $4.25 a pound.
🏠 *500 Sunderland Rd., Amherst 01002, tel. 413/367–9494. Cost: $2; $5 family. Open Memorial Day–Labor Day, weekdays 9–4, weekends 9–5; Sept.–Oct., weekends weather permitting, 9–5.*

New York

The Catskills

👫 9 – 15

The bright, winding, rocky streams of Sullivan County, especially the Beaverkill and Willowemoc Creek, are celebrated for fly-fishing, and even though the banks of these rivers can be packed on a spring weekend morning, it's still a great place for kids to learn how. The friendly, informal **Catskill Fly Fishing Center and Museum** (Old Rte. 17, Livingston Manor 12758, tel. 914/439–4810; open year-round), right on Willowemoc Creek between Roscoe (nicknamed "Trout Town") and Livingston Manor, has information on everything from the best fishing spots that week to trout preserves where your kids won't be frustrated. On four summer weekends it offers instruction (cost: $45) for kids of different age groups in the fine arts of fly-fishing and tying. The platforms above the water for anglers with disabilities are also ideal safe places for little kids to fish. Public fishing throughout the county in lakes and ponds and streams is well marked with bright yellow signs and parking areas. The **Eldred Preserve** (Rte. 55, Eldred, 914/557–8316) is a private resort of log cabins, a restaurant, and nature trails that opens four trout ponds to the public ($2.50 per person), providing rental rods ($5.99) and tackle. When your kids hook a fish, the restaurant will cook it if you wish. The **Beaverkill Angler** (Roscoe, tel. 607/498–5194), is the only spot that rents fly rods ($25 per day).

Rhode Island

Clustered at Point Judith and around Narragansett Bay is the greatest concentration of ocean fishing charter boats in the Northeast. It's much closer to good fishing grounds than places like Montauk on Long Island, so you don't have to spend the whole day on the water motoring to and from the fishing.

Many charter boats welcome kids and structure the day to suit them by fishing for blues off Block Island, taking time to go ashore, and even teaching kids how to fish. The **Rhode Island Party & Charter Boat Association** (Box 3198, Narragansett 02882, tel. 401/737–5812; half-day trip, $250–$300) has 47 boats of all sizes, some of which take just a few passengers. **Rhode Island Yacht Charters** (8 Pond View Ct., West Greenwich 02817, tel. 401/397–9253; $80–$125 per hour), with several boats, including a sailboat, take a personal interest in families and are particularly flexible.

Vermont

Battenkill River

 11 – 15

The other famous trout river in the Northeast is the lively, clear Battenkill in southern Vermont, between Dorset and the New York border, of particular interest to families because one of the best fly-fishing schools in the country, the **Orvis Company** (Rte. 7A, Manchester, tel. 800/235–9763; $340 per person), where my husband and I both learned to fly-fish, is located on the river. I'm still hoping that sometime Gavin will want to attend one of their weekend parent and child courses, which follow a curriculum of fly casting, fly tying, stream ecology, and more, with plenty of field trips on the river.

Hikes, Walks, and Climbs

The Northeast has several thousand miles of trails of all kinds, so the locations and specific hikes below reflect our family's preferences for open vistas, big rocks, waterfalls and ponds, and spots where we're likely to see animals. Picking a hike of reasonable length and difficulty and being willing to stop often make the difference between a pleasant day and one that ends in fights and

grumps. By age 5 many kids can manage a ½- to 1-mile hike or an hour's hike, but before that, you'll probably have to carry them for at least a short bit. When hiking with Gavin in a backpack we learned not to take trails with a steep downhill pitch or streams we had to leap across. Especially important on long hikes with kids is taking extra food, clothing, and a first-aid kit, a flashlight, matches in a waterproof container, a map, and a compass. Make sure your kids have good hiking shoes (sneakers are not recommended). Be aware that weather can change rapidly in this region.

Anyone hiking in the Northeast needs to be concerned about poison ivy and Lyme disease, a bacterial infection transmitted by some but not all deer ticks, which in turn are found on animals, but also on tall grass, moss, ferns, or trees in the deep woods. Deer ticks are very tiny, resembling a small black dot about the size of a pinhead, and are most active during June and July, though prevalent from April through October. They must be on your skin for several hours in order to infect you. If you see one, pull it out gently with tweezers and save it in a jar to show your doctor. Gavin had a textbook case of the disease the summer of 1994: flu-like symptoms for a day or two, then a red rash in the shape of a circle. Our doctor started a regime of antibiotics immediately without even waiting for test results. I was disturbed to learn, however, that about 25% of people never get the rash and that symptoms vary, so if you or your kids don't feel well within a few weeks after a hiking trip, see your doctor and ask about the possibility of Lyme disease. Left untreated, it can cause serious problems. We now try to minimize our chance of exposure by wearing long, light-colored (ticks are easier to spot) pants tucked into our boots, and long-sleeved shirts, using a good insect repellent, and checking our clothing and bodies carefully after hiking. Before using Permanone, a strong tick repellent available at some hiking stores, I'd check with your doctor. The Center for Disease Control recommends that

DEET repellent be applied to clothing and skin (not face!)—but used conservatively and carefully with small children.

For years our hiking bibles have been the excellent "50 Hikes" series published by Backcountry Publications (The Countryman Press, Woodstock, Vermont). Three other superlative guides are *Best Hikes With Children in Vermont, New Hampshire, & Maine, Best Hikes with Children in Connecticut, Massachusetts, & Rhode Island,* and *Best Hikes with Children in the Catskills & Hudson River Valley,* all by Cynthia and Thomas Lewis (The Mountaineers, 1991 and 1992).

In addition to the hikes below, *see* Chapter 10 for state and national parks and forests and other green spaces with excellent trails.

Connecticut

The northwest corner of Connecticut, in the Litchfield Hills, is the most interesting in the state for hikers. It has many short, scenic, easy paths perfect for toddlers, preschoolers, and older kids who enjoy a variety of diversions on a short hike. (See Chapter 10 for information on White Memorial Foundation in Litchfield and the Northeast Audubon Center in Sharon).

Maine

Besides the locations below, *see* Chapter 10 for Baxter State Park, which is good for short hikes by remote ponds where you can swim and spot moose; Mt. Blue State Park, which has easy hikes to mountain summits and rivers for gold panning; and Grafton Notch State Park, which offers hikes to waterfalls.

Acadia National Park

(👪 2 – 15)

The park's free guided hikes and walks for children and families on the enormous network of trails are especially rewarding. We have many favorite hikes here, from the easy

path to Witch Hole Pond to strenuous climbs. The Visitor's Center has good maps. (see Chapter 10.)

🏛 *Superintendent, Box 177, Bar Harbor 04609, tel. 207/288–3338. Park Headquarters, Rte. 233, Eagle Lake (open Nov.–Apr., daily 8–4:30; May–Oct., weekdays 8–4:30). Visitor's Center, Rte. 3, Hulls Cove (open May–Oct., daily 8–4:30). Cost: $5 per car.*

Monhegan Island

(👪 6 – 15)

Remote and beautiful, this small rocky island 10 miles from the mainland is mostly wild, crisscrossed with 17 miles of varied trails that circle the island's rock-and-cliff coastline and traverse the pine woods in its center. It has all the best features of coastal hikes: a pebble-strewn beach with the remains of a shipwreck to explore, views of the open sea, coves with rocks to skip and climb on, plunging cliffs to beware of, grassy spots by rock faces for picnic lunches, and a small village, where the boat from the mainland docks, with ice-cream and souvenir shops. If you have younger kids, don't miss the Cathedral Woods trail, which seemed like a magic forest to Gavin when he was younger because of the tiny huts built at the bases of trees from sticks and bark, a tradition carried on by children on the island and visiting kids. Day-trippers have only a few hours on the island because of ferry schedules; it's most fun to spend the night at one of the island hotels. Ferries from Port Clyde Harbor (*Laura B,* tel. 207/372–8848) run throughout the year. Ferries also depart from Boothbay Harbor and New Harbor (on the Pemiquid peninsula) from late June to Labor Day.

Mt. Kineo

(👪 7+)

This is a relatively short hike, one that even younger kids can do. The trails up Mt.

Kineo, a towering sheer rock face thrust straight up from Moosewood Lake, are only accessible by boat. From Rockwood, on the lake's western shore, it's about a ½-mile canoe paddle (don't attempt it in bad weather). The mountain itself is named for an Indian chief, who, as legend has it, went to live alone here after being banished by his tribe. The Bridle trail is the easiest (about three hours round-trip) climb. Canoes for the trip can be rented at Whitten's Store (Rockwood, tel. 207/534–7778).

Step Falls

🚹🚼 3 – 15

This is one of the most satisfying short hikes we know. It follows a tumbling brook with icy wading pools and granite rocks for climbing for 1½ miles to the dramatic falls. Flat slabs overlooking deep, wide pools make a fine perch for lunch. Be sure to bring bathing suits and towels. (See Chapter 10.)

🏠 Rte. 26, 7.7 mi from Bethel near Grafton Notch State Park (turn right on gravel road just before metal guardrails that border both sides of road).

Massachusetts

When it comes to picking the most enticing hiking for families in this varied state, we're torn between the sheltering forest and rounded hill landscape of the Berkshires and the otherworldly sand dunes and salt marshes of Cape Cod National Seashore (see Chapters 5 and 10 for hiking information) and Plum Island.

Bartholomew's Cobble

🚹🚼 3 – 12

A National Natural Landmark, the Cobble reminds me of a rock garden, with limestone and marble outcroppings (the cobbles) that provide the right environment, unique in the Northeast, for an amazing array of wildflowers and ferns, especially in

the spring and early summer. Within its 300 acres of diverse landscape are many easy trails that even preschoolers we know enjoy. Try the trail along the burbling Housatonic River and a stop at the natural history museum. Each weekend there are many kids' programs and family hikes; the snowshoe treks in winter offer kids' snowshoes for rent.

🏠 Weatogue Rd., Ashley Falls 01222, tel. 413/229–8600. From Rte. 7A, turn right onto Rannapo Rd. and follow it 1½ mi to Weatogue Rd.; turn right, entrance on left. Cost: $3 adults, $1 kids 6–12. Open daily 9–5.

Massachusetts Audubon Society Sanctuaries

🚹🚼 ALL

Wide trails, easy terrain, benches to rest on, bird observation blinds, boardwalks across swamps or salt marshes that make noise as you clatter across them, and well-organized guided hikes are all reasons why hiking in the society's well-run sanctuaries continue to attract us. Ipswich River in Topsfield (see Chapter 10), Wachusett Meadow in Princeton, Laughing Brook in Hampden, and Wellfleet Bay on Cape Cod (see below) all have excellent naturalist-led hikes, many for children. For information contact Massachusetts Audubon Society (208 S. Great Rd., Lincoln 01773, tel. 617/259–9500).

Parker River National Wildlife Refuge

🚹🚼 4 – 13

You're almost guaranteed sightings of deer, rabbits, ducks, geese, and many kinds of birds in the marshes and dunes of this sanctuary. The beach walking is easy and excellent; Hellcat Swamp Trail cuts through a variety of habitats. A plus if you come after Labor Day is picking beach plums and cranberries.

🏠 Plum Island, off Rte. 1A, Newburyport, tel. 508/465–5753. Cost: $5 parking, $1 walkers *or bikers. Open daily ½-hr befor sunrise–½-hr after sunset.*

Wellfleet Bay Wildlife Sanctuary

 ALL

We spied muskrats and all sorts of birds from each of the three trails that wind through the 1,000 acres because well-placed birdhouses and rocks for turtles to sun themselves draw wildlife close to the trails. *West side Rte. 6, Wellfleet, tel. 508/349–2615. Cost: $3 adults, $2 kids under 16. Open daylight hrs.*

New Hampshire

Mt. Monadnock

9 – 15

Mt. Monadnock's huge bald summit, looming over the surrounding landscape of low mountains, is the reason we've climbed it five times and love climbing it more than any other mountain in the Northeast. The last third of each of the six trails to the top is bare, open rock to clamber over. The shortest route, the White Dot Trail, is the toughest, rather like a stone stairway going straight up. The Marlboro trail is the best first-time route (take Rte. 124 5.1 miles from Marlboro; turn left and follow Shaker Rd. .7 mi to the parking area; the trail begins across a gravel road; blazes are white). Be sure to purchase the Monadnock Guide, which includes a map, at the Visitor Center. *Off Rte. 124 (4 mi north of Jaffrey), Jaffrey Center 03453, tel. 603/532–8862. Cost: $2.50 persons over 12.*

Pitcher Mountain

4 – 15

The ½-mile trail up this mountain to a wide, flat, rock-covered summit is the shortest and

easiest one we know to such incredible views of other peaks, lakes, and forests. Thickets of blueberry bushes (see Apples and Berries, *above*), safe ledges to sit on and climb, and a fire tower open to the public are other attractions. *Just off Rte. 123 between Marlow and Stoddard.*

White Mountain National Forest

 ALL

Higher, rockier peaks with more open vistas than any other mountain area in the Northeast, a wide variety of trails from easy to highly challenging, and the Appalachian Mountain Club's guided hikes and system of huts all draw our family here for mountain hiking. The hiking hub of the area, the place to stop for information on trails and trail conditions, is the Appalachian Mountain Club's Pinkham Notch Camp at the base of Mount Washington. The lodge and dining room (not fancy) welcome guests, while the Visitor Center (Rte. 16, Box 298, Pinkham Notch, Gorham 03581, tel. 603/466–2725, for reservations 603/466–2727; programs, $115–$275 adults, $65–$160 kids) has educational displays and a store where you can buy books, maps, and hiking gear. It's the starting point for many of the AMC's family programs (see *also* Camping, *above*).

The Saco Ranger Station (Rtes. 112 and 16) for the White Mountain National Forest also has information. In addition to the guides mentioned in the introduction to this section, The *AMC White Mountain Guide* and *Waterfalls of the White Mountains* by Bruce and Doreen Bolnick (Backcountry Publications) highlight many easy to moderate hikes perfect for families. Maps are also available from the Forest Supervisor (Box 638, White Mountain National Forest, Laconia 03247, tel. 603/528–8721).

👨‍👦 6 – 15

Black Cap Path. On this easy 2½-mile hike you follow stone cairns to a bare rock summit with wide views.
🏯 *3.7 mi from junction of Rte. 16 and Hurricane Mountain Rd., Intervale.*

👨‍👦 5 – 12

Greeley Ponds Trail. Plank walks, bridges, and gravelly beaches around two wilderness ponds, as well as catching frogs and perhaps even seeing a beaver slap the water with his tail keep kids absorbed on this 4-mile, fairly level hike.
🏯 *Off Kancamagus Hwy. (Rte. 112, 9.7 mi east of town at parking lot marked with name of trail), Lincoln.*

👨‍👦 6 – 15

Lonesome Lake Trail. One of the most popular family destinations in the White Mountains is remote and beautiful Lonesome Lake, edged with dark pine trees and in the shadow of the high Franconia Ridge. You can spend the night at the AMC's Lonesome Lake hut. The 3½-mile round-trip hike has some steep parts. Be sure to at least wade in the lake and take the trail around it.
🏯 *Off Rte. 93, Lafayette Campground, Franconia Notch State Park, Franconia.*

👨‍👦 4 – 15

Loon Mountain. If you want to take interesting trails along a mountain summit without having to hike for six hours to get there, Loon Mountain is accessible by gondola. At the top we found boardwalks and trails leading through the nooks and crannies of hollowed-out glacial caves.
🏯 *Loon Mountain Park, Kancamagus Hwy., Lincoln 03251, tel. 603/745–8111. Cost: $8 adults, $3 kids 6–16.*

👨‍👦 3 – 10

Lost Pond Trail. A short 1½-mile (one-hour) round-trip to a scenic wilderness pond with views of Mt. Washington is one of the easiest trails in the Pinkham Notch area. It passes a beaver dam and lodge as well as the pointed stumps of trees chewed by beaver teeth. Gavin at 7 was also captivated by the boulder fields at the far end of the pond.
🏯 *Rte. 16 (sign near pond across from Pinkham Notch Camp).*

New York

Adirondack Park

👨‍👦 8 – 15

More than 2,000 miles of marked trails leading to mountain peaks, ice caves, and waterfalls cross the wild, forested land of this park in northern New York State. Though you can find many easy hikes scattered through the park, it's a place that draws serious hikers and climbers. The High Peaks district near Lake Placid concentrates rugged climbs and challenging trails. Many trails, though well marked, well maintained, and easily accessible from main roads (look for wood signs with yellow lettering), are rough, steep, and rocky, and as we learned on one ill-fated hike, sometimes lead straight up to the summit by way of an old, rutted, rock-strewn streambed. For kids under 13, the **Adirondack Mountain Club**'s (ADK) well-organized family events and guided hikes offer satisfying introductions to the region. They're similar to the AMC's programs in New Hampshire. On the High Peaks Traverse, you get a taste of the wilderness without having to backpack; you hike in 3½ miles to the ADK's fairly comfortable but rustic **Johns Brook Lodge** (contact Adirondack Loj, *below*, for information), and use that as your base for three to five days of hiking. Other family programs originate at their wilderness center on the shore of Heart Lake, **Adirondack Loj** (off Rte. 73, Box 867, Lake Placid 12946, tel. 518/523–3441; summer program, $120–$320 adults, $95–$220 kids), which also has a campground. The ADK in Lake George (Luzerne Rd., Lake George 12845, tel. 518/668–4447) organizes guided hikes as well. The best guidebooks to hiking in the Adirondacks are the ADK's book of day hikes and *Fifty Hikes in the Adirondacks* by Barbara McMartin (Backcountry).

Mohonk Preserve

(👫 3 – 15)

A 5,600-acre nature preserve that surrounds the 2,000 acres owned by the Mohonk Mountain House resort (see Chapter 14), it has easy paths that even a stroller can negotiate, as well as the fantastic rock formations and open cliff hikes that delight our family. The Labyrinth (ages 10–15), with ladders up cliff walls, tunnels and bridges, rock formations, and caves, is both challenging and exciting. The Visitor's Center, ½ mile from the gatehouse, has good trail maps.
🏠 *Mountain Rest Rd., New Paltz, tel. 914/255–0919 or 914/255–1000. $5 parking.*

Vermont

Green Mountain National Forest

In this huge forest we favor the special recreation areas designed to provide easy access to the backcountry. They have many good, short trails with much to see along the way; easy-to-read map brochures highlight sights appealing to kids (see also Chapter 10).
🏠 *Forest Supervisor, Green Mountain National Forest, 231 N. Main St., Rutland 05701, tel. 802/747–6700 for information and maps; Green Mountain Club, Box 889, 43 State St., Montpelier 05601, tel. 802/223–3463 (trail maps: "Day Hiker's Guide to Ver-*

mont" and "Day Hiker's Vermont Sampler" list many trails appropriate for families).

Grout Pond

(👫 0 – 15)

A flat 2-mile loop trail, with camping shelters and picnic tables, circles this pretty pond frequented by canoers and beavers. Swimming is excellent.
🏠 *Kelley Stand Rd. (off Rte. 6 between Stratton and Arlington), Stratton.*

White Rocks Recreation Area

(👫 3 – 15)

Among the most fascinating and easy trails we've hiked anywhere are the White Rocks and Ice Beds Trails in this area. The "white rocks," rock slides of shattered quartzite deposited during the Ice Age, once served as a meeting place for Native Americans. The trail snakes along a ridge past ledge outcroppings and overlooks of the huge boulder fields and eventually comes to the base of the largest rock slide. If you look carefully, you'll be able to see snow and ice in the crevices even in August.
🏠 *Groton State Forest, Wallingford 05773. Take Rte. 140 from Wallingford to Sugarhill Rd., then right on U.S. Forest Service Rd. 52 to White Rocks Picnic Area.*

Horseback Riding

Riding horseback through the woods on a crisp fall day, when the air smells sharp and red and yellow leaves surround you is one of the great pleasures of the region. Five is not too young to begin learning, but many stables will not take kids younger than 8 on trail rides.

Among the best places for families to ride are ranches in New York's Catskills and stables and resorts in Vermont's Green Mountains, as well as the area around Lake

George (see Chapter 6). Horseback riding on cross-country trails is usually also available at ski resorts off-season. Late summer and fall, when days are a bit cooler, are the most comfortable times.

New Hampshire

Castle in the Clouds

👫 8 – 15

Eccentric multimillionaire Thomas Gustave Plant's quirky stone mansion, built high above Lake Winnipesaukee in the Ossipee Mountain Range, is surrounded by 6,000 acres networked with 85 miles of bridle paths and carriage trails on which you can take one-hour guided rides.
🏠 *Rte. 171, Moultonborough 03254, tel. 603/476–2352 or 800/729-2468. Cost: $10 admission, persons over 10; $25 trail rides. Reservations required. Open May–mid-June, weekends 9–5; mid-June–mid-Oct., daily 9–5.*

New York

Ranch resorts lure families with trail rides for all levels of ability, pony rides for kids, and a welcoming attitude toward young kids. Two in the Catskills, Pine Grove Ranch Resort and Rocking Horse Ranch, have a large selection of horses, and trail rides and lessons are included in the price of lodging. They also have many other activities if every child in your family doesn't want to ride (see Chapter 14). **Pine Grove Ranch** (Lower Chestertown Rd., Kerhonkson 12446, tel. 914/626–7345 or 800/346–4626) breeds its own purebred and half-bred registered Arabian saddle horses, of which 65 are available to ride. There are ponies for little kids and western riding lessons eight times a day. **Rocking Horse Ranch** (600 Rte. 44–55, Highland 12528, tel. 914/691–2927 or 800/647–2624) has 90 horses, 500 acres of woods and orchards to ride in, and many half-hour trail rides a day.

Vermont

Kedron Valley Inn and Stables

👫 10 – 15

One of the prettiest villages in New England, Woodstock has been a center for riding for generations and seems, even today, to have more horses than cars. Kedron Valley Stables ranks high for families with older kids who know how to ride. The well-designed itineraries cover an 85-mile network of trails and paths—through flower-filled meadows, by lakes and streams, up and down hills. As trips require five or six hours per day in the saddle, kids should be keen, experienced older riders.
🏠 *Rte. 106, Woodstock 05071, tel. 802/457–1480. Cost: trail rides, $80 per hr for family of 4; lessons available; inn-to-inn treks, $360–$1,100.*

Mountain Top Inn and Resort

👫 6 – 15

You don't have to stay at this resort known for its cross-country skiing to take advantage of their excellent kids' riding lessons and trail rides during the warmer half of the year. Kids as young as 5 can learn to ride; those 8 (at least 54 inches) and up can go on one-hour, half-day, and full-day trail rides on 80 miles of trails. The stable has kid-size boots and helmets. This is a friendly place where kids hang over the fence and help feed the horses.
🏠 *Mountain Top Rd., Rte 108, Chittenden 05737, tel. 802/483–2311 or 800/445–2100. Cost: lessons, $25–$38; trail rides, $25 per hr.*

Vermont Icelandic Horse Farm

(**👫 9 – 15**)

These affectionate, sturdy, pony-sized (12–14 hands) mounts brought from Iceland are less intimidating to kids and easy to ride because of their surefootedness and smooth gaits—you don't have to post. They were brought to Iceland more than 1,000 years ago by the Vikings and are now considered the purest breed of horse in the world. This farm's friendliness to kids is another reason to try a lesson or the one-hour and half-day guided trail rides that climb into high meadows and woods in the Mad River Valley; longer rides make time for a swim. The farm has inn-to-inn treks in the valley, on which kids are allowed to help out with feeding and grooming.

🏠 *R.R. 376–1, Waitsfield 05673, tel. 802/ 496–7141. Cost: $30 per hr; inn-to-inn treks, $335–$1,095.*

Indoor-Action High Spots

Into the life of every family on vacation in the Northeast, unless you are very, very lucky (not us), come those days and weekends when the rain washes out everyone's outdoor plans. Under these circumstances, we've found that a museum will rarely suffice as a substitute for diving off a raft or biking through a campground, but indoor miniature golf or video games may.

Discovery Zone Centers

(**👫 1 – 10**)

Every once in a while I bemoan the fact that something for little kids has been invented too late for my family. That's how I felt when confronted by the 10,000 square feet of foam mountains, rollerslides, tunnel mazes,

giant ball crawls, and bouncy air beds filled with active noisy kids in one of these centers. Tots and toddlers have a miniplay area in each of these indoor playgrounds.

🏠 *Various locations in CT, ME, MA, NY, and RI; tel. 800/386–2368 for center nearest you. Cost: $6.99, 2 hrs; $1.99 each additional hr. Open daily, hrs vary by location.*

Connecticut

Stew Leonard's Dairy

(**👫 2 – 12**)

It's the Disneyland of supermarkets, a cross between an amusement park and a country fair that's now the world's most entertaining and largest (it covers 8½ acres) supermarket. In the parking lot, goat kids amble in the petting zoo; inside, animated milk cartons sing, a mechanical chicken in a cage shoots out plastic eggs, and employees dressed as cows and chickens wander the aisles patting squealing kids.

🏠 *100 Westport Ave., Norwalk 06851, tel. 203/847–7213. Open daily 7 AM–11 PM.*

Maine

L.L. Bean

(**👫 12 – 15**)

Wandering around here on a rainy day or boring evening (it's open 24 hours a day, 365 days a year) is great fun. The store, housed in a rehabilitated version of Leon Leonwood Bean's original boot factory, is still the center of the company's mail-order business. When we tire of looking at canoes and marveling at outdoor gadgets, we hop on the free horse-drawn carriage outside and head for the shopper's theme park of 100-plus factory outlets in town.

🏠 *Rte. 1, Freeport 04033, tel. 207/865– 4761 or 800/341–4341.*

Massachusetts

Cove Lanes

(👫 4 – 15)

We are a family that has driven 45 minutes to play miniature golf indoors in the middle of winter. Rainbow's End, the 18-hole course at this recreation center, has the usual frustrating and crazy holes—there is a waterfall. Downstairs is a bowling center, a pool table, and a game room with the latest in video games.
🏠 *Rte. 7 (just north of town), Great Barrington 01230, tel. 413/528–1220. Cost: $2, golf. Open daily 9 AM–midnight.*

New Hampshire

Funspot Amusement Center

(👫 6 – 15)

The ultimate game and bowling spot in the Northeast for kids, this one has 500 electronic games and both regular and candlepin bowling.
🏠 *Rte. 3 (1 mi north of town), Weirs Beach 03247, tel. 603/536–4377. Cost: 25¢, tokens (discounts for bulk purchases). Open Sept.– June, daily 10–10, July–Aug. daily 24 hrs.*

Perpetual Motion Indoor Playground

(👫 1 – 6)

More like an actual indoor version of an outdoor playground than Discovery Zone centers, Perpetual Motion is also more personal, individual, and charming, with a huge wooden train of four brightly painted cars designed by its engineer-owner. Kids seem to get an extra kick out of the fact that swings, a huge sandbox, and a minicarousel with three horses are all indoors.

🏠 *16 Haverhill St., Rte. 133, Andover 01810, tel. 508/474–4424. Cost: $5. Open Mon.–Wed., Sat. 9:30–4:30; Thurs. 9:30–7:30; Sun. noon–5.*

New York

Doubleday Batting Range

(👫 6 – 15)

Nowhere are kids so much in the mood to test out their own batting and pitching abilities as in Cooperstown, home of the Baseball Hall of Fame. Luckily, right next door to the Hall of Fame is a building filled with batting cages and a machine that measures the speed of your pitch with radar, where kids can indulge their need for action. Although most batting ranges don't have anything for little kids, here the machine in one batting cage pitches just tennis balls and in another soft balls.
🏠 *Doubleday Plaza, Cooperstown 13326, tel. 607/547–5168. Cost: $1–$2 per machine. Open late June–Labor Day, daily 10–5; Labor Day–Columbus Day, weekends 10–5.*

Llama Trekking into the Wilderness

On a guided camping trip on which gentle-natured llamas carry the gear, you can hike over high trails into backcountry that might be too rugged and remote for a family to carry their own equipment. More lovable, friendly, and approachable than packhorses, llamas don't bite or kick, though they've been known to spit.

Maine

Telemark Inn

(👫 4 – 15)

Treks into even wilder country from this remote, rather deluxe Adirondack-style lodge perched in the peaks of the White Mountain National Forest seem designed to make families with little kids feel at home in the wilderness. You hike in along the spectacular Wild River to a base camp with a good swimming hole, then make daily forays up trails that have kid-pleasing features such as bear claw marks on tree trunks. No cramped tents or freeze-dried packets of mystery food on these treks; hot towels greet you in the morning, and food is good. **🏠** *RFD 2, Box 800, Bethel, ME 04217, tel. 207/836–2703. Cost: 3-day trek, $385 adults, $285 kids under 12. Season: May–Sept.*

Mountain Biking: Easy Trails to Thrilling Rides

With easy-to-difficult grassy trails already in place for cross-country skiing, old logging and access roads through the woods, and lifts to take you and your bike to the top of the mountain for thrilling rides down, ski areas offer the most extensive networks of safe off-road mountain bike trails in the region. Many now not only maintain the trails in summer, but also offer rentals, races, guided tours, and instruction (usually for older kids and adults only), in addition to lodging and a host of other activities. Though 7- or 8-year-olds can ride many of the easier trails, kids need to be substantially older to use the high-performance bikes required to ride up or down from mountain summits. All areas below require the use of helmets and rent both adult and kid sizes, along with standard mountain and superperformance bikes. Besides those mentioned below, Smuggler's Notch and Stratton (see Chapter 12) offer trails easy enough for younger kids. State parks and forests also have designated loops of uncharted logging roads and cross-country trails as mountain-bike paths.

New Hampshire

Loon Mountain Park

👫 6 – 15

Located right on the scenic Kancamagus Highway in the heart of the rugged White Mountains, Loon Mountain (see *also* Chapters 10 and 13) in summer feels more like a family and kid place than many other ski resorts with mountain-bike rentals and trails, and is an especially good place if you have children of widely different ages. Its easy cross-country trails near the rushing Pemigewasset River even have picnic tables. The gondola transports more expert bikers to the summit for a not-too-difficult ride down. The shop sponsors an exciting downhill four-hour guided bike tour on the Franconia Notch Bike Path. **🏠** *Rte. 112 (Kancamagus Hwy.), Lincoln 03251, tel. 603/745–8111. Cost: $13 per hr adult bikes, $9 per hr kids 6–16 (kid-size helmets available). Open Memorial Day–mid Oct., daily 8–4; mid-Oct.–late Nov., weekends 7:30–6.*

Waterville Valley

👫 6 – 15

In this ski resort's mountain bike park on Snow's Mountain in the White Mountain National Forest, miles and miles of marked trails and bumps and jumps have been set aside only for bikers, so kids don't run the risk of hitting hikers. All sorts of lessons, tours, and special events are offered throughout the summer (tel. 800/468–2553). **Mountain Valley Bikes** (tel. 802/236–4666; $5–$8 per hr adults, $4–$5 per hr kids) rents bikes as small as 20 inches.

Vermont

Catamount Family Center Endurance Sports

(👫 6 – 15)

Not far from Burlington is a 500-acre family outdoor sports playground where you can do orienteering, cross-country running, nature hikes, and especially mountain biking. Easy to hard trails, mostly pine bed or grass, crisscross the hilly land; once-a-week mountain bike races are held, even for kids in the 8-and-under group. The smallest bike they rent will fit a 6-year-old.
🏠 *421 Chittenden Rd., Williston 05494, tel. 802/879–6001. Rentals: $15 4 hrs; $25 per hr for superperformance bikes for older kids; helmets to borrow. Open weekdays noon–9, weekends 9–5.*

Craftsbury Sports Center

(👫 12 – 15)

This unusual resort sits in northeast Vermont's high, rolling farm country in the midst of miles and miles of winding dirt farm roads and grassy cross-country ski trails perfect for mountain biking. Bikes are rented, self-guided bike tours insure that you won't get lost, and flexible and informal instruction is available. Accommodations at the resort, once a boys' boarding school, are basic (shared baths, simple furnishings) but comfortable, and meals are the healthy yet delicious whole-wheat pizza, homemade pudding kind. It attracts a very broad spectrum of people, from singles to families, serious athletes to grandparents.
🏠 *Box 31–VOE, Craftsbury Common 05827, tel. 802/586–7767 or 800/729–7751. Cost for bikes: $6 per hr; $15 per half day. Open daily 8:30–4:30.*

Mountain Bike School and Training Center at Mt. Snow

(👫 7 – 15)

The words "Training Center" convey well the serious atmosphere of intensive instruction, geared more to highly athletic and competitive older teens and twentysomethings than to families, at this school in a friendly southern Vermont ski resort. It has one of the most varied and extensive mountain biking trail systems in the region, with 140 miles of marked trails, among which are a number at the mountain's base and by the golf course that suit very young kids; one passes a beaver pond. Older kids can join the guided tours, but trail maps for self-guided tours are easy to follow.
🏠 *400 Mountain Rd., Mount Snow, Dover 05356, tel. 802/464–3333 for information. Cost: 2 hrs, $19 adults, $14 kids; full day, $29 adults, $21 kids; helmets included.*

Rockhounding and Fossil Hunting

Abandoned quarries and mines abound in the Northeast, but the safest places to prospect for minerals are at those monitored by a mineral shop or museum or state park, which often rent and sell equipment. (Do not go inside an abandoned mine unless experts have determined that it is safe.) At the least you need a small hammer, several small plastic or cloth bags in which to squirrel away each child's samples, and plastic safety glasses because chips do fly. A mineral pick and chisel are useful additions. Damp surfaces of sharp rock are the norm, so you need jeans and sturdy shoes with rubber soles. You can even pan for gold in a few Maine, New Hampshire, and Vermont streams. A good book for kids 8 to 12 is *Understanding and Collecting Rocks and Fossils* by Martyn Bramwell (Usborne Publishing, 1983).

Maine

For additional sites in Maine, check *Gems & Minerals*, a Maine Geographic guide published by Delorme Mapping Company (Box 298GS, Freeport 04032) or "Maine Mineral Collecting," from the Maine Publicity Bureau (see Chapter 2).

Perham's

👫 5 – 13

In the midst of a region thick with mineral and gem deposits, Perham's, the prime mineral store catering to the state's rockhounders, owns four quarries within 8 to 10 miles that are open to the public and provides a map. The sites are mostly big pits in the woods, each with its own specialty—rose quartz, mica, feldspar, and more. The store sells equipment (also for gold panning) and a guidebook to other quarries in Maine. 🏠 *Rte. 26, Box 280, West Paris 04289, tel. 207/674–2341. Open daily 9–5.*

New Hampshire

Gilsum

👫 5 – 13

Tiny Gilsum, once a thriving mining town, sponsors an annual Rock Swap at the end of June that's great for kids who are serious rockhounders. Though the town library sells maps pinpointing the 60 abandoned mines in the area, the Rock Swap doesn't sponsor mine tours on which you can prospect. If you write, however (Gilsum Recreation Committee, Box 76, Gilsum 03448, tel. 603/352–7435), they may be able to get you permission to visit and prospect at a local one.

Ruggles Mine

👫 6 – 13

At the oldest mine in the Northeast, on top of Isingglass Mountain, caves and tunnels with arched rock formations and floors slick with water lead off from the less eerie open pit. Bring a flashlight. The most common of the 150 different types of minerals and gems that you may find here are mica, feldspar, garnet, and quartz. If you're lucky, you might hit upon some golden beryl or tourmaline. In the small shop where you pay admission, you can buy or rent equipment and buy samples of minerals you want but don't find. 🏠 *Isingglass Mountain (off Rte. 4), Grafton 03748, tel. 603/448–6911. Cost: $9 adults, $4 kids 4–11. Open late June–mid-Oct., daily 9–5.*

New York

Barton Garnet Mines

👫 6 – 13

After a tour of the large open-pit mine where most of the world's industrial garnets (they're a dark red color) come from, you can look for stones yourself. In contrast to other mines, here site guides are available to answer questions about how to find stones. You do have to pay for the gems you take with you. You can also see gem cutters demonstrate how to polish and shape garnets. 🏠 *Rte. 28, North Creek 12853, tel. 518/251–2706. Cost: $3 adults, $2 kids under 14. Open late June–Labor Day, Mon.–Sat. 9–5, Sun. 11–5.*

John Boyd Thacher State Park

👫 8 – 13

This park covers some of the richest fossil-bearing terrain in the world; it's also a prime hunting ground for Indian arrowheads. The trail to take is the Indian Ladder Geological Trail, which is open to kids ages 8 and up. 🏛 *Rte. 157, 15 mi southwest of Albany, 12186, tel. 518/872–1237. Open daily 8 AM–10 PM.*

Rollerblading and Skateboarding

Unlike California, the Northeast doesn't have a skate park in just about every single community. Nonetheless, in-line skating, and to a lesser extent, skateboarding are popular here, especially among teens in cities. On the paved roads in city parks that are closed to traffic we've often seen more skaters than bike riders on a sunny weekend. The big problem elsewhere is traffic; the places below are among the few indoor and outdoor centers in the Northeast strictly reserved for these two sports. Be aware that all require parents to sign a waiver before kids will be allowed to skate, and none will let kids skate without protective gear and a helmet.

Massachusetts

Charles River Esplanade

👫 12 – 15

For the best rollerblading in Boston, try the Esplanade along the Charles River. Skaters also congregate at Frog Pond on Boston Common and at Government Center (Chapter 3). For rentals, the best place is **Eric Flaim's Motion Sports** (349B Newbury St., Boston 02116, tel. 617/247–3284; smallest size, women's 6; $20 per day including protective gear), a shop that specializes only in in-line skates and offers lessons.

Maximus

👫 12 – 15

The atmosphere at this huge, old, 4,000-square-foot warehouse, a mecca for Boston area skateboarders and in-line skaters, is friendly, and older, more experienced skaters offer tips to the younger kids who come in the afternoon. It's primarily a hang-out kind of place for kids serious about the two sports, with a street course of ramps and miniramps and a 10-foot half-pipe. You have to bring your own skateboard or skates, but helmets (required) and pads can be borrowed free. 🏛 *324 Rindge Ave. (off Massachusetts Ave., Alewife stop on Red line T), Cambridge 02140, tel. 617/576–4723. Cost: $10. Open daily 12:30–8, Thurs. 12:30–10.*

New Hampshire

Waterville Valley

👫 8 – 15

Tooling around at a leisurely pace on an extensive network of paved roads, sidewalks, and parking lots with no pass-through traffic is Waterville Valley's big attraction for skaters of all ages. Kids under 12 who aren't yet interested in ramps and half-pipes may have more fun here than at official skate parks. Small size skates (size 1 and 2) are available. 🏛 *Waterville Valley 03215, tel. 603/236–8311. Rentals: $8 per hour includes helmets and protective pads, including small sizes.*

New York

Central Park

👫 8 – 15

New York City's skating mecca is Central Park (see Chapter 4). Streets throughout the park are closed to traffic on weekends; if your kids are younger and just learning, Wollman Rink, which sponsors inexpensive family nights, may be a better bet (see Chapter 4). You can rent skates at **Peck & Goodies** (917 8th Ave. at 54th St., tel. 212/246–6123; 1414 2nd Ave. at 73rd St., tel. 212/249–3178; they also give lessons in Central Park); **Blades West** (120 W. 72nd St., tel. 212/787–3911); **Blades East** (160 E. 86th St., tel. 212/996–1644; they'll give you instructions and a carrying box); or at **Wollman Rink** (midpark at 63rd St., tel. 212/ 517–4800).

🏠 *5th Ave. and 59th St. to Central Park West and 110th St., New York.*

Vermont

Cutting Edge North

(👫 9 – 15)

This skateboard and snowboard shop in an old mill building maintains an indoor skate park adjacent to the shop and an outdoor skate park with a street course in a paved parking lot outside. Both are used primarily by skateboarders, attracting kids from Massachusetts and New York state and kids on vacation as well as a local clientele. Helmets and protective gear are required, and you are expected to bring your own equipment, though a few helmets are available.

160 Benmont Ave., Bennington 05201, tel. 802/447–7570. Cost: $7. Open: Tues.–Sat. noon–8, Sun. noon–6.

Stowe In-Line Skate Park

(👫 10 – 15)

In summer, most of the huge parking lot at the base of Spruce Peak ski area is transformed into the Northeast's only big in-line skate park. The set-up, next to the Alpine Slide, fulfills most skaters' fantasies: It has everything from a half-pipe to ramps, a downhill slalom course served by a lift, and

a snack bar. There's serious attention to safety here; all rentals include helmets, elbow and knee pads, and wrist guards, in-line skates rented are top quality, and certified instructors give group and private lessons.

🏠 *Spruce Peak Base Lodge, Stowe Mountain Resort, 5781 Mountain Rd. (Rte. 108), Stowe 05672, tel. 802/253–3000. Cost: $10; skates and protective gear, $8–$15 (kids' sizes available). Open July–Labor Day, daily 10–7; Labor Day–Columbus Day, weekends 10–7.*

Sailing and Windsurfing

To me sailing is the sport that best captures the essence of the Northeast. As you drive along the coastline of sheltered bays on a summer afternoon, you see harbor after picturesque harbor sprinkled with white sails and beyond, beckoning, open blue water swept by wind. If you want to get out on the waves, the region offers sailing schools, bareboat charters of day sailers and cruising boats, and captained boats of all kinds where you can relax and let a skipper and crew do the work. Besides the ocean sailing areas that most appeal to us, large lakes, such as Lake Champlain and Lake Winnipesaukee, despite heavy powerboat traffic, have active sailing communities. We discovered that the most inexpensive way for a family to learn to sail or rent a boat is through one of the many community sailing programs (see Newport, *below*); the U.S. Sailing Association (Box 209, Newport RI 02840, tel. 401/849–5200) publishes a free directory to all the programs in the United States.

You'll find rental Windsurfers and lessons at many beaches, but not all have conditions appropriate for beginners. What you need to know is that you must have the right angle of wind to windsurf safely and that taking a lesson from someone with substantial experience is important. Beginners (kids as young as 7 can learn if they are strong) need large inland ponds or bays with flat water and steady light winds like the kettle ponds on Cape Cod; those more advanced want the thrill of rolling wave action that you find at ocean beaches. Besides the Cape and Nantucket, Martha's Vineyard and Block Island offer limited but good windsurfing.

Connecticut

Longshore Sailing School

(🚹🚺 8 – 15)

Known for its successful junior sailing program, the largest in the country, this school also offers private sailing lessons for families in a calm, protected bay of Long Island Sound. This is an easy place to learn. They also rent boats and Windsurfers.
🏠 260 S. Compo Rd., Westport 06880, tel. 203/226–4646. Cost: $34 per 1-hr lesson.

SoundWaters

(🚹🚺 8 – 15)

A combination of sailing and environmental education, three-hour trips on this three-masted schooner give opportunities to steer the boat and hoist the sails as well as trawl for sea creatures and learn about the ecology of the Long Island Sound.
🏠 4 Yacht Haven West Marina, Washington Blvd., Stamford 06902, tel. 203/323–1978. Cost: $25 per person.

Maine

Boothbay Harbor

(🚹🚺 5 – 15)

This is boat country; it has the greatest number and variety of pay-as-you-go boat excursions in Maine. Seal watches, puffin watches, lighthouse watches, lobster fishing, up the Kennebec River, out to a misty island, just sailing around the bay, a water taxi from one side of the bay to the other—whatever intrigues you is leaving in just 15 minutes or

half an hour at most. Cruising the coves, circling the islands, rocking on waves brushed with white is the only way to really know Maine, and the trips, as if planned for young children, are mostly short and skirt coastlines with much to see. A boat tour of the harbor and a short sail on a Friendship sloop (a type of one-masted sailboat) are musts. **Cap'n Fish's Boat Trips** (Pier 1, tel. 207/633–3244) offers many one-hour (and longer) choices; **Bay Lady** (Pier 1, tel. 207/633–6990), a 31-foot Friendship sloop, leaves Fisherman's Wharf for two-hour cruises.

Windjammer Cruises

(🚹🚺 12 – 15)

Windjammers are the classic tall ships, schooners rigged with many sails to accommodate the variable winds characteristic of the east coast and to be flexible enough to change course quickly. An impressive fleet of them lies in Camden's picturesque harbor, dwarfing the hundreds of sailboats plying the waters of huge Penobscot Bay. On a three- or six-day cruise on one of them, adventure combines with quiet relaxation, good food, and a chance to explore the pine-covered islands of the rocky coast and bay the way sailors did in the great age of sail more than 100 years ago. Kids can help hoist sails and steer the ship; each night you anchor in a different cove or village harbor. **Maine Windjammer Cruises** (Box 617, Camden 04843, tel. 207/236–2938; $315–$485 per person) has three ships. The Mistress, skippered by a family with two outgoing young girls, is ideal for a large family.

Massachusetts

Cape Cod

(🚹🚺 6 – 15)

What makes the Cape an ideal place for kids to learn to windsurf is the large number of bays and ponds with different angles and intensities of wind. Among the prime places to learn and experiment are large, freshwater kettle ponds, such as Great Pond in Eastham, and protected bays such as Pleasant Bay in Chatham. At calm Gull Pond in Wellfleet (which connects with three other ponds) and Flax Pond in Nickerson State Park (see Chapter 10) numerous different kinds of boats are available to rent. **Jack's Boat Rentals** (Rte. 6, Wellfleet, tel. 508/349–9808; $15 per hr) has concessions at both Gull Pond (tel. 508/349–7553) and Flax Pond (tel. 508/896–8556), offering rental canoes, kayaks, boogie-, sail-, and surfboards, sunfish, and even kid-size Windsurfers that can be used by 6- and 7-year-olds, in addition to lessons. However, private lessons offered by **Fun Seekers** (tel. 508/349–1429), usually held at Great Pond or Pleasant Bay, are much more thorough; a two-hour introductory lesson costs $50 and includes Windsurfer rental.

The Cape's shifting winds require a different kind of sailing. **Arey's Pond Boat Yard** (Arey's La., Box 222, off Rte. 28, South Orleans 02662, tel. 508/255–0994; 5 morning group lessons, $90; private lessons, $40 per hr) is one of the Cape's few sailing schools outside a yacht club; it offers group and private lessons for kids and adults.

Nantucket

👫 7 – 15

The most popular beach on Nantucket for families, Jetties Beach is an easy place to learn to windsurf and sail because windsurfing is safe no matter what the wind direction. Rentals and instruction are right at the beach. **Force 5 Watersports** (Jetties Beach, tel. 508/228–5358; 37 Main St., Nantucket, tel. 508/228–0700; $15–$30 per hr; 1-hr private lesson, $50 including rental) rents kayaks, Sunfish, and Windsurfers. They teach more children than adults, including some as young as 6, and have the small-size windsurfing sails kids need.

Rhode Island

Newport

It's the yachting capital of the world, the site of the America's Cup race, and on a sunny day with the steady southwest breezes for which it is famous, Narragansett Bay is thick with sailboats of every size billowing white sails and colorful spinnakers. Even if you sail for only an hour or two, doing it here is interesting for kids because of the bay full of other boats and the coastline; if you spend half a day or a day on the water, there are easy-to-sail-to destinations such as Block Island, Sakonnet Point, and Cuttyhunk where you can go ashore. If you want to learn to sail, this city has more sailing schools than any other in the Northeast to choose from.

👫 12 – 15

J. World Sailing School. After talking to a number of sailors and yacht clubs, I've satisfied myself that this is the ultimate sailing school in Newport, the one I'd most like my family to attend if I could afford it. They too are flexible, offering weekend, five-day, or two-week instruction for just adults or for a family of four during the day and for several days on a cruising boat. Kids need to be old enough and interested enough to put up with six-hour days on the water.
🏠 *Box 1509, Newport 02840, tel. 401/849–5492. Cost: $255 and up per person.*

👫 7 – 15

Sail Newport Sailing Center. The whole purpose of community sailing organizations such as this one based at Fort Adams State Park is to make sailing more available and affordable, especially for kids and families. Kids 7 to 15 can join a two-week all-day sailing school, adults and kids 13 and up can take a three-day series of sailing lessons, a family can hire a private instructor to teach them all, you can just rent 18- or 22-foot

sailboats by the half or full day, or you can take a sailing tour of the harbor.
🏨 *53 America's Cup Ave., Newport 02840, tel. 401/849–8385 or 401/846–1983.*

Swimming

In the Northeast there are four areas that have the very best ocean beaches: the southern shores of Long Island and Rhode Island, the islands of Nantucket and Block Island, and Cape Cod. Not all beaches are equally safe for kids, however; those with riptides, sudden drop-offs, and heavy surf may be okay for older kids and adults familiar with the ocean, but little kids need shallow water, low wave action, and no undertow. It's important to realize that two beaches only ½ mile apart can have widely different conditions.

As everyone in our fair-skinned family burns quickly and few ocean beaches offer shade, we usually haul a portable umbrella just in case we can't find one to rent. In July and August, the biggest problem at just about any beach in the Northeast is parking. As the parking cost can be as high as $10 per day, whenever possible we stay at a hotel or in a cottage within walking or biking distance of at least one attractive beach.

I should say a word about swimming in lakes and rivers. Maine's Sebago Lake (see Chapter 10 *and* Camping, *above*) is sandbottomed, fringed with pines and sand beaches (though except for the state park, all are privately owned by individuals and resorts), and crystal clear. Lake Champlain's shoreline in both Vermont and New York offers few sand beaches (except in Vermont's Grand Islands area) but clean and delicious water. See also Chapter 10 for state parks with good places to swim.

Massachusetts

Cape Cod

The choice of different kinds of beaches (there are 150) on the Cape overwhelms: on protected Cape Cod Bay, the surf is gentle, and shallow water seems to stretch forever; southside beaches on Nantucket Sound have rolling surf and are warmed by the Gulf Stream; at the round, deep freshwater kettle ponds tucked away behind ocean beaches, water is warm and calm too, like big swimming pools; at open ocean beaches, waves of cold water curl in and slap the beach with force and vigor. A beach sticker is often required for parking; weekly rates are cheaper. (*See also* Chapter 5.)

👫 ALL

Cape Cod National Seashore. The park's ocean beaches are spectacular, but for families, Herring Cove Beach and Race Point Beach in Provincetown (see Chapter 10) are more protected; Race Point Beach is prettier, with more sun, dunes and a feeling of remoteness.
🏨 *South Wellfleet 02663, tel. 508/349–3785. Open weekdays 8–4:30.*

👫 13 – 15

Craigville Beach. With fine sand, gentle surf, and warm water, this beach is extremely popular with teens. Here you'll find volleyball games, food, showers, and bathrooms.
🏨 *Near Hyannis.*

👫 ALL

Flax Pond. In Nickerson State Park (see Chapter 10), this is warm and calm, ideal for toddlers, with a nice beach and picnic areas, lifeguards, a snack bar, a playground, and boat and Windsurfer rentals plus instruction.
🏨 Rte. 6A, Brewster 02631, tel. 508/896–3491. *Free.*

(朴朴 **ALL**)

Old Silver Beach. A long crescent of soft white sand is kept shallow at one end by a sandbar, which makes tidal pools with crabs and minnows. It has lifeguards, bathrooms, showers, a snack bar, and lots of parking. 🏠 *North Falmouth.*

(朴朴 **ALL**)

Sandy Neck Beach. This 6-mile barrier beach between the bay and marshland is one of the Cape's most beautiful, with sand dunes and a sand and pebble beach that looks like it goes on forever. At low tide shallow pools form for splashing and paddling, but stay away from the area where four-wheel-drive vehicles are allowed. Just before dusk musicians, storytellers, and mimes perform around a campfire. It has a snack bar and full facilities. 🏠 *Sandy Neck Rd. off Rte. 6A, West Barnstable. Parking $8.*

(朴朴 **ALL**)

West Dennis Beach. On the warmer south shore, this beach has an open feeling and extensive parking, as well as Windsurfer rentals, bathhouses, a playground, and food. 🏠 *West Dennis.*

Nantucket

Believe it or not, the waters around Nantucket are warm from mid-June through September, and the warmest, calmest water is on the north shore. **Jetties Beach,** where the annual sand sculpture contest is held, has our vote as the best all-around beach for families because of its lively activities—a playground in the dunes, take-out food, swimming lessons for kids in the summer, water-sports rentals and lessons (see Sailing and Windsurfing, *above*), and tennis courts nearby.

New York

Long Island

The traffic on this island drives us wild, especially on summer weekends. The reason everyone, including us, is willing to put up with it is the fringe of magnificent wide beaches along Long Island's south shore that run practically its entire 103-mile length from (incredibly crowded) Jones Beach all the way to Montauk Point. The two areas we head for, for different reasons, are Fire Island and the South Fork, at the tip of the island.

Ocean swimming on these beaches requires some skill (see *below*), so when Gavin was small, we searched out bay beaches and those that border both the ocean and a large pond. A major difficulty is finding a beach where you can park for just the day. While anyone can simply walk onto a beach, parking at many is restricted to Nassau and Suffolk county residents and nonresidents who've paid an expensive full-season fee for a sticker, and this requirement is strictly enforced. Cars are towed. Only state parks and some town beaches have one-day-use parking fees, and lots fill up quickly.

(朴朴 **4 – 12**)

Fire Island National Seashore. Fire Island is the beach area we come to when we want to feel cut off from everything but sand and water and sky. There are no cars here, just boardwalks across the dunes. Two hours from New York City, this 32-mile-long strip of sand, dune, and beach grass no more than half a mile wide lies off Long Island's south shore between the ocean and the Great South Bay. In contrast to driving and driving on the Long Island Expressway to get to the South Fork, you have to take a ferry to get here. For day trips we go to the beach by the Sailor's Haven visitor center, which has a lifeguard, a marina, and an easy-to-get-to snack bar on the bay side. For

older kids, the Watch Hill center has the most active marina. (*See also* Chapter 10.)
🏨 *Park Headquarters, 120 Laurel St., Patchogue 11772, tel. 516/289–4810. Sailors Haven Visitor Center, tel. 516/597–6183.*

 0 – 15

Foster's Memorial Beach (Long Beach). On Noyac Bay, west of Sag Harbor, Long Beach is safe enough for 3- and 4-year-olds to sit in the water with a bucket and shovel while you watch from 5 feet away. Lots of families eat dinner here while watching the sunset.
🏨 *Southampton. Cost: parking $10.*

8 – 15

Hither Hills State Park. Montauk is wilder and more windswept than Easthampton, and this beach is sometimes swathed in mysterious mists (see Camping, *above*).

3 – 15

Main Beach. There's a casual elegance to this white-sand beach on the South Fork that makes it one of the most beautiful in the world; even the weathered wood pavilion has charm. It's also the only beach in Easthampton open to the general public. Everything you want is here—snacks, Windsurfers, swimming lessons—but if you have little kids, you can't let them just noodle about in the water unless you are right next to them.
🏨 *End of Ocean Ave., Easthampton. Cost: permit $10 (at beach or at Easthampton Village Hall, 27 Main St., tel. 516/324–4150). Open weekdays 9–4.*

Rhode Island

South County

The stretch of coastline from Watch Hill at the Connecticut border to Narragansett, which Route 1 parallels, consists almost entirely of town or state-owned sandy beaches, some of which are restricted to

town residents with a sticker. These are mostly wide, flat beaches with the merest hint of dune, more accessible, but not as beautiful as those on Long Island.

 5+

Misquamicut State Beach and Atlantic Beach. For people-watching, teen action, and body surfing, this 7-mile-long, very wide beach park is *it*. There's even an amusement park with minigolf, kiddie rides, and a Ferris wheel right here. Expect crowds and loud music from boom boxes. The water is very clean, although occasionally August can bring in an excess of seaweed. Surf is usually mild to moderate, and there's little undertow.
🏨 *Atlantic Ave. (off Rte. 1; follow signs), Westerly, tel. 401/596–9097.*

6 – 15

Narragansett Town Beach. A highly accessible, yet perfect New England beach of miles of fine white sand that you can walk to from town, it has some of the best surfing on the East coast; for older teens who want to learn, free lessons are given by the pros once a week in summer. There's little undertow and a gradual drop here.
🏨 *Rte 1A, Narragansett, tel. 401/783–3563.*

6+

Ninigret Conservation Area/East Beach. Outstandingly beautiful, this undeveloped barrier beach lies between Ninigret Pond, Rhode Island's largest salt pond, and Block Island Sound and borders the Ninigret National Wildlife Refuge. With few amenities (only a lifeguard and portable toilets in the tiny parking lot), a steep drop-off, and moderate surf, it is best for families who most want a long, uncrowded beach. (*See* Chapter 10.) Ninigret Pond is ideal for windsurfers. (Be warned that on weekends, the lot is filled by 8:30 in the morning.) If you crave more amenities and more kids, go to 4-mile-long **Blue Shutters Town Beach,**

which you pass on East Beach Road, and which has a snack bar and showers; its parking lot ($10) fills about an hour later.
🏠 *Conservation Area, end of East Beach Rd., off Rte. 1, Charlestown 12813, tel. 401/322–0450. Cost: $10 parking.*

(👫 1 – 10)

Roger W. Wheeler State Beach. It is safe for kids to romp in the surf at this clean beach protected by a jetty because there is no rough surf or undertow, and shallow water extends out quite a way. Swimming lessons, a playground, and picnic areas are added family attractions.
🏠 *Off Sand Hill Cove Rd., Narragansett, tel. 401/789–3563. Cost: $10 parking.*

Block Island

In contrast to the flat or rolling landscape of many other beach areas, this one is hilly, with breathtaking bluffs and moors, and small beaches in coves. A long, curved swath of beautiful sand beaches on the island's east side, known collectively as Crescent Beach, runs from Old Harbor to Jerry's Point, an easy walk up Corn Neck Road. All have gradual drops. **State Beach** (tel. 401/466–2611), the most crowded, has lifeguards, a snack bar, and bathrooms, and the gentlest surf, but we favor an unnamed, uncrowded area between it and Scotch Beach, recommended to us by a year-round resident. The prettiest is **Mansion Beach,** just north of the Great Salt Pond, with bayberry bushes, beach roses, and some moderate surf. Rocky areas at **Corn Neck Beach** that attract all kinds of fish are good for snorkeling.

Tennis

In nearly every community we've visited in the Northeast we've tracked down at least one or two tennis courts, and at many resorts (see Chapter 14), tennis is a major

sport, with tennis lessons and clinics for both parents and kids.

Rockywold-Deephaven Camps and the Balsams in New Hampshire, the Sagamore in New York State, and the Tyler Place and Basin Harbor Club in Vermont all have excellent programs. Tennis fanatics who crave a total family weekend or weeklong tennis immersion swear by the summertime tennis programs at ski resorts, especially those in Vermont, some of which offer instruction to very young kids.

Sugarbush Area, Mad River Valley

Two resorts in this serene, untouristy, 7-mile-wide valley with the Green Mountains on the west and the Roxbury Range on the east stand out in the Northeast for their family tennis programs, which are appropriate for kids as young as 3. These resorts also offer easy access to hiking in the Green Mountains and a variety of other sports. At both, small racquets, lower nets, and well-supervised group lessons make a big difference for little ones. For older kids, both have clinics to further skills and also arrange matches and round-robin doubles so kids can meet other kids their own age.

(👫 3+)

Bridges Resort and Racquet Club. See Chapter 14.
🏠 *Sugarbush Access Rd., Warren 05674, tel. 802/583–2922 or 800/451–4213.*

Sugarbush Resort Tennis School and Club

(👫 3–15)

I give the edge in instruction and variety to Sugarbush, ranked among the top six tennis schools in the country, where kids can be involved in as much or as little tennis as they like; for those who want less, a camp program of ropes courses, hiking, swimming, and field trips is the alternative. But I'm convinced the kids' program is so successful because the instructors have been specially trained to teach kids, and lessons, which start with a tiny tots program for 3- to 6-year-olds and continue with junior tennis weeks and round robin matches, have humor and informality.

🏨 *RR1, Box 350, Warren 05674, tel. 802/ 583–2381. Facilities: inn or condominium lodging, half- and full-day kids' camp, nursery, 27 outdoor courts, 3 indoor courts, 18-hole golf course, indoor and many outdoor pools. AE, D, MC, V.*

Stratton Mountain Resort

👫 7 – 15

Huge, sprawly, and open, Stratton is a self-contained resort village overlaid with a country-club atmosphere. If your kids want to split their time between tennis and mountain biking, they ought to be ecstatic here. The biggest advantage for families, however, is the wide variety of discounted lodging choices if you buy a tennis package. The junior tennis program, in which kids play a minimum of 4½ hours per day, is only for 7- to 17-year-olds. The courts are conveniently ringed around the Sports Center at the base of the slopes.

🏨 *Stratton Mountain 05155, tel. 802/297– 2200 or 800/843–6867. Cost: tennis packages, $185–$385 adults, $60–$245 kids. Facilities: many lodging packages, kids' adventure camp, gondola rides, mountain biking rentals and trails, 27-hole golf course, 23 outdoor and 4 indoor courts, sports center with pool. AE, D, MC, V.*

Tubing Peaceful Streams and River Rapids

The kind of tubing our family has done is the easy kind, simply sprawling on an inner tube

in bathing suits and drifting lazily downstream with the current for an hour or two on flat, calm rivers. For that, all we need are basic tubes, life jackets, towels, a pair of old sneakers, a pleasant stream—and someone with a car to pick us up at an agreed-upon take-out point. Even younger kids can manage such an outing if the stream is shallow and slow, with few rocks. Tubing in a Class II river (see White-Water Rafting for explanation of class categories), where you contend with 1- to 3-foot waves, is exciting, but too challenging and scary for those much under 12. Either way, expect to get wet and wear a T-shirt and hat and plenty of sunblock. Go in July and August, when the water is warmer.

Connecticut

Farmington River, New Hartford to Canton

👫 10 – 15

Similar to the Esopus (see below) in exciting rapids, the 2½-mile stretch popular for tubing on this river strikes me as safer because there are fewer rocks, and a lifeguard is stationed at the biggest rapids to ensure that those who overturn get to shore safely. On a hot day, the three sets of rapids are thick with shrieking teenagers, who, we observed, sometimes climb out and hike back to do them again. **Jason's Farmington River Tubing** (140 Main St., Rte. 44 and the Farmington River, New Hartford 06057, tel. 203/693–2598; $7, including life jacket and shuttle) rents tubes with handles. Kids as young as 10 who are at least 54 inches tall can use the 42-inch tubes.

Maine/New Hampshire

Saco River, North Conway to Hiram Falls

👫 7 – 12

The slow-moving Saco, ideal for family canoers (see Canoeing, above) is almost too slow for tubing, though you'll see many trying it. Bring your own tube, as shops in the area do not rent them. There are many entry points along the river; check with **Saco Bound** (Box 119, Rte. 302, Center Conway 03813, tel. 603/447–2177, or Main St., North Conway 03860, tel. 603/447–3801) for information.

New York

Delaware River, Sullivan County

(👫 8 – 15)

Floating and bobbing over a 3-mile Class I section of gentle riffles on this river boundary between New York state and Pennsylvania (*see also* Canoeing, above, and White Water Rafting, *below*) is just exciting enough to be fun, but relaxing compared to tubing the Esopus. With time out for a swim, it takes about two to three hours, and the best time is after lunch. **Kittatiny Canoes** (Dingmans Ferry, PA 18328, tel. 800/356–2852; $14 per day), with six outposts along 135 miles of river, three in New York State, rents their own custom-made tubes and provides life jackets.

Esopus Creek

(👫 12+)

Tubing on the rapids of the fast-flowing, rocky Esopus Creek, a Class II waterway in the Catskill Forest Preserve, is a hot summer afternoon adventure for families with kids over 12 who won't be daunted by the 1- to 3-foot-high waves. You bounce along on huge truck-size inner tubes; if the water isn't high enough (check with the shop below) you're likely to bump on rocks and get a few bruises. A few caveats: Kids under 15 should wear helmets; everyone should wear life jackets and canvas shoes for protection; kids should not be allowed to tube without an adult. **Town Tinker**

Tube Rental (Bridge St., Phoenicia 12464, tel. 914/688–5553; $7 regular tubes, $10 tubes with seats), rents tubes and equipment and provides bus shuttle service regularly on weekends.

Watching for Whales

Whale-watching is a hot activity for adults and families in the Northeast, and you can catch a boat from any number of town wharfs in five states, from the tip of Long Island to northern Maine. Although kids agree seeing a whale is incredibly exciting, especially if it swims under and around the boat, what they don't like is sitting around, gazing out over expanses of water, and waiting, waiting, and waiting some more. A little pre-trip education helps, though whale-watch boats usually carry a naturalist who spouts some amazing facts about whale habits on the way out so kids know what to look for.

Consider trips that take four hours or less, in larger boats to minimize rolling, that guarantee whale sightings (if you don't see one, you get a repeat trip), and offer food, drink, and a sheltered, preferably heated, cabin area. The whale-watching season is April to October, but the best months are the warmer ones, mid-June through September. Only four kinds of whales appear in the Northeast—fin, right, minke, and humpback—and you rarely see all kinds.

Out on the water, the temperature will be at least 10, sometimes 20 degrees cooler, and kids may get wet from the spray. Wear long pants and rubber-soled shoes, and bring sunglasses, sunscreen, a hat, a sweatshirt, a waterproof windbreaker, and binoculars. If kids start to feel sick, stay out in open air; keep eyes on the horizon; nibble on plain crackers. *Where the Whales Are* by Patricia Corrigan (Globe Pequot, 1991) lists all the trips in North America.

Maine

Bar Harbor

When you travel out from Bar Harbor to Mount Desert Rock, where the whales' feeding grounds are, you sail around Acadia National Park. Fewer whale-watch vessels ply these waters than ply the Stellwagen Bank (see below). Dress warmly.

👨‍👦 8 – 15

Acadian Whale Watcher **and** *Sea Bird Watcher.* The *Sea Bird Watcher* is a new, fast 70-foot boat that offers a 3½-hour trip. Both boats have heated cabins and carry naturalists trained by the National Audubon Society. Midweek is busiest.
🏨 *Golden Anchor Pier, 56 West St., Bar Harbor 04644, tel. 207/288–9794 or 207/288–9776. Cost: $22–$25 adults, $14–$18 kids 7–14.*

Massachusetts

Massachusetts Bay

Whales travel the length of the Gulf of Maine, but the greatest number congregate in the Stellwagen Bank, a huge, watery feeding ground of plankton that attracts some 500 whales annually for a summer-long dinner party in Massachusetts Bay just between Provincetown and Gloucester.

This is the prime east-coast whale-watching territory, yet it's only 6 miles from Provincetown harbor. You won't necessarily see more whales than you will in Maine, but it will be warmer on the ocean. Though I've included trips from other points, taking off from Provincetown is ideal for kids; because you're already 30 miles out at sea, it takes far less time before you actually see a whale.

👨‍👦 8 – 15

Captain John Boats. Of the several boats of this modern fleet, one is quite large, with a spacious, enclosed cabin that has seats, tables, and a big snack bar, as well as an upper deck. Onboard naturalists are research scientists who track these whales all year long and know most by name. Though sightings are not guaranteed, in practice the company gives rain checks if no whale is sighted. Trips are four hours long; it usually takes about 45 minutes to an hour before whales are spotted.
🏨 *Town Wharf, 117 Standish Ave., Plymouth 02360, tel. 508/746–2643 or 800/242–2469. Cost: $21 adults, $14 kids under 12.*

👨‍👦 8 – 15

Hyannis Whale Watcher Cruises. The only excursions from the mid-Cape use a large boat that accommodates 300.
🏨 *Millway Marina, Barnstable Harbor, Hyannis 02630, tel. 508/362–6088 or 800/287–0374. Cost: $10–$22; kids under 4 free. Apr.–Oct., 2 to 3 3½-hr trips a day.*

👨‍👦 8 – 15

Ranger V. My pick for the best trip for kids is the *Ranger V,* the largest whale-watching boat on the Cape, which carries 415 passengers. The size guarantees minimal rocking, and virtually eliminates seasickness. Family-owned and run, it appreciates young passengers.
🏨 *MacMillan Pier; ticket office, Bradford St. at Standish St., Provincetown 02657, tel. 508/487–3322, 508/487–1582, or 800/992–9333. Cost: $10–$18; kids under 7 free. Mid-May–mid-Nov., 3 3½-hr trips a day.*

👨‍👦 12 – 15

Voyager. This is a long trip, 5½ hours, but for kids the big draws are the naturalists from the aquarium staff on board, one of whom presides over an on-board tidal pool with creatures that can be touched, plus all the equipment to check out. A radar fish finder, a hydrophone so you can hear what dolphins sound like, an underwater video camera that projects views of whales' actions underwater on the boat's several TV screens, and a computer system keep kids absorbed.

🏛 *New England Aquarium, Central Wharf, Boston, tel. 617/973–5277 for information, 617/973–5281 for reservations. Cost: $24 adults, $16.50 kids.*

White-Water Rafting

White-water rafting can be exhilarating for families without being totally terrifying and can be appropriate for kids as long as they know how to swim, like boats and the water, and are old enough—at least 8 (50 pounds). Some rafting companies will take younger kids; I don't advise it. Rivers differ in how dangerous and difficult they are to maneuver; that depends on both the time of year (wilder in April than in August) and also on the intensity and nature of the rapids. A classification system that ranks their difficulty from I (flat water with no more than riffles, and the easiest) to V (for experts only), gives you some guidance. Kids under the age of 13 should stick pretty much to Class II and III, but even on a Class II river, expect to get wet.

Maine and Massachusetts have the strictest regulations in terms of guide licensing and quality and condition of equipment. All outfitters listed here give safety talks prior to the trip and cater to families. Forget April (the water is too high), May, and even the beginning of June, when the water is still so cold you have to wear a wet suit to stay warm.

Maine

Kennebec River

(👫 8 – 15)

There are two sections to this big, warm river rushing through a landscape of wild northern forest wilderness. In the upper section, Kennebec River Gorge, you'll find water in the Class III and IV categories; adventurous kids 12 and up (weighing 90 or more pounds) are permitted on this part of the trip. Below the Gorge is Carry Brook, 6 miles of easy, gentle rapids even 8-year-olds might enjoy, but with just as much wilderness scenery. Outfitters offer families various possibilities—a split trip for adults and kids or a half-day trip on the easy section. Family-run **Crab Apple Whitewater, Inc.** (Crab Apple Acres Inn, Rte. 201, HC63 Box 25, The Forks 04985, tel. 207/663–4491 or 800/553–7238) has been in the business for 10 years and is very family-oriented, with guides who are especially friendly to kids. **Saco Bound/Down East White Water** (Box 119, Rte. 302, Center Conway, NH 03813, tel. 603/447–2177; *see* Canoeing *in* New Hampshire, *above*), is highly reliable, with considerable experience with families. Both outfitters' trips cost between $60 and $90, including lunch.

Massachusetts

Deerfield River, Fife Brook

(👫 8 – 15)

The 12 miles of fast-flowing river, mostly Class II, with one Class III rapids, that pass through Mohawk Trail State Forest make a good introductory guided raft trip for kids because of the easy rapids, pleasant swimming spots, and abundance of wildlife. Six-hour-long trips include time for lunch and plenty of swimming. **Crab Apple White-**

water, Inc. (see *above*) runs trips for $45 to $60, including lunch.
🏨 *Charlemont.*

New York

Delaware River, Sullivan County

👫 8 – 15

The combination of relatively tame rafting with the spectacular scenery more common to intense gorge rapids draws many families to this wide, swiftly flowing Class I+ and II river, where you need no guide to accompany you. Along the most scenic section, from Pond Eddy to Matamoras, high shale cliffs with ribbon waterfalls and unusual rock formations rise straight up from water so clear you can look down and see fish. Your kids will probably spot beaver lodges and birds of all kinds, from blue herons to bald eagles. **Kittatinny Canoes** (Dingmans Ferry, PA 18328, tel. 800/356–2852; $23–$25 per person; children under 12 free when 4th, 5th, or 6th in a raft) offers continuous daily trips on six-person rafts from three locations on the upper Delaware at bargain prices, especially for families with several children. Shuttle service and life jackets but not lunch are included.
🏨 *Matamoras, PA 18336.*

Sacandaga River

👫 8 – 15

This short, fun-filled, and exciting but not intimidating introduction to rafting takes under two hours and travels 3½ miles over Class II and some Class III rapids. It's for families who just want a taste of white water; the trip doesn't have the wild and adventurous flavor of longer trips on more spectacular rivers. **W.I.L.D. W.A.T.E.R.S.** (Rte. 28, Box 197AHCR01, Warrensburg 12885, tel. 518/494–7478; $12 adults, $10 kids under 12) runs regular trips daily. Reservations are not necessary, though they are advisable.

ON SNOW AND ICE
WINTER SPORTS

13

Winter in the Northeast is usually cold, sometimes brutally cold, and snowy. But the mountain landscape, quaint towns, and cozy lodges of northern New England and New York lend themselves to family vacations that embrace the ice and snow. To us the season means skiing, sledding, ice-skating, and the justly famous snow sculpture contests at the area's winter carnivals. Most downhill areas I've included also offer cross-country skiing, as well as sleigh rides and ice-skating.

I think of a ski trip as an ideal family vacation because skiing is fun for everyone, beginner or expert, young or old. Ski areas automatically provide kids with time with peers and allow parents some time alone together. Ski areas in New England and New York state compete to attract families, offering baby-sitting, discount lift tickets, teen centers, and other lures. One new development in the 1990s that may prove a bargain for families is the multiple-area lift pass (either season, day, or several-day). In 1995, for example, you can buy a book of lift-pass coupons good at Vermont's Killington, Bromley, and Mount Snow/Haystack, New Hampshire's Waterville Valley, and Maine's Sugarloaf. A pass good at Maine's Sunday River is also valid at Vermont's Sugarbush and New Hampshire's Attitash. There are several other linked resorts, and the trend is growing.

Among the nearly 100 downhill ski areas in the Northeast, I've chosen only those that my family or skiing families I know have found particularly family-friendly and that offer the most for families with kids of all ages and abilities. All described here have good nursery facilities and excellent ski school programs designed for children as well as adults, a casual atmosphere, and other family amenities. Most nurseries, for example, rent pagers; if your child is having a hard day, the staff will contact you. The ski schools have teaching programs that rely on games and other tempting activities and have a teacher/student ratio of no more than 1:6 for kids under 7, and no more than 1:10 for kids older than that.

I have to admit that I am prejudiced in favor of ski areas that feature SKIwee programs for kids because I watched my son prosper in this system. SKIwee is an all-day learn-to-ski program (lunch and hot chocolate breaks included) developed by *Ski* magazine in which kids learn through games from instructors who have been specifically trained to teach kids. At the end of the day, what your child has learned is noted on a progress card that you can take with you—and use at any other area with a SKIwee program.

All areas rent ski equipment; areas with ice-skating also rent skates. Remember that it's essential to make reservations for the nursery, children's programs, and children's rental equipment well in advance, especially for holidays and weekends. Although there are many lovely places to cross-country ski, I've deliberately chosen only those that rent kids' equipment, give kids' lessons, and have some super-easy and well-groomed and patrolled trails.

The most complete guide to skiing for families is the biennial *Skiing With Children* from TWYCH (Travel with Your Children, 45 W. 18th St., 7th Floor, New York, NY 10011, tel. 212/206–0688; $29 for non-subscribers, $15 for subscribers). It's also worth taking a look at the September, October, and November issues of *Ski, Skiing,* and *Snow Country* magazines; every year they rate resorts based on readers' experiences and their own and alert you to new bargains.

If your children are just beginning to ski, read *A Very Young Skier* by Jill Krementz (Dial, 1990) or, for kids 8 and up, *The Usborne Book of Skiing* (Usborne, 1986), an illustrated informational guide to equipment, techniques, and history.

Maine

Maine ski areas sometimes have natural snow when others do not, and vice versa. The big pluses are the generally lower prices for everything from lodging to all-day children's programs and, at most areas, smaller crowds and shorter lift lines. These areas' big drawback for many families in southern New England and New York is how long it takes to get to west-central Maine: eight hours by car from New York City, 4½ from Boston, and 2½ from Portland, Maine. The small resorts like Shawnee Peak and Big Squaw Mountain are friendly and rustic—appealing for families—but as most of them have what I call layer-cake skiing—experts at the top, intermediates in the middle, and beginners at the bottom—and limited options for some age groups, I've opted to include only Maine's two major ski resorts.

Sugarloaf/USA

The modern village at the base of Sugarloaf Mountain is the largest on-mountain ski vil-

lage in the Northeast. Architecture here doesn't try to be a contemporary version of a quaint New England town—the dormered six-story hotel is brick and restaurants serving sophisticated food and drink sport greenhouse sections with views of the slopes. The area makes a hit with families because of its convenience—facilities, lodgings, restaurants, and an indoor sports center clustered by the central lifts—and its varied activities. Rock concerts for teens, excellent day care for little ones, a kids-only ski slope, the only above-the-timberline skiing in New England, hard to easy slopes, even half-hour dogsled rides (tel. 207/246–4461) through pines and over mountains pulled by 12 all-white Samoyeds. You can walk or ski almost everywhere.

This is a big area with a lot for all skiers—beginning, intermediate, or expert. Beginners appreciate the novice area around the base where three chair lifts lead to three beginner-only trails. These lifts' $5-a-day ticket for all riders is a special bargain. Ten additional easy slopes are reserved for slow skiers—hot-doggers caught bombing around on them must forfeit their lift tickets until they watch a film on safe skiing—and are ideal for family runs with younger children. More than 60% of the trails are intermediate (long runs wind down the face of the mountain offering wonderful views), but unlike other family-friendly New England areas, Sugarloaf satisfies families that include at least one expert downhill skier, adult or teenager: The vertical is higher than that of any peak in the northeast other than Killington's in Vermont (much more crowded) and Whiteface's at Lake Placid, New York. From the steep, open snowfields that cover the summit you can take some of the most challenging black-diamond runs in the east. If you love bumps, try Sugarloaf's bone-rattling Skidder. The trails, which do include a few easy runs from high elevations, spread out like a fan from the snowfields, but Sugarloaf's scale rules out letting preteens, even good skiers, head off by themselves. Ski together as a family or take advantage of the superb nursery and the ski school.

The best deals for families are the three annual family weeks in January, February, and March; kids 12 and under stay free in their parents' room and get lessons, lift tickets, equipment, and use of the health club free. Musical performances, movies, magic shows, and other evening events also appeal to all ages.

A bright, cheery nursery takes kids from 6 weeks to 6 years daily and Wednesday and Saturday nights from 6 to 10. Three-year-olds who want to try skiing use equipment free. Both 4- to 6-year-olds (Mountain Magic) and 7- to 12-year-olds (Mountain Adventure) can take half- or full-day programs. The intermediate kids' adventure slope, "Moose Alley," has a ½-mile-long trail with its own warming lodge where you can get hot chocolate and cookies.

Sugarloaf's excellent Mountain Adventure is a fast-paced daily ski clinic for 13- to 16-year-olds, who can hang out later at an alcohol-free nightclub, Rascals. The club is primarily frequented by kids who can't yet

drive, and video games and pool are the biggest attractions. One night a week teens take over the health club.

On-mountain lodging includes condos, an inn, and a hotel, which are moderate to very expensive; the older condos are closer to the lifts. Lodging packages include use of the health club. The access road (Rte. 27) has some attractive, informal, friendly, and inexpensive lodges.

🏠 *RR1, Box 5000 (off Rte. 27), Kingfield 04947, tel. 207/237–2000; 207/237–2000 snow report; 800/843–5623 on-mountain lodging; 800/843–2732 area-wide reservations. Facilities: 101 trails, 14 lifts, gondola, 20 restaurants, nursery, ski school, teen center, 3 pools, fitness club, laundromat, hotel, condos, shuttle buses. AE, MC, V.*

CROSS-COUNTRY SKIING. Sugarloaf's **Touring Center** (tel. 207/237–2000) is the terminus for 85 kilometers (53 miles) of cross-country trails along old logging roads, through piney forests, and down an old narrow-gauge railway track, looping through the Carrabasset Valley. Because Sugarloaf gets so much snow, cross-country skiing here is usually good even fairly late in the season.

Sunday River

Maine's other major ski resort is a combination of the West and New England. It's huge, a complex of interconnected trails (including six trails on a mountain developed in 1994) that sprawl across seven mountains with slope-side lodging in modern, low condos and a few country inns. You'll find more diversity of terrain here than at any other ski area in New England: long runs and varied trail configurations for experts and intermediates. New trails and lodging (including a massive four-story wood-frame hotel and conference center that has both old-fashioned shutters and contemporary sleekness) have been added at a rapid pace since the 1980s, but the atmosphere remains low-key and focused on the slopes rather than glitz. Five miles away down a level road is Bethel, a historic New England village so perfect that it was once featured in a Christmas-card commercial, where the *Silver Bullet Express* ski train arrives from Portland. The key attractions for families here are the teaching program at the excellent children's ski school (ranked No. 1 in the east by readers of *Ski* magazine in 1993); the child care; the snowboard park and snowboard clinics for teens; and, for parents, a learn-to-ski program that guarantees you'll be skiing independently on easy trails by the end of the first day. If you and your children are learning to ski or trying to get to the next level, Sunday River is a great place. It is also the place to come if any member of the family has physical disabilities: There is free skiing and instruction (tel. 207/824–3018) for both adults and children.

Though Sunday River can get crowded (it's only about an hour from Portland), there are usually only short waits because lifts are efficiently sited. The majority of the trails are intermediate; some intermediate and a couple of easy trails start from the peaks, but most of the highest trails are for experts. Although the wide variety of slopes spread out over several mountains is a plus, it's also a drawback for families: Lifts start from several different base areas in the valley, making it easy to lose kids unless you all stick together.

The day-care center and nursery for kids 6 weeks to 6 years occupies the ground floor of the Merrill Brook II condominium. Three- and 4-year-olds who want to try skiing can sign up for a one-hour, one-on-one private lesson complete with lift ticket and rental equipment ($28 for kids in the day-care program, $50 for those not in it).

Sunday River's ski school program for ages 3 and up has been so successful that other ski areas (including several in the West) have bought it. The method is adapted from the SKIwee program, but instructors receive extensive training in recognizing different learning styles; they find out just what works with each child and teach accordingly. An instructor in a class of 4- to 6-year-olds demonstrates a turn to one child, draws a diagram of the same maneuver in the snow for another, and gently pushes the legs of a third into the correct position so he can feel the difference—eliciting a shower of giggles. Kids here seem to progress faster because extra instructors shuttle among groups to whisk away those who are about to make the leap to the next level of skill for an hour or two of one-on-one coaching just when they need it.

Kids in SKIwee (4- to 7-year-olds) have their own center in Merrill Brook II, and the Mogul Meister program for 7- to 12-year-olds is adjacent. At night they can gather here for Camp Sunday River, with games, ski movies, supervised sledding, and more. Several nights a week there are sleigh rides (check at South Ridge Lodge, tel. 207/824–3000), ice-skating, or fireworks above the slopes.

The daily MTV (More Terrain and Vertical) ski school program for kids 12 and up tutors pretty good skiers who want to get better; it also hooks kids up with others their age. The popular teen nightclub, MVP, open from 7 to 11:30 PM on weekends and during holiday weeks, offers music, videos, and pizza. At the snowboard park you can take clinics and use the 350-foot-long half-pipe.

On-mountain lodging includes a hotel, trailside condos, and town houses that range from moderate to very expensive, plus an inexpensive inn and ski dorm. Nearby are several inexpensive, old-fashioned ski lodges. The town of Bethel is 5 miles away. ▲ *Box 450, Bethel 04217, tel. 207/824– 3000; 207/824–6400 snow conditions; 800/ 543–2754 lodging reservations. Facilities: 101 trails, 14 lifts, ski school, sleigh rides, 9 restaurants, 7 pools, fitness center (at hotel). AE, D, MC, V.*

CROSS-COUNTRY SKIING. Sunday River Inn and Cross-Country Ski Center (tel. 207/824–2410) nearby has 40 kilometers (25 miles) of groomed trails.

Massachusetts

The Berkshire hills of western Massachusetts shelter a number of friendly ski areas; the hills are gentler than those farther north and offer mostly beginner and intermediate slopes. Several are just right for an introduction to skiing, a family day trip, or a weekend outing, especially when it's very cold up north. An excellent, comprehensive guide to all winter sports in this area, including some wonderful off-the-beaten-path cross-country trails, is *Skiing Downhill and Cross-Country in the Berkshire Hills* by Lauren Stevens and Lewis Cuyler (Berkshire House, 1990).

Butternut Basin

Butternut has neither on-mountain lodging nor the flavor of a charming, cohesive ski town or resort, nor the size and variety of places farther north. But for a day trip or even a weekend it offers a friendly family atmosphere, very clean, modern, attractive and sunny base lodges with old-fashioned, tasty fast food (in the spring bring your lunch and eat on the sunny deck overlooking the slopes), a strong SKIwee program on weekends, and two completely separate beginner lifts and slopes for kids. It's only a two-hour drive from most of Connecticut, Westchester County, and the Springfield area.

The biggest drawbacks are the weekend crowds and lift lines, though kids who are in beginner SKIwee classes won't have to wait long at their lifts. If you can, get here early, ski, and eat lunch by 11:30. There's not much for teens—no night skiing or snowboard park—but the ski shop, where Gavin usually has to spend at least some time, has a wide (though pricey) selection of ski wear and junior racing wear. The trails are mostly broad, open, well-configured beginner and

intermediate runs; my son loves the panoramic view of the Berkshires from the summit.

The best bet here for kids 4 to 12 is the weekend SKIwee program. The beginner area has wide, gentle slopes and is right by the main base lodge, so it's easy to ski over from other slopes periodically to check on how your child is doing. Instructors are warm and friendly. A sweet nursery in a three-room log cabin takes up to 25 kids 2 to 6, but will accept younger ones if you reserve. The number of caretakers varies, but the ratio is one adult to four or five kids.

The area is small and compact enough that kids who are good skiers can explore by themselves; Gavin favors the coin-operated slalom run, where you can race against the clock or another skier on a parallel course.

Motels and inns on Route 23 are closest to the ski area; you'll also find places ranging from moderate to very expensive in nearby Great Barrington, South Egremont, and Stockbridge.

🏠 *Rte. 23 (2 mi east of town), Great Barrington 01230, tel. 413/528–2000; 413/528–4433 ski school; 800/438–7669 snow conditions; 413/528–4006 area lodging (Great Barrington Chamber of Commerce). Facilities: 22 trails, 8 lifts, 2 cafeterias, 7 km (4.3 mi) cross-country trails. AE, D, MC, V.*

Jiminy Peak

Jiminy Peak is small, but its atmosphere and amenities are similar to those at more major resorts in Vermont—and it's only 2½ hours from New York City. We like the convenience of the handsome neo-colonial clapboard condominiums and suite hotel clustered at the base of the lifts, the clean, roomy cafeterias, and the variety of intermediate and black-diamond trails. It's ideal for a weekend, especially for a family of good intermediate skiers who want to ski together. Because of the area's small size, congenial atmosphere, and converging trail layout, this is also a place to let kids explore the mountain on their own. One drawback, though: The slopes here tend to ice up in the afternoon, more so than at Butternut.

The two-room nursery with a staff of one adult for five kids and lots of toys in a big room takes babies from 6 months, and the SKIwee program accepts children ages 4 to 12. Though there's a beginner J-bar lift and a separate beginner slope, I think the beginner area and program at Butternut are superior. The facilities for small ones here are a bit out of the way, and the ski-school meeting area can be congested.

The best bet for kids is the Mountain Adventure program—eight weekends of instruction for 6- to 15-year-olds with the same teacher. Night skiing is about it for teen action, says Gavin, but the black-diamond trails are pretty challenging.

The resort's expensive to very expensive on-mountain lodging hotels and condos (see Chapter 6) is the most convenient; less expensive inns and motels are nearby in Hancock and Pittsfield.
🏠 *Corey Rd., Hancock 01267, tel. 413/738–5500 or 800/882–8859 information and on-mountain lodging; 413/443–9186 or 800/237–5747 area lodging (Berkshire Visitor's Bureau); 413/738–7325 snow conditions. Facilities: 28 trails, 7 lifts, 2 restaurants 2 cafeterias, 1 bar, ice-skating, nursery, ski school. AE, D, MC, V.*

New Hampshire

New Hampshire's White Mountains, dominated by looming 6,288-foot Mt. Washington, thrust up high, beautiful, rugged peaks in the northern part of the state. That's where you'll find the ski areas, many of which are easily accessible from Interstate 93. Direct national flights can land an hour from many of the slopes at Manchester airport. By car, Boston is two to three hours

away from most areas; New York is six. New Hampshire's ski areas usually have a casual, friendly feel, making them great for families.

Bretton Woods

Bretton Woods has the sociable, intimate atmosphere of a small, old-fashioned area, yet it has plenty of family amenities—and spectacular views of Mt. Washington. It's not glitzy or hectic with activities, and it has a variety of gentle yet interesting and winding runs that make it easy for the whole family to ski together or for kids to explore the mountain on their own, sheltered from wind by surrounding mountains. A limited lift-ticket policy keeps it generally uncrowded. Plus it offers convenience, comfort, and good value—an attractive three-level base lodge (which houses a nursery), easy parking and drop-off area, and the good packages for families at the resort's on-mountain town houses. If you have teens, there's night skiing, rare at Northeast ski areas.

During Family Fest Weeks (between Christmas and New Year's and Presidents' holiday week in February) kids can take sleigh rides, play games, and see movies. Most activities are geared to younger kids; except for the snowboard movie hosted by an extreme skier and pizza and sub parties, night skiing is the only choice for teens.

Most of the slopes are beginner and intermediate, among them several long, gentle runs from the top. Try eating at the mountain-top restaurant at the end of the high-speed quad chair lift; glass, china, and silverware are used to cut down on waste.

The Babes in the Woods nursery in the base lodge is open for 2-month-old infants to 5-year-olds from 8 to 5. If your children seem ready, they can spend part of the day in the hour-long snow play and ski readiness program, in which a ski instructor works with just two kids (equipment is included in the price). Children 3 to 12 can attend the excellent Hobbit Ski School's all-day (8:30 to

4) programs that teach through games involving characters from J.R.R. Tolkien's books. Lifts, lunch, equipment, two outdoor sessions, and supervised play are all included. (There's no half-day option, and the day is longer here than at most ski schools; for some younger kids it may be too long.) Kids 5 and under ski free on the T-bar lift. One big bargain for families with kids 6 to 15 who just want to ski rather than take lessons is the regular midweek (including holiday weeks) "pay-your-age" kids' ticket—an 8-year-old, for example, pays just $8 for the whole day.

Convenient on-mountain town houses have good family packages; a lovely, moderately priced lodge and a motor inn owned by Bretton Woods are nearby. You'll find inexpensive, clean, and functional motels in the town of Twin Mountain 5 miles away—some of these offer their own family packages.
🏠 *Rte. 302, Bretton Woods 03575, tel. 603/278–5000; 800/232–2972 information; 603/278–1000 Bretton Woods lodging; 800/245–8946 Twin Mountain Chamber of Commerce. Facilities: 30 trails, 5 lifts, 2 restaurants, 1 cafeteria, 2 bars, ski shop, ski and snowboard instruction, nursery, sleigh rides and ice-skating nearby. AE, D, DC, MC, V.*

CROSS-COUNTRY SKIING. Bretton Woods has superb cross-country skiing on its 90 kilometers (56 miles) of groomed trails. These go through the woods and over bridges, are well maintained and easygoing, and afford great views of Crawford Notch. The cross-country center (tel. 603/278–5181 or 800/232–2972) is a few miles from the base lodge.

Jackson Ski Touring Foundation

In Jackson, New Hampshire, a charming, traditional New England village below Mt. Washington, with a population of about 800, cross-country skiing is as good as it gets. The Jackson Ski Touring Foundation maintains a vast, well-groomed and marked (according to difficulty) trail network surrounding the town. There is a moderate fee for use of the trails, which wander up three river valleys in the White Mountain National Forest. You can set out on a ski tour from the door of your inn or ski to a restaurant for lunch.

The town has a lighted rink. **Nestlenook Farms Recreation Center** (tel. 603/383–0845) also has ice-skating, as well as sleigh rides in the country over arched bridges and along a river. On the sleighs, drawn by Clydesdales, are cushioned benches, brass lamps, and sleigh bells. Kids can feed reindeer in the woods and warm up with hot cider and hot chocolate afterward.

The **Jack Frost Nordic Ski School** (tel. 603/383–9657) schedules lessons for kids 6 and up on weekends. If your kids are too young to cross-country ski, you can rent a pulka (a special kids' sled) and pull them behind you.

The 15 or so places to stay in town range from condos to cozy inns and from inexpensive to very expensive. Some are much more appropriate than others for families, but the local Chamber of Commerce is very helpful and knowledgeable.
🏠 *Jackson Ski Touring Foundation, Box 216, Main St., Jackson 03846, tel. 603/383–9355 or 800/927–6697 information and snow conditions; 800/866–3334 area reservations (Jackson Resort Association); 603/356–3171 or 800/367–3364 (Mt. Washington Chamber of Commerce). Facilities: 156 km (100 mi) trails. MC, V.*

DOWNHILL SKIING. Two small nearby areas are particularly good for families with small children. **Black Mountain** (tel. 603/383–4490) in Jackson has bargain midweek lift tickets and a special weekend family ticket for two parents and two kids 15 or under. **King Pine Ski Area** (tel. 603/367–8896) at Purity Spring Resort (see Chapter 14), 25 minutes south of Jackson, with 50% beginner runs, offers excellent beginner instruction.

Loon Mountain

Just off the Kancamagus Highway only a few miles from Interstate 93 and Lincoln, Loon is a nice, friendly, family mountain that doesn't cost the earth. Condos (and a resort hotel) right on the mountain, some of which really are ski-in, ski-out; the friendly staff (who have a special rapport with kids); the free skiing for kids 12 and under midweek when parents participate in a five-day ski week; and the food on the mountain (especially the barbecue on the deck at Summit Lodge) all contribute to Loon's appeal. A free and funky steam train links one base lodge with the other. Condos and parking lots form a long strip at the foot of the mountain between the two clusters of lifts. You can also ice-skate on the lighted rink by the cross-country ski center, where you can rent skates.

Beginner slopes and trails are set apart here, so slow-skiing families don't have to worry about hotshots, but unfortunately the two beginner areas are at opposite ends of the strip at the base of the mountain. Lots of wide, easy intermediate and beginner trails and even one long, 2½-mile enforced-slow-skiing beginner run from the very top of the mountain make this area a good one for a family of beginning or low intermediate skiers. The expert slopes, accessible from a gondola from the base lodge, carve a separate sector of the mountain.

Loon Mountain limits lift tickets to reduce lines, but this means that unless you order a ticket in advance or stay in lodging that includes a guaranteed lift ticket, you probably won't get one on weekends or holidays. Though the arrangement of the lifts generally spreads skiers well, they end up jostling a bit on big holiday weekends.

The Honeybear nursery takes children from 6 weeks to 6 years; there's SKIwee for 3- to 8-year-olds and a Mountain Explorers program for kids 9 to 12. Three-year-olds staying in the nursery can take one or two short introduction-to-skiing sessions at no extra cost.

Young teenagers may find the Personal Performance Clinics worthwhile; they include two clinics a day, free use of the Nastar (racing) course, and video analysis. Unless your teen is interested in the clinics or just wants to ski and ski, I'd opt for a different area.

The on-mountain lodging includes both condominiums and a hotel with a pool. Accommodation at both ranges from moderate to very expensive and includes guaranteed lift tickets. Nearby Lincoln has inexpensive motels, many of which offer packages that also include guaranteed weekend lift tickets. 🏠 *Kancamagus Hwy., Lincoln 03251, tel. 603/745–8111, 603/745–8100 snow conditions, 800/227–4191 lodging. Facilities: 41 trails, 9 lifts. AE, D, DC, MC, V.*

CROSS-COUNTRY SKIING. Check at Loon's cross-country skiing headquarters near the base lodge for information (and lessons and rentals) on the 35 kilometers (21 miles) of trails. Be sure to try the logging road that parallels the East Branch of the Pemigewasset River, where two kids we know spotted lots of small wild animals and dramatic ice formations. Children under 10 can take a "tag-along" lesson with their parents for a reduced fee.

Waterville Valley

This resort in the White Mountain National Forest (with a 4,000-foot mountain as a backdrop) is one of my choices for the three best ski areas for families in the Northeast. In a cup surrounded by mountains, two of which, Tecumseh and Snow's Mountain, are laced with ski trails, this modern version of a cozy New England town centers on Town Square. Here families climb aboard horse-drawn sleighs for daily afternoon and evening rides, set out on the cross-country trail system, and play hockey or just skate on the big, covered skating rink. The interconnected clapboard buildings around the square house shops, restaurants, lodgings, entertainment, and a sports center; inns, lodges, and condos spread out beyond. Whether you want excellent child care, highly rated ski instruction, snowboard facilities, superb cross-country skiing, kids' and family activities, or plenty for teens to do, all of it is here, and the vacation packages for families with kids 12 and under (weekend, midweek, and weeklong) are a good value. There's even a program for children with physical disabilities. The town recreation department schedules family and children's activities on a regular basis, including regular Sunday night family movies and gym times divided by ages.

The three busiest times are the week between Christmas and New Year's, February President's Day week, and the third week in March. For teens, these weeks are the most fun. There are no special family weeks; five- and seven-day family packages that include nightly entertainment are available from December to March. Children 12 and under ski and stay free with most lodging packages, and the nursery is free when parents purchase a five-day midweek lift ticket.

The one flaw is that lodging is not ski-in, ski-out. No matter where you stay, you have to take at least a short shuttle bus ride to the base lodge; a circular road runs through the valley on which free buses travel all day long picking up and dropping off skiers. With a five-day midweek package, you can store your equipment at the base lodge free.

Most of Mt. Tecumseh's trails are intermediate; it has no long beginner runs, and the expert runs don't offer the variety, challenge, or lengths of those at Sugarloaf or Sunday River. Its trails do converge at the base, making it easy to find your kids, especially as the base lodge houses everything—ski school, nursery, lift ticket office, cafeteria, and pizza corner. Adult and kids' beginning trails and lifts are helpfully set off from the main runs; little kids even have their own easy-to-use surface lift. The widest selection of beginner runs is at Snow's Mountain, 2 miles away, but it has no base lodge, so you have to transport rental skis on the shuttle bus.

Two nurseries take 6-week-old infants to 4-year-olds. Slopeside Nursery in the base lodge has cheerful and well-equipped rooms in an enclave of the basement of the ski school building that opens up onto a children's terrain garden, making outdoor play, weather permitting, very easy. Curious George Nursery, in the village, is where the creators of the Curious George books once lived—a charming cabin whose nooks and crannies are filled with Curious George memorabilia and toys. It's open for kids up to age 9 daily and two evenings a week. The ratio of caregivers at both nurseries is high: one for every three infants and one for every five older kids. Infants and toddlers have their own rooms, and there's even a separate area for nursing mothers at both nurseries.

In the excellent SKIwee program 3- to 12-year-olds have both half- and full-day options that include indoor games. Three- to 5-year-olds have their own ski slope, Kinderpark, accessible only from the ski school. Nine to 12-year-olds (Mountain Scouts) stay with one instructor the entire day, eating lunch in one of the mountain restaurants, or they can sign up for Nastar race clinics.

Unlike most ski areas, Waterville Valley has a discounted teen lift ticket for 13- to 19-year-olds. The ski school offers teen camps during holiday weeks that spill over into after-ski sleigh rides, ice-skating parties, and more. Teens can go everywhere in the village on foot and hang out at Zoo Station, the under-21 club that's connected to the video arcade.

Most of the Valley's lodging is in expensive to very expensive condominiums and all-suite hotels, which have family packages that make them more reasonable, but the town has a few more moderately priced lodges and country inns as well. Nearby Campton has inexpensive bed-and-breakfasts.
🏠 *Waterville Valley 03215, tel. 603/236-8311 or 800/468-2553 information and lodging, 603/236-4144 snow report. Facilities: 53*

trails, 13 lifts, sports center (indoor pool, Jacuzzi, jogging track, indoor tennis courts), 5 restaurants, ski school, ski shop. AE, CB, D, DC, MC, V.

CROSS-COUNTRY SKIING. Waterville Valley's cross-country network, ranked among the 10 best in America by *Snow Country* magazine, has 105 kilometers (65 miles) of graded trails, of which 70 kilometers (43 miles) are groomed and patrolled; the rest are marked wilderness trails. Kids get their own special lessons.

New York

The Catskills and the Adirondacks contain numerous small and large ski areas. For information on small areas that are family-oriented, fun, and inexpensive for a day trip, see *Let's Take the Kids! Great Places to Go with Children in New York's Hudson Valley* by Mary Barile and Joanne Michaels (St. Martin's Press, 1990). In truth, except for Whiteface at Lake Placid, we (and our friends, including New York City residents) would rather ski in New England.

Whiteface/Lake Placid

Yes, Whiteface Mountain is terrific for down-hill skiing—and very uncrowded—but it's pretty cold up here. This classic, rugged eastern mountain, site of the 1980 Olympic Winter Games alpine events, is 965 meters (3,216 feet) high and offers very long (for the East), challenging runs as well as a good beginner area and lower prices than other major Northeast ski areas. Yes, there's a good kids' ski school with a SKIwee program and day-care. But the real reason for families to come here in the winter is that it and the village of Lake Placid 9 miles away are a center for off-slope winter activities that are unavailable at other ski resorts—bobsled rides on America's only Olympic bobsled run (you ride with two or three people, a driver, and a brakeman; it's for adventurous kids 12 and up); luge rides; skating on the

outdoor Olympic Speed Skating Oval (where Eric Heiden won five gold medals in the 1980 Olympic games) and on all the Olympic indoor rinks; and watching such competitions as the World Junior Alpine Skiing Championships. All the facilities used for the 1980 Olympics are still here and in use.

The town, which borders Mirror Lake, has an old-fashioned, European flavor; it's full of restaurants, shops, and movie theaters, yet small enough so that a 12- and a 14-year-old in one family we know could explore the town's many kitschy souvenir shops on their own.

Whiteface has runs spread out over two peaks; many steep, twisting trails lure advanced skiers, but the majority of runs satisfy intermediates or beginners. Nonetheless, this area is best for experts or intermediates (except children under 10) because those are the longer, more interesting trails; the beginner slopes are confined to the bottom of the mountain.

Kids Kampus, a sector of the mountain reserved for kids 1 to 12, has its own base lodge and cafeteria, a snow playground, a chair lift, and a handle tow. You can park here and then, after dropping your kids off, take a lift and ski to the base lodge or catch a shuttle. The nursery is open for children 1 to 6 from 8 to 4; kids 3 to 6 can join a play-and-ski program of indoor and outdoor activities for a half or full day. Kids 7 to 12 can also attend a half or full day, something most areas don't offer.

There is a teen mountain adventure program, but several teens we know prefer the snowboard park and coin-op racing; what they like best, besides just skiing, is trying all the other activities in the area, including shopping and exploring the town on their own.

A wide variety of inexpensive to expensive lodging in individual houses, condos, lodges, hotels, cabins, motels, and B&Bs is available in Lake Placid and as close to Whiteface as across the road from the ski area. But this is one area where I recommend staying in the town, preferably right on Mirror Lake and with indoor parking so you don't have to scrape ice and snow off your car in the morning. (*See also* Chapter 6.)

🔥 *Whiteface Mountain Ski Area, Rte. 86, Wilmington 12997, tel. 603/946–2223 resort reservations and information; Olympic Regional Development Authority, Lake Placid 12946, tel. 800/462–6236 information and ski conditions; Lake Placid Visitors Bureau, tel. 800/447–5224 reservations. Facilities: 65 trails, 10 lifts. AE, D, DC, MC, V.*

CROSS-COUNTRY SKIING. The Mt. Van Hoevenberg Cross-Country Center (tel. 518/523–2811) has 50 kilometers (31 miles) of wide, groomed, patrolled, and marked trails, including many easy but scenic ones good for children. Unlike most areas, the trails here are kept covered with snowmaking equipment. Intrepid families who want wilderness skiing can easily hook up with the Adirondack Park's trails.

OTHER ATTRACTIONS. Bobsled rides are expensive and scary; attending international luge and bobsled competitions is almost as exciting. Two kids we know advise walking up and down the mile-long course so you can watch the starts, see the sleds careen around the Omega Curve, and catch a glimpse of a sled almost upside down. At the Olympic Arena on Lake Placid's Main Street, you can go to figure-skating competitions and ice hockey tournaments. The ski-jumping competitions at Whiteface are thrilling—better live than on TV, according to our teen informants. For information on these events, contact the Olympic Regional Development Authority (tel. 800/462–6236).

In February, a highlight is the nearly 100-year-old Saranac Lake Winter Carnival nearby, which boasts an ice palace you can walk through (tel. 518/891–1990).

Vermont

Most of Vermont's 20 alpine ski areas and most of its cross-country areas are on or not far from Route 100, a north–south highway roughly near the center of the state that parallels the Green Mountains. Keep in mind that there can be great differences in temperature between the most southern resort—Mount Snow—and the most northern one—Jay Peak, almost at the Canadian border. If you have young children, opt for the more southern resorts in the coldest months. For information on Vermont skiing, check with The Vermont Ski Area Association (26 State St., Box 368, Montpelier 05601, tel. 802/223–2439).

Bolton Valley

Low-key, homey, moderately priced Bolton Valley lies in northern Vermont not far from Stowe and Smugglers Notch. It is a compact, self-contained, midsize area that was designed for families by Ralph DesLauriers, a father of 9. Despite its remote feeling, the area is only about 4½ miles from Interstate 89 (but the road is steep and winding, requiring good tires after a big snowfall) and is the ski mountain closest to the Burlington International Airport, about a half-hour away.

Here you don't need to use your car at all because the horseshoe-shape hotel with restaurants and shops below is right at the base of the mountain. The three main-mountain lifts are just up from the hotel, while the cheerful sports center is just down from the hotel. All runs converge at the attached base lodge, which means even young kids can easily come and go from the slopes to where you're staying or to the shops without needing supervision.

The area draws families staying a weekend or longer using Bolton Valley's other attractions—very reasonably priced package vacation plans, an excellent baby-sitting program, and family activities, which range from nightly feature films to sleigh rides to game nights. Unlike most Vermont ski areas, Bolton illuminates night skiing.

In the network of trails on two mountains you'll find gentle slopes designed for beginning and intermediate skiers. Some of the runs from the top of the mountain have spectacular views of Lake Champlain and the Adirondacks. Though you can take steep, short runs at the top and do a bit of glade skiing, a family of expert skiers would probably be bored.

The hotel is warm and cheerful but simple; signs are handwritten; the base lodge (being renovated) was slightly shabby in 1994; the sports center is like a big, friendly, family rec room; the food is simple, too. Kids, especially those under 12, seem happy here, but families looking for sophistication or excitement should go elsewhere.

Free skiing and lodging for kids 6 and under is a regular feature here, and different ski packages may include a two-for-one midweek special and a day-care/ski package in which one low price covers a full-day adult lift ticket and day-care for one child.

At the HoneyBear Child Care Center play and games, indoors and out, are supervised daily for infants from 6 weeks and children up to 6 years. Among the several small, cozy, brightly decorated rooms are, besides play areas, a kitchen and a separate room for infants. Four- and 5-year-olds can take one or two special SKIwee lessons; we liked the fact that instructors pick up kids at the child-care center and return them there. These lessons are shorter than the usual SKIwee sessions and take place in a special protected area with its own slower lift. (Three-year-olds must take a private lesson if they want to ski—a worthwhile rule.) Child care is available three nights a week; baby-sitters (most work at the resort) can be reached through the front desk.

You save money by enrolling your children for five days in SKIwee instruction for 5- to 7-year-olds (Cubs) or 7- to 12-year-olds

(Bears). Kids' Night Out is a three-evening-a-week activity program for 6- to 12-year-olds that includes movies, sleigh rides, scavenger hunts, and more. Families who want to ski together in the afternoon can opt for the half-day morning alternative.

Mountain Explorers (11- to 14-year-olds) and the A-Team (12- to 18-year-olds) challenge intermediate and advanced skiers afternoons (in the morning these kids are sleeping) on all types of terrain. In the evening teens can gather at the sports center, where movies appear on the big-screen TV at 5, 7, and 9 PM every night. Kids hang out at the indoor pool, play video games (not very up-to-date, says my son), ping-pong, and volleyball; on weekends and holiday weeks the center takes a more active role, setting up special game nights.

The best bets for lodging are the moderately priced resort hotel, the on-mountain condominiums, or the inexpensive inn on Mountain Road.

🏠 *Bolton, VT 05477, tel. 802/434–2131 or 800/451–3220. Facilities: 44 trails, 6 lifts. AE, D, DC, MC, V.*

CROSS-COUNTRY SKIING. The cross-country skiing at Bolton is good, with more than 100 kilometers (60 miles) of trails and a touring center behind the hotel where free popcorn is served next to the old potbellied stove. Because of their high elevation, the trails are among the first to open and last to close in the state.

Mountain Top Inn Touring Center

Mountain Top has been a center of ski touring for more than 30 years. Now, with 110 kilometers (66 miles) of wide, double-tracked trails and another 72 kilometers (45 miles) of single-track backcountry trails, it is an outstanding place to learn how to cross-country ski. Families can take advantage of the skating rink, sledding, tobogganing, saunas, a hot tub, horse-drawn sleigh rides, and winter horseback riding. You don't have to stay at the inn (see Chapter 14), but it turns out to be a good deal because all the activities and a ski-touring pass are included in the price.

🏠 Box 521, Mountain Top Rd., Chittenden 05737, tel. 800/445–2100; 802/773–1330 or 800/372–2007 area lodging. Facilities: restaurant, bar. AE, MC, V.

Mount Snow–Haystack

Mount Snow and neighboring Haystack (which Mount Snow owns and operates) constitute the southernmost big ski area in New England, meaning it's easier to get to than are many others: only about four hours by car from New York City and the Connecticut coast, less from Albany, Boston, and Hartford. The southern location also means that in midwinter Mount Snow can be as much as 15 degrees warmer than areas farther north—a real plus for families with small kids—but extensive snowmaking installations give it a long season (November to May).

The atmosphere is comfortable, unpretentious, and family-oriented; the ski school introduced the SKIwee program to the country; and two 15-year-old friends of ours rate the new snowboard park "awesome." Several families we know come here regularly on weekends for the Alpine Training Center, a members-only (about 200 families; anyone can join) lodge on the mountain, where you can store your skis, eat, and get to know other families. It sponsors a race training program for 8- to 18-year-olds and a development program for 5- to 16-year-olds; kids are grouped by age and ability and ski each weekend with the same group and coach.

Families can ski together here because over two-thirds of Mount Snow's trails (and all of Haystack's) are for intermediates, including most of the wide, sunny runs from the summit. Some steep slopes and bump trails do challenge the experts, including the scary Ripcord—at Mount Snow black diamond definitely means most difficult.

The one big drawback at Mount Snow is the crowds on weekends, especially in the cafeterias. If your family plans to ski together, you can go to the Carinthia Base Lodge or head for Haystack. Ideal for families with young children just learning to ski, Haystack has a special learning area with its own lodge and an inexpensive weekend family-of-four lift ticket. Though accessible from Mount Snow by shuttle bus, Haystack does have a condominium village of its own.

The four annual Teddy Bear Ski Weeks include five days of free skiing and special activities each evening for kids 12 and under who bring a teddy bear. During these weeks nearby inns offer a variety of lodging packages—usually free accommodations and meals for children sharing a room with parents, plus discounted lessons.

Next to the main base lodge is the well-equipped 4,500-square-foot Pumkin Patch Day Care Center. Infants (from 6 months) have their own room, as do toddlers. The center takes children up to 8 years old. Kids over 4 play indoors and out. Four- to 6-year-olds join SKIwee classes.

Regular SKIwee is for kids 7 to 12. Ski lessons start out at the Children's Learning Center, a separate, protected area with its own rope tows and terrain garden, and the SKIwee meeting place. Both half- and full-day programs are available for all kids. The children's learning center hosts evening movie and pizza parties for families (Wednesdays) or kids up to age 12 (Saturdays).

The best bet for teens here is being part of the Alpine Training Center. Good skiers also profit from being videotaped on the Lower Exhibition trail and critiqued free of charge. Saturday nights, from 8 to midnight, teens can listen or dance to live music or a DJ at a teen-run, supervised alcohol-free club at Carinthia Base Lodge.

Mount Snow also has a serious commitment to snowboarders, starting with the BOARDwee program for 7- to 12-year-olds.

The full-time staff of snowboard instructors uses the 2,500-acre snowboard park, which has a 135-meter (450-foot) half-pipe, banked turns, jumps, and its own lift. If your teenager is a snowboarder, avoid the college student weeks.

Mount Snow has no central sports facility. Try the outdoor ice skating rink and sledding on the Ski Baba Trail at Carinthia Base Lodge. You can take a 1½-hour sleigh ride at Adams Farm (tel. 802/464–3762) in Wilmington through meadows to a log cabin in the woods where you'll warm up with hot chocolate by an old-fashioned woodstove. Some lodges have their own small pools.

The resort has several on-mountain lodging options, from relatively expensive condominiums (except during special package weeks) to a less expensive lodge with suites. Several inexpensive inns border Route 100 just south of the mountain.

🏠 400 Mountain Rd., Mount Snow 05356, tel. 802/464–3333 information; 800/245–7669 or 802/464–8501 lodging; 802/464–2151 snow reports. Facilities: 84 trails (Mount Snow), 43 trails (Haystack), 24 lifts, 3 restaurants, 7 cafeterias, 5 bars, fitness center (for hotel guests only), nursery. AE, D, DC, MC, V.

CROSS-COUNTRY SKIING. Timber Creek (tel. 802/464–0999) is right across the road from Mount Snow. Nearby West Dover and Wilmington have four cross-country centers: the **Hermitage Inn** (Box 457, Wilmington 05363, tel. 802/464–3511), **Prospect Touring Center** (tel. 802/442–2575), the **Sitzmark Lodge** (E. Dover Rd., Wilmington 05363, tel. 802/464–3384), and the **White House Inn** (Box 757, Wilmington 05363, tel. 802/464–2135).

Okemo Mountain Resort

For families, Okemo's attractions lie in its convenience: All the facilities at the bottom of the mountain are close together so it's easy to drop kids off and to find one another at the end of the day; the 800 slopeside condominiums with their cost-cutting family packages (kids 12 and under stay free) really are ski-in/ski-out. One problem, however, is that the cluster of several-story buildings at the bottom of the mountain and the arrangement of the condos on the mountainside make you feel you're surrounded by high rises instead of out in the wild. Another drawback is that to reach the top, skiers must take a beginner lift and then transfer to other lifts partway up the mountain.

Unlike most other ski areas, Okemo is right next to a town. Ludlow has specialty shops with kid appeal, restaurants and pizza places that deliver, sleigh rides, a cross-country skiing center, lots of lodging choices (if the aesthetics of the on-mountain condos bother you, several old-fashioned, out-in-the-country inns are nearby), and a good program of town activities for kids.

The skiing is also family-friendly, particularly the long, wide beginner slope and two beginner lifts right across from the base lodge. The trails are mostly intermediate, with many long runs that kids and parents can ski together, and even a 4½-mile-long beginner trail from the top of the mountain. Although the fact that all the lifts and trails eventually funnel people into the same small area at the bottom has advantages, when the resort is very crowded, the lift lines are long, and you feel like you're skiing out of and into a traffic jam. One drawback for very good skiers is that many trails have the same configuration. The snowboard park, with a 126-meter (420-foot) half-pipe, has terrain and obstacles for jumps, rail slides, and other challenges.

The nursery, convenient in the lower level of the base lodge, is open daily and on some holiday evenings. Kids 1 to 6 play indoors and out. One bargain: Midweek day care is half price. Three- and 4-year-olds can take an easygoing, very basic—no lift riding—introduction to skiing.

Four- to 8-year-olds join the SKIwee program, which has a half-day option; it includes free play and indoor activities in a large area in a separate building. Beginners learn the basics before they even hit the slopes, then head for the children-only teaching slope and an easy-to-use poma lift—especially valuable when the mountain is crowded. The daylong Mountain Explorer program for 8- to 12-year-olds, for kids with average or better skills, skis the main mountain. All the programs lunch in the SKIwee Center, where there are also after-ski activities. The junior racing team trains competitors ages 8 to 18. The best time to come with teens is on weekends or during holiday periods when the town of Ludlow offers ice-skating, volleyball, and dances.

On-mountain accommodations include hundreds of fairly expensive ski-in/ski-out condos (midweek packages are the best bet) plus a lodge, but there are many inexpensive country inns and motels in Ludlow and within a 10-mile radius.

🏠 *RFD 1, Ludlow 05149, tel. 802/228–4041; 802/228–5571 or 800/786–5366 reservations and area lodging; 802/228–5222 snow conditions. Facilities: 83 trails, 11 lifts, restaurant, 4 cafeterias, bar, ski shop, ski instruction, nursery. AE, D, MC, V.*

Stowe Mountain Resort

Established in the 1930s as one of the country's first ski areas, Stowe is a cosmopolitan village with excellent, challenging downhill skiing and some of the best cross-country touring centers in the Northeast for families. We like skiing here because it's *not* a planned community at the base of the lifts; rather, there's a sense of tradition and history and an almost European flavor to this oldest New England ski town. Mountain Road between the town and the downhill ski area is lined with restaurants, inns, ice-cream parlors, and shops. The Village Trolley travels along it all day long dropping off and picking up people and skis. There's ice-skating at Edson Hill Manor's (tel. 802/253–7371 or 802/253–8954) rink or the town public rink and sleigh rides at Edson Hill Manor, Topnotch Resort & Spa (tel.

802/253–8585), or Pristine Meadows (tel. 802/253–9877).

To me Stowe (for cross-country or downhill skiing) is best for serious skiing families who like a more sophisticated atmosphere and food and whose kids are at least 8 years old. Though it can be expensive, Stowe offers five- and seven-day family ski packages in which kids 12 and under stay free, ski half-price, and get a free ski lesson. Stowe's January winter carnival has lots for kids, such as magicians and jugglers on Village Night and fireworks.

Stowe's downhill skiing area is divided between Spruce Peak, for beginners and intermediates, where the ski school is located, and Mt. Mansfield (1,318 meters/4,393 feet), where trails range from long, easy glides from the summit that families can ski together, to intermediate runs, to the steep front four black-diamond runs. The two base lodges are linked by a shuttle bus.

Kanga's Pocket nursery for 2-month-olds to 3-year-olds, though cozy and cheerful, is very small and somewhat inconvenient—up a steep, winding road from Spruce Base Lodge. I'd go to another area if you need day care. The well-run ski school has instructors hired specifically to teach children. Parents can choose from two-hour group lessons or full-day programs. The flexible Pooh's Adventure (3–5s) program, which uses the Pooh characters in ski learning games, is a combination ski lesson/child-care program (up to four hours of skiing depending on a child's interest and a large toy-filled indoor play area). The separate outdoor area for these beginners is small and not particularly attractive, but there is a kids'-only rope tow on an easy slope. Those beyond that stage use several open, gentle slopes and a slow, close-to-the-ground chair lift. Kids 6 to 8 (Mini-Mountain Adventure) have their own base camp where they eat lunch together and store their equipment if they're skiing all week; 9s to 12s join Mountain Adventure and ski all over both mountains with their instructor.

During holiday weeks intermediate and advanced skiers 13 to 16 have a special full-day program, Extremely Teen; some days they break at five or six for pizza and then ski at night together. Regular lessons, including special clinics, are available for snowboarders.

Stowe has inexpensive to expensive casual to elegant motels, country inns, full-service resorts, bed-and-breakfast options, and even houses to rent within a short drive of downhill and cross-country centers. The best bet for downhill skiers is somewhere along Mountain Road; for cross-country skiers, the Trapp Family Lodge (see Chapter 14).

🏠 *5781 Mountain Rd., Stowe 05672, tel. 802/253–3000 or 800/247–8693 information or reservations, 802/253–2222 snow conditions. Facilities: 45 trails, 11 lifts, 2 restaurants, 4 cafeterias, 3 bars, fitness center, 4 ski shops. AE, D, DC, MC, V.*

CROSS-COUNTRY SKIING. The nearly 200 kilometers (124 miles) of trails at the four cross-country centers—**Edson Hill Manor** (tel. 802/253–7371), **Stowe Mountain Resort** (tel. 802/ 253–3000), **Topnotch Resort and Spa** (802/253–8585), and the **Trapp Family Lodge** (tel. 802/253–8511)—in Stowe are linked (though only experts can really manage to ski from one to another). The best choices for families are skiing Stowe's 3-mile recreational path that meanders through town or the Trapp Family Lodge's groomed, well-patrolled trails on the outskirts of town.

Stratton

I find Stratton expensive and crowded, and its extensive village complex and covered parking lot for 700 cars reminds me of a mall. But my son and his friends love it—and so do a lot of families we know, particularly those that include good intermediate or expert skiers. Why? Because of its warmer southern location, wide variety of slopes (including some super-challenging black diamonds), convenient on-mountain lodging

and sports center, excellent kids' ski school, and a ski learning park for beginners. Young teens can hang out in the 25 shops and restaurants in a minimall at the base as well as use the excellent snowboarding facilities and instruction. This is the birthplace of the snowboard, and the U.S. Open Snowboard championships are held here. Stratton has special packages for families, including a frequent-skier card that saves you money if you ski at least a week during nonholiday times.

Stratton's trails fan out from the summit, the most difficult plunging down the front face of the upper mountain. Several easy long runs wind along either side, and the Ski Learning Park beginner area of 10 trails (and a terrain garden) and several short lifts lies on the lower mountain directly in front of the village square complex. It's easy to ski together as a family or let your kids explore on their own in the learning park, which has its own less-expensive lift ticket. Another good place for families to ski is the less-crowded and sunnier Sun Bowl area on the other side of the mountain; you can ski to it on an easy trail or drive to the Sun Bowl Base Lodge. On the main face of the mountain, the high-speed, 12-passenger gondola is exciting to ride, but lines are generally long on weekends.

The sports center is a bit of a hike from most condos. The country club a mile away has a lighted ice skating rink. Movies (some family-oriented) are shown at the Bijou theater in Village Lodge, but you may see more kids at the big video arcade in Mulligan's restaurant. Don't look for special planned evening activities for kids and families here. Nearby Manchester is filled with sophisticated shopping (including lots of outlets) and restaurants.

A fresh, spacious center in the base lodge for infants and children age 6 weeks to 12 years has a downstairs crib and infant section that includes a private room for nursing mothers; upstairs you'll find a room full of the small tables, toys, and climbers that make toddlers and preschoolers feel at home. The SKIwee Little Cub program (ages 4–6) has its own building on the slopes across from the main base lodge. The flexibility of the combined play-and-ski program is an asset for families. Not only can you choose half- or full-day, but if children don't want to go back out to ski, they can stay inside and paint or play.

The Big Cubs (ages 7–12), including snowboarders as well as skiers, have their own space in the lower level of the main base lodge, equipped with indoor training equipment, picnic tables, videos, and more. For kids who come to Stratton every weekend, the Stratton Mountain Training Center (like the Alpine Training Center at Mount Snow) offers regular recreational and racing training in which kids ski or snowboard with the same group; the snowboard race training here is the very best.

The only special teen programs are through the Stratton Mountain Training Center; good skiers can join one of these just for a weekend. Two serious teen skiers we know praise the two weeklong intensive junior race camps; there are also four three- and eight-day snowboard race camps.

On-mountain lodging includes moderate to very expensive houses, condos, an inn, a lodge, and a hotel. Less expensive motels and lodges are 15 minutes away on Route 11.
🏠 RR1, Box 145, Stratton Mountain 05115, tel. 802/297–2200 or 800/843–6867; 802/297–4211 snow conditions; 802/297-4000 or 800/843-6867 on-mountain and area lodging reservations. Facilities: 92 trails, 14 lifts, 9 restaurants, 7 bars, sports center (75-foot indoor lap pool—no shallow end or lifeguard), fitness equipment, indoor tennis, racquetball), ski instruction, ski shop. AE, D, DC, MC, V.

CROSS-COUNTRY SKIING. Stratton's cross-country center (tel. 802/297–2200) is in the Sun Bowl area; 20 kilometers (12 miles) of trails are groomed; 50 kilometers (30 miles) are backcountry skiing. Three other cross-country touring centers are based nearby: the **Hildene Inn** (Manchester,

tel. 802/362–1788); **Viking Ski Touring Center** (Londonderry, tel. 802/824–3933); and **Wild Wings Ski Touring Center** (Peru, tel. 802/824–6793).

Suicide Six and the Woodstock Inn and Resort

Among the greatest ski bargains for families in the Northeast are the Family Ski Week (offered eight weeks from mid-December through March) and Family Ski Pak (three days, two nights) offered by the plush 146-room Woodstock Inn, which owns this small ski area that's more appropriate for families than its name suggests. The packages are the reason to come here. They include superior lodging compared with most ski-resort hotels (uniquely decorated rooms in various configurations with luxurious marble baths) in the large white clapboard-and-brick, distinctly New England–style inn, as well as free lift tickets, ski rentals, and group lessons for the entire family. The Ski Weeks are a particularly good deal, as you get two connecting rooms, one of which will hold as many as four kids, and free breakfasts and dinners for kids under 14. To take the best advantage of the package, families should have kids over 6 who are beginning or intermediate skiers.
🏠 Woodstock 05091, tel. 802/457–1666; 800/457–1622, snow conditions; information on packages at inn, 802/457–1100; fax 802/457–6699. Facilities: 19 trails, 3 lifts, sports center with indoor pool, fitness center, ski instruction, ski shop, baby-sitting. AE, MC, V.

CROSS-COUNTRY SKIING. The ski touring center has 60 kilometers (37 miles) of trails. Equipment and lessons are available free with the family package.

Village at Smugglers Notch

This self-contained resort village at the bottom of Morse Mountain is simply one of the three best ski resorts in the Northeast for families, with a superb child-care center and children's ski school and programs, rewarding family activities, a well-thought-out teen program, and reasonably priced family packages. Commitment to families is evident in their excellent "Guide to Planning the Perfect Winter Family Vacation" (well worth writing for). Convenience is a huge plus here: The village houses restaurants (you'll see families at all of them), sports facilities, shops, and entertainment, all within walking distance of the condos, slopes, and chair lifts. Kids can walk everywhere. The levels of service (for example, you can reserve cribs, potty seats, high chairs, and so on), friendliness to and enthusiasm for kids, and organization are unsurpassed. You check in and out, register for all lessons and activity programs, and purchase lift tickets in one small building.

The atmosphere, food, and activities, though more sophisticated than Bolton Valley's, are just right for kids. Most of the village and nearby restaurants share the easy tone. A small, lighted outdoor ice-skating rink is just the right size for kids. Across the road from the resort is Vermont Horse Park (tel. 802/644–5347), which offers sleigh rides.

Ski trails spread out over three mountains: Morse for beginners, Madonna and Sterling for experts and intermediates. One drawback is that you have to take a lift to the top of Morse and ski across to the other mountains; you can ski or take a shuttle back to the village. There are several long beginner runs, a trail over the mountain to Stowe (you can purchase a one-time lift ticket there to get back), some challenging bump runs and glade skiing, and a Nastar race course, but an expert might be bored after a few days.

The five- and seven-day family ski packages, available all winter long, are your best bet here: They include lift ticket, accommodations, use of the pool and hot tub, and family and teen evening activities. Smuggler's even offers a Kid's Fun Guarantee (if your kids don't have fun, lesson and program fees are refunded) for 3- to 12-year-olds. During the two annual Family Festival

weeks in February, kids 3 to 12 get free lessons, rentals, and dinners.

The Alice's Wonderland Child Care Center for kids 6 weeks to 6 years is a model to be emulated. Warm and welcoming, its large rooms (one for infants, with a special sleeping room; one for toddlers; and one for older kids) are filled with a pleasant disorder of colorful toys, climbing apparatuses, blocks, fish tanks, and rocking chairs. Kids spend the day both indoors and out. The roomy outdoor playground behind the center is equipped with slides, swings, climbers, and a most beguiling pirate ship.

The kids' ski school is really clued in to what motivates kids to learn. The Mogul Mouse's Magic Lift for beginners is low to the ground and runs at half speed. Some 150 of the 250 instructors, including many men, are specially trained to teach kids. In the Discovery Camp for 3s to 6s, a horse-drawn wagon sometimes takes kids up to the lift, and learning is through fun and games—playing Simon Says on skis, skiing under hoops and in special terrain gardens, and participating in a cookie race at the end of the week. The Adventure Camp for 7s to 12s is similar. There's even a special one-hour family program, "Mom and Me" or "Dad and Me," in which a specially trained instructor shows you how to teach your child to ski.

Evenings bring free family activities—bingo, Pictionary, sledding, ice-skating, fireworks; Tuesday is Parents' Night Out, when kids up to 12 can eat dinner and join in special activities at Alice's.

The teen program here is especially imaginative. The Explorer Ski Program for 13- to 17-year-olds meets afternoons for challenging instruction—racing development or glade and bump ski techniques; during holiday weeks a full-day program includes snowboarding, snowshoeing, and cross-country skiing. Scheduled evening teen activities here (karaoke, sledding, volleyball, dances) actually are well attended because the ski instructors go, too, inviting kids to come along after the ski program ends. The pool table is a big attraction at the alcohol-free teen center Outer Limits (busiest after 7:30, deserted during the dinner hour); it has couches, magazines, video games, and an experienced counselor, who introduces kids to each other and often initiates special activities in which kids have shown interest. Teens who are super-expert skiers or are looking for a sophisticated atmosphere may be disappointed here.

The condominiums on the mountain are the best choice because of the resort's ski packages, but inexpensive lodging is available on Route 108 between the resort and the town of Jeffersonville.

Route 108, Smugglers' Notch Resort 05464; tel. 802/644–8851 or 800/451–8752 information, reservations, snow report. Facilities: 57 trails, 7 lifts, half-pipe, 395 condominiums, indoor pool, hot tub, indoor tennis court, 4 restaurants, 2 cafeterias, 3 bars, ice-skating rink, ski shop, fitness room, teen club, general store. AE, CB, DC, MC, V.

CROSS-COUNTRY SKIING. Smugglers' has 22 kilometers (14 miles) of trails winding through woods and along a stream and up into the Notch itself. On Wednesday and Saturday nights, the Nordic Tour skis the trails and the Owl Tour, on snowshoes or skis, takes you hooting around for owls and into the notch for history about the place.

SADDLE UP, TEE OFF, LIE AROUND
FAMILY FARMS, LODGES, RANCHES, RESORTS, AND NATURE CAMPS

14

We've found over the years that the Northeast has a range of choices from grand, luxurious, and historic resorts with first-class golf courses to tranquil, picturesque farms to ranches with nonstop activities to nature and music camps that provide education as well as entertainment. Resorts, whether luxurious and expensive or informal and a bargain, are usually the easiest vacation imaginable, with accommodations, meals, supervised kids' and adult programs, and extensive sports facilities all included in the price. But it's important to decide just what kind of atmosphere and how much pampering your family wants. We don't like nonstop activities or constant interaction with other adults, for example, and we don't mind roughing it as long as we're in a beautiful place with great views. The family lodges and inns listed below provide amenities similar to those of the resorts but on a smaller scale.

Farms, on the other hand, tend to be quite low-key, a way for families to enter into a simpler way of life that's been an essential part of New England since colonial times. Compared with western states there aren't many ranches in the Northeast, and most are in New York state. (See also Chapter 6.)

Nature camps offer the joy of living close to the wild. In our experience your family will have a good time only at a nature camp that truly understands a kid's way of exploring—these camps do. We learned the hard way to bring exactly what the camp suggests you bring. Hint: To prepare your kids, take a few short local hikes before you go.

I've also put in a couple of very unusual places that we thought were fun—a music camp and a history center where you can experience what life on a farm was like 100 years ago.

For teens to be happy, Gavin has convinced us, the essentials are a large enough group of peers and a space where they can hang out together; they also have to be able to get around easily on their own by bike or foot. Add to that either challenging outdoor activities like rock climbing or waterskiing or organized sports activities. If all this can be near a town with shops too, you've got it made.

It's hard to compare costs, because some places include all meals (EP means no meals, MAP means only breakfast and dinner are included; AP means all three meals), children's programs, and recreational facilities, even the use of boats, in the price, while others do not. The latter may appear less expensive, but in our experience they usually end up costing more when you add up what you spend at the golf course, the tennis courts, and the restaurants. If your accommodations include a kitchen, you can save money by cooking for yourself. Resorts tend to be the most expensive. The price categories below are based on what a family of four with two school-age children would spend on an average day. Very expensive ($$$$) means over $450 a day; expensive ($$$), $350–$450; moderate ($$), $200–$350; inexpensive ($), under $200. Weekly rates are lower. Cribs and cots are available in all the places listed here. Lessons, whether tennis, golf, or sailing, and boat usage usually cost extra.

We've found it's best to stay one week if you're going to sign up for the children's program so you can take advantage of all the facilities and your kids can make some friends. If you stay longer, you may find, as we have, that all the newfound friends leave, and your child is miserable for the following week. Most charge more in July and August, while June and September are bargains. For more ideas, look at *Family Resorts of the Northeast,* by Nancy Pappas Metcalf (The Countryman Press, 1992), *Me & You & the Kids Came Too,* by Dawn and Robert Habgood (Dawbert Press, 1992), and *The Best Bargain Family Vacations in the U.S.A.,* by Laura Sutherland and Valerie Wolf Deutsch (St. Martin's, 1993).

Connecticut

Inn at Lake Waramaug

(👫 3 – 15)

This has been summer-cottage, elegant-antique-store, pretty-country-town territory since the last century, and this 18th-century white colonial country inn, with the requisite green shutters and big front porch and terrace bordered by clipped yews, fits right in. Despite the Oriental rugs, bookshelves, old wing chairs, and other period furnishings, kids we know feel more at home here than at other inns around the lake. Gavin has from the first time we dropped by for one of their many offbeat weekend events—a frog-jumping jamboree, which

took place on the sweeping, maple-shaded front lawn that slopes down to the road (the small beach is on the other side).

Families are likely to feel more comfortable in the motel-style guest houses closer to the road, which are decorated in American colonial-country style (some with fireplaces), because the rooms and baths are very big and don't have that watch-out-for-the-breakable-antiques feel. If you have young children, the one problem here is the narrow road that separates the inn and guest houses from the beach. Be warned that cars sometimes drive fast, and the road is not suitable for young ones to bike on. Your kids may prefer the large oval indoor pool to the small sand beach crowded with pulled-up canoes and Sunfish and lounge chairs.
🏠 *North Shore Rd., New Preston 06777, tel. 203/868–0563 or 800/525–3466, fax*

203/868–9173. 23 rooms (5 in inn and 18 in 2 guest houses) with private bath, air-conditioning; 2 adjoining rooms. Facilities: dining room, swimming beach, volleyball court, tennis court, indoor pool, boating (canoes, rowboats, Sunfish), fishing, exercise room, game room with video games, pool table, ping-pong, snack bar, children's dinner seating, children's portions. AE, MC, V. Rates MAP; discount for kids under 15 sharing room with parents. $$–$$$

Maine

Attean Lake Lodge

☗☗ 2 – 12

These 18 hewn-log cabins and lodge are on Birch Island, a 10-minute boat ride from the shore of pristine, 6-mile-long Attean Lake. Cabins nestle cozily and privately among the trees and afford wonderful views of the lake. Each has a broad, partly screened deck and a woodstove or fireplace. Playing cards at night in front of a fire by kerosene lamplight really makes you feel like you're out in the wilderness; be sure to bring several flashlights and extra batteries. Three meals a day of simple New England fare are served on real tablecloths at the main lodge, but the cookouts twice a week, when you eat at picnic tables overlooking the lake and little kids run around, are more fun. Canoes are stashed conveniently at spots along the shore and by ponds adjacent to the trails so you don't have to portage. For toddlers, the resort's own fairly long, sandy beach, well equipped with sand toys and beach chairs, is right near the lodge. Kids can gather in a games room in the main lodge, but many families tend to spend their days together. ▲ *Jackman 04945, tel. 207/668–3792 (May–Oct.); 207/668–7726 (Nov.–Apr.); no fax. 18 cabins. Facilities: lake beach, boating (canoes, fishing boats), fishing, hiking, library, games, swing set. AE, MC, V. Closed Sept.– Memorial Day. Rates AP. $$*

Chewonki Wilderness Programs

☗☗ 8+

The Chewonki Foundation is dedicated to environmental education and still operates the oldest ecologically oriented kids' camp in the country, once attended by bird expert Roger Tory Peterson. Now it also has weeklong (and sometimes three-day) summer programs for families that teach about the environment through an encounter with nature somewhere in Maine, whether canoeing, hiking, or sailing. What's special is their hands-on way of teaching about the natural world (such as night walks to listen to owls hooting, trees rustling, and raccoons snuffling) and the emphasis on group cooperation. Every trip produces a journal (a compilation of poems, essays, drawings, and accounts of each day's activities by all the adults and kids in the group), which is copied so everyone has a record of the trip. Food is healthy—no yucky dehydrated packets—and even kids learn how to make pancakes and much else over open fires. It's important to know just how much your kids are able to do and not overestimate their capacities. Are they ready for a six-day hiking trip that culminates in a climb of Mt. Katahdin? ▲ *R.R. 2, Box 1200, Wiscasset 04578, tel. 207/882–7323, fax 207/882–4074. Facilities: depends on trip. MC, V. Rates include camping equipment, boats, meals, and instruction; children's rates. $*

Goose Cove Lodge

☗☗ 0 – 12

This secluded, rustic lodge and 11 cottages with a quintessential Maine coastal view of pine-covered islands and the open ocean beyond has been rated one of the best family cabin resorts in the Northeast by *Family Circle* magazine. The combination of the friendly staff, the casual yet sophisticated atmosphere, and the way activities and meals promote intimacy among the guests makes this place special. One advantage if you have small children is that kids eat at 5:30, an hour before the adults. When Gavin was little, we would have found it blissful to be able to gather for drinks and animated adult conversation in a cozy lounge, then consume delicious adult food like white bean and escarole salad or rhubarb pudding in a spectacular, windowed half-octagon dining room overlooking the ocean while the fog rolled in without comments like, "I don't want to eat that yucky stuff." But the truth is that this place is primarily for families with portable babies or kids who love nature. The water at the beach is too frigid for all but the hardiest, and there's no swimming pool. In rainy weather, kids can hang out in the cozy library with its excellent collection of children's books or watch videos or play pool in the large shed that serves as a recreation room. Families are likely to do best in cottages nestled on the hillside and suites in the main lodge's east annex (these have separate living rooms and fireplaces); they're furnished simply with hooked rugs, knotty pine walls, and modest antiques.

🏠 *Goose Cove Rd., Deer Isle, Sunset 04683, tel. 207/348–2508, fax 207/348–2624. 6 rooms with private bath, 6 suites; 11 cottages, most with refrigerator or kitchenette. Facilities: dining room, ocean beach, boating (canoes, rowboats, sailing lessons), marked nature trails, recreation hall with table tennis, pool, VCR and video library, arts-and-crafts center, library with children's books, gift shop, baby-sitting, supervised children's dinner, children's menu. MC, V. Closed mid-Oct.–mid-May. Rates MAP, weekly only July–Aug. $$*

Samoset Resort

👫 3 – 12

This sleekly modern wood hotel and condominiums with gabled roofs is a good place to combine a golf and family vacation: It's set on a couple of hundred acres next to Maine's picturesque Penobscot Bay. Unfortunately, to get from the hotel to the ocean, you have to walk around the golf course on a long public access road. The plush-contemporary condos that have kitchenettes and views of the bay may be best for families. Of all the things for kids to do, fishing off the nearby mile-long lighthouse-tipped granite breakwater stands out. Meals in the formal dining room tend to drag; burgers at umbrella-topped picnic tables outside may be preferable.

🏠 *220 Warrenton St. (off Rte. 1), Rockport 04856, tel. 207/594–2511 or 800/341–1650, fax 207/594–0722. 150 double rooms, 18 suites; 72 time-share condos in 3 buildings. Facilities: 3 restaurants, 1 indoor and 2 outdoor tennis courts, indoor and outdoor pools, fitness center, 18-hole championship golf course, racquetball, shuffleboard, badminton, basketball, horseshoes, volleyball, playground, croquet, fishing (pole rentals), biking (bike rentals), supervised all-day children's program (ages 3–12). AE, D, DC, MC, V. Rates MAP or EP (children's program, bikes, golf not included); kids under 16 free; package plans. $$–$$$$*

Sebasco Lodge

👫 4 – 12

Simple, 1950s-style basic cottage accommodations (lodges are for those with no kids) clustered within walking distance of each other on a rocky and beautiful 700-acre peninsula on the Maine coast, lots of organized family activities from folk concerts to barn dances to bingo games, and reasonable prices draw families back here year after year. You can park your car and not use it again until you leave. This is a very casual and sociable, but not sophisticated place; it's crammed with stuff for kids to do. Everything is easy. When you arrive, you receive a list of all the activities and clear instructions on how to sign up. Two-year-olds wade happily in the shallow end of the saltwater pool that looks out over the bay while 12-year-olds take turns doing corkscrew jumps off the side. *Ruth,* the resort's boat, takes a weekly hour-long "pirate trip" in Casco Bay (about halfway through the cruise, menacing-looking but friendly costumed pirates complete with eye patches board). After dinner, young teenagers can play New England's old-fashioned version of bowling, Candlepins, at the resort's four-lane alley in the funky barnlike recreation building. Don't worry about the food. The blueberry pancakes and lobster are the best, along with the BLTs at the snack bar overlooking the water. If you want more privacy and sophistication, you can stay at the nearby Rock Gardens Inn and Cottages (207/389–1339) and still use the recreational facilities here.

🏠 *Sebasco Estates 04565, tel. 207/389–1161 or 800/225–3819, fax 207/389–2004. 64 rooms in main inn and lodges, with phone, private bath; 20 1- to 6-bedroom cottages, all with phone, some with fireplace, kitchen, TV. Facilities: dining room, outdoor saltwater pool, 9-hole golf course, 2 tennis courts, gift shop, bowling, recreation room with video games and ping-pong, boating (canoes, sailboats, motorboats), playground, private sand beach 1 mi away, weekly boat excursions, supervised kids' morning program (ages 3–7; extra charge). AE, MC, V. Closed early Sept.–late June. Rates MAP. $–$$*

Washburn-Norlands Living History Center

(👫 8+)

If your kids are fascinated by how children lived long ago, they might jump at the chance to live in the year 1870 at a three-day weekend program at this living-history center. Norlands, a traditional Maine farmhouse with a connected cottage, a shed, and an enormous barn, was the summer home of the Washburns, a prominent New England family. All of it is pretty much as it was in the last half of the 19th century. You'll sleep in the attached seven-room, unheated hired man's cottage (the farmhouse in front

is now a museum) under fairly primitive conditions: no private bedrooms, corn husk or straw mattresses resting on rope frames (we guarantee that it's pretty uncomfortable), and an outhouse behind the barn (or the chamber pot under your bed). As soon as you arrive, you are given the name of a real adult or child close to your age in the Pray or Waters families (the Washburns' nearest neighbors), and that's the role you play for the rest of your stay during a make-believe family reunion. The staff and everyone else stays in character as they pitch in together to milk cows, cook meals from recipes used 100 years ago, or play an old-fashioned game. At dinner when the President is discussed, his name is Ulysses S. Grant, and current events means the recent purchase of Alaska. Your assumptions about modern living may be rearranged (toilet paper and window screens are the only contemporary concessions). Staying here can leave a more profound impression about life in the past on your kids than any visit to Sturbridge or Mystic, but it is not for every family. It's best to come in summer or early fall before it gets too cold. Read the information they send before you make reservations.

🏠 *Billie Gammon, R.R. 2, Box 3395, Livermore Falls 04254, tel. 207/897–2236. 5 bedrooms for 16 participants. Facilities: 2 dining rooms. Rates AP; discounts for kids 8–12½. No credit cards. $*

Massachusetts

Chatham Bars Inn

(👫 4 – 10)

A three-minute walk from Chatham village, on a low hill across the road from the beach, sit this gracious, elegant, shingled World War I–vintage inn and a series of gray-shingle Cape-style cottages. To me this luxurious and soothing place feels very much like Cape Cod a generation ago—spacious, quiet, private, with spectacular views of a bay full of fishing boats and clouds and sky. The bay and beach (there's also a beachfront pool) are somewhat sheltered from the open Atlantic by a long outer sandbar across the mouth of the bay. A five-minute trip on the inn's launch brings you to the bar, where the surf crashes in on the ocean side and the currents on the bay side create warm, shallow pools perfect for wading.

Larger cottages can be split into several-room suites; smaller ones can be rented whole. All contain antique wicker, paned windows, and pine furniture. Many of the shore cottages are far enough from the inn that you'll have to drive to meals and activities; even at the closest ones you have to cross a road.

🏠 *Chatham 02633, tel. 508/945–0096 or 800/527–4884, fax 508/945–5491. 44 inn rooms, some with decks (3 adjoining rooms); 103 rooms in 26 1- to 8-bedroom cottages. Facilities: 3 restaurants, private ocean beach, outdoor heated pool, beach house, fitness center, 4 tennis courts, 9-hole golf course, shuffleboard, croquet, volleyball, supervised kids' program (ages 3½–12); teen program in July and Aug. at the beach. AE, MC, V. Rates MAP (includes children's program). $$$–$$$$*

Lighthouse Inn

👫 ALL

The center part of the white clapboard main inn that looks out on Nantucket Sound was once a lighthouse (in 1850), and it's still lit every night. It's small and informal and welcomes children with a miniature golf course and a huge closet downstairs crammed with games, sand toys, and art supplies. The dining rooms are decorated with fishing nets and other nautical gear, lunch is served on a deck, and you can watch sunsets from the porches. For more privacy, families can choose the classic, weathered shake cottages and guest houses where roses climb white trellises and scrubby pines remind you that the ocean

wind here blows hard all winter long. These cottages have a homey decor but come with unexpected conveniences like cable TV and hair dryers in the bathrooms. Though the water at the two small beaches on either side of a long stone breakwall in front of the inn may be warm, kids, including toddlers, like to splash in the solar-heated pool. The snack bar has kid-size tables.

🏠 *Box 128, West Dennis 02690, tel. 508/398–2244, fax 508/398–5658. 32 rooms, 7 suites, 13 cottages. Facilities: dining room; ocean beach; miniature golf; putting green; outdoor pool; recreation room with pool table, video games, ping-pong, large-screen TV; shuffleboard; 2 tennis courts; supervised kids' program (ages 3–9); supervised kids' lunch, dinner, and evening entertainment. MC, V. Closed mid-Oct.–mid-May. Rates MAP or B&B; free for children under 3. $$*

New Seabury Resort

👫 2 – 15

Though we're not fans of planned communities, we have to admit that this complex of tasteful small villages, each with a different architectural style, and private homes on 2,000 acres of a beach-fringed peninsula overlooking Nantucket Sound does evoke something of a Cape Cod feel. Curving roads and secluded paths wind through piney woods out to small beaches and dunes, as well as to a fabulous 3½-mile-long beach. Most of the more than 1,500 houses and attached villas here are privately owned second homes. That and its size mean New Seabury doesn't have the immediate friendly intimacy of many of the Northeast's family resorts. Nor does it have a central dining building to pull people together. On the other hand, as all lodging includes kitchens, this is a good place for a very comfortable extended family vacation at the beach. Kids quickly make friends in the day camp and ride their bikes everywhere. The wide, sandy bathing beach has tame surf, warm water, shady cabanas, and even a beachfront pool. The big plus for teenagers at this resort is the Popponessett Marketplace, a shopping area of weathered shingle buildings, crushed seashell walkways, climbing roses, and most important, a pizza parlor, a Ben & Jerry's, and 21 shops.

🏠 *Box 550, Rock Landing Rd., New Seabury 02649, tel. 508/477–9111 or 800/999–9033; in MA, 800/752–9700; fax 508/477–9790. 165 studio, 1-bedroom, and 2-bedroom villas with kitchens, some with air-conditioning. Facilities: 7 restaurants and snack bars, shops, ocean beach, 2 18-hole golf courses, 16 tennis courts, biking (bike rentals), sailing, nature walks, hiking, fitness center, 2 outdoor pools, baby-sitting, supervised children's program (age 4+), teen activities and center, family activities. AE, D, DC, MC, V. Rates EP (meals available). $$*

Pinewoods Camp

(🧑‍🧒 3 – 12)

Our friends Curtis and Louise, who never miss an opportunity to square dance, have been to this annual family music and dance camp near Plymouth several times with their three children. The camp, one of two in the Eastern United States sponsored by the Country Dance and Song Society, offers accommodations in a variety of buildings from houses with several rooms to individual cabins. Campers age 5 and over help with meals or housekeeping. The buildings stand on 23 acres of pine-covered hills near two lakes; the clear water at the larger (1 mile long) is good for swimming. Everyone gets to know one another here, and a real camaraderie, born of singing and dancing together, develops. One class a day is organized by age, a second is organized by interest, and some are for families together. It's not all music and dance—there are craft classes, for instance—but if you're not serious and enthusiastic about folk music, your kids won't be.

🏠 *Country Dance and Song Society, 17 New South St., Northhampton 01060, tel. 413/*

584–9913, fax 413/585–8728. 140 beds in cabins with private bath or bath nearby. Facilities: dining room; swimming; canoeing; dance pavilions; supervised children's program combining music, dance, crafts, songs, storytelling; family and adult dance programs. MC, V. 2 weeks, July and/or Aug. Rates AP (include all classes, activities). $–$$

New Hampshire

Appalachian Mountain Club Family Education Programs

(🧑‍🧒 5 – 13)

Sleeping in bunks at Lonesome Lake Hut, the AMC's most popular family destination in the White Mountains, was a peak outing for our family. The hike up to it is a short and easy 1.8 miles, but the view made us feel we'd come much, much farther. At the Zealand Falls Hut at the edge of the Pemigewasset Wilderness, you can swim in very cold pools by a waterfall. On the AMC's family weekend camps and 5-day programs staff naturalists lead hikes, teach map and compass reading, and use nature games to help kids—and their parents—learn about animals as well as the importance of treating the earth with respect. One thing John and I appreciate about the AMC huts is the fact that they are a big step up from camping: breakfast and a hot dinner, basic but filling, are provided. The meeting point (and sometimes the main accommodations) for many of the family programs in July and August is the larger Pinkham Notch Lodge, a brown wood building rather like a barn, which has more comfortable rooms than the huts, hot showers, a library and visitor center, and the AMC Trading Post, where you can buy gear and maps. It's essential to reserve, especially for prime times in late July and August. Members of AMC get a discount.

🏠 *Pinkham Notch Visitor Center, Box 298, Gorham 03581, tel. 603/466–2721*

(Appalachian Mountain Club, 5 Joy St., Boston, MA 02108; membership and information, tel. 617/523–0636; reservations, 617/455–2727). Lodge at Pinkham Notch: 23 bunkrooms with sheets and blankets for 2, 3, 4, or 5, 2 large shared baths; snack bar, library, store, visitor center with exhibits. Lonesome Lake Hut: 2 bunkhouses with 9 rooms for 4, 6, or 8; children's program, canoes, some gear on special family weekends. MC, V. Rates include breakfast, dinner. $

Balsams Grand Resort Hotel

(👫 5+)

This huge, gracious 100-year-old resort seems transplanted from a hillside above Lake Lugano in Switzerland next to this perfect lake in the middle of a 15,000-acre New World mountain wilderness. In the late 19th century, when steam trains whisked well-to-do city folk to the mountains each summer, there were dozens of grand hotels like the Balsams in the White Mountains; this is one of the few survivors, and with good reason. It still has one employee for every guest, which means the service is as deluxe as the surroundings, and an Old World, princely atmosphere.

The oldest part, a white frame four-story building with a long wraparound porch, is joined by an entrance portico to a fantasy Mediterranean-style seven-story pale-brown stucco wing, built in 1918, that has reddish-orange tiles on its roofs and cupolas.

Kids love exploring the endless covered porches, corridors, and public rooms filled with ornately carved Victorian furniture and finding a vintage Coca-Cola machine in the game room. In the formal dining room, they can view the entrées at a central table before ordering. Unlike that at most family resorts, the food here is superb. Most rooms are spacious (opt for a renovated one) and have simpler New England–style decor—four-poster beds, wicker chairs, pas-

tel walls, wall-to-wall carpeting, ruffled tie-back curtains, and huge walk-in closets. Many have fireplaces and deep tubs.

Activities for all ages but infants and preschoolers seem limitless. Kids can even take conga lessons from the hotel's ballroom musicians, and you can all catch an evening feature film in the hotel's theater. Rooms come equipped with long lists of activities and careful instructions on how to sign up.

 Dixville Notch 03576, tel. 800/255–0600; in NH, 800/255–0800; fax 603/255–4221. 232 rooms, 75 adjoining rooms; no TV in rooms. Facilities: dining room, outdoor heated pool, lake swimming, 6 tennis courts, volleyball and badminton courts, playground, boating, fly fishing, croquet, 18-hole and 9-hole golf courses (no charge), shuffleboard, hiking trails, game and TV rooms, children's nursery and day camp, supervised children's dinner, baby-sitting, nightclub (ages 12–21), movie theater, gift shops and boutiques; late Dec.–Mar., alpine and cross-country skiing, skating, sleigh rides, tobogganing. AE, D, MC, V. Rates MAP late Dec.–Mar.; AP, end May–mid-Oct. (include all facilities and programs); kids under 18 pay their age times $7 per night. Closed Apr., May, Nov., Dec. $$–$$$$

Inn at East Hill Farm

(👫 1 – 9)

Have your kids ever collected eggs, then brought them into the kitchen to have them cooked for breakfast? They can do this every morning at this unposh working family farm and resort. Quarters range from cottages with knotty pine furniture to motel-type rooms with a basic version of Scandinavian modern to a new five-bedroom house that looks like a reproduction maple sugaring house with a porch at each end. Young school-age kids are free here to explore nooks and crannies and join in making ice cream in an old crank ice-cream maker instead of enrolling in a structured program. They can hang over a wooden slat fence to pet horses, feed chicks, or just poke around one of the many barns even in winter. For toddlers and young school-age kids, it feels very comfortable and down-home, especially with stacks of muffins and cookies and juice waiting just in case they get hungry in the afternoon. 🏠 *460 Monadnock St. (watch for signs to Mt. Monadnock on Rte. 12 in town), Troy 03465, tel. 603/242–6495, fax 603/242–7709. 8 double rooms with bath (2 connect) and deluxe 3-bedroom, 3-bath suite in main inn; 7 2-bedroom cottages; 4 3-bedroom, 2-bath cottages; 18 rooms with bath (all connect) in modern motel-style unit; 1 deluxe 5-bedroom, 5-bath house. Facilities: 2 outdoor pools, indoor pool and sauna, tennis court, barns with animals, pond with paddleboats and rowboats, swings, sandbox, wading pool, 2 whirlpools, waterskiing, pony rides, horseback-riding program, daily organized kids' activities; cross-country skiing, ice-skating, sledding, sleigh rides. D, MC, V. Rates AP (include activities); kids under 2 free, special rates for ages 2–18. $*

Loch Lyme Lodge and Cottages

👫 1 – 13

Families have been coming to this peaceful, relaxing, friendly, and inexpensive resort in the Connecticut River Valley for more than 70 years, many booking a year or more in advance. Though the main lodge is 18th century, this is not a fancy place. The office is in the red barn. The roomy, old-fashioned, stained-lumber-sided cabins with green shutters, screened porches, and fireplaces face the lake or the lawn or nestle in the woods. Cabins facing the lake are booked way, way ahead; one is taken for the first week in August until 2010! As you sit in one of the white Adirondack chairs by the lake at dusk watching your kids catch fireflies in a glass jar or go off to play flashlight tag with a bunch of other kids, you may be gratified to observe that filling unstructured time with country pleasures is just what kids need on a summer vacation. One of those pleasures is talking to the lodge's friendly college-student staff, which usually hails from at least six different countries. 🏠 *R.F.D. 278, Rte. 10, Lyme 03768, tel. 603/795–2141 or 800/423–2141. 4 rooms with shared bath in main lodge, 12 1- to 4-bedroom cabins with kitchens; 12 1- to 2-bedroom cabins with meals or breakfast only. Facilities: swimming beach, biking routes, rowboats, canoes, plastic kayaks, paddleboat, Windsurfer, badminton, 2 clay tennis courts, volleyball, baseball field, playground, basketball, public beach (½ mi away); no TV. No credit cards. Closed Sept.–June. Rates MAP or B&B (include boats); kids 4 and under free, special rates for ages 5–15; other discounts and packages. $*

Purity Spring Resort

👫 1 – 15

This old New England farmstead turned resort on a winding road seems to be exactly what a summer camp for families should be. The onslaught of adult and family events includes canoe races, island breakfast cookouts, Trivial Pursuit tournaments. Everything, from the beaches (three are roped off so it's easy to keep track of kids) to a drop-in child-care center to weekly all-day family hikes in the White Mountains to evening campfires, is all about "family fun." There's nothing fancy about the white farmhouse with green shutters framed by two big maples that serves as the main inn or the cottages and lodges set nearby on the flat expanse of green lawn brightened with flower beds. Rooms are basic and functional. In the lodges, which we liked best, the rooms, each with private bath, have a common lounge with TV and VCR. Kids draped themselves on chairs and the floor to watch together until parents jointly insisted on bedtime. 🏠 *HC63 Box 40, Rte. 153, East Madison 03849, tel. 603/367–8896 or 800/367–*

8897, fax 603/367–8664. 45 rooms, some with shared bath, in cottages (some with fireplace), main inn, and lodges open year-round; 70 rooms at King Pine Ski Area open Dec.–Apr., depending on weather. Facilities: 4 lake beaches, boating (rowboats, canoes), waterskiing, hiking trails, 5 tennis courts, shuffleboard, badminton, basketball, library, indoor pool, fitness center, croquet, game room with pool and ping-pong, VCR, coin laundry, playground, supervised children's programs, daily child care, baby-sitting; skiing, ice-skating, cross-country skiing Dec.–Apr., depending on weather. AE, D, MC, V. Rates AP late June–Aug., MAP Sept.–June; discount for kids. $–$$

Rockhouse Mountain Farm

 3 – 12

This lovely 450-acre farm lies in the foothills of the White Mountains. The old New England farmhouse with small and medium-size rooms filled with Welsh pine is a refreshing contrast to the area's more commercial amusement attractions. A treat for kids six and older is the chance to sleep with other kids in the kids' bunk rooms. They can hang out in the barn, where there's actually a swing hanging from the rafters, and help milk cows, feed chickens and ducks, sit on tractors, and go haying, pat dogs and cats and llamas, and be impressed by peacocks with spread tails strutting about. If your kids are at least 6, don't miss the half-hour hike to an ancient Indian cave on Rockhouse Mountain on the farm's property.

Rockhouse Mt. Rd. (6 mi south of Conway, off Rte. 153), Eaton Center 03832, tel. 603/447–2880. 15 rooms with shared or private bath, 3 kids' bunk rooms (4 bunks per room). Facilities: 2 dining rooms, private lake beach ½ mi away, boating (sailboats, canoes, rowboats), farm activities, recreation room with ping-pong, marked hiking trails on 450 acres, separate kids' dining room. No credit cards. Closed late Oct.–mid-June. Rates MAP (include boats); discount for kids. $

Rockywold-Deephaven Camp

ALL

This is a special place, the only resort on scenic, island-filled Squam Lake, the film site of *On Golden Pond*. Nearly 100 years old, it's always struck me as a quintessentially Yankee resort—a combination of wonderful service (your "cottage girl," read maid, will wash your laundry; a *New York Times* will appear upon request; the kitchen will clean and cook fish you catch), rustic but private accommodations in unique individual green-trimmed cottages of dark, weathered wood along a craggy shore, serious tennis playing and sailing, and a very strong respect for nature. Little changes here: Blocks of ice harvested from the lake in winter are still delivered daily to each cottage and stored in an old wood icebox. Everything is rustic and camplike—no TV, no radio, no phone, just unpainted walls, individual short wooden docks, and the essential screen porch overlooking the lake, where you sit at twilight so you don't get eaten by mosquitoes. Activities are those that have been around forever, like square dances, hikes, fishing, softball games, or capture the flag, and include everyone from infants to white-haired great-grandparents. Food is what I think of as hearty—hot soup, roast beef, tortellini and a big salad bar—but always includes a vegetarian dish. Like Purity Spring, this is a big summer camp, but more sophisticated, intellectual, and upscale despite its underplayed accommodations. Kids over 8 can roam just about everywhere themselves, but there are no lifeguards.

Now for the drawback: It's very hard for newcomers to rent a cottage here, almost impossible in August. Get on the waiting list, accept a late-June or early July week, then keep coming back until you're promoted to high season via their complicated seniority system.

Box B, Squam Lake, Pinehurst Rd. (off Rte. 113), Holderness 03245, tel. 603/968–3313, fax 603/968–3313. 60 cottages. Facilities:

daily housekeeping service, 2 small beaches for toddlers, 2 main docks with diving boards, 8 tennis courts, toddler playground, athletic field, recreation hall, indoor play areas, hiking trails, boating (canoe, rowboat, sailboat, kayak rentals), hydrobikes and mountain bikes (rentals), organized games, outings, activities for all ages, lessons, supervised morning play group (ages 3–5). No credit cards. Closed mid-Sept.–early June. Rates AP (include all activities but boating and bikes); free for kids under 2; reduced rate for kids 2–5. $$$

Waterville Valley Resort

👫 ALL

See Chapter 13.

Whitney's Inn at Jackson

👫 4 – 13

Whitney's, a little more than a mile from the center of town, is a classic mid-19th-century inn, a now sky-blue farmhouse with additions that ramble on and on. The setting, though, reminds us of the Alps, especially in summer, when if you walk up the hill by the pond across the road, you'll be treated to a stunning view of the entire Presidential Range. We know this place best in winter because it's right next to the Black Mountain ski area and is surrounded by one of the best cross-country trail systems in the Northeast, a network that meanders all over this valley; conveniently for families, one trail starts by the pond. Though the inn and service are gracious, it is not at all stuffy. Such thoughtful touches as the huge, three-ring binder at the desk that catalogues all the inn's board games and puzzles by age category or the decidedly informal rec and game room in the big wood barn next door let you know just how welcome families are. Guest rooms in the inn (they're named after trees) are spacious but also filled with breakable-looking collectibles. For families with young children the family suites (like motel

units) and cottages, which also have living rooms with day beds, are more appropriate. **🏠** Box 822, Rte. 16B (about 1½ mi from town and covered bridge), Jackson 03846, tel. 603/383–6886 or 800/677–5737, fax 603/383–8916. 13 rooms (1 suite) in main inn, 8 family suites in chalet, 4 rooms in Brookside House, 2 cottages. Facilities: game room with ping-pong, tennis court, shuffleboard, volleyball, badminton, swimming pond, picnic area, children's program mid-June–Labor Day (ages 5–12), children's dinner; downhill skiing, cross-country skiing, ice-skating Dec.–Feb. or Mar., depending on weather. AE, MC, V. Rates MAP; children under 12 stay and eat free Mar. 26–Sept. 3; discounted family packages. $–$$

New York

Fieldstone Farm

👫 4 – 15

About 9 miles from the National Baseball Hall of Fame (see Chapter 8) is this friendly, informal farm with 170 acres of fields, big ponds with islands, and woods that are safe for kids to explore after a hard day of total immersion in baseball. The fieldstone barn, the house, and the two-story stone townhouse apartments are clustered together by a pond and swimming pool on a huge expanse of mown grass and trees; farther up the driveway past the meadow are the wood-frame cottages, some set back in the woods, some right in a field on top of the hill, with space and light around them. We really felt kids were welcome here when we saw the 80-foot-long rec room on the top level of the barn—some kids were shooting baskets; others had set up a volleyball net for a game. Outside, kids were catching frogs in the pond with a net and petting one of the two cats. Many guests come back year after year, initially because the farm is close to the Baseball Hall of Fame, but then just because it's a place to sink into the natural world.

🏠 *Box 528, Cooperstown 13326, tel. 315/ 858–0295 or 800/336–4629. Rte. 28 north from Cooperstown to Fly Creek, right on Rte. 26 and watch for signs, 9 mi from Cooperstown. 6 apartments, 13 cottages, all with kitchen. Facilities: outdoor pool, 2 fishing ponds, paddleboats, rowboats, hiking, tennis court, shuffleboard, game area, basketball, volleyball, ping-pong, indoor game room (no video games). D, MC, V. Closed mid-Oct.–mid-May; weekly stays given priority July–Aug. Rates EP. $*

Hemlock Hall

👫 2 – 12

As most of what makes this lake special is hiking, canoeing, and fishing, a vacation here is definitely for outdoorsy families. At the end of the only public road that reaches the lake's northern shore is a turn-of-the-century lodge, built by a wealthy shoe magnate, that was restored in the 1950s; it still has a stone fireplace with hearths on three sides and even a fireplace in an upstairs hall. The rooms in the main lodge are more picturesque (marble bedroom washbasins, hooked rugs, and antique furniture), but the no-frills two-room cottages are more appropriate for rambunctious children. Don't expect lots of privacy, however. Families quickly get to know one another at the long family-style dinner tables as assigned seating changes at each meal. The food is good, but for most of the kids, getting a turn at ringing the huge dinner bell is the biggest treat. No alcohol is permitted in the dining room.

🏠 *Box 110, Maple Lodge Rd., Blue Mountain Lake 12812, tel. 518/352–7706 (July and Aug.) or 518/359–9065. 8 rooms (5 with private bath, 3 share) in main lodge, 6 2-room cottages, 4 1-room cottages, 4 adjoining cottages. Facilities: dining room, sand beach, paddle and rowboats, canoes, Sunfish, kayaks, playground, hiking, recreation room. No credit cards. Closed Oct.–May. Rates MAP (include use of boats); inexpensive box lunches available. $$*

Mohonk Mountain House

 👫 ALL

We love staying at this huge, rambling stone and dark-stained and painted wood hotel with towers and cupolas. It was built in the late 19th century and is now a National Historic Landmark and one of the best resorts for families in the Northeast. The gigantic fireplaces, carved dark woodwork, and Victorian antiques everywhere make us feel we're in some grand, European castle. The setting is spectacular too—perched at the rocky edge of a deep, clean, blue mountaintop lake in the Shawangunk range about two hours north of New York City. Most of the rooms have fireplaces and the same sorts of heavy antiques; we prefer the tower rooms, which have fabulous views of the mountains. The hotel does not feel stuffy or formal. There are "a zillion things to do here so it's hard to choose," is Gavin's assessment. You can hike on 85 miles of trails through woods, by ponds, and up to peaks in the 7,700 acres surrounding the hotel. You can have tea on the porch, walk on a bridge to a sunbathing float in the lake, visit the blacksmith shop, hunt for arrowheads, and much more. We still haven't come for one of the themed mystery weekends, but we're going to.

🏠 *Lake Mohonk, New Paltz 12561, tel. 914/ 255–1000, fax 914/256–2161. 281 rooms with bath; 44 adjoining rooms. Facilities: restaurant, swimming beach, boating, 6 tennis courts, hiking trails, nature preserve, croquet, horseback riding, 9-hole golf course, fishing, fitness center, basketball court, volleyball, softball, shuffleboard, snack bar, library, laundry, supervised kids' programs (ages 2–12, Memorial Day–Labor Day and on weekends), teen program (Memorial Day–Labor Day), evening activities for kids and teens, early dinner with children's menu, baby-sitting; cross-country skiing, ice-skating all winter. AE, MC, V. Rates AP. $$$–$$$$*

Pine Grove Resort Ranch

 4 – 15

Of all the dude ranches in the East, we think this 600-acre one run by the Tarantino family in the Catskills' Shawangunk Mountains comes closest to an authentic Old West ambience. Here you can even join a cattle drive, but just poking along on a horse over deserted, dusty trails to an old lime kiln cut into the mountainside seems to capture some of that flavor. The old-time wooden signs, wagon wheels, hand-hewn furniture, and rough-beamed ceilings in the common areas of the main lodge and the barn by the corral perhaps overdo the theme a bit. By contrast, the many spacious but motel-bland rooms are almost a surprise. The down-home jeans-and-a-shirt atmosphere is carried through in evening sing-alongs, square dances, and the general family friendliness here.

There are about 65 horses to ride, including ponies for the kids, and riding lessons eight times a day, plus a huge choice of indoor and outdoor activities. All rooms connect by hallways to the dining rooms, the pool, and the day camp, so the three-ring-circus atmosphere can continue regardless of the weather. We think this is a particularly good place for active teenagers: meals are all-you-can-eat, including free unlimited snack bar food; the indoor basketball and volleyball courts hum nonstop; and kids can even learn to rope a steer. For little kids the chance to play in a teepee village or the playground with kid-size wood vehicles may eclipse the pony rides.
🏠 Lower Chestertown Rd., Kerhonkson 12446, tel. 914/626–7345 or 800/346–4626. 120 rooms with bath, 4 1- to 4-bedroom villas. Facilities: dining room, snack bar, pony rides, indoor pool, lake beach, indoor sports, tennis courts, golf course, boating, fishing, baby-animal farm, playground, horseback riding, nursery, supervised day camp for kids, teen program, evening family entertainment, Indian village with tepees, campfires, dances;

skiing, ice-skating, tubing. AE, MC, V. Rates AP (include all-you-can-eat meals and free snacks); free for kids under 4, ½-price for kids 4–16; many packages. $$

Rocking Horse Ranch

 4+

Despite the deer with antlers over the fireplace and the steer skulls, wagon wheels, and colorful Native American blankets on the barnboard walls in the modern, motel-style main building and rooms, this ranch has more a Long Island or Hudson Valley flavor overlaid with folksiness. It does have the largest stables in the East, with 90 horses; 500 acres of woods and orchards to ride in; and literally hundreds of activities for every age group and interest, from infants up. If you are an experienced rider, you may be able to go on several half-hour trail rides a day. Trail ride sign-up lines are often long. All trail rides are accompanied by several experienced members of the ranch staff; one friend of Gavin's, looking for some excitement, was disappointed by how quickly staffers controlled a beginner's runaway horse.

Younger kids especially enjoy the petting zoo and the shallow kids' pool; older kids go for the video parlor. Supervision of kids is superb, even extending to a "night patrol" program, in which staff members check on sleeping kids while adults party downstairs.
🏠 600 Rte. 44–55 (intersection of Rtes. 44 and 55 off Rte. 9W, 75 mi north of New York City), Highland 12528, tel. 914/691–2927 or 800/647–2624, fax 914/691–6434. 120 rooms with bath and air-conditioning. Facilities: supervised kids' program day and evening, infants' nursery, waterskiing, fishing, hiking, riding, playground, ping-pong, badminton, tennis, hayrides, indoor and outdoor heated pools, kids' pool, paddleboats, miniature golf, petting zoo, bocce courts, fitness center, nightly entertainment for families and teens; skiing, ice-skating. AE, D, DC, MC, V. Rates MAP (include all activities and facili-

ties), free for kids under 4, less than ½-price for ages 4–16. $$

Sagamore Resort

👫 3 – 15

Built in 1883 on Green Island in Lake George, just across a short bridge from Bolton Landing, the Sagamore was restored to grand resort status in the 1980s and came under the management of the Omni chain. A long stairway leads to the porticoed entrance of the Victorian-style hotel flanked by two several-story white clapboard wings. The suites in the new stained-wood-and-glass lakefront lodge buildings (a short walk from the main hotel), which have a more Adirondack-country feel and are filled with sturdy Adirondack twig-style furniture, cushy sectional couches, quilts on the walls, fireplaces, and small kitchens with round wooden tables for eating, are just right for families.

Service is impeccable, food is excellent; younger kids are welcomed with a special kids'-height buffet table at breakfast, stocked with bite-sized French toast, tiny pancakes, chocolate milk, Frosted Flakes, and coloring books. The well-organized children's program is best for preschoolers and school-age children. The lake beach, mostly encircled with a wood deck so it resembles a natural swimming pool, is too deep for very young children; though they can play in the sand behind it, they can't walk into the water themselves. For teenagers, the big attractions are hanging out in the game room, the tennis clinics, and going to the nearby amusement parks.

🏨 *Bolton Landing 12814, tel. 518/644–9400 or 800/358–3585, fax 518/644–2626. 50 rooms, 50 suites in main hotel; 120 rooms, 120 suites in lodges; all with private bath and cable TV; some with fireplace, terrace, or balcony. Facilities: 2 dining rooms, café, grill room, 18-hole golf course, croquet, 5 outdoor tennis courts, 2 indoor tennis courts, gift shop, walking trail, game room with ping-*

pong, video games, volleyball, basketball, indoor pool, lake beach, spa, fitness center, racquetball, supervised all-day kids' program and dinner, tour boat, playground, baby-sitting. AE, DC, MC, V. Rates EP (most activities extra). $$$–$$$$

Silver Bay Association

👫 ALL

This enormous 600-acre national conference center for the YMCA on Lake George is simply an astonishing bargain for vacationing families. Picture long, flat grassy fields, turn-of-the-century Adirondack wood-and-stone buildings, a massive four-story clapboard inn with peaked dormer windows and fronted with a covered porch hung with plants (both on the National Register of historic places), clay tennis courts, a timber boathouse, and many more buildings, all set on one of the most beautiful bays on the lake. The real bargains here are the recreational facilities, which are like those at a grand resort, and the kids' program and playgrounds for infants and up, which are among the best we've seen anywhere. Rooms in the inn are pretty basic: nondescript Scandinavian style with clean, functional bathrooms; the rooms in lodges with shared baths, which are quite large, holding a double and a single bed, have that old-furniture look and are decorated with amateur watercolors painted by guests. On the plus side, if your kids leave their wet bathing suits on the floor, it doesn't matter.

Food is no-frills but includes things kids like. It's an easy drive to Lake George attractions (see Chapter 6), but your kids probably won't want to leave.

🏨 *Silver Bay 12874, tel. 518/543–8833, fax 518/543–6733. 103 rooms (15 adjoining rooms) in main inn, 27 rooms (4 adjoining) in Bayview Lodge, all with private bath; 125 rooms with shared baths in 6 other lodges; 23 1- to 4-bedroom cottages with kitchens. Facilities: 2 beaches (lifeguards); 2 gymnasiums; 6 tennis courts; boating (sailboats, canoes, rowboats); library; arts center; basketball; tennis;*

softball; baseball; crafts workshop; archery; weight and exercise room; nature center; hiking trails; supervised children's programs (infants–high school); baby-sitting; tennis, swimming, and sailing lessons; snack bar; ice-skating, cross-country skiing Dec.–Mar. MC, V. Kids under 4 free, kids 4–12 pay ½-price when sharing room with parents. $

Rhode Island

Weekapaug Inn

(👭👬 3 – 15)

On first sight it looks like an unpretentious, rambling, weathered gray barn with dormer windows and expansive decks. It's set on a flat peninsula poking out into a huge saltwater pond behind a long barrier beach. The simplicity is the sophisticated, proper, old New England–family kind (no bathing suits in the public rooms, please, and jackets at dinner). The inn does not advertise. It is in a very quiet colony of large, privately owned summer cottages on a stretch of beautiful white sand beaches that are as glorious as any in the Northeast. This is not a "family place" in the sense that The Tyler Place or the Basin Harbor Club in Vermont (see below) are. Instead it has room for a few families and extends its warm, personal, attentive service to them. Relaxing, playing tennis, or boating on the big saltwater pond behind the tennis courts, and enjoying the beach, the ocean, and the natural world are the key attractions. The kids' morning program is also low-key, mostly taking them to nearby Fenway Beach, which is shallower and has more kids and better waves for body boarding than the beach in front of the inn. If older kids get bored, you're not too far from Mystic Seaport.

In contrast to the antiques-filled common rooms on the first two floors, which resemble an old private club, the bedrooms are simple, with small baths, but you won't

spend much time in them. For older children and teens who want independence there are 10 reduced-rate small rooms on the top floor with two shared baths that are most often rented to the children of guests. Did I mention that the food is really good, especially the fish?

🏨 25 Spring Ave., Weekapaug 02891, tel. 401/322–0301, fax 401/322–1016. 55 rooms with private bath, plus 6 family suites and 10 rooms that share 2 baths. Facilities: dining room; ocean beach with bathhouse and snack bar; tennis; lawn bowling; shuffleboard; boating (kayaks, canoes, Sunfish, Windsurfers, sailboats, rowboats); library; recreation room with ping-pong; TV room; swing set and jungle gym; supervised program in morning and for lunch and dinner (ages 3–12). No credit cards. Closed mid-Sept.–mid-June. Rates AP, special rates for kids. $$$

Vermont

Basin Harbor Club

(👭👬 3 – 15)

This 700-acre lakefront resort around secluded Basin Harbor on Lake Champlain's eastern shore just oozes the comfortable, conservative New England style and tradition favored by well-to-do families who like to wear blue blazers and bow ties to dinner on their vacations. It really does feel like a club—and you can fly in on your private plane. White sailboats and speedboats dot the lake; brightly painted Adirondack chairs in red, blue, and yellow dot the expansive, well-manicured lawn in front of the main lodge, a red-roofed white farmhouse nestled among colorful flower beds near the lake; families, sometimes three generations, gather on the veranda for a drink. The whole place seems bright and timeless, as though summers here have not changed in the hundred-odd years the Beach family has owned and run it. This is a more formal, upscale place with fewer children than The Tyler Place (see below) farther north on the lake, and not as appropriate for families with toddlers.

The food in the main dining room is good. It includes 20 desserts and a make-your-own sundae bar laid out at the lunch buffet. There's a separate kids' dining room. If you don't want to dress for dinner every night, you can head for the Red Mill, a casual place for hamburger fare with bare wood beams and tables in an old restored barn that also houses a game room, usually full of teens. The airy cottages furnished in pine, wicker, and chintz may be preferable to the slightly stuffier, country-house feeling of the main lodge. All the cottages are different—one- or two-story white frame, some fronted with cut Vermont stone, some with decks or screened porches, some in the woods, by a garden, or even perched on pillars at the edge of the water. The sheltered sandy beaches are much nicer than the one at The Tyler Place; they're better for little kids than the pool. This is a place where it really matters whether children the same age as yours are on hand; to make sure they will be, come during August or over the fourth of July.

🏠 Basin Rd., Vergennes 05491, tel. 802/ 475–2311 or 800/622–4000, fax 802/ 475–2545. 43 hotel rooms in 2 main buildings; 77 cottages, all with phone, most with refrigerator, ½ with fireplace. Facilities: 3 restaurants, snack bar, game room, library with children's books, outdoor pool, beach, playground, biking, hiking, nature trails, golf, tennis, badminton, croquet, volleyball, ping-pong, waterskiing, windsurfing, sailing, boating, babysitting, supervised morning kids' program (ages 3–10) and kids' dinner, afternoon crafts, family activities, private airstrip. AE, MC, V. Closed mid-Oct.–June. Rates AP (include all facilities); kids' rates and packages. $$$

Bridges Resort and Racquet Club

👫 3+

This is a condo-land (individually owned, so the furnishings are fairly diverse) with a mountain backdrop and towering pines near the Sugarbush ski area, but in summer it becomes a tennis-playing family's heaven. It's my pick for a strictly tennis destination because of the well-run, extensive program that even teaches tennis to 3-year-olds, using regular junior racquets but a lower net (see also Sugarbush Resort in Chapter 13). Youngest kids in families of tennis players often feel left out, I've observed—here they don't.

🏠 Sugarbush Access Rd., Warren 05674, tel. 802/583–2922 or 800/451–4213, fax 802/ 583–1018. 100 1-, 2-, and 3-bedroom condominiums. Facilities: 2 indoor tennis courts, 10 outdoor tennis courts, outdoor tennis stadium, 1 indoor and 2 outdoor heated pools, fitness center, game room, playground and children's activity center, supervised children's programs and tennis instruction, volleyball. AE, MC, V. Rates EP. $$

Mountain Top Inn and Resort

👫 ALL

Though this is a small country inn, it has as many things to do as a much bigger, more expensive, even grand resort and absolutely sensational views of the Green Mountains and the Chittenden Reservoir. The real draw for us are the extensive cross-country ski trails on the inn's 1,300 acres, but horse-loving friends tell us that this is also an especially good place to introduce young (7 and up) kids to horseback riding. In winter, it's most convenient to stay at the main inn, a modern post-and-beam farmhouse with comfortable sofas and stacks of board games in the two main sitting areas, even though the rooms, unfortunately if your kids are noisy, could use more soundproofing. In summer, try one of the cottages just up the hill; they're close to the kidney-shaped pool, but you'll still have to drive to the beach.

 Mountain Top Rd., Rte. 108, Chittenden 05737, tel. 802/483–2311 or 800/445–2100, fax 802/483–6373. 33 rooms, 22 cottages and chalets. Facilities: restaurant, sauna, whirlpool, outdoor heated pool, tennis, 5-hole golf course, shuffleboard, croquet court, boating, fly fishing, horseback riding, sand swimming beach with snack bar and toys; cross-country skiing, ice-skating, sledding. AE, MC, V. Rates MAP (include all activities without instruction); free for kids under 6; discount for kids under 18. $$$

Rodgers' Farm Vacation

(**††** 3 – 9)

In the high, rolling country of northeastern Vermont, down a rutted dirt road, is this small off-the-beaten-path farm. It takes only two families at a time, so coming here is more like visiting an aunt or a grandma than going to a resort. For city-bred kids it's a peaceful, quiet place where they can take a break from their over-scheduled lives and easily entertain themselves with all the animals they'd like to have but don't. They can gather eggs and pet goats as well as 10 or so cats and kittens. Hayrides let them discover how prickly hay is when you lie back on it.

 R.F.D. 3, Box 57, West Glover 06875, tel. 802/525–6677. 5 rooms with shared bath. Facilities: hayrides, swing set, sandbox, swimming 4 mi away. MC, V. Closed Nov.–June. Rates AP or B&B; discount for kids under 12. $

Trapp Family Lodge

(**††** 4+)

If you and your kids have seen the movie or musical, The Sound of Music, you know the story of the von Trapp family, who left Nazi-occupied Austria in 1938 on a professional singing tour, eventually coming to America.

They made their farm in Stowe into a lodge in the late 1940s and introduced cross-country skiing in the Northeast (see Chapter 13). This is a rebuilt and expanded version of that Stowe original, which burned down in 1983, but to me its gables, carved balconies, steep sloping roofs, and bell tower still make it look like an Austrian-style wood chalet built into a hillside. Stay on the third floor, where you can walk out a back door and be right on a ski trail. From the balconies you have a spectacular view of the Stowe Valley.

The large rooms with heavy, dark European lodge-type armoires, the dormer windows on the higher floors, the comfortable living rooms downstairs with carved fireplaces and big sofas, the tables with games set out in the card room, and the live music in the dining room all contribute to the plush, homey atmosphere. For the kids, the connection with the Trapp Family Singers makes it very special, not just any old hotel. Staying here in summer is also popular, especially as a base for hiking and exploring the area around Stowe.

 Stowe 05672, tel. 802/253–8511 or 800/826–7000, fax 802/253–7864. 73 rooms, 6 suites, varying number of 2-bedroom time-share guest houses. Facilities: dining room, tearoom, indoor and outdoor pools, fitness center, tennis courts, gift shop, sports shop, supervised children's programs, ping-pong, library, summer concerts, children's menu; cross-country skiing, including children's instruction and rentals, sledding. AE, DC, MC, V. Rates MAP; free for kids under 13. $$–$$$

Tyler Place

(**††** 0 – 13)

You feel as though you're at a cheerful, simple, and informal (but not rustic) summer cottage colony at this terrific 60-year-old resort. It holds about 50 families and is spread out along a mile of Lake Champlain's wooded shoreline. All the lodgings are different: Some are basic square white frame

1930s-style cottages with a fireplace, chenille bedspreads, painted old furniture, and a screen porch, overlooking the lake or set back on the lawn; others are suites in a Victorian farmhouse with its own small playground or in the big, modern stained-wood inn that also houses the two-story dining room hung with patchwork quilts. All provide separate bedrooms for parents, something we've always viewed as important. Infant care in the form of mother's helpers and the structured, well-supervised morning and evening programs for six separate age groups of kids from 2 to 17 led by adventurous and wonderfully outgoing and nurturing college students draw families back year after year. This is one of the few places that really caters to people with infants and toddlers, but for many kids over 14 it may be too sedate.

It's not a place for an intimate family vacation—kids eat lunch and dinner with their peers and counselors (a nice touch for teens is the extra-late breakfast), and parents eat at tables of six in the adult dining room. Whatever kind of sports activity you want, it's here. The only drawback is the lack of a good beach for small children; use the L-shaped lifeguarded pool and the little kids' wading pool instead.

🏡 *Highgate Springs 05460, tel. 802/868–4291 or 802/868–3301, fax 802/868–7602. 27 3- to 6-room cottages with fireplace, 23 suites. Facilities: supervised children's programs (infants–teens), mother's helpers, heated pool, 6 tennis courts, biking, boating, fishing, swimming, volleyball, softball, preschoolers' center and dining room, kids' recreation center, evening entertainment, adult activities, separate children's and teen dining with separate menu, family picnic baskets, baby-sitting, family events. MC. V. Closed Sept.–May. Rates AP (include all sports and lessons); special rates May, June, Sept. $$–$$$*

Directory of Attractions

Here is a list of the attractions covered in this book, each one followed by a **boldface** age range and the *italic* number of the page on which you'll find a description.

Connecticut

Barnum Museum, Bridgeport, **3–13**, *174*

Beardsley Park Zoological Gardens, Bridgeport, **All**, *190*

Bruell's Orchard, Eastford, **4–13**, *232*

Children's Museum of Southern Connecticut, Niantic, **2–7**, *174*

Discovery Museum, Bridgeport, **3+**, *174–175*

Gillette Castle State Park, East Haddam, **All**, *157*

Farmington River, Avon–Simsbury, **4–15**, *240–241*

Farmington River, New Hartford–Canton, **10–15**, *265*

Hartford Whalers (hockey), Hartford, **8+**, *223*

Housatonic Meadows State Park, Cornwall Bridge, **7–15**, *236–237*

Housatonic River, Falls Village–Cornwall Bridge, **8–15**, *241*

Hungerford Outdoor Education Center, Kensington, **3–12**, *190*

Inn at Lake Waramaug, New Preston, **3–15**, *290–291*

Lake Waramaug State Park, New Preston, **0–12**, *203*

Lime Rock Park (auto racing), Lakeville, **5+**, *223*

Longshore Sailing School, Westport, **8–15**, *259*

Maritime Center at Norwalk, Norwalk, **All**, *190–191*

Mystic Marinelife Aquarium, Mystic, **All**, *191*

Mystic Seaport, Mystic, **All**, *158*

Old Newgate Prison and Copper Mine, East Granby, **7–15**, *158*

Peabody Museum of Natural History, New Haven, **4–15**, *175*

Rocky Neck State Park, Niantic, **2+**, *203, 237*

Science Center of Connecticut, West Hartford, **3–12**, *191*

Sharon Audubon Center, Sharon, **4–12**, *203*

Sheffield Island Lighthouse, Norwalk, **6–13**, *158–159*

SoundWaters (sailing school),Stamford, **8–15**, *259*

Stew Leonard's Dairy, Norwalk, **2–12**, *252*

USS *Nautilus* Memorial Museum, Groton, **6–15**, *175*

White Memorial Foundation, Litchfield, **3–12**, *203–204*

Maine

Acadia National Park, **2–15**, *204–205, 233, 246*

Acadia Toddler Tromp, Acadia National Park, **1–5**, *237*

Acadia Zoological Park, Trenton, **1–12**, *191–192, 218–219*

Acadian Whale Watcher and *Sea Bird Watcher* (whale watching), Bar Harbor, **8–15**, *267*

Attean Lake Lodge, Jackman, **2–12**, *291*

Baxter State Park, Millinocket, **3+**, *192, 205*

Boothbay Harbor, **5–15**, *259*

Chewonki Wilderness Programs, Wiscasset, **8+**, *291*

Desert of Maine, Freeport, **5–14**, *205*

Ft. Knox State Park, Prospect Harbor, **3–15**, *1159*

Ft. Popham, Phippsburg, **4–13**, *159*

Ft. William Henry/Colonial Pemaquid Restoration, New Harbor, **5–12**, *159*

Goose Cove Lodge, Sunset, **0–12**, *291–292*

Grafton Notch State Park, Newry, **7+**, *206*

Kennebec River, **8–15**, *268*

Lily Bay State Park, Greenville, **5+**, *206, 237*

L.L. Bean, Freeport, **12–15**, *252*

Lumberman's Museum, Patten, **6–15**, *175–176*

Maine Aquarium, Saco, **2–14**, *204*

Maine Department of Marine Resources Public Aquarium, West Boothbay Harbor, **2–12**, *192*

Maine Maritime Museum, Bath, **4–15**, *176*

Monhegan Island, **6–15**, *246*

Mt. Blue State Park, Weld, **6+**, *206, 237*

Mt. Desert Island, Acadia National Park, **9–15**, *241*

Mt. Desert Oceanarium, Southwest Harbor, **All**, *192–193*

Mt. Kineo, **7+**, *246–247*

Pemaquid Point Lighthouse and Fisherman's Museum, Pemaquid, **5–15**, *159–16-*

Perham's (rockhounding), West Paris, **5–13**, *256*

Railway Village, Boothbay, **3–9**, *176*

Reid State park, Georgetown, **All**, *206–207*

Samoset Resort, Rockport, **3–12**, *292*

Scarborough Marsh Nature Center, Scarborough, **7+**, *193, 207*

Sebago Lake State Park, Naples, **All**, *207, 237–238*

Sebasco Lodge, Sebasco Estates, **4–12**, *292–293*

Step Falls, Bethel/Grafton Notch State Park, **3–15**, *247*

Sugarloaf/USA, Kingfield, **All**, *271–272*

Sunday River, Bethel, **All**, *272–274*

Telemark Inn, Bethel, **4–15**, *253–254*

Washburn-Norlands Living History Center, Livermore Falls, **8+**, *292*

White Mountain National Forest, Bethel, **7+**, *207*

Windjammer Cruises, Camden, **12–15**, *259*

Massachusetts

Actor's Theater of Nantucket, Nantucket, **4+**, *115*

Aery's Pond Boat Yard (sailing), South Orleans, **6–15**, *277*

African Meeting House/Black Heritage Trail, Boston, **10–15**, *32*

Animal statues, Boston, **2–12**, *32*

Arnold Arboretum, Boston, **All**, *37–38*

Bartholomew's Cobble, Ashley Falls, **3–12**, *129, 247*

Basketball Hall of Fame, Springfield, **5–15**, *176*

Bassett Wild Animal Farm, Brewster, **2–10**, *100, 193*

Battle Green, Lexington, **8–15**, *34*

Battleship *Massachusetts*, Fall River, **7–15**, *176–177*

Beartown State Forest, Monterey, **All**, *128–129*

Berkshire Botanical Garden, Stockbridge, **0–8**, *126*

Berkshire Hiking Holidays, Lenox, **8+**, *124*

Berkshire Museum, Pittsfield, **4–12**, *126*

Berkshire Opera Company, Lenox, **12–15**, *135*

Berkshire Scenic Railway and Museum, Lenox, **5–10**, *126*

Berkshire Theatre Festival, Stockbridge, **8–14**, *135*

Berkshire Tour Company, Pittsfield, **All**, *124*

Blue Hills Reservation, Milton, **All**, *39*

Boston Ballet Company, Boston, **5+**, *55*

Boston Bruins (hockey), Boston, **9+**, *40, 225*

Boston by Little Feet (tours), Boston, **7–12**, *29*

Boston Celtics (basketball), Boston, **8+**, *39, 224*

Boston Children's Theatre, Boston, **5–12**, *54*

Boston College Eagles (football), Brookline, **7+**, *40, 224*

Boston Common, Boston, **All**, *31, 38*

Boston Harbor Islands State Park, Boston, **All**, *38, 208*

Boston Harbor Tours, Boston, **7–15**, *29*

Boston Marathon, Boston, **6+**, *40, 225–226*

Boston Pops, Boston, **8+**, *55*

Boston Public Garden, Boston, **All**, *31, 38*

Boston Public Library, Boston, **3–6**, *53–54*

Boston Red Sox (baseball), Boston, **7+**, *39, 223*

Boston Symphony Orchestra, Boston, **5–12**, *55*

Boston Tea Party Ship and Museum, Boston, **4–10**, *35, 177*

Boston University Terriers (football), **All**, *40*

Boston Waterfront, Boston, **All**, *32–33, 160*

Brewster Mill, Brewster, **3–8**, *99–100*

Bunker Hill Monument, Charlestown, **6+**, *34, 160*

Butterfly Place at Papillon Park, Westford, **4–12**, *193–194*

Butternut Basin, Great Barrington, **All**, *274*

Cape Cod Baseball League, Harwich, **3–14**, *109, 224*

Cape Cod Museum of Natural History, Brewster, **3–12**, *99*

Cape Cod National Seashore, South Wellfleet, **All**, *100–101, 208–209, 261*

Cape Cod Scenic Railway, Hyannis, **4+**, *97*

Cape Playhouse, East Dennis, **4–10**, *106*

Captain John Boats (whale watching), Plymouth, **8–15**, *267*

Charles River Boat Company Tours, Boston, **4–15**, *29*

Charles River Esplanade, Boston, **12–15**, *257*

Charlestown Navy Yard, Charlestown, **All**, *34*

Chatham Bars Inn, Chatham, **4–10**, *292–294*

Chatham Band Concerts, Chatham, **All**, *106*

Chatham Fish Pier, Chatham, **All**, *100*

Children's Museum, Boston, **All**, *35, 55, 177*

Children's Theatre in Residence at Maudslay State Park, Newburyport, **6+**, *54*

Christmas Stroll, Nantucket, **All**, *109*

Computer Museum, Boston, **8+**, *35, 178*

Cove Lanes, Great Barrington, **4–15**, *253*

Craigville Beach, near Hyannis, **13–15**, *261*

Cranberry World, Plymouth, **5–13**, *35, 160–161*

Dance Umbrella, Cambridge, **9+**, *55*

Deerfield River/Fife Brook, Mohawk Trail State Forest, **8–15**, *268–269*

Discovery Days Children's Museum, Dennisport, **0–9**, *99*

Discovery Museums, Acton, **All**, *36*

Drumlin Farm Education Center/Wildlife Sanctuary, South Lincoln, **2–11**, *37, 194*

Essex Shipbuilding Museum, Essex, **6–13**, *178*

Faneuil Hall Marketplace (Quincy Market), Boston, **All**, *33, 56, 161*

Fairfields Dairy Farm/Bed & Breakfast, Williamstown, **2–10**, *1127*

First Congregational Church (Old North Church), Nantucket, **8–12**, *109–110*

Fisheries Aquarium, Woods Hole, **3–12**, *99, 194*

Five-Minute Train Ride, Boston, **3–10**, *31*

Flax Pond, Brewster, **All**, *261*

Force 5 Watersports (sailing/windsurfing), Nantucket, **7–15**, *277*

Fourth of July, Nantucket, **All**, *109*

Fourth of July, Tanglewood (Lenox), **5–15**, *125*

Franklin Park Zoo, Dorchester, **All**, *37, 194*

Freedom Trail, Boston, **7–15**, *29, 33, 161*

sports), Lake Placid,
7+, *148–149, 229*

Olympic site
(tour/events), Lake
Placid, **6–15,** *139*

Painted Pony Rodeo,
Lake Luzerne, **5–15,**
138

Paper Bag Players,
Manhattan, **4–9,** *90*

Paul Smiths
Adirondack
Interpretive Center,
Paul Smiths, **4–15,** *139*

Philipsburg Manor,
North Tarrytown, **All,**
167–168

Pine Grove Resort
Ranch, Kerhonkson,
4–15, *301*

Prospect Mountain,
Lake George, **8+,** *142*

Prospect Park,
Brooklyn, **All,** *73*

Prospect Park Wildlife
Conservation Center,
Brooklyn, **0–12,** *72*

Puppet Playhouse,
Manhattan, **3–10,** *90*

Puppetworks,
Brooklyn, **3–7,** *90*

Queens Wildlife
Conservation Center,
Queens, **0–12,** *72*

Radio City Music Hall,
Manhattan, **All,** *66, 92*

Rockefeller Center,
Manhattan, **All,** *66, 168*

Rocking Horse Ranch,
Highland, **4+,** *301–302*

Roosevelt Island Tram,
Manhattan, **3+,** *65*

Sacandaga River, **8–15,**
269

Sagamore Resort,
Bolton Landing, **3–15,**
302

Saranac Lake and
Indian Lake Islands,
5–15, *239, 242*

Saratoga Performing
Arts Center, Saratoga
Springs, **8+,** *147*

Saratoga Racetrack,
Saratoga Springs, **6+,**
138, 228

Silver Bay Association
(resort), Silver Bay,
All, *302–303*

Ski-jumping
competitions,
Adirondacks, **All,** *147*

Small Journeys, Inc.
(tours), Manhattan, **5+,**
62

Soho, Manhattan, **All,**
65

Sony 84th Street
Theater, Manhattan,
6+, *89*

Sony Theatres Lincoln
Square, Manhattan, **6+,**
89

South Street Seaport,
Manhattan, **All,** *66, 70,
92, 168*

Staten Island Children's
Museum, Staten Island,
1–10, *70–71, 95*

Staten Island Ferry,
Manhattan, **All,** *64–65*

Statue of Liberty,
Manhattan, **All,** *66–67,
1168–169*

Studio Museum of
Harlem, Manhattan,
7+, *70*

Subways, Manhattan,
2–13, *65*

Summer Stage,
Manhattan, **10+,** *92*

Sunnyside (historic
house), Tarrytown,
6–14, *169*

Swedish Cottage
Marionette Theater,
Manhattan, **3+,** *90–91*

Tada! Youth Ensemble,
Manhattan, **4+,** *91*

Taipei Theater,
Manhattan, **7+,** *91*

Theatreworks USA,
Manhattan, **6–12,** *91*

Theodore Roosevelt
birthplace, Manhattan,
9+, *67*

Ukrainian Museum,
Manhattan, **3–10,** *70*

United Nations,
Manhattan, **10+,** *67*

U.S. Open (tennis),
Flushing, **10+,** *74, 229*

Urban Park Rangers
(tours), Manhattan, **5+,**
62–63

Van Cortlandt Manor,
Croton-on-Hudson,
3–14, *169–170*

West Point (U.S.
Military Academy),
West Point, **7–15,**
170, 227–228

Whiteface Mountain,
Adirondacks, **All,**
139–140, 279–280

Winter Carnival,
Saranac Lake, **3+,** *137*

World Financial
Center, Manhattan,
All, *67*

World Trade
Center/Observation
Deck, Manhattan, **All,**
67, 170

Rhode Island

Astors' Beechwood
(historic house),
Newport, **8+,** *170*

Block Island Historical
Society, Block Island,
5+, *117–118*

Block Island National
Wildlife Refuge, Block
Island, **4–12,** *118, 217*

The Breakers (historic
house), Newport, **8+,**
170–171

Brown University
(football), Providence,
6+, *230*

Burlingame State Park,
Charlestown, **All,** *217,
239–240*

Burton Island State
Park, St. Alban's Bay,
All, *240*

Children's Museum of
Rhode Island,
Pawtucket, *187*

Empire Theater, Block
Island, **3–15,** *122*

Flying Horse Carousel,
Watch Hill Lighthouse,
and Napatree Point,
Watch Hill, **3–10,** *171*

Ft. Adams State Park,
Newport, **3+,**
217–218

Fourth of July, Block
Island, **All,** *117*

Great Salt Pond
Channel, Block Island,
4–14, *117*

Green Animals
(topiary garden),
Portsmouth, **2–12,**
218

J. World Sailing School,
Newport, **12–15,** *259*

Misquamicut State
Beach/Atlantic Beach,
Westerly, **5+,** *218, 263*

Museum of Natural
History, Providence,
9+, *187*

Narragansett Town
Beach, Narragansett,
6–15, *263*

Ninigret Conservation
Area (East Beach),
Charlestown, **6+,** *218,
263–264*

Norman Bird
Sanctuary, Middletown,
7–12, *218–219*

North Light/North
Light Interpretive
Center, Block Island,
All, *118*

Pawtucket Red Sox
(baseball), Pawtucket,
4+, *229*

Roger Williams Park
and Zoo, Providence,
All, *199*

Roger W. Wheeler
State Beach,
Narragansett, **1–10,**
264

Sail Newport Sailing
Center, Newport,
7–15, *259–260*

Southeast
Light/Mohegan Bluffs,
Block Island, **4–15,**
118

Taste of Block Island Seafood Festival and Chowder Cookoff, Block Island, **All**, *117*

Weekapaug Inn, Weekapaug, **3–15**, *303*

Vermont

Basin Harbor Club, Vergennes, **3–15**, *303–304*

Battenkill River, **5–15**, *243, 245*

Ben & Jerry's Ice Cream Factory, Waterbury, **3–15**, *171*

Billings Farm and Museum, Woodstock, **All**, *171, 200*

Bolton Valley, Bolton, **All**, *280–281*

Bridges Resort and Racquet Club, Warren, **3+**, *264, 304*

Burton Island State Park, Alban's Bay, **All**, *219*

Catamount Family Center Endurance Sports, Williston, **6–15**, *255*

Craftsbury Sport Center, Craftsbury Common, **12–15**, *255*

Cutting Edge North (skateboarding), Bennington, **9–15**, *258*

Emerald Lake State Park, East Dorset, **0–13**, *219*

Fairbanks Museum and Planetarium, St. Johnsbury, **5–13**, *187*

Green Mountain National Forest, **All**, *220, 250*

Grout Pond, Stratton, **0–15**, *250*

Kedron Valley Inn and Stables, Woodstock, **10–15**, *251*

Merck Forest and Farmland Center, Rupert, **3–12**, *220*

Montshire Museum of Science, Norwich, **2+**, *188*

Mount Snow-Haystack, Mount Snow, **All**, *282–283*

Mountain Bike School/Training Center at Mt. Snow, Dover, **7–15**, *255*

Mountain Top Inn and Resort, Chittenden, **6–15**, *251, 304–305*

Mountain Top Inn Touring Center, Chittenden, **All**, *281–282*

Okemo Mountain Resort, Ludlow, **All**, *283–284*

Quechee Gorge/Quechee State Park, Quechee, **6+**, *220–221*

Rock of Ages Granite Quarry, Barre, **6–13**, *171–172*

Rodgers' Farm Vacation, West Glover, **3–9**, *305*

Shelburne Farms, Shelburne, **2–10**, *200*

Shelburne Museum, Shelburne, **5+**, *188*

Stowe In-Line Skate Park, Stowe, **10–15**, *258*

Stowe Mountain Resort, Stowe, **All**, *284–285*

Stowe Recreation Path, Stowe, **5–15**, *235–236*

Stratton Mountain Resort, Stratton Mountain, **7–15**, *265, 285–286*

Suicide Six and the Woodstock Inn and Resort, Woodstock, **All**, *286*

Sugarbush Resort Tennis School and Club, Warren, **3–15**, *264–265*

Trapp Family Lodge, Stowe, **4+**, *305*

Tyler Place, Highgate Springs, **0–13**, *305–306*

UVM Morgan Horse Farm, Middlebury, **4+**, *200*

Vermont Icelandic Horse Farm, Waitsfield, **9–15**, *252*

Vermont Institute of Natural Science, Woodstock, **3–15**, *200–201*

Village at Smugglers Notch, Smugglers Notch Resort, **All**, *286–288*

White Rocks Recreation Area, Wallingford, **3–15**, *250*

Index

INDEX

NOTES

NOTES

NOTES

NOTES

Fodor's Travel Guides

Available at bookstores everywhere, or call 1–800–533–6478, 24 hours a day.

U.S. Guides

Alaska	Las Vegas, Reno, Tahoe	Philadelphia & the Pennsylvania Dutch Country	USA
Arizona	Los Angeles	The Rockies	The Upper Great Lakes Region
Boston	Maine, Vermont, New Hampshire	San Diego	Virginia & Maryland
California	Maui	San Francisco	Waikiki
Cape Cod, Martha's Vineyard, Nantucket	Miami & the Keys	Santa Fe, Taos, Albuquerque	Walt Disney World and the Orlando Area
The Carolinas & the Georgia Coast	New England	Seattle & Vancouver	Washington, D.C.
Chicago	New Orleans	The South	
Colorado	New York City	The U.S. & British Virgin Islands	
Florida	Pacific North Coast		
Hawaii			

Foreign Guides

Acapulco, Ixtapa, Zihuatanejo	The Czech Republic & Slovakia	Japan	Provence & the Riviera
Australia & New Zealand	Eastern Europe	Kenya & Tanzania	Rome
Austria	Egypt	Korea	Russia & the Baltic Countries
The Bahamas	Euro Disney	London	Scandinavia
Baja & Mexico's Pacific Coast Resorts	Europe	Madrid & Barcelona	Scotland
Barbados	Florence, Tuscany & Umbria	Mexico	Singapore
Berlin	France	Montréal & Québec City	South America
Bermuda	Germany	Morocco	Southeast Asia
Brittany & Normandy	Great Britain	Moscow & St. Petersburg	Spain
Budapest	Greece	The Netherlands, Belgium & Luxembourg	Sweden
Canada	Hong Kong	New Zealand	Switzerland
Cancún, Cozumel, Yucatán Peninsula	India	Norway	Thailand
Caribbean	Ireland	Nova Scotia, Prince Edward Island & New Brunswick	Tokyo
China	Israel	Paris	Toronto
Costa Rica, Belize, Guatemala	Italy	Portugal	Turkey
			Vienna & the Danube Valley

Special Series

Fodor's Affordables

Caribbean

Europe

Florida

France

Germany

Great Britain

Italy

London

Paris

Fodor's Bed & Breakfast and Country Inns Guides

America's Best B&Bs

California

Canada's Great Country Inns

Cottages, B&Bs and Country Inns of England and Wales

Mid-Atlantic Region

New England

The Pacific Northwest

The South

The Southwest

The Upper Great Lakes Region

The Berkeley Guides

California

Central America

Eastern Europe

Europe

France

Germany & Austria

Great Britain & Ireland

Italy

London

Mexico

Pacific Northwest & Alaska

Paris

San Francisco

Fodor's Exploring Guides

Australia

Boston & New England

Britain

California

The Caribbean

Florence & Tuscany

Florida

France

Germany

Ireland

Italy

London

Mexico

New York City

Paris

Prague

Rome

Scotland

Singapore & Malaysia

Spain

Thailand

Turkey

Fodor's Flashmaps

Boston

New York

Washington, D.C.

Fodor's Pocket Guides

Acapulco

Bahamas

Barbados

Jamaica

London

New York City

Paris

Puerto Rico

San Francisco

Washington, D.C.

Fodor's Sports

Cycling

Golf Digest's Best Places to Play

Hiking

The Insider's Guide to the Best Canadian Skiing

Running

Sailing

Skiing in the USA & Canada

USA Today's Complete Four Sports Stadium Guide

Fodor's Three-In-Ones (guidebook, language cassette, and phrase book)

France

Germany

Italy

Mexico

Spain

Fodor's Special-Interest Guides

Complete Guide to America's National Parks

Condé Nast Traveler Caribbean Resort and Cruise Ship Finder

Cruises and Ports of Call

Euro Disney

France by Train

Halliday's New England Food Explorer

Healthy Escapes

Italy by Train

London Companion

Shadow Traffic's New York Shortcuts and Traffic Tips

Sunday in New York

Sunday in San Francisco

Touring Europe

Touring USA: Eastern Edition

Walt Disney World and the Orlando Area

Walt Disney World for Adults

Fodor's Vacation Planners

Great American Learning Vacations

Great American Sports & Adventure Vacations

Great American Vacations

Great American Vacations for Travelers with Disabilities

National Parks and Seashores of the East

National Parks of the West

The Wall Street Journal Guides to Business Travel

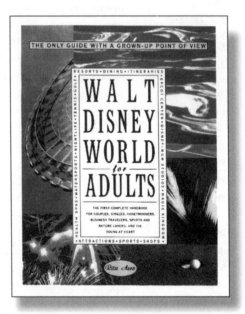